CURRENT APPROACHES IN DRAMA THERAPY

Second Edition

CURRENT APPROACHES IN DRAMA THERAPY

Edited by

DAVID READ JOHNSON, PH.D., RDT-BCT

and

RENÉE EMUNAH, PH.D., RDT-BCT

CHARLES C THOMAS • PUBLISHER, LTD.
Springfield • Illinois • U.S.A.

Published and Distributed Throughout the World by

CHARLES C THOMAS • PUBLISHER, LTD.
2600 South First Street
Springfield, Illinois 62794-9265

ISBN 978-0-398-07847-8 (hard)
ISBN 978-0-398-07848-5 (paper)

Library of Congress Catalog Card Number: 2008039991

With THOMAS BOOKS *careful attention is given to all details of manufacturing and design. It is the Publisher's desire to present books that are satisfactory as to their physical qualities and artistic possibilities and appropriate for their particular use.* THOMAS BOOKS *will be true to those laws of quality that assure a good name and good will.*

Printed in the United States of America
MM-R-3

Library of Congress Cataloging in Publication Data

Current approaches in drama therapy / edited by David Read Johnson and Renée Emunah.–2nd ed.
p. cm.
Includes bibliographical references and index.
ISBN 978-0-398-07847-8 (hard)–ISBN 078-0-398-07848-5 (pbk.)
1. Drama–Therapeutic use. I. Johnson, David Read. II. Emunah, Renée. III. Title. [DNLM: 1. Drama. 2. Psychotherapy–methods. 3. Models, Psychological. 4. Psychodrama–methods. WM 420 C9747 2009]

RC489.P7C86 2009
616.89'1523–dc22 2008039991

*The book is dedicated to Penny Lewis (1946–2003),
whose inspiration and leadership produced the first edition of this volume,
and whose many contributions to drama therapy and the creative arts
therapies will be long remembered.*

CONTRIBUTORS

Sally Bailey, MFA, MSW, RDT/BCT is Associate Professor of Theatre at Kansas State University in Manhattan, Kansas where she directs the drama therapy program and teaches playwriting, creative drama, and drama therapy. She is a past president of the National Association for Drama Therapy and recipient of the 2006 Gertrud Schattner Award and the 2005 NADT Service Award. In addition to two books, *Wings to Fly: Bringing Theatre to Students with Special Needs* and *Dreams to Sign,* and a number of book chapters on drama therapy, she has written many plays with clients.

John Bergman, MA, RDT/MT works in New Zealand, Romania, Australia, England and the United States. He has worked for 28 years doing drama/drama therapy and psychoeducational drama in criminal justice. He is the founder/artistic director of Geese Theatre Co USA, and the former artistic director of Geese UK and current president of Transcena, Romania–all theatre and theatre therapy-based companies working exclusively in prisons. He has received a BAFTA for his original show *Lifting The Weight* (for young offenders) as well as awards from the American Correctional Association and the National Association for Drama Therapy. He is the clinical supervisor for *Aware,* a therapeutic neurological program for adolescents in Melbourne. He has written numerous chapters as well as a training video, *An Introduction to Drama Therapy with Juvenile and Adult Sex Offenders* (Safer Society Press). His book (with B. Hewish), *Challenging Experience: Experiential Exercises for the Treatment of Violent and Sexually Violent Men* is now used in 15 countries.

Dale Richard Buchanan, Ph.D., LICSW, TEP, CGP is the Executive Director and former Chairperson of the American Board of Examiners in Psychodrama, Sociometry and Group Psychotherapy. He is a founder and former Chairperson of the National Coalition of Arts Therapy Associations. He was the Chief Psychodramatist (1977–1987) and Director of Clinical Therapies (1987–1998) at St. Elizabeth's Hospital in Washington, DC, where he supervised and managed 18 creative arts therapists and over 150 students completing year-long stipended internships. He is the author of 20 published articles, two book chapters, and co-editor of *The Badge and the Battered: A Manual for Family Crisis Intervention Training for Law Enforcement Officers.* He has received the J.L. Moreno Lifetime Achievement Award, the Scholar's Award, the Collaborators Award, the Hannah Weiner Service Award, the Neil

Passariello AIDS Service Award, and the President's Award from The American Society of Group Psychotherapy and Psychodrama. He also served on their Executive Council and as Vice President. In 1992, he served on the Joint Commission of Accreditation of Healthcare Organization's Biopsychosocial Rehabilitation Task Force.

Pamela Dunne, Ph.D, RDT-BCT is the Director of the Drama Therapy Institute of Los Angeles. She directs a summer program for the Institute in Europe as well as opening a recent branch of the Institute in Italy. She is a Professor at California State University in Los Angeles, and a past President of the National Association for Drama Therapy. She directs workshops and trainings in Australia, New Zealand, Hong Kong, Europe and the Middle East. She has published over eight books, including *The Narrative Therapist and the Arts: 2nd Edition,* and *Narradrama: Integrating Drama Therapy, Narrative and the Creative Arts: 2nd Edition.* She has also produced a film, *Exploring Narradrama.*

Renée Emunah, Ph.D., RDT-BCT is the Founder/Director and Professor at the graduate Drama Therapy Program at the California Institute of Integral Studies in San Francisco. She is the author of the book, *Acting for Real: Drama Therapy Process, Technique and Performance,* which has been translated into Chinese and Japanese. She was the recipient of the Gertrud Schattner Award for Outstanding Contribution to the Field of Drama Therapy in 1996. She is a past president of the National Association for Drama Therapy. She is the author of many book chapters and articles, and served on the Editorial Board of the *International Journal of the Arts in Psychotherapy* from 1985–2002. For 15 years, she worked in psychiatric facilities with groups of adults and adolescents; more recently she has worked individually with children and adults, and in private practice. She has been invited to present her work at conferences, universities, and trainings internationally with a recent focus on teaching in Japan. In 2006, she was a keynote speaker at the Arts in Hospitals Conference in Hong Kong, and in 2008, the keynote speaker at the National Association for Drama Therapy Conference. She is listed in the 2009 edition of *Who's Who in America.* She is the co-editor of this edition of *Current Approaches.*

Diana Feldman, MA, LCAT, RDT-BCT serves as the Executive Director of ENACT, which she founded in 1987. As the developer of the ENACT Method, she has led workshops at national conferences on education, drama therapy and arts in education. In 2004, ENACT was awarded a Ford Foundation grant to further its research and evaluate the ENACT method. She is currently completing a book of short stories about her years working in classroom settings. Diana earned an MA in Educational Theatre from New York University.

Antonina Garcia, Ed.D., LCSW, TEP, RDT/BCT, CGP trains psychodramatists nationally and internationally and is in private practice. She is co-author with Patricia Sternberg of *Sociodrama: Who's in Your Shoes? 2nd Edition* (Praeger Press). Formerly she was Coordinator of the Creative Arts in Therapeutic Settings Option at Brookdale Community College and currently teaches at New York University in the Drama Therapy Masters Program. She is past executive editor of the *Journal of Group Psychotherapy and Psychodrama.* She is a Fellow of the American Society of Group Psychotherapy and Psychodrama, and past Chair of the American Board of Examiners in Psychodrama. She is also a recipient of the ASGPP J.L. Moreno Lifetime Achievement Award, the Scholar's Award and is a two-time winner of the Collaborator's Award. Dr. Garcia also appears in the DVD, *Three Approaches to Drama Therapy,* produced by Robert Landy, Ph.D.

Eleanor C. Irwin, Ph.D., RDT is one of the founding members of the National Association for Drama Therapy and a recipient of the Gertrud Schattner Award for Outstanding Contribution to the Field of Drama Therapy. She is certified as a Trainer, Educator, Practitioner in Psychodrama, and is a Licensed Clinical Psychologist. Dr. Irwin is a teacher and supervisor in the Department of Psychiatry at the University of Pittsburgh where she is a Clinical Assistant Professor. She is a past president and current Chair of the Child Analysis Committee of the Pittsburgh Psychoanalytic Center, a certified Child and Adult Psychoanalyst, and a Training and Supervising Analyst. Dr. Irwin has published articles and chapters in books on the clinical and creative use of drama, play, and expressive therapy; and with Judith A. Rubin, Ph.D., ATR-BC, she is the co-founder of Expressive Media, Inc., which is dedicated to the production and distribution of videos that support and encourage the use of the creative arts in mental health.

David Read Johnson, Ph.D., RDT-BCT is Director of the Institutes for the Arts in Psychotherapy, New York; Co-Director of the Post Traumatic Stress Center, New Haven, CT; and an Associate Clinical Professor, Department of Psychiatry, Yale University School of Medicine. He was a founding member and past President of the National Association for Drama Therapy, former Chairperson of the National Coalition for Arts Therapy Associations, and former editor-in-chief of the *International Journal of the Arts in Psychotherapy.* He currently trains students in Developmental Transformations and treatment methods for posttraumatic stress disorder. He has written numerous articles and book chapters, and the books: *Waiting at the Gate: Creativity and Hope in the Nursing Home* (with Susan Sandel), *Essays in the Creative Arts Therapies: Imaging the Birth of a Profession,* and *Trauma-Centered Group Psychotherapy for Women* (with Hadar Lubin). He has been the co-editor of both editions of *Current Approaches.*

Fara Sussman Jones, MA, RDT, LMSW is presently a senior social worker at the Jewish Board of Family and Children's Services (JBFCS), where she provides outpatient individual and family counseling to adolescents. She also conducts groups for teens in mainstream and alternative high school settings. At JBFCS, Fara facilitates staff development trainings and provides consultations to other professionals on the use of creative art therapy interventions and techniques. Fara received her MA in Drama Therapy from New York University in 1997, where she wrote her Master's thesis on the application of role theory with patients who suffer from chronic schizophrenia. She previously worked with ENACT as a Program Manager, Staff Development Trainer and Teaching Artist with at-risk teens, families and educators in the New York City school system, and provided clinical supervision to student interns.

Fionnuala Kenny graduated from University College, Dublin and was a member of the Abbey Theatre Company, the National Theatre of Ireland. She appeared frequently on Irish radio and television, and played distinguished Irish actor Siobhan McKenna's daughter in the centennial RTE presentation of J.M.Synge's *Riders to the Sea.* Following work in London at the Old Vic, the Royal Court (with Alan Simpson and the Dubliners) and with Mike Alfred's Shared Experience company at the Roundhouse, she completed post-graduate work at London University and began a career as an adult educator at West Thames College where she was the Head of Faculty for Arts and Communication Studies from 1993–1997. In 1997, she joined STOP-GAP as a Director.

Don R. Laffoon, MA, RDT-BCT, the co-Founder and Executive Director of STOP-GAP, is an internationally recognized theatre director who has lectured extensively and toured plays he has directed to Germany, Wales, Iran, and Australia. After receiving his M.A. in theatre (directing) at Purdue University, he had the honor and challenge of being asked to create the National Children's Theatre of Iran (having learned Persian as one of the first Peace Corps Volunteers to go abroad). He is the past-Chairperson of the National Coalition of Arts Therapies Associations and is a past president of the National Association of Drama Therapy. In addition to his numerous publications on theatre and drama therapy, he translated from Persian *The Butterfly,* a play written for him by Iran's greatest playwright, Bijan Mofid.

Robert J. Landy, Ph.D., RDT-BCT, LCAT is Professor of Educational Theatre and Applied Psychology, and Director of the Drama Therapy Program at New York University. A pioneer in the profession of drama therapy, he lectures and trains professionals internationally. As researcher and writer, Landy has published and produced numerous books, articles, films and plays in the fields of drama, drama therapy, musical theatre and related topics. He has been featured in the media in the CBS-TV series *Drama in Education,* the award-winning documentary film, *Standing Tall,* and his own production, *Three Approaches to Drama Therapy.* Landy has more than 40 years of clinical experience, having treated children and adults with a wide range of psychiatric, cognitive and adjustment problems. Recently he co-founded the Institute for Drama Therapy in New York City, offering workshops and trainings to both professionals and students. He has also worked in prisons, developing programs to treat mentally ill offenders as well as the general population within New York State correctional facilities. His latest book is *The Couch and the Stage: Integrating Words and Action in Psychotherapy,* published in 2008.

Penny Lewis, Ph.D., ADTR, RDT-BCT was Senior Faculty at Antioch University's Antioch-New England Graduate School, and Co-Director of the Certificate Program in Transpersonal Drama Therapy (with Saphira Linden), for many years. She authored many books including *Creative Transformation: The Healing Power of the Arts.* She served as the Chair of Alternate Route Training in the National Association for Drama Therapy, where she authored *The Alternate Route Training Handbook.* She was formerly a Special Guest Editor for the *International Journal of the Arts in Psychotherapy* and a co-editor of the first edition of this book. She lectured, presented, and published internationally from 1970, and maintained an active private practice in Amesbury, Massachusetts until her untimely death in 2003.

Saphira Barbara Linden, MA, RDT/BCT, LCAT, CP is co-founder and Director of the Omega Transpersonal Drama Therapy Certificate Program in Boston. She trained with Jacob and Zerka Moreno, is a Certified Practioner in Psychodrama, and is adjunct faculty, Lesley University. Since 1967 she has created and produced numerous award-winning original plays and arts events, including *The Cosmic Celebration,* a transformational theater pageant performed throughout the United States and Europe for 11 years. Her artistic work on participational theater was the subject of a half hour film on the National PBS Series, *Artists in America.* She has trained hundreds of professionals in the arts, mental health, education, and organizational development. Ms. Linden has a private practice in Boston, where she has worked since 1971 as a transpersonal psychotherapist, a Sufi meditation teacher and guide, and a management consultant. The author of numerous articles and book chapters, she is currently writing, *The Soul of Drama Therapy: A Comprehensive Guide to Transpersonal Drama Therapy in Theory and Practice.*

Nisha Sajnani, MA, CCC, RDT is Director of Creative Alternatives, Montreal; Drama Therapist, Post Traumatic Stress Center, New Haven, Connecticut; Ethics Chair of the National Association for Drama Therapy; and past president of the Creative Arts in Counseling Chapter, Canadian Counseling Association. Nisha has worked across diverse communities in both clinical and community settings with individuals, couples, families, and groups for the last 15 years.

Jo Salas, MA is the co-founder of Playback Theatre, and has been the artistic director of Hudson River Playback Theatre since 1990. Her publications include *Improvising Real Life: Personal Story in Playback Theatre,* now published in seven languages, and a second book, *Do My Story, Sing My Song: Music Therapy and Playback Theatre with Troubled Children,* as well as numerous articles. She is a core faculty member of the Centre for Playback Theatre and teaches internationally. She holds a Master's degree in music therapy from New York University and was certified as a music therapist by the American Association for Music Therapy.

Stephen Snow, Ph.D., RDT-BCT is co-founder of the Drama Therapy Graduate Program at Concordia University, where he is presently Associate Professor, Chair of the Department of Creative Arts Therapies, and Director of Creative Arts Therapies at The Center for the Arts in Human Development. Since 1985, he has worked in geriatrics, psychiatric rehabilitation, with the developmentally disabled, and in private practice. He has presented internationally on therapeutic theatre, having directed 30 theatre productions with people with special needs. His has written numerous articles and book chapters on drama therapy, and is the co-editor of *Assessment in the Creative Arts Therapies* (Charles C Thomas, Publishers). Dr. Snow received the Gertrud Schattner Award for Outstanding Contribution to the Field of Drama Therapy in 2001 and the Research Award in 2004. He was co-recipient of the Innovation and Research Award from the American Association for Intellectual and Developmental Disabilities in 2006. Most recently, he has created *The Initiative for the Advanced Study of Culture, Conflict and the Arts Therapies* at Concordia University.

Patricia Sternberg, Ph.D., RDT-BCT is a recipient of the Gertrud Schattner Award for Outstanding Contribution to the Field of Drama Therapy. She is Professor Emeritus of the Theatre Department at Hunter College in New York City, where she led the Developmental Drama program for many years. She is a playwright with over 25 plays produced and/or published and the author of eight books including *Sociodrama: Who's in Your Shoes?* (with Antonina Garcia), and *Theatre for Conflict Resolution.* She is a well-known trainer, presenter, and workshop leader nationally and internationally. Dr. Sternberg is a practicing drama therapist who has worked with a variety of populations in both psychiatric and educational facilities.

Armand Volkas, MFA, MA, MFT, RDT-BCT is a psychotherapist and drama therapist in private practice. He is Clinical Director of the Living Arts Counseling Center in Oakland, California where he directs a training program for students, interns and licensed psychotherapists who want to integrate drama therapy into their practice. He is an Associate Professor in the Drama Therapy Program at California Institute of Integral Studies. Since 1988, he has been Artistic Director of The Living Arts Playback Theatre Ensemble. For many years, Mr. Volkas has developed innovative programs using drama therapy for social change, intercultural conflict resolution, reconciliation and intercultural communication, such as *Healing the Wounds of History,* which has received international recognition for its work in bringing groups in conflict together.

Emilie Ward, MA, LCAT, RDT received her B.A. from Sarah Lawrence College and her Masters degree in Drama Therapy from New York University. She is the Director of Training and Research for ENACT, training and mentoring teaching-artists and running workshops for students, staff and parents for 11 years. She has led workshops at national conferences on education, drama therapy and arts in education. Her drama therapy background includes working in Child Life at the Brooklyn Hospital Center and with a formerly homeless and mentally ill population at Goddard Riverside Community Center's outpatient rehabilitation program, The Other Place.

Daniel J. Wiener, Ph.D., RDT-BCT is a Professor of Counseling and Family Therapy at Central Connecticut State University, and in private practice in West Hartford, Connecticut and Leverett, Massachusetts as a licensed psychologist and marriage and family therapist. He is a Diplomate in Family Psychology, an AAMFT Approved Supervisor and a Certified Group Psychotherapist. Having founded Rehearsals for Growth (RfG) in 1985, he has presented numerous workshops, nationally and internationally. In addition to authoring numerous professional articles and book chapters, Dr. Wiener has published two books: *Rehearsals for Growth: Theater Improvisation for Psychotherapists,* and *Rehearsals for Growth: Collected papers, 1991–2004,* and has edited /co-edited three others: *Beyond Talk Therapy: Using Movement and Expressive Techniques in Clinical Practice; Action Therapy with Families and Groups: Using Creative Arts Improvisation in Clinical Practice;* and *Interactive and Improvisational Drama: Varieties of Applied Theatre and Performance.* He is the recipient of a number of teaching awards, the 1997 Zerka T. Moreno Award by the American Society for Group Psychotherapy and Psychodrama, and the 2006 Research Award by the National Association for Drama Therapy.

PREFACE

This second edition of *Current Approaches in Drama Therapy* provides a comprehensive compilation of the primary drama therapy methods and models that are being utilized and taught in the United States and Canada. This edition offers experienced practitioners and board certified trainers of drama therapy, as well as students and newcomers to the field, an updated articulation of theoretical and clinical approaches to drama therapy practice. This volume is therefore recommended as a basic text in the field of drama therapy. Every aspect of the book has been updated and revised, including a comprehensive bibliography on drama therapy. We have added four new approaches in this edition: "Healing the Wounds of History," by Armand Volkas; "Rehearsals for Growth," by Daniel Wiener; "Performance in Drama Therapy," by Sally Bailey; and "Theatre of the Oppressed," by Nisha Sajnani. Their addition is a good indication of the continued vivacity and growth of our profession.

The approaches were selected on the basis of the fact that they have been taught in universities and institutes, presented at national conferences, and published in professional journals. Each of the chapters is authored either by the founder or a key proponent of that approach to drama therapy. Each author accepted the discipline of writing the chapter within a prescribed format, including updated theoretical and conceptual premises, as well as one or more case examples. Authors were encouraged to compare their approach to that of other primary approaches in the field, and evidence of this dialogue is much more present in this edition. It is important to note that we do not presume that this book includes all approaches in the field, nor were we able to include the work of many gifted clinicians who have yet to articulate a particular model or approach. Further editions will continue the process of expanding the body of knowledge in the field.

Section I provides a context for the state of the field of drama therapy in North America. The first chapter describes the history of the field. The second chapter discusses stages in professional development and theory building. A third chapter examines advances in clinical practice, especially over the past decade, emerging areas of interest, and challenges for the future. Section II contains 14 specific approaches to drama therapy. Section III describes four related approaches–*Psychodrama, Sociodrama, Playback Theatre,* and *Theatre of the Oppressed,* each of which has had significant influence on drama therapy practice despite their founders not identifying as drama therapists. A separate index of key concepts in drama therapy is included in this new edition, demonstrating the consolidation and breadth of theory in the field.

We are aware that this second edition of *Current Approaches* is part of a continuous professional challenge: to articulate the similarities and differences among various methods within one discipline. Each approach in this book is at the same time a unique set of ideas and methods, and a variation of the fundamental processes that underlie drama and psychotherapy. It will be through an active dialogue among these perspectives that our profession will continue to mature. The rapid transformation of our local and global cultural environments will continue to challenge our creativity and flexibility in adapting drama therapy methods to the changing needs of our clients and society.

DAVID READ JOHNSON AND RENÉE EMUNAH, EDITORS

ACKNOWLEDGMENTS

We wish to thank the contributing authors who graciously and enthusiastically joined with us in the preparation of this volume. Support for this effort also came from the National Association for Drama Therapy and Sally Bailey, who aided in the updating of the drama therapy bibliography. We appreciate the assistance of Sarah Harkness in editing of text and preparing the index and Beth Van Buecken in updating the bibliography. Our publisher, Michael Thomas, offered continuous support and patience throughout the entire process. Finally, we thank the clients whose courageous journeys are reflected in the many case examples throughout the book; it is you that have given the authors the inspiration and motivation to develop these approaches to healing.

CONTENTS

SECTION III: RELATED APPROACHES

CURRENT APPROACHES IN DRAMA THERAPY

Section I

THE STATE OF THE FIELD

Chapter 1

THE HISTORY AND DEVELOPMENT OF THE FIELD OF DRAMA THERAPY IN NORTH AMERICA

DAVID READ JOHNSON

THE CREATOR

In the beginning, there was Moreno. This visionary single-handedly discovered drama therapy in the 1920s. His theatre of spontaneity, use of improvisation, and theatrical sensibility make him the original drama therapist (Moreno, 1946). Though there were others who used drama as therapy (including de Sade, Evreinov, Iljine–see an excellent review by Phil Jones, 1996), none had any substantial influence on the future of the field since there was no transmission of their work to others. Moreno, on the other hand, did nothing less than expand forever the boundaries of what was possible in psychotherapy.

Moreno trained as a psychiatrist, but his longstanding interest and activities in theatre led him to the discovery of *Psychodrama* by the early 1920s. In 1925, he emigrated to the United States, where he revolutionized the practice of psychotherapy until his death in 1974. While he was at St. Elizabeth's Hospital in Washington, he influenced Marian Chace, the originator of dance therapy, as well as many art and music therapists. In New York during the 1950s, hundreds of therapists attended his workshops and presentations, many of whom later became leaders of the humanistic and encounter movement (e.g., Fritz Perls–Gestalt Therapy; Eric Berne–Transactional Analysis; Arthur Janov–Primal Scream).

Moreno's psychodramatic writings provide a strong foundation for drama therapy, and for some time it seemed that no more needed to be said: How could anyone imagine a drama therapy that was not Moreno's? However, in the late 1960s, a new group of theatre artists entered the mental health field–partly as a result of the cultural changes evoked by the Vietnam War, and partly due to the expansion of art, music, and dance therapies. As these theatre people encountered psychodrama, they found it wanting. Because Moreno had intended to influence his psychiatric colleagues, he had encapsulated his methods into a structured form, reminiscent of an enacted psychiatric interview. As a result, his method began to stray from the aesthetics of its theatrical roots. Increasingly, his audience had become mental health professionals rather than theatre people, so theatre training was not incorporated into the required training of a psychodramatist. A breach had developed between psychodrama's theatrical roots and its actual practice, a breach into which a number of drama therapy pioneers leapt.

THE TITANS

There were five of them. Each contributed in a special way to the creation of the field of drama therapy. Though by the 1960s there were many people practicing some form of drama therapy, these five had an influence that reached out beyond their immediate areas, inspiring others to move toward drama therapy. Each one embraced this new entity of drama therapy; without them, drama therapy as a profession may never have been born.

Eleanor Irwin received her degree in speech therapy, but found herself at the Pittsburgh Child Guidance Clinic under the tutelage and mentorship of Marvin Shapiro, a gifted psychiatrist who encouraged Ellie and other future creative arts therapists. Out of that clinic came Judith Rubin, Penny Lewis, as well as Ellie, all who have become leaders in their respective fields. Ellie Irwin published the first articles on drama therapy in the early 1970s, and soon they found their way into the hands of other drama therapists, inspiring us greatly (Irwin, Levy, & Shapiro, 1972; Irwin, 1977). Her work was characterized by careful, rigorous clinical descriptions of cases, clear articulation of a theoretical base, and a delight in the play of children. Her psychoanalytic background (she later become a psychoanalyst) served her well in rooting her work in a widely accepted area of scholarship. As a link between drama therapists and the psychiatric community, Ellie Irwin was far ahead of everyone else in her integration of these perspectives. Her articles provided deep reassurance that we had the capacity to stand up to the scrutiny of psychiatrists.

Marian (Billy) Lindkvist founded the Sesame Institute in 1964 in London, which integrated psychiatric principles and research with movement, art, and drama (Wethered, 1973). She established a full-time course in drama therapy in 1974. Both Renee Emunah and Lynn Temple studied with her in London at Sesame. She also made several trips to the United States during which I and others were profoundly impacted. Marian was influenced by the British tradition of drama-in-education of Brian Way (1967) and Peter Slade (1954), in which guided play was used to explore topics of both social and personal importance. She also did much work on shamanic ritual, particularly in African cultures, which drew her to Jungian concepts of archetypal expression. She extended her own and Sesame's work with children to the elderly, adult psychiatric patients, people from various cultures, and even "normal" people (Pearson, 1996). Sesame had a serious research interest, and one of the first outcome studies in drama therapy was done with chronic schizophrenic adults with Sesame clinicians (Nitsun et al., 1974). Though Slade had written about drama therapy much earlier, he always had his feet planted on educational soil. Billy took a bold step over the line, committing herself entirely to the therapeutic arena.

Sue Jennings wrote *Remedial Drama* in 1973, one of the first books on drama therapy. She later started a course in drama therapy at St. Albans, University of Hertfordshire, and helped to create the British Association of Drama Therapy in 1977. Since then she has developed training programs throughout Europe, Greece, and Israel, and has written numerous books and journal articles. She has been the Johnny Appleseed of our profession, always traveling, sowing seeds of inspiration and wisdom on her way. Sue also emerged from the drama-in-education tradition in England, though she has preserved the influence of the professional stage and the literature of Shakespeare in her practice. She has remained a powerful influence on the professional development of drama therapy internationally. United States and Canadian drama therapists were well aware of her work, which provided a strong impetus to us as we gave birth to a new profession.

Richard Courtney was steeped in the drama-in-education tradition of Britain, but was able to extend the field far into psychology and psychotherapy in his book, *Play, Drama, and Thought,* which was published in 1968 and spurred many of us on. This book established once and for all the links between drama and psychology. He later helped Gertrud Schattner finish editing her book on drama therapy. Richard was a man of immense breadth of knowledge and interest, who effortlessly wove intellectual themes among fields of great diversity. He became fascinated by the potential of drama for personal growth–at first from an educational point of view, and then later from a psychotherapeutic point of view. The essence of a British gentleman, mediated by years of living and teaching in Canada, he brought an air of gentility, perspective, and worldliness to the beginnings of the drama therapy movement. He died in 1997.

Gertrud Schattner spent much of World War II in Switzerland with her psychoanalyst husband. After the war, she used drama with concentration camp survivors. She came to this country and trained in the Karen Horney Clinic in psychotherapy. For years she taught drama and then drama therapy workshops and courses, settling in at Bellevue Hospital and Turtle Bay Music School in the 1960s. Her life mission was drama therapy. Trained professionally as an actress in Europe, even working with Otto Preminger in prewar Austria, she became influenced by Viola Spolin (1963) and creative drama approaches including improvisation. Her work grew out of theatre games, movement exercises, and improvisational role-playing. After the war she had developed a clear vision of drama therapy which she embraced without an ounce of misgiving. Though she was not a writer, she initiated the project of an edited book that brought all of us together, and was instrumental in bringing the National Association for Drama Therapy into being. Her fiery commitment to the field was the match that lit the smoldering doubts of others, igniting us into action. She died in 1994.

These were our Titans. Though few of them were friends, each cast a large shadow, providing a protective shade for the developing profession.

OUT OF THE DESERT

By 1974, many people were experimenting with what we now know as drama therapy: Don Laffoon at Stop Gap in Los Angeles; Janet Goodrich with addicts in Washington, DC; Margaret Ladd and Imagination Workshop in New York; Rosilyn Wilder, Toddy Richman, Naida Weisberg and Rose Pavlow with children and the elderly; Renee Emunah with psychiatric patients; Elaine Portner with families; Barbara Sandberg at William Paterson College; Ray Gordon with ex-prisoners at the Cell Block Theatre; John Bergman at Geese Theatre; and myself at the Yale Psychiatric Institute. Numerous psychodramatists such as Adam Blatner, Nina Garcia, and Jonathan Fox were rediscovering the theatrical roots in Moreno's teachings. Others, such as Lynn Temple, Pat Sternberg, Pam Dunne, and Bernie Warren, were also winding their way from creative drama to drama therapy.

In 1974, with some trepidation I presented a workshop on "drama therapy" at the Psychodrama Conference. Previously, drama therapists cloaked their presentations under the term, *Sociodrama*. After my talk, a short, older woman approached me, and without speaking, handed me a slip of paper. It read: "Hello, I am Gert Schattner. I am editing a book on drama therapy. Would you like to contribute a chapter?" In this way she had been collecting drama therapists all across the country. Even then she had a clear idea that we needed an association, though she thought that a book should come first. During the years 1974 to 1978, due to the need to develop the book, a network began to develop among nascent drama therapists. As Gert had good friends in New Haven, she and I took many train rides together between New York and New Haven, debating and dreaming about our profession-to-be. Finally, in 1977, Gertrud and I decided it was time to begin the association, so we invited Eleanor Irwin, Barbara Sandberg, and Ray Gordon to join us for a weekend in February, 1978, in order to decide if drama therapy existed as a separate field. Not surprisingly, in about five minutes we had decided that it did exist, and spent the rest of the weekend planning the association. We wondered how psychodramatists might respond to the announcement of our existence. We recognized that each of us had gained much from our psychodrama training, and had always been welcomed into the psychodrama world. Ultimately, we realized the anxiety was ours, not theirs. We then jointly invited 17 drama therapists to join us as a Steering Committee to form the association.

ESTABLISHING BOUNDARIES

The Steering Committee met in Ray Gordon's Cell Block Theatre in New York City on April 9, 1978. The meeting was audiotaped and transcribed, and even now makes fascinating reading for anyone interested in the issues we struggled with then. The Steering Committee met three more times, elected a Board of Directors, and incorporated the National Association for Drama Therapy in June, 1979.

The main issue was boundaries. If we were carving a new territory out of theatre, creative drama, psychodrama, psychotherapy, and play therapy, where were the lines? We needed to define ourselves specifically enough to have a meaningful identity, but if we drew the lines too narrowly, few present would qualify! As each person spoke, their definition of drama therapy inevitably left someone else out, who then became upset. At one point in the proceedings, someone said, "If you insist that to be a drama therapist you have to have two years of clinical practice, then that immediately excludes me and it excludes other things that I'm doing with the people I work with." Another countered, "Until there are qualifications, we don't know if any of us are qualified to be drama therapists." "Are we talking only about severely disturbed people in hospitals or does drama therapy also include the normal neurotic?" There were people with little clinical training, people who had been drama therapists and were no longer working, and people with little theatre training. Everyone understood what a real drama therapist should be, but no one matched the description entirely! It certainly would have been silly to form an association that no one would be allowed to join, but that is how we often made ourselves feel during those fretful meetings.

The Steering Committee was an effective transitional structure in which to begin the sorting out process. Fundamentally, people who were there for more peripheral reasons dropped out, while those who found themselves closer to the center of an emerging vision, remained. Though there was tremendous dissension and distress, we emerged without a major split in the organization at its birth. Gertrud became the first president, and I became the vice-president. Ironically, the book (Schattner & Courtney, 1981) that had pulled us together was not published until two years after the association was incorporated.

ESTABLISHING LEADERSHIP

The next three years were a period of establishing the initial leadership and control of the organization among the different interests represented on the steering committee and in the field at large.

The view that the organization should be a formal one, with standards, in compliance with the structures of other arts therapy associations, versus a more entrepreneurial, albeit nonprofit, model was now played out within the Board. The need to remain open to new members and not be too exclusive was paramount in order to facilitate an energetic recruitment. How could this be done without inviting too much diversity that might fragment the organization? In the beginning, the more clinical, psychiatric values represented most by Ellie and myself came to dominate the Board. Later, as basic standards had been established, a need for recruitment of new members and integration of related people led to finding ways of being more flexible.

The Board proceeded to establish standards of practice, registration, grandparenting, and ethical guidelines. As each standard was discussed, the fears that a new boundary was being erected that would eliminate people had to be dealt with. There were esteemed practitioners and authors who for one reason or another did not satisfy one or more of the requirements, or, alternatively, practitioners who did qualify but had not chosen to join us. Conflicts within the Board leadership were usually generated by these concerns. A great deal of elbow grease was used to navigate through these difficult personal and political waters during these early years. Fortunately, no major breaks occurred.

ESTABLISHING PROGRAMS

Meanwhile, two Masters Degree programs were being established by two leaders in the field, Robert Landy and Renee Emunah, neither of whom was a part of the founding group, but who had been actively involved in drama therapy for years. Robert Landy began the drama therapy program in the Educational Theatre department at New York University in 1982. Renee founded a drama therapy program in the Psychology Department at Antioch University West in San Francisco in 1983 (the program moved to the California Institute of Integral Studies in 1989). The stability of these two professional programs over the years has provided the field with a rich network of relationships among students, faculty, and related professions, anchoring us in a constantly changing and challenging healthcare environment. Within a few years it became apparent that the future of the field was dependent upon these two programs, and others to be established. For the first time, in addition to independent pioneers each of whom had invented drama therapy, we now had students who were asking questions such as: what is our body of knowledge?

The very act of establishing a Masters Degree program raises the question: what are we teaching? We had barely begun to share our different perspectives on drama therapy; barely decided that it was not psychodrama, and we were supposed to have a curriculum based on a body of knowledge for our students! What proportion of courses should be psychology or psychotherapy-based? What drama therapy techniques should be taught, or could be taught? Should psychodrama be taught? How much previous theatre training should be required, and how much ongoing performance or theatre work should be integrated into the Masters? What about internships, and jobs beyond internships? Generally, neither program had enough money to hire many full-time drama therapy faculty, or invite many visiting drama therapists to teach, leaving their programs vulnerable to a lack of diversity. The Association's role was to develop standards of training, evaluate, and finally approve Masters programs without unnecessarily constraining them. Too vigorous an approach might strangle the very beginnings of our own profession! Despite these challenges, there was good communication and support among all involved to encourage the growth of these two programs. For example, with input from the two program directors, the standards for approval of graduate programs were implemented in 1986 with a strong consensus.

REACHING OUT

Development of professional standards and masters programs, as well as furthering our networking through national conferences, continued during the period 1982–1985. We became active in the efforts of the newly formed National Coalition of Arts Therapy Associations, becoming a member in 1983, and participating in the first National Coalition of Arts Therapy Associations Conference in New York City in 1985. We found ourselves thrust among larger, more established creative arts therapy associations. Our eyes were opened to legislative, legal, ethical, and professional dilemmas. We began to understand that we were part of a larger effort. We found ourselves on committees studying state licensure of creative arts therapists, regulatory agencies, and third party insurance reimbursement. We were represented in state coalitions of creative arts therapists. We learned how other associations were dealing with malpractice issues, sexual indiscretions, taxes, and lawsuits. These experiences were both exhilarating and intimidating, given our level of development.

The conference also gave us the opportunity to integrate another awkward split between American and British drama therapists. Many of us had trained in England, and some, like Renee Emunah, Lynn Temple, and others, had worked directly with Marian Lindkvist or Sue Jennings. Increasingly, students and faculty from the States visited England for training, and both Sue Jennings and Marian Lindkvist presented at our conferences. Currently, there remains strong impetus for international participation in our conferences and educational events, and links with the international drama therapy community continue to grow.

SCHOOLS OF THOUGHT

By 1985, however, there still were only beginning efforts to conceptualize approaches to drama therapy. Until that time, one could identify a psychoanalytic approach, represented by Eleanor Irwin and her Pittsburgh colleagues; a psychodramatic approach, in which drama therapists applied

Moreno's theories; a performance approach, based on theatrical traditions but without a significant theoretical basis; and a somewhat generic improvisation or theatre game approach, based on Viola Spolin's work.

The years 1985 to the present have seen the development of more sophisticated schools of thought emerge within the drama therapy field. Robert Landy developed distancing theory and in his book, *Drama Therapy: Theory and Practice,* (1986) provided the most in depth conceptual framework for drama therapy yet published. Now he has deepened this perspective further with role method, which he has elaborated in *Persona and Performance: The Use of Role in Therapy and Everyday Life* (1993). As the head of the New York University Program, he has been very influential in creating a group of students who are grounded in the same approach. Renee Emunah has developed her Integrative Five Phase approach based on humanistic and developmental principles, presented in her book, *Acting for Real* (1994). Her model is generally viewed as the most sophisticated integration of various drama therapy processes and techniques available today. I worked on an approach called *Developmental Transformations* (Johnson, Forrester, Dintino, James, & Schnee, 1996), which is now taught through a three-year postgraduate institute training program. Pam Dunne developed a narrative approach to drama therapy based on postmodern theories (Dunne, 1992), and Jonathan Fox greatly refined and extended his *Playback Theatre* model and training program (Fox, 1994). Other models, most of which are included in this book, have continued to emerge and are increasingly being recognized in publications and conferences.

As the number of discrete models grows, it is critical that meta-analyses be conducted to compare and contrast them on fundamental principles relevant to drama therapy. Phil Jones contributed greatly to this effort in his book, *Drama as Therapy* (1996). Penny Lewis and I continued with the first edition of *Current Approaches to Drama Therapy* (2000), and Robert Landy has recently contrasted three approaches in drama therapy in his book, *The Couch and the Stage* (2008).

A FAMILY TREE

It is important to understand these approaches from an historical standpoint, to know from what roots we have sprung. As a step in that direction, I have outlined the general family tree of drama therapy approaches in Figure 1.1. Certainly it should be stressed that this diagram is greatly simplified in order to identify the major traditions that have influenced the development of drama therapy. In actuality, most approaches have been influenced by many factors, and are increasingly overlapping as they integrate each other's insights. The turn of the century produced three movements that made possible the creation of drama therapy: psychotherapy, occupational therapy, and the acting training of Stanislavski.

Psychotherapy

Freud's contribution to the development of drama therapy cannot be overestimated. The very possibility of psychotherapy exists due to his insights, and concepts such as the unconscious, projection, transference, and symbolism, now taken for granted, are psychoanalytic in origin. Carl Jung, Melanie Klein, Anna Freud, Erik Erikson and Jacob Moreno developed his ideas further, producing the methods of active imagination, play therapy, and psychodrama, from which many branches of drama therapy emerge, as indicated in Figure 1.1. Margaret Mahler's developmental perspective and Donald

Winnicott's notion of transitional space have also been very influential among drama therapists. Jungian influence has brought an interest in myths, rituals, culture, and spirituality into the psychotherapeutic arena, offering a welcoming environment for many drama therapists.

Occupational Therapy

Occupational therapy began as a profession at the turn of the century because nursing had become professionalized to the point that nurses no longer cared for the recreational needs of psychiatric patients. Occupational therapists used the arts in their work, and indeed there are several articles published early in the century entitled drama therapy. By the 1940s however, occupational therapists had also turned to more specialized pursuits, opening up the way for the new profession of activities therapies, which then divided in the 1970s into recreation therapy and the creative arts therapies (Mosey, 1973). Drama therapy as a professional identity was formed largely through the transformations in these disciplines, and many drama therapists today are hired in job lines that go back in history to activity therapists, occupational therapists, and even nurses. Nevertheless, when the drama therapy association formed, the field of creative arts therapies was ready to accept it, and our profession was modeled after those of art, music, and dance therapies. In terms of employment, this was our initial home. Many drama therapists working in this tradition of psychiatric care have naturally adopted integrated and eclectic models, and it is of no surprise that the most sophisticated of these, Emunah's *Integrative Five Phase Model* (Emunah, 1994) was developed in this context.

Theatre

Stanislavski was pivotal in linking theories of acting to the personal, psychological realm of experience (Stanislavski, 1961). From this critical shift, Artaud later developed the ideas of suffering, emotion, and physicality, while Brecht explored the concepts of distance, cognition, and insight. Each of these orientations to theatre were developed further in the 1960s by Grotowski and Beckett, respectively, influencing many drama therapist's orientations (e.g., Brecht on the Role Method; Grotowski on Developmental Transformations). Separately, the emphases on stage performance and on improvisation continue to provide a methodological basis for many drama therapists, who may create therapeutic productions with clients, or who use improvisational theatre games and other exercises in their sessions. The relative absence of theoretical refinements in these areas is balanced by the well-established power of these primary theatrical experiences on participants. Finally, the drama-in-education movement in England produced a large number of practitioners who became interested in drama for personal growth, a tradition that has influenced many drama therapists. Today these models might be called play process models, since they retain much of the developmental qualities of the earlier work with children.

The Boundary of Drama Therapy

The 1960s gave the creative arts therapy movement a tremendous impetus, and practitioners in all areas–psychotherapy, theatre, and psychiatric care–were tiptoeing up to the idea of drama therapy, often without calling it by name. By the beginning of the 1970s, however, the time was apparently ripe for people to move over the line into drama

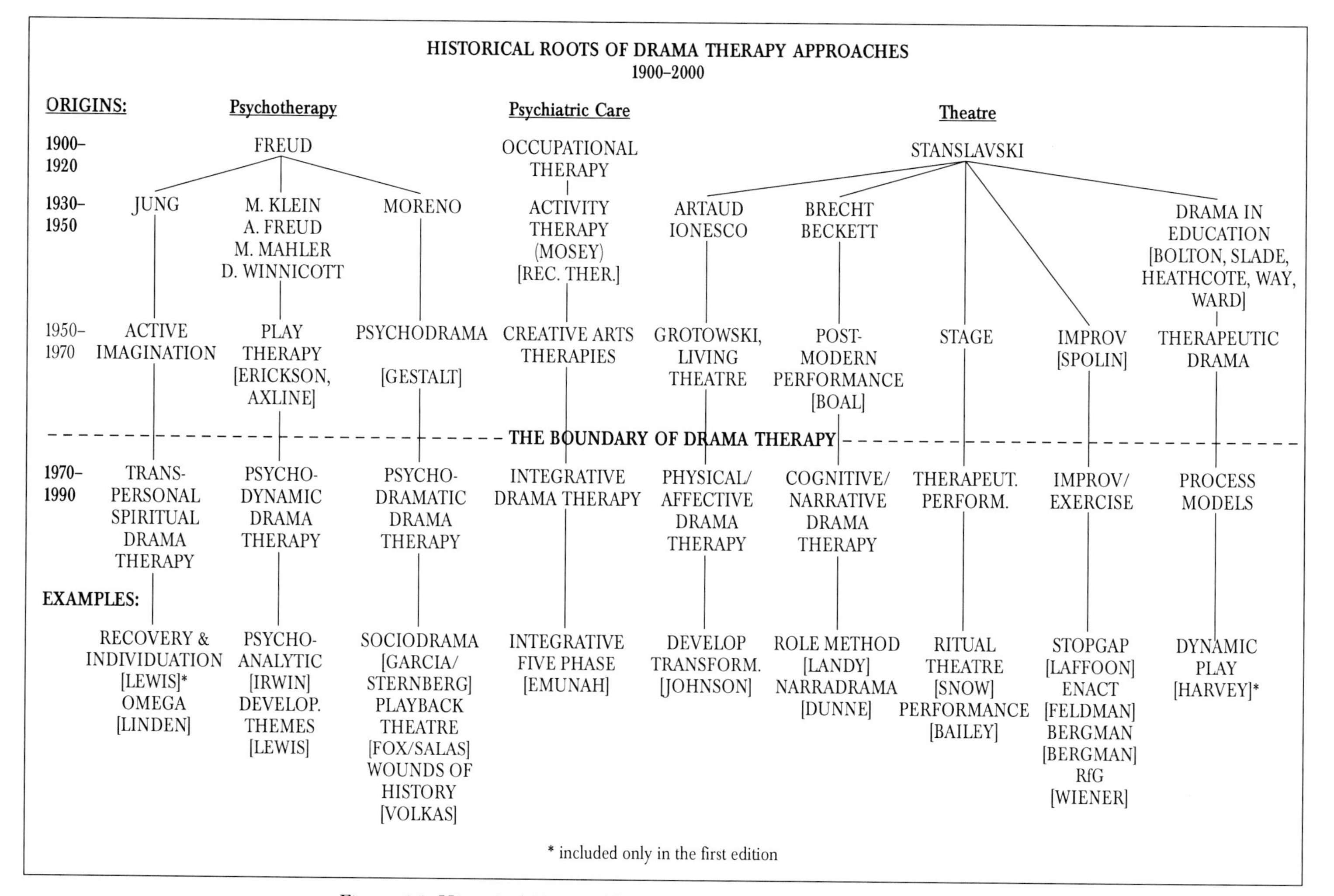

Figure 1.1. Historical Roots of Drama Therapy Approaches, 1900–2000.

therapy proper. Most practitioners were influenced by many of these approaches and have integrated them in their own ways. Some drama therapy methods, however, have retained their links to a particular tradition. I have listed some examples of these approaches in Figure 1.1.

Though there are only a few schools of thought in the field of drama therapy, we are now on the edge of a more sophisticated dialogue among them and within them. Until recently, the field has been characterized by a panoply of techniques, approaches, and personalities; a wonderful collection of creative and unique people. Now as distinct approaches are articulated, differences can be examined, preferences debated, and loyalties tested. The result will certainly be further clarification of approaches, deepening of the clinical work, and maturing of the profession.

STUDENTS AND MENTORS: A PROFESSION

We are now faced with our future. As a small profession we have both the capacity to make changes rapidly, as well as the vulnerability to influences from our environment. It is crucial that we continue to articulate our specific vision. Four challenges in particular loom large on our horizon. First, we need to develop new university programs, to expand beyond the three approved ones (Stephen Snow directs the program at Concordia University in Montreal, Canada, founded in 1997). We need to supply the field with a larger flow of students. The recent initiation of the Alternative Training program has allowed new institutes to form, providing more training opportunities to potential students. Second, we need to expand opportunities for advanced training beyond the internship and Masters degree, to allow apprenticeships under caring mentors to help students internalize an identity as a drama therapist. Otherwise, we will be vulnerable to professional drift, where students move into other more established professions after training in ours. The establishment of Ph.D. programs will eventually be necessary. This advanced training will also allow for the dialoguing and colleagueship necessary for each school of thought to deepen and become more sophisticated. Third, we need to write books. The production of excellent books will attract new students into our programs, as well as establish our field within academic circles. In this way we also contribute to the overall health care system. Finally, we need to participate with the other creative arts therapy organizations in legislative and regulatory arenas, both in order to protect our professional interests, and to protect the needs of our clients. Essential to that process will be the willingness to join with others in coalitions or a multidivisional National Creative Arts Therapy Association (Johnson, 1999). The recent approval of the Creative Arts Therapy license in the State of New York has been a tremendous accomplishment for the field. Many other states now allow Masters trained drama therapists to become licensed as Professional Counselors or Marriage and Family Therapists, which many in the profession have achieved. The constant challenges presented to us by managed care, the recent hegemony of cognitive-behavioral forms of treatment, and the culture of the Internet will be important issues for our profession to face in the coming years.

Our field will be a temporary one unless we are able to manage the organizational demands of a maturing profession, and articulate our specific contributions to health care. This is not done through advertising or impression management. It is accomplished by attracting students of excellence, providing effective training, and creating an environment of exploration, depth, and focus. Through the efforts of many individuals over half a century, drama therapists have laid a foundation upon which we can build an enduring profession.

REFERENCES

Courtney, R. (1968). *Play, drama, and thought.* New York: Drama Book Specialists.

Dunne, P. (1992). *The narrative therapist and the arts.* Los Angeles: Possibilities Press.

Emunah, R. (1994). *Acting for real: Drama therapy process, technique and performance.* New York: Brunner/ Mazel.

Fox, J. (1994). *Acts of service: Spontaneity, commitment, tradition in the nonscripted theatre.* New Paltz, NY: Tusitala Publishing.

Irwin, E., Levy, P., & Shapiro, M. (1972). Assessment of drama therapy in a child guidance setting. *Group Psychotherapy & Psychodrama, 25,* 105–116.

Irwin, E. (1977). Play, fantasy, and symbols: Drama with emotionally disturbed children. *American Journal of Psychotherapy, 31,* 426–436.

Jennings, S. (1973). *Remedial drama.* London: Black Publishers.

Johnson, D., Forrester, A., Dintino, C., James, M., & Schnee, G. (1996). Towards a poor drama therapy. *The Arts in Psychotherapy, 23,* 293–306.

Johnson, D. (1999). *Essays on the creative arts therapies: Imaging the birth of a profession.* Springfield, IL: Charles C Thomas.

Jones, P. (1996). *Drama as therapy: Theatre as living.* London: Routledge.

Landy, R. (1986). *Drama therapy: Concepts and practices.* Springfield, IL: Charles C Thomas.

Landy, R. (1993). *Persona and performance: The use of role in therapy and everyday life.* New York: Guilford.

Landy, R. (2008). *The couch and the stage.* New York: Jason Aronson.

Mahler, M. (1968). *On human symbiosis and vicissitudes of individuation.* New York: International Universities Press.

Moreno, J. (1946) *Psychodrama. Vols. I–III.* Beacon, NY: Beacon Press.

Mosey, A. (1973). *Activities therapy.* New York: Raven Press.

Nitsun, M., et al. (1974). Movement and drama therapy with long-stay schizophrenics. *British Journal of Medical Psychology, 47,* 101–119.

Pearson, J. (Ed.). (1996). *Discovering the self through drama and movement.* London: Jessica Kingsley.

Schattner, G., & Courtney, R., (Eds.), (1981). *Drama in therapy, Vols I & II.* New York: Drama Book Specialists.

Slade, P. (1954). *Child drama.* London: University of London.

Spolin, V. (1963). *Improvisation for the theater.* Evanston, IL: Northwestern University.

Stanislavski, S. (1961). *Creating a role.* London: Methuen.

Way, B. (1967). *Development through drama.* London: Longman.

Wethered, A. (1973). *Movement and drama in therapy.* London: MacDonald and Evans.

Winnicott, D.W. (1971). *Playing and reality.* New York: Penguin Books.

FOR FURTHER INFORMATION:

National Association for Drama Therapy
21991 Sunstone Court
Ashburn, VA 20148
Tel.: 571-333-5725
www.naat.org

Chapter 2

THE DEVELOPMENT OF THEORY AND METHODS IN DRAMA THERAPY

David Read Johnson, Renée Emunah, and Penny Lewis

The primary bond among drama therapists is a general sentiment that theatre processes have healing potential; surprisingly, we are linked less by our theories and methods. Our profession has emerged out of direct clinical experience, and only now are we developing and articulating theories and methods that support this experience. This book intends to provide a detailed view of the state of our developing profession in the United States and Canada. (Similar reviews of models in the United Kingdom can be found in Jennings, 1987; 1992; 1997; Jones, 2007.) Each of the key approaches in drama therapy presented here has something of value to contribute to the understanding and practice of drama therapy. For the most part, these theories and methods are still closely linked to their originators, as training programs that disseminate these knowledge bases have existed for a relatively short time.

Phil Jones (1996) has warned us about the proliferation of approaches which tend to highlight their uniqueness, thereby overlooking the tremendous overlap among them. Indeed, as one reads the chapters in this book, one can readily see similar themes, concepts, and principles, often named differently or justified by different psychological theories.

THE LEVEL OF AUTONOMY IN DRAMA THERAPY THEORY

Most drama therapists began their careers as doers, as actors or clinicians, who discovered for themselves the exciting possibilities of linking drama with healing. Indeed, that is the nature of this field. Our convictions regarding our work have usually been founded on experience, not theory. As the field has developed, however, the need to ground our work firmly in theory has been increasingly appreciated. But theories of what? There are several conceptual levels at which theory can be directed: (1) a theory of the therapeutic effects of drama therapy, (2) a theory of psychotherapy in general, (3) a theory of theatre/drama, or (4) a theory of the self and human experience. Certainly at a minimum every approach needs to articulate a theoretical framework at the first level, the therapeutic basis of drama therapy.

Beyond this, however, there is wide variation in level of theory development among the chapters in this book. For example, *Psychoanalytic Drama Therapy* (Chapter 11) articulates a theory of drama therapy that is based on a theory of psychotherapy and a theory of human experience, namely psychoanalysis. Likewise, *Role Method* (Chapter 5) articulates theories at all four levels derived from sociological role theory. Other methods, however, may present theoretical material at only one or two levels. Most drama therapists rely on theories from other fields for theories of the self, such as developmental psychology, existentialism, psychoanalysis, or postmodernism. So far only Moreno has created an autonomous theory of self/society (see Chapter 18).

Because drama therapy is so interdisciplinary in nature, it is possible to trace the justification for our methods to basic concepts in psychotherapy, theatre, religion, and philosophy (Landy, 1994). Yet, our reliance upon other fields for our foundations has been of some concern to creative arts therapy scholars, who on the whole have expressed strong desire for independent theories for our disciplines. For example, Jones seeks a drama therapy "which can be understood within its own parameters, which does not need to look to models of analytic therapy or to psychodrama for the justification of how change and personal development occur. Too often in the past theorists and practitioners have had to look outside drama therapy itself to try to justify its relationship to change, to find clothing which is made up of items from others' wardrobes" (1996, p. 292). Robert Landy, in his book that describes in detail the interdisciplinary nature of drama therapy, also meditates on this question of the dependence/independence of our discipline: "if the drama therapist is conflicted as to which psychotherapeutic model to apply in formulating objectives, it is possible that he needs to discover a new or more comprehensive model which reflects the creative, expressive nature of drama therapy. Objectives which ignore this crucial reality will compromise the therapist's work in a modality that is inherently dramatic. . . . A therapist who works through the media of drama/theatre needs to formulate goals that are based in the art of drama/theatre" (1994, p. 44).

Shaun McNiff, in a similar vein, calls for "a theory indigenous to art. Art is the primary process of the profession and its power cannot be fully realized within theoretical systems and approaches to therapy that approach art as an adjunctive mode of operation" (1986, p. 7). He links theoretical independence to professional independence: "the creative arts therapy profession must realize that it has the ability to take on a primary role within the health field. . . . If we perceive ourselves within adjunctive and secondary roles, we will create this destiny for the profession. . . . In this respect, our conceptualization of the profession should become more empirical and primary rather than derivative" (1986, pp. 7–8).

In a previous article, one of the editors (Johnson, 1984) provides an alternate view of maturity as a profession, not based on the development of entirely independent theories, but in the capacity through our discoveries to improve upon and contribute to the specific theories within which we work. Perhaps we unnecessarily place a burden upon ourselves and our students to suggest that we must create a "new and comprehensive model," dealing with issues others have worked on for centuries. Should we not be thankful that others have mapped out some of the terrain for us, to free us to focus on the drama therapy process itself? Certainly that seems an imposing enough project!

Nevertheless, the impression still remains that we are a profession who know *what* we are doing, but not sure *how.* Thus many in our profession may refer back to early shamanic practices as a basis for our model of healing, while at the same time referring to the latest research in neuroscience. Shape shifting and the amygdala may be mentioned in the same article, surely an indication that we are at an early stage of theory development!

In any case, as one reads the chapters in this book, one will encounter an interesting dialectic between the unique and the dependent, the creative spark and the derivative, the apparently new and the very old.

PHASES IN PROFESSIONAL DEVELOPMENT

Fortunately many professions have traveled the journey we are on, and there is much information about how professions develop and the stages they traverse. Perhaps the most comprehensive source of information on professional development as it relates to the creative arts therapies is Shaun McNiff's book, *Educating the Creative Arts Therapist* (1986). Cathy Malchiodi's recent *Expressive Therapies* (2005) also addresses many current professional issues. Let us briefly outline the phases of development that typically characterize a profession such as ours.

First, in order for substantive progress to be made, it is critical that the originators of methods be steeped in direct experience, exploring the variations and nuances as they encounter their clients, populations, and settings. Theory and methods arising out of serious study and intense practical work are bound to last. Perhaps the best example of this is Jean Piaget, who revolutionized developmental psychology through the study of only about six children; but oh, what study! The direct, personal engagement with the relevant phenomena provides the immediacy, the concern, and the meaning required for any work of importance. Though this process initially links the method with the personality of the originator (Corsini & Wedding, 1989), subsequent development will extract what is generalizable from the initial birth.

The second phase is the publication and dissemination of detailed case studies using the particular method. The case study is a long-revered and very important phase in professional development. In England, for example, Steven Mitchell (1996) contributed a whole volume on the case study in drama therapy; and in this country several of the authors in this book have produced case studies. More are needed, however, especially studies that depict treatment over time. In reviewing the publications of drama therapists, there are not many true case studies in the literature; usually what are presented are modified case vignettes. The case study provides an opportunity for the step-by-step exposition of the therapeutic process, constrained as it must be by the particulars of the specific client, disorder, therapist, and setting. The phenomenological texture of the case study allows for a naturalistic testing of hypotheses, expansion of concepts, and discovery of new possibilities. The intrinsic complexity of real events curtails the impulse toward reduction implicit in most theory-building.

The third phase involves published case studies from a variety of clinical populations and different clinical settings. A theory or method designed in only one setting or with one population typically goes under radical transformation when tested in new areas. Some methods may in fact be found to be appropriate only for a particular client population.

The fourth phase involves publication of comprehensive descriptions of the theory and method by the originator, and again there is a wide discrepancy among the approaches in this volume on this score. Some approaches are supported by numerous articles and/or books; others only by a few. The act of writing often reveals new aspects or challenges to the author, who in the process of attempting to articulate the approach to a wider audience, discovers limitations or new directions. Publication provides organized feedback from a broader, more diverse audience than one's students or clients. Landy (Chapter 5), for example, gives an excellent example of how feedback from colleagues stimulated a significant revision in his theory.

The fifth phase involves training others in the approach. If the approach is only effective when used by its creator, its impact will be small. What is transferable to others with different personalities, sensibilities, and styles must be identified. Do others embrace the excitement and charm of the approach enough to desire to specialize in it, to further its development, and to contribute to its study? Thus one expects to see publications about the method by people other than the creator. For the most part, the methods in this book have not achieved this level of development: publications are still written largely by their originators. Developmental Transformations, Chapter 6, may be one exception as a number of articles have been published by other authors). The transmission and continued life of a method is directly dependent upon the degree to which students become committed to it, gain independent mastery, and then extend the method themselves.

The relative lack of transmission of models and methods in our field is of some concern. Certainly this is partly due to the youth of the profession. Many of the models presented here have only recently been articulated. On the other hand, perhaps our difficulties in mentoring, an expression of the artist's passion for autonomy, are also at work (Johnson, 1999). Clearly, without a continuous practice and study of an approach by a committed group of people, the method cannot deepen in sophistication. Paradoxically, our passion for autonomy casts its shadow in the reverence given by many of our methods to age-old traditions (i.e., Zen, shamanic ritual, Sufi practice, psychoanalysis) that require years of mentorship and apprenticeship in highly specific practices.

Finally, a profession arrives at a phase in which publications about the method are produced by others not trained in the method. Here one enters the realm of commentary, analysis, and participation in the general scholarly debates within the larger intellectual and clinical community. Here one's world views are tested according to diverse criteria, stretched and linked to domains and processes not imagined by the originator, such as historical and cultural contexts. Only at this point can one say that a profession has matured; for in a mature profession, the various methods and theories are in some sense shared by all, through interactive discourse involving comparison and analysis among different approaches. Toward this end, two recent books have made significant progress: Robert Landy's *The Couch and the Stage* (2008) presents an in-depth comparison of psychodrama, role method, and developmental transformations. Phil Jones' *Drama as Therapy,* 2nd edition, (Jones, 2007) also contains numerous dialogues among drama therapy practitioners.

In the first edition of *Current Approaches* (Lewis & Johnson, 2000), the chapters made almost no references to each other's work. Examination of references revealed recognition of major theories of psychology and psychotherapy, theatre traditions, and philosophical or spiritual works, rather than other drama therapists. This was interesting because these authors are members of the same small profession, are very familiar with each other, have attended each other's workshops, and read each other's publications. Without question they have influenced each other. Why was there no indication of this contact? Presumably a good way to identify the uniqueness of an approach is to differentiate it from other drama therapy approaches. Apparently this was being done indirectly and left for the reader to surmise. There may be a number of reasons for the surprising lack of mutual referencing. First, it may reflect the early stage of work within which many of these authors are operating, where much attention is placed on articulating self-consistent principles. It takes time to look outward. Second, because of the extremely small size of our field, concerns about competitive issues may govern the authors' reluctance to contrast their methods with each other. Third, if Jones is correct, then there may also be concerns that if one were to compare methods, one might discover how similar indeed one's method is with those of many others, undercutting the precious commodity of uniqueness that provides some of the impetus for the work.

The absence of noncompetitive dialogue in the literature among drama therapy practitioners and scholars remains a significant reminder of how early in development the profession is. In this new edition, chapter authors were asked to include comparisons to other methods within the field. While these sections on comparison are for the most part in beginning stages, we feel it is an effort toward mutual referencing, acknowledgment of influence, and respectful dialogue about our similarities and differences.

EVALUATING VALIDITY IN DRAMA THERAPY

Aristotle said that theories must be based on formulations that are "primary and true." Internal validity of an approach is based on the consistency of its concepts and postulates, its plausibility, comprehensiveness, and congruence with known facts and phenomena. One desires a theory to make implicit sense. External validity is based on the degree that what the theory predicts or claims to achieve does indeed occur. Questions relevant to external validity include: How is the approach utilized and experienced in the actual process of drama therapy? How are the concepts actualized within the therapeutic process? How sensitive is this approach to diverse world views and cultures? How does the approach play out with different conditions, such as gender, ethnicity, socioeconomic status, location, and therapist personality?

Once theories and techniques have been developed, it is important to establish whether claims of effectiveness have any basis. Typically external validity has been determined by standards established by the scientific community. The basic principle of the scientific perspective is that judgment should be based on observations of phenomena, as opposed to earlier criteria such as the opinion of the authority (e.g., King, Pope), dogma (Bible, Koran), or opinion of the majority. In contrast to common belief, the scientific model does not subscribe only to controlled quantitative studies as the means for establishing efficacy. The scientific spirit advocates that consistent observations from diverse sources are required before claims of efficacy by one practitioner should be deemed reliable, and that these observations should be made with great care and rigor. Quantitative, empirical studies are only one means by which these criteria can be satisfied.

In other health fields, criteria have been established for what are termed standards of evidence. The Agency of Health Care Policy and Research (1994) has developed a set of guidelines for classification of the level of evidence for particular therapeutic interventions. These are:

Level A: randomized controlled clinical studies
Level B: well-designed clinical studies without randomization or placebo comparison
Level C: naturalistic clinical studies and observations sufficiently compelling to warrant use of the technique
Level D: long-standing and widespread clinical practice
Level E: long-standing practice by circumscribed groups of clinicians
Level F: recently developed treatment not subjected to widespread clinical practice

Clearly many of our approaches satisfy the requirements of Levels D and E, and some are still at Level F. However, given the publication of detailed and carefully observed case studies, some are at Level C. The field unfortunately has few rigorous empirical studies of treatment outcome. Nevertheless, it is important to note that a majority of clinical methods used in medicine are also at level C, as are many other methods of psychotherapy (AHCPR, 1994). This analysis therefore supports the importance of good, detailed case studies in establishing the validity of our approaches. Such practice is well within what can be considered a scientific paradigm.

DIVERSITY AND INCLUSION IN THE FIELD OF DRAMA THERAPY

The field of drama therapy at this point is also limited by the lack of culturally diverse representation in the originators and primary theorists. Indeed, nearly all the authors in this book are Caucasian, and the percentage of men is much higher than in the field at large. Yet we live in a multicultural world, and we serve clients of all races and backgrounds. Our work has much to do with expanding perspective, and yet we cannot encompass a broad range of perspectives when our leaders are all of the same dominant ethnicity. We are painfully aware of this limitation in our profession. It is important to acknowledge this fact, and to take steps toward becoming a more inclusive field. We are heartened that a new generation of drama therapists and students of drama therapy are more diverse, and that more attention is being paid within the field to the significance of diversity.

REPRESENTING DRAMA THERAPY IN THE WRITTEN WORD

A further challenge for our field is how to make such a lively mode of therapy speak to a reader on paper. Our work bursts with energy, our teaching is experiential, and we are passionate about action. Can this passion be translated to the written word? Can we bring the work to life in a book? Can we maintain our essence, our life force, as we verbally articulate theories and methods? Can you, the reader, picture the work–cinematically, dramatically–as you read the case stories? Writing about our work, articulating our theories and methods, is critical to the development of our field. Yet it is also important to find other methods besides writing to communicate our work. Video documentation, especially of treatment over time, is a relevant (though currently underused) method of transmitting information in our field. Robert Landy has contributed to this endeavor in his recent film depicting three sessions with the same client, utilizing Developmental Transformations, Role Method, and Psychodrama (Landy, 2005). One of the editors (Emunah, 1990) has produced several videotapes over the past decades illustrating her work with clients over 20–32 sessions. Another method–more unusual and yet intrinsic to our medium–is theatrical performance. Drama therapists have created powerful, informative, and poignant theatre performances about their work with clients, their challenges in becoming the therapist they wish to be, and transference and countertransference issues. The editors of this book invite readers to find embodied and innovative ways of reflecting on and communicating their experience as drama therapists, in addition to contributing to the written body of knowledge in our field.

CONCLUSION

Hopefully in perusing the riches in this volume, readers will find theories, methods, and styles that are compatible with their own personality and world view, and with the particular clients they serve. Many have noted that the best theoretical model and method to adopt is often the one that resonates with one's own personality. Others may choose a model that reflects their shadow side, and pulls them toward the person they wish to be. Whatever the outcome, we hope that this book stimulates questions, discussions, and contact among all who believe in the therapeutic value of drama and theatre.

In this chapter, we have summarized the current state of development of theory and methods in drama therapy. We have found trends both toward specialization into identified approaches, and toward exploration of common processes underlying all approaches. We have found a diversity in the degree of dependence upon theories from other disciplines, as well as a sentiment directed toward the discovery of autonomous artistic models. We have found that the field is still in the early stages of professional development, in which the need for intensive case studies is paramount. We have examined central components of theory building.

These 18 chapters will reveal a dynamic, rich field–deep in its process of becoming. Each author, in his or her own way, is challenged by the simultaneous demand for inner- and outer-directed reflection: in expressing a unique perspective on drama therapy and at the same time being able to communicate effectively with the broader community. Balancing these demands successfully will indeed be the path toward further maturity of the profession.

Despite these challenges, we firmly believe that as drama therapy continues to develop, a mature professional community will emerge. Such a community will be characterized by close contact and continuous dialogue, cross-fertilization, and feedback, where all of the theories and methods arising out of this creative medium will be experienced as belonging to the field as a whole. By writing, training and dialoguing, the originators share their offspring with the wider field. We thank each one of them, and we welcome those who are to come in our burgeoning field.

REFERENCES

Agency of Health Care Policy and Research, (1994). *Standards of evidence in the health care professions.* Washington, DC: AHCPR.

Corsini, R.J., & Wedding, D. (1989). *Current psychotherapies.* Itasca, IL: F. E. Peacock Publishers.

Emunah, R. (1990). Caring for the Inner One: Self-Expression and Self-Acceptance in Drama Therapy. Filmed by and Co-produced with Brandy Brawner. Available from author.

Jennings, S. (1987). *Dramatherapy: Theory and practice 1.* London: Jessica Kingsley.

Jennings, S. (1992). *Dramatherapy: Theory and practice 2.* London: Jessica Kingsley.

Jennings, S. (1997). *Dramatherapy: Theory and practice 3.* London: Jessica Kingsley.

Johnson, D. (1984). Establishing the creative arts therapies as an independent profession. *The Arts in Psychotherapy, 11,* 209–212.

Johnson, D. (1999). The challenge of mentoring. In *Essays in the creative arts therapies: Imaging the birth of a profession* (pp. 59–65). Springfield, IL: Charles C Thomas.

Jones, P. (1996). *Drama therapy: Theatre as living.* London: Routledge.

Jones, P. (2007). *Drama therapy: Theory, practice, and research,* 2nd Edition. London: Routledge.

Landy, R. (1994). *Drama therapy: Concepts, theories, and practices,* 2nd edition. Springfield, IL: Charles C Thomas.

Landy, R. (2005). *Three approaches to drama therapy.* Video and DVD. New York: New York University.

Landy, R. (2008). *The couch and the stage.* Lanham, MD: Jason Aronson.

Malchiodi, C. (2005). *Expressive therapies.* New York: Guilford.

McNiff, S. (1986). *Educating the creative arts therapist: A profile of the profession.* Springfield, IL: Charles C Thomas.

Mitchell, S. (1996). *Dramatherapy: Clinical studies.* London: Jessica Kingsley.

Chapter 3

THE CURRENT STATE OF THE FIELD OF DRAMA THERAPY

Renée Emunah and David Read Johnson

At the time of this revised edition of *Current Approaches,* the profession of Drama Therapy approaches its 30th birthday. Our field is now entering a more full-fledged, committed adulthood, a stage of bringing forth into the world the discoveries–born out of passion and dedication–made in the prior decades. It is a time to take stock of our varied efforts, identify our core foundations and contributions, and consolidate our collective energy–in order to forge into the breach of this still new and turbulent millennium.

In our field's first decade, we were busy establishing ourselves as a profession, defining and distinguishing ourselves, ensuring that we could train people, developing jobs, and serving clients. In the second decade, we branched out into work with more populations and contexts, and we trained people who could then supervise others. By the third decade, particular approaches had emerged in the field, and these have gradually became more pronounced, articulated and developed. In this edition, the originators present them–refined and updated. The collection of chapters in this book offers novice, experienced, and prospective drama therapists alike with a sense of how drama therapists practice their craft. This edition of *Current Approaches* provides the essential layout of the state of the field of drama therapy in North America.

A number of influences have brought greater coherence to the field. There has been increased interaction and sharing of ideas among the originators, in person and in publication. Students of the various schools have eschewed fragmentation and have integrated aspects of several approaches in their professional work. As a result, a number of concepts developed within specific approaches have spread out into wider usage and application.

The background for this coherence lies in the "Psychoanalytic Model" of Eleanor Irwin (Chapter 11), and Moreno's "Psychodrama" (Chapter 18), both of whom have contributed so many ideas, concepts, techniques, and wisdom to the drama therapy enterprise that much is taken for granted. Whether *tele, role reversal, transference,* or *projection,* these ideas continue to be our Procrustean Bed. Augusto Boal and Jonathan Fox have also provided additional impetus for drama therapists through their contributions in social applications of theatre. Penny Lewis, whose passing ended a long career of creative work, has left us with enduring concepts such as the *somatic countertransference,* as well as many important concepts from Jungian and developmental object relations theories (Chapter 12).

This book represents an endeavor to look more deeply into the heart of our own work, and to appraise each other's works in their similarities and differences. Regardless of method, one thing is clear: In helping people through dramatic action, we nurture presence, expression, and transformation.

POPULATIONS AND CONTEXTS

Nearly all the approaches in this book are suitable for a wide range of populations and age groups, and are not population-specific. Nearly all the approaches use group work. With the exception of some performance-based approaches, nearly all are also applied on an individual therapy basis. Many approaches are also used in family, couples, and organizational work. The key, of course, is adapting the approach, method, and techniques to the particular needs of a given population, age group, culture, and context–and even within those categories there is a infinite range . . . as each client is unique and multifaceted.

ADVANCES IN CLINICAL PRACTICE

Improvisation has long been at the heart of drama therapy, and all drama therapists believe in the healing properties of play and spontaneity. Over the past decades, David Read Johnson has been the forerunner in examining the inner workings of improvisation and the nature of play, as well as the potential for intimacy between therapist and client. His term *playspace*–defined as the mutual agreement among participants that what is occurring is imaginary, therefore demarcating the boundaries between play and reality, is now a widely used term in the field of drama therapy. Johnson's concepts of *Intimate Play*–when the client's improvisational material is fueled by thoughts and feelings about the relationship with the therapist–and *Deep Play*–when the play content arises from aspects of interpersonal presence –are beginning to be more generally used in the field. "Developmental Transformations" (Chapter 6) challenges drama therapists to re-think what is possible and permissible in a session, regarding the live engagement of the therapist in the play, the use of physical touch and proximity, and the attainment of a state of presence with another person.

All drama therapists believe in creating a safe environment for their clients. Over the past decades, Renee Emunah has examined the way an ongoing drama therapy series of sessions (whether brief or long-term) progresses over time, and the ways in which a drama therapist can intentionally balance safety and challenge. The analysis of the evolution of drama therapeutic work has created a foundation for drama therapists, regardless of method. Her term *culminating enactments*–the personally intimate and intricate scenes that can place during Phase Four of the "Integrative Five Phase Model" (Chapter 4)–is becoming commonly used in the larger field. *Self-revelatory performance* (a process Emunah distinguishes from its sibling, autobiographical theatre)–a theatrically-honed culminating enactment, in which one dramatically grapples with and heals core and multileveled current struggles–has also become widely utilized in the field. The relationship and interplay between *expression and containment,* long a central focus of Emunah's work, has also become infused into general drama therapy discourse.

All drama therapists believe in the importance of examining roles and expanding role repertoire. Robert Landy's painstaking analysis of role, including his *taxonomy of roles,* has influenced and strengthened the field's understanding of character and role play, regardless of whether a practitioner is specifically using Landy's "Role Method" (Chapter 5). His terms *counter-role*–the shadow, denied, or avoided figure on the other side of the conscious role–and *guide*–the transitional figure between role and counter-role that serves as a bridge to the other–are becoming integrated within the larger field of drama therapy practice. His articulation of the significance of tolerating ambivalence and paradox, from the perspective of role theory, has deepened our understanding of healing through drama therapy, and his evolving views on core self (or lack thereof) have instigated important dialogue and debate. Landy's long-term exploration of Thomas Scheff's concept of *aesthetic distance* has been a mainstay for all drama therapy practitioners, regardless of method.

All drama therapists believe that live, embodied enactment of new stories and new roles can promote hope and change. *Story* has long been a central passion and focus for Pam Dunne. Dunne's "Narradrama" (Chapter 9) approach has honed and highlighted the creative ways and projective techniques in which clients can restory their lives, reinvent themselves, review their issues from different vantage points and find the personal agency necessary to invoke real change. Through her work, narrative and postmodern family therapy concepts, such as *re-storying, externalizing conversations,* and *problematized stories,* have entered the drama therapy lexicon.

Saphira Linden has continued to deepen her exploration of the transpersonal dimensions of drama therapy, integrating her years of experience in improvisation, performance-based theatre, psychodrama, educational, and social intervention methods. In a world rushing toward the concrete, the immediate, and the electronic, Saphira's "Omega Transpersonal Drama Therapy Approach" (Chapter 10) holds to the importance of the inner journey, and achieving contact with such things as the *soul,* the *collective presence,* and the *spiritual essence* within each of us.

Daniel Wiener, whose "Rehearsals for Growth" (Chapter 16) is new to this edition, brings many family systems concepts to his model of working with couples. Integrating playful exercises, paradoxical interventions within the playspace, and family systems perspectives, RfG has added an important new dimension to drama therapy practice, which otherwise has emphasized individuals and groups.

ADVANCES IN PERFORMANCE-BASED INTERVENTIONS

Many newcomers to the field of drama therapy ask about the use of performance in drama therapy. As evidenced in this book, performance is alive and well in the field of drama therapy, and is used in a multiplicity of ways. Stephen Snow's scholarly and clinical work in "Ritual/Theatre/Therapy" (Chapter 7) has deepened our considerations of performative drama therapy, particularly in repairing the weak self-images of many of our clients. His investigation of the relationship between dramatic performance, ritual, and shamanism has contributed to the ongoing exploration of our field's deepest and most ancient origins. He has introduced the term *performance ethnography* into our drama therapy lexicon, which provides a bridge between the imaginative and the cultural perspectives.

Sally Bailey, new to this second edition, has built on the work of earlier drama therapists and articulates the power for clients in performing original theatrical productions (Chapter 17). She highlights the personal, social, and cultural impact of performance on the experience of living with disability, illness, or oppression. Her work is influenced by narrative therapy, with an emphasis on helping clients find alternatives to destructive patterns through story-making and performance.

All drama therapists believe in the power of storytelling. "Playback Theatre" (Chapter 20)–in which personal stories of participants or audience members are shared and then played back, typically by a trained troupe that aesthetically and theatrically reflect the essence of the story in a way that validates the *Teller*–has expanded our understanding and appreciation in the field for telling and listening to stories, in their complexity and simplicity. Playback Theatre has experienced rapid and widespread growth over the past decades. Most academic drama therapy programs now include Playback in the curriculum and there are numerous Playback companies throughout North America and the rest of the world.

ADVANCES IN SOCIAL INTERVENTIONS

In addition to the traditional emphases on clinical work and performance, many forms of drama therapy are focusing on social problems, reflecting shifts in the wider culture. Pat Sternberg and Nina Garcia review the origins of this approach in their chapter on Moreno's "Sociodrama" (Chapter 19), which established early on the conceptual and methodological bases for social interventions. Sociodramatic methods have been widely incorporated by drama therapists in many different contexts, including non-clinical arenas such as corporate consulting, diversity training, and education.

For many years, both "STOP-GAP" (Chapter 14)-originated by Don Laffoon, and "ENACT" (Chapter 13)–originated by Diana Feldman, have used specifically designed performances and exercises (conducted by actors and drama therapists) to impact underserved community and school-based settings. Their passion and dedication to social change helps to boost the self-esteem of their urban, in-need populations. The Southern California-based STOP-GAP, founded in 1979, and the New York-based ENACT, founded in 1986, serve thousands of participants each year.

John Bergman's "Drama Therapy Approach" (Chapter 15) has also focused on an important social area of prisons. His emphasis on organizational consultation and understanding the wider cultural and ideological constraints on change in institutions have been very influential in the drama therapy field. Many drama therapy approaches remain focused on an individual model of change. Bergman powerfully illustrates how individual change can often not come about without sophisticated and patient intervention at the much broader level of institutional and even political processes. In this way, Bergman joins Augusto Boal in directing the field's attention to larger, sociopolitical dynamics.

Drama therapy's developing emphasis on social justice brings new author but long-time practitioner Armand Volkas, who has developed a method called "Healing the Wounds of History" (Chapter 8). Using both process and performance formats, Volkas brings together groups of people with a legacy of historical trauma–such as children of

Holocaust survivors and children of Nazis–in an effort to promote new understanding and healing. As a supervisor, teacher, and trainer, Volkas has brought many drama therapy students into increased awareness of the importance, and opportunity, of drama therapy in working toward social justice.

Augusto Boal's work in "Theatre of the Oppressed" (Chapter 21) and its variants such as Forum Theatre and the Rainbow of Desire, is newly described in this book by Nisha Sajnani. Boal's work uses the boldness of the theatrical medium to help people address pressing social issues related to their oppression by others, and of others. The work largely intends to open spaces of dialogue and inquiry into the forces that allow each of us to tolerate and enable collective suffering. Though Boal's work was initially best categorized as Applied Theatre, over the past decade his work has been increasingly viewed from therapeutic and transformational frameworks, and thus increasingly incorporated into drama therapy practice.

Collectively, the work of Laffoon, Feldman, Bergman, Volkas, and Boal reflect a growing realization of drama therapy's potential for contributing to the wider society, extending the influence of the more traditional, clinical practices of Irwin, Johnson, Landy, Emunah, Lewis, and Dunne.

IDENTIFYING DIFFERENCES AMONG THE APPROACHES

As greater integration occurs, important differences are easier to identify. These appear to be: (1) the degree of engagement by the therapist in the dramatic action; (2) the use of physical touch and proximity; (3) the balance of cognitive versus emotive forms of expression; and (4) the emphasis on the past versus the present. These polarities have superceded previous issues such as: use of objects and props versus free interaction; use of myths, stories and plays versus improvisational material; and the use of interpretation versus client-centered reflection.

Degree of the Therapist's Engagement in the Drama

In all forms of drama therapy, the drama therapist must remain an ethical, responsible, and skillful guide. However, there is a significant variation in the role of the therapist between the different approaches to drama therapy. In Developmental Transformations, for example, the therapist is an active co-player, an actor within the play, and even a play object for the client (though s/he also serves at times as witness). On the other extreme is Psychodrama, in which the therapist is clearly a director. In Landy's Role Method, the therapist is a guide, most often serving as director and witness, though s/he at times takes on an auxiliary role in the client's drama. In the Integrative Five Phase Model, the therapist is an active co-player early on, and gradually shifts to assuming a greater directorial role, facilitating interventions within the dramatic mode. Stephen Snow, whose work revolves around performance, speaks of the equal attention given to the roles of theatrical director and facilitator of the process. For the most part, current drama therapy methods maintain a clear boundary between the play action and the therapist, who serves as director, side coach, and facilitator. Johnson, Lewis, Linden, and Bergman's approaches, in contrast, are more likely to encourage active immersion on the part of the therapist in the dramatic action.

The Use of Touch and Physical Proximity

Though all drama therapy methods involve some degree of physicalization and touch, the general trend has been toward less use of physical touch and proximity. Only Developmental Transformations and Lewis' Developmental Themes approaches incorporate physical touch as a major element in their work. Omega Transformational, Integrative Five Phase, Rehearsals for Growth, and Bergman's Drama Therapy Approach utilize specific touch methods when appropriate. The other approaches for the most part use only incidental physical touch.

Balance of Cognitive versus Emotional Expression

As in the wider culture, toleration of strong affect and catharsis, essential components of both psychoanalysis and psychodrama, has diminished in our twenty-first century. Most methods attempt to maintain a balance of cognition and emotion in the sessions. Psychoanalytic, Developmental Transformations, Psychodrama, Integrative Five Phase, Bergman's Drama Therapy Approach, and Healing the Wounds of History are more likely to evoke strong emotional release. Role Method, STOP-GAP, ENACT, Playback, and Narradrama are more likely to emphasize cognitive awareness.

Emphasis on the Past versus the Present

Differences between approaches also lie in the degree of exploration of past childhood experiences, wounds, and traumas. The more clinically-oriented approaches typically investigate the past–at least in long-term therapeutic contexts. These include: Psychoanalytic, Role Method, Integrative Five Phase, Developmental Transformations, Omega Transformational, Psychodrama, and Developmental Themes. Narradrama and Rehearsals for Growth, though clinically-oriented, typically do not dwell on the past, focusing rather on present issues. Sociodrama, STOP-GAP, and ENACT also do not focus on individual pasts; in fact these approaches take special care that the focus is on relevant but not specifically personal issues of individual clients. Performance-based approaches–Ritual/Theatre/Therapy such as typically emphasize the client's self-mastery and achievement rather than exploration of the past. Societal and systems-oriented approaches–Bergman's Drama Therapy Approach, Playback, and Healing the Wounds of History–give equal weight to past events and attempts to transform people's attitudes about them in the present.

Interestingly, these four issues may all be variations on a significant trend in the wider mental health culture toward cognitive-behavioral modes of intervention. Such a culture privileges interpersonal distance and caution on the part of the therapist, restraint from physical touch, avoidance of overwhelming emotion, and emphasis on the present rather than the past. Many of the methods in drama therapy were created within the cultural environment of the 1960s with its appreciation for experimentation, emotional release, and risk-taking. We are now living in more conservative times, and this shift in the society has affected the ways drama therapists speak about their work.

DRAMA THERAPY AND THE URGENT ISSUES OF OUR TIMES

Drama therapy will continue to address the many personal and social issues that have been its focus in the past. However, there appear to be a number of areas in which drama therapy may be able to make unique contributions in the near future, based on the shifting needs in the world today. We believe these include: (1) the treatment of the traumatized child, (2) prevention of interpersonal violence, and (3) appreciation of cultural and ethnic diversity.

The Traumatized Child

As evidence of the epidemic of childhood maltreatment is recognized, more resources are being directed to the treatment of abused, traumatized, and neglected children. In this arena, the use of artistic, playful, and nonverbal methods has received wide acceptance. Children need help to express the unspeakable, to externalize what has shut down their psyche, and find means to gather resilience. Trauma, violence, pain, love, and all powerful experiences are felt and recalled in the body. The awareness of the interconnection between body, mind, and emotion has been increasing, especially in its impact on children's development. It is likely that drama therapy, as well as the other creative arts therapies, will be sought out in the future specifically for this population.

Addressing Interpersonal Violence

Violence continues, and grows–in our homes, in our communities, between nations. How do we prevent it from spreading further? Can we reach out to troubled youth, preventively? If aggression, frustration, and anger are expressed in play–in a way that does not overwhelm or exacerbate anxiety, and if fantasy expression is encouraged in childhood and beyond, and if it is contained, witnessed, distinguished from reality, played with and transformed, can this be one step in thwarting violence?

Inherent in drama therapy are two critical elements: the interplay between *expression* and *containment,* and *perspective.* The very nature of drama therapy induces experiencing from another's perspective, seeing oneself in perspective, and changing one's perspective. Experiencing from another's perspective promotes understanding, empathy, and insight. Seeing oneself in perspective implies creating some distance and objectivity that can prompt change and self-mastery. Changing one's perspective–so difficult to achieve in real-life–is eased in the fluid and permissive dramatic realm. Viewing from a broader perspective enables one to look backward and forward in time, understanding the forces that shaped who one is, the way one's actions have a ripple effect in the world, and the multiple roads that lay ahead. It is possible that our combined focus on expression/containment and engendering perspective can provide a major contribution to preventing violence on all scales. We believe that drama therapy may become an integral part of Violence Prevention and Anger Management programs in agencies and schools.

Appreciation of Cultural and Ethnic Diversity

We live in an increasingly multicultural world community, in which respecting difference is paramount. Increased global awareness, intermingling of races and cultures, and a sense of moral responsibility have united to create a tremendous interest and need in addressing diversity issues. The component of *perspective* in drama therapy is relevant here. Gaining experience–via a dramatic enactment (such as role play) or intervention (such as doubling)–from someone else's viewpoint and perspective promotes empathy, understanding, and compassion. Drama therapy interventions and theatrical performance can help to raise consciousness, sensitivity, and emotional connectedness to complex and deep-seated issues revolving around difference. The pain of oppression, the impact of privilege, and the ways in which unintentional and unconscious racism and intolerance occur must not only be intellectually understood but also felt in the gut.

Drama therapy may provide important and effective tools to help communities and groups open themselves to question their own assumptions about the world, and the Others whom they feel are oppressing them, or whom they may be unconsciously oppressing. Placing strongly-held and often unquestioned ideas into the performative playspace establishes possibilities for flexibility and transformation. The mutuality required in improvisation and in sustaining a performance provides a bridge between groups over which aspects of experience previously tied down by oppressive frameworks can migrate. In a theatrical performance framework, there is a paradoxical provision of distance for the audience (who can sit back and witness issues that may otherwise be overwhelming) and a breaking down of distance, affording both containment and an outlet to experience and feel strong emotions.

Increasingly, we believe, drama therapists will be utilized to aid in Diversity Training Programs, cross-cultural exchanges, and Conflict Resolution efforts. Much can and needs to be done in this arena, as class, race, gender, religious, and cultural intolerance and inequality continue to affect our world.

FACING THE CHALLENGES OF THE FUTURE

The world appears to be moving rapidly in new directions. Technology and computer/internet connectivity, genetics and medical advances, fitness, cosmetic surgery, and marketing increasingly pervade our daily lives. These developments give rise to images of greater longevity, greater global connection, and greater personal power. At the same time, concerns about the deteriorating climate, pollution, and species extinction offer more sobering images of global vulnerability and fragility. In the early years of the creative arts therapies, the 1950s through the 1970s, our work was largely designed to uncover the unconscious desires and fantasies held back by a repressive culture. Today, we worry less about what is harbored in our unconscious, and more about the threats to our existence in the real world, including the environment, the economy, terrorism, and globalization. Being together, celebrating and performing, telling and listening to our stories, seem increasingly from a different time. The interest in the role of the shaman, mentioned by many of our authors, received intense interest in the 1960s and 1970s. Now, young people seek a different metaphor to build their lives upon. The magical power of the shaman/doctor/therapist has been surpassed by the magnetic pull of the Internet and the personal computer. We are on the edge of a collective fantasy of merging human and machine, of genetics and silicon chips, of the imagined longevity that bionics will bring. What will be left out, perhaps, is living well. It will be essential for leading drama therapists to address these changes in our world and to find ways of adapting our approaches to these changes, in order for our field to remain relevant and viable, if not cutting edge.

Forms of personal expression are being revolutionized. Instead of canvas, stage, and concert hall, young people today have access to new creative platforms to express themselves and to gain access to huge audiences. YouTube, MySpace, Twitter, and other forums are the new playspaces for millions of people. Here is the potential drama therapy of our time, minus the embodied encounter. Today people are being stimulated by fantastic forms of free expression on their computers and cell phones without the opportunity of physical release or connection. The anonymity and distance of the interaction prevents each person from receiving the embodied responses to their communication that makes it authentic and intelligible. The burgeoning interest in bodywork and body therapies, such as massage, Somatic Experiencing, Reiki, and Hakomi, for example, may be the counterpart to our digital, disembodied age.

Drama therapy involves the encountered body within the *as if* frame. How can we negotiate a relationship with the electronic media? Devising creative means for integrating traditional forms of embodiment and performance with those provided by the Internet *is* the challenge facing us. Indeed, drama therapy methods may be ripe for offering people means of extending their online experimentations with performance into the real embodied encounter. For example, can the videotaped performances by children in a school program concerning important social issues be uploaded to a specially devoted MySpace page each day, and responses to it be used in the next session? Can programs that examine and prevent racism, violence, or abuse use live text messaging as a way for a group to communicate with a person playing the role (via cellphone) of someone in pain or trouble? Can a Playback team respond to Tellers' stories who are around the globe via live streaming video?

It will be critical that drama therapists do not distance themselves from the digital media simply because of the limitations on embodied encounter. Rather, we encourage drama therapists to use their creativity to find ways of transforming our work to engage with these new developments in self-expression. The Internet offers the possibility of greatly expanding the exposure and dissemination of creative expression, largely by providing access to a much larger audience than that which we have been used to. Viewing the Internet as a performative frame, its audience of much greater diversity and global reach, may stimulate drama therapists to find a new avenue for the field of drama therapy.

CONCLUSION

Our field is about relationship, intimacy, creativity, action, interaction. The perspective-inducing element in our work, in conjunction with the qualities we focus upon, can help propel the world toward the change–on personal and global scales–that is becoming essential. There is a profound call in this millennium for an expansion of perspective; a reworking of the ways we have lived. It is a time to respond to Robert Landy's invitation to examine our roles, Pam Dunne's invitation to change our stories, Renee Emunah's invitation to access our internal nurturing parent, Armand Volkas' invitation to heal ancestral wounds, and David Johnson's invitation to play in a way that counteracts rigidity, beckons fluidity, and releases our capacity for transformation.

There are now several generations of drama therapists practicing, in all types of settings, throughout North America (and the world), most of them trained by the authors in this book. We propose taking hold of our similar and different approaches to drama therapy–not competitively but rather in a spirit of embracing, dialoguing, challenging, and developing each other's work. At the heart of our field is action. We propose using our combined energy and insight, in a consolidated and focused manner, toward fulfilling the imperatives of our still-new century.

This is an academic book, but underlying each author's work is passion for theatre and healing, and deep desire to enable people to lead more emotionally healthy, joyful, engaged, and enriched lives.

Section II

CURRENT APPROACHES IN DRAMA THERAPY

Chapter 4

THE INTEGRATIVE FIVE PHASE MODEL OF DRAMA THERAPY

Renée Emunah

Both drama and therapy are richly layered, multitextured endeavors; both involve a process of gradual unfolding. Both entail risk-taking, which can evoke resistances and fears as well as instill trust. As a drama therapist, I am interested in creating a gentle unfolding–promoting trust and minimizing fear, and creating a solid container–that can hold many layers of exploration and revelation. I am interested in how an aesthetic flow, that is, a quality of seamless, organic progression of the work/play, furthers the therapeutic process. I am interested in the subtle interplay between leading and following, between creating an engaging structure and following the participant's cues.

This interplay between leading and following parallels the nature-nurture mirroring dance of parenting from the very beginning. Parenting involves following a baby's lead, observing her modes of communication, sensing her needs and preferences, learning who she is, responding to her subtle cues. But it also involves facilitation, setting a kind of structure, offering particular realms of experience to which the baby may respond. This continues throughout childhood: responding to the child's particular needs, interests, sensibilities, and inclinations. At the same time, the parent intentionally sets the stage for the kind of experiences s/he wishes the child to have. The *Integrative Five Phase Model* is both a way of facilitating an intentional drama therapy process and a way of understanding the clients' leads and identifying their cues–enabling the drama therapist to situate, respond to, and maximize the potential of each unique client's and group's multifaceted therapeutic journey.

THE INTEGRATIVE FIVE PHASE MODEL

The Integrative Five Phase Model of drama therapy represents a developmental course of treatment, in which the therapeutic journey is paced and progressive, offering a sense of unfolding. Each phase paves the way for the next stage, spiraling a series of sessions toward deeper levels of play, intimacy, and self-revelation. The work progresses from interactive dramatic play

(Phase 1), to developed theatrical scenes (Phase 2), to role play dealing with personal situations (Phase 3), to culminating psychodramatic enactments exploring core themes (Phase 4), and ending with dramatic ritual related to closure (Phase 5). The fictional mode provides a protective safeguard as well as a means of expanding one's capacities for, and range of, expression. But eventually the roles are shed, the masks unraveled, and the fictional scenarios give way to life scenes (Emunah, 1998).

The shift from the fictional to the personal is influenced by the clients; it is an organic process, in which the therapist is attentive to the clients' natural and spontaneous connections to the fictional enactments. This point signals the end of Phase Two; the clients are on the verge of readiness to explore their real lives more directly. The first two phases afford a sense of liberation and expansion, and also elicit the clients' more healthy selves, as their spontaneity, creativity, imagination, and resourcefulness are evoked. The personal work that follows emerges from the fictional scenes and the clients' associations to these scenes, thereby circumventing the pitfall of having preconceived notions of issues as one embarks on specifically personal, psychodramatic work. The personal material is connected to the fictional material; indeed it is an outgrowth of it.

Based in humanistic psychology, the model elicits and expands the healthfulness of the person. The model is also guided by central concepts of psychodynamic, existential, and cognitive-behavioral approaches to psychotherapy. Emotional catharsis and mastery, cognitive insight and behavioral change are all essential and intertwined parts of the therapeutic process. The expansion of one's sense of self, role repertoire, freedom and possibility, along with an awareness of limitation, underlie this approach to drama therapy.

The Integrative Five Phase Model is eclectic, encompassing the wide array of processes, techniques, healing properties and possibilities inherent in the medium of drama therapy–in a sequenced fashion, involving careful reflection and perception on the part of the drama therapist. The five phases are linked to the five conceptual sources that I find most primary to drama therapy. While elements of all five conceptual sources are evident in each phase, each source corresponds to a particular phase. Phase One is most influenced by dramatic play, Phase Two by theatre (acting), Phase Three by role theory and role play, Phase Four by psychodrama, and Phase Five by dramatic ritual. The phases are not separate blocks, but rather fluid and overlapping stages. The model is about fluidity, not rigidity; it is about facilitating a seamless flow and subtle progression, deepening both the aesthetic and therapeutic possibilities of the clinical encounter.

I believe that therapeutic work in drama therapy can have an aesthetic sensibility that enriches healing, and that the coinciding of aesthetic/theatrical and therapeutic goals ignites the life force of our modality. As drama therapists we can take hold of the aesthetic in all that we do, not only in directing performances, but in the sense of wholeness within a session, the poetic interventions within a deeply cathartic Phase Four scene, the quality of ritual bringing closure to sessions and to a treatment series. Drama therapy emerged from the art form of drama, and aesthetics are at the root of the Integrative Phase Five Model.

The Integrative Five Phase Model grew out of extensive observations of drama therapy groups rather than from preformulated structures or designs. Early videotapes of my work documenting long-term drama therapy treatment with emotionally disturbed adults actually illustrate the phase progression, even though I had not yet developed this model (Emunah, 1979, 1990). The development of the model was based on articulating and conceptualizing what I was witnessing and instinctively facilitating. Over the years, the model has been expanded upon and refined, and used with many different populations and within a wide variety of contexts.

While the nature and course of the therapeutic journey are obviously influenced by each unique client and each group, the movement from one phase to the next tends to signify the development of the therapeutic process. The initial playful stages of the Integrative Five Phase Model form a backbone for the later intensely personal stages of work. The early phases remain present even as a group progresses to later phases. Clients relish re-experiencing the earlier work, and this creates a more continuous and cumulative process. The model is thus not strictly linear: each stage encompasses and builds on elements of the prior stages; and the final phase is reminiscent of the first phase, bringing the journey full circle.

Basic Concepts

The model is based on the following premises:

1. The therapeutic journey is eased and strengthened by a sense of gradual unfolding, in which the work is paced and progressive, creating in the clients a sense of readiness at all times for the next step/level.
2. Beginning the therapeutic process within the creative drama mode is liberating, enabling clients to experience a sense of freedom from the constraints of everyday life and from engrained patterns. The engagement in the fictional realm also circumvents the tendency to immediately rehash predictable, familiar life issues. Over time, the associations clients have between the fictional scenes and their real life lead to a more direct working through of real life issues, but from a fresh, often unexpected perspective.
3. The fictional realm is protective, at the same time that it enables self-revelation, in a safe and distanced manner. Over time, the need for safeguards diminishes. Just as theatre director Joseph Chaikin (1984) poetically described the way the wearing of a mask changes the actor's face, so too the process of taking on roles impacts the client's self image and perception. When the time comes to discard roles and unravel layers of masks, the person is not the same as s/he was prior to these acting processes.
4. The building of trust and interrelationship/s within the group (or between therapist and client) provides a critical foundation to the later personal, emotional work. The therapeutic value of an individual's psychodramatic scenework is integrally linked to the depth with which other group members witness, support, empathize with, and thereby help contain that person's work (Emunah, 1994). Additionally, clients will play auxiliary roles in a fellow member's psychodramatic scene with greater commitment once they have established a caring relationship with that person.
5. Developing an ease with (and skills in) drama/acting leads the eventual personal/psychodramatic scenes to be performed with greater authenticity. The more authentic the enactment, the more deeply the client/actor is affected. A familiarity with dramatic processes also reduces self-consciousness and the cognitive distance/disruption that can occur when one is adjusting to various interventions within emotional scenework.
6. Intense and varied emotions can be safely expressed in the context of fictional roles, scenarios, and acting processes. Through these drama therapeutic processes, the therapist comes to know the client's capacity and tolerance for emotional expression, and the degree of containment s/he needs, information that is very useful in terms of guiding the client and making interventions when the client later engages in the deeply personal scenes.
7. In drama therapy, the client's creativity,

expressiveness, spontaneity, playfulness, and imagination are accessed, qualities that enhance self-esteem and self-image. Experiencing, and having others witness, one's strengths enables a person to feel freer to later disclose and grapple with material/parts of the self that are frightening, shameful, or painful.

8. The Integrative Five Phase Model is emotionally and relationally based. That is, of central concern and priority are: (a) the capacity to express, release, contain, master, transcend, and transform familiar, new, and deep-seated emotions; and (b) the capacity to experience play and self-revelation in the context of a meaningful relationship with the therapist and with others in the group. For these reasons, most of the early processes and techniques are geared toward interaction and emotional expression.

9. Techniques used in a session are never isolated, but always interrelated, creating a sense of nondisruptive flow, gradual progression (even within the session), and aesthetic cohesion.

The Therapeutic Process

Phase One: Dramatic Play

The first phase lays the foundation for the work that is to follow. A nonthreatening, playful environment is established. Processes include versions of creative dramatics, improvisation, interactive techniques, and theatre games. These processes and techniques have been adapted and honed over many years for therapeutic purposes to further the goals of Phase One (see Emunah, 1994, Part II). In a group therapy context, many of the techniques are physically active, and most are socially interactive. Individual and group skills are developed. These skills, in turn, promote self-confidence and self-esteem, along with an awareness of and appreciation for the qualities of co-participants. This phase is based on a health model. The strengths and healthy parts of the client are elicited; in keeping with the humanistic paradigm (Maslow, 1968; May, 1975; Rogers, 1961), qualities such as expressiveness, playfulness, creativity, spontaneity, humor and aliveness are nurtured. These qualities develop the clients' ego-strength, enabling them to tolerate the more intense work, often involving painful self-examination, later in the treatment series.

Trust begins to develop–trust in one's own capacities, trust between group members, and trust in the therapist. Acceptance of self and others, a growing connectedness between group members, and group cohesion are central features of a successful group process. Although these features evolve naturally over a period of time, following an often slow and rocky course, drama offers specific means of accelerating and strengthening this course. Interaction between members, which can be so awkward or minimal in beginning phases of verbal groups, is facilitated by drama therapy. Drama is a collaborative art form. This aspect of drama is central to the work in Phase One. The unifying capacity of drama is drawn upon; collective creativity is encouraged. In individual drama therapy, the interactive dramatic processes in Phase One facilitate the development of the relationship with, and trust in, the therapist.

Dramatic play, the most influential conceptual source of Phase One, generates spontaneity and facilitates relationship and interaction. Participants play out personally or socially significant themes symbolically, creatively, and collaboratively. Familiar themes and issues are also left behind, as participants enter the world of the imagination.

Phase One can be the most or the least structured part of the treatment series. It is the least structured when working in a mode of free-associative and nondirective play. By observing and participating in the client's dramatic play, the therapist gains a deeper understanding of underlying issues and themes. Phase One is the most structured part of a treatment series of sessions when the therapist takes the role of active facilitator, easing the clients into the drama therapy mode and treatment process, rather than prioritizing diagnosis or interpretation. Structured dramatic play and theatre games tend to diminish potential reluctance, fear, and self-consciousness, especially with adult clients who have lost touch with the dramatic play of childhood.

It is important that initial activities are simple, engaging, failure-proof, and age-appropriate. The use of unsuitable techniques at this early stage may increase the clients' inhibitions and resistances, which often results in wavering commitments and dropouts. In addition to the fears associated with beginning any therapy process and of joining a group, there are particular fears associated with drama therapy. These include the fear of appearing childish, of having to perform (and failing), and of being asked to be other than oneself (or other than how one actually feels). The therapist should avoid any techniques that might confirm these fears. The trust of the clients needs to be earned during Phase One; the establishment of a positive therapeutic relationship is paramount. Later in the series, the clients' commitment and connectedness to treatment is sustained by peer relationships and the overall sense of group identity.

With sensitive leadership during Phase One, clients experience a sense of permission, freedom, and joy, reminiscent of the experience of dramatic play in childhood. This sense of permission expands into a sense of liberation in Phase Two, with the more developed dramatic acting and scenework.

Phase Two: Scenework

Phase Two progresses from the spontaneous improvised play and structured dramatic processes in Phase One to sustained dramatic scenes, composed of developed roles and characters. The primary dramatic process in this phase is scenework, which is generally improvised (although some drama therapists use existing scripts). Though the link to dramatic play remains present, the conceptual source at the heart of Phase Two is theatre.

In contrast to psychodrama, in which protagonists play the roles of themselves in a variety of situations, the scenework of Phase Two involves playing roles other than those reflecting one's own life. This allows for greater role distance and less immediate self-disclosure, a useful step in the development of trust and spontaneity.

The aspect of drama central to Phase Two is the notion that acting gives permission to be different. Diverse scenes and roles afford clients the opportunity to experience and exhibit new sides of themselves. Within the dramatic context, latent aspects of the self emerge and suppressed emotions are expressed. Wished-for qualities or characteristics can be tried on and embodied. The shadow part of the person can be tolerated and given voice through the sanctioned theatrical role.

The critical point of awareness for the therapist at this stage is to ensure the freedom that promotes self-expression and role-expansion. More specifically, the therapist should not insist on verbal processing or ownership. Urging the person to analyze everything that emerges spontaneously or within the context of the role can be inhibiting. The beginning of Phase Two should be one of liberation, not inhibition. It is important not to destroy the very context that is enabling the transformation to take place.

By the middle of Phase Two, clients begin naturally to comment on or to discuss their enactments. Concurrently, the scenes typically take on greater depth and complexity. Early Phase Two scenes generally involve more superficial, though often humorous interactions and plots, but gradually both acting and content become more multidimensional, nuanced, realistic, and emotionally-laden. Following the scenes, there may be manifestations of surprise at the emotion displayed in the scene or the type of character played. Frequent types of remarks are: "I can't believe how much anger I expressed in that role," "I've never acted like that in my life," "that's so different than the way I usually behave," "I loved playing the rebellious child because I was always so good in real life." Toward the latter part of Phase Two, clients relate more personally to their enacted roles. Comments here may be: "That's a pattern of mine, so it felt familiar to play that role, and I became more aware of the way I deal with conflict," "that part helped me express the grief I have suppressed," or "I just got an insight into how my behavior as a teen affected my whole family." This is an exciting point in the series, for here clients really make the connection between drama and therapy. This connection is often expressed as an "aha!" experience. For the first time, they simultaneously experience this activity as both drama and therapy.

The end of Phase Two is marked not only by the responses of the actors but also by those of the audience. Clients watching the scenes begin to express associations they had to the scenes and feelings or memories that are evoked. An improvisation about a couple arguing might remind someone of their divorce; a scene about loss might elicit sadness and even tears, in much the same way that watching a movie or play affords cathartic release. Scenes also help people to recall positive moments in their lives and give occasion for these to be shared with the group. This verbal processing is not forced but spontaneous; clients manifest the desire to review and discuss the scenes.

Because of the personal disclosures and potentially intense emotional reactions arising at this point, it is important that Phase Two occur only after some degree of trust within the group and with the therapist has already been established.

To summarize, in the first two stages of drama therapy, the dramatic medium provides the safeguard, or disguise, that enables self-revelation. In this context, participants often seem to both expose more of themselves and to feel safer than in normal everyday encounters. Gradually, as trust continues to develop between group members and towards the therapist, the need for safeguards dissolve, and what is exposed can be consciously tolerated and integrated. The verbal processing at the end of Phase Two steers the scenework in a more personal direction.

Phase Three: Role Play

Phase Three is marked by the shifting of the dramatizations from the imaginary to the actual: clients are now ready to use the dramatic medium to explore situations in their own lives. Current predicaments, conflicts, and relationships are presented and examined. The thin line separating drama and real life is particularly apparent at this point. The scenes, based on real life, seem so real. Yet the fact that they are enactments rather than real life occurrences is of critical significance in terms of therapeutic possibilities. The stage becomes a laboratory setting in which real life can be explored and experimented with safety. Central to Phase Three is the notion of drama as *rehearsal for life.*

The primary dramatic process in Phase

Three is role play. Clients replay confusing or disturbing interactions with friends, express feelings to significant people in their lives, confront people with whom they are angry, and practice for anxiety-producing events. Common themes shared by a particular group are often explored. A group of recovering substance abusers, for example, may enact scenes related to the challenges of sobriety. The drama therapist uses many psychodramatic techniques such as doubling, playing with time, role reversal, along with theatrical techniques such as adding or eliminating characters, or highlighting particular moments.

The dramatic examination of interpersonal issues within the group is also largely the domain of Phase Three, a phase that incorporates many aspects of psychodrama and sociodrama. Often the joy and freedom, interaction and collaboration of the first two phases highlight the group's commonality, and contributes to a honeymoon period. But in Phase Three, which typically occurs in the middle of a treatment series, differences within the group are apparent, and conflicts may emerge. Many of my groups explore not only personal but sociocultural dynamics. For example, racial dynamics and tensions within the group, which are often unspoken, can be brought to dramatic light in an attempt to raise the group's consciousness about race, privilege, power, and the complexities of oppression, intermingled with individuals' intra-psychic issues and interpersonal styles.

By the time a group reaches Phase Four, interpersonal issues within the group are typically resolved and a sense of support and respect for difference predominates, a necessary component for the content of the work to deepen. By the end of the Phase Four, the deeper quality of therapeutic/ aesthetic work takes the interrelationships within the group to a new level. Clients often feel profound respect, awe, and love as they witness and hold one another in the latter stages of the therapeutic journey.

Role play and role theory are the most influential conceptual sources of Phase Three. Through dramatization and ensuing discussion, clients gain a clearer view of the roles they play in life and the patterns that emerge in their interactions. Moments from real life are magnified and elucidated under the illuminating lights of the theatrical stage. Clients simultaneously act and watch themselves in action, a feat difficult to accomplish on a regular basis in real life. The measure of distance from reality afforded by drama stimulates the functioning of the self-observing ego. This distance can be capitalized upon by pausing in the midst of a scene or just after the scene ends; at this point the players examine each person's role and behavior, how each interpreted and was affected by the other's role and behavior, and how effective each person was in his or her role. The drama therapist gradually makes interventions, under the auspices of theatrical directions, which facilitate awareness and change, rather than needless repetition.

Clients play not only themselves, but also other people in their lives. For example, adolescents may be interviewed as their parents, followed by enactments of relevant parent-teen conflicts. In playing the role of others, the client gains perspective; the responses and motivations of others are better understood. Taking on the role of another person in one's life relating to oneself (for example, if I play the role of my brother while someone else plays me) enables one to encompass and assimilate the multitude of roles and facets of self that are manifested in relation to others.

One technique I developed for work with my graduate students as they enter Phase Three in a course entitled, "Drama Therapy Process and Technique," is a "support group for close ones of students in the first year drama therapy program." We sit in a circle, and each student plays the role of someone s/he is very connected to (i.e., a parent, sibling, spouse, friend), while I facilitate a meeting beginning with how people are related to the person they know in the program, and feelings they have about the person being in the program. This process eases people into personal role play within a group format, enables people to get to know each other more intimately, within the context of their outside relationships, and begins to stir up individual issues and (future) enactments. For example, this session is sometimes followed by sessions in which the students (as themselves) make phone calls (using a phone as a prop) to the person they played in the support group. The support group enactment also indicates the range of readiness for more personal disclosure: some students play more evocative roles that have a deeper bearing on their real life relationships and concerns, while others choose more distanced roles.

Work in Phase Three often occurs on a behavioral level; role play in assertiveness training or conflict resolution, for example, is considered Phase Three material. However, through skillful intervention on the part of the drama therapist, insight into roles and behavioral patterns is also achieved. The drama therapist at this point needs to pay careful attention to the direction of the scenes, ensuring that the client is taken further, toward understanding or discovery of options, rather than simply repeating real life actions. Verbal processing is generally very integrated with dramatic work at this point. Dramatization and discussion help clients not only vent feelings and practice new behaviors, but also understand and change underlying dynamics. Most importantly, at this stage clients experience themselves not only as actors, but as directors, playwrights, audiences, and critics of their own life dramas.

It is toward the end of this phase that clients often begin to experience a sense of hope for change in their lives. The hope comes as a result of experiencing (as opposed to only imagining) themselves responding (via the dramatic mode) to personal situations differently from the nonconstructive patterns of response they fall prey to in reality. The implication is that if they could act that way in scenes that are almost real, perhaps they could act that way for real. The importance of the development of acting skills in Phases One and Two must be reemphasized here. Without a certain level of dramatic proficiency, the scenes are not real enough for this dynamic to take place. It is at this point, too, that clients frequently report that they responded to a difficult real life situation in a new or uncharacteristic way. Many clients have told me that this was accomplished by pretending they were acting in a scene. Put in other terms, these clients made use of the capacities they had manifested in drama to cope more effectively and healthfully with the trials of real life.

Phase Four: Culminating Enactment

The examination of roles, relationships, and conflicts in current life situations gradually leads clients to a deeper level of introspection. The increased level of consciousness regarding role and life patterns achieved in Phase Three facilitates entry into the subconscious. Phase Four is marked by the shift from concrete, present-day issues to more core issues in clients' lives. The past comes closer to the surface, and unconscious material becomes more accessible. Memories, dreams, associations, and images–involving family constellations, childhood traumas, significant events–shed light onto unresolved issues, recurrent themes, and ongoing struggles. Scenes frequently revolve around experiences that have affected or disturbed the person's present. Some scenes entail revelations that were until now kept hidden from the group, the therapist, or even from oneself.

The primary conceptual source of Phase Four is "Psychodrama" (Chapter 18) and the primary dramatic processes are psychodramatic. There is an increased focus on the individual within the group, as the inner life of protagonists are dramatically explored and their stories relived. Many of Moreno's (1946) psychodramatic techniques, such as *doubling,* are vital early in Phase Four. By the middle of Phase Four, clients are enacting what I call *culminating scenes.* The culminating scenes are elaborations and deeper explorations of themes that have emerged during the preceding phases.

Though the culminating scenes resemble psychodramatic scenes, they have two unique features. First, the scenes are performed only at a point at which clients have already developed proficiency in drama, as well as a high level of trust in the group. Second, the content of the scenes is emergent, growing out of the process thus far. These features enable a degree of depth, subtlety and complexity that is often not possible when one begins a treatment series with psychodrama. The scenes are enacted with a particular sense of authenticity and possess intense power on a theatrical as well as a therapeutic level. In performance-oriented drama therapy groups, *self-revelatory performances* (Emunah, 1994) are usually based on culminating scenes.

There is an evolution to Phase Four as the degree of self-exposure and emotional intensity interweaves with the level of group cohesion and support. The gradual, paced process in drama therapy, in which significant issues (which cannot be predicted or prescribed in advance by the client or the therapist) emerge, facilitates a journey of surprise and discovery. The notion that to pretend or be disguised enables revelation and exposure, a notion capitalized upon in the early stages, is important to reemphasize here. In drama therapy one begins by acting rather than by reenacting. This process of acting steers the client away from initiating therapeutic work around predictable and familiar issues that may be unconsciously presented as a shield against dealing with more authentically significant issues. The gradual, paced process enables the therapist both to gauge and to develop the client's tolerance for emotionality and self-exposure before embarking on the intense culminating scenes of Phase Four.

The culminating scenes are a climactic point in the group process. Revelation, disclosure, and sharing are heightened; insight is deepened. As buried emotions emerge and are given an outlet for expression, a powerful experience of catharsis occurs. The therapeutic intensity is matched by the theatrical power of the scenes; both are matched by the level of group support and cohesion. Inner resources, creative reserves, and untapped strengths are drawn upon in developing these scenes. There are often various stages and levels of exploration: one client's culminating scene may have several parts and take more than one session to unfold. The enactments result in a unique sense of artistic achievement and personal mastery over often very painful content.

The immediacy and potency of this kind of dramatization tend to heighten the empathy of the other group members and the therapist. In this process of sharing and showing one's internal world, a burden is lifted, an inner weight removed. What was private is now witnessed. This often leads to an experience of intense acceptance and forgiveness, as clients expose what had previously been hidden, even from themselves. A sense of exoneration and of communion ensues–in individual therapy by and with the therapist, in group work within the group, and in performance-oriented drama therapy with the outside world–reminiscent of the ritual purging ceremonies of indigenous cultures, in which evil spirits were expelled in the presence of the entire tribe (Collomb, 1977). The ritualistic aspects of drama pervading the end of Phase Four create a transition to the final stage of the drama therapy treatment series.

Phase Five: Dramatic Ritual

After the climactic, culminating scenes of Phase Four (the duration of which varies widely), the series begins to come to a close. This closure is in itself an important developmental process, facilitating the integration and assimilation of the therapeutic progress made in the preceding phases. The work of Phase Five assists clients in carrying the changes made within the context of drama therapy into the outside world. At the same time, the multiple and complex feelings regarding termination are explored. Phase Five is about transition and closure.

Phase Five is conceptually linked to ritual, and primary dramatic processes are dramatic rituals. In early societies, dramatic rituals were ways in which communities marked points of transition, shared fears, sorrows, wishes and successes, and celebrated events. The celebratory aspect of drama is central to Phase Five. Dramatic rituals are incorporated to help clients review the treatment series, evaluate progress, give each other feedback, experience the rewards of accomplishment, and express both the sadness and joy of completion. The processes also serve to reflect and intensify the sense of unity and kinship within the group. The unique entity formed by the group and the particular interrelationships within the group are acknowledged and honored.

The intense feelings evoked by the therapy process and its imminent conclusion, along with the deep level of intimacy that has been experienced within the group, can sometimes be best conveyed via dramatic ritual. Collectively developed and repeatable group creations, composed of powerful images, metaphor and story, rhythmic sounds, and poetry and movement, enable the expression of a seldom-mentioned dimension to the therapy process: the spiritual dimension. I am referring to the sense of awe one encounters during a process that entails uncovering layers, discovering what was previously unknown, accessing the unconscious, and transforming pain into art. In the course of treatment, there have been transformations, on small and large scales, witnessed in others, experienced in oneself, and shared with the group (or in individual therapy, with the therapist). These transformations can be perceived not only from psychological and aesthetic standpoints, but from the spiritual perspective.

Much of the description of Phase Five applies also to the final phase of each session within the series. Closure of the treatment series and of each individual session is not a matter of implying that there has been resolution. Rather, closure provides an arena for reviewing what has transpired, recognizing the steps that have been taken, and making the transition from the drama therapy session to outside reality. The drama therapist devises and utilizes creative techniques to facilitate this review of the process. In work with one 10-year-old girl, at the end of each session I became her secretary, jotting down notes as she recalled what was significant about that session. This became a closing ritual to our sessions, helping her to digest and integrate our work.

Significant points in time, powerful scenes, trying periods, critical conflicts or challenges, and important insights are all recalled and reviewed in Phase Five. This retrospection deepens the level of awareness of all aspects of the process. The entire journey is, in a sense, encapsulated, helping the client to grasp and own the experience, with all its impact. The rituals in Phase Five provide a kind of framing of the treatment session and series.

By the end of Phase Five, clients tend to feel validated for the process they have been through. The dramatic rituals help achieve this for, like all rituals, they mark life events, rather than letting events fade into oblivion. In this way, there is a sense not only of loss for what is over, but rather of appreciation for what has been gained.

The intensive and carefully designed process of closure not only helps clients reflect on and integrate the past, but creates a sense of opening to the future–pointing to the steps that lie ahead, the possibilities, and the hope as one continues the journey. (See Figure 4.1 for a summary of the phases.)

Practical Applications of the Phases

The five phases are best viewed not as rigid entities, but as an analysis of the gradual unfolding of a therapeutic process. The phases are fluid and often overlapping. Phase One, for example, remains present on some level throughout the series; it is important not to drop the playful component, even as the clients enter more emotional terrain. Elements of several phases are often present within a single session.

The phases are not intended to be prescriptions for drama therapy, but rather helpful guidelines, which can assist the drama therapist in pacing, identifying needs, assessing progress, and determining appropriate techniques and interventions. Beginning drama therapists, in particular, may be unsure how to assess the degree of containment that is needed, how much and how far to develop therapeutic material, how much to encourage verbal processing after dramatic enactments, whether to interpret scenes or to encourage the client to make personal connections to fictional enactments. Identifying the phase the group or client is in helps make informed therapeutic decisions.

The model is suited to work with any population. However, some populations may be best served by an emphasis on a particular phase. For example, some groups of children or of people with a developmental disability may benefit most from Phase One work. Phase Three work, on the other hand, may be most appropriate for support groups (dealing with specific issues) composed of high functioning adults. If a group is already openly talking about a given issue (for example, achieving sobriety, or living with HIV), that group should begin in Phase Three. However, after some time, dipping backwards into Phase Two can help clients experience respite from real life concerns and permission to act in new ways.

The model is especially relevant to groups with a fixed membership. With rolling group membership, there is an increased fluctuation in the phases (as the group dynamics and needs shift from session to session) rather than the more steady progression typical of fixed membership groups. With changing membership, Phases Four and Five are rarely apropos. My own preference is for fixed group membership, even in brief treatment, to allow for progression, and to foster the interrelationships and group cohesion that I believe play a most significant role in the journey toward health and well-being.

This phase-oriented model is based on work over a period of time, but this period of time has a wide range–typically, from eight sessions to several years. Brief drama therapy that entails at least eight sessions can generally follow the evolutionary course from

	Phase One	Phase Two	Phase Three	Phase Four	Phase Five
Primary conceptual sources	Dramatic Play	Theatre (scenework)	Role Play	Psychodrama (culminating enactments)	Dramatic Ritual
Primary dramatic processes	Creative drama Improvised play Theatre games & D. T. techniques	Scenework (fictional)	Role Play role reversal replays of life scenes	Exploratory reenactments Culminating scenes	Dramatic Rituals
FOCUS	Humanistic/ Health Model	Experimentation/ Liberation	Explore, rehearse preview & review current issues	Core themes	Embracing the whole
Objectives	Trust Interaction & Relationship Spontaneity & Creativity	"Selves"–expression Role–expansion Emotional expansion	Self/role-awareness (self-observing ego) Role flexibility Perspective	Emotional catharsis Insight Empathy & Intimacy	Integration Review & Transition Acknowledgment & Celebration
Therapeutic Progression	Spontaneity & Freedom	Liberation & Expansion	Behavioral Change & Hope	Catharsis & Insight	Integration

Figure 4.1. Integrative Five Phase Model.

Phase One through Phase Five outlined in this chapter. However, I have found that even in briefer intensives such as three-day workshops, the evolution of all five phases often occurs, though with more active facilitation on the therapist's part. The ascertainment of phases is especially important in brief drama therapy (Emunah, 1996), because the drama therapist often needs to be a more active facilitator, gently encouraging the group or client to move forward through the phases. In longer-term work the therapist is more of a witness to and follower of the group's pace and evolution.

There is no set formula for the way in which a group progresses through these five phases. In some cases, the first two phases may be very brief; in others they may comprise the bulk of the series. In many forms of brief drama therapy each of the phases may not be lived out. Rather, the drama therapist determines which phase is most appropriate for and useful to the client or group, and focuses the limited work within that mode. Phase Three is typically the most applicable phase to brief drama therapy. Clients tend to enter brief therapy in order to deal with a particular problem, and are prepared to tackle specific issues, feelings, and conflicts related to this problem directly–all of which point to Phase Three work. The work of Phases One and Two is often too indirect and circuitous for brief drama therapy. While some of the playful and fictional components of these phases can be incorporated, lingering in these phases can lead clients to feel that their presenting problems are not being taken seriously enough. On the other hand, the work of Phase Four, revolving around deep-seated material, is often also beyond the realm of brief therapy. Phase Four relies on preparedness and the gradual unfolding of layered therapeutic material; moving into this phase in either a premature or a superficial manner can be countertherapeutic. In that Phase Five represents a culmination and integration of the other four phases, it, too, is less applicable to brief therapy. In general, Phases One and Five tend to be least incorporated phases in brief therapy. Phase Two is incorporated primarily as a prelude to Phase Three, and Phase Four is incorporated selectively and carefully, in accordance with the emotional readiness of the particular client or group. A particular phase may not only be most suitable given the length of treatment provided, but also may be influenced by the therapeutic orientation of a particular facility (Emunah, 1996).

Despite the limitations of the use of all five phases in some forms of brief drama therapy, elements drawn from each phase are incorporated to enhance the Phase Three-oriented course of treatment, with the following primary objectives: Phase One for building interrelationships and individual strengths; Phase Two for expanding role repertoire and creating a sense of permission and possibility; Phase Four for deepening the level of catharsis, insight, and intimacy; and Phase Five for supporting integration and closure. Different drama therapists, because of their own orientation and skills, may feel more affinity with a particular phase, and their work may incorporate little of the other phases. Those with a stronger creative drama background or belief in the importance of play and spontaneity, for example, may lean toward Phase One work, and an entire series with such a therapist may remain in this phase. Drama therapists with a stronger background in psychodrama and a preference for in-depth psychotherapeutic work may focus on Phase Four. Those who are more comfortable with here-and-now, concrete approaches to psychotherapy will probably make most use of Phase Three. Theatre-oriented drama therapists may find Phase Two the most natural and interesting. Thus the phases can be viewed not only as stages of group development, but rather as models of practice.

In my own practice, I have made equal use of all phases, with different phases being emphasized with particular groups. My groups with emotionally disturbed and acting-out adolescents (Emunah, 1985, 1990, 1995) centered on Phases Two and Three. With high-functioning adult clients the emphasis leans toward Phase Four. In my individual work with children, Phase One is the most primary and extended phase, developing into Phase Two, and with older children the latter phases are also a significant part of the overall treatment process. Of course, it is not only population that determines emphasis, but the unique configuration of clients within a given group, or the dynamics of an individual in one-to-one therapy. In the majority of cases, I find in retrospect that all five phases have been present to a surprisingly equal degree.

Although the Integrative Five Phase model was developed in the context of group drama therapy with emotionally disturbed adults, I have found that the model is equally applicable to high-functioning adults, and in a wide variety of contexts. Students and colleagues have applied the model in work with a range of populations, age groups, and treatment contexts, including very specific treatment issues such work with male veteran survivors of sexual assault (Mulkey, 2004).

Interventions in Phase Four

Within Phase Four, skillful intervention on the part of the therapist is paramount. One scene may unfold through a series of directions/interventions. These may be numerous and complex, but they are also subtle and discreet, not breaking the flow of the action or the client's immersion in the scene. The focus is on sustaining and deepening the emotional richness of the work. The risk in direction/intervention is that the client's emotional engagement will be disrupted, and s/he will become self-conscious or too cognitively oriented. On the other hand, the therapist's directions are an essential means of steering the work toward the heart and essence of the client's issues and therapeutic needs, prioritizing authenticity and ultimately healing. The original content often shifts and transforms, as the work spirals toward issues of greater meaning that are closer to the client's core life themes.

The interventions involve a trusting dance between therapist and client, who are in close connection with one another. Any resistances, impasses, fears, impulses, and images of the client are respected and incorporated, as part of the unfolding process. Both therapist and client need to have faith that going further and deeper into the heart of an issue, even if this leads to feeling more pain, will also be the way through the pain, into some kind of clarity, release, oasis, or hope. The way out is not easy, and does not involve a quick fix or superficially represented change; the way out is by going deeper in, and eventually through. This deep entry into the heart of an exploration must not, however, involve any retraumatization. The drama therapist's choices in intervention involve working something through dramatically, authentically, and often aesthetically, but without reliving past wounding experiences that could retraumatize the client.

Early objectives in intervention often revolve around heightening and/or containing emotion. For example, the client may say a certain line that evokes a great deal of feeling, or is significant, and the therapist's direction to repeat this line amplifies the emotion. *Doubling* or expressing underlying feelings can also heighten emotion. Physicalizing a dilemma, or having hurtful thoughts or memories dramatically represented (though avoiding having these played out in a realistic fashion that could be retraumatizing), can heighten emotionality and immediacy. Stepping back from the action, expressing feelings about the process as it is unfolding, sculpting others to depict and externalize one's emotions, and reversing roles are potential ways of containing emotion. There is often a back and forth between heightening and containing emotion within the work; once containment is offered, the client feels ready for another level of emotional expression and exploration.

Another important objective involves clarifying, exploring the origins of, and distilling important issues. The questions how and why are often asked, without necessarily stopping the action. Insight is gleaned through the work, but within an emotional playing field. Thus the probing and reaching for deeper understanding is not only a cognitive endeavor. As the issues become more clear, distilled, and understood, the directions toward healing can become more specifically tailored and distinctive.

I believe that we cannot change the past; we can only work through it, and try to heal ourselves. I therefore avoid psychodramatic scenes that involve asking clients to depict how they would have liked things to be. A client exploring psychological damage from (a past with) abusive or neglectful parents will not be asked what kind of parents she would have liked to have or how she would have preferred her childhood to be. I believe that such an intervention can lead to post-enactment longing and unnecessary sorrow, or even further wounding. However, I might well steer a scene toward recontacting the pain in that past, followed by easing the client into becoming a parent to herself, tending to that wounded child. And this leads to a key objective in many Phase Four scenes: *finding an internal nurturing parent.* The internal nurturing parent, who can be a source of great comfort and healing, emerges within the emotional framework of the scene, and develops through the therapist's interventions. Thus, at the same time that the client may be immersed in primal pain, s/he is also drawing on and activating her own self-healing capacities.

Concurrently, the protagonist is no longer alone in his or her pain, but rather is supported and witnessed by the therapist and other group members. Often group members will be called upon as a double for the protagonist, or simply to have physical connection (such as hands gently touching the protagonist's back or shoulders). Clients who take on the role of the protagonist's wounded child usually feel deep empathy, and their own well of emotions is evoked. The experience of another's empathy (and I believe that empathy is heightened in witnessing personal material in this dramatic form) is another aspect to the multifaceted healing. Group members may also be called upon to become a chorus. People watching sit close by, minimizing distance, sometimes even forming a circle around the client.

In directing Phase Four scenes, the drama therapist uses his or her own intuition, creativity, and contemplation, but is always in close contact with the client, and makes use of the client's particular imagery and language. The therapist needs to remain open to surprises, new information, shifts and turns in the progress of the enactments, and also needs to feel some spaciousness around possibilities of intervention, incorporating aesthetic and often poetic and metaphorical elements. Aesthetic notions in directing/intervening, and therapeutic orientations in directing/intervening, often coincide and support each other (Emunah, 1994).

Prolonged and emotionally deep Phase Four scenes bring both protagonist and group to a somewhat altered state of consciousness, and switching to a verbal mode afterward for processing can be jarring and at times counterproductive. It is best to linger in the emotional realm, and yet still offer some time for reflection and integration. This can be in the form of dramatic rituals, nonverbal exchanges, or simply asking participants to say one word or phrase from the enactments that personally touched them. Somatic or action-oriented work, such as falling and being caught in a circle (typically beginning with the protagonist in the center, followed by others) with the group as a chorus uttering affirming words, offer other possibilities for further support and closure. The Integrative Five Phase Model is based on an organic flow, avoiding harsh disruptions; this includes sensitivity to shifts from emotional, dramatic work to verbal discussion, and in many cases an avoidance of such a shift. Processing can also take place during the scene, and in action, serving to stay in touch with how the protagonist is faring during the Phase Four enactments, reinforce important moments, and attain a meta-level awareness of the impact of the work. More cognitive and verbal reflection often occurs at the start of the following session, rather than immediately after the emotional, dramatic work.

Example of a Phase Four Scene

The following was an early Phase Four scene, occurring at the fourteenth session in a group of high-functioning professional people. Names, facts, and some of the dialogue have been changed to ensure confidentiality. To help keep track of the multiple interventions, and turns within the scene, I have listed each step, even though in reality it was one fluid sequence.

1. Larina, a 45-year-old Mexican woman who has lived in the U.S. for the past sixteen years, and works as a human resources manager of a large company, creates a *Self-Sculpture* (Emunah, 1994, 1999), placing four people from the group in positions to represent the parts of her that: (a) "need to work hard and be successful," (b) "want to rest and hibernate," (c) "are struggling to control it all," and (d) "feel ugly and incapable." When I ask her if she wants to further refine the images, she places the part that needs to be successful on one side of the room, the part that wants to hibernate on the other, and the struggle to control it all in the center. The ugly/incapable part is placed huddled in the corner, back turned away from the group.

2. I ask her to give lines that represent each stance. We then have the action come alive. There is feisty dialogue: "Work overtime! This needs to get done, now! Fatso! You can't keep up. Shut up, I need a long sleep." The centerpiece of trying to hold it all together just grunts in a tense and constricted way, while being pulled by an imaginary rope on both sides, and struggling to hold herself together. This part is played by a male group member, Andreas. Larina watches and then freezes the scene.

3. I stand next to Larina and ask what she is feeling. She is especially focused on and emotional about the part Andreas is playing. I ask her to take over this role. This is clearly a challenge for her, and takes some courage. In this role, Larina's grunt begins in a constricted way, but soon becomes an intense wail, releasing frustrated anger and hurt. I can see her body move from a tightness to a release, and along with the release come tears.

4. I ask Andreas to go behind Larina, as a kind of support and double, enabling Larina to stay longer with this release/expression.

5. Larina is now sobbing and, standing beside her, I ask her to call for what she needs, from within this emotional state. She says, "friends and courage."

6. I ask her to pick someone to represent

Friends, and another Courage. I place Maria who she has representing Friends, at the opposite end of the room, facing Larina. I place Lia who represents Courage, also at some distance, on the other side of the room.

7. I ask Larina to call out to Maria/Friends (from across the large room) for support. I continue to stay at her side. She calls forth, adding the lines through her tears, "I can't do it alone." Spontaneously they walk toward each other. She begins speaking to Maria in Spanish, and hugging her.

8. I notice that those watching seem deeply moved and engaged. I ask everyone in the audience to come up and also be Larina's friends, along with Maria (thereby magnifying the sense of support, and underscoring that support exists within this actual group).

9. I now ask Larina to call for Courage. She does so loudly and forcefully. Maria is behind her, offering a supportive presence (the rest of the group has sat down again as witnesses to the scene). I quietly ask Lia not to budge until the call is strong enough to propel her to respond. Finally, Lia walks forward and says, "Thank you for calling for me. I am here."

10. I walk with Larina, who now also has Friends (Maria) and Courage (Lia) behind her, with their hands on her shoulders, toward the part of herself in the corner that feels ugly and incapable, played in a cowering way by Mirta. As I look at Larina, a very beautiful and competent woman, I gently ask her how this part came to be. She says it is what she was told. "By who?" I ask. She thinks for a moment, and then says, "by my father, my ex-husband, and society."

11. I pick three people to play out these roles, and ask her to give them one or several lines: She starts with *Society:* "you should be home baking cookies." *Ex-husband:* "you need to lose weight. I'm not attracted to you." *Father:* "you are fat and ugly." Sadly, she adds more lines for her father, which clarify and intensify the content we are working with: "you're nothing, no good for anything. You're a piece of shit." I ask the three men playing these roles to stand close to each other, but at a distance from Larina, and with their backs toward her, reiterating that these are voices from the past but ones she, Larina, still carries inside her (this structure also creates some distance, during an obviously painful sequence).

12. As the three lines are voiced, in all their harshness, I stand near Larina. Larina is crying as she listens to this chorus of painful lines. I now ask her to respond, with the support of Maria and Lia (who still stand behind Larina, and now serve as *doubles,* repeating what Larina says). Larina, along with Maria and Lia, tell the voices they are not fair or true, and gradually their responses to the voices include anger, aimed primarily at the father.

13. I direct her, along with her doubles, to walk over to the voices and push the group of male voices further away (with the help of Maria and Lia). (This heightens emotionality and immediacy at the same time that it accesses her agency. I notice that nearly all the people watching are now in tears.)

14. I reiterate that Larina is battling the voices of the past. But there are also voices of the present, and the future, which I now suggest we represent, facing her, in a different part of the room. She gives the lines: "you are beautiful, you are capable, you are loveable," as three people who have been watching the scene spontaneously and eagerly come up to play out these supportive lines. I direct the voices of the past to continue to be heard but more faintly, and from a greater distance, with the ones of the present/future heard more fully.

15. This is a very poignant moment as Larina listens to and looks at these voices. There is some choice, of which voices to lis-

ten to, which ones to face. Her supporters are still present, behind and around her, touching her shoulders. She is deep in tears at this point. Her gaze is toward the present and future.

16. I now ask Larina to attend to the part of herself cowering in a corner, who feels ugly and incapable, assumed by Mirta. For a moment she spontaneously looks back at Lia, who is a double/supporter, but also represented Courage, and says, "I need you." Lia responds, "I am here, totally. Feel me." Larina cries more deeply as she looks at Mirta. I ask her how old this part of herself is. She says, "very old, and very young. She has always been there. She took in my dad's abuse. At her most destroyed, she is twelve."

17. I ask Larina to address this 12-year-old self. She sits next to her on the floor, and tries to speak. Finally she says, slowly and gently, "what he told you about yourself was not true. He was fighting his own battles, and he laid them on you. You are not ugly. You are not a nothing. I know how hurt you are. But you are something, someone special. Do not hold onto the things he calls you. They are not true. I have come back to tell you that. I am here for you. I have come back for you." Both Larina and Mirta are sobbing through this exchange.

18. After this tearful monologue continues for awhile, switching into Spanish for some time, I motion to Larina to be the 12-year-old self (switching places with Mirta), and Mirta to play the part Larina just played, repeating the lines Larina has just spoken. Mirta does so, in English and then in Spanish, as Larina takes in the soothing and nurturing words which just minutes ago were hers. Then, I ask her to return to her adult self (for the ending of the scene). She reaches out to hug her younger self. As the two women embrace, I discreetly ask the group to come around them in a small circle.

19. After a long silent pause, in which we all let out some deep breaths, I have the group circle around Larina, everyone standing, placing their arms on her shoulders and back, and softly muttering spontaneous words of support. People say, "we are your friends, Larina; we are here for you; you are beautiful; you are capable; you can rest here" and so forth. Next I invite Mirta into the circle. The process transforms into a falling in the center of the circle, with the group catching and softly repeating lines the person in the center instructs us to say, the lines s/he needs to hear at this moment. Eventually everyone in the group takes a turn.

Phase Four and Self-Revelatory Performance

The fact that many Phase Four scenes have such theatrical power and richness led me to consider their use in performance. I conceived of *self-revelatory performance* (Emunah, 1994) as a process of taking hold of core themes and fashioning this material into a multilayered theatrical piece. The central differences between autobiographical theatre and self-revelatory performance are that the latter: (1) involves current issues (though these are often rooted in the past) that the performer is in the midst of grappling with, and (2) focuses on healing and transformation, rather than simply sharing the story or depicting the issues. Self-revelatory performances tend to be theatrically riveting because of their immediacy as the actor works through something of critical importance live, on stage, with the audience as witness. My students have greatly developed this form, creating full-length performance pieces, many of which are remarkably aesthetic and transformative for both actors and audiences. One former student now teaches this form and has written about it (Rubin, 2007). Self-revelatory performance presents another opportunity for drama therapists, either as performers, in which they use their theatre/performance background for personal inquiry, or as directors, which requires skills in directing Phase Four scenes along with a keen aesthetic sensibility.

Individual Therapy and Single Sessions

How does the Integrative Five Phase Model apply to work with individuals? The following is an example drawn from ongoing work with an individual client in which elements of various phases, as well as premises of the Integrative Five Phase Model, are apparent within each session. Elements of the work and facts about the client have been changed to ensure privacy and confidentiality. I will briefly describe parts of the fifth and sixth weekly sessions. The client, Don, is a very bright, competent, socially skilled, Caucasian-American 34-year-old poet who came to therapy because of his uncertainty and confusion about his choice of both career and male life partner. Early sessions revealed the extent to which he absorbed other people's opinions about his life choices, leaving Don feeling anxious and distraught, out of touch with his own desires, and unable to trust his own decisions.

Excerpt of Two Sessions with an Individual

In our fifth session, Don speaks of hearing and replaying other people's perspectives in his mind, and not being sure what is his own voice. We begin tossing a ball back and forth, each time stating one of these perspectives/lines (of others in his life). I repeat some of the lines he says, or add ones he has talked about. There are lines such as, "you could be doing better," "you are so capable . . . ," "you went to the best schools, you should get into a more traditional field," and so forth. We then walk around the room, stating these lines. My intention is to get these lines out into the *playspace,* to externalize the voices, as well as to energize the body and free up the emotional psyche.

The line that seems to have the most charge, "you can do better," is then used in the format of a *Line Repetition* technique (Emunah, 1994). I repeat this line, and he responds with, "But I'm doing what I love." We improvise as we dramatically play out these lines, and then we role reverse.

To my surprise, Don begins crying for the first time since he began therapy. He says that his tears come from "being able to hear these lines I rarely say or hear, said back." I sit next to him, and after awhile ask him what images came up as he repeated the two lines. "I felt like cement when I said, 'you could do better,' and I felt like there was quicksand when I said, 'but I'm doing what I love.'" So we begin walking around the room, both of us repeating each line, the former with a feeling of walking over cement, and the latter, trying to get over/through quicksand, naming other thoughts and images as they come up. Not stopping the quicksand action, I ask him what we can do, and he says, "find a tree branch." He briefly speaks to and then as the tree branch, creating an anchor for himself.

Recalling how much hearing the line "I'm doing what I love" moved him, and wanting him to have the opportunity to linger with and develop this line/perspective, I say we are both going to be lawyers giving our final summation to the jury. First he sits down as jury member, while I plead for practicality and "you can do better," offering arguments (drawn from what he himself has said in sessions). Then it is his turn to give his final summation, representing doing what one loves. He comes up with a very moving monologue, ending with "you only have your heart." I ask him to join me as jury member, and we both sit quietly for a moment, absorbing the impact of these last lines.

In our next session, we walk around the room, and I ask him to throw out any images. He says, "static . . . the static of other people's voices and opinions." We walk, magnifying the somatic feeling in our bodies of having other's voices inside us, then let this feeling go, then walk silently in our own thoughts and wishes, while still being in close relationship with each other. I ask him what images arise when we remove the static. He pauses, and finally responds: "a molecule or atom."

"A single unit," I say.

"Yes," he responds, visibly moved. "There are electrons around it but it doesn't absorb these."

He walks around as a molecule/atom, and I buzz around him as the electrons. [We joke about we how we never know how high school science will come back to us.]

I ask him to sit, internally holding onto the image of himself as the atom. He is calm, but then adds, "It feels like me. Like this is who I am. But I'm embarrassed."

R: "To tell me?"

D: "No, I feel so safe with you. I don't know why but I feel embarrassed. It is just that it is me, to the core, without the fluff around, and no one sees that."

I recall an earlier session in which he had created a Self-Sculpture that included an embarrassed part. He had represented this part of himself with a ball behind a curtain. I put this ball back in the same spot behind the curtain, and now ask him to move there, and to speak as the embarrassed part of himself. He utters quietly, "just me, just me, just me" over and over, and soon is cradling himself.

We sit down. He is emotional and shaken. "That was some deep shit."

I think about what a perfect image (the atom) he has come up with for individuation. I recall the work we have done around his relationship with his mother, with whom he has always had a very loving and close relationship, and yet whose opinions and responses have at times overwhelmed him and overshadowed his own sense of self.

His father, a successful lawyer, had wanted him to pursue a more traditional career, and had been struggling with Don's homosexuality. I place a rolled-up blanket to represent the embarrassment/"just me," and ask Don to speak to this part of himself. He gently touches the blanket and says, "you, you, you, just you, you are fine, as you are, as you are." I repeat these words softly, as a kind of echo, "fine, you are, as you are. . . ." I notice there is a sense of syncopated poetry in our utterances.

He says he wants to go to a lake; lakes have always been a source of comfort to him. He has positive memories of hiking around lakes with his mother in his childhood, where they picnicked and then just sat quietly together. We go to a lake in our imagination, on the other side of the room. As he faces a beautiful crystal blue lake, I ask him to speak his mind. He says, "I feel at peace here. No one to interrupt my thoughts." But then it looks like his thoughts have been interrupted. And sure enough he says, "but images of my father's wishes for me are interrupting the peace." I ask how and where his father enters this space. He says he is on a huge rock to the right. So we inch over to the right, face the rock, and he speaks to his father: "Dad, I love you. And I cannot be who you thought I would be. I am different. I love men, I love a man. Dad, let me be. This is me. Let me be. This is me. Let me be." I encourage him to say these lines now louder, and in different ways. Soon he is shouting, in a deep stormy voice I have not yet heard, over and over: "THIS IS ME, LET ME BE."

He is quivering and teary-eyed. We move over to the lake at the left. He says, "I need you lake, I need your comfort, I need your words." This last remark prompts me to suggest he become the lake. The role reversal happens effortlessly. As the lake, he speaks softly and evenly: "Here you can just be. Feel my stillness. My stillness is inside you too. In the stillness you know what is true for you. Go for the stillness, go for the truth. Come closer, and put your feet in me. I will cleanse you and release you." He responds to my suggestion to switch back to himself in almost a trance-like state, rolls up his pants, and places his bare feet in the water. I can feel the water as clearly as he does.

The Role of the Therapist

The drama therapist working within the Integrative Five Phase Model must be flexible in her own role repertoire as a therapist, as the different phases call for varying styles in leadership. Typically in the early phases the drama therapist is very much of a co-player, helping to invigorate a group, or join with an individual client, and promote in action a playful, permissive, and interactive environment. Beginning in latter Phase Two through Phase Four, s/he gradually assumes more of a director role, as s/he makes interventions within scenes, stays in close proximity to protagonists, coaches the group, facilitates dialogue, and insures safety. Because so much attention is needed to oversee the direction of scenes, especially in Phases Three and Four, the therapist becomes less of a co-player. Even in this directorial role, however, the therapist is very close to the action, never directing from a (literal or metaphoric) distance. The more active participation of the therapist returns in the dramatic rituals of Phase Five, and is also naturally present on some level (often in beginnings and ends of sessions) throughout.

In order to achieve the progression of the Integrative Five Phase Model, the drama therapist also creates a balance between offering energy and a strong presence in leadership, but at the same time being discreet (while following the flow of the client/s); leadership can be both strong and subtle, allowing the session/s to unfold in a way that feels very organic, with the therapist's role melding with the underlying energy of the group or the individual client.

COMPARISON WITH OTHER DRAMA THERAPY METHODS

I have been influenced and inspired by the powerful, poetic and clearly articulated work of my colleague David Johnson. The Integrative Five Phase Model and "Developmental Transformations" (DvT) (Chapter 6) share similarities in the developmental, process-oriented evolution of the work into increasingly deep realms. The playful work in Phase One and the beginnings of even later sessions, especially in work with individual clients in which imagery is very central, appears at times similar to DvT. However, DvT goes deeper into the heart of transformational play, whereas in the Integrative Five Phase Model the play eventually builds into sustained scenes, which eventually become reality oriented. In DvT, everything is playable and the therapist becomes the client's *playobject,* whereas the therapist in the Integrative Five Phase Model is more rooted in the role of guide.

Robert Landy's "Role Method" (Chapter 5) has also been influential in my thinking about roles; I particularly appreciate and resonate with his well-honed explication of the importance of embracing ambivalence and paradox. His thoughts on role repertoire are in keeping with my notions of multidimensionality. The work at the end of Phase

Two of the Integrative Five Phase Model, in which clients connect to the fictional roles they played, bears similarities to Landy's Role Method. However, in the Role Method, the client begins with invoking a role, and after several steps, s/he is asked to relate the fictional role to everyday life. In the Integrative Five Phase Model, the drama therapist waits until the clients spontaneously make such connections, lingering first in the fictional realm without requesting any analysis. Later on in Integrative Five Phase Model, the fictional realm and projective techniques are left behind, as clients tackle real life more directly (without the earlier distancing mechanisms), whereas Role Method remains focused on projective techniques and roles, along with reflection on how these relate to real life. Also, drama therapy work in the Integrative Five Phase Model does not typically begin with (or ever focus upon) creating a role or character, but is rather more immediately (and generally) relationally/interactively and emotionally oriented.

The *internal nurturing parent* role in the Integrative Five Phase Model is similar to Landy's *guide.* In Phase Three scenes, clients often respond to their own questions via a role reversal, in which they take on an older, wiser figure or part of themselves. The role of the internal nurturing parent, however, develops gradually, and typically emerges fully in the context of emotionally-laden Phase Four scenes.

In Role Method, clients engage in verbal reflection following their role explorations. In the Integrative Five Phase Model, much of the reflection happens in action, or through further dramatic scenes or rituals, though at other times the reflection takes place verbally. Reflection in Developmental Transformations occurs within the playspace; there is no interpretation or verbal analysis following the play.

"Psychodrama" (Chapter 18) is of course a major influence on the Integrative Five Phase model, and Phase Four of the Integrative Five Phase model is based on psychodrama. Elsewhere I have written about the integration of drama therapy and psychodrama (Emunah, 1997). The work of "Playback Theatre" (Chapter 20) has also inspired aspects of my process-oriented work, especially in the way Playback elicits concise aesthetic responses that reach for essences.

Although there are similarities between Phase Three work and "Narradrama" (Chapter 9), in that both involve helping clients achieve new perspectives, reframe life issues, and embody future wishes, the Integrative Five Phase model places greater emphasis on directly delving into and healing past wounds that affect or interfere with the present.

CASE EXAMPLE

I worked with Shawn twice a week for a year, in four three-month series. Shawn was among the more socially interactive, verbally sophisticated, and creative members of the adult psychiatric day treatment center. At 32, she was an exceptionally bright, sensitive, and attractive white Australian woman. Long, wavy red hair framed her strikingly beautiful and expressive face. Shawn was divorced; she had been married for four years during her mid-twenties to an artist who was 15 years her senior. She had a seven-year-old son, who lived with his father during the week and with her over the weekends.

Shawn lived in her own apartment, had an advanced degree in Art History, and had achieved some success as the assistant curator of a small museum. She also had undergone two brief psychiatric hospitalizations for suicide attempts. At times she was anorectic, and even more frequently gave in to impulses of self-mutilation in the form of cutting herself. Her psychiatric diagnosis was Borderline Personality Disorder. Shawn came from a wealthy, professional family. Both of her parents had been alcoholic and incapable of providing her with sustained care. Her mother, now deceased, had been neglectful and emotionally unavailable, and her father, a radiologist, had been emotionally abusive as well as seductive with her. (There had not been explicit sexual molestation.) She had an older sister who was a talented musician and also a drug abuser, and two younger brothers–one an alcoholic and the other a successful attorney. One set of grandparents was still alive and seemingly supportive, but lived in Australia, where Shawn had spent the first ten years of her life.

In our early work, Shawn was depressed, but the sessions brought out her natural though rather buried playfulness and spontaneity. For the duration of each session, at least, the depression lifted. Her skits during Phase One (Dramatic Play) were wonderfully imaginative and creative, and she was surprised by the validation she received from others for her skills. She was drawn especially to dramatic play that allowed her to express anger safely and playfully, such as *Gibberish* (using sounds or made-up language instead of actual words), and this expression of anger further reduced her depression.

But as the group moved into the more developed improvisational scenes of Phase Two (Scenework), associations and feelings related to Shawn's childhood were easily triggered, and she quickly became overwhelmed. For example, after another client played an alcoholic stepmother in a fairytale scene, Shawn grew silent, and later I found out that that night she cut her arm with a razor. Her cutting seemed to be a way of inducing physical pain to distract her from emotional pain, and also to make the emotional pain more tangible and palpable. At this point in treatment (after approximately eight sessions over a month period), I began encouraging her to identify feelings as they came up in the session. This was difficult for her because she tended to have a delayed reaction; she put feelings aside and later felt devastated. In childhood, Shawn had never been allowed to express feelings, nor had she witnessed her family express feelings directly. Rather, her parents had used drinking as a way of avoiding and denying feelings. I tried to check in with Shawn frequently during the session and to give her extra support at the end of the session. Any feelings she acknowledged were validated. This process also served to develop her trust in me and in treatment.

But as her trust in me increased, so did her fear of abandonment. Her transference toward me was manifested by the degree of her upset and the feelings of abandonment she expressed when there was a change in schedule. For example, when I announced that I needed to end one session 15 minutes early in order to catch a plane or when, a month in advance, I announced that we would not meet the Friday after Thanksgiving, Shawn accused me of not caring about her or the group. Rather than interpreting the transference, I chose to reassure her, in an attempt to provide some consistent support and care.

Much of the work as the group moved into Phase Three (Role Play) revolved around helping Shawn predict the situations that would precipitate overwhelming emotion and thus the cutting. She either had little sense of when this might happen, or did not care enough to try to protect herself. For example, she had been planning a trip at Christmas to see her father, whom she had not visited in several years. I had her direct other members of the group in an enactment of what the visit might be like. As she watched the playing out of her father's drinking and seductiveness, two things gradually became clear to her. First, dealing with the feelings evoked by the enactment was difficult enough and she was far from ready to cope with this visit in reality. Second, she realized that her anorexia and self-punishing behavior were linked to guilt over her father's stated preference for her over her mother, and specifically his sexual comments about her body.

At this stage, I followed any scene evoking past feelings with a scene about how she could deal with these feelings. After the scene about the visit with her father, we enacted a scene about how she might feel alone that very evening and what she could do to cope without resorting to the cutting. This served to help her anticipate her reactions, as well as practice new ways of responding to her pain.

Insight into the cutting deepened in an exercise entailing the creation of a sculpture depicting parts of herself. The dominant role in Shawn's sculpture was the punishing part. I had her enter the sculpture and assume this part. While playing the role, she surprised herself and the group by spontaneously exclaiming, "I'm your mother!" At the following session, she made a dramatic phone call to her deceased mother, whom she contacted in Hell. Using humor as a distancing device, she confronted her mother's negative and punitive attitude toward her. She also addressed her mother's self-destructiveness and the feeling she had that her mother wanted her (Shawn) to emotionally die with her. Shawn reported at the next session that as the impulse to cut herself had arisen, a stronger impulse had taken over, which she had succumbed to: to buy herself a doll. It was to be her first doll. As a child, she said, she had never wanted dolls; she hadn't known what to do with them.

By the end of our fourth month, the self-mutilating and self-destructive behavior had ceased. The work from this point on centered largely on the theme of nurturing herself. Her rejection of her inner sad and wounded child was linked to the self-mutilation; she had wanted to get rid of this child. As she started to understand and accept this part of herself, and to experience the empathy that others had for this part of her, she began, via scenework, to find ways of taking care of herself. A great deal of sadness was expressed for the way she had been abandoned and the ways she had abandoned herself. Now she struggled to reach this child inside her. There was a scene in which she desperately tried to place a long-distance phone call to her inner child, insisting on getting through despite the difficulty or cost. There was a scene in which she used her creativity and imagination to devise a planet in which people cared for themselves, or as she put it, there were no self-child abusers. There were many scenes in which she played the role of a child needing care. She was increasingly able to play a nurturing parent, albeit in scenes of other members of the group.

There were still days of hopelessness, or times in which emotions overwhelmed her. Any pain of the present triggered tremendous pain from the past. On one occasion, she had just found out that a neighbor had been diagnosed with AIDS. At this time, as at other times of increased emotional stress, she was asked to identify and direct others to play out all the feelings she had. She watched and conducted, which helped her to develop an observing self and to acknowledge and contain all of her emotions. This process also helped her to make the distinction between present stress and feelings leftover from her past. I gradually encouraged Shawn to make modifications in the scene, for example, to direct the anger outwardly, instead of inwardly toward herself, or to introduce a nurturing part that could tend to the sad child part of herself.

One day I had Shawn enter the scene and assume the role of this sad child part of herself. I, along with two members of the group, sat next to her. Doubling for her, we repeated and added to the feelings she was expressing. Our presence enabled her to relive some of the desolateness she experienced in her childhood, but this time with supportive, understanding people at her side.

As the contact with her neglected inner child developed, Shawn was also drawn to examine her relationship with her son. Through role play, she reviewed challenging interactions with him and practiced communicating more openly and expressing her love more fully. Her skills at mothering her son clearly surpassed her skills at mothering herself, but Shawn was as motivated to enhance the former as she was to discover the latter.

The more playful work also continued and she manifested an increasing zest for improvisation. She seemed to be using this aspect of the group process to experience a childhood she had never really had. Shawn proved to be remarkably expressive. The roles and characters she improvised became increasingly strong and assertive. I directed her in scenes to apply the qualities displayed in character roles, such as assertiveness, toward situations in her own life that were difficult for her. Dramas were enacted in which she had to turn down requests for help by her peers at times in which she really needed all her energy to take care of herself, or in which she had to politely refuse men's invitations that did not interest her.

By the end of our seventh month Shawn was able to perceive her own strengths. She was also able to trust me and her peers without excessive fear of abandonment. Despite anxieties, especially about separations and endings, she experienced more hope and optimism for the future. She began enacting in scenes (and thereby visualizing and emotionally preparing for) some of the future work and life situations for which she yearned.

In emotionally-laden scenes, Shawn no longer needed to stay in the role of director. The observing part of herself was internalized enough that she could now be the actor. She could handle emotionality, without the need for distancing, though she still needed some help taking hold of her pain. For so long she had had a punitive attitude toward herself, and her inner child. Now she needed to embrace this child, with all the gentleness and compassion that she was so able to manifest toward other people in the group.

One of Shawn's *culminating scenes* in Phase Four was about saying good-bye to her mother, and not saying good-bye to herself. In the scene, she played herself expressing a multitude of intense feelings toward her mother, including rage and love and disappointment, all of which she could now tolerate. Her capacity to be in touch with and express emotion was matched by her capacity to contain emotion.

"I don't understand why you never lived," Shawn said, gazing toward the empty chair. "You've been dying for as long as I knew you. With the smoking and the drinking and the running and everything. And now when you're dying you don't want to die. It's a little late, don't you think? I don't want to be here watching you die. I've spent my life watching you die."

The tone of sadness transformed to anger. "Why couldn't you ever live, damn it? And why couldn't you ever see me? Why did you leave me in a car because you couldn't remember I was there? And leave me in a store, and do all the other shit you did."

Now the sadness again, embedded in rage and hurt. "Was I that bad?"

There was a long pause, and I could see that an inner turn was being made. My directions were minimal because by this point in treatment Shawn was remarkably self-directed; the self-actualizing impulse within her, which Maslow describes as an innate force (that is often inhibited by fear), was clearly manifested–Shawn wanted to get well. "But the fact that you're going to die doesn't mean I have to die. The fact that you spent your life dying doesn't mean I have to make the same choice." I asked her to repeat this last line, to underscore the insight embedded in it. She did, and then thoughtfully added: "I've sort of done that in the last two years, but I don't have to keep doing it. I'm learning to have my feelings now. Something you never did. That's what everyone in the family was afraid of–all the drinking, all the suicide–running from feelings. But now I'm having mine, and it's not easy. But it doesn't have to kill me to have my feelings."

I then asked Joanne, a very sensitive member of the group with whom Shawn was close, to assume the role of Shawn's neglected inner child. This was the part that Shawn had tried in the past to destroy. Gently, I directed Shawn to take hold of this part of herself. She did so physically, holding Joanne in her arms. Soon she did so with her tone and her words. "You're very special and you're very loveable. Sometimes I have trouble seeing that, but it's getting easier. When I have trouble it isn't because of anything you've done. It's just that I learned things a whole lot differently, and it's hard doing them the new way. But you're an important and special part of me. And you deserve to be held. And you deserve to be loved. And you deserve to have all the feelings you have."

Without interrupting the scene, I softly suggested to Shawn that she assure her child that she will never say good-bye to her again. There was a very long silent pause as Shawn struggled with this direction. This was by far the most difficult challenge yet: to promise never to abandon herself again. But slowly she reached inside, until she found the words. "I know we had to say good-bye to a lot of people in our life, and there will be a lot more. But there is one good-bye I don't ever have to say. And that's to you."

In the closing rituals of Phase Five of her final series of drama therapy, Shawn was able to say good-bye to me and to the group without the sense of abandonment she had experienced in previous endings of our group series. At this ending, what she expressed was gain rather than loss, because this time she was taking herself with her.

CONCLUSION

The Integrative Five Phase model embraces the wide gamut of properties within the field of drama therapy, drawing from sources in dramatic play, theatre, role play, psychodrama, and ritual. The model follows a gradual progression, from fictional to real-life material, and from safety to risk-taking, with an emphasis on increasing connectedness to emotions, others, and oneself. Expression, relationship, and reflection are all central components. As in any form of therapy, I believe the quality of relationship between therapist and client/s, along the therapist's attunement to the client/s, are more important than the theoretical constructs.

There is no dearth of pain and suffering–individual, social, and planetary–that needs addressing. Given the vast and dire needs ahead, drama therapists are still at the beginning of exploring how our unique skills and perspectives can contribute to healing and transformation in far-reaching ways. There is also no dearth of joy and beauty, play and possibility, and our work already helps people access and revel in this part of life experience.

REFERENCES

Collomb, H. (1977). Psychosis in an African society. In C. Chailand (Ed.), *Long-term treatment of psychotic states.* New York: Human Sciences.

Emunah, R. (1985). Drama therapy and adolescent resistance. *The Arts in Psychotherapy, 12,* 77–84.

Emunah, R. (1990). Expression and expansion in adolescence: The significance of creative arts therapy. *The Arts in Psychotherapy, 17,* 101–107.

Emunah, R. (1994). *Acting for real: Drama therapy process, technique, and performance.* New York: Brunner/Mazel.

Emunah, R. (1995). From adolescent trauma to adolescent drama: Group drama therapy with emotionally disturbed youth. In S. Jennings (Ed.), *Dramatherapy with children and adolescents* (pp. 150–168). New York and London: Routledge.

Emunah, R. (1996). Five progressive phases in dramatherapy and their implications for brief therapy. In A. Gersie (Ed.), *Dramatic approaches to brief therapy* (pp. 29–44). London: Jessica Kingsley.

Emunah, R. (1997). Drama therapy and psychodrama: An integrated model. *International Journal of Action Methods,* 108–134.

Emunah, R. (1999). Drama therapy in action. In D. Wiener (Ed.), *Beyond talk therapy* (pp. 99–124). Washington, D.C.: APA Publications.

Maslow, A. (1968). *Toward a psychology of being.* Princeton, N.J.: Van Nostrand Reinhold.

May, R. (1961). *The courage to create.* New York: Norton.

Moreno, J. (1946). *Psychodrama: Vol. 1.* Beacon, N.Y.: Beacon House.

Mulkey, M. (2004). Recreating masculinity: Drama therapy with male survivors of sexual assault. *The Arts in Psychotherapy, 31* (1), 19–28.

Rogers, C. (1961). *On becoming a person: A therapist's view of psychotherapy.* Boston: Houghton Mifflin.

Rubin, S. (2007). Self-revelatory performance. In A. Blatner & D. Wiener (Eds.), *Interactive and applied drama* (pp. 250–259). Iuniverse.

BIBLIOGRAPHY

Emunah, R. (1983). Drama therapy with adult psychiatric patients. *The Arts in Psychotherapy, 10,* 77–84.

Emunah, R., & Johnson, D.R. (1983). The impact of theatrical performance on the self-images of psychiatric patients. *The Arts in Psychotherapy, 10,* 233–239.

Emunah, R. (1985). Drama therapy and adolescent resistance. *The Arts in Psychotherapy, 12,* 71–79.

Emunah, R., & Lo Presti, T. (1985). Theatrical performance in drama therapy. *National Association for Drama Therapy, Monograph, #1.*

Emunah, R. (1989). The use of dramatic enactment in the training of drama therapists. *The Arts in Psychotherapy, 16,* 29–36.

Emunah, R. (1990). Expression and expansion in adolescence: The significance of creative arts therapy. *The Arts in Psychotherapy, 17,* 101–107.

Emunah, R. (1994). *Acting for real: Drama therapy process, technique, and performance.* New York: Brunner/Mazel.

Emunah, R. (1995). From adolescent trauma to adolescent drama. In S. Jennings (Ed.), *Dramatherapy with children and adolescents* (pp. 150–168). New York/London: Routledge.

Emunah, R. (1996). Five progressive phases in drama therapy and their implications for brief therapy. In A. Gersie (Ed.), *Dramatic approaches to brief therapy* (pp. 29–44). London: Jessica Kingsley Publishers.

Emunah, R. (1997). Drama therapy and psychodrama: An integrated model. *International Journal of Action Methods,* 108–134.

Emunah, R. (1999). Drama therapy in action. In D. Wiener (Ed.), *Beyond talk therapy* (pp. 99-124). Washington, D.C.: APA Publications.

Emunah, R. (2005). Drama therapy and adolescent resistance. In A. Weber & C. Haen (Eds.), *Clinical applications of drama therapy in child and adolescent treatment* (pp. 107–121). New York: Brunner-Routledge.

Videotapes

Emunah, R. (1979). Individual progression in a drama therapy group. Available from the author.

Emunah, R. & Brawner, B. (1990). Caring for the inner one: Self-expression and self-acceptance in drama therapy. Available from the author.

FURTHER TRAINING

The California Institute of Integral Studies in San Francisco offers one of three NADT approved graduate training programs in Drama Therapy, and incorporates specific training and experience in the Integrative Five Phase model. The program is housed within a graduate department of Counseling Psychology, leading to an M.A. in Counseling Psychology with a Concentration in Drama Therapy.

For more information, contact:
Renée Emunah, Ph.D., RDT-BCT, Director
California Institute of Integral Studies
Drama Therapy Program
1453 Mission Street, San Francisco, CA 94103
www.ciis.edu
415-575-6230

Chapter 5

ROLE THEORY AND THE ROLE METHOD OF DRAMA THERAPY

ROBERT LANDY

INTRODUCTION

Role theory has a history throughout the twentieth century in the fields of psychology, sociology and anthropology. It was developed by a number of theorists and practitioners who believed that the dramatic metaphor of life as theatre and people as actors could be applied to an analysis of social and cultural life and inner psychological processes. Those most associated with its early development include William James (1890, 1950), Charles Cooley (1922), George Herbert Mead (1934), and Ralph Linton (1936).

In the 1950s, two prominent role theorists, Theodore Sarbin (Sarbin & Allen, 1968) and Erving Goffman (1959), further developed the metaphor and offered complex social psychological views of life as performance. Goffman's book, *The Presentation of Self in Everyday Life,* became required reading in many psychology and sociology courses since its publication in 1959. The idea of life as performance influenced many social scientists throughout the 1960s and 1970s who analyzed everything from cab-drivers and their fares to gynecological examinations from the perspective of role theory (Brissett & Edgley, 1975).

Somewhere on the fringe of scholarly acceptability lurked another theorist with a more direct and insistent message. The theorist was Jacob Moreno (1946, 1947, 1960) and his message was that life is not like theatre; life is theatre. Moreno was less patient and precise than his fellow role theorists. Rather than refining his theoretical speculation, he worked hard to apply his almost theological beliefs to the development of whole systems of therapy, social and cultural analysis and even means of dialoguing with God.

Moreno's work is significant to drama therapists and psychodramatists alike because it is practical. He created a role method of treatment even though his intention was to create both a theory and a practice. Although there have been attempts to glean psychodramatic role theory from Moreno's voluminous and redundant opus (see Fox, 1987), it seems clear that the theory remains in the shadow of the practice.

Drama therapy as a profession developed

in a way similar to psychodrama although a number of individuals are responsible for pioneering the field. Since its inception, it has been a practical approach concerned more with the playing of roles than the thinking about roles. Although a number of methods have been developed in the past 30 years, many of which are represented in this book, little attention has been focused upon theory. Why is this?

It could be that drama therapists, like their counterparts in other applied forms of therapy, are oriented toward practice and less concerned with theoretical issues. Some with strong backgrounds in the arts and alternative modes of healing tend to value action more than reflection. Others might simply question the value of theory or ignore it altogether, trusting in the power of the spontaneous healing moment. Many of the leaders of the field came of age during the cultural wars of the 1960s when stodgy systems of academic thought were pushed aside to yield practical ways of solving profound and frivolous problems.

As one of the leaders, I realize that in the '60s my goal was not Maoist in nature–attempting to destroy all traditional cultural systems–but rather an attempt to integrate ideas that were worth conserving with those that needed to be changed. Although I thought that theory had to go and direct action had to be taken, I have come to change my view and to even understand that I misunderstood my metacognition at the time.

Well into the twenty-first century, I fully embrace the necessity of theory and the traditions of role that have been established by my predecessors. However, I also believe that role theory is not just based upon recent trends in social science, but also in ancient healing traditions that point to the dramatic and therapeutic qualities of shamanic healing (see Eliade, 1972; Landy, 2008). I further embrace the insights offered by critics and philosophers writing about the meaning and purpose of theatrical performance. Examples include the work of Aristotle and Cicero, Goethe and Nietzsche, Walter Benjamin and Northrup Frye, Martin Buber and Victor Turner. But more so I have turned to the thoughtful theatre directors and writers for a deeper understanding of the meaning and function of role. My theatre mentors include Stanislavski and Brecht, Gordon Craig and Peter Brook, all of whom have been able to practice a theatre aesthetic and to reflect upon it with an equal measure of excellence.

From these and many other sources I have learned that the act of taking on and playing a role is mysterious and complex. I have learned that it occurs in many contexts–in everyday life, in artistic performance, in education, in therapy and in prayer, communing with one's god. In this chapter, I will try to clarify my understanding of role and to offer my version of role theory as it relates to drama therapy. Like my most respected theatre mentors, I will offer an application of my theoretical approach to drama therapy–the *Role Method*. The Role Method is not a theory, but a practical application of role theory. Like any other approach to drama therapy or any other healing practice, the method will be most effective if it can be understood and validated within the context of its theory. My aim in writing this chapter is to demonstrate the continuity of role theory and Role Method and to make a strong case for a sound intellectual foundation for the still nascent field of drama therapy. When I speak of role theory in the following pages, I am referring to my version as it applies to drama therapy.

THEORY AND PRINCIPLES

Role Theory Assumptions

There are several assumptions that lie at the heart of role theory. The first is that human beings are role takers and role players by nature. That is, the abilities to imagine oneself as another and to act like the other are essentially unlearned and genetically programmed. Further, human behavior is highly complex and contradictory and any one thought or action in the world can be best understood in the context of its counterpart. Human beings strive toward balance and harmony and although they never fully arrive, they have the capacity to accept the consequences of living with contradiction and paradox. It is not ultimately the need to resolve cognitive dissonance that motivates human behavior, but the need to live with paradox.

A further assumption is that the personality can be conceived as an interactive system of roles. This notion is close to other models that attempt to create a taxonomy to classify personality structures. Philosophically, role theory is more akin to archetypal systems, such as that offered by Jung (1964) than to more reductive behavioral systems, such as that offered by Bloom and his colleagues (1956).

When I published my book on role theory, *Persona and Performance* (1993), I stated emphatically that there was no room for the concept of self. I argued that the Self was a problematic, tired term too easily linked to modern, humanistic models and that role theory offered a more post-modern understanding of human existence as multidimensional. Many of my students and colleagues have challenged me on this point and accused me of creating a reductive system, flawed largely by my rejection of some form of observing ego and some essential core construct (see, for example, Meldrum, 1994). As I have continued to work through role theory in practice and thought, I have been able to respond to that criticism by offering a new concept, that of the *guide,* which I will describe below. This part of the personality, a transitional figure that stands between contradictory tendencies and leads one on a journey toward awareness, is not quite the same as the self, although it serves some similar functions.

Basic Concepts in Role Theory

Role, Counterrole and Guide

Human experience, according to role theory, can be conceptualized in terms of discrete patterns of behavior that suggest a particular way of thinking, feeling or acting. *Role* is one name for these patterns. Each role, although related to other roles, is unique in terms of its qualities, function and style. Role is not necessarily a fixed entity, but one that is capable of change according to the changing life circumstances of the individual role player. However, like Jung's notion of archetype, each role is recognizable by virtue of its unique characteristics. For example, when one plays the role of mother, certain discernable qualities will be expressed, including a sense of nurturing and care-taking of another. Although the archetypal nature of the role will remain constant over time, certain specific qualities may change as, for example, one in the mother role expresses the desire to be mothered herself or to abrogate her responsibilities toward her child. Even in the extreme, as a mother engages in fantasies of infanticide, Medea-like, she still maintains the essential qualities of mother. Each role can therefore be identified by its archetypal qualities and its degree of deviation from those qualities, as long as the deviance is understood in relation to the norm.

The primary source of role is the theatre where an actor takes on a role as a means of signifying a particular character with a particular set of qualities and motivations. The metaphor of life as theatre has been so powerful throughout history because so much of human existence concerns a struggle between opposing desires and opposing levels of consciousness. The dramatic structure of antagonist vs. protagonist is played out time and again in everyday life in social interactions and in the struggle with dissonant cognitions. In fact, one way of conceptualizing thought is as an inner dialogue among discrepant points of view (see Moffett, 1968).

When a client begins drama therapy, the drama therapist working from the point of view of role theory often assumes that at least one role the client needs to play in life is either unavailable, poorly developed or inappropriately aligned with other roles or other people in their roles. The initial task of therapy, then, is to help the client access that role and identify it.

In theatrical terms, the role is the protagonist in the client's drama, even though this figure might not yet be aware of the struggles it will undergo in its search for awareness and connection. The *counterrole* (CR) is the figure that lurks on the other side of the role, the antagonist. It is not necessarily the opposite of the role as evil is to good, but rather other sides of the role that may be denied or avoided or ignored in the ongoing attempt to discover effective ways to play a single role. CR is not necessarily a dark or negative figure. If one plays the social role of mother, the CR might be brother or daughter or father. Or it might be something more particular to a client's issues, like helper. For such a client, mother might represent a punitive or abusive figure.

The CR has no independent existence outside of the role. Role appears to have an independent existence and many clients hope to find a way to enact a given role with a degree of competence. Yet even role seeks connection to its counterparts. To be a truly moral person demands an ability to acknowledge and make peace with the immoral or amoral qualities that lurk on the other side.

Role and CR often shift, so that role reversals occur with some regularity. In struggling with moral issues, a client can choose to work with the role of saint or sinner and allow for a shift as one role moves from foreground to background.

The *Guide,* as mentioned above, is the final part of the role trinity. The guide is a transitional figure that stands between role and CR and is used by either one as a bridge to the other. One primary function of the guide is integration. Another is to help clients find their own way. As such, the guide is a helmsman, pilot and pathfinder, a helper who leads individuals along the paths they need to follow. In its most basic form, the guide is the therapist. One comes to therapy because there is no effective guide figure available in one's social or intrapsychic world.

The following story illustrates the notion of therapist as guide. It was October and eight baseball teams were vying for a spot in the World Series. At the beginning of one session, Joe, a man in his mid-40s whom I had been treating in drama therapy for a number of years, asked me whether I had seen the Mets game the previous night. He told me that he watched the game intently so that he would be able to talk with me about it. He knew that I was an ardent Mets fan. The game had been particularly exciting and we chatted about it for a few minutes. Then he told me, with some sadness, that his father never took him to a baseball game.

During the session, we worked on a number of issues, one concerning his relationship with his adolescent nephew, whom he treated in a fatherly way on a recent visit. He worked very deeply with material concerning his relationship to present and absent family members, especially his father who had died 20 years earlier. At the end of the session, Joe quite spontaneously took my hand and said: "Thanks for taking me to the game." He embraced me, as if to say goodbye, a usual ritual for our closure. I held him for a moment and sang:

> Take me out to the ball game,
> Take me out to the crowd,
> Buy me some peanuts and cracker jacks,
> I don't care if I never get back . . .

When I reached the chorus he joined in:

> For it's one, two, three strikes you're out
> At the old ball game.

We looked at each other and laughed and then he left.

In that session, I became not only Joe's transferential father, but also his guide. Although his real father did not take him to a real ball game, his guide could take him to a virtual one. Our therapy session was a ball game in that we were able to share an intimacy painfully denied by his father. In the moment of intimacy, with the help of the guide, the past rejections of the father were corrected.

The guide figure is first visible as existing in the world outside the client. It takes many forms in everyday life including: parent, sibling, special relative or friend, teacher, coach, religious leader, media personality, criminal, demon and God. The guide can be moral, immoral or amoral.

Although drama therapy begins with the tacit understanding that the therapist will take on and play out the role of guide, the process moves toward a different aim–that clients will internalize the guide and discover, ultimately, a way to guide themselves.

Another way to look at the same internal understanding of guide is that clients enter therapy with all kinds of potential inner guide figures. For many, these figures are hard to access. Through the process of drama therapy, clients are challenged to recreate their inner guides which, once developed, can lead them through difficult territory.

Role and CR are more clearly properties of the client. They are revealed through behavior and thought. Like the guide they, too, will serve as internal figures that seek balance within the psyche. Joe seeks such a balance between the part of him that is a child, longing for a father's love, and the part of him that is a grown-up, capable of fathering others even as he fathers himself.

When the three parts of the psyche are intact, the inner guide will facilitate the connection between child and father. It will allow Joe to feel loved and loving at the same time. It will allow Joe to feel the pain of the missed moments of fathering without shame.

Role Types and the Taxonomy of Roles

For many years I asked the question–if it is true that the personality is a system of interactive roles, what are the specific roles within that system? In looking for answers, I turned to others systems. From Jung (1971) I learned about the attitudes of the extrovert and introvert and the four functions of thinking, feeling, sensing and intuiting. For a more archetypal understanding of role, I also looked toward Jung's notion of anima and animus, of shadow and persona and puer. From latter-day Jungians such as Campbell (1949) and Hillman (1983), I discovered a more contemporary way to understand role types.

I looked at less conventional systems such

as the spiritual enneagram that proposes nine personality types: the reformer, the helper, the status seeker, the artist, the thinker, the loyalist, the generalist, the leader and the peacemaker (Riso, 1987). I also looked at more literary systems such as that offered by Carol Pearson (1989) who envisions personality structure as comprised of six types: innocent, orphan, magician, wanderer, martyr and warrior.

Although all these systems were valuable and revealing, none led me to the essential source of all work in drama therapy–the theatre. Having realized that the one unique feature of drama therapy, distinguishing it from all other healing forms, is its theatrical underpinnings, I turned directly to theatre.

It occurred to me that the one indivisible element in theatre is role. Many plays have neither plot nor spectacle nor even language. But all share the basic premise that actors take on roles to create a character. Starting with this premise, I began to look at the many roles available in theatrical plays since the beginning of recorded history. I limited myself to an exploration of Western dramatic literature as I was unfamiliar with the Eastern traditions. In recent years as I became more aware of such Eastern theatrical forms as Japanese Noh theatre, Peking Opera and Indian Kathakali, I have come to realize that these traditions, free from the modern Western influence of psychological realism, lend themselves more easily to classification according to character type. But this must remain the subject of another study.

As I searched the dramatis personae of many hundreds of Western plays, I became aware of a repeated pattern of character types that seemed to transcend time, genre and culture. They included heroes and villains, nobility and commoners, victims and survivors, wise fools and ignorant kings, deceivers and helpers and lovers of all kinds.

The repeated role of hero, for example, from the Greek Oedipus to the British Lear to the American Willy Loman, embodied certain archetypal qualities and I began to specify them. They included a willingness to confront the unknown and to journey forth on a spiritual search for a meaning just beyond their grasp (Landy 1993, p. 230). I also noticed that all heroes serve a common function within the drama–taking a risky psychological and spiritual journey toward understanding and transformation (Landy 1993, p. 230).

Finally, I became aware that each role type, consistent with its aesthetic form and genre, tended to be enacted within a particular style. I provided two primary styles, the presentational, a more abstract form removed from the trappings of real-life speech and action, and the representational, a more reality-based form. Given my understanding of *aesthetic distance,* I postulated that presentational styles are linked to more cognitive modes of expression, and representational styles are linked to more affective modes. In playing a role, the actor achieves the desired aesthetic effect, whether comic or tragic, whether melodramatic or farcical, by playing with the level of distance. However, the role that an actor takes on is in itself determined by its aesthetically-based stylistic tradition. While it is true that the modern Willy Loman is a kind of anti-hero popular in mid-twentieth century literature, he still is typically measured against the classical tragic hero from whom he derives. Although many actors play him in a realistic manner, attempting to discover the emotional depths of his suffering, he was written by Arthur Miller within a presentational style, consistent with the traditions of the role type, hero.

Parallel to the stage actor, the client in drama therapy is led through particular levels of cognition and affect as the drama therapist introduces more or less stylized roles and activities. The drama therapist facilitates the client's play with style in order to help her discover a balance of affect and cognition so that she might be able to work through a dilemma with the capacities to feel and to reflect intact. Style is the distancer in drama therapy, a way to move a client closer or further away from a role that she needs to play in order to discover balance.

In completing the *taxonomy of roles,* I listed 84 role types and a number of sub-types. My main criterion for choosing a role type was its appearance in at least three historical periods, e.g., classical, renaissance and neoclassical, or repeated use throughout one particular period and/or genre. In recent years I have refined the taxonomy, eliminating redundancy, especially for the purpose of developing an assessment instrument, to be discussed below.

It should be noted that all roles in the taxonomy work within the triadic system of role, counterrole and guide. Any one role type, such as the child, can serve as protagonist (role), antagonist (CR) and/or guide within an individual's therapeutic drama.

Role System

In developing the taxonomy of roles, I made the assumption that all human beings have the potential to take on and play out all the identified roles plus others not specified. The quantity of roles available will be based upon many factors including biological predisposition, social modeling, psychological motivation, environmental circumstance, and moral judgment, as well as such secondary factors as readiness and will. The totality of roles available at any one moment is known as the *role system.* Role system is another way of thinking about personality structure. It is the container of all the intrapsychic roles. Within the role system are those roles that are available to consciousness and that can be played out competently. But there are also dormant roles within the role system that have faded from consciousness because of neglect or abuse or lack of need. Roles that are not called out will not be played out, even though they may exist within. They will be activated when given the proper social or environmental circumstance.

As an example, Jill was repeatedly told by her family that she was dull and unimaginative. She was discouraged from continuing her education beyond the age of 16. After her minimal schooling, she took on a series of menial and unfulfilling jobs. After a brief time in drama therapy, she enrolled in a continuing education course in art history. She recalled that her hand shook as she filled out the registration form. During the first class, when slides were shown of classical paintings, she was overcome with emotion and had to leave the room. She secluded herself in the bathroom and sobbed. The next class, for the first time in her life, she discovered that she had something to say about the paintings. She dared to speak up and was acknowledged for her insightful comments.

With my encouragement, Jill began to do her own drawings, very intimate images concerning her abusive past. Although the creation and dialogue with the images was very painful, she took great pride in discovering that a whole new role–that of artist–was suddenly available. During one session she exclaimed: "I think the artist has been there all the time. It was just asleep."

The structure of the role system is dynamic. When one role is called into the foreground, others fade into the background. One way of viewing the structure is as a staged scene in a play. When one actor speaks, the others on stage need to listen and react appropriately. Some remain silent and unseen, playing out their roles as supports and extras.

Within the structure of the role system, roles tend to seek balance with their counterparts. This is especially true in a healthy, integrated personality. Such a personality is also one in which a variety of roles from a variety of domains are prepared, if called, to take a leading part in an individual's life drama.

Story

As the role in its triadic expression is the form of one's dramatic expression, *story* is its content. While in role, the client tells and/or enacts a story, which can take both verbal and nonverbal forms. The story is the client's narrative of events past, present, and/or future. It can be told in both presentational and representational styles, even though, in Role Method, the client most often creates a fictional story, which eventually becomes a mirror reflecting actual life dilemmas. Many stories told and enacted in drama therapy recapitulate classical myths and tales of heroes' journeys, with the hero or protagonist representing the role, the villain or antagonist representing the counterrole, and the guide as a helping figure, representing the reparative function of the therapist as well as the potential inner integrity of the client. In drama therapy, role is the essential form, preceding story. Story is its outer shell, containing the role and its manifestations. Without role, there can be no story, as all stories require a storyteller and a potential story listener. Without story, role exists, but as a mere form in search of a content.

Distancing Theory

Role theory, based in the aesthetic form of theatre, is best understood in terms of *aesthetic distance.* Theatre is a mirror of or frame around reality and, as in all forms of art, is marked by its separation from and representation of everyday reality. Aesthetic distance in the theatre is a marker of the relationship between an actor and a role, a group of actors and its audience. In the most distanced forms of theatre, those that are highly stylized, as in ancient Greek drama, modern forms of epic theatre, and contemporary post-modern presentational forms, the actor plays a role as an abstraction, removing oneself from an emotional identification with the character. In the least distanced forms, as in the early days of the Moscow Art Theatre, directed by Stanislavski, and contemporary forms of method acting, the actor merges with the role, presenting oneself as the character.

In role theory, I base my understanding of distance both in the aesthetic traditions of theatre and the work of the sociologist, Thomas Scheff (1979), who speaks of one's presentation in everyday life along a continuum of overdistance, an overabundance of thought; aesthetic distance, a balance of feeling and thought; and underdistance, an overabundance of emotion. With an understanding of emotion and distance according to this theory, the drama therapist has a model through which to gauge a client's need for expression and repression. Given that dramatic media are more or less inherently distancing, the therapist can make a choice of technique based upon the need of the client for greater or lesser degrees of expression. For one who has experienced trauma, for example, an approach that affords greater distance is often indicated. For a more neurotic person fearful of direct expression, an approach that generates greater emotion is often indicated.

In distancing theory, as derived from theatre and sociology, the optimal form of expression is the midpoint of aesthetic distance. This point is noted by one's ability to express feeling without the fear of becoming overwhelmed, and to reflect upon an experience without the fear of completely shutting down emotionally. In relationship to other forms of drama therapy, aesthetic distance can be seen as closely related to the *playspace* in "Developmental Transformations" (Johnson, Chapter 6), the imaginal realm between everyday reality and dramatic expression, and *catharsis* of integration in psychodrama, the moment of integration between feelings and thoughts (Moreno, 1946/1994).

View of Health and Illness

The healthy person, from the point of view of role theory, is noted by an ability to live with ambivalence, contradictory tendencies and paradox. In a previous book of essays (Landy, 1996a), I refer to this person as one who is effectively able to live a double life. The image does not refer to schizoid splits but to an acknowledgement that the human condition is in part one of living simultaneously within paradoxical realms of mind and body, thought and action, subject and object, actor and observer, a role and its counterpart. The healthy adult person who functions responsibly has found a way to live with the contradictory tendencies to act up like a child and to act out like an adolescent. The role and CR are in balance and when the need arises to play the child or adolescent, the individual can do so without the fear of losing all sense of maturity and judgment.

When out of balance, that is, when too much the child or too much the adolescent, the healthy person is able to draw upon the wisdom of a guide figure to help move back toward the center. The guide might be a friend or a therapist or it might be an inner figure that signals a time for reflection and a time for a shift of behavior.

The healthy person is also noted by an ability to take on many, if not most, of the roles in the taxonomy and to play them out in everyday life with some degree of proficiency. Very few people, the best character actors notwithstanding, are able to enact all 84 roles with a full measure of competency. Proficiency and competency are often hard to measure. However, these traits are generally present when one is able to behave in role and reflect upon that behavior in a balanced way, that is, with feeling and with understanding. The competent role player is also one who is able to articulate in words and/or action the appropriate qualities, function and style of any given role. Health, then, is a measure of both the quantity of roles one internalizes and plays out and the quality of the role enactment.

The unhealthy person, from a role perspective, is one who has given up the struggle to live with contradictory tendencies and has, instead, embraced one role or a cluster of related ones, at the exclusion of all others. Feeling overwhelmed by complexity, the unhealthy person finds ways to limit the quantity and quality of roles within his inner and outer world. This is the domain of fundamentalists who worship one belief system as they reject all other forms of belief or ways of seeing the world. This is the domain of the autistic whose world is limited to a very small private set of thoughts and behaviors. In most forms of extreme mental illness marked by obsessional or delusional thinking, the role system is severely limited.

From a social point of view, the unhealthy person is marked by an inability to take on the role of the other and thus to empathize with another. We find that narcissistic individuals, for example, live in a very narrow universe of roles. Each social encounter that offers a possible means of taking on a new role becomes a distorted mirror. Instead of looking at the other and seeing a reflection of what they might become, narcissists look at the other and see a reflection of how they are. For the narcissist, the other cannot mediate or represent any new ways of being. In offering a fixed mirror, the other becomes the pool of water that ultimately drowns the mythological Narcissus.

The unhealthy person is also marked by an inability to internalize and enact a number of roles competently. In the extreme, these people find many of the roles listed in the taxonomy foreign and distant. Further, they find it difficult to attribute qualities, functions and styles to those roles with which they identify.

Methods of Assessment and Evaluation

In applying the taxonomy of roles to clinical work in drama therapy, I have developed two assessment instruments. The first, called *Role Profiles,* began as a simple pencil and paper test that offered a modified list of the roles within the taxonomy and asked the subject to rate each one on a Likert-type scale from 0–4 according to two measures: how much one acts like the role in one's everyday life and how much one plays out the role in one's imagination. Role Profiles evolved into a card sort test where the subject is given the following directions:

> This experience is intended to explore your personality as if it were made up of characters commonly found in plays, movies, and stories. You will be given a stack of cards. On each card is the name of a role, which is a type of character you have probably seen in movies and plays or read about in stories. Please shuffle the cards thoroughly. Place each card in one of four groups that best describes how you feel about yourself right now. Each group is labeled by a large card which says: This Is Who I Am; This Is Who I Want To Be; This Is Who Is Standing In My Way; This Is Who Can Help Me. Try to group the cards as quickly as possible. Any questions? When you are ready, begin. Be sure to place each card in one group only.

Following the card sort into the four categories, the subject is asked a number of questions in order to ascertain the quantity and quality of her roles. Criteria applied in Role Profiles refer directly to role theory. Several Master of Arts level research studies have been done (Bikki Tam, 2004; Clayton, 2000; Fistos, 1996; Florin, 2001; Raz, 1997; Rosenberg, 1999; Tangorra, 1997; Tranchida, 2000), attempting to establish reliability and validity and other benchmarks of research. Two descriptive studies have been published (Landy, 2001a; Landy, Luck, Conner, & McMullian, 2003), explaining the efficacy of viewing an individual's role system in terms of the quantity and quality of roles taken and played. Further research needs to be done to provide evidence of the effectiveness of Role Profiles in assessment and treatment.

The second instrument developed from role theory is called *Tell-A-Story.* Its aim is to assess an individual's ability to invoke a role, CR and guide and to move toward some integration and connection among the roles. Through Tell-A-Story, the subject is given the following task: "I would like you to tell me a story. The story can be based upon something that happened to you or to somebody else in real life or it can be completely made-up. The story must have at least one character."

The tester is instructed to provide any prompts necessary to help the subject tell the story. The tester encourages those who are not very verbal to tell the story through miniature objects or puppets. Following the story, the subject is asked to specify the characters in the story, limited to three, and answer a number of questions concerning their qualities, function and style of presentation. The subject is also asked to specify the theme of the story and comment on the connection between the fictional roles and everyday life. This assessment instrument requires further research and refinement before it is applied to a broad clinical spectrum, although two descriptive studies have been completed (Seitz, 2000; Landy, 2001b).

In evaluating change, the therapist looks for a shift in the quantity and quality of roles taken and enacted, as well as an ability of the client to identify and work through role, CR and guide figures. To determine the effectiveness of the treatment the therapist asks several questions:

1. Is the client able to identify a problematic role(s) and to take it on and enact it with a degree of competency? Competency means an awareness of the qualities, function and style of role presentation and an application of that awareness to effective social interactions in role.
2. Is the client able to identify a CR and take it on and enact it with a degree of competency?
3. Is the client able to identify a guide figure and use it as an aid in moving through a crisis?
4. Is the client able to integrate contradictory roles?
5. Is the client able to take on and play out a range of roles throughout the six domains of the taxonomy of roles?

The therapist can evaluate a client's progress at the end of each session, at the conclusion of a given number of sessions or at the termination of the treatment. At any juncture, having made the evaluation, the therapist can share their observations and offer suggestions to the client. They can also help the client evaluate their progress by sharpening the ability to identify roles, counterroles and guide figures.

METHOD AND TECHNIQUE

The Therapeutic Process: Role Method

Role theory is applied to treatment by means of the Role Method (RM). In *Persona and Performance* (1993), I specified the method as proceeding through eight steps:

1. Invoking the role.
2. Naming the role.
3. Playing out/working through the role.
4. Exploring alternative qualities in subroles.
5. Reflecting upon the role play: discovering role qualities, functions and styles inherent in the role.
6. Relating the fictional role to everyday life.
7. Integrating roles to create a functional role system.
8. Social modeling: discovering ways that clients' behavior in role affects others in their social environments.

The model still holds although I have revised Step Four to accommodate my understanding of CR and guide. During the working-through stage, the client is presumably working with a single role that he has identified and named. For example, George, a visual artist in his late '50s, came to therapy because he felt like a professional failure. I pointed out that failure was more a quality than a role and helped George discover that the failed role was that of artist. We worked with the artist role through stories and dreamwork and role play. Soon we discovered that it was not the artist part of George that felt like a failure, but its counterpart whom George first named the banker and then the businessman.

In identifying his problematic role as the businessman, George did not appear to be exploring a subrole of the artist but in fact discovering a counterrole. When George acknowledged his feelings of incompetence concerning the sale of art, he was able to reclaim the artist on the other side of the businessman and work toward integrating the two with the help of several guide figures whom he identified and named.

There is an intermediary step between three and four. This is the step of de-roling which generally applies to a shift in realities from the dramatic to that of everyday life. In this first instance of de-roling, however, the client distances himself from one role, enters for a moment into a neutral position associated with everyday life, and then prepares to take on the CR.

De-roling also occurs between Steps 4 and 5 as the client moves fully out of the imaginary realm, leaving the fictional roles behind, and prepares to reflect upon the fictions just created. De-roling signals the essential paradox of the dramatic experience–that of the continuity of the me and not-me, of the actor in relation to the role. In leaving the dramatic role, the actor resumes a life in a parallel universe that is less obviously masked and stylized. Because drama therapy treatment in role can become quite complex and confusing, the therapist needs to insure that the client de-roles each character and each object. While under the spell of the role, the client loses distance and has difficulty reflecting upon the drama.

There is no such rarified position as a fully de-roled human being. Behind all masks are more masks. The aim of de-roling is not to fully transcend one's personae, but to shift from one reality, that of the imagination, to another, that of the everyday, for the purpose of reflection. Another way of looking at de-roling is as a shift from a more effective, physically active mode to a more cognitive, reflective one.

The steps in the Role Method do not necessarily proceed in a linear fashion. As a client works with a problematic role, he might discover, as George did, that the problem really lies on the other side. The CR then becomes the role and needs to be clearly named and worked through in itself. At the place marked as Step Four, the client is encouraged to locate a guide figure. Many, however, begin therapy with a guide figure intact or temporarily lost, one that usually is based upon a nurturing or idealized parent.

Steps Five and Six of the Role Method are reflective and point to a cognitive component of the approach. Following enactment in the imaginal realm clients are asked to derole and to reflect upon the roles they have played and then to link the roles to their everyday lives.

Some approaches, such as Developmental Transformations, view reflection as occurring within the playspace (Landy, 2008). Even Moreno (1946/1994), the founder of "Psychodrama" (Chapter 18), "Sociometry and Sociodrama" (Chapter 19), spoke of the importance of a form of action reflection. However, following the action phase of psychodrama, as in Role Method, clients de-role and engage in a verbal process of reflection. I believe most drama therapists would agree that reflection, whether in words or action, is important. The differences in approach lie in whether the reflection occurs within the enactment phase, as in Developmental Transformations, or following the enactment, as in Role Method and psychodrama. Emunah's "Integrative Five Phase Model" (Chapter 4) seems to embrace both points of view, with reflection in words and/or action occurring sometimes within the drama and sometimes from without.

One strong justification for a verbal form of reflection outside the enactment is in recent research in neuroscience (see, for example, Demasio, 1994, 1999: van der Kolk, 2002a; van der Kolk, 2002b) offering a holistic, integrative model of the brain. For optimal therapeutic benefits to occur in recovery, for example, from trauma, both hemispheres of the brain need to be activated. Working entirely through nonverbal means, as in working entirely through verbal means, mitigates against a holistic conception of psychological healing. There are certainly exceptions to the use of verbal processing in working with certain populations with limited insight and verbal capacities such as autistic children and severely mentally ill or developmentally disabled adults. However, with most populations, some form of reflection at least through action is well indicated.

The final step, that of social modeling, implies that once a role or configuration of role-CR-guide has been changed, clients become models for others within their various social environments of home, work, and play. When George goes to an upscale cocktail party given by wealthy art dealers, many of whom he has encountered previously, feeling insecure each time, he is fearful that they will see him as a failed artist. But since therapy has helped him to revise his self-conception, he is able to go as a competent artist whose business and self-promotional acumen is a work in progress. The dealers react positively to his altered self-perception and engage him in conversation. At the same time, peers at the party who think of themselves as failed artists see George in a more relaxed state and wish they could be more like him. George then, in his transformed state, becomes a role model for them.

I begin both a group and an individual session in a variety of ways. Most often, I greet my clients and wait for them to verbalize or nonverbally indicate their present state of being. Sometimes, especially with a new group, I will lead them through a physical warm-up and help them locate a role. One exercise I use often is to ask the group to move through the room and let go of tension through breathing and stretching and extending. I ask them to focus upon one body part and allow a movement to extend from, for example, their belly. I ask them to play with the movement, adding a sound and letting a character emerge. Once the character is established, I help the group develop it further through improvisational interactions in role, brief monologues, and finally, a naming of the role.

Once individuals in the group are warmed up to their roles, we work through these roles by means of storymaking or sculpting or free play in small groups. As we do so individuals are encouraged to locate counterroles and guide roles and to play them out within their dramatizations.

The form of identifying the three roles is generally effective, especially in higher functioning groups. This approach can become more confusing with low functioning or highly medicated groups. In that case, I generally begin work with a single role. If and when there is an opportunity to move to the other side of the role, I will ask individuals or a full group to locate and take on the counterrole.

With this model in mind, I utilize a range of techniques, generally staying within the scope of projective techniques (Landy, 1994). With individuals as well as groups, I use sandplay and free play, mask and puppets, drawings and sculpts, storytelling and storymaking and playback theatre. Most recently, I have found that work with stories provides a clear structure within which clients can locate and work with their roles and subsequent counterroles and guides. If any of the three are missing, the story structure provides a frame in which to locate the missing pieces. I generally work with the structure of a hero's journey, in which the hero is on a search toward a destination. The journey is blocked by one or more obstacles, which serve as counterroles. Because the journey is difficult, the hero needs a guide. I help the clients locate the figures of hero/role, obstacle/counterrole and guide through movement, guided imagery, story or drawing. Then I ask the client to direct his story with chosen members of the group in those roles.

In treatment, I also make use of psychodramatic techniques including doubling, role reversal, mirroring and sharing during closure. I try to avoid the direct reality orientation and intense cathartic nature of Psychodrama unless I sense that clients have distanced themselves too much from feeling and need to tell a direct story with a maximum of affect. In groups I also make use of sociometry in order to discover certain underlying dynamics and to encourage members to make more risky choices.

With some clients who have difficulty organizing their lives because of borderline tendencies or addictive dependencies, I will use a modification of cognitive-behavioral approaches. My aim is to help them develop effective coping strategies. In terms of a role approach, I often ask them to identify a role that they need to play and to specify its behavioral qualities. I help them practice playing the role in therapy as a rehearsal for moments in everyday life. I model this kind of work on the approach of George Kelly (1955) who developed a form of treatment called fixed role therapy, and on that of Wolpe and Lazarus (1966), who developed an approach of behavior rehearsal, based upon their notions of behavioral therapy.

In working cognitively, my goal is to help individuals reconstruct their mental schemas and find appropriate roles and counterroles to structure their lives. Through this work, a conscious effort is made to locate an inner guide figure, a kind of reliable central intelligence that can effectively direct the show.

The Role of the Drama Therapist

The drama therapist working through the Role Method needs to be flexible and responsive, engaging directly in the relationship with clients. Generally speaking, the drama therapist serves as guide, standing apart from the client, sometimes as witness, other times as coach, encouraging him, finally, to find his own guide. It is inadvisable for the drama therapist to become too distanced as this may objectify the client, or too enmeshed, as this may subvert the client's need for safety and clear boundaries. When moments of transference occur, the drama therapist can take on the transferential role and engage with the client, encouraging him to take on an appropriate counterrole. In the example I offered above of Joe, both therapist and client enter the domain of father and son as they visit a metaphorical baseball game and sing the evocative song, *Take Me Out to the Ballgame.*

In general, the drama therapist neither encourages nor discourages transference. When it appears, the drama therapist should be prepared to do one of two things. In the first instance, the therapist takes it on in the form of a role and encourages the client to take on the counterrole. Then, in their respective roles, they enact a brief drama. Following the enactment, they de-role and discuss the experience. In the second instance, often in a group process, the therapist helps the group to shift the transference from the therapist to the group thus empowering the group to work through the drama of transference on its own. For a full discussion of this second approach, see Eliaz (1988).

The model of distancing very much guides the interaction of therapist and client (Landy, 1983, 1993, 1994, 1996ab, 2007). The therapist assesses each moment and makes instantaneous judgments as to how close and how distant to be with the client. The determination is based upon two primary factors:

1. the client's diagnosis and ability to handle closeness and/or separation;
2. the therapist's ability to contain emotion and to deal effectively with countertransferential reactions within a session.

Although therapists must be willing to take on various counterroles to the client's roles and engage in a direct form of play, they will most of the time serve more as director and witness to the play of the client(s). One exception is when working with children through play therapy. In this case, the drama therapist most often engages directly in the play unless the child clearly indicates a wish to play alone. In playing with the child, the therapist works toward establishing open communication and trust, setting limits, containing emotion, and helping to clarify the theme of the play. The therapist works through the structure of role-CR-guide to help the client find a way in and out of each.

When taking a more distanced stance, the therapist guides the enactment and encourages the client to take on and play out the necessary roles. As an example, George comes into a session and tells me a dream. It is about a villain who sits in a room at the top of a tall tower. He has killed George's wife and George goes up to confront him. The villain transforms into many shapes. In one, he is driving George's car and George puts his hands over the villain's eyes so he will crash. In the front seat is a tough, sexy woman. In the end, George is with his wife who has come back to life. They are both descending the stairs of the tower. The villain is above and spits down at them. It is hard to avoid the spit. The villain is captured and sent to jail.

In working with the dream, I ask George to assume all the roles. He plays the villain, the wife, the sexy woman in the car, the car, the tower and the spit, giving a first person monologue for each role. He also identifies himself, George, as the protagonist. I watch George work. I am fully engaged in his drama, although I do not participate directly. I guide him from role to role, sometimes asking questions so that he will deepen his connection to a particular role or amplify a theme. After his enactment, I lead him through a discussion of the roles and their connection to one another. Finally, I ask him to link the roles in the dream to his everyday life.

Through our work together, George has learned to make the connections, to expand his repertory of roles, to deepen his commitment to several key roles and to find a way to guide himself without the fear of crashing. As therapist, I remain present as guide, reminding him to remove his hands from his eyes while he is driving, encouraging him to explore all the dark rooms at the tops of towers, urging him to look at ways to exist as a man among men and among women. In the end, George is able to accept all the dream images as parts of himself–the villain and the hero, the feminine and the masculine, the terrorist and the lover.

Populations Best Served through the Role Method

I began experimenting with drama therapy in the mid-1960s when I was a teacher of emotionally disturbed adolescents. My task was to teach English and drama, but many of my students were too disorganized and did not have the inner controls to learn how to scan poetry or to memorize lines in a play. Their pathologies ranged from learning disabilities and neurological impairments to severe mental illness and trauma. It took me several years of trial and error to begin to feel any sense of competence. I was learning the ropes, making up the work as I went along. For my students I was a guide of sorts, although very much a work in progress. I was not much older than some. Many had more life experience than I would ever have. Yet, I knew something about the theatre and had a great faith in its healing power. My years as an actor were more therapeutic than aesthetically gratifying as I found a form through which I could express and work through my pain. I was passionate about sharing my experience with others.

Twenty-five years passed before I developed role theory and the Role Method, and yet the seeds of my work as a drama therapist were planted at that time. I learned how to reach people who were unable to think and feel in a traditional way, who were unable to trust and to communicate and to empathize.

As I have developed drama therapy approaches over the years, I have kept my early experiences very much alive. The emotionally disturbed people I initially worked with remain my models, and when I speak of role-CR-guide or the taxonomy of roles or the Role Method, I still reflect upon my early work with them. It made sense that when I started to treat individual clients in drama therapy, the first population I worked with was learning disabled adolescents.

During the past 30 years I have worked with many people, including those with the following diagnoses: attention deficit hyperactive disorder (ADHD), alcohol and heroin addiction, eating disorders, post-traumatic stress disorder (PTSD), bipolar disorder, conduct disorder and sociopathy, sexual disorders, borderline and schizophrenic disorders, physical and developmental disabilities and normal neurotics, among others. My students trained in Role Method have applied the principles of role theory to the treatment of these and a range of other populations including incarcerated adolescents and adults, war veterans, sexually abused children, homeless mentally ill and frail elderly.

It is difficult to say which groups respond best to this treatment. On one level, it appears that the higher functioning normal neurotic population is most responsive in that this group can easily verbalize and reflect upon their enactments in role. Yet, there is growing evidence that the Role Method is also effective in treating lower functioning mentally ill individuals. One recent study (Sussman, 1998) offered evidence, primarily anecdotal, that a group of schizophrenics could effectively invoke and work through a number of roles, then relate these figures to their everyday lives.

It remains speculative as to which groups are best suited to Role Method as there are no empirically-based outcome studies. The evidence that abounds is largely anecdotal and based in process recordings and clinical observations. The exception is the development of systematic case studies that provide a view of the therapeutic process in terms of the role theory paradigm. Case studies include those of Michael (Landy, 1993), Hansel and Gretel (Landy, 1993), Kerry, Lena and Walt (Landy, 1996a), Sam (Landy, 1996a), Fay (Landy, 1999), and Derek (Landy, 2008). The latter can be viewed in the film, *Three Approaches to Drama Therapy* (Landy, 2005), which contrasts Role Method with Psychodrama and Developmental Transformations.

Limitations and Challenges

There are a number of limitations to role theory. Like any other theory, it is limited by its own set of assumptions concerning epistemology and such psychological issues as personality structure, health and wellness, therapeutic goals and processes. It challenges the humanistic, existential, modernist assumptions that underlie much of drama therapy, moving drama therapy discourse into a cognitive, constructivist, post-modernist realm. Some practitioners find this particular orientation too theoretical and intellectual.

Role theory does not sufficiently address issues of human development. It relies on a model of the human personality–the taxonomy of roles–that is derived from an art form and has very little scientific basis. The taxonomy itself, no matter how flexible and fluid, remains a reductive system, not easily applicable to the fluid and spontaneous movement of individuals from role to role in everyday life and in therapy.

Role theory tends to have more of a literary than social scientific focus and thus does not lend itself to the development of a substantial empirically-based research literature. Even as modeled in dramatic literature, it relies more upon role and character than on theme and plot, sound and sense.

The other side of this argument is that the part of role theory that is derived from sociology and symbolic interactionism has too much of a scientific focus as noted in the development of a substantial research literature (Brissett & Edgley, 1975; Serifica, 1982). As such, it remains limited in the minds of those who insist on a fully aesthetic perspective.

The Role Method is also limited in that it is based in a single theory that is limited in at least the ways mentioned above. If it were linked more clearly with other approaches it might allow the practitioner more leeway in treatment and analysis. Although Role Method practitioners do make use of techniques associated with play therapy, Developmental Transformations, the Integrative Five Phase Model, "Playback Theatre" (Chapter 20), Psychodrama, Gestalt Therapy and related approaches, their primary means of treatment is through projective techniques. This can be a limitation, especially when clients need to work in a direct manner, unmediated by role.

There are two challenges to this and indeed to any method and/or theory of drama therapy. The first is to verify its efficacy through carefully designed research studies. Through research, the method/theory will assert its uniqueness among others. The second is to demonstrate its common bonds with other approaches to drama therapy, which would, in a broad sense, further establish the credibility of the entire field of drama therapy. The latter challenge is met, in part, through the film, *Three Approaches to Drama Therapy* (Landy, 2005), and the book, *The Couch and the Stage: Integrating Words and Action in Psychotherapy* (Landy, 2008).

CASE EXAMPLE

The experience I will describe took place during an intense two-day workshop in Israel. I think that it well represents both the philosophy of role theory and the practice of Role Method. The focus of the workshop was to explore the spiritual dimension of life. In the beginning, as the group was warming up, it became clear that many were uncomfortable with the topic. The group was comprised mainly of therapists and artists, who primarily considered themselves to be secular Jews. They harbored open resentment toward the ultraorthodox whom, they thought, tried to impose strict spiritual and moral guidelines upon their everyday lives.

After some heated debate, I helped the group identify several roles: the spiritual searcher, the doubter, the object of the search and the guide. Although I had intended to limit the role choice to three, I recognized the group's need to distance itself from associating God with the object of their search. The fourth role of guide was acceptable to the group because it felt more neutral than God and stood outside the object of the search.

As I reflected upon the choice of roles, I thought that the literal guide was redundant and that the object of the search would easily stand in for the guide. More than that, I imagined that any of the roles could be guide, although the searcher and doubter felt like a clear representation of the role and counterrole.

Following a complex process of storytelling, drawing and improvisational enactment, I asked the group to choose one story to dramatize. They chose Judah's story. Judah was an anomaly in the group–a businessman among therapists and artists. He had never attended a therapeutic or creative workshop of any kind. He remained quiet and withdrawn throughout the first several hours of the experience. On a number of occasions I wondered if he would be able to complete the tasks and enter fully into the process. Yet his story was extraordinary in some way. This is Judah's story:

> A man comes home from work early and lies down on the couch to take a nap. He wakes suddenly, as if from a dream, to find the light from the TV blinding him. He tries to turn it off, but he cannot. He is disoriented and in order to regain his balance, he must determine the time of day. He picks up the phone and calls an old girlfriend named Rona. He identifies himself as Robert. He asks her urgently: "Is it 6 o'clock in the morning or 6 o'clock in the evening? Please tell me. I must know!" There is no answer. The man cannot rest. He is desperate to know the answer to his question. The question remains unanswered.

The story baffled and intrigued me and probably the others in the group, for they chose it among many highly imaginative and poetic stories. I noticed that there did not seem to be a guide in the story. Although the man turns to Rona to answer his question, she is unable to answer. I wonder why Judah identified the man as Robert. Was this some form of transference? Did he think that I could help him answer his question or, better yet, understand what the question means? Was I supposed to be the guide for Judah who takes on my name in order to search for a sense of balance?

In terms of role theory, my speculation made sense. Judah, a man who has never experienced therapy or a creative arts experience, felt off balance in his life and his wife, a creative arts therapist, suggested that he attend this workshop. In search of a guide to help him find his balance, he takes on the role of the leader whom he imagines is powerful and wise. Judah hopes that the guide role will help him find the clarity and balance he so desperately seeks. In this example, the role and the guide are merged although, as we shall see, they soon become separate. The counterrole appears to be the ex-girlfriend, Rona, the one who cannot answer the question, the false hope, as many ex-lovers come to be.

After the group chose Judah's story, Judah read the story aloud. Unsure of how to proceed with the dramatization, I asked Judah: "Who is telling the story?" As the words came out of my mouth, I realized that I had no idea why I asked this question.

"Leonard is telling the story," Judah replied.

Something was happening that felt unexpected and exciting. Other presences were about to be revealed.

"Who is Leonard?" I asked.

"I am Leonard," said Judah.

Then Judah told the story behind the story. He was born Leonard in Poland. He immigrated to Israel when he was five years old. At the border, the immigration officer told him that Leonard, literally, the Lion, was not a proper Jewish name. As he was about to enter his new land, he was given the name Judah, the Jew.

An important part of the Role Method concerns the naming of roles. I recognized that Judah's drama would be based upon discovering the right names for his roles and working them through. In discovering the twin names of Leonard/Judah, a significant role-CR relationship was present. On a whole other level, however, I recognized that Leonard would be Judah's guide, just like Robert. Judah seemed to need several guides. He was in foreign territory. By engaging in this workshop, he had stepped over another border.

I asked Judah to tell Leonard's story. He stumbled but managed to tell this:

> There is a little boy. He is not alone. He is with a group of human beings. I think they are grown-ups but they could be children. Or I think they are childlike. The human beings help Leonard to grow.

I ask Judah to choose three people as the human beings and one as Leonard. He chooses Avi, a very playful and dramatic member of the workshop, to be Leonard. Taking their cue from Avi, the group becomes light and playful. The human beings engulf Leonard, and Leonard loves the attention. They circle the room, arm in arm, singing and dancing. They are connected and happy. Judah stays by my side. He tells me that he is happy watching the drama.

I noticed that the human beings are easy guides for the little boy to follow. There does not appear to be a counterrole in the story. There is no tension, no strife. It appears to be a picture of the boy before he crosses the border, before the fall, before he was forced to change his identity and be a man.

I asked Judah if he was ready to enact Judah's story. He became more serious as he said "Yes." He chooses Dahlia to play himself. I ask him to help Dahlia enter into her role. But as he begins to instruct her, she stops: "Who am I supposed to be?" she asks. "Am I Judah or Leonard or Robert?"

Dahlia raises a very important question. In terms of role theory, is she to be the role, the CR or the guide? Judah, the spiritual searcher, seems to be the protagonist of the story, the central role figure. Leonard could be either a CR or guide. Robert would appear to be a guide figure.

Who is guiding whom, I wonder? Then I remember the four roles the group had specified at the beginning of the workshop. The first, the spiritual searcher, is well exemplified by Judah. The doubter could also be Judah in the guise of the storyteller or when he returns home from work, so weary that he falls asleep. The object of the search is unknown, but appears to be the one who can answer the man's question. It might be Rona. The guide appears to be Robert, the workshop leader whose name is taken on by Judah.

With all the potential role confusions it is no wonder that Dahlia is confused. Then she questions why Judah picked a woman to play a man. Dahlia is stuck and I ask Judah to choose someone else from the group to help her find her way. He immediately chooses Avi who again takes on the childish energy of Leonard and starts to wail: "I want my Mommy! I want my Mommy!"

Dahlia is energized and plays with Avi. They encircle each other as she tries to contain his energy, his mock expression of fear. Role and CR are finally present, the child in pain and the mother attempting to contain. They have transcended the story line, but something very important is happening and we all feel it. I bring Judah directly into the drama, having him reverse roles with

Dahlia. Judah tries to calm the child. He pets Avi and says: "It's OK. You will be alright. You are such a good boy."

I tell Judah to try to reach Rona and ask her the question. He picks Roni from the group to play Rona. But as moves toward her, Avi holds on to him tightly. Judah struggles to break free. He finally manages to pull away, but loses a shoe to Avi.

Judah asks the question: "What time is it? I have to know."

She replies: "It is six in the morning."

But I feel she is the wrong object of Judah's search, the wrong guide, and so I ask him: "Did you ask the right question?"

He replies: "No."

I invite others in the group to enter the drama as Judah/Robert and attempt to find the right question. No one is successful. Judah is not able to accept any of their questions.

Again, I am stumped. How do I end this enactment? What needs to happen? Then I realize that the role-CR tension needs some resolution. The drama now concerns Judah, the searcher, and Rona, the object of the search. I ask all in the group to touch the person with whom they most identify–the searcher or the object of the search. Most all choose Judah. They, too, are searchers who are not clear as to their spiritual questions. How different they are from the beginning of the workshop when most openly identified with the role of doubter.

Needing to integrate the two roles, I ask Avi and Roni to attempt to touch one another. When they do, the drama will end. I ask the group to ensure that the moment of touch does not happen too quickly. They take hold of Avi and Roni and pull them in different directions. I then ask Judah to stand in for Avi. Judah and Roni struggle to break free from the group.

Finally, exhausted, the group allows them to touch. The drama ends, and I work hard to de-role all the participants. Judah is in a heightened state and has trouble letting go of the extraordinary roles of the man who wakes up, of Robert and Leonard, of searcher, guide and child. This form of experience in role is so new to Judah. The full group helps him to breathe, to shake off the magic, to come back to the present moment in time. It is a hard journey back for all.

As we discuss this experience, many levels of role-CR-guide unfold. On the level of the dramatic reality, Robert and Rona become role and CR, the searcher and the object of the search. The question of time is never properly answered and doesn't even seem to matter since it might have been the wrong question to ask in the first place. What seems to matter most is the touch, the integration of the roles. Judah reports that this moment was the most satisfying of all. This might be so because of the integration of role and CR which, according to role theory, should have some relationship to Judah's everyday life.

That relationship is discovered when Judah explains that Roni, whom he chose to play Rona, the ex-girlfriend, is in reality his wife. On another level, then, this was a drama about Judah's connection to his wife. The figure of the ex-girlfriend becomes a kind of counterrole that leads Judah back to the strength of his current relationship. Incidentally, I recall that Roni led Judah to the workshop in the first place, hoping that it would move him out of his lethargy and imbalance.

On another level, Judah makes a conscious association of Robert as guide. He becomes aware that he took on this guide role as a means of searching for an answer to his burning question. I ask him to consider ways to hold on to this role as he reenters his everyday realms of love and work and play.

Finally we are left with the theme of the workshop, exploring the spiritual realm through drama therapy. At the beginning of the experience, I mentioned to the group that I was in the process of researching ways that children see God. It was at that moment that several group members expressed their uneasiness with the topic of spirituality in general, and the concept of God, in particular. I chose not to deal with God in any direct way, but here we were at the end of the workshop and I had a need to link our work with the central theme.

"Was Judah's story dramatization spiritual in any way?" I asked. Many nodded in the affirmative and tried to articulate the mysterious quality of Judah's story and the search for love as a spiritual theme. Some spoke about the question of time and related this to the timelessness of the divine. But the most striking comment was made, finally, by Avi, the one who was able to so easily take on the role of the child, Leonard, before and after the fall. He informed us that God is referred to in Hebrew as *Hashem,* literally, the name. There is a prohibition in the orthodox Jewish faith about speaking the name of God directly. Thus God is referred to as Hashem. Avi said that he saw the drama therapy experience as focused upon naming. Judah's search for the right name and Dahlia's confusion over the names was like the Jew's search for the right name for God. Then Judah recognized that the prohibition against speaking the holy name of God connects to his own prohibition against speaking the name of Leonard, the child that he was a long time ago.

Upon further reflection I became aware that Judah was a man very much in search of a guide, one who could help him integrate not only the name he lost as a child, but also the lost qualities of the child. In the end, he recognized that the playful qualities of the child could guide him in so many ways: to get him through his work, to allow him a restful night's sleep, to keep him focused in the present moment in time, to keep him connected to his wife. The implications of the name, Leonard, remained with Judah. Leonard is not only the child but also the lion, the king of beasts, the one in control of the jungle without and the jungle and playground within.

As the group was disbanding, we all also recognized a final political level. Judah's story is the story of a nation of immigrants who left behind their names, their original roles, to take on new identities and to build a nation in and among hostile forces. For many who have shut out the old roles, the counterroles they have taken on have seemed somehow incomplete. Although the state of Israel has had many powerful guides, no one has been universally accepted. Israel is a country of splits and it has been difficult for many to find integration and balance. Judah found his balance having rediscovered Leonard through the help of a guide, Robert, as well as the guiding figures provided by Avi and Roni.

The final step of the Role Method concerns social modeling. As Judah takes his new awareness into the many realms of his everyday life, he has the opportunity to affect the lives of others. He has taken one large step toward assuming the qualities and function of the guide.

CONCLUSION

Role theory and Role Method in drama therapy are separate but intimately connected. Role theory concerns a way of understanding the origins and goals and processes of drama therapy. It is derived in part from the social sciences but primarily from traditional healing forms and the art form of theatre. As such it provides the field with its central and unique focus first as an art form and then a science. As a theory, it gives a framework in which to make sense of all other aspects of the clinical and research branches of drama therapy.

Role Method is an extension of the theory to clinical practice. Although I have attempted to outline the approach in a sequential fashion, I feel that the actual process of therapy moves along a curve or circle rather than a straight line. In the example of Judah we see evidence of invoking roles, working them through, discovering counterroles and guides, reflecting upon the roles and connecting them with everyday life roles, integrating role-CR-guide and speculating among the possibilities of social modeling. Yet, I hope it is clear that the actual process is in many ways murky. In this case, the most important element, the actual turning point, seems to be the naming. In other cases, the key moment appears in the invocation or working through or reflection. Each case is unique.

Drama therapy is a very small field, a subset of psychotherapy or the art of drama/theatre or the creative arts therapies. Or perhaps drama therapy is a field in itself, derivative as much as all fields, yet indivisible. I think the field is too young to proclaim its independence. But then again, the same had been said about Israel and for that matter, about the United States of America.

If the field is to survive well into the future and if it remains alive as more than a footnote in a textbook of psychotherapy or theatre or creative arts therapy, then it will need a solid foundation in theory, in clinical practice grounded in theory, and in research. Role theory and its concomitant Role Method is one attempt to do just that–to organize discrepant concepts, techniques and practices into a coherent system, one that has the weight and the lightness to travel through time.

REFERENCES

Bikki Tam, J. (2004). *A survey and study of Role Profiles of the Hong Kong Chinese mentally ill rehabilitation population.* MA thesis, New York University.

Bloom, B. et al. (1956). *Taxonomy of educational objectives, handbook I: Cognitive domain.* New York: David McKay.

Brissett, D. & Edgley, C., Eds. (1975). *Life as theatre: A dramaturgical sourcebook.* Chicago: Aldine.

Campbell, J. (1949). *The hero with a thousand faces.* New York: Pantheon Books.

Clayton, S. (2000). *Role Profile of an adult with chronic depression.* MA thesis, New York University.

Cooley, C. (1922). *Human nature and social order.* New York: Scribner's.

Demasio, A. (1994). *Descartes' error: Emotion, reason and the human brain.* New York: Putnam.

Demasio, A. (1999). *The feeling of what happens: Body and emotion in the making of consciousness.* New York: Harcourt Brace & Co.

Eliade, M. (1972). *Shamanism: Archaic techniques of ecstasy.* Princeton, NJ: Princeton University Press.

Eliaz, E. (1988). *Transference in drama therapy,* Ph.D. dissertation, New York University.

Fistos, J. (1996). *Role Call: The development of a card sort assessment based on the role method of drama therapy.* MA thesis, New York University.

Florin, N. (2001). *Role Profiles 2000: The many roles of mother.* MA thesis, New York University.

Fox, J., (Ed.), (1987). *The essential Moreno.* New York: Springer.

Goffman, E. (1959). *The presentation of self in everyday life.* Garden City, New York: Doubleday.

Hillman, J. (1983). *Healing fiction.* Barrytown, New York: Station Hill.

James, W. (1890/1950). *The principles of psychology.* New York: Dover.

Jung, C.G. (1964). *Man and his symbols.* Garden City, New York: Doubleday.

Jung, C.G. (1971). *Psychological types.* Princeton: Princeton University Press.

Kelly, G.A. (1955). *The psychology of personal constructs.* Vol. I. New York: Norton.

Landy, R. (1983). The use of distancing in drama

therapy. *The Arts in Psychotherapy, 10,* 175- 185.
Landy, R. (1993). *Persona and performance.* New York: Guilford Press.
Landy, R. (1994). *Drama therapy: Concepts, theories and practices.* 2nd ed. Springfield, IL: Charles C Thomas.
Landy, R. (1996a). *Essays in drama therapy–The double life.* London: Jessica Kingsley.
Landy, R. (1996b). Drama therapy and distancing: Reflections on theory and clinical application. *The Arts in Psychotherapy, 23,* 367–373.
Landy, R. (1999). Role model of drama therapy supervision. In E. Tselikas-Portmann, (Ed.), *Supervision and dramatherapy.* London: Jessica Kingsley.
Landy, R. (2001a). Role profiles–An assessment instrument. In *New essays in drama therapy–Unfinished business.* Springfield, IL: Charles C Thomas.
Landy, R. (2001b). Tell-A-Story–A new assessment in drama therapy. In *New essays in drama therapy–Unfinished business.* Springfield, IL: Charles C Thomas.
Landy, R. (2005). *Three approaches to drama therapy.* Video and DVD. New York: New York University.
Landy, R. (2008). *The couch and the stage: Integrating words and action in psychotherapy.* Lanham, MD: Jason Aronson.
Landy, R., Luck, B., Conner, E., & McMullian, S. (2003). Role profiles–A drama therapy assessment instrument. *The Arts in Psychotherapy, 30,* 151–61.
Linton, R. (1936). *The study of man.* New York: Appleton-Century-Crofts.
Mead, G.H. (1934). *Mind, self and society.* Chicago: University of Chicago Press.
Meldrum, B. (1994). A role model of dramatherapy and its application with individuals and groups. In S. Jennings, A. Cattanach, S. Mitchell, A. Chesner, & B. Meldrum. *The handbook of dramatherapy* (pp. 75–92). London: Routledge.
Moffett, J. (1968). *Teaching the universe of discourse.* New York: Houghton Mifflin.
Moreno, J.L. (1946/1994). *Psychodrama.* Vol. 1. Beacon, NY: Beacon House.
Moreno, J.L. (1947). *The theatre of spontaneity.* Beacon, NY: Beacon House.
Moreno, J.L., Ed. (1960). *The sociometry reader.* Glencoe, Il. The Free Press.
Pearson, C. (1989). *The hero within.* New York: Harper Collins.
Raz, S. (1997). *Psychological type and changing acting personas–A hypothetical model of role theory in role acquisition among performing artists.* Ph.D. dissertation, Miami Institute of Psychology.
Riso, D. (1987). *Personality types.* Boston: Houghton Mifflin.
Rosenberg, Y. (1999). *Role theory and self concept.* MA thesis, Lesley College, Israel.
Sarbin, T. & V. Allen. (1968). Role theory. In G. Lindzey & E. Aronson, (Eds.), *The handbook of social psychology,* 2nd ed. Reading, MA: Addison-Wesley.
Scheff, T. (1979). *Catharsis in healing, ritual and drama.* Berkeley: University of California.
Seitz, P. (2000). *Drama therapy storytelling assessment: A comparison of mentally ill and normal neurotic stories.* MA thesis, New York University.
Serafica, F. (1982). *Social-cognitive development in context.* New York: Guilford Press.
Sussman, F. (1998). *Application of role theory and myth to adult schizophrenics in a continuing day treatment program,* MA thesis, New York University.
Tangorra, J. (1997). *Many masks of pedophila: Drama therapeutic assessment of the pedophile role repertoire.* MA thesis, New York University.
Tranchida, J. (2000). *Open domains: Comparing the domains and classifications of role theory's taxonomy with the role-groupings of undergraduate drama students.* MA thesis, New York University.
van der Kolk, B. (2002a). Posttraumatic therapy in the age of neuroscience. *Psychoanalytic Dialogues, 12,* 3, 381–92.
van der Kolk, B. (2002b). Beyond the talking cure. In F. Shapiro, (Ed.), *EMDR: Towards a paradigm shift.* Washington, DC: American Psychiatric Press.
Wolpe, J. & Lazarus, A. (1966). *Behavior therapy techniques: A guide to the treatment of neuroses.* New York: Pergamon Press.

Video

CBS-TV (1980). *Drama in Education.* New York, New York.

Chinese Theatre Association. (1996). *Drama Therapy in Taiwan.* Taipei, Taiwan,

Fanlight Productions (2004). Peggy Stern, Director. *Standing Tall,* Boston, Massachusetts.

TransVideo, Inc. (1987). *Reach for Speech: the Use of Sociodrama to Teach Oral Communication Skills.* New York, New York.

FURTHER TRAINING

Master of Arts Degree in Drama Therapy
Approved by the National Association for Drama Therapy and
New York State Department of Education
New York University
Steinhardt School of Culture, Education, and Human Development
Director: Robert Landy, Ph.D., RDT-BCT, LCAT
35 West 4th Street
Suite 777
New York City, New York 10012
212-998-5402
www.nyu.edu/education/music/drama/dramther.html

Training in Relational Drama Therapy
Institute for Drama Therapy
Directors: Robert Landy, Ph.D., RDT-BCT, LCAT, and
Emily Nash, LCAT
212-579-3034
www.Institutefordramatherapy.com

Chapter 6

DEVELOPMENTAL TRANSFORMATIONS: TOWARDS THE BODY AS PRESENCE

DAVID READ JOHNSON

Developmental Transformations is a form of drama psychotherapy that is based on an understanding of the process and dynamics of free play. The essence of Developmental Transformations is the transformation of embodied encounters in the playspace. These four components: *transformation, embodiment, encounter,* and *playspace,* will be described in detail later. Important aspects of this approach include: (1) the sessions consist entirely of dramatic, improvisational interaction between the therapist and client(s); (2) the therapist is an active participant in the play and intervenes through his/her own immersion in the client's playspace; (3) the process of play is used to loosen or remove (i.e., deconstruct) psychic structures that inhibit the client(s) from accessing primary experiences of Being (i.e., Presence); and (4) the client's progress in treatment is believed to follow natural, developmental processes that in themselves will lead to greater emotional health. Technically, Developmental Transformations is a treatment for disorders of embodiment, encounter, and play.

GENESIS

Developmental Transformations (DvT) is based on the theatrical ideas of Jerzy Grotowski (Grotowski, 1968; Johnson, Forrester, Dintino, James, & Schnee, 1996) and Viola Spolin (Johnson, 1982; Spolin, 1963). Over the course of development of this approach, numerous theoretical perspectives have been incorporated to understand the processes involved. These have included the psychological perspectives of cognitive development (Johnson, 1999; Piaget, 1951; Werner & Kaplan, 1963), psychotherapeutic perspectives of psychoanalysis, particularly free association (Freud, 1920; Kris, 1982), object relations theory (Jacobson, 1964; Klein, 1932), client-centered therapy (Rogers, 1951; Gendlin, 1978), authentic movement (Whitehouse, 1979), and dance therapy (Sandel, Chaiklin, & Lohn, 1993); philosophical perspectives of existentialism (Sartre, 1943), postmodernism (Deleuze & Guattari, 1987; Derrida, 1978), and Buddhism. These widely divergent sources have been used to understand aspects of the therapeutic method, concepts of the self-structure, and images of Being.

DRAMA THERAPY FRAME OF REFERENCE

Basic Concepts

The Instability of Being

The essential proposition of DvT theory is that Being is unstable. The universe is not at rest, we are not at rest, and whatever frame, form, awning, shelter, floor, ground, or shield we build or hang on to that gives us the temporary illusion that life is stable, will yield to transformation, change, and eventually disappearance. Business contracts, national boundaries, marriage vows, and self-representations all serve for a time to bring order and give form, but all eventually give way to new forms that arise.

DvT theory therefore is in alignment with the first and second of Buddha's Three Signs of the Dharma. All forms of life are impermanent and turbulent. Where DvT theory departs from traditional Buddhism is that DvT does not expect that there is a way to bring it to an end in nirvana, at least any time soon enough for DvT practitioners. Rather, DvT attempts not to quell this turbulence, but to reduce our fear of it. DvT helps us to feel comfortable on the swaying boat in a rough sea, not only to walk on solid ground. Most relationships between people appear to be more like rough seas than solid ground, so perhaps DvT has some relevance for helping us in intimate relationships.

The instability of Being derives from the experience of *difference:* the discrepancies and incompleteness we encounter when we sense the world and struggle to comprehend it by stabilizing concepts, ideas, and repetitions. Thus, at heart, the human struggle is intimately engaged with variance, multiplicity, and unpredictability, all of which are also the essential components of improvisation.

It is not difficult to find evidence that the world is turbulent, especially human life: everywhere things arise, come forth. There is an outflow from one thing to another, in birth, in bloom, in stars, in ideas, in our bodies. If life were not turbulent, in tension with itself in some way, there would be no impetus for such outflows, for development. So turbulence gives us emanation, and emanation development, and development, transformation. And that is the reason our practice is called Developmental Transformations. And this is the basis for the first principle of DvT: *transformation.*

Emanation theory suggests the world is naturally given, rather than willed. Emanation theory therefore diverges from the implications of a constructivist model, that through an act of will we can reconstruct (or *restory*) our lives. In parallel fashion, Developmental Transformations is more interested in the process through which roles and images arise and then transform in the client, rather than what these roles are or how they are structured. Thus, we believe the best way to produce a large array of flower (i.e., expand the role repertoire) is to feed the root (i.e., connect to the embodied impulse).

If things arise, then there is *Source,* for the very presence of arising brings with it, Source, from which it or we have sprung. DvT theory does not specify the nature of this Source, which presumably lies within each of us, within the universe, and therefore out of which everything has come. The nature of this Source is completely up to each person to believe in. It is in fact possible that just as what arises emerges from the Source, so the notion of Source emerges out of the act of arising, and that source and arising are the same thing. Nevertheless, DvT does not adhere to the idea that there is no source, that things arise randomly or out of nothing, that anything goes, or that our egos can decide what goes. Rather, being out of touch with the Source, with the outflow that arises from within our Bodies, is a sign of ill health, and conversely, that bringing ourselves more into contact with this or these Sources is natural and a sign of health.

Let me use a metaphor of the Earth: At its center, the Earth remains a boiling hot piece of the Sun, without form, in turmoil. The surface of the Earth has cooled, forming a crust, which has the appearance of solid ground but in fact is built out of huge tectonic plates that slowly rise up from and fall back into the depths. The crust has cooled because the Universe is cold, yet there remains strong pressure from the center to push material up from below.

It can be imagined that the Self has a similar structure: its surface has the appearance of solidity, but is in fact constantly changing; its crust, made up of large tectonic narratives, is used to locate oneself in the cool social world within which we live; our identity is constructed of these roles which form what we call our persona. Yet underneath there remains the pressure of Desire, and at our center, let us call it the Source, is a turbulent, heated core, without form. To some, the absence of form at our center is a reason to proclaim that we have no core. But if we have no core, what then is *this* which rises up? The pathway through which the Source emerges within us is our Body. By Body we mean both our physical and energetic presence. Thus, as the Source is expressed, it cools and forms into desires and impulses, thoughts and perceptions, images of self and other, roles and identities. Health is understood to be the continued natural unfolding of this developmental process. Ill health is understood to be the stifling of this process when already-created forms block the emergence of new forms. This is often due to protective responses to painful encounters with other human beings. The result is a division among Other, Self, and Source.

Developmental Transformations intends to facilitate a renewed flow or link between Source, Self, and Other (not a withdrawal from others or attainment of a selfless state). It does so through the use of free play as a tool for continuous transformation. As one experiences embodiment, opens oneself to the encounter with others, and embraces continuous change (i.e., play), one finds oneself reconnected to one's Source. This is what we mean by *Presence.*

One of the reasons concepts such as Source has been questioned is that what seems to emerge from it is steeped in paradox, seemingly irresolvable paradox. But if the Source is turbulent, then these paradoxes are to be expected, and in fact I would suggest that any irresolvable paradox is a sign of proximity to the Source. These paradoxes, which have plagued philosophy from the beginning, include the apparently simultaneous connection and difference between mind and body (or energy and matter), between subjectivity and objectivity, between the finite and the infinite, and between reality and imagination. Every attempt to clarify these dilemmas has failed. And each of these dilemmas serves as another source of instability in our lives: being a mind and a body, being a subject and an object, living in a real and imagined world at the same time. Each of us struggles with bringing quiet to these dialogues within ourselves and between ourselves, with little success. Therefore it is likely that much of what is played with in the playspace will be these paradoxes.

Emanations of Body

DvT proposes that the emanation that each human being is may be best characterized as *Body,* in both its material and energetic forms (the word body, uncapitalized, refers to the physical body). We arise into this world as Body, with consciousness being its energetic limb and our physical body being its material limb. Its first manifestation is simply *Presence,* with its turbulent but minimal form. The next manifestation may be called Body as *Desire,* in that our presence coalesces into impulse and desire. Next is Body as *Persona,* in which our experience and desires form further into notions of Self and Person. (In this sense, DvT is also aligned with the third of Buddhism's Three Signs: that the Self is a composite of impersonal elements.) Finally, our emanation forms further into Body as *Other,* in which we organize ourselves in the larger world and clothe ourselves with social roles and identities. All of these manifestations are active simultaneously: I am a white, male, drama therapist in the east coast of the United States, I am David Read Johnson, a member of my family, having various personal characteristics; I am at this moment tense and my stomach is growling for no apparent reason; and I am simply here. Yet these layers are not equal: each one lays close on top of the other. Generally I spend too much energy on myself for Others and keeping up my Persona, rather than attending to my desires or to my presence.

Yet to be both conscious and material, to have two forms of presence, is deeply paradoxical and anxiety-provoking. My consciousness is unbound; my imagination free. My physical body on the other hand limits me; I can be located (and hurt). I wake each morning *here,* with *this.* Sartre has called this dilemma *nausea:* I am this body and yet I look at this body as if it were an object, a dizzying prospect to be sure. I spend too much time attempting to change, reshape, undo, or hide my body. We puncture, cut, pierce, color, suck out, and strangle our bodies, in secret, in front of the mirror, for others, for our imaginations . . . in endless ways. And the tension never ends, for our energetic and material presence are tied together. To not fear this conflict, to be able to play with consciousness' disdain for the body, for example, or our ability to be located by the Other, is an aim of DvT and its emphasis on *embodiment.*

Proximity to the Other

Managing these paradoxes and layers of Being is sufficiently challenging, but all the more so when I am in *proximity* to other people. If I am a source of turbulence, interacting with another source of turbulence greatly increases my sense of instability. No wonder that we long to look out to sea, to work the land, to go to bed, and to be left alone! Our intimate relationships with each other are highly unstable, and all too often our repeated attempts to stabilize them lead to their death and encrustation. If DvT intends to help us reduce our fear of the instability of being, then it is clear that this is best tested where this instability can most be found: in close proximity to others, not alone or with objects. Learning in the proximal environment is likely to be long lasting and readily applicable. This is the basis for the third principle of DvT: *encounter.*

Encountering another person is an awesome event. Perceiving the gaze of the Other, we can feel our freedom constrained, invaded (Sartre, 1943). We can respond by becoming silenced, shamed, or disempowered. It seems almost impossible for such a meeting to be neutral, something always appears to be at stake. If object relations theorists are correct when they claim that the Self is built up out of others' perceptions of us, then each encounter risks shaking that foundation (Klein, 1932). Perhaps Sartre is right, when he claims that we experience ourselves as an object in the Other's view, questioning our own sense of personal freedom (Sartre, 1943). In any case, to be seen, to be known, when it leads to being hurt, results in protective measures. These often include controlling or narrowing the experience of encounter with others, crippling our efforts at intimacy. Simply being in a room alone with another person, especially when they are not located in a chair or behind a desk and can move freely, can bring up intense memories of encounters with others, as well as the protective measures against them. The only things available to cloak the encounter are the dramatic roles and actions of the play, and indeed these are initially quite well-developed, clear, and "story-bound." Plot keeps an order to time, character orders self, story gives predictability to the ending. All of these pass away during our therapeutic work, as client and therapist allow themselves to be with each other with fewer and fewer intermediary veils; they fill their dramatic playspace with references to their in-the-moment feelings and perceptions of each other, and thus time loses its linearity, roles become collages, and the next act cannot be predicted.

Thus our general theory relies on the notion that life is unstable and that our fear of this instability can be reduced. Our fears of change and impermanence, of our presence as a body, and of our proximity to others are the three significant existential challenges we face, and that DvT attempts to address.

Playspace

The *playspace* is a mutual agreement among the participants that everything that goes on between them is a representation or portrayal of real or imagined being. The playspace is the container of the entire therapeutic action in Developmental Transformations. It consists of three essential components:

1. *Restraint against harm*–the playspace is a restraint against harm. Play does not continue if a party becomes hurt. If the possibility of harm arises, the participant's playspace will quickly become restricted and lose energy, leading to leaving the playspace altogether if the threat continues. The playspace can only be maintained when all parties understand that their intention is only to represent harm, but not to commit it. Paradoxically, the playspace tends to reveal harm or evil or perpetration exactly to the extent to which the participants feel confident of each other's ability to restrain any potentially harmful enactment. To the observer, it may appear that horrors have been unleashed into the world, when in fact they have only been released into the playspace.
2. *Discrepant communication*–the playspace consists of discrepant communications, in which the parties indicate that they are enacting representations of reality or imagination, and that the boundary between the playspace and the real world is portrayed along with the content of the representations. Thus, the playspace, like theatre, is a lie that seeks to reveal itself as a lie, and therefore, is honest. At different times and with different people, the amount of discrepancy that is required to maintain a sense of the playspace will vary. As the practice progresses, participants require less discrepancy in their communications in order to maintain the playspace.
3. *Mutual agreement*–the playspace is an inter-subjective experience mutually understood by all participants. This mutuality is communicated when each

> party indicates a recognition of the discrepancy in the others' communications, that is, a recognition that the others' behavior is a representation, a portrayal.

The playspace is therefore a moral and ethical relationship among the participants exactly because of its three components. The playspace is a restraint against harm, it honestly marks the boundary between reality and fantasy, and it is a mutual relationship. Restraint, honesty, and mutuality form the basis for the claim that the playspace, unlike other forms of play, has a moral foundation.

Purpose of Theory

The main purpose of theory in DvT is to help the therapist/leader empty themselves of restrictive theoretical thoughts that will interfere with their open response to the client. Therefore, theory needs to be as streamlined as possible, with all unnecessary elements removed. Second, the theory needs to be self-negating, in that it needs to act in such a way as to remove itself from the foreground of thought. Third, the theory needs to act on other theoretical propositions that emerge in the therapists' mind in such a way as to remove them from any foundational position and shifting them–in this case via the playspace–into *playobjects* within the playspace. I have found that when the therapist acts on the basis of any preformed agenda, framework, or theory, s/he almost always misses important elements in the client's behavior, thereby reducing the impact of DvT. This, however, in no way is meant to discourage DvT practitioners from having a theory of the human being, or life, or truth, or whatever, as long as while they are acting within the playspace in DvT, they are able to place that theory into the playspace as a playobject, subject to transformation with everything else.

Therapeutic Process

The kind of play that takes place in the playspace is free improvisation, in which clients are asked to play out dramatic movements, sounds, images, and scenes based on thoughts and feelings they are having in the moment. Thus, as these thoughts and feelings change, the scenes, characters, and actions change. Similar to meditative practice, the client is asked to allow thoughts and feelings to arise, to contemplate them, and then to let them go as others arise. In Developmental Transformations, this process takes place in an embodied, interactional, and dramatic form, rather than sitting in silent meditation. Verbal discussion or processing occurs within the playspace, not at the end of the session outside the state of play.

Inevitably, thoughts and feelings arise that do not seem playable to the client. The therapist's job is to help the client maintain the state of play through these moments, often by shifting away from them. Over time, the goal is for the client to be able to play with the unplayable, for it is the unplayable that blocks our way to the Source. This process is essentially what Grotowski referred to as the *via negativa,* the negative way, being a process of removal of blocks. The play process serves the via negativa, or if you will, the deconstructive process, largely through repetition. As difficult issues repeatedly arise, are then avoided, then addressed again, the client and therapist find ways of playing with different aspects of the issue, until, with time, the issue becomes like a cliché to them, and loosens its grip on the client, who eventually lets what is to come next arise. In this way, client and therapist descend together through increasingly intimate stages of play.

The beginning phase of the work, which corresponds to the level of Body as Other, is *Surface Play,* in which the client and therapist play with the social stereotypes and issues that first come to mind. Soon, however, as their encounter shifts onto that of Body as Persona, the client(s) begins to play with images, characters, and stories from their life and history, as well as aspects of their personality. Scenes with their parents, children, friends, and lovers, parts of themselves, fantasies of all kinds, are played out over and over in increasingly varied ways during this *Persona Play.* Every possible action toward significant people in their lives and themselves are portrayed, including those secretly held for years as well as new ones, never before conceived.

As this work proceeds, client and therapist begin to open themselves to the experiences of Body as Desire, and the play shifts into *Intimate Play,* where the client's thoughts and feelings about the therapist begin to fuel the dramatic action. The play now becomes about the client's relationship to the therapist and again all possible and impossible situations are portrayed. At first the scenes consist of what might happen between them, or what did happen in the past between them. Increasingly, however, the play is about the here-and-now relationship between them and what is occurring at the moment. As always, the unplayable feelings remain one step ahead of the playspace.

Eventually, the playing out of their relationship gives way to greater ambiguity and even mystery. They become acutely aware of each other's presence in the room with the other person/body/consciousness. Scenes devolve into silent gestures or mutterings, long pauses and glances, or simple bodily contact. Both client and therapist are aware of all the various stories, scenes, and actions of past sessions, but a feeling of not needing to play them out again, only making passing reference to them, seems strongest. In these states of *Deep Play,* client and therapist are intensely aware of each other and their bodies, and are freed up enough to work on their feelings of being bound or restrained by each other in the play. This level of intimacy is not available if there are still strong desires for each other as individuals; what desire is present might best be described as passion, the passion that has thrust them out into this life, and which is shared between them with a certain sense of irony.

It is not necessary for all clients to reach Deep Play in order to be helped. The playing out in Surface Play of many possibilities of being is a powerful way of increasing one's role repertoire and spontaneity. Persona Play, in which personal issues are explored, is the arena of many forms of drama therapy, and can have significant effects on a person's self-understanding, flexibility, and adaptive functioning. Intimate Play can be immeasurably helpful in increasing a person's tolerance of interpersonal encounters, openness to intimacy, and lowering fearfulness of others.

Role of the Therapist

The Developmental Transformations therapist takes the role of the guide with the client, demonstrating comfort and confidence in entering the imaginal realm of the playspace (see my discussion of therapist roles in Johnson, 1992). The therapist does not act as a sidecoach or director, but as an actor from within the play. As the client's playobject, the therapist becomes an animated presence that the client must contain; the roles of container/contained are therefore partly reversed in this method of therapy. Important in this process is the healing charisma of the therapist, who by showing spontaneity, creativity, and humor, encourages the client to continue his or her journey.

Developmental Transformations is a relational approach, and the intersubjective encounter between client and therapist is a central component. Following Grotowski's *poor theatre* notions, all obstacles to encounter are removed from the session room, including projective objects and preset exercises (Grotowski, 1968). The client has nothing to play with except the therapist. The therapist's job is to attend to the client, and to become their playobject in the playspace. In so doing, the therapist attempts to reveal the client. The therapist does so largely through a process called *Faithful Rendering,* in which s/he plays out what the client's play "calls for." It is the equivalent of Rogers' empathic technique, of placing oneself in the frame of reference of the client, only now in dramatic form (Rogers, 1951).

The therapist's main task is to help the client enter and remain in the playspace. The therapist accomplishes this by demonstrating the containing power of the playspace, through interweaving the dramatic scenes with the client's personal material, here-and-now processing, and previously unimagined possibilities.

The therapist must keep his/her attention on the client(s), be open to their communication on all levels, and then faithfully render in dramatic form the feelings, images, and scenes that are evoked by the client. In many therapeutic forms, the therapist gives empathic feedback to the client, usually in verbal form. Developmental Transformations is in many ways a form of client-centered therapy in which the therapist gives empathic feedback in embodied, imaginal form.

Finally, the therapist attempts to establish nonlinear norms, so as to be able to facilitate the via negativa/deconstruction process. Thus, typical dramatic structures such as plot, consistency of character, storyline, ending, moral, and climax-denouement, are intentionally disrupted through such methods as repetition, transformation of the scene, introduction of divergent elements, and shifting attention to discrepant elements within a scene. This work facilitates a tolerance for what we call *emergent elements,* as opposed to *existent elements,* which means that the client begins to place his/her attention on what feeling is emerging within, rather than what is currently being played out in action.

General Clinical Principles in Individual Therapy

Individual therapy is initiated with a series of verbal sessions in order for the client to inform the therapist of problems, personal history, previous therapies, and goals, as well as for issues of touch and personal boundaries to be discussed. The Developmental Transformation sessions occur in an empty, carpeted room with a few pillows and a circular carpet called the *Witnessing Circle.* After stretching and warming up, the client and therapist begin to move, or make a sound, or create a scene, which soon transforms into other images and scenes. The therapist at times sits in the Witnessing Circle and watches the client continue the play, and then returns to the play. This gives the client an opportunity to explore being witnessed by, as well as being with, the therapist. *Transforming to the Here-and-Now* is a particularly powerful technique in which the therapist and client transform the scene into "reality" and discuss something going on between them while still in the playspace. This allows the client to integrate his observing self with his self-in-action, rather than splitting them by processing the session afterwards.

The therapist generally begins with *mirroring* the client's actions, and then shifts to *faithful rendering,* in which the therapist plays out the complementary role required by the scene created by the client. This is followed by the use of *emergent rendering,* in which the therapist uses observed discrepancies between the client's behavior and that expected of their role to transform the scene into that which is emerging from the client. Later, the therapist may use *divergent rendering,* also known as *sway,* to subtly introduce variance within the embodied enactment, which allows the client to practice tolerating states of instability.

The session continues until the therapist remarks, "take a minute," and leaves the room, giving the client a few minutes to silently reflect on the session. There is no verbal discussion of the session at the end, unless the client asks for it. Often the client will spend a few minutes at the beginning of the session to inform the therapist of events of the past week, and of course if there is a crisis, the entire session may be devoted to a verbal discussion. The purpose of not including a set-aside time for de-roling or verbal commentary is consistent with the overall goals of this therapy, which are to become present, rather than to gain insight. An embodied presence, necessarily ambiguous, at the end of the session is viewed positively, just as it is after meditation.

Since each individual's unique personality and expressive inclinations spring forth in these sessions, it is impossible to describe patterns or stages. One person's Developmental Transformations sessions are completely different in appearance than another's: some lay on the floor face down, others run around and scream, some exercise or perform dances, others play children, others play with mimed body parts. The therapist will always attempt to respond to these "playthings" as if they are the client's "toys" and the room is the client's "playroom." Nevertheless, it does not take long for clients to open their "toy chest," find something that scares them, and not want to play with it. Eventually, with the help of the therapist, they do find a way to play with it.

Transcripts of individual therapy sessions can be found in Johnson (1991; 1992), Johnson et al., (1996), and later in this chapter.

General Clinical Principles in Group Therapy

Developmental Transformations group work follows the same principles as individual therapy, with the additional challenge of managing the greater complexity inherent in a group. For many populations, being in a group is especially unplayful, and the therapist must find ways of engaging the group members in the play. The therapist accomplishes this task through interventions within five dimensions of play behavior: ambiguity, complexity, media of expression, interpersonal demand, and affect expression (see Johnson, 1982). These are based on developmental principles described by Piaget (1951) and Werner and Kaplan (1963). *Ambiguity* is the degree to which the therapist has not determined the spatial configuration, tasks, or roles in the group at a given moment. *Complexity* is the degree to which these space, task, and role structures include multiple elements (such as numerous, different roles). *Media of Expression* refers to whether the action is being expressed along the developmental continuum of movement, sound, image, role, or word. *Interpersonal Demand* is the level of interaction required among members, as well as whether the roles are expressed in inanimate, animal, or human form. *Affect Expression* is the degree to which the action and imagery is personal, and/or intense.

In general, the group session begins at the earliest developmental level, which means clearly-directed, unison sound and movement, with little interaction and impersonal, nonintense imagery. The therapist slowly makes interventions that increase the developmental level of one or more of these dimensions toward greater ambiguity, complexity, interpersonal demand, and intense, personal imagery. The therapist will use the group's involvement in the play, that is, its energy or flow, as a signal of whether to continue on or to linger at a particular level. It is important to understand that the therapist's attention is on these developmental dimensions, not on the content of the client's imagery or scenes, nor on introducing preset exercises or structures. This is because the Developmental Transformations therapist is managing the state of play, not the content of the play.

For many clinical populations, typical stages of the group session include Greeting, Unison Movement and Sound, Defining, Personification, Structured Role Playing, Unstructured Role Playing, and Closing. A more detailed description of these stages is included in Johnson (1986). Suffice it to say that group work usually begins by inviting the group members into the playspace (Greeting), and then engaging in unison movement in a circle (Unison Movement). Over a period of time images begin to arise (Defining), followed by more organized roles (Personification), which are then worked on through the play (Structured Role Playing), only to dissolve into more free-flowing improvisation (Unstructured Role Playing). A departure from the playspace occurs during the Closing ritual. We have found that as groups become more familiar with the method, and as the therapist becomes more seasoned, these stages become less distinct.

Transcripts of group sessions can be found in Johnson (1986), James and Johnson (1996), Dintino and Johnson (1996), Forrester and Johnson (1995), and Schnee (1996).

Populations Served

Developmental Transformations has been applied for the past 30 years in a wide variety of settings, including inpatient hospitals, outpatient clinics, substance abuse and rehabilitation programs, nursing homes, and a private practice clinic. Both group and individual work has been conducted over both extended and extremely short (even one session) time periods. Populations served include schizophrenia (Johnson, 1984), affective disorder and substance abuse (Forrester & Johnson, 1995), posttraumatic stress disorder (Dintino & Johnson, 1996; James & Johnson, 1996), sexually abused children (James, Forrester, & Kim, 2005); homeless mentally ill (Galway, Hurd, & Johnson, 2003; Schnee, 1996), elderly (Johnson, Smith, & James, 2002; Johnson, 1986; Sandel & Johnson, 1987; Smith, 2000), violent men (Landers, 2002), and the normal neurotic (Johnson, 1991; Johnson et al., 1996; Porter, 2000). The goals of each treatment need to be tailored to the specific population, time frame, and nature of the clinical setting, though the method remains essentially the same.

In contrast to cognitive-behavioral treatments, Developmental Transformations is not best suited for addressing highly specific symptoms or issues (e.g., obsessive-compulsive disorder, phobias, psychotic symptoms, achieving sobriety, decision-making around divorce). Being an indirect process approach, existential, relational, and personal issues tend to be revealed and reflected by the therapist. The therapist does not take a structuring or advice-giving stance.

Clients whose behavior is violent, out-of-control, or floridly psychotic are usually not able to engage in the playspace and thus are not recommended for this approach. Clients whose intense dislike for play, drama, or body movement prevent them from participating should also be considered for other forms of treatment.

COMPARISON WITH OTHER DRAMA THERAPY APPROACHES

Developmental Transformations has great overlap with many other drama therapy approaches that utilize improvisation in a developmentally-informed manner that matches the dramatic expression with the abilities and needs of the clients. DvT departs largely in the degree to which the therapist immerses him/herself in the dramatic playspace and intervenes from within the dramatic play. DvT also has eschewed the format of a series of exercises, however subtly or spontaneously chosen, (such as that in the "Integrative Five Phase Model," Chapter 4; "ENACT," Chapter 13; or "Rehearsals for Growth," Chapter 16) and instead engages the clients in an ongoing flow of action and image, as does the "Psychoanalytic Approach" (Chapter 11) and the "Developmental Themes Approach" (Chapter 12). Another major difference lies in DvT's view that roles and stories are solidifications at the end of the creative process, rather than being building blocks of that process, a view held by "Role Method" (Chapter 5), "Narradrama" (Chapter 9), and "Psychodrama" (Chapter 18). DvT, ironically like Moreno himself, places itself more on the side of Spontaneity, than the Cultural (or Role) Conserve, such as that listed in Landy's Taxonomy of Roles. Landy (2008) has recently published an excellent and indepth comparison of DvT with Role Method and Psychodrama.

On the other hand, DvT's concept of *playspace* is essentially the same as Role Method's concept of *aesthetic distance;* the role of the therapist is not unlike Boal's Joker; and its evocation of the perpetrator not unlike that achieved in "Healing the Wounds of History" (Chapter 8). DvT's performative emphasis is also in line with other "Performance Models" (Chapters 7, 10, and 17). Finally, DvT shares with "Narradrama," "Role Method," "Theatre of the Oppressed" (Chapter 21), and "Rehearsals for Growth," especially, a postmodern sensibility that life is a multitextured weave of desires, thoughts, and roles, being constantly shaped and reshaped by the combined forces of the body and the cultural surround. Indeed, this sensibility is increasingly evident in all approaches to drama therapy.

CASE EXAMPLES

Persona Play

The following is a transcript of a drama therapy session from my private practice (adapted from Johnson, 1992) that illustrates Persona Play. Parts of the session have been revised to protect the client's identity. Elaine is a 32-year-old woman employed as a therapist, who had come to me because she felt depressed, had a problem with overeating, and had lost interest in sex with the man she had been living with for several years. She had been sexually abused once by her father when she was about ten. She had no children, but had had two abortions about which she felt very ambivalent. I had been meeting with her for several months, and she had become very comfortable with the transformations. She had made substantial progress and at the time of this session was feeling much less depressed. Our sessions had evolved in structure so that the transformations began as I opened the door to the office.

The Session

Knock on door. Therapist opens door.

Elaine: My word!

Therapist: My word!

Elaine: *My* word. (Entering room).

Therapist: (laughing to self) No, no, it's *my* word.

Elaine: No it's not, that's *my* word (pointing to a spot on the floor).

Therapist: That? Are you kidding? That word there, is *mine.* I put it there only yesterday.

Elaine: Then what about *that* word?

Therapist: No, mine.

Elaine: Or that? (going around the room frantically)

Therapist: Nope.

Elaine: Then where is my word?

Therapist: (shrugs shoulders)

Elaine: I can never find the right word.

Therapist: For what?

Elaine: For it (makes large, vague gesture).

Therapist: For *it?*

Elaine: Yes, for it. (look at each other mysteriously)

Therapist: Well, what *is* the word for *it?*

Elaine: (shrugs shoulders and opens mouth)

Therapist: (opens mouth, tries to talk. Nothing comes out.)

Elaine: (whispers) I'm speechless!

Therapist: Me, too.
(Therapist and Elaine try talking, showing distress that they cannot speak. They begin to signal each other with their hands in strange ways. Gradually, guttural sounds begin to emerge, gibberish that grows to sound like bubbling noises. Their hands move like they are swimming, then like they are treading water.)

Both: Ohhhhhhh!

Elaine: It's hot!

Therapist: It's boiling!

Elaine: Oh my god, we're being cooked!

Both: Help! help!

Therapist: What's this? (holds up something)

Elaine: It's a potato.

Therapist: You mean we're soup? . . . Whose soup?

Elaine: Hers. (pointing in corner)

Therapist: (transforming to witch) Ha, ha ha, my my my, aren't you going to spice up my brew, honey! [Elaine often played these masochistic, victimized roles.]

Elaine: Oh please, Gertrude, please don't cook me!

Therapist: Why not, you little twirp?

Elaine: I haven't done anything.

Therapist: Oh yes you have! (Therapist puts spices into pot and stirs)

Elaine: Oh! Oh! (in different tone, more enjoyable, she wriggles comfortably) What have I done to deserve *this?* [This was an advance for Elaine, who had had difficulty turning negative, victimized images into positive ones. In this case, it even had a sexual connotation.]

Therapist: (changing tone) Why, honey, just being you.

Elaine: (smiling) This feels wonderful.

Therapist: I knew you'd like the jacuzzi, isn't it great?

Elaine: Can you put a little more bubble bath in, dear?

Therapist: Sure. (Goes to other side of room to put away bubble bath.)
Elaine: I'm done. What should I do with the bath water?
Therapist: Oh just throw it out.
Elaine: (picks it up and throws it in corner.) I hope I didn't throw the baby out with the bath water! (laughs)
Therapist: (turning, looking very serious) Honey, did you throw the baby out with the bath water?
[Elaine had worked on her feelings about the abortions many times, and had felt terribly guilty about them. Her humorous way of bringing them up was striking, so the therapist decided not to let it pass.]
Elaine: Oh, I, oh, I . . .
Therapist: You didn't! (rushes over to corner with Elaine; both gasp.) You DID! [The therapist felt it was important to acknowledge the act, so that the full intensity of the experience could be evoked.]
Elaine: I'm so sorry!
Therapist: I can't believe this, this is the fifth time you've done this. Look at all of those dead babies. You should feel ashamed of yourself!
(both now walk around the room in despair.) What are we going to do?
Elaine: I just had to do it.
Therapist: You had to do it. Really, and what do *they* think about *that?*
Elaine: I don't know.
Therapist: Well, then, why don't you go over to that dead baby corner and find out! (Elaine goes over, and therapist leaves to the witnessing circle.)
[Having evoked the anxiety situation and the internal self-criticism, the therapist heightened the tension by leaving her alone with her "deed." He wondered what she would do.]
Elaine: (Turns around in middle of room, sighing.) Ohhhh, (drops down onto floor) I'm dead. She killed me. (Silence.) I'm dead. She killed me. (Long silence. Turns on floor, sighing.) Please! Please. Take me back, mommy! (begins to reach out into space, her eyes are closed) Pleeaasee, take me back mommy! (Turns again toward therapist, and reaches out toward him.) Please, please, take me back, take me back. (She cries, while still reaching toward the therapist, the reaches now turning into grabbing motions, which she expands into a motion of grabbing food and stuffing it into her mouth. She continues this with great energy, stuffing herself more and more, grunting, acting as if she is growing fatter and fatter. She leans back and rubs her tummy as if it is huge, and lets out a monstrous growl, standing up with arms out, and begins to stomp around the room.)
Elaine: Pow, pow, boom boom,

(laughs) I am a GIANT, take that (stomps on floor–clearly an image of stomping on little people).

[The transformation from guilt over the abortion into reaching out for her mother, into filling herself up with food, to becoming a powerful mighty giant showed a great deal of flow, indicating minimal inhibition. This was the first time she had actually played the babies. The therapist decided to join her after the scene had transformed. He was particularly taken with her willingness to represent the issue of fatness/pregnancy/female power.]

Therapist: (Enters also as giant) Pow, booom, (Elaine: laughs) Hi Bertha!
Heh, this is fun . . . squish!

Elaine: Yeh, boom, boom.

Therapist: Boy, are you FAT! I've never seen you looking so good.

Elaine: Yeah, and aren't you FAT, god you look great.

Both: (laugh)

Therapist: Oh, we're FAT! (begins to sing, Elaine joins)

Both: Oh we're fat, oh we're fat, it's so great to be fat . . . if we weren't fat, we'd have to be bad . . . (they dance together in a ridiculous way, then begin to hum) mmmm, mmmm, bad!
(The tone begins to change into a lower pitch, which quickly becomes more ominous. As they keep moving back and forth, holding each other by one hand, they begin to look over their shoulders furtively) Mmmm-mm, oooooohhhh, oh! (they look and see something horrible) Ahhhhh!

Therapist: Run for it!

Elaine: Hide, hide, it's going to get us!

Therapist: Where are we going to hide?

Elaine: I don't know, we can't hide from ourselves.

Therapist: (Stops and motions Elaine over; whispers), you don't mean that this improvisation really represents our running away from the fat, ugly, or destructive parts of ourselves, do you?

Elaine: Could be.

Therapist: Oh, I don't think so. How can you hide from yourself?

Elaine: I've been doing it for years.

Therapist: (Turning outward to room) Ladies and gentlemen, I would like to introduce to you, the one the only, a spectacle beyond belief, yes, the woman who can hide from herself! (applauds)

Elaine: (Runs around, turns around quickly in place, puts hands over eyes, puts head under a pillow, crosses her arms over her genitals.)

Therapist: Yes, ladies, and gentlemen, this woman has been hiding important parts of herself, from herself, things so obvious to you and me, things anyone should know, but no, she hides from them, yes, she hides them *from* . . . whom? But why? Why, ladies and gentlemen? Well, let's ask her . . . (he turns and pretends he doesn't see her, she moves around room as if to avoid him. He begins to stalk her) Where is she? Where are you? You, who, where are you? (Elaine now sits in a corner of room, fiddling with the carpet.) Where are you, Suzy? (pretends to knock on door) Suzy, let me in so we can play.

[The imagery of hiding developed a sinister quality that evoked in the therapist a feeling that he was the evil one she was hiding from. He realized this might be related to the father-image and the sexual abuse.]

Elaine: I don't want to, Daddy.

Therapist: Come on, Suzy, let Daddy in, he wants to play with you.

Elaine: (Both as Suzy and herself) We always get back to this.

Therapist: (Both as Daddy and therapist) Yes, that's true. This is what is called an "early childhood trauma," Suzy. [This interpenetration of dramatic role and real self is characteristic of a successful creation of a transitional space, in which the drama is sustained and at the same time the therapist and client are talking directly to each other.]

Elaine: I know, Daddy, but do I have to go through it again?

Therapist: Don't worry, Suzy, you will be able to work it through in your therapy years from now. You'll want to have enough material for the sessions won't you? [Through this somewhat provocative humor, the therapist communicates that trauma is part of any human life. He also makes reference to an earlier concern of hers, that she wouldn't have enough to say in their sessions.]

Elaine: That's outrageous! (Comes to the pretend door, opens it.) Listen, you daddy-therapist you, you think I make these things up just to entertain you? Well, leave me alone with my own traumas, I can deal with them myself!

Therapist: (Leaves to the witnessing circle.)

Elaine: Good riddance. (Wipes hands, looks down at them.) Blood. Blood on my hands. (looks over at therapist) Blood everywhere. A bloodbath. Hum. Maybe it's my blood. (Goes over to wall and rubs hands on wall, then rubs both hands at once, then begins to hug the wall softly, places her cheek against wall. Silence.) I want to go back in. I am going back in. (Turns and crawls under a big pile of pillows. Silence. Then peeks out at therapist, then extends a hand through the hole like a tentacle, then retracts it. Long silence. Therapist enters quietly and sits near the pillow pile.)

[Elaine again shows a remarkable ability to stay with her associations, and again the image of a retreat to a mothering presence emerges. The therapist sensed her wish to have him come to her rescue, an often repeated pattern.]

Therapist: Hmmm (sternly). My client has gone back to the womb. As a result of my work, she has regressed terribly. I therefore have failed.

Elaine: (Begins humming to herself, obviously trying to drown out the therapist.) Hmmm-mm, hmmm!

Therapist: It must be safer in there than out here with me, can you believe that? Where did I go wrong? How have I frightened her? Answer me, someone, give me some advice!

Elaine: I want you to take care of me, but you are my therapist, so I have to take care of myself.

Therapist: Hmmm. That's probably good judgment. I have another interesting clinical case to present to you today, of a therapy that's reached an impasse. This is a woman who takes complete care of herself because she can't get what she wants from her therapist. Every time she wants him, he reminds her of terrible people.

Elaine: That's right! (Elaine gets up holding several pillows around her "for protection" and walks around the room.)

Therapist: You can see, for example, that she carries her nurturance around with her. (Elaine has trouble holding all of the pillows, and drops several, picks them up) With difficulty. Let's see what happens when someone offers to help her. Maam, may I help you with your nurturance?

Elaine: No thank you, I'll keep my nurturance to myself, if you please.

Therapist: I beg your pardon. Where did you get all this self-nurturance?

Elaine: Why, at mother mountain.

Therapist: Really, can you take me there?

Elaine: Sure, follow me. (They walk around and then go to the pillow pile. Elaine puts the rest of pillows together and sits on top.)

Therapist: Can I join you?

Elaine: Sure, come up here.

Therapist: Wow, you can see a lot from here. It's nice to know that there is a solid place like this around. How long has this been here?

Elaine: For generations. My grandmother lived here for many years, and I came to her when I was frightened or worried, and she comforted me. She was like a mountain! [This was new information for the therapist, who had not known of the positive influence of her grandmother.]

Therapist: What's that place? (pointing to the corner where she had hidden)

Elaine: Oh, that's the hideaway, that's a great place, where I can go to get away from it all. Works like a dream.

Therapist: And that?

Elaine: Oh, that's the dead baby corner.

Therapist: It's so dark there.
Elaine: Yeah, not as dark as it used to be. A sad place, for sure, but I realize it's a part of me.
Therapist: What do you mean?
Elaine: Well, these are all parts of me (gestures to the room).
Therapist: Noo! You mean mother mountain, the hideaway, and the dead baby corner are parts of you? Forget it. They are *out there,* not *in here!* (pointing to her).
Elaine: I wish you were right, but it is an inescapable conclusion.
Therapist: I thought we just made it up. . . . Well, then how are they related to each other?
Elaine: I'm not sure exactly, that's why I came to see you. (laughs)
Therapist: Okay, hmm, we could measure them.
Elaine: Great idea. (leaps off pillows and goes over to hideaway and pretends to measure it with a tape measure. Therapist follows, and they both scurry around taking measurements, mumbling numbers to themselves, and then both begin to write numbers and strange symbols on the blackboard, until there is a messy, complicated diagram) [Jointly client and therapist are making fun of their own attempts to understand, and in so doing acknowledging the limitations of their profession, and more specifically, that Elaine is not ready to connect these parts of herself without intellectualizing.]
Therapist: Well, there it is.
Elaine: Perfect understanding.
Therapist: It's amazing that we achieved so much after, literally, *minutes* of psychotherapy!
Elaine: Yeh. Really, you know, I'd like to hear you summarize it for me, you know, your *formulation* (sarcastic).
Therapist: No, I think that's something that you would gain a great deal from, since you're the client.
Elaine: But I'm paying *you,* and I want a report, doctor.
Therapist: Okay, after all, it shouldn't be much trouble. Hum, (looks at diagram) well, let's see, I (laughs) can say that, uh, (becomes silent, mouth opens but nothing comes out)
Elaine: My word, he's speechless (laughs)
Therapist: Nope, that's *my* word ! (both laugh) . . . take a minute.

Discussion

Throughout this session the therapist acted as a guide who traveled with the client through her inner landscape, which consisted of memories of the past, current conflicts, and feelings about her therapist. The therapist tried to help her keep in touch with her stream of consciousness, at times underscoring and intensifying images, at times helping her to link different meanings between themes, and always trying to increase the depth and breadth of her experiencing–to allow the most enriched and variegated world to emerge. Maintaining a playful, humorous, and intimate environment sustained the "transitional space" in which inner and interpersonal worlds combine (Winnicott, 1971). Merely by allowing these processes to continue most freely, the healing message is given: you are all right, you are filled with many things, good and bad, and you can live with them all. The discovery of oneself and achieving forgiveness for being human is the intended result. Elaine used this and other sessions to acknowledge her feelings about not having children, about her fears that such a decision would be a rejection of her mother and grandmother, and about her doubts whether her career was the right one for her. In this session, the roles projected onto and played out by the therapist generally represented aspects of her persona. Later, as their work moved into Intimate Play, the client was able to play with her feelings and perceptions of the therapist's persona.

Deep Play

The following example is a complete Developmental Transformations session with a 36-year-old woman. I have disguised or altered parts of her history as well as sections of dialogue to preserve her privacy. I saw her weekly in hour-long sessions for three years. This is her 107th session, near the end of her treatment. She had come into treatment because she was concerned about her capacity for intimacy with a man. She was an elementary school teacher, unmarried and not in a relationship for several years, though she had dated numerous men through her twenties and early thirties. She had developed a very strong desire to have a child and to find a man to marry. She was the oldest of three children. Her father died of cancer when she was only seven years old (he was about her present age, 36) and she initially spoke about him in idealistic terms. Eventually she shared her concern that he may have abused her when she was three or four years old, though she had no specific memories. This concern was explicitly linked to her attempt to find an explanation for her difficulties with intimate relations with men. She reported no other traumatic events in her life. She had been in verbal therapy for several years with two separate therapists prior to working with me. In both cases she developed strong positive transferences to her (male and female) therapists. She was interested in drama therapy because she felt it might help "my body reveal what's holding me back."

In the following session, actions and speech of the therapist and client are followed by notations (made after the session) of the therapist's associations. As this is an example of Deep Play, the session is highly embodied and relational, and these associations are quite personal, though not the therapist's real feelings, rather those evoked by being with the client. They are purposefully presented with a poetic turn, because that more closely communicates how they were experienced. Numerous double entendres occur between therapist and client, including references to her history, past sessions, and transference fantasies. Hopefully, by including them the reader may gain a better understanding of the material the therapist uses to motivate his/her actions in the session. In this sense, we say that the actual session consists of the co-occurring associations of client and therapist, not the actions or words that would be seen or heard by an outside witness. These expressions are the crystallizations of emergent, bodily impulses; as such, they are best understood as the *wake* of the session.

Session #107

They begin wandering around the room, looking down at the floor, moving their arms somewhat aimlessly.

T: ca, cann, canntt, can't believe, can't

believe, can't be *leave* . . .
[can't believe that he is dead, can't believe she is staying in the therapy, can't believe a word we say, can't believe I'm not falling in love with you]

C: some, somer, summer, somerly, southerly, . . .
[some not all, sum it all up, its summer in the south and I am warm, there is a warm southerly breeze on my face]
(movements slow down, turn to each other)

T: caa . . .

C: ssss . . . (slowly collapses into ball in front of T)
[she is closing in, she is asking me to embrace her, to enclose her, the egg again, the egg and shell again]

T: (slowly descends over her so close but not touching)
[I am around you, I can hurt you or love you, hurt you with my love, but I won't, I won't touch you, so nothing will pierce your shell]

C: I . . . I . . . I am lost
[what's happening to us, come and find me, beauty and the beast, the darkened forest and the treasured gem, I will continue the search for you]

T: (hovering over her), what if I find you?
[what if, what if, what if you let me in and we are together]

C: (long pause) . . . find me
[I am coming]

T: (slowly lowers body onto hers, touching softly)

C: (long long pause)
[I feel so close, I can stay here forever, will she turn toward me, what is there to discover, the egg again, so many sessions of this image, I am being allowed to make contact, what new form is being created, or will she kill us]

C: I thought you are dead
[I am dead, I am not making love to her, I am scared to go further, her father died and she feels abandoned, I am her father, she was never sure if her father abused her, am I abusing her? don't know, do know I am me and I am definitely alive]

T: (long pause), I can be dead and I can be alive
[am I your dead abusing or nonabusing father or am I me]

C: I think I want to be with you, not him
[so I am me, and you are with me, but what would your father say about this?]

T: Ewe, wood, lite, mee? (a play on "you would let me?")
[who is she letting in, suddenly I feel something of a wood sprite, a hare, a skipping stone, I am a sprinkle!]

C: You can find me or you can lose me
[oh no she mentions losing, I am going to lose her, I have to prove it to her, like in so many past sessions, I have to prove my worth]

T: I don't want to lose you
[her father didn't want to for sure but he did, her lover to be won't want to for sure, I think I am going to]

C: Don't lose me (both begin to sink)
[we are together in sinking, the scene is slipping, like before, things slip away, we know it and it is so much fun to know it]

T: Slip away, slip away
[like oil, like skin, she is part of me, I feel her body as she leaves me]

C: (moving out, very slowly along his

legs)
[we are leaving each other in a way that brings her close, the end of making love, the tingle on the skin]

T: Can't believe you are slipping away
[can't believe in you, your father's dying in the hospital, blind with pain and painkillers, your seven-year-old self's abandoning lover as he slips away]

C: (stops, leaning away on all fours)
[I want her, I can't stand this distance, this distance makes me ache for her]

T: (reaches out with hand toward her, she can't see but probably senses)
[I reach out as my desire, as her future lover will desire her, as her child will desire her, despite this terrible distance that defeats me, with her back to me my desire knows no bounds]

C: (long long pause)
[an aching, a reaching]

C: I want a baby
[she wants a baby wow, I am your baby, we will make love and I will give you a baby like we played out before, no, I want you like I want my own baby, yes, she wants me, I am your baby]

T: I am your baby
[remember all the mother scenes you have played–now is the time to care for your child, here I am take care of me! Forget the babies you have accidentally killed in our improvs, or stolen like Rumpelstiltzskin . . .]

C: Give me a baby
[yes she remembers, we are reading each other's minds, we are like one mind, it doesn't matter who is the baby]

T: You are my baby
[you are my baby, I have worked with you for nearly three years, you are my work, my labor, my love]

C: I am your baby
[I will protect you like my own, I own you, I can control you and destroy you, but I won't make love to you or eat you]

T: (long long pause, as both move slightly side to side, as if to play with the idea that they might be able to see one another)

C: I like this . . .
[I can't stop thinking or feeling and I feel proud of her that she is here so long with me, she likes this, what?, what is she doing?]

T: What is happening between us?
[look at me]

C: (They look at each other, she turns, both move ever so slightly towards each other)

T: (They get very close, half inch cheek by cheek, long long pause)
[I have no words for this, I smell her hair, I see the outlines of her face and eye, half a blur, and I imagine I am in a forest, the left side of my face is misshapen or removed, I am awaiting the arrival of another animal, I sense the slightest twitch, an eyelid blinks in the distance, an opening that I enter, willingly, filled with anticipation]

C: Maybe under everything there is love, not death
[is she saying she loves me, yes, me? not me, who am, I, rather this!]

T: Yes, love
(long pause as they remain a half inch apart)

C: Will it slip away
[the slope, the oil, the tension, the relief, the grief, her story of everything slipping through her fingers,

yes it will slip away or we will imagine it slipping away]

T: It can slip away or not slip away
[play with me]

C: Seems inevitable
[she understands herself so well, she is joking, smiling to herself, to ourselves, about this Self that is wrapped around her and oh what it will do, but for the moment let us savor this weightless knowledge, here in this nameless place]

C: (Slowly lowers head onto T's shoulder, then slowly slips down his chest, T's arm wraps around her and she slowly slips through along his body. They pause, legs overlapping, facing away from each other)
[we play at missing each other and leaving each other while we play at making love which means mourning our not making love]

T: Who is dead and who will grieve?
[no one helped you grieve your father's death, no one helped you name what you lost]

C: I will grieve; you are dead
[don't mix her up I am the father and she is the daughter, "you keep switching roles on me!," she can do it]

T: I am dead (he slowly turns and moves toward the witnessing circle but so slowly he will never make it)
[OK I am the role, you have expelled me, so I am going to pretend to go to the witnessing circle like I have so many times and upset you, only I don't need to go there I just need to pretend to go there, and you will not get upset but you will remember getting upset and that is my little joke that I make, because I love you]

C: There will be no witnesses to my death
[she gets the joke and thanks me for not going into the witnessing circle but, guess what, her life is her own and we will not be together for ever and besides she can be the dead one and switch roles on me, so there!]

T: (holds still with arms up in air)
[you have caught me I am yours]

C: My baby
[you are mine I have you I love you can I come over and take you, will you the therapist allow it, of course you will, so now is the time for me to, now is the time for me to . . .]
(long long pause)

C: (She comes over and puts arms around him and he turns and lays on her lap)
[I am possessed, do with me as you wish, I feel like you are a mother, I wish my mother had been able to do this to me, she has not held me for years]

T: You hold me

C: You are holding me
[you me you me you me, how long will this last, what is this her inner space has become so wide and luminous, what warmth I feel]
(long long pause)

T: This time you will not sleep away
[you have let me in and I will carry this forever in my heart even though we will part. what time is it? probably the end of the session]

C: (smiles) Yes I will not slip/sleep away
[she smiles because she knows it is the end of the session and we both are keeping track, even though we now exist in a timeless place beyond reckoning]
(long long pause)

T: So near the end of the session and

yet something is about to happen
[one of us might initiate a departure or entrance or embrace or kindness]

C: Yes something will happen
[yes to all of the above which we both know are possible, thus we have done them together anyway, even though her father did die and she has been sad for 16 years]

T: What's going to happen with us?
[us, us, uh, ssss, uh, ssssssss]
(pause)

C: Yes! (she silently strokes his hair)

T: Take a minute (T departs the room)

Discussion

This is a good example of a Deep Play session between a therapist and client who have developed a high level of trust. This client also demonstrates a great deal of courage to stick with very upsetting issues. Viewed from the outside, this session appears to have little action and nearly meaningless dialogue. From within the session, I can say that it was an extremely powerful, tense, focused encounter with each other, and with ourselves. The session demonstrates how the here-and-now dialogue that had previously occurred out loud in the Persona and Intimate Play phases, has now descended underneath and between our vocalizations. The client, who has read this transcript, shares this view. The vocalizations and actions of the session of course were immensely meaningful and important, both as means of grounding our ongoing flow of associations and as markers of shifts in our imagery.

The issues of intimacy with men, concerns regarding her father's relationship with her, feelings of gratitude to me, and anxiety about termination, all were explored in the session. A feeling of tolerance for the complexity of life, of the ambiguity surrounding her childhood, and of joy for being with someone, mixed in this very large playspace we had created. The miracle of the transitional space occurred here, for we thoroughly enjoyed that I was pretending to be her father, pretending to be her lover, pretending to be her. Yes, only pretend, but what pretend! She had recaptured a child's eye on life: knowing the truck is not a real truck but feeling as though it is.

This client responded well to the treatment and had resumed dating during our work together. Two years after termination she married and I learned recently has had a child, fulfilling her longstanding dream.

Ethical Considerations

In a therapeutic method such as Developmental Transformations, which involves body movement, physical touch, intimate encounter, and play, ethical issues and professional boundaries are clearly paramount. The basis of any ethical practice is the therapist's intention to do no harm and that of course is essential in the training of our therapists. In addition, we attend to ethical principles in the following ways.

Informed Consent

Clients are clearly informed about the nature of the therapy and the possibility of both physical touch and playful rendering of upsetting issues. Previous experience in psychotherapy is elicited and direct inquiry is made about any improper behavior of previous therapists. Life history of psychological trauma and especially childhood sexual abuse is also taken and discussed with the client. An informed consent "contract" is then signed by the client, therapist, and supervisor, indicating the nature of the treatment, stating that the therapist will be following the American Psychological Association Ethical Guidelines at all times, that the therapist will have no outside social contact or relationship with the client and does not intend to engage in any behavior of an aggressive or sexual nature with the client. The client is instructed in what steps to take if he/she ever feels intimidated or concerned about the nature of the treatment on any issue.

Physical Touch

Developmental Transformations therapists are neutral regarding physical touch between therapist and client; there is nothing in our method that prescribes touching. Touching occurs because it is a natural human act. Complete absence of touch is unnatural. Inappropriate touching is unnatural. One of the crimes of incesting parents is that they cross the boundary between natural and unnatural touch, confusing the issue for the victim. In the early phases of Surface and Persona Play, physical touch is highly contextual, occurring as needed by the scene or role. The therapist only engages in pretend touch, that is, will never grab the client and really hold on, and will never kiss the client or touch any sensitive area of the body. In the later phases of treatment during Intimate and Deep Play, touch that occurs will often be decontextualized, that is, touch not derived from a role, but merely touch. Examples include leaning against each other, sitting on the client, pushing against each other on all fours, being pressed up against a wall by the client. Always, if there is a concern about the client's experience of touch, the therapist will address it, usually by Transforming to the Here-and-Now, and sometimes after the session.

Playing with the Unplayable

Some issues are so painful to the client that permission must be obtained, during the play, in order to proceed. Typically the therapist will Transform to the Here-and-Now and inquire if the issue emerging is something better left alone. Often this leads to a playful interaction about the decision itself rather than the issue, which may free the client to muster the courage needed to address it directly. If not, the therapist and client will move away from it, only to return at a later point.

Countertransference

It could be said that DvT involves the therapeutic use of countertransference, for certainly the degree of involvement with the client is high. The therapist attempts to use the evoked images that arise in working with the client in responding dramatically within the playspace. As the client's playobject, the therapist brings all of his unique personal qualities into the play. That the therapist has personality quirks, issues, deficits, and conflicts is assumed; in this way, the therapist is like a child's *broken toy*. Interestingly, however, children often have no problem playing with their broken toys, as our clients do with DvT therapists. The therapist just has to be mindful not to refuse to play with these aspects of him/herself. In this way, DvT does not seek to restrain the client's exploration of the deficits of the therapist by claims of privilege or the illusion of an objective stance. In this work, for therapist as well as client, there is nothing to hide behind; what we seek is to reduce the need to hide.

DvT does not attempt to perfect a person, eliminate neurotic conflict, or repair character flaws, rather these pernicious aspects of our lives are revealed more fully. Instead, responses of shame, embarrassment, deceit, and anxiety over their revelation are replaced by responses of insight, humor, acceptance, forgiveness, and "oh, well!" Like all playobjects, or toys, we eventually break, and are broken through mishandling by others. We have missing parts, we can't turn or talk like we used to, our batteries are low, and buttons do not work. Yet, though imperfect as we are, the desire for play overcomes, and we can be held and played with, be cared for and given pleasure to, and be kept in the playroom or bedroom or toychest for many years, just as we hold our loved but broken ones close to us. This is what being here is all about.

REFERENCES

Deleuze, G., & Guattari, F. (1987). *A thousand plateaus.* Minneapolis: University of Minnesota Press.

Derrida, J. (1978). *Writing and difference.* Chicago: University of Chicago Press.

Dintino, C., & Johnson, D. (1996). Playing with the perpetrator: Gender dynamics in developmental drama therapy. In S. Jennings (Ed.), *Drama therapy: Theory and practice,* Vol. 3 (pp. 205–220). London: Routledge.

Forrester, A., & Johnson, D. (1995). Drama therapy on an extremely short term inpatient unit. In A. Gersie (Ed.), *Brief treatment approaches to drama therapy* (pp. 125–138). London: Routledge.

Freud, S. (1920/1966). *Introductory lectures on psychoanalysis.* New York: Norton.

Galway, K., Hurd, K., & Johnson, D. (2003). Developmental transformations in group therapy with homeless people with a mental illness. In D. Wiener & L. Oxford (Eds.), *Action therapy with families and groups* (pp. 135–162). Washington, DC: American Psychological Association.

Gendlin, E. (1978). *Focusing.* New York: Bantam.

Grotowski, J. (1968). *Towards a poor theatre.* New York: Simon & Schuster.

Jacobson, E. (1964). *The self and object world.* New York: International Universities Press.

James, M., Forrester, A., & Kim, K. (2005). Developmental Transformations in the treatment of sexually abused children. In A. Weber & C. Haen (Eds.), *Clinical applications of drama therapy in child and adolescent treatment* (pp. 67–86). New York: Brunner Routledge.

James, M., & Johnson, D. (1996). Drama therapy in the treatment of combat-related PTSD. *The Arts in Psychotherapy, 23,* 383–396.

Johnson, D. (1982). Developmental approaches in drama therapy. *The Arts in Psychotherapy, 9,* 183–190.

Johnson, D. (1984). The representation of the internal world in catatonic schizophrenia. *Psychiatry, 47,* 299–314.

Johnson, D. (1986). The developmental method in drama therapy: Group treatment with the elderly. *The Arts in Psychotherapy, 13,* 17–34.

Johnson, D. (1991). The theory and technique of transformations in drama therapy. *The Arts in Psychotherapy, 18,* 285–300.

Johnson, D. (1992). The drama therapist in role. In S. Jennings, (Ed.), *Drama therapy: Theory and practice,* Vol. 2 (pp. 112–136). London: Routledge.

Johnson, D. (1999). Refining the developmental paradigm in the creative arts therapies. In D. Johnson, *Essays on the creative arts therapies* (pp. 161–181). Springfield, IL: Charles C Thomas.

Johnson, D., Forrester, A., Dintino, C., James, M., & Schnee, G. (1996). Towards a poor drama therapy. *The Arts in Psychotherapy, 23,* 293–308.

Johnson, D., & Lubin, H. (1997). Treatment preferences of Vietnam veterans with posttraumatic stress disorder. *Journal of Traumatic Stress, 10,* 391–405.

Johnson, D., Smith, A., & James, M. (2002). Developmental transformations in group therapy with the elderly. In C. Schaefer (Ed.), *Adult play therapy* (pp. 78–103), New York: Wiley& Sons.

Klein, M. (1932). *The psychoanalysis of children.* London: Hogarth.

Kris, A. (1982). *Free association: Method and process.* New Haven: Yale University Press.

Landers, F. (2002). Dismantling violent forms of masculinity through developmental transformations. *The Arts in Psychotherapy, 29,* 19–30.

Landy, R. (2008). *The couch and the stage.* New York: Jason Aronson.

Piaget, J. (1951). *Play, dreams, and imitation.* New York: Norton.

Porter, L. (2000). The bifurcated gift: Love and

intimacy in drama psychotherapy. *The Arts in Psychotherapy, 27,* 309–320.

Rogers, C. (1951). *Client-centered therapy.* Boston: Houghton-Mifflin.

Sandel, S., & Johnson, D. (1987). *Waiting at the gate: Creativity and hope in the nursing home.* New York: Haworth.

Sandel, S., Chaiklin, S., & Lohn, A. (Eds.), (1993). *Foundations of dance/movement therapy.* Columbia, MD: American Dance Therapy Association.

Sartre, J.P. (1943). *Being and nothingness.* London: Methuen.

Schnee, G. (1996). Drama therapy with the homeless mentally ill: Treating interpersonal disengagement. *The Arts in Psychotherapy, 23,* 53–60.

Smith, A. (2000). Exploring death anxiety with older adults through developmental transformations. *The Arts in Psychotherapy, 27,* 321–332.

Spolin, V. (1963). *Improvisation for the theatre.* Chicago: Northwestern University Press.

Werner, H. & Kaplan, S. (1963). *Symbol formation.* New York: Wiley.

Whitehouse, M. (1979). C.G. Jung and dance therapy. In P. Lewis (Ed.), *Eight theoretical approaches in dance/movement therapies* (pp. 51–70). Dubuque: Kendall/Hunt.

Winnicott, D.W. (1971). *Playing and reality.* New York: Basic Books.

BIBLIOGRAPHY

Articles and Chapters

Sandel, S., & Johnson, D. (1974). Indications and contraindications for dance therapy and sociodrama in a long-term psychiatric hospital. *American Dance Therapy Association Monograph, 3,* 47–65.

Johnson, D., & Munich, R. (1975). Increasing hospital-community contact through a theatre program in a psychiatric hospital. *Hospital and Community Psychiatry, 26,* 435–438.

Johnson, D., & Sandel, S. (1977). Structural analysis of group movement sessions: Preliminary research. *American Journal of Dance Therapy, 1,* 32–36.

Johnson, D. (1979). Drama therapy. In R. Herink (Ed.), *Psychotherapy Handbook.* New York: Aronson.

Johnson, D., & Quinlan, D. (1980). Fluid and rigid boundaries of paranoid and nonparanoid schizophrenics on a role-playing task. *Journal of Personality Assessment, 44,* 523–531.

Johnson, D. (1980). Cognitive organization in paranoid and nonparanoid schizophrenia: A study of self-other representations. *Dissertation Abstracts International, 41,* No. 5.

Johnson, D. (1981). Effects of a theatre experience on hospitalized psychiatric patients. *The Arts in Psychotherapy, 7,* 265–272.

Johnson, D. (1981). Diagnostic implications of drama therapy. In G. Schattner & R. Courtney (Eds.), *Drama in Therapy, Vol. 2* (pp. 13–34). New York: Drama Book Specialists.

Johnson, D. (1981). Drama therapy and the schizophrenic condition. In G. Schattner, & R. Courtney (Eds.), *Drama in Therapy, Vol. 2* (pp. 47–66). New York: Drama Book Specialists.

Johnson, D. (1982). Principles and techniques of drama therapy. *The Arts in Psychotherapy, 9,* 83–90.

Johnson, D. (1982). Developmental approaches in drama therapy. *The Arts in Psychotherapy, 9,* 183–190.

Johnson, D., Sandel, S., & Margolis, M. (1982). Principles of group treatment in the nursing home. *Journal of Long-Term Care Administration, 10,* 3–11.

Ryan, E., & Johnson, D. (1983). Freedom and discovery within the therapeutic bond. *The Arts in Psychotherapy, 10,* 3–7.

Sandel, S., & Johnson, D. (1983). Structure and process of the nascent group: Dance therapy with chronic patients. *The Arts in Psychotherapy, 10,* 131–140.

Johnson, D., Sandel, S., & Eicher, V. (1983). Structural aspects of group leadership styles. *American Journal of Dance Therapy, 6,* 17–30.

Emunah, R., & Johnson, D. (1983). The impact of theatrical performance on the self-images of psychiatric patients. *The Arts in Psychotherapy, 10,* 233–240.

Johnson, D. (1984). Drama therapy. In T. Karascu (Ed.), *Manual of Psychiatric Therapies, Vol. 2* (pp. 767–775). Washington, D.C.: American Psychiatric Association.

Johnson, D. (1984). The arts and communitas. *Design, 86,* 36–39.
Johnson, D. (1984). Establishing the creative arts therapies as an independent profession. *The Arts in Psychotherapy, 11,* 209–212.
Johnson, D. (1984). The representation of the internal world in catatonic schizophrenia. *Psychiatry, 47,* 299–314.
Johnson, D., Sandel, S., & Bruno, C. (1984). Effectiveness of different group structures for schizophrenic, character-disordered, and normal groups. *International Journal of Group Psychotherapy, 34,* 413–429.
Johnson, D. (1984). The field of drama therapy. *Journal of Mental Imagery, 8,* 105–109.
Johnson, D. (1985). Expressive group psychotherapy with the elderly. *International Journal of Group Psychotherapy, 35,* 109–127.
Johnson, D. (1985). Envisioning the link among the creative arts therapies. *The Arts in Psychotherapy, 12,* 233–238.
Johnson, D., & Quinlan, D. (1985). Representational boundaries in role portrayals among paranoid and nonparanoid schizophrenic patients. *Journal of Abnormal Psychology, 94,* 498–506.
Johnson, D. (1986). The developmental method in drama therapy: Group treatment with the elderly. *The Arts in Psychotherapy, 13,* 17–34.
Johnson, D. (1987). The role of the creative arts therapies in the diagnosis and treatment of psychological trauma. *The Arts in Psychotherapy, 14,* 7–14.
Johnson, D. (1988). The diagnostic role-playing test. *The Arts in Psychotherapy, 15,* 23–36.
Johnson, D. (1989). Melody and rhythm of the creative arts therapies. *Music Therapy, 8,* 8–16.
Johnson, D. (1989). The theatrical dimensions of psychotherapy. In A. Robbins (Ed.), *The Psychoaesthetic Experience* (pp. 77–92). New York: Human Sciences Press.
Johnson, D., & Eicher, V. (1990). The use of dramatic activities to facilitate dance therapy with adolescents. *The Arts in Psychotherapy, 17,* 157–164.
Johnson, D. (1990). How the arts are used in therapy. In *Health and Medical Horizons* (pp. 80–91). New York: MacMillan.
Johnson, D., Agresti, A., Nies, K., & Jacob, M. (1990). Building a therapeutic community in a nursing home through specialized groups. *Clinical Gerontologist, 9,* 203–217.
Johnson, D. (1991). On being one and many. *The Arts in Psychotherapy, 18,* 1–5.
Johnson, D. (1991). The theory and technique of transformations in drama therapy. *The Arts in Psychotherapy, 18,* 285–300.
Johnson, D. (1991). Taking the next step: Forming the National Creative Arts Therapies Association. *The Arts in Psychotherapy, 18,* 387–394.
Johnson, D. (1992). The drama therapist in role. In S. Jennings, (Ed.), *Drama therapy: Theory and practice, Vol. 2* (pp. 112–136). London: Routledge.
Johnson, D. (1993). Marian Chace's influence on drama therapy. In S. Sandel, S. Chaiklin, & A. Lohn (Eds.), *Foundations of dance/movement therapy* (pp. 176–192). Columbia, MD: American Dance Therapy Association.
Johnson, D., & Quinlan, D. (1993). Can the mental representations of paranoid schizophrenics be differentiated from those of normals? *Journal of Personality Assessment, 60,* 588–601.
Johnson, D., Feldman, S., Southwick, S., & Charney, D. (1994). The concept of the second generation program in the treatment of post-traumatic stress disorder among Vietnam veterans. *Journal of Traumatic Stress, 7,* 217–236.
Johnson, D. (1994). Shame dynamics among creative arts therapists. *The Arts in Psychotherapy, 21,* 173–178.
Johnson, D., Feldman, S., Lubin, H., & Southwick, S. (1995). The use of ritual and ceremony in the treatment of post-traumatic stress disorder. *Journal of Traumatic Stress, 8,* 283–299.
Feldman, S., Johnson, D., & Ollayos, M. (1994). The use of writing in the treatment of PTSD. In J. Sommer & M. Williams (Eds.), *The handbook of post-traumatic therapy* (pp. 366–385). Westport, CT: Greenwood Publishers.
Sandel, S., & Johnson, D. (1995). Theoretical foundations of the Structural Analysis of Movement Sessions. *The Arts in Psychotherapy, 23,* 15–26.
Morgan, C.M., & Johnson, D. (1995). Use of a drawing task in the treatment of nightmares in combat-related PTSD. *Art Therapy, 12,* 244–247.

Forrester, A., & Johnson, D. (1995). Drama therapy on an extremely short term inpatient unit. In A.Gersie (Ed.), *Brief treatment approaches to drama therapy* (pp. 125–138). London: Routledge.

James, M., & Johnson, D. (1996). Drama therapy for the treatment of affective expression in post-traumatic stress disorder. In D. Nathanson (Ed.), *Knowing feeling: Affect, script, and psychotherapy* (pp. 303–326). New York: Norton.

Dintino, C., & Johnson, D. (1996). Playing with the perpetrator: Gender dynamics in developmental drama therapy. In S. Jennings (Ed.), *Drama therapy: Theory and practice, Vol. 3* (pp. 205–220). London: Routledge.

Johnson, D., Forrester, A., Dintino, C., James, M., & Schnee, G. (1996). Towards a poor drama therapy. *The Arts in Psychotherapy, 23,* 293–306.

Johnson, D. (1997). An existential model of group therapy for chronic mental conditions. *International Journal of Group Psychotherapy, 47,* 227–250.

Lubin, H., & Johnson, D. (1997). Group therapy for traumatized women. *International Journal of Group Psychotherapy, 47,* 271–290.

James, M., & Johnson, D. (1997). Drama therapy in the treatment of combat-related PTSD. *The Arts in Psychotherapy, 23,* 383–395.

Johnson, D. Lubin, H., Hale, K., & James, M. (1997). Single session effects of treatment components of an intensive inpatient PTSD program. *Journal of Traumatic Stress, 10,* 377–390.

Lubin, H., & Johnson, D. (1998). Healing ceremonies. *Family Therapy Networker, 22,* 39–42.

Johnson, D. (1998). On the therapeutic action of the creative arts therapies: The psychodynamic model. *The Arts in Psychotherapy, 25,* 85–100.

Johnson, D. (2000). Grotowski's influence on psychotherapy in the United States and Britain. Translated into Polish by Jaroslav Fret. *Pamietnik Teatralny, 49,* 230–244.

Johnson, D. (2000). Creative arts therapies. In E. Foa, T. Keane, & M. Friedman, (Eds.), *Effective treatments for posttraumatic stress disorder* (pp. 356–358). New York: Guilford.

Johnson, D., Smith, A., & James, M. (2003). Developmental transformations in group therapy with the elderly. In C. Schaefer (Ed.), *Play therapy with adults* (pp. 78–106). New York: Wiley & Sons.

Lubin, H., & Johnson, D. (2003). Use of ceremony in multiple family therapy for psychological trauma. In D. Wiener & L. Oxford (Eds.), *Action therapy with families and groups* (pp. 75–102). Washington, DC: American Psychological Association.

Galway, K., Hurd, K., & Johnson, D. (2003). Developmental transformations in group therapy with homeless people with a mental illness. In D. Wiener & L. Oxford (Eds.), *Action therapy with families and groups* (pp. 135–162). Washington, DC: American Psychological Association.

Johnson, D., & Forrester, A. (2004). Creative arts therapies in the treatment of incest. (In Hebrew). In Z. Seligman & Z. Solomon (Eds.), *Critical and clinical perspectives on incest* (pp. 334–348). Tel Aviv: Hakibbutz Hameuchad Ltd.

Johnson, D. (2007). British influences on Developmental Transformations. *Journal of the British Dramatherapy Association, 29,* 3–10.

Books

Sandel, S., & Johnson, D. (1987). *Waiting at the gate: Creativity and hope in the nursing home.* New York: Haworth.

Johnson, D. (1999). *Essays on the creative arts therapies: Imaging the birth of a profession.* Springfield, IL: Charles C Thomas.

Lubin, H., & Johnson, D. (2008). *Trauma-centered group psychotherapy for women.* New York: Haworth.

FURTHER TRAINING AND RESEARCH

Training in Developmental Transformations currently occurs within the Institute for Developmental Transformations, progressing through three levels. The first level involves a 400 hour internship under supervision, including individual and group work, seminar, and workshops. Level Two training includes a personal psychotherapy (minimum 80 hours) in Developmental Transformations, seminar, supervision of clinical work, assisting in teaching, and written papers. Level Three includes intense supervision of individual psychotherapy clients, seminars, teaching experience, and written work. Generally, full training takes three-four years after basic training and employment in drama therapy. Training centers are in New Haven, New York, San Francisco, Israel, and The Netherlands.

The Institute's research program has largely relied on intensive case study, which provide valuable data with which to examine the therapeutic process and therapist technique. In addition, clients in our psychotherapy clinic are periodically asked to rate their improvement anonymously, and results from these questionnaires indicate substantial satisfaction with the therapy method and with their therapists. On average, after six months of treatment, symptoms such as depression, anxiety, self-esteem have shown significant improvement (defined as greater than one standard deviation change). Finally, in a treatment outcome study with Vietnam veterans suffering from posttraumatic stress disorder, the Developmental Transformations group was rated by the veterans as one of the most beneficial treatments (out of 24) they received during a four-month inpatient program (Johnson & Lubin, 1997). This data has been especially promising. More rigorous research studies are planned in the future.

The Institute for Developmental Transformations
526 West 26th Street, Suite 309, New York, NY 10001
www.artstherapy.net
email: artspsychotherapy@sbcglobal.net
212-352-1184

Chapter 7

RITUAL/THEATRE/THERAPY

STEPHEN SNOW

The therapeutic impact of performance is different from, and often greater than, process-oriented drama therapy. Renee Emunah (1994)

Persons in the psychotic episode tell us they are participating in a ritual drama emerging spontaneously from the psychotic depths. John Weir Perry (1974)

[Creating the theatrical production gave the participants] opportunities to deconstruct the current disabling constructions and to reconstruct new and more powerful identities. Amorim & Cavalcante (1992)

THE THERAPEUTIC AND TRANSFORMATIONAL POTENTIAL OF THE PERFORMATIVE FRAME

Drama Therapy as a field, or a praxis, can be divided into two fundamental forms: (1) process-oriented and (2) performance-based or focused. The latter approach deals with drama and theatre as means to the creation of a performance that constitutes the therapeutic frame. Most of the well-known methods of drama therapy fit into the former category. In essence, they are deconstructions of dramatic processes and media, synthesized with various established psychological theories and psychotherapeutic perspectives: Irwin (psychoanalytic object relations theory), Landy (social psychology and role theory), Emunah (humanistic and developmental psychology), Johnson (developmental and self psychology, object relations theory), Dunne (narrative psychology). They represent sophisticated integrations of psychological theory and dramatic method that define process-oriented approaches.

The subject of this chapter is drama therapy within the *performative frame*[1], that is, drama therapy that takes place within the special time and space of the creation of a performance which eventually has an audience and a post-performance review. This is mostly a theatre-based approach to drama therapy, although it could include other media such as film, radio, video performance and performance art. In the following pages, I aim to authenticate this performance-based approach as a legitimate form of drama therapy and to demonstrate the deep roots of healing though performance in human history and culture. I will review anthropological theory in regards to dramatic healing rituals. Elsewhere, I have theorized that this ancient background of healing via dramatic ritual has established an innate healing function within the processes of drama and theatre (Snow, 2005).

I have gone through several phases in the development of my own theatre-based approach to drama therapy. I began in 1985, in a nursing home in Brooklyn, New York with a method known as "Living History Theatre," created by Susan Perlstein (Charnow, Nash & Perlstein, 1988). Basically, this is a dynamic combination of life review, reminiscence therapy, ethnography, playwriting and theatrical performance. It gives the elderly a chance to share their treasured life stories by creating a theatrical performance. I developed several productions with the nursing home residents using this method (Snow, 1989).

My second phase of working dramatherapeutically within the performative frame was at Bronx Psychiatric Centre (1986–1992). There I worked with individuals with chronic psychiatric disabilities, sometimes with severe psychopathologies. This work was heavily influenced by my Jungian background, especially inspired by the writing of Jungian psychiatrist John Weir Perry (1953, 1974, 1976), whose theories on archetypal symbology and ritual process in psychosis were very appealing to me. I have published on this work in several places (Snow, 1983, 1991, 1996a).

My third phase of development (1994–2006) was the creation of *therapeutic theatre* practice at The Centre for the Arts in Human Development, which I co-founded as part of my work as a professor of drama therapy at Concordia University (Montrèal). This performance-based drama therapy has focused on adults with a wide variety of developmental disabilities who are the core clientele of the Centre. I have written about this work for *The Arts in Psychotherapy* (Snow, D'Amico & Tanguay, 2003) and will use several case examples in this chapter. My present work at the Centre has taken a turn in a new direction, combining therapeutic theatre with *performance ethnography*. This defines a fourth phase of development.

There have been several major influences on my development of the *Ritual/Theatre/Therapy* approach. There has been my deep and long-term experience in and study of Jungian archetypal psychology. My background in performance studies (Ph.D, 1987), including explorations of the ethnography of ritual practices and shamanism, has been very significant. Finally, my life-long experience in theatre, as an amateur, educator and practicing professional theatre artist, has enormously impacted my vision of theatre as a potential form of therapy.

In terms of drama therapy, the biggest influence on my thinking was probably the early work of Emunah and Johnson, especially their seminal article on "The Impact of Theatrical Performance on the Self-Images of Psychiatric Patients" (1983) as well as Emunah's chapters on her own vision of "Theatre and Therapy" (1994, Chapters 9–11). I certainly consider Robert Landy an early mentor and have always been grateful for his sound advice and his clearly articulat-

1. Performative is a term from Performance Studies, suggesting a depth-oriented framework for the construction and understanding of performances in their personal, interpersonal, and collective cultural meanings. See Denzin (2003), *Performance ethnography: Cultural pedagogy and the politics of culture.*

ed and pragmatic approach to drama therapy (1986, 1993). Especially significant for me has been Penny Lewis's work on shamanism, ritual, archetypal psychology and the imaginal realm (1988, 1993). Shortly before her premature death, we found ourselves to be quite kindred spirits. In Canada, with my friend and colleague drama therapist Barbara McKay, we developed the graduate drama therapy program at Concordia University. There was a welcomed sharing of knowledge, especially in regards to her work on *Collective Creation* (1996). On the British side, I have been most influenced by Mitchell's writing on *Therapeutic Theatre* (1992) and, more recently, by Jones's historical rendering of the development of *Theatre as Therapy,* as well as his own brilliant process approach to drama therapy (1996, 2007).

Reviewing some of the other drama therapists included in this volume, probably the most obvious parallel with my own work in therapeutic theatre is Saphira Linden's "Omega Transpersonal Approach" (Chapter 10). We were both influenced by the experimental theatre of the '60s, as well as being shaped as drama therapists by our backgrounds in Jung, ritual, shamanism and the power of transpersonal symbology. In terms of theatre as a therapy praxis, Laffoon and Kenny (Chapter 14), Bailey (Chapter 17), and Feldman, Sussman Jones, and Ward (Chapter 13) all express ideas similar to my own point of view regarding the essential therapeutic potential of theatre. *ENACT's* documented results of theatre practice with adolescents is similar to what I have recorded in this chapter in regards to adults with developmental disabilities. Finally, I was heartened to discover Bergman's emphasis on *therapeutic community* in his Geese Theatre Company's international work in prisons (Chapter 15). This concept is extremely important to our work in therapeutic theatre at The Centre for the Arts in Human Development (Snow et al., 2003).

Perhaps it is important to point out that, like many of the drama therapists mentioned above, our work at the Centre includes both process-oriented and performance-based drama therapy. The theatre productions are the tip of the iceberg. The clients participate in at least a year and a half of process-oriented drama therapy groups twice a week, before we begin to develop the therapeutic theatre production. A complex web of social relations, psychological and emotional development, and growing expressive and artistic skills underlie the surface of the final performance and help define the performative frame.

So, how and why can a theatrical performance, that whole complex framework of creating, rehearsing, performing and letting go of a performance, be shaped in a way to have a therapeutic and transformational effect? What are the ritual elements, the rites of passage, that ultimately make it so? What are the aspects of identity deconstruction and reformation that can take place in the performative frame? How does transpersonal and archetypal symbology factor into this process? And, finally, where does the profound potential for psychological healing in the performative frame come from? Let us begin to answer these important questions with an overview of a 30,000 year-old tradition of ritual dramatic healing.

THEORY

Roots of Drama Therapy in Shamanism

After more than 30 years of studying the scholarship on and the traditions of shamanism, I am convinced that drama therapy is based upon the essential structures of shamanic healing rituals, as they have evolved in human experience over the past 30,000 years or so. I will bypass the thorny questions in regards to cultural evolution and transmission of cultural knowledge and psychological structures that are implied in this point of view, and instead focus on the fundamental correlations between shamanism and drama therapy.

My first real insights into this relationship came with the reading of a cross-cultural study by Lucile Hoerr Charles, entitled *Drama in Shaman Exorcism,* in which the author clearly demonstrates that "the shaman's chief function in exorcism of the sick is psychotherapeutic; his method is dramatic" (1953, p. 97). The shaman's ritualized psychosomatic healing of the sick is, in fact, a performance that, according to Charles, includes:

> . . . impressive setting and lighting, costume and make-up, theatrical properties and sound effects . . . possession of or battle with the shaman by the spirits through ecstacy and frenzy which may be considered a supreme example of dramatic improvisation, often with elaborate use of voice, dialogue, and body pantomime. . . . (1953, p. 96)

I was, at that point in time, quite familiar with the literature that related shamanism to the origins of theatre and theatrical acting (Bates, 1987; Cole 1975; Kirby, 1975; Schechner, 1977), but my real interest was the investigation into how and why the ritual performances of shamans were and are psychotherapeutic. Ellenberger's (1970) excellent essay on *The Ancestry of Dynamic Psychotherapy* was very helpful in this direction. Besides being a kind of protoactor, the shaman was also a protopsychotherapist. Roots of the use of dramatic means for psychotherapeutic purposes are very ancient (Snow, 1996b). Another drama therapist, exploring similar territory, was able to articulate this concept quite succinctly: "Shamans seem to be aware of the fact that that which is performed in the imaginal world has a healing potential, while actors generally do not make much of this potential. In this regard, drama therapists may be more like shamans than actors" (Pendzik 1988, p. 83). It seemed to me that this realm of healing through dramatic ritual, which for millenia had been owned by shamanic practitioners, was being reclaimed, reconstructed and reconstituted by contemporary drama therapists.

"Demon Exorcism" in a Contemporary Psychotherapeutic Context

I had been working therapeutically with the demon fantasies of a person with schizophrenia in a present-day psychiatric hospital (see first case study). Meanwhile, the fundamental pattern that I understood from Charles and others as the basis of shamanic healing was the exorcism of evil disease-causing spirits. Exorcism is, of course, an extraordinarily loaded term in our culture. Images of spinning heads, pea soup spray from horror films immediately come to mind. However, one only has to briefly peruse the ethnography of shamanism to realize how common the experiences of possession and exorcism are in tribal cultures.

According to Ellenberger's (1970) model of primitive disease theory, the two most common psychosomatic illnesses were *loss of soul* and *spirit intrusion.* In regards to the first of these, he makes an intriguing comment:

> Could not the therapist who gives psychotherapy to a severely disoriented schizophrenic patient by trying to establish a contact with the remaining healthy parts of the personality and to reconstruct the ego be considered a modern successor to those shamans who set out to follow the tracks of a lost soul, trace it into the world of spirits, and fight against the malignant

> demons detaining it, and bring it back to the world of the living? (Ellenberger 1970, p. 9)

Spirit intrusion is, of course, possession. The entry of a disease-causing spirit into the soul of the sick person is a phenomenon reported on, worldwide, by shamans and ethnographers of shamanism (Halifax, 1982; Harner, 1980; Keeney, 2005; Lommel, 1972; Shirokogoroff, 1935). However, in tribal societies, the two etiological concepts are often blurred; the quintessential idea is that a demon or malignant spirit has somehow mastered the spirit of the patient. Here is an eyewitness account of shamanism practiced amongst the Tungus in the early twentieth century:

> A man over forty is affected by an unknown spirit. He himself has made several attempts at shamanizing but . . . he cannot master the spirits, while the latter master him. The performing female shaman is a young but experienced shaman. The aim is to find what kind of spirit is doing harm. For the purpose, she introduces into herself spirits: she becomes possessed by her "helping spirits." By drumming and singing–she brings herself into a state of ecstasy and the spirits enter her. Through her spirit the shaman wants to find the road to the spirit that affects the client. She goes [trance flight] to the yurt of the family. . . . During the performance the shaman fell down several times at the moment when the spirit entered her [possession]. The people who were near her support her and lifted her up, just like a piece of wood . . . the body and limbs were rigid. Before the entry of the spirit, she increased the intensity of the singing and drumming and began to tremble; when she was travelling [her spirit], she jumped and beat the drum with great force. (Shirokogoroff, 1935, pp. 311–312)

Herein, we discover the image of the shaman as the *Master of Spirits* (Eliade, 1964) and the *Wounded Healer* (Halifax, 1982). But how can we locate this shamanic functioning in the practice of a modern drama therapist? I have purposefully italicized words in order to emphasize that the shaman is utilizing a dramatic ritual performance to accomplish her therapeutic efficacy. I would like to point out a few key themes that begin to constitute a formula for shamanism as a precursor of drama therapy: (1) The shaman is performing. Kirby (1975) has clearly demonstrated how the shaman's therapeutic enactment is the beginning of theatrical role playing. Like the shaman, an actor can become possessed by his or her role (Bates, 1987); (2) the healing ritual is a performance. Drumming and singing are included in the example above; movement is also intimated. Charles (1953) also cites the use of puppets, masks, storytelling, ventriloquism and prestidigitation. Cole (1975) compares the trance flight of the shaman to a spiritual realm (an *illud tempus*) with the actor's entry into the mythological and symbolic work of the play script. In fact, Cole defines theatre by what he designates as the *rounding;* for the actor like the shaman must make a trance flight to a spirit world, and allow him or herself to become possessed by the spirit of his or her role (1975, p. 15). The actor does this in service of the audience. In the example above, the shaman performs both functions (trance flight and possession) in the service of healing her client; (3) The shaman journeys in the imaginal realm; (4) allows herself to become possessed without getting sick; and, ultimately; (5) masters the disease-causing spirit through a dramatic ritual performance. A pattern begins to emerge that directly correlates shamanic ritual performance with the performative frame of drama therapy (Figure 7.1). In this formulation, the structures and processes of ancient shamanism are paralleled by those of contemporary drama therapy, especially regarding the use of a ritual performance. For insightful commentary on the correlations of drama therapy playspace and shamanic ritual healing space, see Blair

Glaser's (2004) article "Ancient Traditions within a New Drama Therapy Method: Shamanism and Developmental Transformations."

The Theory of Archetypes

> Modern psychology has the distinct advantage of having opened up a field of psychic phenomena which are themselves the matrix of all mythology–I mean dreams, visions fantasies, and delusional ideas. Here the psychologist not only finds numerous points of correspondence with myth motifs, but also has the invaluable opportunity to observe how such contents arise and to analyze their function in a living organism. (Jung 1956, p. 390)

Jung established his theory of the archetypal contents of the psyche, in part based on observations he made early in his career, of the psychotic ideation of schizophrenic patients ([1936] 1970). He postulated that in the depths of the human psyche there is a matrix of extraordinarily powerful symbols or symbol-engendering structures that have the potential to catalyze transformations in the individual's experience of himself and the world. He states in "The Psychology of the Child Archetype:"

> Archetypes were, and still are, living psychic forces that demand to be taken seriously, and they have a strange way of making sure of their effect. Always they were the bringer of protection and salvation, and their violation has as its consequence the "perils of the soul" known to us from the psychology of primitives. Moreover, they are the infallible causes of neurotic and even psychotic disorders, behaving exactly like neglected or maltreated organs or organic functional systems. (In de Laszlo 1958, p. 119)

In this same essay, Jung also describes the archetypes as psychic organs–I will pick up this theme, later–but, notice how the potentially demonic quality of the eruption of an archetype, like the shamanistic "disease-causing demon," might easily master the soul of the neurotic or psychotic individual. The course that an archetype imposes on an individual might well be described as a rite of passage and, for many Jungians, the process of psychotherapy is exactly that: a rite of passage that takes one into the depths of the unconscious and then out again; a death and rebirth, so well depicted in the famous mythological image of the "dark night sea journey." Barbara Sullivan, in her essay, *The Archetypal Foundation of the Therapeutic Process* equates the Jungian tradition with the symbolic practices of primitive societies and correlates these with Campbell's well-known model of the *Hero's Journey;* all three constituting ritual processes in which there is a psychological death and rebirth (Sullivan, 1987).

John Weir Perry, a Jungian psychiatrist, has developed a formidable theory as to how and why ritual dramas are spontaneously played out in the psychotic episodes of persons with schizophrenia (1974, 1976, 1987). He discovered the parallels between the inner process of acute psychosis in his patients and the ancient Hebrew New Year's ritual (a basis for the messianic myth in the Judeo-Christian tradition). Perry designates this course as "the reconstitution process as deriving from the archaic ritual dramas of renewal" (Perry 1974, p. 3). Through his research on this ritual tradition from the times of King David, Perry found this myth/ritual system to be filled with powerful archetypal symbols, including that of the divine kingship (later to become the image of Christ the King). He writes:

> These archetypal affect-images mobilized, governed, and directed the emotional energies of the people through their expression in dramatic form. As history moved on, however,

SHAMANISM

(1)		(2)		(3)		(4)		(5)
Patient enters the Ritual Performance Space with Shaman	>	Entry into the realm of spirits (Powerful images of demons/spirits)	>	Performative elements are put into effect by the Shaman	>	Through Ritual Performance the patient is helped to master spirits/spiritual state	>	Ritual Performance Space is discontinued

DRAMA THERAPY

(1)		(2)		(3)		(4)		(5)
Patient enters the Ritual Performance Space with Drama Therapist	>	Entry into the "imaginal realm" (Powerful archetypal images)	>	Performative elements are put into effect by by patient *and* the Drama Therapist	>	Through Ritual Performance the patient is helped to master psychological states	>	Ritual Performance Space is closed; therapy is terminated

Figure 7.1. Ritual Performance in Shamanism and Drama Therapy

> the imagery changed and the role of the sacral king evolved into that of a particular kind of hero and savior. (Perry, 1974, p. 61)

Theatre Evolved From Dramatic Ritual

I was very fortunate during my graduate studies to have studied with Richard Schechner, and also for a very brief time with Victor Turner. These two great scholar/writers helped me to gain an appreciation for the intricate ways in which ritual and the other performative modes in culture are interconnected. Schechner has written brilliantly about various kinds of cultural performances, including Asian and Native American ritual performances (1977, 1981, 1985). Schechner was very influenced by Turner (actually they mutually influenced each other up until the time of Turner's death in 1983). Both men were fascinated with the possibilities of cultural transmission and saw performance as a potential source for a "new transcultural communicative synthesis" (Turner 1982, p. 19). Turner, of course, developed the concept of (and coined the term) *liminality* (a term used pervasively today by creative arts therapists, especially in relation to the concept of the therapeutic playspace). Turner was very keen to identify ways in which the liminal genres of tribal societies were reflected in contemporary culture. As he wrote in *From Ritual to Theatre:*

> Just as when tribesmen make masks, disguise themselves as monsters, heap up disparate ritual symbols, invert and parody reality in myth and folk tale, so do the genres of industrial leisure, the theatre, poetry, novel . . . play with the factors of culture, sometimes assembling them in random, grotesque, improbable, surprising, shocking, usually experimental combinations. (1982, p. 40)

I see drama therapy as one of these experimental combinations, rooted in the healing traditions of ritual performance and shamanism. I have written elsewhere (Snow, 1996a) of my debt to Schechner's development of what he calls "Turner's Talmud" on Van Gennep's conceptualization of the liminal phase of rites of passage and its connection to Bateson's "Play Frame" (Schechner 1981, pp. 2–45). My own interest turned away from the analysis of cultural performances and, in the early 1980s, I began to focus on how ritual performance was used for healing. As in Perry's study, I was especially interested in how collective forms of ritual drama sometimes functioned as community therapy in certain cultures. I must have watched Bateson and Mead's *Trance and Dance in Bali,* their documentary film on a very special Balinese ritual dance drama, over 100 times! My essay, *Rangda: Archetype in Action in Balinese Dance-Drama* (1983) was an attempt to articulate how the archetype of the *Devouring Mother* (Rangda) operates psychologically in this ritual performance. It is clear from this documentary that, at least in the 1930s, this performance was still a very dynamic community ritual and, according to Bateson and Mead, the embodied archetype, the demonic Rangda, has the power to cause a large number of the ritual participants to fall into trance. This film made me very curious about how an embodied archetype in a ritual drama can affect both actors and audience in such a psychologically dynamic way. I became aware of psychologist Stephen Larsen's notion of the *mythic seizure,* which is constituted by a deep emotional experience of what Perry has called the *archetypal-affect images.* Larsen theorizes:

> The mythic seizure, sought in its terrifying immediacy as in shamanism, is still bound to forms of an orthodox mythological tradition. The relativity that accompanies contacts of the personal with the numinous, and produces

> those intensely private mythologies which are incomprehensible to others and are labeled as madness, is here constrained by the forms of the traditional mythology. (Larsen, 1976, p. 56)

Larsen is here speaking of Haitan Voudon, but he could just as easily be talking about the ritual performances of Rangda in Balinese culture, for the whole dance-drama is contextualized with traditional Bali Hindu mythology. Even from Bateson and Mead's film, it is possible to get a sense of how powerfully the dramatic embodiment of Rangda affects the participants–one might even say in a therapeutic way. For at the conclusion to this ritual enactment, audience and actors all appear to be relaxed and calm, as if they had been exorcised by their trance possession.

These were some of the experiences, some 25 years ago that began to point me in the direction of developing a form of ritual theatre therapy based on constructing and performing plays.

David Read Johnson and Renee Emunah (1983) have written about the therapeutic efficacy of theatrical performance. These two pioneering drama therapists have investigated the significant effect that rehearsing and performing plays can have on the self-images of psychiatric patients. I was inspired by their work and in the mid to late 1980s began to create therapeutic play productions in the psychiatric hospital where I was employed as a drama therapist (Snow, 1991, 1996b). Some of these were real explorations of ritual dramas that, in Perry's words, had emerged "spontaneously from the psychic depths" (1974, p. 54). I especially remember one performance that evolved out of a patient's story about an "Energy Creature." This central figure in the narrative was a kind of fairy tale archetypal image of an immortal being who could "appear and disappear anywhere in the universe at will . . . (with) no physical needs and . . . (who) will live as long as God" (Script A, 1991). This being was locked and frozen (image of mental illness) in his own super high tech orbit, yet he yearned to become human (a metaphor for mental health). One day the Energy Creature lands in Central Park and a cast of characters (all played by psychiatric patients) debate the pros and cons in regards to living on planet Earth. In response to his request to do so, one of the characters responds "Are you crazy? Disease–Poverty–Homelessness –Drugs–Crime!" and goes on to enumerate all the undesirable qualities of life on Earth. Finally, after witnessing the gentle caring of two young lovers, the Energy Creature makes his decision. He decides to give it a try and, in that moment, he is transformed. Theatrically, in front of everyone, he was literally changed from his mechanical, computerized, robot-like suit to everyday normal street clothes. This moment was very moving to both the staff and patients in the audience, and they responded with a standing ovation for the patient/actors who created and performed this play, called "The Energy Creature and His Friends."

Here, an archetypal image was embodied and a metaphorical death and rebirth were enacted. The patient/actors had developed their performances out of improvisations on themes and images (some text was finally set for raps and songs), so this experience fits within the model delineated by Emunah and Johnson:

> The self is the material of the creation, and the self is applauded. The impact on self-image is extraordinarily powerful. The fact that the achievement is shared with one's group of patient-actors strengthens and intensifies the impact. The reaction is one of exhilaration, pride and affirmation of identity. (1983, p. 236)

A shift in one's perception of self can be actualized through the performance, which almost always carries in its process the sense of a rite of passage. Fears must be overcome, obstacles surmounted and the threshold towards a new self-concept, potentially crossed. All of this can be enormously therapeutic for an individual who has been stigmatized with a mental health disability.

PRINCIPLES OF THE RITUAL/THEATRE/THERAPY APPROACH

As Emunah states in her excellent textbook on drama therapy:

> . . . the other important dimension to drama therapy is public performance. Performance transforms notions about theatre and about therapy. The setting of the therapy scene changes from the closed room to the public stage; the cast changes from client and therapist to client/actor, therapist/director, and outside audience. The therapeutic impact of performance is different from, and often greater than, process-oriented drama therapy. (1994, p. 251)

Out of my own experiences producing therapeutic theatre over the past 23 years, and taking into consideration the therapeutic effects of the archetypal imagery evoked in the process of theatrical performance, I have delineated a model that demonstrates how and why the performative frame of drama therapy is different from and often greater than the process-oriented mode of drama therapy.

Basic Concepts

Health

The essential paradigm for mental health here is a Jungian one, based on the fundamental concept that health is wholeness or balance, especially in relationship to the archetypal components of the unconscious. Sullivan (1987) suggests that "the psyche rests on the archetypes" (p. 27). The point of view taken is also in alignment with that of Neumann. "The archetypal structural elements of the psyche are psychic organs upon whose functioning the well-being of the individual depends, and whose injury has disastrous consequences" (Neumann,1954, p. xv).

It is my belief that one of the reasons that the experience of theatrical performance is often innately healing is because it evokes the positive healing energies of the archetypes. This is congruent with Cole's theory concerning the actor's journey to and experience of the mythological realm of numinous symbols (Cole, 1975). Everything in performance-making is intensified because of this. Many of my former drama therapy students have told me how they intuited the healing function of theatre and how specific performances have served as therapy for them (a good number of them came to drama therapy from professional theatre). I believe that they are rediscovering what Bates calls the "Lost Tradition" in which "The shaman actor . . . in performance dips into the timeless ocean of human concerns, and intervenes in the conduct of life by incarnating the spirits and their wisdom" (1987, p. 23). Just making contact with this spiritual dimension can have a salubrious effect. However, many of the psychiatric patients with whom I have worked are extremely out of balance, sometimes being totally overwhelmed by such mythological content. In these cases, "the complexes take on in the unconscious an archaic-mythological character and an increasing numinosity through the enrichment of their contents, as can be easily observed in the case of schizophrenia (Jacobi, 1959, p. 11). Here there is the need to develop a very contained ritual drama of renewal in order to bring the client back into balance and help them to detach from the mythic seizure that possesses them.

Thus, a great deal in this model depends upon the ego's relationship to the archetypes.

Another extremely important factor in mental well-being is the quality of the self-concept. Everyone who enters into the performative frame risks injury to their self-concept. This is especially true for individuals who have been highly stigmatized and marginalized by their society. As Emunah and Johnson (1983) point out: "The negative self-images of psychiatric patients undermine the stability of every self-presentation, and make every interpersonal interaction a potentially dangerous event" (p. 233). But in this very risk is also the potential for positive transformation of the self-concept.

Dysfunction and Spiritual Emergencies

In Jung's early writing on schizophrenia, he defines the grandiose delusions of his patients in terms of a compensatory function, related to profoundly wounded self-images ([1936] 1970, p. 136). Perry has further developed this perspective in his own work:

> From observing the behavior of the archetypal affect-images in schizophrenic episodes, the impression has grown on me that the syndrome revolves around the problem of self-image . . . the self-image of that of being faulty, undesirable, unworthy and unpromising. . . . Close behind these feelings are the fantasy ones–from the compensatory archetypal affect-image–of being superlative, more than human, a genius, or a person of momentous importance in the world. Thus, when the personal self-image is severely debased–as it usually is in the pre-psychotic make-up–the archetypal image is in the same measure exalted. (1974, p. 26)

The patient who created the role of the Energy Creature saw himself as being omnipotent and immortal, having no limiting human needs and being able to live "as long as God." The great transforming symbol in the play was his de-roling from this grandiose state and accepting his human limitations.

Patients may present their fantasy material in very different styles, according to the nature of their psychopathology. Perry worked with first-onset psychotic episodes of persons with schizophrenia in their twenties or early thirties (1974, p. 25). I have worked with one schizo-affective patient (the same individual who created the Energy Creature) in a period of extreme decompensation (Snow, 1991, 1996a). For Theo (see Case Studies), mythological fantasies were mostly long-term defenses, protecting him against any real contact with the world. Psychiatrist Stanislav Grof (Grof & Grof, 1986) has discerned another type of psychotic state which he defines as a "spiritual emergency" or "transpersonal crisis." Often these are a kind of shamanistic initiatory crisis. This is exactly how psychologist David Lukoff describes his personal experience of a psychotic episode at the age of 23: "My shamanistic initiatory crisis awakened certain healing abilities in me that contribute to my work with psychotic patients" (1990, p. 26). This type of intensive inner voyage is certainly not unlike that which Jung underwent, after his break with Freud, around 1912. It is why Laing (1967) points to Jung as having opened up the territory for exploring the organic healing process involved in contacting the archetypal domain of the psyche.

In terms of psychiatric rehabilitation, the drama therapist must work in consultation with the treatment team in order to determine a reliable assessment of the type of psychotic experience which a specific patient is undergoing. Many projective techniques, such as mask-making, puppets and scripting, can be utilized as assessment tools. Johnson (1988) has also developed an instrument based on improvisational role playing, which he calls the *Diagnostic Role-Playing Test* (1988).

In terms of developing performance as the therapeutic modality, understanding the nature of the damage to a client's self-concept is of paramount importance. This applies to all potential participants, not just those with severe psychopathologies. I borrow a very basic definition of self-concept from Ross (1992, p. 3): "The self-concept is no more than the concept a person has of him or herself. That concept represents how one thinks and feels about oneself–how one perceives oneself." This relates directly to the issue of self-esteem, for if one feels badly about oneself, then that individual has low self-esteem. This is especially true for persons who are members of a highly stigmatized group. As Fishman, Scott and Belof state in regards to individuals with intellectual and cognitive handicaps:

> . . . when someone is diagnosed as mentally retarded, he is thrust into a hall of mirrors. The label creates a special contact with other people: expectations are scaled down; people no longer call upon the retarded person to use daily skills that would ordinarily be expected were he not retarded. The way normal people assess and treat him affects his self-image. (Klepac, 1978, p. 343)

Another possible purpose for the performative frame in drama therapy is to improve the self-image of the patient/actor, through the construction and performance of a play, so at the end, like Emunah and Johnson's clients, they can say to the world: "See, I'm able!" (1983, p. 236).

The central notion here is to utilize the full force of a theatrical production as a vehicle for therapy. The intention of the performance is to help in the reconstruction of self-image through the various media of drama, including the final performance and cool down period. As Amorim and Cavalcante (1992) describe in their process of developing a puppet play to be performed for the public by young adults with developmental disabilities, the whole procedure gave the participants "opportunities to deconstruct the current disabling constructions and to reconstruct new and more powerful identities" (p. 154).

Therapeutic Process

The essential formula for the use of the Ritual/Theatre/Therapy approach takes into consideration both the nature of the damage to self-concept and the dynamic of the relationship of ego to archetype (Figure 7.2). In the process of constructing the performance, the injured self-image is put in contact with the archetypal image or story. There is an intention to help balance the relationship of ego and archetype, either by working through an embodied archetype (as in the case of persons in psychotic episodes) or by using an archetypal role as a catalyst to assist the client in developing a more positive self-image. Either way the ritual construction of the performance leads towards a sense of mastering, like the shamans who master the spirits, one's out-of-balance psychological state. The realization of the performance enhances this sense of mastery. As Emunah and Johnson (1983) comment: "Members usually sense the development of their self-images as a result of the group's work in rehearsal, but the brutal and exciting confrontation with the audience is seen as a confirmation of it" (p. 236). Landy also helpfully points to the necessity of creating a support system for the patient/actors as they move through ritual performance process. He writes:

> . . . in order to facilitate the development of positive self-concept and social interaction

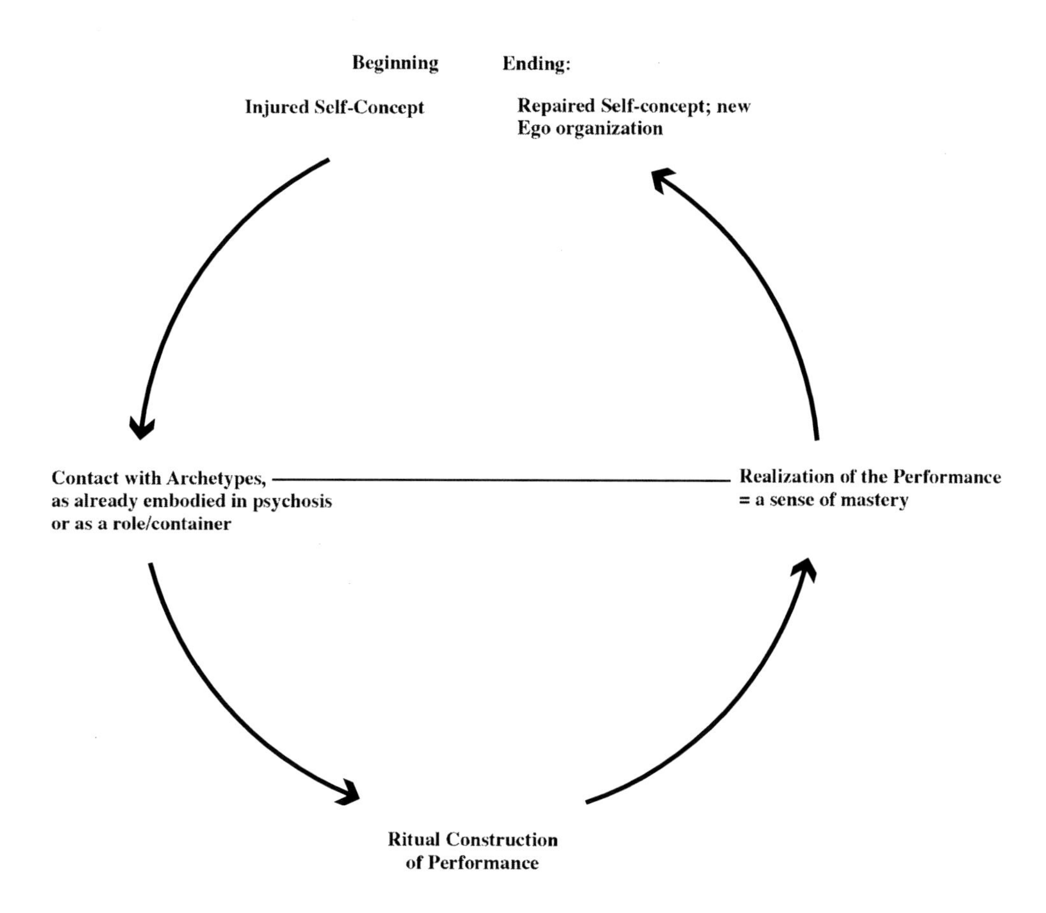

Figure 7.2. Therapeutic Formula for Ritual/Theatre/Therapy.

through the theatre experience, the drama therapist must develop support groups both during and following the performance experience and must not lose sight of the therapeutic needs of the performers through focusing on the entertainment needs of the audience. (1986, p. 153)

Of course, having to focus on the therapeutic needs of the performers and other desideratum for the positive outcome of the performance (so that it will, in fact, have a beneficial effect on the actors' self-images) can put an inordinate degree of pressure on the therapist/director.

Reviewing the work of Emunah, Johnson, Landy and others, it seems that there are several prerequisites for performance to have maximum therapeutic effect:

- clients' therapeutic needs must be placed first and foremost before aesthetic or entertainment values
- all roles must be appropriate for the physical, psychological and emotional needs of the clients
- improvisationally-developed and self-revelatory performances hold the most therapeutic value

- support groups must be in place during and after the performance experience

METHODS AND TECHNIQUES

The whole spectrum of drama therapy techniques is available to the process of constructing a performance. The choice of methods, of course, depends on the intentions regarding the manipulation of *distance.* Landy, who developed the theory of distancing for the field of drama therapy, writes: ". . . the drama therapist draws upon a wide range of psychodramatic and projective techniques that implies a variation of relationship between self and role, self and other" (1983, p. 175).

Mask Work, Scripting, and Puppets

I have used mask work to help embody a powerful archetype emerging from the patient's creative expression (Fig 7.3). I have guided the scripting process to help contain the overflow of psychotic ideation. With groups in geriatrics and psychiatric rehabilitation, and with developmentally disabled adults, I have employed puppets to establish

Figure 7.3. Mask Design for Ancient God of Rock 'n Roll (Collaboration of Theo and Art Therapist, Sam Sherrod).

contact or to set a frame of *aesthetic distance.*

Role Selection

I have utilized various role methods to help seniors process painful memories, and also to bring out blocked or repressed memories that might become the basis for scene work. Certainly, one of the major considerations is always the choice of role. When the right role is chosen, following the client's lead, its performance has the most likelihood of being a therapeutic experience. The right role helps to empower the client in a way that often brings balance to an otherwise chaotic, disorganized and conflicted personality.

Ritualization

Finally, a ritualization within the rehearsal-performance-closure process is another important issue. For persons with severe psychopathologies, ritualizing the time and space of the production helps give structure and a sense of security. This can be as simple as using the same song to welcome everybody, each day, or implementing the same opening and closing exercises at every rehearsal. In a production with developmentally disabled adults, entitled "Oh! That Aladdin . . . ," the music therapist/musical director devised a wonderful, short welcoming song that always helped to promote the unity of the group. It became a kind of musically ritualized group identity. In the same production, the drama therapist/director instituted the same closure techniques at the end of each rehearsal. Participants will quickly show when they desire the repetition of such actions and when they prefer a change. For many, the repetition of activities in time and space is an important structure to experience the environment of the play production as safe and holding. I have written elsewhere of how the drama therapist needs to be a ritual specialist, especially in work with psychotic episodes, creating and sustaining a transitional space in which clients can deconstruct and reconstruct themselves (Snow, 1996a).

Role of the Therapist

The role of the drama therapist in this performative frame is multifocal and multidimensional. The single most important function is integrating the therapeutic and the aesthetic, sacrificing neither for the other. The art product must become the context for an important experience of mastery for the client, and, at the same time, the "exquisite attention to the person"[2] must never be lost. The therapeutic process must constantly parallel the creative process, and sometimes be the same thing. To do this work effectively, it is to the advantage of the drama therapist to have a strong background in a number of areas: play directing, dramatic construction, and dramaturgy; comparative mythology and symbology, ritual theory and practice; psychodrama and sociodrama; videography; and, of course, improvisational role-playing.

Populations Served

This type of work is open to all populations. I have practiced therapeutic ritual performance, in different styles, with youth-at-risk, seniors, persons with mental health disabilities and persons with developmental disabilities. This is a very human process, with deep phylogenetic roots. As Joseph Campbell (1949) suggested some years ago:

2. A definition of therapeutic focus that was given by a member of a panel at the NADT Conference at Yale University, in 1995. I'm quite sure that this phrase was coined by Remi Barclay Bosseau, RDT.

"It has always been the prime function of mythology and rite to supply the symbols that carry the human spirit forward. . . . In fact, it well may be that the very high incidence of neuroticism among ourselves follows from the decline among us of such an effective spiritual aid" (p. 11).

Challenges

I have attempted to build a case for how Ritual/Theatre/Therapy can offer such a process, especially for persons with extremely wounded self-concepts. Perry has even suggested that such rituals of renewal will emerge spontaneously, when the psychic pressure is too great. In these situations, the drama therapist can serve as guide, facilitator and ritual specialist who helps the suffering individual to greater health through drama.

Probably the greatest single challenge in doing therapy within the performative frame is the lack of time and focus to allow for the working through process. In other words, it is important to not allow the client to get stuck in their defense mechanisms so that they use the ritual performance merely to recycle their repetition compulsion or the psychotic fantasies that form their psychotic prison. For instance, I thought I was making great progress–even incredible progress–with a psychiatric patient with a schizo-affective disorder. I had actually been his guide through a number of therapeutic performances. Without a doubt, he was replacing large areas of psychological disorganization and fragmentation with genuine creativity. He was out of the hospital, living on his own, and had even applied and been accepted to graduate school. Then, on his first day at his new graduate program, he completely decompensated. Recidivism is, of course, a norm in psychiatric rehabilitation, but this came as a shock to me, and I had to humbly admit that all my work with this patient had had only minimal effect. He could not seem to integrate and sustain new levels of balance and health.

Most of the work in the context of performative drama therapy is, by its very nature, brief therapy. How can it be expected to induce long-term structural changes in the personality? Perhaps all it can do is point the individual patient in the right direction. The short-term intensive work of creating a performance can be a boost to the individual's self-image, but an enduring restructuring of the personality takes a long period of working through (Epstein, 1995). However, there is some evidence to contradict this point of view. Mehl-Madronna (1997) clearly states his belief that short, intensive work, like three-day, all-day sessions, can produce more therapeutic results than a year of once or twice per week psychotherapy. This model is closer to the kind of intensity evoked by the performative frame of drama therapy. At the Centre for the Arts in Human Development at Concordia University in Montreal, where we conduct research on the effectiveness of the creative arts therapies in helping adults with developmental disabilities, it has been quantitatively demonstrated that, for some clients, the peak of therapeutic effectiveness during the year is when we produce our theatrical productions (D'Amico et al., 1998).

Summary

Why, then, is it possible for a performative frame in drama therapy to sometimes be more effective than process-oriented drama therapy? I believe it is because the intensity and concentration, which I just described as a possible weakness, can be also be a great strength, creating the frame for a very effective, focused rite of passage. The creative intensity of preparing and performing a piece of theatre offers a context for the kind of liminality that is conducive to the deconstruction and reconstruction of the personality; the performance offers a whole new role, and perhaps a whole new way of viewing life. Sometimes, that which is performed in the liminal, imaginal realm can get carried over into real life and be maintained as a new component of the personality. Such results of performances can definitely be described as the therapeutic consequences of this style of drama therapy.

CASE STUDIES

An Adult with Paranoid Schizophrenia

Theo was one of the most withdrawn patients I had ever observed on Ward 13. Then in his late twenties, he had been hospitalized, or in special schools, since the age of six. Very early on, he had been diagnosed as a paranoid schizophrenic of the chronic type. He was a somber figure on the ward. During that period, he spent a large amount of time in the dayroom, sitting next to a table, with his head resting on his folded arms. In fact, when I first met him, he always had a mark on his forehead, which I assumed came from the impression made by holding his head on his folded arms for such a length of time. His eyes were deeply sunken in their sockets, and with his black shock of hair and goatee, he seemed like some kind of occult persona, with the look of someone like Edgar Allan Poe.

As might be expected, Theo was filled with fears and terrible hallucinations. He saw dead people hanging in trees, outside his window, on the hospital grounds. Once, he saw his father who died of cancer when Theo was five, standing in his closet, wearing a long cape, and peering out with the face of a cat. Theo believed the world was filled with vampires. He was very hypochondriacal, often making statements like "I have cancer in my chest" or "I have a tree in my brain." It was believed that he may have been molested by male staff in one of the special schools for emotionally disturbed children. He was highly homophobic. When he was 17, he tried to kill his mother by kicking and beating her, so he had been hospitalized on a chronic psychiatric unit since that time.

In April of 1988, after I had directed a ward play, entitled *New Faces of 1988,* I first made contact with Theo. I cannot remember whether he first spoke to me or I to him, but I do recall he had a story or a script that he wanted to share with me. The more I listened to Theo's description of his tale, the more I became fascinated with it as an allegory of Theo's mental illness.

I saw, right away, that this script represented a kind of ritual drama that came from Theo's psychopathology, but that it also contained his dream for a healthy life. So I thought that it just might be therapeutic for Theo to embody this ritual drama through a video production, a movie. Theo was extremely excited by this concept. We agreed to make a movie of this narrative, in which he would write the script and the songs, and also star as the central character. I received the permission of the unit chief, who was also enthusiastic about the project, and we began the work on *Rocky Roads,* also known as *Elvis Presley's 34th Film.* (Theo was also very identified with Elvis, whom he considered a vampire–one of the Undead–and whom he had incarnated between 1954 and 1960.) In brief, the script was framed as a dream, in which the hero, Tom (Theo), who leads a very normal life with his wife and child in their lovely country house with a white picket fence, falls into a dream state (Theo's psychotic world view). In his dream,

Tom is captured by demons and taken to the "Kingdom of the Ancient Demon Worshipers of Rock 'N Roll." The Demon God asks Tom to sing for the multitudes in his kingdom. Tom does so and, then he awakens to find himself back in his '57 Chevy, with his dear wife, Beth, who tells him that he had fallen asleep for the past three hours. As the movie ends, they pull into the driveway of their pretty little house with the white picket fence.

The whole process of embodying, enacting and catching this ritual drama on film took well over a year. All the procedures involved with this production are much too complicated to go into here, but the effect on Theo was truly amazing. It was as if he gradually came alive. He was always ready and prepared to play his role. His level of concentration was as good as many professional actors with whom I have worked. He constantly made very creative suggestions, many of which were incorporated into the work. He developed excellent connections with all the members of the production team; and this carried over into his forming some new relationships on the ward, for example, with the ward custodian whose helper he became. Theo was definitely no longer the withdrawn, seemingly fatigued figure, slumped over the table in the dayroom.

This was the beginning of my work in exploring the embodiment of ritual dramas, symbols and inner mythology of schizophrenic patients in drama therapy. I was, at that time, very influenced by David Read Johnson's work with schizophrenic patients at the Yale Psychiatric Institute and felt that my success with Theo was an exemplification of Johnson's perspective that:

> The nature of the drama, with its tolerance for the unreal and the imaginative, entices the inner self of the schizophrenic, which is occupied in fantasy, to reveal some part of itself. The patient finds he can explore with some freedom the various fragments of himself while, at the same time, actualizing them for others. In this way, the inner self makes contact with the world, and the individual's fantasies become part of objective existence. (Johnson in Schattner & Courtney, 1981, p. 60)

The process of this performance/ production, and how it related to the transformative power of the embodiment of symbols within ritual, seems linked to the historical background of ritual healing performances. For instance, one of the symbols that we actualized in the movie was the Demon-god or Demon-king of Rock 'N Roll. Theo made a preliminary sketch of the face of this archetypal figure and then, the art therapist, Sam Sherrod, who was part of the production team, collaborated with him on a design for a mask to be worn by the actor who played this role in the film (see Figure 7.3). All the talk about demons got us into a bit of hot water with other staff on the ward. One of the occupational therapists took it all quite literally and perceived us as practicing some form of modern-day demonology. Although I truly regard my creative arts therapies work as taking place in what Penny Lewis calls the "transitional space of the imaginal realm" (1988, 1993), I have to admit my colleague on Ward 13, unawares, may have been pointing in the right direction–the shamanic background of demon exorcism in shamanic healing rituals.

With the film production that actualized the mythic content of his fantasies, Theo became more energized and more socially interactive. His creativity and self-expression were enhanced, and he seemed to have less fear of the world. He co-wrote and acted in scenes; he wrote and sang seven original songs. His lyrics were plaintive, poignant, haunting. He seemed to be reaching out to the world, trying to make contact. The ritual performance of the film-making served as a bridge. The scenes were ritualistically enacted. For instance, in the role of the film's protagonist, Tom, Theo was tied up by the demons, released, and then tied up again. Finally, sitting, bound with ropes on the top of a hill, he sang:

> I'm stuck on a mountain
> Dreaming of you . . .
> I'm stuck on a mountain
> Waiting for you . . .
> And if you ever dare
> You will see me there.
> Then, I'm stuck on the mountain
> Dreaming of you . . .
> (filmscript A)

A sense of Theo's inner landscape is embodied, exteriorized and frozen in time in this film. His performance allowed him to externalize some small piece of his inner world. This contact, on the plane of fantasy, was repeated in the everyday reality of the ward: he made friends with the ward custodian. A little progress in a life that had been harshly isolated and profoundly defended by paranoid ideation.

Although this example represents only partial success, it seems to suggest the potential efficacy of the performative drama therapy model defined in the previous section. The contact with and embodiment of the archetypal affect-images appeared to guide this patient towards decreasing social isolation, better communication, increased reality testing and improvement of self-image through the completion of the task of performing what he had created. As Jacobi writes:

> The motifs of the archetypal images correspond to the part of man's make-up that is conditioned by phylogeny, and they are the same in all cultures. We find them recurring in all mythologies, fairy tales, religious traditions and mysteries. . . . In every single individual psyche they can awaken new life, exert their magic power, and condense into a kind of 'individual mythology'. . . . To open upon this store in one's own psyche, to awaken it to new life and integrate it with consciousness, means nothing less than to save the individual from his isolation and gather him into the eternal cosmic process. . . . The archetype as the primal source of all human experience lies in the unconscious, whence it reaches into our lives. Thus it becomes imperative to resolve its projections, to raise it contents to consciousness. (1962, pp. 47–49)

For individuals possessed by the mythic seizure, the embodiment of the archetype, framed in a ritual dramatic performance, can serve to structure and organize the psychotic experience that threatens to tear them apart. For people who have had their self-image wounded by social stigmatization or neglect, the contact with the powerful archetypal symbols, especially when contained in a performance, can lift them up and empower them.

Developmentally Disabled

Timothy had been an extremely abused child. Born with a developmental disability, he had been rejected by parents whom he had never known. He had been placed in a number of foster homes and, on several occasions, he was beaten by his supposed caretakers. By the time he was an adolescent, he was almost completely shut down emotionally. When I first met him, he was terribly insecure, with a constant need to prove himself. However, I noticed he also had a genuine aesthetic sensibility and a real talent for dramatic improvisation. I cast him in the lead role in a production called *Oh! That Aladdin . . .*, the culmination of a drama workshop that was part of the Drama Experiences for Special Populations course at Concordia University. This course brought together 20 university students and

20 developmentally disabled adults.[3] I believe that Timothy's contact with the numinous symbols of the great Persian fairy tale, on which the play was based, had a truly transformative effect upon his self-image. This ancient story embodies the essential hero myth that is at the heart of so many of the classic fairy tales. As Bettelheim (1975) tells us, ". . . fairy stories represent in imaginative form what the process of healthy human development consists of . . ." (p.12). This story is particularly inspiring and hopeful. In the beginning, Aladdin is a selfish little wretch, a street rat, laughed at and scorned by his neighbors. However, through his own courage and hard work, he is elevated to the position of a prince. This story seems to be the perfect therapeutic vehicle for persons with developmental disabilities, who are often themselves the object of scorn and ridicule. Timothy was truly beautiful in this role. He paralleled Aladdin's bravery and industriousness with the enormous amount of hard work and commitment he put into developing his performance. This subtext played to the audience. In the first performance, in 1994, after Aladdin defeats the Evil Magician and wins back his princess, Timothy sang the following song:

> I am someone
> Can you see
> I am someone
> Special
> . . . Maybe you
> Know someone too
> . . . And I see
> You are special and I see
> We are all so special."
> (Oh! That Aladdin . . . , 1994)

Although this was not the end of the play, the entire audience of about 400 people spontaneously stood up after the song was over, and gave Timothy and the cast a standing ovation. Five years later, Timothy reflected on this moment as a powerful validation of his personhood. He had been opened emotionally for singing through his work with the music therapist/musical director, in her role as vocal coach. The authenticity with which he sang this song was remarkable. The story of this hero, who begins in the gutter, perseveres and, finally, finds his true happiness showed Timothy that real change was possible in his own life. He stated: "It shows that you're able to change the situation that you are in. You can actually reverse it, from being bad to being good. Show people you're actually capable of doing . . . by expressing yourself, telling or showing people" (Interview, October 1999).

The standing ovation at the end of the song was a confirmation of the therapeutic exclamation: "See, I'm able!" Certainly, it imprinted that message in the consciousness of Timothy and the rest of the cast.

I suggest that this theatrical embodiment of the powerful archetypal symbols and meanings in Aladdin go far beyond the verification of capability, the *reality principle* which, in Bettelheim's view, stories like this make manifest: "Fairy tales depict an ego integration which allows for appropriate satisfaction of id desires" (1977, p. 41). Genuine fairy tales can serve as powerful agents of healing. Well-known storyteller and author Clarissa Pinkola Estes (1992) made the claim that these stories are actually medicine. In his essay on *The Phenomenology of the Spirit in Fairy Tales,* Jung describes the spiritual presence of the archetypes of the Spirit in fairy tales and the life-enhancing power of these

---

3. Also known as the Aladdin Project (www.cahd.net), this was the beginning of the Centre for the Arts in Human Development at Concordia University (Montreal).

affect-images (in de Laszlo 1958, pp. 61–112). This force is even more potent when the images are embodied through the drama. I think of Timothy in the "Cave of Wonders," that brilliant symbol for the unconscious, and how that symbol must have resonated with his own courageous adventure as a neophyte actor, his own exploration of himself as a hero. The experience of entering this role as the container for the archetypal motif of the hero's journey must have carried for Timothy a little of what Jung meant when he said, "Experience of the archetype is not only impressive, it seizes and possesses the whole personality, and is naturally productive of faith" (1956, p. 232). It surely provided Timothy with what Jacobi describes as ". . . awakening of new life," in experiencing a whole new sense of self.

The Wizard of Oz Production

Perhaps there is no more archetypal story among modern-day fairy tales than L. Frank Baum's *The Wizard of Oz.* As Madonna Kolbenschlag (1994) writes in her wonderful book about the orphan archetype: "The Wizard of Oz is exceptionally endowed with an intuitive representation of both psychological and cultural myth–it has a power of metaphor and symbol that derives from unconscious rather than conscious design. Indeed, it is an extraordinary metaphor for transformation, and Dorothy is the classic archetype of the spiritual orphan" (p. 18).

The Oz books, especially the second, became the material for the first therapeutic theatre production at the Centre for the Arts in Human Development at Concordia University in Montreal. The image of the orphan swept up in a cyclone and carried on an incredible hero's adventure seemed to be another ideal vehicle for a therapeutic exploration via theatre. The orphan archetype has great resonance for many of our developmentally disabled clients at the Centre.

We began our process with improvisations on images and themes in the story. I wanted to see which characters clients would take; also what kinds of imaginary additions might be made by the participants. I will report briefly on two successful examples of role-taking and how and why these roles were particularly therapeutically valuable for one individual.

Autism

Jane was an extremely anxious person. Diagnosed with autistic features (there had been an earlier diagnosis of schizophrenia), she periodically had major panic attacks, even going so far as to strike herself in the face. She could become hysterical and scream and shout. Interestingly, it was her creativity in improvisation that led us to discovering the central metaphor for our play production. Through improvisation, Jane created a new character, not found in the original stories of Oz. Her name was Winda, Queen of the Wind. As director, I began to see how the image of the wind guided the whole story. Jane's contribution to the development of the production was essential and her invented character became a cornerstone of our new version, entitled *The Winds of Oz.* Winda brought on the cyclone, blew the Wizard away in his hot air balloon and helped Dorothy return to Kansas. It was a very empowering role for Jane and she really enjoyed making a unique creative contribution to the ritual process of constructing the play. She reports in an interview (November 1997):

Q: Is there anything about the experience you think changed you?

A: It made me a calmer person. . . . It made me happy, feel good, give a good performance, loving it so much, liking it.

Q: And that made you feel calm?

A: Yup.

Q: Would you like to do a play, again?

A: Yup. But not the Wind. I want to be Fire.

Jane has a wonderful sense of humor and this role gave her a chance to express herself (even to the point of improvising some bawdy puns concerning the wind), and to be in a symbolically empowered position. She felt very confirmed in her talents and uniqueness.

Williams Syndrome

Laura was a special case, as her syndrome, besides bringing her some intellectual and cognitive challenges, also brought her a gift. It seems that many individuals with Williams Syndrome are musically talented (Levitin, Cole, Chiles, Lai, Lincoln, & Bellugi, 2004). At the age of seven, she still had trouble tying her own shoelaces, but she could hear a melody on the radio and immediately play it back on the little keyboard her parents had given to her. She was blessed with a great musical ear and a fine singing voice. By the age of twenty, when she entered the Centre, she had decided she wanted to sing and perform for the public. So, for our production of *And Alice Dreams* (2000), we cast Laura in the role of Alice and gave her fictional character the same desire she had in real life. Laura gave an outstanding performance. Here are some of her responses to her performance in *And Alice Dreams . . .*, taken from a recent interview (July 2007):

Q: Did it [playing the role of Alice] help you in becoming a singer?

A: It was a little scary at first, but I got through it . . . to recognize what songs I'm doin', what stuff I have to memorize . . . the role of what I have to, you know . . . and people like Julie Andrews, okay, she had to memorize *hers* because she can't sing anymore, poor soul . . . I think I was nervous going on the stage.

Q: Did it help you to become more confident playing that role?

A: Yup. It has because . . . 'cause it helped me a lot of what, like what kind of am I doing as Alice. How am I doing this right? How am I doing it wrong?

Q: Since playing that role, way back in June 2000, you went on to sing in Hollywood and Las Vegas. Did playing the role of Alice help you?

A: It did . . . to make sure I know the words right, to know the way *why* I am doing this song. 'Cause I wanna do it for some people that I know . . . I just think it was just scary at first, but I was just calm and just went on the stage. I mean that was a fun role for me . . . being so happy to be on the stage. Yep! . . . Like I could put a smile on peoples face in knowing what I wanted to do!

Indeed, in the months following the performance, Laura did what she wanted to do. She went on to sing in Hollywood and Las Vegas for benefits for the Lilly Claire Foundation, an organization that raises money for Williams Syndrome. Laura also went on to study music at the Berkshire Music Academy, a school in western Massachusetts that specializes in young people who have cognitive impairments and a talent for music. Laura has been the subject of a number of TV specials, such as David Suzuki's *The Nature of Things,* and has also been working with a neuropsychologist at

McGill University who does research on Williams Syndrome. Equally important, she has been pursuing her dream of singing and performing for people, studying with an excellent professional voice coach and singing at every possible opportunity, including a benefit concert with professionals like the Savoy Ellingtons, Livingston Taylor and Ranee Lee. She is living proof of what is possible when a person believes "I Can!"

Severe Anxiety

Nancy's is a success story of a different kind. She entered The Centre for the Arts in Human Development with a bundle of fears, suffering from severe anxiety, and with a very rigid personality. She couldn't be in spaces where there were fresh-cut flowers. They made her anxious. She expressed fear and hostility towards the participants with Down's Syndrome, because "the way their eyes look" made her believe they were making faces at her. She did not identify with her peers in the program. Cast as the Blue Fairy in the Centre's 2002 therapeutic theatre production, *The Legend of Pinocchio,* she made great progress (Figure 7.4):

> . . . by the end of the play production, she felt the experience had taught her that she "can be friendly and helping towards others." She loved the fact that, as the Blue Fairy, she was the one that finally helped Pinocchio to become "real." She became a fully integrated member of the cast and made notable improvements in her spontaneity, creativity and self-expression. (Snow et al., 2003, p. 78)

The therapeutic goals set for her, after her initial interview and assessment at the Centre, were accomplished through her participation in the theatre production: improved social skills, gains in self-esteem, learning to set boundaries, and developing and maintaining friendships.

So for Jane, Timothy, Laura and Nancy,

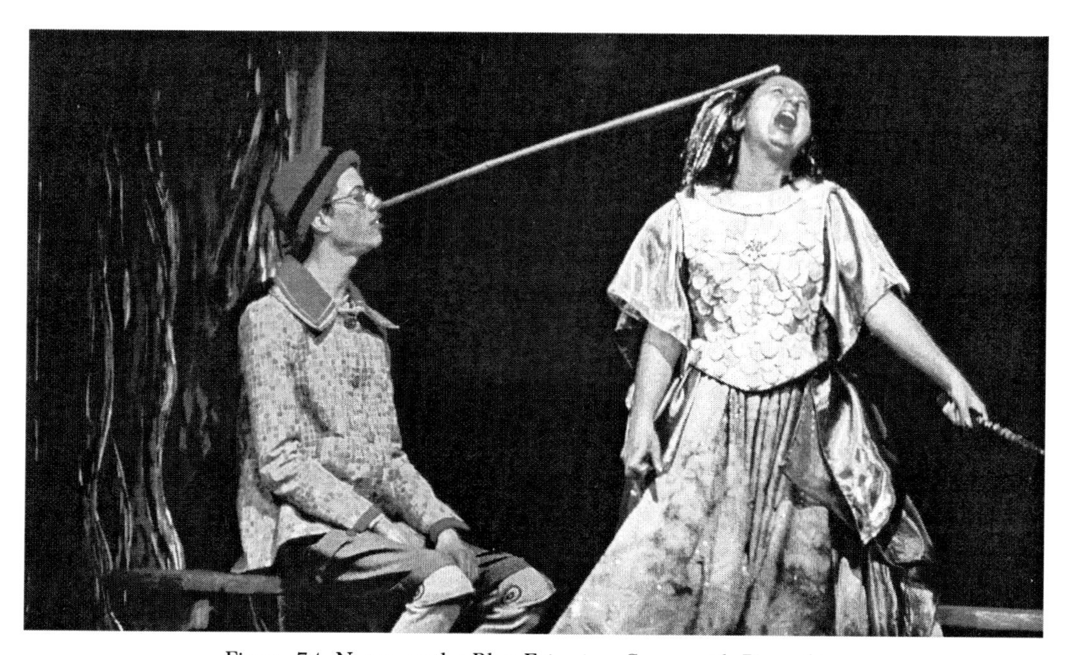

Figure 7.4. Nancy as the Blue Fairy in a Scene with Pinocchio.

their roles became a way to ameliorate negative self-images, as well as cognitive and psychological challenges.

For those in our society who have been severely stigmatized, the applause at the end of a theatrical performance has a special meaning. As Emunah and Johnson (1983) have clearly demonstrated, performances can have a powerful positive impact on the self-images of performers. Emunah states elsewhere:

> For the actors, the sense of kinship and shared emotionality with the audience brings about a sense of connectedness. The connectedness is especially significant for those who have experienced themselves as different or alien, who have been institutionalized or segregated. The combination of the feelings of connectedness, accomplishment, and acceptance, in conjunction with the ensuing rush of love for one's fellow actors and director with whom one has shared the entire journey, is awesome. As the actors walk off stage, with the applause of the audience still flooding their ears, they experience a rare and sacred sensation: glory. (1994, p. 294)

This is the culmination of all the hard work and all the unique contributions that every individual has given to the production. It has been a journey and a rite of passage. The applause is a confirmation that it has been worthwhile, and that the parts of oneself that one has shared with the world have been accepted. Fortunately, as we developed this therapeutic theatre work at the Centre, we also evolved methods of assessing its efficacy. For the 2002 production of the *Legend of Pinocchio,* we implemented both ongoing documentation and pre- and post-interviews. The results of this qualitative evaluation demonstrated that many of the therapeutic values we wished to instill through our *therapeutic theatre* work had, indeed, been realized (Snow et al., 2003, p. 83).

CONCLUSION

The roots of the therapeutic uses of performance are ancient and go deep into the history of our collective human experience. Theatre has its origin in ritual, most especially in the shamanic dramatic rituals in which disease-causing spirits were embodied and exorcised. In many cultures, shamans were and are known as the "masters of spirits." Actors who become possessed by the spirit of a character are also a kind of master of spirits, but their function is aesthetic, educational or for the purpose of entertainment. As Pendzik (1988) has pointed out, drama therapists are more like shamans because we assist our clients to master spirits through the various media of drama and theatre. One approach is through performance itself. I have defined this as the performative frame of drama therapy. Emunah (1994) has commented that the use of performance in drama therapy can at times be even more effective than process-oriented drama therapy. This chapter has attempted to demonstrate a theoretical basis for why this is so, at least within a style of practice that I have developed over the past quarter century. One of my major themes has been to elucidate how the evocation and embodiment of archetypes in the construction and enactment of various kinds of performances can serve as healing ritual dramas for patient/actors. I believe that the spontaneous archetypal material that sometimes emerges in persons undergoing psychotic episodes can be contained and restructured through the process of performance-making. I also maintain that archetypically symbolic roles can serve as containers and assist to some degree in the reconstruction of wounded self-concepts. Performative drama therapy, within a Ritual/Theatre/Therapy context, is a viable therapy for many different populations.

Certainly, I am not the only drama therapist to use theatrical performance and theatrical methods to assist clients in developing themselves and to work through the pathological aspects of their personalities. The work of Emunah, Johnson and Landy has already been cited. I would also like to mention the important work of British drama therapist Steve Mitchell whose Therapeutic Theatre is modeled on the paratheatrical explorations of Grotowski (Mitchell in Jennings, 1992, Mitchell, 1996, 1998). Drama therapists Miller James and Cecilia Dintino have also effectively utilized theatre productions as therapy with veterans with posttraumatic stress disorder. Finally, my colleague and friend, the Canadian drama therapist Barbara Mackay has made use of ritual and performance in her work with different populations (Mackay, Gold, & Gold, 1987; Mackay in Gersie, 1996; Mackay, 1989).

As the field of drama therapy develops, increasingly refined perspectives and methodologies emerge in the use of drama as a therapeutic tool. I have attempted to articulate the context for and the application of my own particular approach to performative drama therapy. It is still in a process of evolution. My hope is that my words will be both evocative and provocative for the reader: evoking the genuine powers of our ancient heritage in the human utilization of drama for healing, and provoking the reader to think deeply about how we can further develop the dramatic tools we have inherited for the future benefit of human beings in need of healing.

I am still very excited about the many ways in which performance and the development of theatre productions can be shaped as vehicles for therapy. I am presently looking forward to developing therapeutic theatre in relation to *performance ethnography* at the Centre for the Arts in Human Development at Concordia University. Our most recent production (June 2007) of a *musical ethnodrama* has shown great promise in integrating the therapeutic goals of performative drama therapy with the emancipatory goals of ethnodrama. I am looking forward to what may evolve as we explore, as co-researchers, therapists and theatre artists, the narratives of clients' lived experience, by way of developing a ritual of renewal via the construction of a dramatic performance.

REFERENCES

Amorim, A.C., & Cavalcante, F.G. (1992). Narrations of the self: Video production in a marginalized subculture. In S. McNamee, J. Gergen, (Eds.). *Therapy as social construction* (pp. 149–165). London: Sage Publications, Ltd.

Bates, B. (1987). *The way of the actor: A path to knowledge and power.* Boston: Shambhala.

Bettleheim, B. (1977). *The uses of enchantment: The meaning and importance of fairy tales.* New York: Vintage Books.

Campbell, J. (1949). *The hero with a thousand faces.* Princeton: Princeton University Press.

Charles, L.H. (1953). Drama in shaman exorcism. *Journal of American Folklore, 66,* 95–122.

Charnow, S., Nash, E., & Perlstein, S. (1988). *Life Review Training Manual.* Brooklyn, N.Y.: Elders Share the Arts, Inc.

Cole, D. (1975). *The theatrical event: A mythos, a vocabulary, a perspective.* Middletown, CT: Wesleyan University Press.

D'Amico, M., Barrafato, A., & Varga, S. (1998). The Centre for the Arts in Human Development. Unpublished progress report 1996–1998. Montreal: Concordia University.

Denzin, N.K. (2003). *Performance ethnography: Critical pedagogy and the politics of culture.* London: Sage Publications.

Eliade, M. (1964). *Shamanism: Archaic techniques of ecstasy.* Princeton: Princeton University Press.

Ellenberger, H. (1970). *The discovery of the unconscious.* New York: Basic Books, Inc.

Emunah, R., & Johnson, D.R. (1983). The impact of theatrical performance on the self-images of psychiatric patients. *The Arts in Psychotherapy,*

10, 233–239.

Emunah, R. (1994). *Acting for real: Drama therapy, process, technique and performance.* New York: Brunner/Mazel Publishers.

Epstein, M. (1995). *Thoughts without a thinker: Psychotherapy from a Buddhist perspective.* New York: Basic Books.

Glaser, B. (2004). Ancient traditions within a new drama therapy method: Shamanism and developmental transformations. *The Arts in Psychotherapy, 31,* 77–88.

Grof, C., & Grof, S. (1986). Spiritual emergency: Understanding and treatment of transpersonal crisis. *Revision, 8,* 7–20.

Halifax, J. (1982). *Shaman: Wounded healer.* London: Thames and Hudson, Ltd.

Harner, M. (1980). *The way of the shaman: A guide to power and healing.* New York: Bantam Books.

Jacobi, J. (1959). *Complex/archetype/symbol in the psychology of C.G. Jung.* Princeton: Princeton University Press.

Jacobi, J. (1962). *The psychology of C.G. Jung.* New Haven: Yale University Press.

Johnson, D.R. (1981). Drama therapy and the schizophrenic condition. In G. Schattner & R. Courtney, (Eds). *Drama therapy, Vol. 2* (pp. 47–64). New York: Drama Book Specialists.

Johnson, D.R. (1988). The diagnostic role-playing test. *The Arts in Psychotherapy, 15,* 23–36.

Jones, P. (1996). *Drama as therapy: Theatre as living.* London: Routledge.

Jones, P. (2007). *Drama as therapy: Theory, practice, and research.* London: Routledge.

Jung, C.G. ([1936] 1970). *The psychology of dementia praecox.* New York: Johnson Reprint Corp.

Jung, C.G. ([1956] 1970). *Symbols of transformation.* Princeton: Princeton University Press.

Jung, C.G. (1958). The phenomenology of the spirit in fairy tales. In V. De Laszlo (Ed.), *Psyche & symbol* (pp. 61–112). Garden City, N.Y: Doubleday Anchor Books.

Jung, C.G. (1958). The psychology of the child archetype. In V. De Laszlo (Ed.), *Psyche & symbol* (pp. 113–131). Garden City, N.Y: Doubleday Anchor Books.

Keeney, B. (2005). *Bushman shaman: Awakening the spirit through ecstatic dance.* Rochester, VT: Destiny Books.

Kirby, M. (1975). *The ur-drama: The origins of the theatre.* New York: New York University Press.

Klepac, R. (1978). Through the looking glass: Sociodrama and mentally retarded individuals. *Mental retardation, 16*(5), 1343–345.

Kolbenschlag, M. (1994). *Lost in the land of Oz.* New York: Crossroad.

Laing, R.D. (1967). *The politics of experience.* New York: Ballantine Books.

Landy, R. (1983). The use of distancing in drama therapy. *The Arts in Psychotherapy, 10,* 175–185.

Landy, R. (1986). *Drama therapy: Concepts and practices.* Springfield, IL: Charles C Thomas Publishers.

Landy, R. (1993). *Persona and performance: The meaning of role in drama, therapy and everyday life.* New York: Guilford Press.

Larsen, S. (1976). *The shaman's doorway: Opening the mythic imagination to contemporary consciousness.* New York: Harper Colophon Books.

Levitin, D.J., Cole, K., Chiles, M., Lai, Z., Lincoln, A., & Bellugi, U. (2004). Characterizing the musical phenotype in individuals with Williams Syndrome. *Child Neuropsychology, 10*(4), 223–247.

Lewis, P. (1988). Transformative process within the imaginal realm. *The Arts in Psychotherapy, 15*(4), 309–316.

Lewis, P. (1993). *Creative transformations: The healing power of the arts.* Wilmette, IL: Chiron Publications.

Lommel, A. (1972). *Masks: Their meaning and function* (N. Fowler, Trans.). New York: McGraw-Hill.

Lukoff, D. (1990). Divine madness: Shamanistic initiatory crisis and psychosis. *Shaman's Drum, 22,* 24–29.

Mackay, B., Gold, M., & Gold, E. (1987). A pilot study in drama therapy with adolescent girls who have been sexually abused. *The Arts in Psychotherapy, 14,* 77–87.

Mackay, B. (1989). Drama therapy with female victims of assault. *The Arts in Psychotherapy, 16,* 293–300.

Mackay, B. (1996). Brief drama therapy and the collective creation. In A. Gersie (Ed.), *Dramatic approaches to brief drama therapy* (pp. 161–174). London: Jessica Kingsley.

Mehl-Madronna, L. (1997). *Coyote medicine.* New York: Scribner.

Mitchell, S. (1992). Therapeutic theatre. In S. Jennings (Ed.), *Dramatherapy: Theory and practice 2* (pp. 51–67). London: Routledge.
Mitchell, S. (1996). (Ed.). *Dramatherapy clinical studies.* London: Jessica Kingsley.
Mitchell, S. (1998). The theatre of self-expression. *Dramatherapy 20*(1), Spring 1998.
Neumann, E. (1954). *The origins and history of consciousness.* Princeton: Princeton University Press.
Pendzik, S. (1988). Drama therapy as a form of modern shamanism. *Journal of Transpersonal Psychology 20*(1), 81–92.
Perry, J.W. ([1953] 1987). *The self in psychotic process: Its symbolization in schizophrenia.* Texas: Spring Publications, Inc.
Perry, J.W. (1974). *The far side of madness.* Englewood Cliffs, N.J.: Prentice-Hall, Inc.
Perry, J.W. (1976). *Roots of the renewal process in myth and madness.* San Francisco: Jossey-Bass.
Pinkola Estes, C. (1992). *Women who run with the wolves: Myths and stories of the wild women archetype.* New York: Ballantine Books.
Ross, A. (1992). *The sense of self: Research and theory.* New York: Springer Publishing Company.
Schechner, R. (1977). *Essays in performance theory 1970–1976.* New York: Drama Book Specialists.
Schechner, R. (1981). Restoration of behavior. *Studies in Visual Communication, 7*(3), 2–45.
Schechner, R. (1985). *Between theatre and anthropology.* Philadelphia: University of Pennsylvania Press.
Shirokogoroff, S.M. (1935). *Psychomental complex of the Tungus.* London: Kegan, Paul, Trench, Tauber & Co., Ltd.
Snow, S. (1983). Rangda: archetype in action in Balinese dance drama. In J. Redman (Ed.), *Themes in drama 5* (pp. 273–291). Cambridge: Cambridge University Press.
Snow, S. (1989). *Theatrical outreach by the elderly: The value of sharing life stories through Living History Theatre.* Unpublished manuscript.
Snow, S. (1991). Working creatively with the symbolic process of the schizophrenic patient in drama therapy. In G. Wilson (Ed.), *Psychology and the performing arts* (pp. 261–268). Amsterdam: Swets & Zeitlinger.
Snow, S. (1996a). Focusing on mythic imagery in brief drama therapy with psychotic individuals. In A. Gersie (Ed.), *Dramatic approaches to brief therapy* (pp. 216–235). London: Jessica Kingsley.
Snow, S. (1996b). Fruit of the same tree: A response to Kedem-Tahar and Kellermann's comparison of psychodrama and drama therapy. *The Arts in Psychotherapy, 23*(3), 199–205.
Snow, S., D'Amico, M., & Tanguay, D. (2003). Therapeutic theatre and well being. *The Arts in Psychotherapy, 30*(2), 73–82.
Snow, S. (2005, September). The evolution and emergence of drama therapy. Paper presented at the XIII World Congress of Psychiatry. Cairo, Egypt.
Sullivan, B. (1987). The archetypal foundation of the therapeutic process. In N. Schwartz-Salant & M. Stein (Eds.), *Archetypal processes in psychotherapy* (pp. 27–50). Wilmette, IL: Chiron Press.
Turner, V. (1982). *From ritual to theatre: The human seriousness of play.* New York: Performing Arts Journal Publications.

BIBLIOGRAPHY, VIDEOGRAPHY, ARCHIVAL, AND INTERVIEWS

Scripts

Filmscript A (1988). *Rocky Roads.* Bronx Psychiatric Centre. Bronx, New York.
Playscript A (1990). "The Energy Creature and His Friends." Bronx Psychiatric Centre, Bronx, New York.
Snow, S. (1994). *Oh! That Aladdin!* (All lyrics by Roger Jay). The Centre for the Arts in Human.Development, Concordia University, Montreal.
Snow, S. (1997). *The Winds of Oz* (All lyrics by Roger Jay). The Centre for the Arts in Human Development, Concordia Universtiy, Montreal.
Snow, S. (2000). *And Alice Dreams* (All lyrics by Roger Jay). The Centre for the Arts in Human Development, Concordia University, Montreal.
Snow, S. (2002). *The Legend of Pinocchio* (Lyrics by

Jeremy Bouchard, Gillian Street and Stephen Snow). The Centre for the Arts in Human Development, Concordia University, Montreal.

Videography

Documentary: The Centre for the Arts in Human Development at Concordia University. Producers: Frank Roop and Stephen Snow. Montreal, 1996.

Archival: *Oh! That Aladdin.* 1994, 1995. Concordia University, Montreal

Archival: *The Winds of Oz.* 1997, 1998. Concordia University, Montreal

Archival: *And Alice Dreams.* 2000, Concordia University, Montreal

Archival: *The Legend of Pinocchio.* 2002, Concordia University, Montreal

Documentary: *The Alice Project: Creative Arts Therapy in Action.* Producer/Director: Phil Herbison, 2003, Montreal. Distributor, Films for the Humanities and Sciences at: www.films.com.id/13314/The_Alice_Project_Human_Development_in_Action

FURTHER TRAINING

Stephen Snow, Ph.D., RDT-BCT, Co-founder
Chair, Department of Creative Arts Therapies
Drama Therapy Graduate Program
Concordia University
1455 de Maisonnueve Blvd. West
Montreal, Quebec H3G 1M8
Program Inquiry: 514-848-2424 Ext. 5214 or
infodt@concordia.ca
Program website:
http://creativeartstherapies.concordia.ca

Chapter 8

HEALING THE WOUNDS OF HISTORY: DRAMA THERAPY IN COLLECTIVE TRAUMA AND INTERCULTURAL CONFLICT RESOLUTION

ARMAND VOLKAS

In 1995, fifty years after the end of World War II, I made a pilgrimage to Auschwitz concentration camp where both of my parents had been imprisoned for more than two years. I saw Block 10, where sterilization experiments had been performed on Jewish women, including my mother, by the infamous Dr. Klauber. I saw the location where my father had worked processing the confiscated clothes, shoes and other belongings of people sent to labor camps or to their death by the Nazis. I visited the gas chambers. In the adjacent Birkenau concentration camp, I wandered around the area they call "the burning fields." At a point near the end of the war, there were so many transports bringing in Jews to be exterminated that the gas chambers were operating 24 hours a day. The crematoria couldn't dispose of the corpses fast enough. The Nazis ordered the camp inmates to create huge mountains of bodies and set them on fire. The bodies burned for weeks. The ashes were put in the nearby ponds and spread around the surrounding terrain. What struck me, wandering around the former burning fields in the summer of 1995, was the fact that they were alive with the most beautiful wildflowers I had ever seen. I was moved by the way that nature was able to transform the results of such horror into beauty. This transformative principle that I observed so profoundly in nature guides my work as a drama therapist.

In my journey to reconcile my own past as the son of Jewish WWII resistance fighters and survivors of Auschwitz concentration camps, I have sought to understand how nations and cultures integrate a heritage of perpetration, victimization and collective trauma. I have endeavored to comprehend how collective trauma is passed from generation to generation. I have also committed myself as a psychotherapist to developing an arts-oriented approach to working with intercultural conflict resolution in which collective trauma plays a primary role. Considering the number of seemingly intractable intercultural conflicts that plague the world, it is critical that we find innovative ways to address the impact that this trauma has on the personal and collective psyche. The techniques of drama therapy, with all of their transformative potential, are powerful tools in moving towards ending the cycle of re-traumatization and perpetration.

Healing the Wounds of History (originally called *Acts of Reconciliation*) began as a drama therapy process in which I used theatre techniques to work with a group of participants from two cultures with a common legacy of conflict and historical trauma. I first used this process in 1989 with sons and daughters of Jewish Holocaust survivors and Nazis. I subsequently used it with many other cultures in conflict, most recently with Israelis and Palestinians, Armenians and Turks on the legacy of genocide, and Japanese, Chinese and Koreans on the impact of Japanese perpetration during WWII. This work has evolved into several related applications: a workshop that focuses on a single trauma and its impact on a group of people or nation, a more general workshop open to persons of diverse cultures who wish to explore their legacy of historical trauma, therapeutic sessions with an individual, couple or family for whom historical trauma is a defining event, a process lasting several days bringing together participants from two cultures with a shared legacy of conflict and trauma and lastly, a *Playback Theatre* (Fox, 1986; Chapter 20) performance that follows such an intensive workshop in which workshop participants and audience volunteers share personal stories related to the historical trauma in question. This chapter will focus on the latter two applications.

THEORY AND PRINCIPLES

Healing the Wounds of History (hereafter HWH) is based on several premises:

1. Collective trauma is a psychological state shared by any group of people and can affect even an entire society. Examples in the United States include the events of 9/11, Hurricane Katrina and the Vietnam War. The impact of collective trauma is carried in our psyches in the form of images, stories, sense memories, spoken and unspoken messages transmitted by parents, teachers and the media. Ultimately, this process evolves into a collective narrative. This narrative is absorbed unconsciously through a process akin to osmosis and has an impact on the cultural and national identity of the individual and the group.
2. The transgenerational transmission of trauma is a real phenomenon observable in the United States in cultures such as African-Americans and Native Americans where the continuing destructive impact of slavery and genocide is visible centuries after the original atrocities took place. Historical trauma is also transmitted intergenerationally from parent to child where a father's alcoholism or depression, for example, may be directly due to the unresolved PTSD of his experience in the Vietnam War, but the historical and collective aspect of the trauma is never fully addressed. The inheritor of such a legacy receives the parent's trauma as a burden of unexpressed grief, often out of their conscious awareness (Ancelin Schutzenberger, 1998).
3. Historical trauma can also have negative effects on cultural and national identity and self-esteem. Human beings are tribal in nature and have a need to feel good about the tribe to which they belong. When this pride of association is disrupted through a history of war trauma, humiliation, defeat, or subjugation, it negatively affects the collective self-regard in the form of in-

ternalized oppression. This can influence the way individuals view or value their own culture (Grier & Cobbs, 1968; Klein, 1980).

4. Healing the Wounds of History takes the view that there is a potential perpetrator in all of us and that under certain circumstances every human being has the capacity for dehumanization and cruelty.
5. There can be no permanent political solutions to intercultural conflict until we understand and take into consideration the needs, emotions and unconscious drives of the human being.

By working with the specific participants who are representatives of their cultures, I seek to make a therapeutic intervention in the collective or societal trauma. In this way my work is related philosophically to *Psychodrama's* founder Jacob Moreno's idea that, "A truly therapeutic procedure cannot have less an objective than the whole of mankind." (Moreno, 1953; Chapter 18). HWH, which takes a psychological approach to conflict, provides a map to help polarized groups traverse the emotional terrain to reconciliation. In this sense the approach is a form of social activism.

THERAPEUTIC GOALS

This work has five important therapeutic goals: The first involves recognizing and deconstructing cultural or national identity. I support workshop participants in reflecting on their cultural identity or identities with the goal of working through obstacles to their self-esteem. Within each person's constructed identity lie cracks that hold the fragments of their collective story. Feelings, associations, formative sense and affective memories emerge from its deconstruction. Often it is the member of the family who has been designated consciously or unconsciously as the carrier of the family legacy who shows up in the workshop. In other cases, the collective trauma has gone underground. Due to the assimilation or the silence of a traumatized parent, the family legacy is hidden from the participant's awareness. In the end, my goal is to help participants uncover the collective story of perpetration or victimization they may be carrying and help them integrate their legacies in a more generative way.

The second goal involves intercultural conflict resolution and teaching intercultural communication. Often there is a taboo against speaking to the other. People from polarized cultures so stereotype, dehumanize or demonize each other that the simple act of talking can be an important step towards healing. There can also exist a lack of authentic understanding of the other culture or empathy for their emotional or political stances. Through the self-revealing, storytelling and playful aspects of the Healing the Wounds of History process the tension between the opposing groups is momentarily eased. Enemies are humanized. This creates enough emotional generosity and psychic space to allow participants to begin to make cultural adaptations with the help of mediation. For the facilitator, all of the principles and elements of conflict resolution come into play at this stage, including effective listening, an empathetic and nondefensive stance and an understanding of the art of apology.

The third goal is to help participants move deeply into and experience their personal and collective grief and mourning. As I guide participants through the HWH process there is a well of grief that will eventually be tapped into. Even if not displayed or acknowledged at the beginning of a workshop, I am always aware of its presence. The collective grief of the participants' parents, grandparents, ancestors and culture as a whole is implied by the very act of our coming together. This grief may be related to victimization or to perpetration, or, more likely, both. Each traumatized group has a need to experience this inherited pain as unique. The added dimension of groups in conflict, sometimes perpetrators and victims grieving together, can have a profound, cathartic effect. Participants, as representatives of their cultures, are given the opportunity to give shape and expression to this collective grief, the principle being that, until that pain is grieved fully, the legacy will continue to be passed on to the next generation (Kellermann, 2007).

The fourth goal is to create a culture of empathy. At its core, HWH is about teaching empathy. Workshop participants develop the capacity for feeling compassion for the pain of the other group and transcend the impulse to view one's own suffering as superior. This helps to create paradoxical feelings that participants must resolve. How can I hate this person and have empathy for him or her at the same time?

The fifth goal is to create meaning out of suffering. A healthy human being needs to create purpose and meaning out of his or her life (Frankl, 1984). Suffering is a great teacher. When there is a legacy of trauma, shame, guilt and humiliation, the task is to transform it into meaning. This is a spiritual task. How can one create meaning out of the meaningless events such as the Holocaust? The way to master suffering is to create acts of service and acts of creation.

METHODS AND TECHNIQUES

Drama Therapy in Intercultural Conflict Resolution

In working with polarized groups over the last 18 years I have identified six phases that can develop in a multiday workshop. These phases do not necessarily emerge in a progressive way but depend on the given circumstances of the group process including a feeling of safety, cultural influences and the amount of emotional and aesthetic distance from the collective trauma.

Phases of the Process

The first phase in bringing cultures in conflict together is breaking the taboo against speaking to each other. Often there is an invisible barrier preventing contact. Speaking to the enemy is often perceived as a betrayal. But when two polarized groups break the taboo and engage in honest dialogue, they can begin to work through the layers of unresolved feelings they carry about each other. I work first with the emotional pioneers who pave the way for others to follow. The second phase involves humanizing each other through telling our stories. When members of cultures in conflict listen deeply to each other's stories and hear each other's pain, they begin to care about one another. Their feelings of empathy and friendship become more powerful than the historical imperative to hate one another.

When there is enough trust, I move into the third phase of exploring and owning the potential perpetrator in all of us. In order to reconcile, people need to acknowledge that under extreme circumstances, we all have the capacity for cruelty. Accepting this truth is the great equalizer. It levels the playing field.

The fourth phase is moving deeply into grief. Grieving together and giving each other permission to grieve is essential. People carry their parents', grandparents' and ancestors' pain, and that pain needs to be grieved in order to break the generational transmission of this pain.

The fifth phase moves towards creating integration, performances and rituals of remembrance. When groups in conflict create commemorative rituals and performances, privately and publicly, to acknowledge the complex, difficult history they share, they provide a way for people to channel their feelings in an aesthetic form. Public presentations serve to extend the healing effects of the reconciliation into society by touching the lives and consciousness of others who did not participate in the workshops.

The final phase of this process extends the learning achieved in the workshop out into the world, making commitments to acts of creation or acts of service. Creation can mean sharing stories, creating poetry, art, theatre and somehow transforming the pain of the past into an aesthetic form. Another mode is to channel the participants' energy into service: working with political refugees, helping survivors of rape, or doing other work that helps to end injustice or make reparation.

Breaking The Taboo Against Speaking To Each Other

The taboo against speaking to one another often comes into play prior to the beginning of the HWH encounter. Taking the step of meeting together is frequently seen as an act of defiance against the status quo. This stance requires courage on the part of participants. I describe these people who are willing to be the first to come to an encounter with the *other* as emotional pioneers paving the way for others to follow. The image of the Healing the Wounds of History facilitator as resistance fighter is apt here, for he or she is symbolically leading an insurgency movement against an entrenched and oppressive fear that is preventing reconciliation or peaceful co-existence.

When members of groups in conflict come together it can, in fact, involve real danger. In the early 1990s while working with a group of Palestinian and Israeli students at UC Berkeley, it was important to hold our meetings clandestinely. The Palestinians feared, if it were discovered by militant forces in the West Bank or Gaza that they were meeting with Israelis, that their families back home would be ostracized or killed. Similarly, in 2007 I recruited Turkish people to participate in a workshop and Playback Performance with Armenians on the legacy of the Armenian genocide. Turks feared that their government would arrest them for anti-Turkish activities when they returned to Turkey. The very act of meeting with Armenians around the issue of genocide might put them in violation of Article 301/1 of the Turkish Penal Code that outlaws public denigration of the Turkish Republic or "Turkishness." Facilitators must recognize the courage and danger sometimes involved in bringing together polarized groups and proceed ethically to protect participants from harm or at least ensure their informed consent to the risks involved.

My strategy as a drama therapist entering into a potentially explosive environment is to first develop the spontaneity and imagination of the group as a warm-up to the dramatic processes that will soon follow. The techniques I use correspond roughly to Renée Emunah's (Chapter 4) Phase I (dramatic play) and Phase II (scene work) of her *Integrative Five Phase Model*. The play has many functions in the context of intercultural conflict. It allows participants to connect as human beings and brings out their child ego state. They find commonalities in the state of play and communicate in nonthreatening ways. This starts to develop the bonds I will build upon later in the process.

Beginning to play can sometimes feel awkward for the facilitator to initiate in this context, as we are working with serious themes such as genocide and war trauma. However, generating playfulness in groups in conflict is an obligatory first step in establishing a beachhead in territory occupied by fear and mistrust. For many, permission to play is the perfect antidote to the burden of the imagery of collective trauma they have inherited. The parentified children within them are partially liberated by the process of reclaiming their lost innocence.

The techniques in this phase are familiar to most drama therapists and facilitators of theatre improvisation. A few are worth describing as their function changes in the context of working with collective trauma and intercultural conflict. I might begin a group with the simple name game in which participants say their names and articulate a movement at the same time that expresses how they are feeling in the moment. This might be followed by more sound-making exercises such as *Sound Ball* in which imaginary balls are thrown around a circle accompanied by creative sounds or *Sound and Movement Transformations,* originally described by Viola Spolin (1968), which allows sound and motion to transform into a new sound and motion which passes from one person to the next until everyone has had a turn.

These structured exercises prepare the participants for more challenging improvisations to come. They are also diagnostic of the group, for as facilitator I am assessing which of my arsenal of techniques participants will be able to tolerate and when. Improvisational space work, pantomime and sense memory are also important skills to develop early in the process. The act of taking an internal image and embodying it is an important building block in the development of a drama therapy process. Adult non-actors are often rusty at engaging in the activity of play that once flowed easily for them as children. Developing their ability to create imaginary external environments playfully also indirectly prepares them for "Psychodrama" (Chapter 18) or "Developmental Transformations" (Chapter 6) in developing the idea of a surplus reality or play-space.

Dramatic play evolves into scenework through exercises such as *Cross from Here to There* in which people cross the room one at a time and then two at a time using sound, movement, words and breaking into spontaneous scenes. The *Role Circle* divides participants into dyads and archetypal issues of power and powerlessness are introduced, to explore roles of authority and submission: Policeman and speeder, parent and adolescent, headmaster and delinquent student, captain and private. These give way to more psychodramatic scenes in which inanimate objects or abstractions can talk to each other: Person on a diet and piece of chocolate cake, cocaine and cocaine addict, writer with writer's block and blank page. Slowly I begin to introduce scenes that reflect the theme or issue we are gathered to address which are more sociodramatic in nature. For example, an Israeli soldier and Palestinian encounter at a checkpoint, a Japanese tourist meeting an elderly Korean woman who remembers the Japanese atrocities in her country during World War II, or two adolescent daughters of Holocaust survivors speaking to each other in the middle of the night because their survivor mother has had yet another nightmare about her experience in a concentration camp.

Many intercultural conflicts involve a spoken demand or unspoken longing for apology. *Line Repetition* (Emunah, 1994), in which participants in dyads repeat lines and explore the emotions behind them such as "You hurt me/I'm sorry" take on special meaning in relationship to Japanese and Chinese, Palestinians and Israelis, Turks and Armenians and Germans and Jews.

In this context, a simple playful activity can propel the group into the heart of their conflict. Even in this warm-up phase a seemingly benign exercise like passing imaginary objects can trigger a powerful emotional reaction based on the tension in the room. In a Palestinian and Israeli workshop in 2004 in Berkeley, California, passing an imaginary lit match and ladybug around the circle gave way to passing a mimed symbolic concretization of hope. There had been another bus bombing in Jerusalem the day of the workshop and the group immediately tapped into the pain and grief about the event that was right under the surface. This exercise provoked a Palestinian and Israeli woman to physically struggle with each other, in a playful way, over the tiny and elusive thread of hope that kept escaping both of them. The playful laughter of the group response to this spectacle evolved into the anguished sobs of the Israeli woman who expressed her feelings of hopelessness about the Middle East conflict. The Palestinian woman comforted her in her pain and despair. This moving scene occurred in the first 30 minutes of the workshop and set the course of the work together.

Humanizing Each Other Through Telling Our Stories

By the time the participants have entered the room the intercultural conflict between them has evolved into mutual stereotyping and profoundly different historical narratives. But instead of arguing over whose version of history is correct, we focus on sharing personal stories. While it might be acceptable to refute someone's version of history, it is almost impossible to claim that someone's feelings and personal stories are untrue. It is for this reason that I move quickly towards sharing affective memories and life stories. My goal is to build mutual empathy and strengthen the bonds between participants. These bonds will be put to the test later when sensitive issues arise.

In setting up the workshops, I often ask participants to bring personal objects related to their collective story. I use these objects to launch the journey into the depth of emotions we are gathered to explore. These objects could include a photograph of an ancestor, a book related to the subject, a piece of jewelry from a grandparent–something that evokes personal and collective memory. In the absence of objects, I ask participants to pantomime them using their imaginations to bring something personal from their past into the room. The pantomimed sense memory of the object can be powerful and evocative. I ask participants to briefly share the significance and meaning of their object with the group. When they have finished sharing, participants place the objects on an altar that has been created in advance of the workshop by me or my assistants. Each participant then takes a stone from the basket of stones that have been provided and encapsulates the story they are carrying, saying, for example, "I carry the story of my father's exile." Participants hold on to their stones throughout the workshop and only return them to the basket at the very end of our encounter. The stones function as a container for all that will happen during our time together. Carrying these stones throughout the workshop sets up a central idea of HWH, that we all carry the stories of our ancestors whether we are aware of them or not.

Certain events such as the Holocaust, the Armenian Genocide and The Middle Passage (the horrific transportation of Africans across the Atlantic), have resulted in forced mass migrations, immigrations and fleeing refugees. In these instances, I might begin a workshop by creating a map of the world on the floor with masking tape. I ask participants to silently move around the map in response to specific directions. For example, move to a place on the map:

Where you were born?
Where your mother was born?
Where your father was born?
Where your mother's father was born?
Where your mother's mother was born?
Where your father's father was born?
Where your father's mother was born?
Where an unknown ancestor was born?

In a large group it is powerful to watch participants move silently around the room. Each change of location on the map implies a personal story of transition, trauma or displacement that workshop participants might be carrying. Some participants know their family history. Others do not know it but only have a vague notion of what occurred. Either way, the exercise evokes memory and feelings about history and identity. I might choose to enter into a sociometric discussion in action to explore the feelings aroused by this exercise or channel the emotional tension built up into another exercise leading to personal story.

One exercise that I often use to mark the transition from warm-up to personal storytelling is "My name is ______. I am a ______". It is a core exercise in the HWH process and begins the deconstruction of the cultural identity of the participant. Each participant stands alone in front of the group and I ask the person to speak his or her full name, either in English or in the person's language of origin. This is followed by a statement of nationality, ethnicity, religion, gender, or sexual preference, depending on the theme of the workshop. For example, a Jewish participant standing in front of a group of children of Holocaust survivors and the Third Reich may state "My name is Sonja Goldstein and I am a Jew." Or, "My name is Jurgen Doering and I am a German." A moment of silence follows each statement. Then the participant is asked by the facilitator to reflect upon and share the feelings or images that come up as they make this public statement. Feelings evoked by these statements are complex and multilayered. "I am a Jew" may have a different resonance for a participant than "I am Jewish" or "I am a Jewish American." A German participant saying his name in German "Ich bin ein Deutsche," has a different feeling than the same statement in English. This is a purposefully provocative exercise that helps participants access the memories that shape their cultural identity.

At times I choose to deepen the exploration of cultural identity by using an adaptation of psychodramatic sculpting to flesh out positive and negative cultural messages. I call this exercise a diagram of roles and messages. This form is essentially a sculpture of the internalized spoken and unspoken messages that a workshop participant received from parents, ancestors, society, educational institutions, authority figures, governments or God, which affect that person's beliefs, identity, and self-esteem. It is sometimes first sketched out on paper before being moved into action.

To illustrate this technique I will describe what happened in a workshop I conducted in October of 2007 with a group of Armenians and Turks during a politically explosive time. Turkey had recalled its ambassador from Washington after a US congressional committee voted to recognize the mass killing of Armenians during World War I as genocide. Turkey continued to deny claims it was genocide, while Armenia welcomed the vote. In response, Turkey threatened to withdraw its support for the Iraq War. In this political climate, Armenians and Turks gathered to face each other in dialogue.

I asked the members of the two groups to

create human sculptures and diagrams of the messages they received from their families, governments, religious institutions about being Armenian or Turkish. Following are two images that emerged from this process:

> An Armenian man shapes a physical representation of the burdens on him as an Armenian, by placing participants in various physical poses and giving them lines to say. In the sculpture, the Armenian man reaches out to Turks with an extended hand but the millions of dead, mangled bodies of the genocide, visually represented by participants from both groups, cry out for revenge. The Turks in the image look towards a clock hoping that time will fade the historical memory of the massacres of Armenians so they won't have to face the culpability of their ancestors. Enraged members of the Armenian community block his reaching out gesture and prevent him from speaking to Turks imploring him to hold on to and remember the trauma of the genocide.

> A young Turkish woman, who happens to be pregnant with her first child, volunteers to create a map of messages she received from her family and Turkish culture. In the sculpture, her father lectures her, warning her not to deviate from the patriotic image of her people. Her mother pleads with her to not get involved with the Armenian/Turkish dialogue as it is dangerous. The Turkish government delivers a nationalistic message reminding the woman of the greatness of modern Turkey and its founder Ataturk. The Turkish educational system teaches history but does not mention the suffering of the Armenian people. In the sculpture, the Turkish woman is shocked to learn about the Armenian genocide. The woman's Turkish friends express their hatred of Armenians with a nationalistic fervor that stuns and disappoints her. The sculpture culminates in a brief psychodramatic enactment in which the woman speaks of her fears and hopes for Turkey to her unborn child. She expresses her commitment to teach her child the truth about history no matter how painful it may be.

This kind of sculpting serves to deconstruct cultural and national identity and make participants aware of the unconscious collective forces that shape their behaviors, opinions and feelings. I use this exercise as a stimulus to move into more intensive emotional work. Often an emotional leader emerges from the participants who can carry the issue or theme of the workshop to another level. When the emotional intensity reveals itself, I shape it in various ways: as a Psychodrama, Playback Theatre, "Sociodrama" (Chapter 19), improvisation or creative ritual.

Towards the goal of intensifying and deepening the group process I ask participants to share formative or transformative stories related to their historical trauma or cultural identity. Participants are drawn to HWH workshops because they want to have their story–their pain, burden and the grief of their legacy–witnessed. Asking participants to share formative or transformative personal stories helps them focus on stories that shaped who they are or that can never be erased from their memories. Following are brief examples of formative stories from previous HWH processes.

> A Palestinian man shares how in 1967 as a ten-year-old boy during the Six Day War he sees Israeli soldiers come into his mosque without removing their shoes. He describes the disrespect and humiliation of that experience. He recounts his profound sadness at leaving Jerusalem, driving towards Jordan and knowing he may never see his homeland again. His story is enacted through Playback Theatre.

> An Israeli man in the same workshop, while in the military, is charged with guarding the northern border of Israel and his unit kills a Palestinian man who was trying to infiltrate the border. The story evolves into a psychodrama in which the Israeli re-enacts the dialogue he had alone with the dead Pale-

stinian man. His words express his profound desire to understand why this Palestinian man risked his life in such a way. It was in this moment that this man decided to get involved with the Israeli Peace movement.

A German woman recounts the story of sitting on her father's lap at age 11 in Germany watching the Eichmann trial. The father had been a member of the Nazi party but watches the proceedings in silence. In her child's mind she becomes Eichmann. It is she who is on trial. A psychodrama ensues in which we explore her burden of guilt as a child of the Third Reich.

A Jewish man remembers when he was ten in Frankfurt, the Gestapo came in during dinner and took his father and uncle away to Dachau at gunpoint. He decided in that moment that the grown-up world was out of control, could not protect him and was not to be trusted. He decided never to grow up. His spirit is still age ten. This scene is "played back" through Playback Theatre and then evolves into a psychodramatic enactment in which the man, as an adult, comes in to rescue his 10-year-old self.

A Japanese man, as a four-year-old boy, witnessed and survived the atomic bomb blast in Hiroshima. In recounting this memory from his 4-year-old perspective he says, "It was the day that the sun fell out of the sky." The man's story is witnessed and honored through a ritualized Playback Theatre enactment.

A Chilean exile and social activist describes her escape from her beloved Chile as a young woman during the military coup in 1973, expresses her longing for reconnection, her lost youth and the grief of her exile. A moving psychodramatic dialogue with a workshop participant playing the role of the country of Chile ensues.

A black woman shares the story of her experience in elementary school when her white teacher who, in a class art project drawing of a human hand, insisted that the girl color her hand Caucasian flesh color instead of brown. In a reparative psychodrama the woman speaks to her teacher and the little girl she once was, reclaiming her right to be seen and valued for who she is.

In entering into these formative and transformative stories with a group of people who have little exposure to action methods, as well as differing cultural values around self-revealing, it is important to prepare them for the more complex dramatic structures that will follow. An adaptation of the Playback Theatre form becomes a useful tool in creating competence and trusting intuition among workshop participants. I conduct a story related to their collective trauma in front of the group and then ask members of the group to step inside the story. Stepping inside someone's personal story necessitates people taking on roles in the *Teller's* narrative. Since the workshop participants generally have little acting experience, I, as facilitator, deconstruct the story into actable elements for them. I am careful to help people succeed in this exercise. Stepping inside others' stories requires two types of risk-taking. First, it is scary for novices to be thrust into a psychodramatic acting exercise that requires an aesthetic sense. But even more threatening is the challenge and responsibility of stepping authentically into the story of an enemy.

To mitigate the potential humiliation of the actor, the Teller of the story needs be coached to restrain his or her natural impulses to critique the enactment. This restraint is necessary in view of the larger good: building trust, intuition, and empathy. Facilitators also need to concern themselves with the safety and emotional needs of the Teller. Stories that are told at this early stage often take on archetypal significance for the group. There is a kind of self-sacrifice taking place by the storytellers, in which personal needs are set aside in the interests of the group.

A recent example of the usefulness of this technique in developing a HWH process occurred at a conference in Tel Aviv, Israel in 2006. My Palestinian-American colleague Amal Kouttab and I co-led a workshop with a group of Israelis and Palestinians on the use of drama therapy in intercultural conflict resolution. The Palestinian participants were mostly mental health workers from Gaza who had received permission from the Israeli government to cross the border to attend the conference. After guiding the group through a brief warm-up we invited participants to share a formative or transformative memory connected to their identities as Palestinians and Israelis. Two personal stories emerged from this request.

A Palestinian mental health professional shared an incident that happened to him on the way to the conference. He had been waiting in line for hours to cross the border from Gaza into Israel. While waiting he witnessed a disturbing scene. A mother holding a distressed 3-year-old boy was attempting to pass through a metal detector to be screened for weapons as required of Palestinians by Israel at checkpoints and border crossings. An Israeli soldier was communicating with the woman through a loudspeaker from a bullet-proof booth commanding her to go through the metal detector separately from her child. The child, hysterically crying with fear of the proceedings, clung to his mother in desperation, refusing to cooperate. In tears, the mother pleaded with the soldier, saying that she would go so far as to take the child's clothes off to prove that her 3-year-old son had no weapons. The soldier, insisting on his authority, refused to make any exception for the mother and the child. Witnessing this humiliation, a wave of seething rage came over this man. He could not express this rage at the border crossing, but was willing to quietly share it with the Israelis present. For him, the humiliation of this young boy was symbolic of the humiliation of all of the Palestinian people. It was a kind of scene that he witnessed every day. It also recalled his father's trauma, who as a young boy in the Israeli War of Independence (*The Catastrophe* for Palestinians) fled with his family from his home in what is now Israel.

Deciding which roles we wanted the participants to play, Amal and I invited workshop participants to bring different aspects of the Palestinian man's story to life through soliloquy, character monologues and fluid sculptures. Israelis were able to embody the roles of the Palestinian boy and his mother with deep empathy. Palestinians were willing to step inside the role of the Israeli soldier revealing his possible feelings and motivations. The complexity of the mental health professional's rage at witnessing the boy's humiliation was explored through fluid sculptures. For a brief moment the Palestinian man felt seen. A culture of empathy prevailed in the group. The Palestinian historical narrative revealed itself through this man's story. The archetypal nature of the story as the common experience of Palestinians made this story ripe to work with and develop in the group.

In response to the Palestinian man's enactment, an older Israeli woman insisted on telling her story. Her *act hunger* prevailed in the group process. She was a Holocaust survivor and described her experience of standing on the selection platform in Auschwitz seeing her grandmother holding her infant sister as they were led to the gas chambers. The story took place in her imagination. The woman visualized what her grandmother might have done to comfort her infant granddaughter as the Zyklon B gas began to fill the death chamber. In a lullaby voice the woman imagined hearing her grandmother saying, "It's all right sweet little one. We're going home now." The Israeli woman explained that her sister's rights as a child were also violated like the boy at the border crossing. She ended her story by passionately expressing the need for Jews to have a state to protect themselves. This story contained the classic Israeli historical narrative and was very provocative for the Palestinians in the room to hear. Palestinians feel that they are constantly being asked to set aside their suffering and their rights to a homeland because of the Holocaust. I could feel the tension in the room around this issue. I chose to meta-communicate with the group about what was happening in the room. I named the triggering elements of the story and asked the group if they were willing to set aside their reactions for a moment and empathize with the Israeli woman's story since this had been our agreement. I promised that we could enter into a discussion after we had honored the story. The group agreed. And, through improvised monologues, fluid sculptures and enactments, the Israeli woman's narrative was fleshed out. In an act of emotional generosity, Palestinians were able to empathize with the Holocaust survivor, including her profound longing for security for herself and her people.

As the workshop was relatively brief, we were not able to move beyond the phase of humanizing each other through telling our stories. Although our intervention did not produce major breakthroughs in the impasse between Palestinians and Israelis, it did open up an emotional space where Palestinian rage, hurt and humiliation and Israeli fear, grief and longing were expressed and witnessed in a contained and respectful way. The heated discussion that followed the enactments created a quality of direct and honest dialogue that had been missing from the conference up to that point and had an important impact on other parts of the proceedings.

These examples serve to illustrate how personal stories can reveal historical narratives. These narratives, when presented side by side, can be explored effectively using dramatic structures including adaptations of Playback Theatre and Psychodrama. Emotional and archetypal themes can emerge from these stories and be developed in the course of a workshop. Their primary result is to create the emotional double bind that short circuits hatred and dehumanization and fills the vacuum with mutual empathy.

Exploring and Owning the Potential Perpetrator in All of Us

In 1975, I began leading drama therapy groups at Chino Men's Prison, in a Los Angeles psychiatric hospital and at California Institute for Women at Frontera. I was interested in understanding the potential perpetrator in all of us. The legacy of the Holocaust had left me with the drive to grasp how human beings can dehumanize others enough to torture, rape, or gas them. On a personal level, if in some way I could humanize the sadistic Nazis of my childhood nightmares, they would be less frightening to me. As a therapist, understanding the human impulse towards cruelty would help me in working with intercultural conflict. Although prison inmates are not Nazis, their crimes involve a violation of human rights. I wanted to deconstruct and understand the dehumanization process that occurs in a cruel act. A prison was an apt laboratory for this kind of emotional and existential research.

In 1986, I was asked by a public defender to work as a drama therapist with a 21-year-old man who had murdered two adults and an 18-month-old child by stabbing them with a knife. Over the course of a year I worked intimately with this man, and in so doing, immersed myself in the mind of a perpetrator. In a dramatic affective memory re-enactment, I accompanied him into the moment he took the knife and stuck it into the bodies of his victims. After he was found guilty, I testified on his behalf at the sentencing phase of his death penalty trial. When the members of the jury were interviewed after having decided that the defendant should get life in prison, they said that it was my testimony that humanized this "monster" enough to save his life. In my capacity as a therapist who deeply empathized with his client, a murderer, I also needed to face the part of me that could commit the same crime.

After working with this man for more than a year, I felt compelled to continue my work understanding the concept of the *perpetrator.* I also felt driven to understand the evil behind the Holocaust and knew that the closest I could get to working with former Nazis was to work with their children who knew them intimately. It was this experience that led me to bring together the sons and daughters of Jewish Holocaust survivors and the Third Reich in the United States, Germany and France. With these two groups and later with Japanese, Chinese and Koreans on their legacy of WWII, and other polarized groups, I explored the archetypal human impulse to commit evil acts.

Guiding groups in intercultural conflict towards exploring the potential perpetrator in each of us is a delicate task. It is a journey into the underworld to grapple with aspects of human behavior that few people want to face. Both perpetration and victimization bring up feelings of tremendous personal shame and judgment for workshop participants. The primary reason that I explore this theme in the context of intercultural conflict is that it humanizes the perpetrator. It is easy to write off criminals and Nazis as monsters and believe that the monster does not inhabit us but resides in the *other.* However, if we hold as true that all human beings are capable of being oppressors, given certain conditions, then it allows us to view perpetration as a human act not just a heinous one. It removes the burden of the perpetrator role from belonging to only one group assembled in the room. Recognizing the perpetrator within each of us allows participants to examine the forces and drives that create perpetration and cause us to engage in violence, commit racist acts or be part of a murderous mob. It permits participants to do this without shame or judgment (Naor, 1998).

However, because of the triggering elements inherent in this kind of emotional investigation, I only venture down the path of exploring the perpetrator when there is enough time, trust and a collective agreement about the value of taking the journey. I must also assess whether the group is ready to tolerate such a potentially divisive endeavor and consider their emotional state and their capacity for aesthetic distance, which this work requires.

I often begin the exploration into this phase by bringing out historical photographs that evoke the collective trauma being explored. I choose participants and ask them to place themselves into physical postures based on the elements in the photograph, including body language, facial expression and emotion. I switch the cultural groupings, for example, I choose a Jew to play a Nazi and a German to play a Jew. Then I ask participants to enact the photograph, bringing the human sculpture to life.

Other theatre conventions I use to explore the photograph include improvising monologues based on characters in the photographs. These photo enactments immediately immerse the participants in the world of the historical trauma. Using their intuition and taking cues from the sensory details of the photograph, the enactments become very real and often frightening. The participants can be triggered by playing the victim and oppressor roles. Germans, for example, enter into the exercise, scared that it will prove their worst irrational fear: that they carry the evil of Nazism in their bloodlines. Jews sometimes point their finger accusing their counterparts of being personally responsible for the Holocaust, needing a target for their collective rage at their victimization.

In an exercise I call *Master/Slave* I break up the group into pairs, each pair with representatives of the different groups. I ask each dyad to assume the roles of master and slave, taking turns at playing both parts. The master must order the slave around in a degrading fashion exploring the power of their role. Sometimes after this exercise we move into expressive arts processes to channel the feelings being stimulated. The art inspired by this undertaking can take the form of visual art, poetry or mask-making that moves into enactment. This helps in processing the experience while simultaneously allowing participants to de-role.

With more time, trust and group cohesion I move into the sharing of personal stories of times participants have been a perpetrator in their lives. Sense memories and affective memories of moments when group participants have dehumanized, devalued or abused someone are explored fluidly through Playback Theatre, sociodramatic, and psychodramatic processes. These activities further universalize the role of perpetrator.

Stepping into the perpetrator role, in the end, becomes a great equalizer. It allows participants to develop a compassionate stance towards the victims and perpetrators of a historical trauma. From this position they can deeply empathize with and humanize both roles as they accept that both are within them. Exploring the role of perpetrator in these direct and provocative ways can be emotionally draining. At these times I move towards the aesthetic distance that playful approaches to thematic exploration allow. Although humorous and sometimes quite irreverent, given our serious theme, these more distanced explorations of historical trauma are no less useful and profound than exploring them directly.

One of the distanced sociodramatic exercises I sometimes use is an improvised performance by each national or ethnic group, entitled *The History of My People* (in five minutes). Each ethnic group is given only a few minutes to prepare an enactment of their people's history from ancient times to the present. The only guideline is that the enactment must be brief. This is a purposefully impossible task. Members of each ethnic group must decide how to include the important elements of their history and how to incorporate the perpetrator or victim aspects in the performance. In the pressured, chaotic and playful preparation for the presentation, the participants tap into their society's cultural training to retrieve the internalized messages and collective narrative of their people. The light-hearted enactments often give way to profound revelations about how each group holds its history within their personal and collective identities.

Another variation on this theme is facilitating the method of Developmental Transformations where the perpetrator role is explored, played with and deconstructed. Also, groups may enact stereotypes of their own cultures, sharing the impact of the internal and external projections.

The emotions and images stimulated by these powerful exercises become a point of departure for discussion and group process integrating the reflections and insights discovered during these explorations. I believe there can be no political solutions to intercultural conflict unless we come to understand and tame the darker emotional and psychological drives of the human being. This is a guiding principle in my Healing the Wounds of History approach to working with groups in conflict.

Moving Deeply into Grief

In the grieving process, waves of strong emotion, often triggered irregularly and unpredictably, wash up on the shores of consciousness and are worked through in various ways. In individualistic cultures, the emotional attachment to the deceased is experienced as a personal loss. In collectivist cultures, the emotional attachment is shared with the family, community and society. Mourning processes guide the group towards a repair of the social fabric that has been torn by the loss of the individual. In the context of my work, I deal with grief caused by a traumatic event, especially a collective trauma, such as disaster, war, genocide or displacement. In such events, large groups of people are impacted and the traumatic event becomes part of the collective narrative and identity.

During a time of trauma, such as war, those who survive are focused on staying alive; they cannot take the time to fully grieve their losses. Once the trauma is over, the focus becomes building a new life and so the trauma is moved into the background, because its impact is so overwhelming and painful. The result can be that entire cultures reconstruct their societies on the unresolved rubble of the trauma.

In the intercultural conflicts that I have dealt with, I have seen members of the first, second, third and even fourth generations struggle under the weight of the unexpressed emotional burdens of their ancestors. For example, the six million Jews who perished in the Holocaust represent both the loss of entire families, towns and generations, but six million individual lives as well. Each lost life was someone who was known and loved: a sister, aunt, grandfather, teacher, neighbor, or first love. The societal trauma is so huge that one cannot grieve all of these lives and losses at once. But drama therapy and expressive arts approaches are able to contain deep wells of emotion through symbolic processes, aesthetic distance and their capacity to work through grief. The HWH model can guide participants on the journey through an archaeological dig of buried memories and emotions. This can happen in small group encounters and large group gatherings and could even lead to national commemorations.

There is no single map to uncover the underlying grief inherent in a historical trauma. Specific exercises to achieve this cannot be listed here. Of paramount importance are the facilitator's intuitive skills. This phase requires the facilitator to tune in and make decisions about therapeutic interventions and track the group's process while at the same time seeking out the emotional leaders whose stories will carry the group into the catharsis of grief that it needs. Psychodrama, more often than not, is the structure I choose to help give shape to the complex stories of grief and mourning. However, unlike in a classical psychodrama, I am not just looking for the most warmed-up person to do a piece of therapeutic work, but tracking and choosing the protagonist who will express the larger collective story that needs to be told to move the group forward in developing the theme of the workshop. One must strike a balance between the personal and collective story in order to achieve a meaningful release.

In a workshop I conducted with descendants of Holocaust Survivors and the Third Reich, a moving example of such a personal/collective story emerged. A German American woman, Hilde, who grew up in the US, had an American GI father and a

German mother. Hilde's mother's parents had been members of the Nazi party. Hilde's mother, Netta, had grown up as part of the Hitler Youth. As a young woman during the war, Netta experienced multiple traumas: the Allied bombing destroyed her home and killed her grandmother, her brother came back from a Russian POW camp a shattered shell of himself, and she was raped by the conquering Russian soldiers. After the war, she met and fell in love with an occupying US soldier. At the age of 20, she moved to the US with her American husband and gave birth to a daughter, Hilde. Netta suffered from post-traumatic stress disorder, dark depressive episodes and a tremendous guilt and feeling of responsibility for the Holocaust. When Hilde was an adolescent, Netta committed suicide.

As the protagonist of the psychodrama, Hilde expressed both rage at her mother's self-destructive act and grief at her loss and the pain that she had inherited. This story was enacted with the help and tender support of both the German and Jewish workshop participants. There was enough compassion created in the room that the Jewish participants set aside their vengeful feelings towards the Germans and were able to empathize with Hilde's pain without judgment. Even though this was the story of a particular woman, echoes of similar losses were shared by the other German women in the room, many of whom were from the same generation as her mother. When the protagonist was reduced to sobs, instinctively all the German women in the room surrounded her and began to sing her a German lullaby (the same one her mother used to sing.) The work of this protagonist tapped into the German participants' need to grieve and reclaim a positive relationship with their identities as Germans. Even though the Germans had been the cause of WWII and their people had been responsible for the deaths of millions of Jews, it did not negate their emotional right to grieve their own losses.

In a HWH process, several workshop participants can experience this kind of meaningful release of grief as we cycle through the various phases of the work. Like the natural ebb and flow of the ocean, when a large wave of grief appears, the facilitator needs to step back and allow it to engulf the group. As the wave recedes, there is a cleansing and integrative effect. As participants share their personal responses, the group is able to sculpt meaning out of these stories of suffering.

Creating Integration, Performances, and Rituals of Remembrance

At the end of a HWH workshop there is a need for closure, integration and assimilation of the feelings and insights that were explored during the group encounter. This segment of a HWH group process is conceptually similar to Renee Emunah's dramatic ritual phase of a drama therapy progression. The participants review what they have experienced, acknowledge what they have learned and decide what they will take with them back out into the world. This is accomplished through creative means and often contains ritual elements.

One example of a ritual of integration that I devised took place at the end of a three-day workshop I conducted in Berlin in the early 1990s with descendants of Jewish Holocaust survivors and the Third Reich. The workshop was held on the beautiful grounds of an ancient castle that had been the quarters of important Nazi officials during WWII. Our time together had been rich in the deep exploration of our mutual pain as inheritors of the legacy of the Holocaust. Dividing the participants into small groups, I asked the teams to imagine that it was 500 years from now and the events of WWII and the Holocaust had become an official day of commemoration observed by both Jewish and German cultures. I instructed them to either create a ritual that they would present to the gathered assembly, or to direct the larger group to be part of a progression they devised.

There were certain elements that I required them to include in their presentations. Each group was to go out into the nature that surrounded the castle grounds and find elements (leaves, branches, stones, flowers, etc.) that they could incorporate into their enactment. Workshop participants also had *sacred spaces* on the grounds of the castle where they could use expressive arts processes of visual art, journal writing and poetry to reflect on their experience and incorporate their results in the final presentation. Finally, I asked each group to include a brief enactment of the story of the Holocaust from the future projection perspective of 500 years in the future.

Filled with the images and emotions of our three days of work together, the German and Jewish participants fully invested themselves in preparation for the final ritual. Through the aesthetic distance of creating and performing the ritual, the groups were able to integrate their complex workshop experiences in a satisfying and meaningful manner.

Another way to culminate a HWH process is to close with a public performance or commemoration. This allows what happened in the workshop to be shared with and experienced by a larger group of people who would never sign up for a drama therapy process themselves, but who would be willing to come to a performance. In my first experiments, I conducted three-day workshops with Germans and Jews and then spent weeks directing the participants in creating self-revelatory performance pieces. Using the Playback Theatre form as a frame, these self-revelatory pieces were interwoven into public Holocaust commemorations. My Playback Theatre company enacted the personal stories of workshop participants in a public forum and we interspersed the self-revelatory pieces throughout the presentation.

As this process is time-consuming and it is not always possible to work with workshop participants in depth to develop theatre pieces, a simplified structure evolved over time. My company, The Living Arts Playback Theatre Ensemble, which I have directed for 20 years, has become seasoned in performing personal stories of trauma and historical complexity related to HWH events. A public Playback Theatre performance is organized and promoted in advance. The workshop participants are not pressured to share their stories although most elect to do so. After the completion of a HWH process with groups in conflict, I invite two participants to share a personal story related to their historical legacy or their experience in the workshop. This serves as a warm-up for the audience, develops the theme of the evening, and functions as a bridge between the closed private workshop and the open public assembly. I then open the Playback process to the public, inviting audience volunteers to come on stage and share a personal story triggered by the intercultural conflict being witnessed on stage. Often, the Tellers are themselves members of the cultures in conflict who, for one reason or another, did not participate in the preceding workshop. In addition, I facilitate the audience in Playback Theatre short forms (Salas, 1993) such as *Fluid Sculptures, Pairs, Narrative V,* as well as engage them with sociodramatic and "Theatre of the Oppressed" techniques (Boal, 1979; Chapter 21). This further deepens the audience exploration of the social, existential and political dilemmas provoked by the performance. It can be argued that this approach to performance effectively functions as a large group drama therapy process in which society is the client.

An innovative use of this large group drama therapy approach to intercultural conflict resolution was initiated by drama therapist Stephen Snow, Director of the Concordia University Drama Therapy Program in Montreal. In October 2003, I was invited by Professor Snow to intervene in the aftermath of a conflict between pro-Israeli and pro-Palestinian students at Concordia University as part of a Peace and Conflict resolution program. A pro-Palestinian faction had won the student government elections in 2001. This had set off a chain reaction that culminated in a violent protest in September 2002 against Benjamin Netanyahu, the former Israeli prime minister, who, as a result of the violence, had to cancel his planned speech on campus. This was a traumatic and polarizing event that captured the attention of the entire country.

In 2003, Stephen Snow organized a week-long workshop for Palestinians and Israelis in Montreal, which I facilitated, and assembled a Playback Theatre ensemble made up of Montreal actors to perform in a culminating event. The public performance was well-attended and the Playback actors were able to give emotional shape to the complexity of the Palestinian and Israeli crisis and engendered compassion for both sides of the conflict, including the felt but unexpressed Palestinian rage. What struck me most was the enormous amount of attention from print and broadcast media that this event received (the CBC, the London Times, French television coverage). As a social activist, I was inspired by the tremendous potential a drama therapy intervention can have on society as ripples of influence turned to waves. News stories and sound bites extended well beyond the Palestinian and Israeli workshop and theatre performance. The possibility of changing perceptions, creating empathy and instilling hope, where none existed previously, seemed momentarily possible.

In recent years I have gone on to produce more performances: *Mapping the Emotional Terrain of Peace,* 2004 (with Palestinians and Israelis), *Hiroshima Stories,* 2005 and *Facing the Mountain: Armenians and Turks in Dialogue,* 2007. I have found that creating workshops, events, rituals and commemorations around a focal point such as an anniversary date (November 9, 1938, Kristalnacht; April 24, 1915, Armenian Genocide; or August 6, 1945, Hiroshima Day) can mobilize latent emotional energy. These are times when the memory of the trauma rises to the surface.

In 2005, for the 60th anniversary of the bombing of Hiroshima and Nagasaki, I organized a day-long workshop at International House in Berkeley, California with Japanese participants and an evening commemoration open to the public. The performance/commemoration featured an Okinawan music ensemble, a troupe of Taiko drummers, a Playback Theatre performance and an art installation. Audience members participated in an interactive public forum and finally placed a thousand origami cranes on a "peace tree." At the heart of the evening were the testimonies of Hiroshima and Nagasaki bomb survivors, whose stories were honored by the Playback Theatre enactments. With Japanese and American cultures as my ultimate clients, I chose to organize the event to help release the unexpressed grief and outrage about this traumatic event and motivate the audience to take social action.

Not only is there a role for drama therapy in guiding meaningful commemorations for significant dates but for creating new dates that need to be acknowledged by society. In the early 1990s I became involved in the public discourse in Germany on the need for Germany to have a Holocaust Commemoration day. There was ambivalence about creating such an annual day of observance as German leaders had difficulty imagining what shape the commemoration rituals would take. At a conference in Berlin, with the help of a group of Germans and Jews who had just completed a workshop with me, we performed a ritual before the politicians and the leaders of the German Jewish community. They eventually established January 27, the day Auschwitz concentration camp was liberated, to be observed annually.

My impulse towards taking a deeply personal process such as working with collective trauma and intercultural conflict and turning it outward came out of my social activism. Although working with group participants can be very meaningful, the impact it has on society is limited. By bringing the essence of what happened in the workshop to the public, I am able to share our experiences with a wider audience. In this way, a whole community can witness these stories, be touched and have its attitudes transformed. Creating a documentary film or having print and broadcast media cover the event further extends its impact.

CASE EXAMPLE

In May 2007, I was invited by Professor Haruhiko Murakawa and Ritsumeikan University in Kyoto, Japan to conduct a series of workshops and performances addressing the Japanese legacy of WWII. Working with my expressive arts therapist colleague and collaborator, Aya Kasai, who also functioned as my interpreter, I facilitated two workshops in Kyoto, one in Hiroshima and another in Tokyo. I also worked with two separate Japanese Playback Theatre companies and conducted performances in Kyoto on the aftermath of Japanese militarism in other Asian countries during WWII. In Hiroshima, I facilitated a workshop and conducted a Playback Theatre performance on the emotional impact of the atomic bomb on the survivors, their descendants and the identity of the city of Hiroshima itself. I will give some background to help the reader understand the historical context in which I intervened and then describe a workshop followed by the description of a performance in Kyoto. (For the sake of confidentiality, some of the details in the workshop have been changed.)

WWII in the Pacific ended with the dropping of the atomic bombs on Hiroshima and Nagasaki, and the surrender of Japan in August of 1945. Japan had occupied and committed atrocities in other Asian countries and subjugated the populations to brutal forced labor, medical experiments and sexual servitude. Because of the emergence of the threat of the Soviet Union, and later Red China, the United States needed Japan as an ally in the fight against communism during the Cold War. Although the United States and its allies formed a tribunal in which many major military and political figures were prosecuted, they were reluctant to bring shame on the Emperor and the postwar Japanese government by making them fully accountable for their "crimes against peace and humanity."

The Japanese economic miracle, the historical phenomenon of Japan's record period of financial growth, propelled it onto the world stage as an economic superpower. The country focused on the future. School history books avoided lingering on the Japanese militarism of the 1920s through 1940s. With the bombing of Hiroshima and Nagasaki, Japan struggled with its role as victim as well as perpetrator. Some Japanese government administrations took steps towards apologizing for past actions, while others awkwardly moved towards retractions of the apology. These behaviors reflected the national ambivalence about accepting responsibility for war crimes. It was too humiliating and brought shame upon the collective. The cultural values around saving face prevented Japanese society from direct reflections on its legacy.

Set against this historical backdrop, my invitation by Ritsumeikan University in Kyoto to address these issues itself was a controversial act. Ritsumeikan University is home to one of a handful of Japanese Peace Museums where Japanese militarism and the events of WWII are presented in an unflinching way. In the museum are artifacts, documents, photographs, and installations that educate students on the details of WWII, including the Japanese invasion of other countries, the use of "comfort women" by Japanese soldiers, forced slave labor and use of prisoners of war for medical experiments. The ultimate goal of the museums is to educate and help people understand the nature of all wars and conflicts.

My workshop, which was to bring Japanese students and students from other Asian countries together to address the unexplored history between them, took place within the museum itself. Although Ritsumeikan University has a large population of foreign Asian students, and the two-day workshop and subsequent Playback performance were widely publicized, in the end, the only participants who registered for the workshop were Japanese. Accepting that this was the reality of Japanese/Asian relations on campus, it was collectively decided that it was important to hold the workshop anyway, so that the Japanese students could confront their legacy.

Fifteen participants attended. They were asked to bring objects or photographs that had some meaning for them, which were related to their personal legacy of WWII. After a brief discussion, we launched into a drama therapy warm-up which included improvisational techniques. We then moved into the opening ritual of our work, where participants presented the objects that they had brought to the workshop, shared a little of their meaning, and placed them on a makeshift altar. One woman placed a photo of her uncle who had died during the war as a Japanese soldier, and tearfully stated, "I carry the ghost of his death." Another placed a photo of herself and her grandmother with whom she had been very close, and said, "I carry the story of the little child that took on my grandmother's pain of the war." Another placed an abstract art object that he had created, and shared, "I carry my emptiness as a Japanese person in relationship to this war."

The group then needed to address their disappointment that the other Asian students did not feel safe enough to attend the workshop. I placed a series of empty chairs in the room facing the participants and asked them what nationalities they would like to address in a sociodramatic dialogue. The nationalities the group chose to embody as victims of Japanese oppression were Filipinos, Chinese, Koreans, Americans and Okinawans. The participants took turns sitting in these chairs and expressing the imagined feelings of the absent voices. It was clear that they understood and empathized with the mistrust that the Asian students felt towards them. Having worked on their disappointment and unresolved feelings, the participants were better able to commit to looking at their own legacies without the benefit of having the victims of their country's atrocities present.

Holding the workshop in a Peace Museum enriched the experience. There were films, artifacts, tactile and sensual stimuli that opened the collective memory files of the participants. I divided them into four groups and asked them to wander around the museum for an hour and a half. Each group was to agree on a single image that they would later bring back and present to the entire group. The four groups all chose photographs that they found compelling. Each group created a human sculpture of its photograph and then brought it to life in an enactment.

One group picked a photo of comfort women being rescued and protected by Allied forces in Burma, empathizing with the women's plight as sexual slaves. Another group selected a picture of Kamakazi pilots eating their last meal before they went on a suicide mission. Through inner monologues the actors revealed that one of the Kamakazi pilots proudly embraced his fate that he was going to die for the Emperor. Another pilot expressed his ambivalence and fear of dying. The third group portrayed a humiliating scene in China, where Japanese soldiers walking on the sidewalk forced Chinese citizens to bow down to them in the gutter. The last group brought to life a scene from the occupation of Korea where a Japanese school teacher forcibly coerced young Korean students to speak Japanese.

This last scene seemed to carry the most charge for the group. A sociodrama emerged out of this enactment where the entire group took turns doubling and role reversing with the students and the teacher. One workshop participant played the character of the teacher with such commitment that the chilling, authoritarian timbre of his voice triggered many of the workshop participants–some needing to put their fingers in their ears to protect themselves from its frightening quality. It became clear that this controlling voice belonged to a Japanese archetypal figure present in various forms in Japanese culture. This voice came to represent the perpetrator, a theme that kept resurfacing during our time together.

The next day, after checking in with the group, a pivotal story emerged. One of the participants shared his experience going home on the bus the previous evening. A developmentally disabled man had gotten on and started disturbing a woman on the bus. The woman reported this incident to the bus driver. It was clear that the man did not have his full capacities. The driver yelled at the man in a very demeaning way, humiliating him and telling him to get off the bus in the same authoritarian voice that had been expressed in the workshop. The participant struggled with the decision of whether to speak up in defense of this mentally challenged man. The fact that no one had stood up to authority had haunted him. The Japanese value of obedience was evident. He finally found the courage to speak out against the oppression he felt he was witnessing as the other passengers looked on. The participant and the bus driver entered into an argument and the participant threatened to report the driver's behavior to his superiors. Hearing that, the bus driver immediately took a more conciliatory tone. The participant experienced some redemption in the fact that he had spoken up in the face of oppression. This felt like a direct response to what had happened in the workshop the previous day.

The story on the bus was then fleshed out by the workshop participants through Playback Theatre techniques and a sociodramatic exploration. The group made the connection between the bus driver and the teacher in Korea and realized that both of them had the authoritarian voice of the archetypal perpetrator. I guided the participants towards attempting to understand the societal forces that had given rise to Japanese authoritarianism in the 1930s and the reasons why the echoes of this voice still exist in Japanese society today.

Gradually I became aware that I was

standing in a cultural minefield: Here I was in a university in Kyoto, Japan, the only Caucasian in the room. Yet my role as teacher and therapist accorded me great respect in the Japanese culture. I realized I needed to move delicately and respectfully through the process of uncovering a potentially shameful side of the Japanese character. I felt that it was important that we humanize and deeply empathize with all of the perpetrator roles we were exploring. I believed that this would help counter the collective inclination to turn the group's gaze away from such shameful images. I introduced the idea of the *wounded child* within the perpetrator. Although a Western psychological construct, the wounded child concept took hold. The group then took turns dialoguing with the perpetrator as well as stepping inside the role. In the integration phase following the enactment, participants shared their insights about the ways that society's messages about obedience and respect for authority had impacted them in their family, school and work.

This process evolved into a more in-depth examination of Japanese identity and the way it is constructed. Using the "My name is . . . I am a . . . " technique described earlier in the chapter, I had the participants sort out the feelings that came up for them as they publicly stated their national identities in various ways. Two Japanese participants exposed their hidden Korean and Okinawan bloodlines in the process of doing this exercise. Korea and Okinawa have both been dominated by Japan in the past. Even in a seemingly homogenous country such as Japan, these revelations demonstrated that there exists a complex web of cultural identity under the surface.

Participants further explored their Japanese identity, first on paper by diagramming and then through the technique of sculpting the significant internalized spoken and unspoken messages from parents, ancestors, society, and authority figures. A Japanese man who had lived in the United States for many years volunteered to do this exercise in front of the group. The roles he chose to portray in his diagram of societal messages were: his father, his mother, school, America and Japanese society. Each one gave him messages that were enacted by members of the group. The strongest charge came from the role of Japanese society insightfully acted by another participant and a moving psychodramatic dialogue ensued between them. The psychodrama unearthed the conflict that existed within this man between the traditional Japanese values of loyalty to the group, politeness, harmony, and indirect communication and the Western values of directness and open emotional expression. In the post-psychodrama sharing the theme of the collision between Eastern and Western values in Japanese culture resonated with the majority of the participants. The point came up that this internal cultural conflict might have had its roots in the history of Japanese modernization, the end of World War II and the injection of Western values caused by the post-war occupation of Japan by the United States.

In a continuing exploration of Japanese history and identity I asked the group to prepare a five minute enactment of their people's history from ancient times to the present. I gave them only 15 minutes to prepare. The group welcomed the comic relief of a playful examination of a serious topic. The light-hearted improvisational presentation fast-forwarded through the creation of the Japanese Islands, the movement of tectonic plates, the period of the Japanese as hunters and gatherers, the influence of Chinese culture, the succession of Shogunates, the opening of Japan by Commodore Matthew Perry, the Sino-Japanese War followed by the Russo-Japanese War, the elevation of the

Emperor to god-like status, the military build-up to World War II, culminating with the atomic bomb and the end of the War followed by the American occupation. Using chairs and other objects in the room, the participants started to symbolically build skyscrapers on the shaky foundation of the rubble and destruction of their country. The group, as if with blinders on, cried out: "Stay focused on the future!" Exhausted, they stopped to view and take stock of the society that they had created. In a synchronistic moment, through the open window of our workshop space, the tall skyscrapers of the city glistened in the sun. Slowly, the group began to dismantle the sculpture of chairs representing the society they had created. Underneath the foundation of these buildings was the unexpressed grief of the Japanese people symbolized by a black scarf.

The workshop closed with an improvised story theatre allegory that was collaboratively created and enacted by the group. In the story, a character that the group named Akira went on a journey in search of the meaning of WWII. Akira was troubled by his legacy and could not make peace with it. He drowned his sorrows in sake and found himself wandering around a peace museum after hours trying to find answers to his quest in the darkened exhibits. Suddenly a group of angry people from Asian countries that had been oppressed by Japan appeared and started to chase him. They were accusing him of not admitting to war crimes. In the midst of the chaos, the Asian people caught Akira and they abruptly started to drink sake together. Once they joined him in drinking, they all became friendly. The scene transformed from one of anger into camaraderie. Akira's conclusion was that the search for the meaning of WWII is very simple: we must find our common humanity. In the playfulness of the improvised story, the group had projected all its fear, sorrow and hope.

In the final ritual, we ended as we had begun. The participants returned the stones they had been holding as symbols of their personal and collective WWII stories. Each participant put their stone on the altar, stating, "I place this stone in honor of . . ." Each participant ended the sentence with a heartfelt sharing of the person they were honoring and what they were taking with them from their experience. A Playback Theatre performance was held two days after the workshop at a lecture hall on the Ritsumeikan University campus. Playback Theatre AZ ensemble from Tokyo, directed by Kayo Munakata, came to Kyoto to perform the stories and support the HWH event. I conducted the performance, interviewing the Tellers with the help of an interpreter. That night the lecture hall was filled to capacity with students and members of the community. The actors began by sharing their own stories related to the legacy of WWII, the advertised theme of the performance. This functioned as a warm up for the audience. As I came on stage to introduce myself, facing a sea of Asian faces, I again became profoundly aware of being an outsider asking the audience to share their inner secrets. I knew that I would need to gain their trust.

I began as I often begin an evening of Playback, by referring to the theme of the evening and the opening stories shared by the actors. Then I asked the audience for feelings and images related to the theme and explained that the actors will respond with fluid sculptures. The first respondent said in an angry voice, "Why do you come to Japan? Why are you speaking English; why aren't you speaking Japanese? You come to Japan, you should learn Japanese." I responded. "These sound like angry questions. Can we play back your anger?" He agreed and the Playback ensemble played back his outrage. I asked him if we had captured the essence of his anger. He said, "Only 50 percent of it." I thanked him for his honesty and moved on to the next person.

I responded to the next raised hand. An older gentleman with white hair stood up and began to rant at the top of his lungs, "How dare you come and speak to us about Japan?" I recognized that voice–it was the harsh controlling voice of the bus driver, the voice of the teacher, the voice of the perpetrator from our workshop. It turned out that this man belonged to the right wing nationalist movement and had come to sabotage the event. I decided to stay with him and to take an empathetic stance towards his rage. "Look at what the United States did to Japan in Hiroshima and Nagasaki," he continued. "Look at China–they've killed thousands of their own people. You must face the facts; you must tell the truth!" He went on in this manner for two minutes.

When he finally paused, I said, "I want to explain that I have not come here as a colonialist power trying to tell Japan what to do. I have come with humility and with empathy. I feel your anger and your passion, sir. Will you permit us to play it back?" He nodded silently. The ensemble played back the man's anger and passion. He was calmed by the aesthetic response of the actors and, with a strange smile on his face, sat down. We were then able to proceed. I then invited someone to be the first Teller of the evening.

My request was met with tense silence. I asked again. Finally, someone from the workshop raised his hand and I invited him up onstage. It was the man who had intervened with the bus driver and he told that story again, but this time in public. In sharing the story again he seemed more empowered and his message to the audience was that we all have a strong voice inside that can be used to fight oppression and promote peace.

The next story was told by a Japanese woman who had visited the Hiroshima Peace Memorial Museum with an American and a Korean friend. They all wandered around the museum, looking at the aftereffects of the atomic bomb. Then the Korean and Japanese friends found themselves outside, waiting for their American friend. He did not emerge from the museum until several hours later. They asked him why he had spent so long in the museum. He replied, "As an American whose country dropped the bomb, I have a heavy conscience. I wanted to carve the images into my brain and heart so as never to forget." The Japanese teller questioned herself: "Do I feel the same guilt and responsibility for what Japan did in Korea and China and other countries?" She had to admit that she did not.

Following these two moving stories I thought that it was important to allow the audience to process what had been stirred up. So I asked people in the audience to turn to a neighbor to discuss the themes from the first two stories. I then invited people to share their feelings and played them back with Playback Theatre short forms. The man who originally challenged me about what I was doing in Japan speaking English said that the first two stories had cleared the air and he now felt that we were all standing on common ground. Another man said he was impressed with the integrity displayed by the first two Tellers.

I asked for another Teller to come up and share a story. Once again, the man who had ranted at me before stood up and started ranting again, this time about the Korean War. Trying to feel compassion for what was driving this man, I sensed a deep hurt within him. I said, "I feel your anger and your hurt and your sense of feeling wronged." I asked the ensemble to play these feelings back. They did a Narrative V monologue driven by a powerful drumbeat created by the Playback musician. Finally, the man seemed to feel seen and understood. He smiled and sat down and we didn't hear from him again the rest of the evening.

A young man came up next and related his memory of being a fourth grader and having a school assignment to go home and ask his family members about WWII and then write a report. First, he asked his grandparents. His grandfather had been too short to be a soldier in the Japanese Imperial Army and felt enormously ashamed that he had not gone to war. His grandmother was conflicted: glad that her husband was alive but also ashamed that he had not been in the army. These sentiments puzzled the boy. Next, he asked his uncle, who had been a soldier in China during the war. The boy knew that his uncle had killed a lot of people and asked him about it. Hearing his question, his uncle hit him hard across the face and said, "Don't you ever ask me about that again!" Shocked at his uncle's reaction, the boy was thrown into a sea of confusion. He felt the profound differences between the experience of his generation and the generations that had lived through the war. He felt the "shame of the gutter" and couldn't make sense of his complex legacy. In a Hamlet-like soliloquy, the Playback actor who had been chosen to portray the young man movingly captured the essence of the boy's confusion and the man's struggle with his conscience and the Japanese soul.

I invited a final Teller to come up on stage and share a personal story. A woman stood up in the audience and started to speak with great passion from her chair as if she could no longer contain herself. She identified herself as a Korean student studying Peace Education at Ritsumeikan University. She thanked the actors and the people who had produced this public forum on the legacy of the war. She thanked the Tellers who had so courageously shared their stories. The Korean woman's family had suffered greatly at the hands of the Japanese during World War II and she felt that it was important to speak about the truth in such bold and honest ways. It gave her hope. She saw the potential of this kind of theatre to heal. A descendant of Japanese victimization had finally felt safe enough to speak up. The audience acknowledged her with warm applause for her courage in expressing herself. The Playback Theatre ensemble honored her by playing back the essence of her experience through a final fluid sculpture.

As the audience filed out of the lecture hall, I was approached by several Chinese and Korean students, some trembling with emotion, sharing their appreciation for the event. A Chinese student whose grandmother had been a comfort woman during the War confided in me. Whispering through her tears she said, "I wanted so much to tell my story. But, I couldn't. I was too afraid." Profoundly moved by this encounter I saw that I might have made a small crack in the silence around this war.

CONCLUSION

Making Commitments to Acts of Creation and Acts of Service

The last phase of the HWH approach actually takes place out in the world, after the workshop is over. Many people participate in HWH workshops hoping that somehow the burden of their historical legacy can be magically lifted from their shoulders. Often inheritors of a historical trauma feel locked in an unfortunate cycle of rage, shame and guilt with no release from their suffering. They attempt to cope by ignoring or avoiding the issues arising from the trauma and its aftermath. Then a film image, news story or an encounter with the enemy reawakens their awareness that there is ultimately no escape from the ghosts of the trauma. Most people live their lives unconscious of the role that history plays in the present. In American society, for example, the impact of slavery can be felt every day if one chooses to see it and feel it. HWH is founded on the premise that historical trauma needs to be worked through in a personal way in order to be truly understood and reintegrated into a life-affirming sense of self. This process provides a bridge between personal and collective experience. First, we need to face history and uncover our unconscious emotional reactions and beliefs. We can then give ourselves the opportunity to transform the trauma through acts of creation or acts of service.

The principle behind encouraging HWH participants to use the traumatic images, memories and messages they have inherited to create art or take social action is that this is the most powerful way to ultimately master the trauma. Though trauma will never disappear and one has a permanent relationship to it, the inheritor can be liberated from a tortured denial or rejection of its existence. Embracing the legacy allows the constrained and unexpressed emotional energy to begin to untangle.

Acts of creation can involve all of the expressive arts (visual art, poetry, music, dance, and theatre) to transform the pain of the past into an aesthetic form. In this way, the person's experience of the trauma can be witnessed and their soul soothed. The empowerment of taking social action can counter the overwhelming helplessness that inheritors of a trauma feel in the face of an unbearable legacy. The HWH approach models the synthesis of art and social action, when workshop attendees become involved in new HWH initiatives or move back out into the world having been transformed by their experience. A German and a Jewish poet collaborated and toured reading their poetry, an Armenian created an ongoing Turkish-Armenian dialogue group, in Montreal a Palestinian-Israeli reconciliation group was formed, a German dancer performed dance rituals in Berlin on Holocaust commemoration day, a Japanese man was inspired to create reconciliation groups with Chinese and Koreans, a Jewish Holocaust survivor created a theatre piece about her story.

As a drama therapist, I do not judge the form that the transformation of the inherited pain takes. I assist in helping the participants find their own paths. I trust in the profound healing and transformative principles I found in nature when I made my pilgrimage to Auschwitz in 1995–the horror of the ashes of the cremated bodies scattered around the burning fields transformed into transcendently beautiful wildflowers.

REFERENCES

Ancelin Schutzenberger, A. (1998). *The ancestor syndrome.* Hove and New York: Brunner-Routledge.

Boal, A. (1979). *Theatre of the oppressed.* New York: Theatre Communications Group.

Emunah, R. (1994). *Acting for real: Drama therapy process, technique, and performance.* New York: Brunner/Mazel.

Fox, J. (1986). *Acts of service: Spontaneity, commitment, and tradition in the nonscripted theatre.* New Paltz, NY: Tusitala Publishing.

Frankl, V. (1984). *Man's search for meaning.* Washington: Washington Square Press.

Grier, W., & Cobbs, P. (1968). *Black rage.* New York: Basic Books.

Kellermann, P. (2007). *Sociodrama and collective trauma.* Philadelphia: Jessica Kingsley Publishers.

Klein, J. W. (1980). *Jewish identity and self-esteem: Healing wounds through ethnotherapy.* New York: New York Institute on Pluralism and Group Identity, The American Jewish Committee.

Moreno, J. L. (1953). *Who shall survive?* New York: Beacon House.

Naor, Y. (1998). The theater of the Holocaust. In Levine, S., & Levine, E. (Eds.), *Foundations of expressive arts therapies* (pp. 223–240). London and Philadelphia: Jessica Kingsley.

Salas, J. (1993). *Improvising real life.* Dubuque, IA: Kendall/Hunt.

Spolin, V. (1968). *Improvisation for the theatre.* Evanston, IL: Northwestern University Press.

FURTHER TRAINING

Armand Volkas teaches a course in Drama Therapy and Social Change at California Institute of Integral Studies in San Francisco CIIS Drama Therapy Program. He also offers professional training and apprenticeship opportunities in his *Healing the Wounds of History* approach through The Living Arts Counseling Center in Oakland, California.

Armand Volkas, MFT, RDT/BCT
Healing the Wounds of History
4000 Broadway, Suite 4
Oakland, CA 94611
Telephone: (510) 595-5500, Extension 11
Email: avolkas@aol.com
Website: www.livingartscenter.org

Chapter 9

NARRADRAMA: A NARRATIVE APPROACH TO DRAMA THERAPY

Pamela Dunne

Once upon a time there was a little girl who loved stories. She would sit on her mother's lap and listen in a mesmerized rapture whenever her mother began telling a story. Her mother's stories always began with "Back in the days . . ." The little girl decided she wanted to be a storyteller when she grew up. She became a storyteller groupie and followed her favorite storytellers. She learned that stories can say things that cannot be said any other way. Of course the little girl is me, and that was the beginning of my journey. Wherever that journey has taken me, from storyteller groupie to children's theatre regular to passionate drama therapist, my zest for stories: their drama, emotion, transformation and healing, are what have always given me my inner smile. I'm still having my life-long love affair with stories.

THEORY AND PRINCIPLES

Narrative Therapy

Story, or *narrative,* shapes how we interpret life events, according to Narrative pioneers Michael White (1989, 1998, 2000), David Epston (1998) and Karl Tomm (1988, 2007). The stories we tell ourselves about our own lives determine which events we consider important. Our self-narrative determines how we interpret our experiences. "It is the stories that persons have about their lives that determines both the ascription of meaning to experience and the selection of those aspects of experience that are to be given expression. It follows therefore that these stories are constitutive of shaping persons' lives." (White 1989, pp. 6–7). As people become aware of different stories in their lives, they decide which stories to hold on to and build their lives on. Through the process of re-authoring, people reinvent their lives.

Stories both describe and shape peoples' lives. People tell stories in their internal dialogue and in social communications about themselves and others. Personal and relationship stories come in many forms. Some are tragic, comic, or romantic, others are mundane or repetitive. Some are startling. Some inspire, others accuse or degrade.

While no one story can hope to completely capture the complexity of lived experience, what we emphasize or omit has real effects on the teller and often on the listener (Freeman, Epston, & Lobovits, 1997).

We all continuously organize and give meaning to our lives through the storying of experience. Dominant, *problem-saturated* stories restrict the roles and actions we perform, because they filter problem-free experiences from our memories and perceptions. We tend to ignore even positive instances in which the problem is overcome or alleviated, when and if these instances don't fit into our internal narratives.

A person may be unable to see alternatives to a solution because his or her creativity and imagination are overshadowed by the problem-saturated story. As experiences that do not fit with the problem-saturated story are filtered out, so are resourcefulness, ability, hope, and affirmation. Finding alternative stories expands the player's repertory of roles. Actions and self-descriptions interact as circular closed systems: actions influence our self-descriptions and our self-descriptions shape our actions.

Narrative Therapy, often referred to simply as *Narrative,* is primarily talk therapy, while *Narradrama* is a form of drama therapy. Narradrama adds varied means of communication to traditional Narrative Therapy: art, poetry, music, dance/movement, and electronic media (photography, video and film). A traditional Narrative therapist explores the alternative story by talking with the participant, while the Narradrama therapist/facilitator encourages the participant to take on different roles and dramatize the alternative story. Narradrama action techniques, concepts, and principles not only pertain to a participant in a therapeutic setting, but to an educational setting as well. The use of the term therapist/facilitator encompasses both education and therapy.

No conflict exists between traditional Narrative Therapy and Narradrama. Traditional Narrative therapists have already begun to use the creative arts as a means of communication, and so Narrative therapists are readily able to adapt and incorporate Narradrama methods into their sessions.

Narrative always emphasizes collaboration and respect between participant and therapist. In their training, Narrative therapists examine how their own cultural values may influence how they think and interact with participants. Narrative therapists set aside their own values and beliefs so these will not intrude on the therapy space. Narrative Therapy invites the voice of the participant to emerge in an atmosphere of mutual respect and understanding.

Narrative inherently fosters respect for cultural minorities, children, and women. Narrative therapists try to be very aware of the effects of privilege in marginalizing and diminishing the voices of participants. In Narrative, meaning and values emerge through the interaction between participant and facilitator, so the Narrative therapist endeavors to not reinforce the dominant culture or system. Every participant expresses different needs as well as different values, and these needs and values deserve respect until or unless the participant chooses to question them. Narrative facilitators work at being flexible, collaborative and open-minded, thereby adapting readily to different cultural and ethnic contexts.

Because each individual is unique, Narrative does not rely on traditional psychological analysis and assessment. Viewing a person in a pathological or dysfunctional way marginalizes the individual and leads to labeling. Narrative strives to be helpful without being judgmental, and this is another way in which Narrative fosters respect and trust.

Outsider Witnesses, Participant Consultants, and Experience Consultants

The idea of outsider witnesses–a *reflecting team*–trained observers who assist in either Narrative Therapy or Narradrama–developed out of honoring and respecting participants' wisdom, culture, and insider knowledge. The reader is referred to Russell and Carey (2004, citing White's work) and Andersen (1991). The outsider witnesses observe part or all of a session and then engage in a conversation with each other exploring how their own experiences connect to what they have just witnessed in the session. They may talk about images or moments of appreciation or express curiosity about something that has occurred. The outsider witnesses speak with each other and do not look directly at the participant or group that they are reflecting about. After the outsider witnesses complete their reflections, the participant or group reflects on these reflections. Outsider witnesses consist of other professionals, paraprofessionals, and persons with insider knowledge–special knowledge gained from personal experience.

Narrative Therapy and Narradrama may also include participant consultants and experience consultants. Participant consultants may be either former participants who have successfully concluded therapy or volunteers who have completed special work in an educational setting and desire to serve others. Participant consultants may be invited to attend therapy/school sessions/meetings or to be outsider witnesses. Former participants might also introduce new participants to their own videos and other forms of expression that helped them effect change in their own lives. Experience consultants, on the other hand, are not volunteers: experience consultants are paid mental health professionals whose life experience may be of value to the participant. Experience consultants may also be members of reflecting teams or attend sessions/meetings. Narrative rethinks mental health services as partnerships built on a combination of professional knowledge and experience knowledge.

Important Narrative Concepts

Double Listening

The principle of *double listening* suggests that there is a duality to all descriptions of experience, and that all descriptions of experience are relational. A singular, problem-saturated description of an experience functions only as a starting point, revealing that which is already visible. Double listening helps uncover things that are not readily visible. The therapist/facilitator listens for clues or actions that reveal what is hidden, and then offers questions or reflections to help uncover it. Borrowing from the French philosopher Jacques Derrida (1978), Michael White (2000) refers to this as "the absent but implicit."

The engagement with this interest in the absent but implicit requires and reinforces a double listening on behalf of the therapist. It is in the context of this double listening that people experience being doubly or multiply heard. This is the context in which people find that there is space for them to express their experience of whatever it is that troubles them. This context provides them the opportunity to explore the unstated: that is, whatever it is that this discernment speaks to. In this way, the engagement with this interest in the absent but implicit contributes to therapeutic conversations as double or multistoried conversations.

White agrees with Derrida that words are signs that construct boundaries between specific concepts. These signs (words) establish borders between privileged meanings and other meanings that are subordinated rather than explicit. By closely listening to people's expressions and forming questions, the therapist/facilitator may be able to open up the part that has been absent. For example, in looking at a participant under the influence of despair, there might be a trace of hope. A question like, "How did you manage to hold onto hope despite your despair?" might bring hope into the picture. Just as negative space is important to visual artists, whatever remains implicit but unsaid is important to Narrative therapists.

"When these negative identity conclusions are more enduring, people experience them to be quite capturing of their lives. Such conclusions are often found to be paralyzing of action in regard to the predicaments of people's lives and can contribute to a strong sense of one's life being held in suspense, of one's life being frozen in time. I believe that one of the primary achievements of externalizing conversations is this unpacking of the thin conclusions that people have about their own and about each other's identity." (White, 2004)

Whenever new descriptions of identity and values emerge, participants experience the transformative power of personal agency stories, a power that can help them change their lives. They see new alternatives, and may choose to move or act proactively in preferred ways. At the same time, discovering hidden descriptions can reverse assumptions of deficit and incompetence, offering participants a potent source of increased confidence and self-esteem.

Re-membering Conversations

Michael White (1989) introduced *re-membering* into narrative therapy by calling attention to the idea that people's identities are shaped by what he referred to as a "club of life." The idea is that members of our club introduce how we come to experience ourselves. The person or persons whose views matter most to us influence our identities most significantly. Those we don't give much credibility to have lower membership status.

Re-membering conversations function not as passive recollections, but purposeful engagements with the significant figures of one's own life history. These significant figures continue to speak to us throughout our lives, even when they are no longer physically present. White invites participants to choose the persons (real or fictional) we allow into our club of significant figures. Positive voices and opinions from the past are sometimes drowned out by newer, louder, and more insistent negative voices. As the gatekeepers to our own club, we can choose to let in the voices we want to listen to and refuse admittance to unhelpful voices. The significant figures may be important people in our lives as well as authors, poets, or fictional characters in literature, movies or comics. Even a stuffed toy or a favorite pet may be part of the club of significant figures who make positive contributions.

First, the therapist focuses on how the significant figure has influenced the person's life. The therapist might ask the participant to assume the role of the significant figure in order to reveal the participant's identity through the eyes of the significant figure. For example, "What sorts of things did you like best about John (the subject's name)? When did you experience John as most confident? What is one of the things that touched you most about John? What strengths do you see in John?"

Next, the therapist turns the frame around and asks questions about the participant's impact on the significant figure. The participant might be asked to describe the ways in which their relationship impacted the significant figure's sense of who they were and what their life was about. For example: "What are some of the ways that John has helped you to grow? Are there things that you have done that you would not have done without John's influence? What contribution has John made to you that he would be surprised to hear?"

Reauthoring Conversations and Reauthoring Conversations Map

When therapists and participants engage in a *reauthoring conversation,* the hope is to discover alternative story lines. The practice of reauthoring presumes that no single story can explain the totality of a person's experience. There will always be other story lines implicit within the randomness and jumbled unfolding of our lives.

As a guide to re-authoring conversations, Michael White developed the "reauthoring conversations map" (White, 2004). The *reauthoring conversations map* divides the questions into two categories. The first category involves questions about the *landscape of action,* and the second category involves questions about the *landscape of identity.* Asking these questions invites the participant to bring forth and expand the alternative story.

Landscape of action questions occur after a unique outcome has been identified. A few examples might be, "Can you tell me more about what happened? What steps did you take to get you ready to do what you did? Can you tell me more about those steps?"

Landscape of identity questions encourage participants to reexamine their own identity. Such questions might include, "When you told me about the times you outsmarted the problem, what do you think this says about you as a person? When you held firm in refusing to let the problem influence you, what were you hoping for? What does this action say about your hopes for your life?"

Hopes, beliefs, dreams, and visions can be linked to new descriptions of identity, allowing participants to see themselves and their actions from different perspectives, and thereby to free themselves from the problem-saturated stories that have held them back.

Narradrama: Narrative Therapy and Drama Therapy Working Together

Narradrama combines Narrative Therapy with drama therapy. Drama therapy helps participants connect emotions, body, and intellect. It helps them explore personal, social and psychological problems. By encouraging creativity as well as imagination and role-playing, drama therapy helps participants reexamine or redefine their self-descriptions and internal narratives. Drama therapy leads to new insights through artistic expression and expansion of roles. The ability to participate in pretend or transcendent activities (Stanislavski's *as if*) helps participants to open doors and move away from problem-saturated descriptions. By functioning in the *as if,* participants can transcend immediate reality and transport themselves in time and space. Roles offer empowerment to the role-player. Describing sights, sounds, and smells help engage participants as the story thickens and becomes multidimensional. By functioning in the *as if,* participants start reverberations that transcend life circumstances, generating a sense of competence and agency. In Narradrama, theatre and role-playing are the core of the process, although other creative forms of expression may be employed to help a participant further explore or expand a story, issue, or problem.

Narrative Therapy maintains multiple perspectives. It rejects external value systems: truth is socially determined and negotiated. Similarly, drama contains multiple voices. Drama has always contained multiple perspectives and embraced the complexity and contradictions of life experience. Both drama therapy and Narrative maintain an evolving, relational view of the self that is continuously developing in different social contexts. In drama therapy the self continues to be revealed through the roles played as well as the interrelationship between the roles. Through narrative the participant tells different stories. How participants perceive their life roles becomes profoundly influenced by their evolving personal narratives.

In both Narrative Therapy and drama therapy, it is important to discover, reveal, and challenge restraints. Individual, family and cultural restraints sometimes limit personal potential and growth. Drama throughout the ages has always sought to expose political and social restraints and to serve as a means of protest. A drama therapist using Narradrama utilizes the concepts of *physicalization* and *concretization* to free participants from restraints and to assist them in discovering new meanings. *Physicalization* is the process whereby participants communicate and experience emotions and ideas through their bodies. *Concretization* is a similar process: conceiving and giving physical form to the otherwise amorphous patterns that restrain the participant.

Narrative therapists utilize *double descriptions* to enable participants to compare the outcomes of problem-saturated stories to the outcomes of alternative stories. Double descriptions provide a means to illuminate and contrast the dominant problematic story against the alternative resourceful story. With improvisational role-playing, stories can be enacted and participants can experience their stories from different perspectives: as actor, director, or audience.

Both Narradrama and traditional Narrative Therapy make use of audiences. In addition to the therapist and other participants in group therapy, outsider witnesses may be brought in to observe. Similarly, the Narrative therapist and drama therapist utilizing Narradrama may invite an audience of the participant's friends and family to witness new meanings, as a formal or informal ceremony to mark moments when participants have made decisions to follow new paths. In Narradrama, participants continuously serve as an audience to each other. In drama therapy, the participants are observers as well as participants. In Narradrama groups, the other members of the group are usually the principal audience for each other's stories, though stories can even be shared with other groups both nearby and far away. Narradrama groups grow to depend on the sustenance and reassurance they receive from each other. Even when the members of the audience simply observe, they participate in the dramatic action and provide reflection as they observe the story being performed.

Drama requires collaboration. Narrative Therapy fosters a collaborative process between therapist and participant. Narrative Therapy rejects the idea of therapist as authority figure. Instead, Narrative Therapy emerges from a collaborative experience between therapist and participant, emphasizing the expertise of the participant and allowing that expertise to emerge. True collaboration in Narrative Therapy requires respect and a joint effort to make things happen. Collaboration in Narrative Therapy and in Narradrama engages all participants in meaning-making and supports the participant, family or group as the primary authors of meaning.

Because of the special moral and ethical responsibilities associated with being a therapist, there is an implicit and unavoidable power differential between therapist and participants. Nevertheless, because equality is essential to effective Narradrama collaboration, it becomes essential to minimize any power differential.

Both drama therapy and Narrative seek to encourage spontaneity. In improvisation, actors respond to each other spontaneously, without scripts, planning, or preconception. Even with scripted traditional theatre, no two performances are ever exactly alike. The Narrative therapist comes to the therapy space without an agenda, as an empty canvas, and allows events to emerge spontaneously. Spontaneous interaction and respect between participant and therapist fosters collaboration and enlivens the therapeutic process. In both Narrative Therapy and Narradrama, the participant compares the old story with the new and decides on what direction to take, building on exceptions and reassembling a new and preferred story. The therapist/facilitator does not direct the course of events or judge the participants' decisions, but invites and encourages the participants to make their own choices and decisions. The therapist/facilitator works in a nondirective way to help the participants expand awareness, express emotions, and discover alternative problem solutions within a supportive, playful, and creative environment.

METHOD AND TECHNIQUES

Narrative and Narradrama Techniques

Externalization

Drama therapy and Narrative both use the process of *externalization,* which may be summarized by the maxim, "The person isn't the problem; the problem is the problem." Taking a curious, open stance, the traditional Narrative therapist invites the participant to externalize through language with the idea of freeing the person from the grip of the problem. This externalizing process helps participants to separate themselves from the problem and offers new perspectives.

> Through *externalizing conversations,* the problem is to an extent disempowered, as it no longer speaks to persons of the truth about who they are as people, or about the very nature of their relationships. This opens new possibilities for action. In the evolution of these externalizing conversations, persons continue to revise their relationship with their problems. (White, 1998)

In traditional Narrative Therapy, externalizing conversations allow participants to distance themselves from the problem. Through externalizing conversations the problem becomes disentangled from the participant's identity and is perceived as something external to the person. As the externalizing conversation continues, participants revise their relationship with the problem. Externalizing encourages participants to objectify problems and enables participants to open space around the problem and see it from various perspectives. This enables participants to escape the problem-saturated stories that have been affecting their lives and relationships. New perceptions of their life experience begin to emerge.

To encourage externalization, a traditional Narrative therapist might ask, "What is your relationship with anger?" This kind of verbal externalization invites participants to actively discuss how they have been influenced by or were able to overcome the influence of the problem. Contrast this with Narradrama, where a problem like anger can be externalized by embodying anger as an object or person, perhaps by taking on the role of anger. "Anger, please tell me about your relationship with Mary (the subject's name).

What is your secret in your ability to influence her?" Alternately, in Narradrama a participant might be invited to construct a collage or a living sculpture to express his or her relationship with anger.

Externalization helps families as well as individuals. When a family confronts an externalized problem and exposes its hidden agenda, family members quickly motivate themselves to develop cooperative strategies to challenge and defeat the problem. Attributing malicious intent to the problem rather than to another member of the family increases the family's cohesion and encourages the members of the family to view themselves and each other in new ways (Wiener & Oxford, 2003).

Through externalization, the participant begins to be aware of choices and roads not taken. The participant contrasts and visualizes the results of continuing on his or her present path while comparing it to a new path or paths opened by the externalization process. Together, the therapist and participant look at the effect of the problem on the participant's life and relationships. The Narrative therapist might typically invite the participant to look at what his or her life will look like in five years if he or she continues to remain in the problem-saturated story. The therapist invites the participant to look at alternative life stories in which the participant functions in a preferred way and does not give so much power to the problem. The participant considers whether to keep things the same, oppose the problem, and whether to defeat or redefine his or her relationship with the problem. The Narradrama therapist might suggest looking at the effects of continuing to give the problem power by facilitating a *problem effects scene* (an improvised scene showing the effect of continuing to give into the problem) or *living sculpture* (a static posed body composition by a group or individual showing the effect of the problem). With a problem effects scene, the participant begins to visualize possibilities for change, examining and enacting turning points, departures, and embarkation and disembarkation.

Michael White's writings discuss the significance of preferences, such as a preferred way of living, a preferred way of relating to a problem, a preferred way of interacting with others, or a preferred self-narrative. Externalizing invites participants to become more aware of these preferences. Externalizing also helps participants to distance themselves from the problem and perceive their relationship to it. Externalization helps participants exercise increased objectivity when deciding whether to challenge the problem, or change their relationship to the problem, or restructure the way they relate to the problem.

Although Narrative externalization is a kind of distancing, drama therapist Robert Landy uses the word *distancing* differently (Landy 2008, p. 101, & 1985, p. 98–101). Landy uses distancing to refer to the emotional immersion of the participant in a role. Landy defines *overdistance* as being distant and unemotional, while *underdistance* as being immersed and highly emotional. Playing a real and vulnerable role in a realistic scene encourages underdistance, because the player tends to get emotionally involved, while playing a fairy-tale character encourages overdistance because the situation is clearly not real, and therefore provides more safety for the participant. Landy considers the healthy state to be a balance between overdistance and underdistance. In Narradrama, externalization is actively sought because it facilitates separating the participant from the problem.

To begin facilitating externalization, a Narradrama therapist might ask participants whether they would like to assemble a *photo problem collage* to illustrate their relationship to the problem. In this exercise, participants take a photo or a symbol of themselves and place it in relationship to a photo or images representing the problem. Afterward, the participant might refer to the photo problem collage for inspiration in putting together a living sculpture with other group members, choosing an auxiliary to play their role and using other group members to portray the problem. Seeing themselves in a photo problem collage helps participants visualize their relationship to the problem, which in turn often encourages participants to either change their relationship to the problem or to protest against it. This might be followed by a *preferred relationship sculpture,* in which the participant is depicted in a preferred relationship with the externalized problem, i.e., defeating or dealing with the problem.

Externalization may also be encouraged through the use of objects, puppets, masks, life-sized dolls, artwork and other media. A teenage boy might create a *small objects projection sculpture* in a sandtray using a miniature lion to represent the problem and a car with a broken wheel to represent himself. An adult might create an *externalized problem mask* such as "Busy Frenzy," to identify the problem and thereby separate himself /herself from the problem. By creating a *personal agency mask* such as a "Spirit Guide Mask," the participant may discover personal resources to use when dealing with the problem.

Externalization can be taken further with a living sculpture or dialogue. A *unique outcome* from the past may become apparent in a *unique outcome scene* (a scene depicting an alternative to the problem-saturated story), which may lead to another unique outcome. If a participant experiences difficulty coming up with an actual unique outcome scene, then a hypothetical or imaginary scene can be created. Either way, the participant becomes more familiar with ways to challenge the problem. Using the personal agency mask and unique outcome scenes to facilitate externalization encourages participants to embrace alternative narratives and to discover strengths and potential resources.

For children, using objects makes externalization captivating and fun: children naturally enjoy playing with puppets, life-sized dolls, masks and other creative materials, especially when the objects are varied in texture, shape, weight and kind. The child experiences empowerment as he or she becomes the author of the world created. New possibilities emerge in the creation of a miniature world, a world that the child can control while exploring characters and stories. Children often choose or make puppets to represent externalized problems. An *externalized problem puppet* might be a tarantula named "Mad Anger," or a sad clown named "Soulful Sadness." This helps children create space between themselves and the problem and to understand how the problem affects them.

Externalizing also helps children overcome the stigma of labeling. For example, children who exhibit ADHD symptoms are referred to as ADHD, as if the child has become the disorder. All sorts of behaviors, regular and irregular, are attributed to the disorder, often at the expense of the child's creativity and ability to cope. By naming and separating the problem of ADHD as an external problem, the therapist becomes aligned with the child. As the child becomes the expert about the problem, the therapist becomes the curious investigator. The pathological and negative description of ADHD begins to lose its weight as the child, family and therapist work together to undermine its influence (Nylund, 2000).

Narradrama Techniques for Young Children

The Wonder Space

Narradrama, like all forms of drama therapy, invites curiosity, wonder, and reflection. The *wonder space* is a special space, designated by a fabric mat. When a child enters the wonder space he or she may draw, talk or create a scene with small objects about something the child wonders about. At any time in the therapy session, a child or therapist/facilitator may go to the wonder space. Alternately, the wonder space could be a wonder chair, wonder hat, or wonder box. An older child might write down "wondering questions" in a creative journal. In the wonder space children may draw, write, create something, or ask a question.

Transformational Circle and Transformational Ritual

Young children enter the transformational circle, which could be a large circular mat, chalk outline, or loop of rope. As children become aware that they have or want to hold onto something–a changed feeling, attitude or behavior–or become aware that they want to change something, they enter the *transformational circle.* A special transformation ritual, spontaneously and collaboratively developed, helps to mark this change. A photo may be taken to capture a key moment. This assists young children to become aware of alternative stories and inner resources and strengths.

Techniques Suitable for All Ages

Role-Playing and Improvisation

Narradrama, like all approaches to drama therapy, utilizes role-playing as the core. Impersonation, the taking of a role, becomes central to the dramatic experience. The ability of the person to take on a role ("I am me and not me") enables simultaneous engagement and separation (Landy, 1991). Taking on a role separate from the self opens up possibilities for viewing experiences from countless perspectives. The role serves as the single most significant feature that distinguishes drama therapy from other forms of psychotherapy and healing. Encouraging participants to assume different roles expands their world and their understanding of others. Taking roles allows participants to enact important stories from their lives and through enactment the meaning and usefulness of the story becomes clearer. The therapist/facilitator using Narradrama strives to engage participants in expanding their role repertoire through the active playing of roles.

Internalized Other Interviewing and Active Role Interviewing

A Narrative technique called *Internalized Other Interviewing* (Tomm, 1988) is a form of role playing in which a person takes on the role of someone from his or her life and responds to questions from the therapist. Internalized other interviewing works well with couples, where one partner takes on the role of the other partner. In observing this technique, the other partner usually becomes extremely attentive and interested in what the other person feels and thinks about them. The person playing the role looks inside himself or herself to find how the other would answer, thus the term internalized other interviewing. In traditional Narrative therapy, participants do not take on the physical mannerisms or the emotions of the person being portrayed.

Active Role Interviewing in Narradrama in contrast, involves inviting the participants to portray the role of the other not only verbally but also physically and emotionally. This involves an engagement of the mind, body and spirit, inviting a deeper understanding, empathy and connection to the person being portrayed.

Deconstruction and Reconstruction of the Alternative Story

A Narrative therapist utilizes *deconstruction* and *reconstruction* to take a problem apart and explore presuppositions. Following deconstruction, the therapist and participant collaborate to reconstruct an alternative story by examining situations in which the problem might have influenced the participant, but did not. The Narradrama therapist and participants seek to dramatically enact these exceptions, to expand them so participants become more familiar with them. Just as playwrights break down stories to expand and refine characters and situations, Narradrama therapists and participants break down or deconstruct problem scenes and put them back together in preferred ways. As part of reconstruction and role retraining, participants reexperience previously enacted or experienced events in a preferred way, reliving difficult circumstances but getting an opportunity to play the scene over. Likewise, participants may enact complete alternative stories, enabling them to reauthor their life experiences. Enacting a reconstructed story or moment helps the participant reshape and retain new strategies or a new relationship to the problem. Deconstruction also assists the participant in observing the most problematic parts of the problem which then helps with developing new strategies to defeat these problems.

Identifying and Dramatizing Unique Outcomes

An actor in a traditional play enacts the lines written by the playwright, portraying a single fixed story. In Narradrama, the improvised and evolving story invites the participant to discover alternatives and exceptions. Uncovering alternative stories assists participants to *restory* their lives. This act of spontaneous creation helps participants to move forward. Situations in which the problem was overcome are referred to as *unique outcomes.* Through unique outcomes, participants can be encouraged to enact performances that change their perceptions of life and weave these into an alternative story.

Dramatizing and enacting unique outcome stories opens space for more awareness and options. A unique outcome may be embodied in a photo sculpture, improvisation, mime vignette or other dramatic form. By constructing alternative stories with unique outcomes, participants begin to become more familiar with alternative choices. By inviting personal creativity in the mapping and acting out of the alternative story, the participant becomes more in touch with other possibilities and begins to experience a shift. Dramatizing unique outcomes assists the therapist and participant in creating a new landscape of action and identity.

Action-Oriented Interventions for Remembering Conversations

As part of Narradrama's action techniques for remembering conversations, a group member volunteers to serve as a scribe/photographer, writing down and recording or photographing new descriptions of identity as important moments occur in the action exercises. A storyboard may be helpful as a warm-up to draw significant figures or symbolic images of figures.

When listening to the significant figures from one's internal club, a circle of empty chairs represent the significant figures chosen (*significant figures chair sculpt*). The participant arranges the chairs according to the figure's importance to the participant. The participant sits in each chair in turn and takes on the role of each of the significant figures as they describe their relationship to the participant and some of the strengths or characteristics of the participant that they appreciate. Transitioning from the significant figure chair sculpt into an active interview can expand the dialogue.

Other options include enacting a significant scene between the participant and one of the influential figures, or writing an analogous story such as a fairy tale: "Once upon a time there was a. . . ." A visual story (using a storyboard) about the relationship between the participant and the influential figure could also be created and enacted. Another exercise involves establishing a "hall of fame" by asking group members to pose as significant figures with the participant playing the role of tour guide and introducing each of the figures and their significance to the participant.

The Role of the Therapist: Challenges and Pitfalls

By privileging the expertise of the participant and acting spontaneously in the moment, a therapist using Narradrama encourages the creative spirit to come forth. Creativity invites the alternative story to emerge and graces the emergence of the story with energy and hope.

At times participants may fail to exercise the strategies that they have developed to move their lives forward as they desire. They may fall back into old patterns and routines. Planning a comeback strategy ahead of time helps participants develop the means for dealing with this eventuality. Putting the comeback strategy in place in advance helps participants to anticipate and overcome setbacks.

The other challenge, as previously noted, involves therapists/facilitators actively trying to find ways to diminish the inherent power differential between themselves and the participant. For effective collaboration, the therapist/facilitator needs to avoid leading the participant. Holding back expertise allows the participant to take the lead and fosters a collaborative effort. The therapist/ facilitator needs to keep these three goals in mind: to foster collaboration, to let curiosity take its course, and to be gentle and invitational in approach.

Narradrama's Eight-Step Process

I have found it helpful to organize Narradrama sessions into eight steps. Narradrama sessions are usually spread over several weeks, and each step may include one or more sessions and steps may change order.

The eight steps are:

1. Warming up to New Descriptions of Self Identity and Environment
2. Externalizing the Problem
3. Possibility Extension (This step is optional.)
4. Externalizing Choices
5. Invite Personal Agency
6. Alternative Stories and Unique Outcomes
7. Restory Life
8. Closure, Reflection and Rituals

Step 1: Warming Up to New Descriptions of Self Identity and Environment

Participants coming for therapy often experience themselves as trapped in negative descriptions of their own identity. They feel powerless and locked into their problem-saturated story. Often they do not experience their environments as nurturing. Starting with some simple exercises to explore preferred and safe environments and alternative descriptions of identity helps to provide a foundation for future growth.

One of the exercises I have found most useful as a warm-up and introduction to Narradrama is the *preferred environment* exercise. I suggest to the participant(s): "Think about different environments where you feel really whole and safe places that you prefer to be. It might be a special room in your home, or at the beach or in a favorite café. Imagine a place where you feel connected, a place where you can be yourself. Take a few moments to visually see the place and take it all in. What are the colors of that place? Take in the colors. What are the sounds? Pause to listen to the sounds. Where do you see yourself in that place, and what are you doing? What are the important things in the environment?"

After the visualization, the participants use colored markers, pastels, paints, and crayons to sketch their preferred environment or use fabrics and objects in the room to create their environment. Afterward, it may be helpful to explore differences between their daily environment and their preferred environment. Participants begin thinking about ways in which their preferred environment might be brought into their real environment. Sometimes they create their preferred environment in the therapy space with whatever materials are available (i.e., colored scarves, fabrics, pillows) and then enter and experience that environment. This not only serves as an introduction to Narradrama, but it also helps the therapist/facilitator and participant explore modes of expression with which the participant feels comfortable.

One exercise, which playfully explores descriptions of identity, is the *self commercial*. The participant creates a video commercial in which s/he takes on the role of the product being advertised. Props, costume pieces, sound and other helpful items may be used. The participant may perform solo or with others. The process of directing the commercial and viewing it afterward often helps the participant gain a new perspective.

Step 2: Externalizing the Problem

In this step, the participant uses objects, fabrics, drawings, puppets, dolls and symbols to externalize personal problems, discovering the mode of expression that feels natural to the participant.

Externalization invites the participant to consider choices: (1) Things stay the same; (2) The participant chooses to oppose the problem; or (3) The participant develops new strategies to defeat the problem or redefine his or her relationship to the problem.

Scenes or living sculptures may be enacted that explore the participant's relationship with the problem, or how others perceive the problem and the participant's relationship to it. As previously mentioned, living sculptures are particularly effective in embodying specific problems, such as being dominated or overwhelmed by anger or sadness.

Step 3: Possibility Extension

A *possibility extension* involves exploring a particular theme like nature for a longer period of time, sometimes over a series of meetings. The possibility extension helps to free the participant from a fixed position or viewpoint, inviting a multistoried perspective. In some cases this step is not necessary and the participant may continue directly into Step Four, Externalizing Choices.

Using images from nature in the warm-ups can sometimes stimulate new and transformational ideas, and this may lead into more extended activities. For example, the therapist/facilitator might suggest the participant picture himself/herself as a tree. "What kind of tree are you? Draw yourself as that tree. Would you be a palm tree, weeping willow, fir or maple?" Then the therapist/facilitator might inquire: "Tree, tell me about your strengths. Why do you think you were chosen to represent Mary (the participant's name)? What qualities make you special and unique?" The participant might develop and enact a dialogue with the tree, or a mythological story about a tree.

Step 4: Externalizing Choices

Once the problem has (1) been externalized through an object, sculpture, drawing, puppet, mask or other creative arts technique; and (2) a possibility extension has been chosen and expanded, then (3) the participant can begin to formulate new strategies for dealing with the problem and outsmarting it. This can be aided by examining the effects of the problem using Michael White's technique of double description in which the effects of keeping on one's present course are contrasted with the effects of changing course. The effects of keeping on (with relationships, work, and so on) are described and contrasted with the effects of changing course and what changing course might do to relationships, work, and so on. This double description helps participants to see how the problem is affecting their lives and to decide on which path to take.

Once the problem becomes clear to the participant, action exercises utilizing drama and the arts may be helpful in discerning potential paths and choices. One technique, the *storyboard crossroads,* uses a movie production storyboard, a series of drawings resembling a comic book that is ordinarily used to plan the shots in a movie. A crossroads is drawn in the middle of a piece of paper. On each side of the crossroads there are a series of blank picture frames to fill in. The storyboard on the left depicts the effects of continuing to follow the status quo for the next five years, while the storyboard on the right visually demonstrates the effect of taking a different relationship to the problem. There are two different futures, two different movies, and two different storyboards. The participant physically moves along both paths, improvising scenes suggested by the pictures. In addition, the therapist/facilitator invites the participant to create both environments suggested by the storyboard and to enter and travel along both roads, using members of the group to play auxiliary roles, objects, and obstacles. To help clarify a preferred pathway, a drumming warm-up exercise might be used. The warm-up begins with the whole group drumming to a simple beat with the words "walking," in unison. Then, participants divide up into two's with each person creating a preferred rhythm which they teach to their partner, and each pair drums the rhythm together.

Step 5: Invite Personal Agency

A participant might begin by creating a *personal agency mask,* or begin by looking at his or her journal notes or pictures to review unique outcomes and personal strengths. Photos of preferred relationships to problems will often help stimulate the imagination. Allow plenty of time for the participant(s) to warm up to the idea of a personal agency mask. Not everyone is immediately ready to enter the creative frame of mind essential to this sort of exercise. Far from being simple or childish, created objects like the personal agency mask can be imbued with so much symbolic significance that the mask can become truly magical, recalling a spiritual tradition that predates scholarship and civilization. By interviewing the personal agency mask and moving, enacting and creating scenes suggested by the mask, participants make discoveries about their strengths and abilities.

Here is another technique for inviting personal agency: participants choose a moment in which they made a decision that they liked, or acted in a way that they preferred, or were able to access inner wisdom. The participants choose a mode of expression that helps recall the moment. As participants observe their creations each of them might: (1) become a newspaper reporter and describe this as an event worthy of being on the news, or (2) become the curator of an art gallery and describe the portrayal of the moment as if it were a prized piece in the gallery; or (3) take on the role of a significant other who is supportive and speak from that perspective. Expanding personal agency enables clients to embrace alternative narratives and become more familiar with strengths and potential resources.

Another discovery of personal agency may become more visible in asking the participant to take on a role of an important person in the past or a fictional role of an admired hero or heroine in a novel or favorite character in a storybook. The therapist/facilitator interviews the participant in role to learn more about the qualities that these characters recognize in the participant.

Step 6: Invite Alternative Stories and Unique Outcomes

A unique outcome from the past might become apparent through an exercise that uses objects, symbols, or art. This could be expanded, through Narradrama, into a unique outcome scene: a scene (or story, poem, sculpture) illustrating an alternative way a problem might be solved. Dramatizing a unique outcome scene can have a rippling effect that leads to the discovery of additional unique outcome scenes. A unique outcome scene might be either a real-life scene or an imaginary scene (from movies, fiction, comic books or from one's imagination) that helps put the participant in touch with inner resources that could be utilized in showing actions of strength against the problem. These scenes which suggest new descriptions of identity and actions become part of the new landscape of action and landscape of identity. In situations in which persons experience difficulty in finding a unique outcome scene or alternative story, remembering conversations from significant figures from the participant's life may be helpful. The significant figures may assist the participant in discovering alternative descriptions identity.

Step 7: Restory Life

One of my favorite ways to restory life is when participants create a *life story picture book* that portrays aspects of their lives and journeys. This is followed by an enactment of that picture book either through the use of living sculptures or through improvisation. This really helps to honor each individual. Participants can develop a *re-storied script scene* in a number of different ways: by creating a poem, picture book, dance, radio program, and monologue or through digital storytelling.

Here is a list of exercises I have found useful for step seven:

Preferred Future Poem. The participant creates a poem that reflects some important images about his or her preferred future. The participant enacts the poem using colored fabrics to suggest the images and environments.

Life Story Picture Book. The participant creates an expandable picture book of his or her life with drawings, photos, and collage and enacts a significant moment.

Affirmation Dance. The participant creates an affirmation dance and chooses a piece of music to accompany the dance. The participant makes a statement through expressive movement.

Radio Restoried Scene. The participant creates an old-fashioned radio show about a restoried scene using dialogue, sound effects, or musical interludes.

Restoried Monologue. The participant creates a restoried scene about himself/herself in which he or she imagines the other people who are in the scene and reacts to them in such a way that it is clear what his or her reactions and responses are.

Digital Storytelling. The participant chooses pictures (from past and present) as well as posing group members in pictures that represent his or her restoried life. The participant creates a digital presentation with music and narration (live or taped) of this story. After seeing the story of the participant, a reflecting team responds by sharing their connections.

Step 8: Closure and Reflection Rituals

Options for closure may involve rituals, drawings, letters, group dances, songs, murals, or any other appropriate activity. It is important that there is an action closure for each meeting.

In the regular group weekly meetings, the session begins and ends in a circle with each person sharing something they bring into the meeting and something they are take out. Sometimes passing a magical object such as a talking stick, or a small musical instrument like a triangle or bell may be helpful in creating a sense of ceremony and sharing. This sharing could also be shown through an action. For example, at the beginning of a meeting a woman might be experiencing confusion, looking in different directions for different choices and not knowing which way to turn. At the end of the meeting this woman might choose to share "clarity," demonstrated by looking in different directions and then choosing one direction and beginning to move down that path, mirrored and followed by the other members of the group. Other options: a group, or even just the facilitator and participant, might collaborate on a song to be sung at the end of each meeting. A large mural, to which additions are made each week, could be used as part of the closure process. A specific ritual could begin and end each meeting, such as lighting a candle and stating a hope for the meeting.

At the conclusion of the eight steps the closure needs to feel like a culmination. With a group, one possible closing ritual consists of having each group member write *appreciation letters* to one or more of the other members of the group, noting and reflecting on a strength, development or special moment in the meeting. Reading the letters out loud in pairs and then to the whole group serves as a very affirming and honoring closure. Readers who would be interested in learning more about the eight-step process are referred to my book *Narradrama* (Dunne & Rand, 2006).

Comparing Narradrama with Other Forms of Drama Therapy

Narradrama is both similar to and different from other approaches to drama therapy. In this section it will be compared to Landy's "Role Method" (Chapter 5) and Emunah's "Integrative Five-Phase Model" (Chapter 4), and then very briefly to Linden's "Transpersonal Drama Therapy" (Chapter 10). Narradrama will also be briefly compared to Expressive Arts Therapy. Narradrama acknowledges the contribution of drama therapy's pioneers, including Robert Landy (1985, 2008), David Johnson (Chapter 6), Renee Emunah (1994), Eleanor Irwin (1993, 2000; Chapter 11), and many others, all of whom have contributed greatly to drama therapy's growing and evolving body of knowledge.

Role Method and Narradrama Compared and Contrasted

Robert Landy's Role Method and Narradrama share many common concepts. Landy's *Taxonomy of Roles* helps in identifying archetypal roles that a participant might choose to play. Similarly, Landy's different role categories provide options a participant might be interested in exploring. In Landy's Taxonomy of Roles (Landy, 2008, p. 105), he identifies and categories 84 role types and 74 subtypes. These roles were organized first according to their distinguishing characteristics, function and style. Style is the behavior form in which the role is enacted, whether representational, abstract or somewhere in between. The Taxonomy of Roles can be used to identify the various roles (archetypal or otherwise) that a participant might choose to play. These categories become especially useful for Narradrama therapist/facilitators who might seek to open up more possibilities for participants. In Narradrama, roles may also be defined as *problem-saturated roles, unique outcome roles, alternative roles,* and *preferred roles.* These broad role categories may be fictional, realistic or archetypal. Exploring roles in this way encourages the search for alternative solutions, new possibilities, and preferred paths and futures.

Role Method's inner *guide* is consonant with Narradrama, which also seeks to help participants develop a sense of agency. The difference is that the inner guide in Role Method functions as a transitional figure that integrates the role and counter role. Narradrama's guide, in contrast, offers help and support, encouraging the participant to explore possibilities, but the guide does not necessarily integrate shadow roles. In Narradrama, a personal agency mask of an inner guide created by the participant helps participants more clearly engage those stronger parts of themselves and embark on a new life path. Role Method focuses on encouraging the participant to integrate problematic roles with the help of the guide figure, while in Narradrama, participants seek and choose among the roles they prefer to exercise in their lives.

Landy's postmodern view of the self parallels Narradrama's concept of constantly changing and evolving identity. Expanding one's role repertoire and exploring different roles can open ways of thinking and relating to others in healthier and preferred ways. Landy states: "The individual is not one thing, a core self, but a multitude of roles that exist in relationship to their several counterparts. Thus Role Method is more postmodern than humanistic. . . . There is a principle, to create new life out of old, to create something of nothing through the action of the imagination" (Landy, 2008, p. 103).

An important distinction when contrasting Role Method with Narradrama is that Role Method focuses on role, while Narradrama focuses on story. For drama to occur in Role Method, the "participants take on a role and in most instances once the role is taken on it is expressed in a role-bound story. As the role is the form of the dramatic action, story is the content, although role precedes story, it takes on a fuller meaning and fulfills its social function when it moves into story" (Landy, 2008, p. 107).

Landy states, "As my work has evolved, role is the focus but as it relates to story" (Landy, 2008, p. 1). Narradrama, in contrast, focuses on preferred choices and a new landscape of identity and action. The playing of roles assists the participant to begin to question their choices, enlarge their perspectives, discover new identity descriptions, and experience what it would feel like to move forward in their lives in preferred ways toward their hoped-for futures.

Narradrama encourages participants to project their stories forward into the future and predict what is going to happen with relationships, social networks, and jobs if they continue to repeat the same patterns and roles. In Narradrama, participants take on roles in order to tell their stories, while Role Method begins with the role, which sometimes develops into a story. Narradrama participants are encouraged to embrace roles that move their lives forward in desired ways. In both Narradrama and Role Method, playing a large variety of roles expands choices, and choices help enable the participant to escape problem-saturated roles.

In Role Method, the therapist functions as a director, maintaining empathy and aesthetic distance while encouraging clients to play out all the roles themselves. If the therapist/facilitator does move into role, according to Landy, the therapist/facilitator should remain a "mutual player, not a mutual client" (Landy, 2008, p. 108). This contrasts with Narradrama, where the therapist/facilitator may also play a role in the story, but then returns to being a collaborator, rather than a director.

Role Method delineates a number of polarities: emotion and distance, fiction and reality, verbal and nonverbal expression, action and reflection, and directive and nondirective action. Landy (2008) discusses contradictory tendencies and paradoxical roles and the human struggle for balance and integration. This parallels Narradrama's double listening, which acknowledges duality and that all descriptions of experience are relational. It is common for a participant to present a limited problem-saturated description of an experience where things that lie underneath the surface remain unperceived, therefore invisible. Just as Role Method seeks to balance and integrate polarities, Narradrama seeks to balance the seen with the unseen, permitting the invisible to become visible.

Integrative Five Phase Model and Narradrama Compared

The improvisational processes described in Renee Emunah's Integrative Five Phase Model create a safe, creative space for the participant, while fostering trust, social interaction, spontaneity, and creativity. Emunah stresses the importance of establishing a nonthreatening and playful environment: "The strengths and healthy parts of the client . . . qualities are elicited such as expressiveness, playfulness, creativity, spontaneity, humor and aliveness. . ." (Emunah, 1994, p. 35). A nonthreatening and playful environment is just as important to Narradrama. In Narradrama, a participant stuck in a problem-saturated story often loses touch with his or her creativity. A person who loses creativity may feel isolated, fearful, and unable to move or progress. Using games and activities to invite creativity is almost always welcome. The improvisational games and activities used in Narradrama assist participants to find new descriptions of self and identify personal qualities they can appreciate. Their landscape of action and landscape of identity changes: instead of seeing themselves as inadequate, they begin to see themselves as adequate and centered. This continual emergence of new identities and actions continues throughout the process of Narradrama. Unlike the Integrative Five Phase Model, the improvisational games and exercises in Narradrama are not only used in Phase One, but continue throughout the entire process.

Narradrama's eight-step procedure shares some similar goals and concepts with the Five Phase model, but the eight steps of Narradrama do not progress in a sequential way through a series of levels. In Narradrama, the particular steps can occur in any order. Narradrama might very quickly take a person from externalizing a problem to restorying how they view their life, restorying might begin on day one, even though restorying is step seven.

Narradrama and the Integrative Five Phase Model share similarities in that they both invite participants to consider possibilities. Changes in behavior often accompany a change of meaning. For Narradrama this change of meaning most often occurs in the landscape of action and the landscape of identity. The participant becomes aware in unique outcome scenes of new possibilities for action and new actions bring forth new identity descriptions. In the Five Phase Model (Emunah, 1994, p. 40–41) the participants experiment with alternatives, and hopefully this leads to the discovery of options, which is similar to the discovery (in Narradrama) that a participant makes when acting out a unique outcome story. Both the Integrative Five Phase Model and Narradrama are humanistic in orientation. Likewise, both approaches are intended to strengthen the individual and foster creativity.

In Narradrama, just as in the Integrative Five Phase Model, the participant may work with realistic or fictional roles, myths, legends, and/or fairy tales, hypothetical, future or actual scenes, any of which may be appropriate to the task at hand. In Narradrama, however, these different kinds of stories can be used in any order, whereas in the Integrative Five Phase Model, the progression typically goes from the fictional to the actual. In Narradrama the moment a new preferred action/idea enters the system a whole new set of possibilities may emerge. This could occur with fictional or realistic roles. The Integrative Five Phase Model emphasizes, particularly within Phase Three work, experimenting with alternatives, discovering new options, and enabling the participant to become the director of his or her own life drama. In this sense, both approaches emphasize the hope that people begin to experience as a result of replaying experiences in new ways. The Integrative Five Phase Model, however, relies more heavily on the enactment of real life, psychodramatic material, while Narradrama relies more on story and creative drama. The Integrative Five Phase model has a more psychodynamic orientation, in which primal woundedness is also actively explored, whereas Narradrama is more strength-based and centers on finding alternative preferred stories, thereby opening up new possibilities for change.

The Integrative Five Phase Model's psychodynamic journey leads participants from the fictional to the actual, from expansion to behavioral change, to catharsis and insight to integration. In Narradrama, participants begin with externalization of the problem and are concurrently invited to discover alternative stories, preferred outcomes and new identity descriptions (which invites participants to restory their lives and their relationships with their problems). Renee Emunah regards Narradrama as most similar to Phase Three of the Integrative Five Phase Model, a phase in which clients review and revise their current life issues. It should be clarified however, that in the Integrative Five Phase Model, client and therapist can begin in Phase Three (or any of the phases that are appropriate to that client's needs), rather than starting in the earlier phases.

Narradrama also agrees with the Integrative Five Phase Model on the importance of ritual. Ritual in Narradrama marks significant events and important transitions. The celebratory aspect of ritual, and its use in closure, is central to both Narradrama and the Integrative Five Phase Model. A Narradrama sequence of six to ten weeks will end with a special celebratory ritual. My film "Exploring Narradrama" (Psychotherapy.net, 2006) shows how a group of teens and the staff of their group home participate in an honoring ceremony. The participants honor each of the other members of the group with an appreciative statement and each member of the group receives a colored scarf. Narradrama, like the Integrative Five Phase Model, uses ritual to mark important events, so they will not fade into oblivion. "Rituals . . . enable us to take hold of our experience, rather than letting experience slip through our fingers unrecognized, unacknowledged and unassimilated" (Emunah, 1994, p. 45).

Narradrama, Integrative Five Phase Model and Role Method all acknowledge the importance of witnessing, but each model describes this process in different ways. In the Integrative Five Phase Model, Emunah states: "In dramatizing, the internal is externalized. In this process of sharing and showing one's internal world, a burden is lifted and an inner weight removed. What was private is now witnessed. This often leads to a process of intense acceptance and forgiveness" (Emunah, 1994, p. 43). Landy (2008) defines the role of the director as a witness: "the director is not only a guide figure, helping clients integrate discrepant roles, but also a witness, one who uncritically stays with clients, validating all their struggles with roles and counterroles" (p. 109). Narradrama emphasizes that people's stories need to be witnessed and honored through telling and retelling processes, not only through the voices of group members, but also through the voices of experience consultants, participant consultants, and a reflecting team including insider witnesses.

Narradrama and Transpersonal Drama Therapy

Narradrama also shares some connections with Linden's "Transpersonal Drama Therapy" (Chapter 10), particularly in the awareness of finding one's strengths and evoking stronger parts of the inner self, such as the spirit guide. The strong focus in the Transpersonal of going on a personal journey toward a fuller and more preferred life parallels Narradrama's reauthoring and restorying. According to Saphira Linden, the Transpersonal approach begins with an assumption of a human being's fundamental health and wholeness rather than pathology first. Narrative and Narradrama wholeheartedly agree.

Narradrama and Expressive Arts Therapies

Narradrama often invites participants to explore all the art forms as a lead-in for beginning the process of externalizing, or expanding an alternative story or unique outcome, or focusing on a preferred moment or marking a new path in a closure. In Narradrama, enactment and role playing, not creative arts expression, are the defining and necessary activities. Expressive Arts Therapy, with its broader sensibility, emphasizes the use of art for its own intrinsic therapeutic value, as a container for suffering, for catharsis, and for getting in touch with one's authentic self. Enactment and role playing, although not a part of Expressive Arts Therapy in general, are unique to drama therapy and Narradrama.

Sometimes in Narradrama a particular form of artistic expression may assume unusual importance when it is the preferred voice of the participant. An example would be a participant who is comfortable expressing feelings through movement but uncomfortable expressing them verbally. To honor such a participant, the therapist/facilitator may choose to invite the participant to begin sessions with Narradrama movement warm-ups that may eventually lead to an enactment phase. With such a participant, even the initial enactments might be nonverbal, i.e., played out in pantomime and movement.

CASE EXAMPLES

Amy's Experience with Narradrama

In the following case example, the techniques of externalization, landscape of identity, landscape of action, unique outcomes and double description are illustrated. This case also demonstrates how Narradrama uses the creative arts to expand possibilities and communication.

Amy, age 17, lives in a group home where she had been placed when she was a young child. Amy's mother had been addicted to drugs. Amy's father is in prison, convicted not only of illegal drug use but physical abuse. Amy's three sisters and two brothers are all in foster care. Amy feels betrayed and alone. She speaks passionately about her past as well as her wish to graduate from high school and go to college. As I connect with Amy's situation, I begin to appreciate and applaud her determination to change her life, as well as feeling real admiration for her life's dream of graduating from college and opening a home for runaway teenagers.

Amy tells me about her love for writing and photography. I ask whether she is interested in exploring writing and photography as part of her therapy. Amy seems reluctant–her previous experiences with therapy have not always been positive–nevertheless, she seems intrigued and decides to try.

This begins our year-long experience with Narradrama. In our first meeting, using Amy's interest in writing, I invite Amy to express different kinds of words–adjectives, nouns, emotionally loaded words, significant words, scary words, favorite phrases, conflict words, action words, preferred words, funny words. Amy shouts out "rage, soul, heart, spirit, coldness, body, light, funny, and God." She writes these words on 3 by 5 cards after physicalizing each word with her whole body through different movements, gestures and sounds. I ask her to complete this sequence with a sculpture that expresses a phrase of her preferred words. I notice that Amy appears both comfortable with and capable of moving and expressing meaning through her body.

I notice that Amy communicates happy emotions by using outstretched arms, open gestures, and body-reaching-outward movements. Amy communicates sad emotions by closing up her body, clutching herself, dropping her head and sinking slowly to the floor. During the first month, Amy externalizes depression, which she calls "Black Depression," as physically overpowering her. In later sessions she externalizes anger as "Rage Anger." Through externalizing she begins to explore the influence that Black Depression exerts. This invites her to question her relationship with Black Depression in a series of living sculptures which each show a different relationship to Black Depression. She asks me to photograph these sculptures to remember the kind of relationship that she wants with Black Depression. Discovering the power of words and her ability to choose words empowers Amy to stand up to Black Depression, and she tells Black Depression in an *empty chair scene* that she is going to take her life back. Amy diligently writes in her journal about her changing relationship with Black Depression and marks important scenes, moments and symbols that she wants to hold on to. All this she records with words and photographs. I invite Amy to take photographs on her own, outside the sessions, to show ways her life might be different when Black Depression no longer rules her life.

During the second and third month of therapy, Amy creates a pictorial history of her life from birth to the present. She draws and paints pictures or selects photographs to capture important life moments ranging from traumatic events to problem stories to alternative stories. As part of restorying, she keeps adding and changing her pictorial history to include pictures and photos that represent what she wants to claim from her own history. This is part of the restorying process. The pictures in Amy's pictorial history contain strong emotions, attitudes, views and postures, and alternative stories frequently emerge (Figure 9.1).

Figure 9.1. Amy's Pictorial History.

In a particular session, I notice that Black Depression seems to have returned. Amy acts despondent, apparently under the influence of Black Depression. I ask her if any of the pictures or photos from her pictorial history seem appropriate to describe the way she is feeling. She creates a *feeling collage,* showing a toilet scene with red drops of blood all around her. Amy seems unable to talk about this picture, and with curiosity I inquire about the possibility of having her write and enact a *story personalization* by personalizing some of the objects in the environment and letting the objects speak. Amy's story of "The Invisible Girl" results from this process:

The Invisible Girl

> The invisible girl walks through the hallways of her high school with her hands sweaty and tears in her eyes. "The tears want to tumble down her cheek like a river," she hears voices saying from behind the paper-thin walls.
>
> Some of the other girls who only pretend to really care say, "there she goes trying to hide her face." Of course everybody says things to make her feel better and tell her that they all "care about her." Of course they think all she wants is attention and they whisper among themselves, "She can't help it any more." She starts to cry uncontrollably and runs into the bathroom stall and slams the door and flushes the toilet to drown out the noise of her crying. She sits on the floor in the bathroom, the closed door behind her for the rest of the day. Her tears are making a puddle around her. Nobody understands her. She doesn't understand herself either, and you can read it in her red, blurry eyes that are swelling up more by the second. She cannot take it any more. Slowly the clear puddle of tears becomes diluted. Large dark red drops fall from her, as she wills her heart to not beat any more.

Amy vividly remembers the scene from her pictorial history a few weeks ago, based on a true incident from her life about two years ago, when she tried to cut herself, a death wish. She describes this time as one of the lowest in her life and one in which Black Depression kept her down. She insists that Black Depression keeps trying to get her down. I am curious about how she was able to pull herself away from Black Depression two years ago to claim a different life. "God helps me in the hardest moments. He takes my hand in his and I feel safe." She sculpts the moment of God reaching out to her hand to ward off Black Depression, and I capture the moment in photographs for her photo journal. Amy impersonates herself and uses a life-sized doll with a mask to signify God (Figure 9.2). This leads into exploring double description: alternative paths, each created by arranging fabric and objects, along with sounds. One of the two paths allows Black Depression to take control of her life. As she walks on that path she experiences the rhythms, sounds and heaviness of Black Depression. The other path, which Amy refers to as God's path, is bright with light rhythms, colors, and sounds. On this path she experiences not only lightness but also warmth and sounds of safety and peace. Amy seems surprised by the emotional impact of experiencing the two paths. The session concludes with Amy tracing her hand and filling it with the images of the preferred path and of her preferred sculpture. Amy then embodies two of the images she most connects to: rain and wavy lines. As the session concludes, I invite Amy to take photographs during the week that represent her preferred path.

In another session later in the month Amy continues to find a way to change her relationship with Black Depression. Because she has just broken up with her physically and verbally abusive boyfriend, I invite Amy to create a *tissue paper emotion collage* out of the emotions she feels, which leads her to

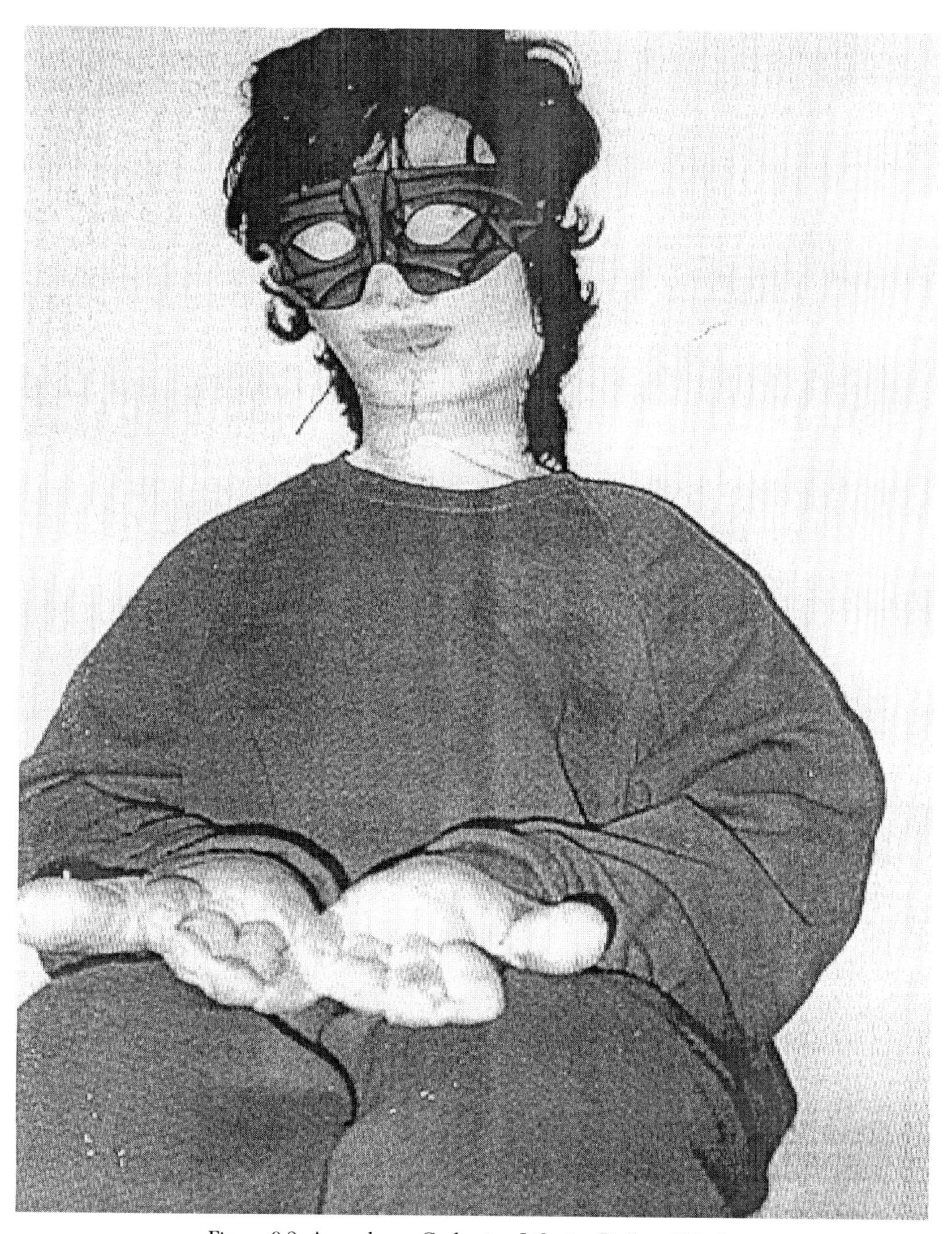

Figure 9.2. Amy shows God using Life-size Doll and Mask.

write a poem in her journal called "Scared."

Scared

The soul is weak and so is the body
Not much more can it take
Looking into the low tide of the water
I imagine myself upon it
The legs move into the water
Led by the heart
Which cannot hold up any longer
The arms work with the legs to make the body move
Across the silvery water
Into the land without him and nobody.

Amy confesses suicidal thoughts triggered by the breakup with her abusive boyfriend but assures me she will not act on these thoughts. I become curious about how Amy finds ways to resist her suicidal thoughts and how she continues in high school substance-free. This leads to exploring a new landscape of action and landscape of identity. New descriptions of Amy as "preserving," "holding out," and "resisting drugs," contrast with negative descriptions of her as "weak," "loser," and "hopeless." These new identity descriptions connect to new actions evidenced in alternative stories of Amy making good decisions and choices. She recalls how she called her best friend when she was feeling suicidal and kept the suicidal thoughts from becoming predominant. She recalled saying "No" to drugs and walking away. Enacting these scenes as the main part of the session strengthens them and makes them more visible and real, enabling her to consider descriptions of herself as "courageous," "preserving," "holding out for good things" and "looking out for her own future." She begins to experience what it's like to embody these new landscapes of identity descriptions. Further, she discovers how to use her writing to make her preferred future real. Amy shows conviction when she says that God and dancing nurture her and give her strength in hard times. In ending the session, Amy draws a picture of herself dancing, with God's presence surrounding her (Figure 9.3). This exhilarating moment represents a unique outcome scene and alternative narrative.

One month later, the building blocks of earlier sessions become even more visible as Amy exercises more control with Black Depression. She joins a recreational drama class, and continues passionately writing her own scene studies, which she performs in the class. She continues with photography and finds that her photos help her to become clearer about herself and her preferred path in life. In her journal she draws a picture of herself in a large rainy field surrounded by daisies and poppies to illustrate this story, "Undone."

Undone

I sit on the ground surrounded by lots and lots of flowers: mostly roses, but some daisies, poppies and daffodils. They scramble together to form zillions of subtle and vivid colors. I usually go there in the rain. When the drops glide though the flowers blending them all together I sit with the blanket over my head and body, the rain pouring down on my head. I go there to think, scream, cry and just stare at the world surrounding me. I am always alone, although I dream of him there sometimes. Nobody can hurt me or blame me or yell at me for reasons I do not understand. The rain gives me answers to my questions where other times it makes the tears come down faster on my face. Everything around me is beautiful and nothing will ever change that. And when I come home, drenched with water and tears, shivering from the coldness and returning to the realities surrounding me, I know . . . I just know. . . .

As her therapist, when I read this story I feel real hope for Amy. It reveals new unique outcomes and alternative narratives. My curiosity prompts me to ask Amy about the rain, a major unique outcome character as

Figure 9.3. Amy's Abstract Cutouts Showing Dancing in God's Presence.

well as the flowers. I invite Amy to expand this story further by telling it through dance. She uses long sheets of colored fabric to create the flowers and blue chiffon to show the rain that covers her body. A definiteness, strength and assuredness break forth and in the last moment of the dance ("when I come home, drenched with water and tears, shivering from the coldness and returning to the realities surrounding me, I know. I just know"), she wraps herself in a cocoon of multicolored fabrics, a peaceful refuge. Running around the room taking photographs while Amy dances, I endeavor to capture these moments. This unique outcome story, discovered through Amy's journals, further expanded through dramatization and experienced more deeply in dance strengthens Amy's journey on what she describes as God's path. Amy's self-narrative has been communicated through writing, drama, photography, and art. To close the session, Amy holds the photograph of the cocoon close to herself and writes in her poem/photo journal about her connection with the caterpillar who begins to open up to a new life of possibilities.

In the next session, Amy brings in a mask which she has created of her strong emotions (emotion mask), and a poem called "Love," which personifies the emotion.

Love

Anything I whisper you will not repeat
When I cry
You embrace me
And promise not to leave.
When I scream you scream with me
Instead of covering your ears and walking away.
You are always there when I need you
And protect me from the evil world
Surrounding us both.
As I sit with the pills
Clutched in my hand
You hold the other
And eventually I drop them.
You take off my mask
And see all of me
Hear all of me
And know all of me.
But still you say
I'm beautiful

Curious about the meaning of the poem for Amy, I inquire about the most striking images in the poem. She identifies the three most striking images as "the mask," "know all of me," and "I'm beautiful." The mask holds multiple meanings like, "hidden parts of the self that want to speak," "hidden parts that want to be unknown," "monster parts," "hero parts," "social" and "personal" parts. Amy's mask symbolizes all of these. In a creative mime vignette, Amy explores some of these roles from behind the safety of the masks, using different masks to signify different characters and moments. "All of me" and "being beautiful" represent what Amy wants to hold on to, but they have been hidden behind her mask.

In another central activity, Amy arranges small objects in a circle around her. Each of these objects represents a new-found identity from one of her alternative stories or unique outcomes. She places an object in the center of the circle (a marble) to represent herself. Then she takes on the role of each of the objects and speaks from the object's point of view. For example, she holds the miniature ladder and says, "I am Amy's perseverance. She discovered me when she played the scene of saying 'No' when her friend Gina tried to convince her to try drugs." Amy's story takes on a new landscape of action and landscape of identity which Amy internalizes as she continues along God's path into her preferred future.

A Woman's Group Discovers Narradrama

The following case study illustrates the Narradrama adaptation of a Narrative Therapy intervention, *The Tree of Life,* developed in 2005 by Ncazelo Ncube and David Denborough (Ncube & Denborough, 2005). Working with children in a Masai Camp in Zimbabwe, Ncube and Denborough developed The Tree of Life as a means to enable these children to talk about their lives without being overwhelmed by their problems, helping them examine and choose among the alternatives that were available to them.

This case study focuses on three women, aged 30 to 50, from a group of seven women who had been meeting for two months to explore personal issues. Sarah, a nutritionist, experienced an impasse in making some difficult career and personal changes. Mary, a high school teacher, experienced problems with anxiety. Brittany, a computer programmer, hoped to develop more assertiveness because she sometimes felt invisible.

On this particular day, I ask the group whether they would be interested in drawing The Tree of Life as a warm-up to exploring their special knowledge, hopes, and strengths. [As these women preferred visual art, the Tree of Life served as a bridge into Narradrama action work]. I begin by handing out large sheets of paper and colored marking pens, and inviting each participant to draw a tree.

Each of the trees looks different. Mary's tree has graceful and feminine curving lines. Brittany's tree has long roots and tall branches that reach upward into the sky. Sarah's tree has a solid trunk and bears abundant fruit.

As soon as they finish their drawings, I ask the participants to picture their lives within their trees, beginning with the roots. "In the roots, draw or write some important parts of your family history, including those who have taught you and been most significant in your life."

This leads into a *living slide show:* each participant enacts scenes about important people from their roots. In previous meetings, the women had already experienced restorying, taking preferred stories from history. Their slide shows include the people and moments from their restoried narratives. The subject of Brittany's slide show is her relationship with her grandmother. Brittany's grandmother recognizes qualities in Brittany that Brittany herself fails to see. As director, Brittany chooses specific theme music and places group members in statue-like poses to portray significant moments with her grandmother. The group members practice transitioning smoothly from one slide to the next.

After her living slide show, I interview Brittany (in role of her grandmother) about what she admires about Brittany. As her grandmother, Brittany says, "I always admired Brittany's dedication to the piano. As a little girl, she used to practice her piano without ever being asked. She just kept at it. Sometimes when I got discouraged I thought about Brittany at the piano, playing all those wrong notes, but not giving up." (This is an illustration of a remembering conversation.)

A reflecting team member remarks, "I was wondering how Brittany's ability to keep at something plays out in her life today? I was curious if keeping at it might kindle her hopes or dreams for her life."

Brittany, in reflecting on the reflections, admits that she has never considered her ability to keep at it as an important factor in her present life. She seems very moved by the revelation that her grandmother and others consider her to be a person who keeps at it. She reflects that she perceives herself more as "failing to follow through," and "nonassertive."

Returning to our drawings of trees, we continue upward from the roots. "On the trunks, I suggest you draw or write about your skills, abilities and competencies. On the branches, draw or write about your hopes, dreams and wishes for your future." I then invite the group to choose one particular ability, skill or competency they had first learned of in childhood and show its development in three scenes: one past, one present, and one future. A cross section of Mary's Tree (Figure 9.4) shows its solid trunk where she illustrates her skills and competencies. Each participant directs her own scene with the other members of the group as actors.

Mary focuses on her empathy. Her first scene shows her in elementary school. She depicts herself as a quiet child who shares her lunch and befriends a new girl at school. The second scene shows her in a private meeting in the present day, with an aide who has doubts about being a teacher. The third scene shows Mary with her younger sister, who is suffering from a recent breakup with her fiancé. (This is an example of reauthoring leading to landscape of action and landscape of identity).

A reflecting team again observes the scenes. One of the members of the team expresses curiosity: "I was curious who in Mary's life most noticed her empathetic listening abilities. I was also curious who might be least surprised by Mary's empathetic listening abilities." Another remarks, "I noticed that Mary in many of her scenes played the role of someone who others could talk to and feel comfortable. I wonder if she would describe herself as a person who was valued in that way?"

Mary, in reflecting on the reflections, comments that valuing herself as an empathetic listener was something she never really considered as an important skill in her life. She notes that she has always chosen to focus on negative descriptions of her "ability to speak out" and "anxiety about her abilities."

We conclude our weekly meeting by forming a circle. "Think of a moment today that you found especially meaningful. Now, I want us all to share that moment with each other." We pass a fabric around the circle, and whoever has the fabric uses it to enact a living sculpture that shows their chosen moment. After being shown how, the others mirror that person's pose.

The following week, it was time to add the ground, the leaves, and the fruit. "The ground represents your daily life and its activities. Draw or write about some of those activities. The leaves represent important people in your life, people who are precious to you, both living and departed. The fruit represents the gifts you have received: emotional support, love, encouragement, education, and wisdom." We focus on each area at a time, writing and drawing symbols on the branches of our trees.

After that, the women expand the responses in their leaves by creating a *Hall of Fame.* Mary arranges a Hall of Fame with special areas set off by pieces of fabric. Each area becomes the locale for a scene between Mary and one of her significant figures. For Mary's husband, she creates an intimate candlelit dinner in a special restaurant, using fabric and chairs. She poses members of the group and uses life-sized dolls to represent this scene. Later, the participants and life-sized dolls become other significant figures in Mary's Hall of Fame. Mary takes the role of a tour guide and escorts our group around. As each figure and scene comes into view, she takes on the figure's voice. Each figure speaks about Mary's contribution to his or her life and what Mary means to them.

Mary finds it difficult to take on the roles of her significant figures and talk about herself. She explains: "I have a problem accepting compliments or hearing good things about myself." She asks another group participant to play the role of the tour guide, and Mary creates a short script for each of her significant figures. From that more distant perspective, Mary begins feeling more comfortable hearing what her significant figures say about her (an example of a Narradrama use of remembering conversation).

The trees are placed around the room to create a uniquely colorful forest. Each of the participants sees the richness and beauty of their own lives, dreams, and skills, as well as the beauty of the other participants' lives.

Figure 9.4. Mary's Tree.

The therapist/facilitator invites the group to show their connection to the trees by inviting two kinds of reflections, one through movement and the other through writing.

"What a beautiful forest! Lovely trees, colorful and bright. Now, I am inviting all of you to reflect on one tree at a time by forming a *living reflection sculpture.* The creator of each tree stands by her drawing. The group faces the participant and creates a living reflection sculpture of connections to the tree and to the participant who created it. Every participant receives a living reflection sculpture pertaining to their specific tree.

The participants each write reflections on the other participants' drawings, and after that the group splits up into pairs. Each member of the pair reads the reflections about his or her partner's tree to the partner. Then each participant reads the reflections out, thereby repeating and strengthening the experience. Here are some of the reflections about Sarah's tree:

"Your tree reminds me of the creation of the universe, something that involves all parts, past, present and future." "There are so many layers in this tree that she seems to be able to tell stories for many, many years to come. Thank you for the abundance and the giving." Another reflector comments: "How deeply rooted–reaching out gracefully to the unknown and embracing it."

For closing, we celebrate through a ritual of receiving the fruit of our trees, our gifts. Small drums of different kinds are handed out to each member of the group. Sarah has an idea; she gathers and ties fruit-sized bundles of fabric to represent each of her gifts. She explains to the rest of us what we are to do: "The person receiving the gifts goes to the center of the circle, while the people on the outer perimeter tap their drums with their fingers."

Sarah goes first. When the drumming starts, Sarah goes to the center of the circle where a different person presents her with each of her gifts. As she receives each gift, Sarah unfolds the fabric and wraps it around herself until she is left standing in the center of the circle wrapped in all her gifts. After the members of the group have all received their gifts, the session ends.

At the end of their work on The Tree of Life, the participants plan and participate in a Tree of Life celebration ritual. The participants each receive an individual certificate printed with miniature copies of their trees, with a list of their new skills and new knowledge.

CONCLUSION

The stories of our lives are the framework through which we interpret life's events, and we can change our lives by changing the way we interpret our own stories and which stories we choose to privilege.

Stories are our houses made of words. We live inside our stories and they give meaning to our lives. As I travel daily through the world of drama in therapy, my heart stays open to the stories. Sometimes I get lost, but when I set my compass to the sound of a story, I usually find my way home. I wish I could sit on my mother's lap and hear her stories again.

REFERENCES

Andersen, T. (Ed.). (1991). *The reflecting team: Dialogues and dialogues about the dialogues.* New York: W.W. Norton.

Derrida, J. (1978). *Writing and difference.* Chicago: University of Chicago Press.

Dunne, P., & Rand, H. (2006). *Narradrama: Integrating drama therapy, narrative and the creative arts: Second edition.* Los Angeles: Possibilities Press, Imprint of the Drama

Therapy Institute of Los Angeles.
Dunne, P. (2006). *Exploring narradrama* (DVD). Psychotherapy.net.
Emunah, R. (1994). *Acting for real.* New York: Brunner-Mazel.
Epston, D. (1998). *Catching up with David Epston: A collection of narrative practice-based papers published between 1991 and 1996.* Adelaide, Australia: Dulwich Centre Publications.
Freeman, J., Epston, D., & Lobovitz, D. (1997) *Playful approaches to serious problems.* New York: W.W. Norton.
Irwin, E., & Curry, N.E. (1993). Role play. In C.E. Schaefer, & K. Gitlin (Eds.), *Play diagnosis and assessment* (pp. 157–187). New Jersey: Jason Aronson.
Irwin, E.C. (2000). The use of the puppet interview to understand children. In C.E. Schaefer & K. Gitlin (Eds.), *Play, diagnosis and assessment* (pp. 682–703). New York: John Wiley and Sons.
Landy, R. (1985). *Drama therapy: Concepts and practices.* Springfield, IL: Charles C Thomas.
Landy, R. (1991). The dramatic basis of role theory. *The Arts in Psychotherapy, 18,* 29–41.
Landy, R. (2008). *The couch and the stage.* New York: Jason Aaronson
Ncube, N., & Denborough, D. (2005). *Tree of life* (DVD). Adelaide, Australia: Dulwich Centre Publications.
Nylund, D. (2000). *Treating Huckleberry Finn: A new narrative approach to working with kids diagnosed ADD/ADHD.* San Francisco: Jossey-Bass.
Russell, S., & Carey, M. (2004). *Narrative therapy: Responding to your questions.* Adelaide, Australia: Dulwich Centre Publications.
Tomm, K. (1988). Interventive interviewing: Intending to ask linear, circular, strategic, or reflexive questions? *Family Process, 27,* 1–15.
White, M. (1989). *Selected papers.* Adelaide, Australia: Dulwich Centre Publications.
White, M. (1998). *Papers by Michael White.* Adelaide, Australia: Dulwich Centre Publications.
White, M. (2000). *Reflections on narrative practice: Essays and interviews.* Adelaide, Australia: Dulwich Centre Publications.
White, M. (2004). *Narrative practice and exotic lives: Resurrecting diversity in everyday life.* Adelaide, Australia: Dulwich Centre Publications.
Wiener, D., & Oxford, L. (2003). (Eds.). *Action therapies with families and groups.* Washington, DC: American Psychological Association.

BIBLIOGRAPHY

Barragar-Dunne, P. (1992). *The narrative therapist and the arts.* Los Angeles: Possibilities Press, Imprint of the Drama Therapy Institute of Los Angeles.
Barragar-Dunne, P. (1993). *Drama therapy activities for parents and children: An exercise handbook* (2nd ed.). Los Angeles: Drama Therapy Institute of Los Angeles.
Barragar-Dunne, P. (1995). *The creative journal.* Los Angeles: Possibilities Press, Imprint of the Drama Therapy Institute of Los Angeles.
Dunne, P. (1993). *The creative therapeutic thinker* (2nd ed.). Los Angeles: Drama Therapy Institute of Los Angeles.
Dunne, P. (1996). *Double stick tape: Drama, poetry and narrative as therapy for adolescents.* Los Angeles: Possibilities Press, Imprint of the Drama Therapy Institute of Los Angeles.
Dunne, P. (1997). Catch the little fish: narradrama with young children. In C. Smith, & D. Nylund, (Eds.), *Narrative therapies with children and adolescents* (pp. 71–110). New York: Guilford Press.
Dunne, P (2003). Narradrama: A narrative action approach with groups. In D. Wiener, & L. Oxford (Eds.), *Action therapies with families and groups* (pp. 229–265). Washington D.C.: American Psychological Association.
Dunne, P., & Rand H. (2003). *Narradrama: integrating drama therapy, narrative and the creative arts,* (1st ed.). Los Angeles: Possibilities Press, Imprint of the Drama Therapy Institute of Los Angeles.
Dunne, P. (2006). *The narrative therapist and the arts,* (2nd ed.). Los Angeles: Possibilities Press, Imprint of the Drama Therapy Institute of Los Angeles.

FURTHER TRAINING

Pam Dunne, PhD, RDT/BCT
Certificate Program in Drama Therapy
The Drama Therapy Institute of Los Angeles
1315 Westwood Boulevard
Los Angeles, CA 90024-4901
Tel: 310/226-2865 Fax: 310-589-0209
Website:dramatherapyinstitutela.com
Email: pamdunnedtila@mac.com

Chapter 10

OMEGA TRANSPERSONAL APPROACH TO DRAMA THERAPY

SAPHIRA BARBARA LINDEN

GENESIS

In this chapter, parallel histories of the formation of an experimental theater and work with clinical populations are woven together. They served as the foundation for this model of *Omega Transpersonal Drama Therapy*. What follows is a selection of experiments, productions, and processes, which illustrate, each in a particular way, how the vision evolved and became more multidimensional.

The avant-garde theater of the 1960s shook people up. Plays were created to hit people over the head with everything that was wrong. People needed to be shaken out of their complacency, their indifference to the incredible number of injustices around them. Just talking about what was wrong was no longer effective; and so the age of multidimensional expression was born, the world of environmental theater, which drew actors and audience into a more intense intimate relationship. Theater Workshop Boston, Inc. was created to develop original plays about timely important issues and create new forms of audience/actor relationships within the 'environmental theater' genre. We felt well aligned with the work of The Living Theater and The Open Theater in New York. A couple of years later, the three theaters all received grants from the new experimental theater division of The National Endowment of the Arts.

Drama Therapy with Special Needs Children and Institutionalized Adolescents

In the late 1960s, I took a job teaching inpatient schizophrenic and developmentally delayed adolescents in Boston State Hospital, through the Boston School system, which was run by a female supervisor in the "physically handicapped" department. There were no books, no supplies, no curriculum, nor assistance of any kind. Theater became the therapeutic and educational form. In this hospital's adolescent unit, there were two classrooms, both composed of long-term institutionalized schizophrenic patients. One of the classes had relatively normalintelligence learners, while the other, which I was given, had a range of developmentally delayed learners from severely autistic to learning disabled. I was told, "They need to be prepared with the basic academic skills as well as practical life skills to make it in the world if they ever leave the hospital."

The only learning materials were my student-patients and myself. Using the tools of what we now call drama therapy processes, many of these patients exceeded their expected learning capacities. Making learning fun through the use of creating a special engaging environment and simple theater games became a key to working with our challenged hospital students. A sterile state mental hospital classroom was transformed into a magical theater store. Every shelf had products that utilized different levels of math and reading skills. These mentally challenged adolescents learned basic math skills at their own level without embarrassment. They were either working in the produce department (with simple arithmetic) or the canned goods section (with algebra), while enjoying taking on the roles of shopkeepers, clerks, or consumers in the food section that corresponded to their level of learning. Thus, an initiation into the connection between theater, therapy and education evolved organically. Using the environmental theater model, we had discovered a new classroom process, called E.T. Theater.

E.T. Theater

	nvironmental		heater
E		**T**	
	ducation		herapy

To
Help
Educate
Adolescents
Through
Reconstruction of
Environments

Later, at Kennedy Memorial Hospital for handicapped and emotionally challenged student-patients, what now would be called a drama therapy program was created, using role playing, theater games, and in particular, the use of puppets. The power of puppets to gain the trust of these student-patients, who had lost their trust in adults, was revealed to me, while engaging them in profound emotional dialogues about their illnesses.

Drama Therapy in Environmental and Participatory Theater

What I knew best was theater. I had been exposed to Grotowski's (1968) *Towards a Poor Theatre* which encourages the use of the actor for everything including being sets and props, and also Viola Spolin's (1963) *Improvisation for the Theatre,* which similarly demonstrates how actors can create images of people, places, and things using themselves. Spolin's work introduced me to theater games and inspired me to teach cognitive material in that modality.

In Theater Workshop Boston's first play, *Riot* (Portman & Rollins, 1968), a total environment was created in a church basement in which the audience had the experience of being in the center of an actual riot, of being trapped, of being unable to get out. There was no audience/stage separation. Rather than just watching a riot, they became part of one, reproduced through sound, movement and light.

Inspired by the power of creating a theater environment, where the boundaries between actors and audience were designed to catalyze intimate actor-audience relationships, our theater experiment was taken one step further with young people. Since children had fewer expectations about what theater was, we experimented with creating a meaningful educational experience and environmental form, where the young audience members became active participants throughout a well-crafted and structured play. While adults may need to be shaken out of their complacency, children often needed to become more aware of what was happening in the world.

In *Tribe* (Linden, 1969), children in the audience became active spectators. As soon as they entered the theater, they were immediately initiated into one of three tribes of Native Americans. In this way, they experienced the beauty and the joy of these cultures; then they experienced the injustice of being pushed off their land. In theatrical terms, they were forced to leave beautiful, spacious, colorful environments, in which they experienced interesting, creative rituals. They were then ordered to travel in a dark, cold, empty space, ending up being shoved together onto a crowded dark gray platform, which represented the reservation. The adults, who brought the children in the audience to the theater, were seated as elders of these tribes and experienced being left behind.

The next experiment in our Theater Workshop Boston's playwriting process was to create a play about pollution for adults and children. In *Creation* (Linden & Rosenberg, 1970), adults were seated in a harried city environment exemplifying polluted values and the children physically became part of a beautiful country world of new values and natural living. There was also a third environment, between the city and country environments, a factory run by a bureaucrat, who represented the voice of selfish capitalism. Children and adults experienced their environments being taken over by a river filled with waste. The children were driven back to the city to take responsibility to work for change. They begged the adult audience to look at the dying world around them and listen to their pleas for action.

Toward the One, a Family Board Game (Linden, Dym, & Hallowell, 1974), was a participatory theater piece for families that created a safe, fun environment in which family members made new discoveries about each other through improvisational play. Using many art forms within a theatrical setting, a people-sized board game was created. Each family formed their bodies into some kind of vehicle to move between experiences. A family therapist took the role of Game-Guide and was assisted by actor-facilitators. We utilized many different expressive arts therapies within the context of a family theater experience.

Sunsong: A People Puppet Pageant for Children (Linden & Sonneborn, 1976) was a participatory children's play that combines both psychological and spiritual disciplines in a healing experience, originally created for special needs students in the Boston schools. The play integrated a family systems therapy model with a Sufi Healing breath practice, based on the healing energies of earth, water, fire and air, as an underlying framework for change. In a delightful musical piece, the whole audience became members of one of four element groups and participated in creative warm-up exercises, dancing and singing. By identifying with the qualities of one of the four elements, children began to discover new potential to heal others and in the process themselves. They worked together to develop creative healing rituals for one of the two puppet children, in the form of songs, dances, improvisations and rituals. The audience children enacted roles of one of these elements of nature in the earth, water, fire or air groups and became the healers of the people puppet family. The two puppet children received the creative gifts of healing and learned that they could be empowered to change their family's dynamics, by making healing changes in themselves. The concept of a systems theory of family dynamics (the underpinnings for most family therapy today) was the basis for the psychological changes taking place in the troubled puppet family. This approach helped children to realize that change was possible and that change in one family member (in this case a child) could help growth happen in the whole family.

Drama Therapy in Organizational Development and in the Corporate World

The earlier sociopolitical theater of the 1960s rejected government, big business and corporate America, as though it were all one entity to be scorned and destroyed at all costs. At some point we realized that in order for significant change to happen, it was necessary to recognize our collective responsibility in the government we have and in the capitalistic system that we have created. Working with people in positions of power could foster significant change. We realized that there was no "them" and "us." It's a rationalization of our mind. The sacredness of life is about realizing our essential connection to all of life's creation.

When the President of our theater's Board of Directors, George Litwin, an experienced leader in the Management Training field, strongly encouraged us to bring our skills and extensive teaching and facilitating experience into the corporate world, we welcomed the opportunity. He was a master at what he did and was a personal guide to many top executives in large Fortune 500 companies. He had experienced much of our work personally and assured us that we had much to offer these organizations. Over a period of several years, we were invited into select client jobs with him and together we co-created what we called transformational learning experiences. We wrote a paper together on Visioning: A Transformational Process (1988). The essence of it was about left-brain strategic planning coming out of right brain visioning processes with the goal of building a world-class company, by thinking out of the box. Drama therapy processes were interwoven into these training programs.

For over two decades within the corporate world we have worked with many of the same educational principles and values in designing creative transformational learning programs in leadership training, visioning, creative problem solving, goal setting (examining the company's goals in the context of one's life ideals and goals), corporate culture change, empathy training, communication, conflict resolution, team building and company review processes.

Examples of Drama Therapy in Corporate Systems

The following is an example of an innovative corporate format: Our core theater company, who were trained facilitators and teachers, were brought into one of the largest banking organizations in the world. They observed a meeting of corporate managers. The actors (unknown to the managers) were each assigned one manager to observe. At a certain point, I stopped the meeting and invited the actors to take the seats of the managers. The actors then assumed the role of the manager they had observed. They role played the subtext of the perceived feelings and thoughts that were not being expressed. The managers were totally astounded at the accuracy of the portrayals. This helped motivate them to try to engage in much deeper and more honest communication. We then worked with the managers in a workshop in which the personal dynamics and communication that surfaced in the role plays were explored and worked through.

In that same corporation, a bank-wide

training program was created called *Managing People.* We were charged with the task of creating a videodrama for the Vice President's Annual Meeting. Many of the Vice Presidents had 5,000 people working under them. In one case, a very bright, charismatic V.P. had just gone through a corporate disaster. In the process of creating a mass change, he had neglected to attend to the people issues that arose in the process. People were burned out, felt devalued, and as a result, a host of other things happened that produced chaos and a major financial disaster. We identified the principles behind what happened and created a script with a different situation and characters that made the point about how important it was to be conscious of the people resources and their feelings and needs. The video production was created as a major learning vehicle that demonstrated that bottom line success necessitates a real consciousness about our human resources, i.e., people sensitivity is good business.

In another very large old Fortune 500 company, a team building retreat was created. First, some old-timers were interviewed, some who had been in the same jobs for 40 years and in some cases had never left the small town in which they lived and worked. They were to fantasize about an ideal job. What would they do if they could do anything that would really inspire them and make them feel that they were being well used? They visualized this and then told the story of what it would be like. This was done to help them stretch their limited self-concept about their work. Then, during the weekend training, a number of exercises were created to help these managers connect with deeper parts of themselves in order to be more effective on the job. We worked on relating to others more effectively and being more honest about what they were feeling. We did psychodramatic role plays to help them in this process. Finally, they were helped to integrate their goals and they were encouraged to take risks, be more creative and do things that expanded their thinking and possibilities in their current jobs. They were also to do the same with the people who report to them.

A marketing consultant for a large food corporation client elicited our help in designing a training program for their marketing staff on empathy. The idea was to give them an experience of empathy personally with themselves, their families and co-workers in order to develop empathy for their consumers. Several drama therapy exercises were created to accomplish this, culminating in the creation of scenes, playing the roles of the consumers (children, men, women, athletes, etc.) of their different food products. Out of this work, new marketing strategies were developed.

Another application of drama therapy in business was the development of a vision process for a small high-tech start-up company. The two founders were about to have a strategic planning meeting with the new CEO who had just joined the company. We suggested creating a shared vision first, out of which the strategic planning could more clearly evolve. They agreed and so a right-brained visioning process was designed and implemented. Listening to soothing music, the three men closed their eyes and were taken through a relaxation and guided visualization process, which culminated in each drawing an image that crystallized the essence of their visioning process. This was accompanied by writing a poem or a succinct piece of prose that expressed their vision. The men shared their drawings and writing with each other and then tried to distill the best from each and integrate their collective images into one vision that felt good to all of them. Finally, at a company-wide meeting off-site, all of the employees were introduced to the collective vision of the three executives and invited to participate in the same process. This time, after drawing the vision, people were instructed to gather in small groups in which they were to collaborate in creating a dramatic skit that reflected their group's shared vision. All of the skits were performed. Out of the richness of their collective creativity, a mission statement was created along with some guiding principles that included much of the company-wide input. This process allowed everyone to take some ownership of the vision, mission and guiding principles of the organization, which served to motivate people and ameliorate the particular challenges that face a start-up company, whose employees work long hours under a lot of pressure.

Diversity Training, Community Healing and World Issues

Coming Home

In a multi-ethnic community our theater company created and produced the opening participatory theater event for Jamaica Plain's new art center, entitled *Coming Home* (1987), in which families moved through three floors of different Ethnic Arts processes that represented the community's diverse ethnic heritage.

The First Earth Run for Peace

In the larger Boston Community, a city wide multicultural arts event was orchestrated in 1986, to be the first receivers of the torch from the runners of *The First Earth Run,* a global torch relay, in commemoration of the United Nations International Year of Peace, beginning at the United Nations and continuing around the world.

Religious Diversity: The Cosmic Celebration

The *Cosmic Celebration,* originally called *The Cosmic Mass* (Khan & Linden, 1973–1983), was a large scale mythic pageant, celebrating the unity of the human family, through its many diverse religious traditions. It was produced for 11 years in several cities in the United States and Europe. As many as 350 people in each production were cast into roles that reflected and helped to develop some aspect of their core self. The purpose was to help the participants transform their limited sense of self to their essential self by role playing an archetypal character that represented that higher or essential part of them, as a spiritual healing practice. This large pageant form reflected ancient Greek theater, where the plays served as healing and educational celebrations for the entire community.

Ethnic Diversity: A Festival of Light

A *Festival of Light* (1997, 1999) at Concord High School was a healing arts event celebrating the ethnic diversity of the entire school community, involving the students, faculty and staff and families.

The Omega Arts Network

World Symposium On Humanity was produced in 1979 in three countries, hooked up by satellite, to facilitate communication between leading thinkers in the fields of science, education, public health, politics, and religion to foster serious discourse on the future of humanity. We had an opportunity to suggest that artist-healers had a valuable role to play in such an important event. We accepted the invitation to organize simultaneous Transformational Arts Festivals in Toronto, Los Angeles, and London.

In the process of creating the guidelines for what kind of visionary and transformational artists and artistic work the arts festivals would present, we created The Omega

Arts Network of Artist-Healers, who saw themselves as vehicles for transformation and healing.

The Omega Arts Network is an expression of the principles of Omega Transpersonal Drama Therapy. Our vision was "To unite artists of all cultures who are consciously working toward creating a vision of a better world with works that are healing, transforming and uplifting for the spirit."

Revisioning a New World: SEJECHO–Voice of the Earth

Through The Omega Arts Network, we encouraged artist-healers in all art forms, to re-envision "a new world" during the 1992, 500th anniversary of Columbus' journey. We created a weekend event that included a multi-ethnic concert/theater evening, a juried exhibition of contemporary transformational art called *Visions of a New World,* and an original participatory sacred musical theater event for planetary unity for people of all ages, called *The Finding Place* (Linden, Grant, & Gebel, 1992). Part of our purpose was to help call forth a new myth and a positive vision for a new world. All generations were invited to experience these artistic-healing events together.

Women's Issues

Eartheart, an original theater piece about the stories of two Jewish women as children, adolescents and adults, reflects the larger story of the earth. As female drama therapists, we wanted to share our perspective of the feminine voice, needing to be heard at this time for conscious healing.

Motherblood, a ten-minute play, is an encounter between two mothers; one who is Israeli, the other is Palestinian, both of whom have survived significant losses. The play was created to be a powerful educational and transformational vehicle for learning about the major issues in the Middle East conflict from both the Israeli and Palestinian perspectives, inspiring people to experience that it is possible to make a difference with global issues one woman to one woman.

OMEGA TRANSPERSONAL DRAMA THERAPY FRAME OF REFERENCE

Psychodrama Origins

In the second year of my job at the state hospital, another teacher was hired, Ildri Bie Ginn. She and I decided to train with Jacob Moreno, the founder of "Psychodrama" (Chapter 18), to help us in this challenging clinical/education situation. With Moreno and his wife Zerka's inspiration, we began to experiment in our clinical setting with the psychodrama techniques we were learning. We were experimenting with the same techniques to explore highly-charged emotional issues in our personal lives.

Working with traditional psychodrama and cathartic experience alone was often insufficient to get the needed insight or perspective. In one such psychodrama, I connected with the light in a lamp in the room. I began to identify with the light and internalize it. I closed my eyes and essentially role played, becoming the voice of that light, or as I understand it now, the voice of my soul or higher wisdom self that is always clear. In this way, I was able to view the world and my life more clearly from a mountaintop perspective. Each time I did this, I was able to gain insight and clarity in a way that astounded me. This became the beginning of my understanding and work in developing methods of accessing and identifying the parts of one's being that have the answers, that know what is best, and that can offer specific advice to the part of one who is in emotional turmoil and confusion. The development of our therapeutic approach includes many ways of accessing the essential self or source of one's strength and clarity beyond the client/patient's limited view of him/herself. This has become the foundation of The Omega Process.

Sufi Origins and the Omega Process

The therapeutic disciplines in our actor, teacher and manager training allowed our students, clients and audiences to be more honest and direct about their feelings and to find solutions to their immediate concerns. At the same time, we were gaining insight about how the childhood experiences of our clients (and ourselves) have affected everyone's adult lives. Through this work, our actors and teachers became more aware of their bodies, and learned to discover where fears and tensions were stored. We noticed that as the psychological work deepened and intensified, a focus on a self-centered ego perspective tended to prevail. We felt a need to expand our consciousness and our awareness of who we really were. We turned to meditation.

Many of us were attracted to the Sufi path, known as the *path of the heart.* This tradition has a long history of integrating spiritual perspectives with expression through the arts: poetry, music, dance, architecture, and the visual arts. Maybe that is why it is also known as the path of the metaphysics of ecstasy. Today, the path of the heart has captivated readers and audiences all over America. In fact, Jelaludin Rumi, a sixteenth century Sufi poet, has in recent years been recognized as the most widely-read poet in the world. These are some of the Sufi themes that appealed to us in our work: the search for truth through experience of the inner nature of reality; consciousness of a larger reality beyond our immediate selves; and unity within the diversity of creation. The teachings and practices evolved from the mystical branches of many ancient traditions (including the early mystery schools), providing an energy source for opening individuals and communities to the potential for dynamic change. The emphasis is on practicing inner discipline while working in the world, with the goal of experiencing states of increased joy, strength and peace. The work includes meditative practices based on breath, light and sound vibrations (mantram or wazifa), sacred dance and walks.

I had been introduced to the powerful role of archetypes in transformation and healing and what could happen when people truly identify with an archetype that is resonant with who they are in their essence. Viewing the soul, pure in itself, as the "I" clothed in the personality, our theater company and I began to understand how people become trapped in a limited perspective or a negative self-image by a mistaken identification. Since we already viewed healing as one of the main purposes of our theater, the Sufi teachings we had experienced helped expand our perspective. We learned that the healing process involves awakening to the eternal qualities of the soul, one's essential self, rather than identifying with the limitations of the personality. We wanted to create in theater, with our students, clients and audiences, an experience of the total human condition in which emotional, social, political and spiritual goals unite in a new vision of what is possible.

Processes within transformational theater work and individual client work evolved to help people identify with the cosmic view. From this vantage point one is able to view more clearly the essential self, one's true nature, beyond one's limited view of identity. We called this the Omega process, taken from a phrase of the Christian Mystic,

Teilhard deChardin's: Omega consciousness, moving from Alpha, which is the cause, through one's history to Omega, which views the larger purpose toward which we are heading.

PRINCIPLES OF OMEGA TRANSPERSONAL DRAMA THERAPY

Transpersonal Psychology: A Definition

The transpersonal approach begins with an assumption of a human being's fundamental health and wholeness, rather than pathology first. Whatever the problems and challenges in one's life, they can be viewed within the context of a larger identity individually and within the greater consciousness of humanity. The following is a definition from John F. Kennedy University's Graduate School for the Study of Human Consciousness:

> Transpersonal Psychology includes the developing wisdom and methodology of psychoanalytic, behavioral and humanistic psychology and expands beyond these approaches to incorporate an understanding of the spiritual aspects of human experience. It addresses attention to experiences in which one's sense of self extends "trans-," meaning beyond and through, the personal or social identity of the individual to connect with a greater whole. This state of being which lies beyond the encultured personality–call it Consciousness, Spirit, Higher Self–is of special interest to transpersonal psychologists. (Walsh & Vaughn, 1980)

The following 11 principles underlie the ideal practice of *Omega Transpersonal Drama Therapy* in all of its many forms:

1. Assuming health rather than pathology. As Transpersonal drama therapists, we assume the innate health and wholeness of our clients, rather than focus on pathology. Whatever our clients' problems and challenges, we view them in the context of a larger identity that is whole, balanced and pure, both individually and in the greater consciousness of humanity. The Transpersonal drama therapist supports the individual's transcendence from all identification, lifting the individual from his or her own world view to one in which "the individual would presumably identify with both everything and nothing" (Walsh & Vaughn, 1980).

2. Shifting the identity from a limited sense of self to the essential Self. We aspire to help our clients shift their identity from a limited sense of self–e.g., from an identification as wounded, a victim, an addict, worthless, inept or other negative qualities, to an identification with the essential Self, higher Self, authentic core Self, or soul. We do not deny human experience, and in fact help people honor these experiences. However, while the trauma and abuses our clients have experienced may be terrible, we help them understand that this is not who they are, but rather what has happened to them. If they can come to identify with who they are in their essential soul self, the source of their innate strength, they can heal more quickly. When our clients learn to identify with their soul's essence, they begin to overcome a personal sense of limitation and low self-esteem and work through their limited self images from early and later conditioning. As they go more deeply into the traumas and challenges of their lives, an identification with soul or "best self" qualities–compassion, beauty, love, intuition, humor, wisdom, joy, empathy, spontaneity, creativity, peace, and many others–serve as sources of strength. From this perspective, and relying on essential soul qualities, the individual is far less defended and blocked in examining painful experiences and aspects of the limited or conditioned self.

Using the methods of ancient esoteric and contemporary spiritual traditions, clients learn the tools taught in other cultures, such as meditation and breath work, to access and identify with this essential Self. There is a variety of theater and meditation exercises that help people access this part of themselves.

3. Embodying the therapeutic issues. By using action methods that embody the emotional issues through movement and enactment, clients are able to recall memories through feedback from the body and senses. Kinesthetic, proprioceptive, visual, auditory and touch senses are used as tools to reveal more information. Transpersonal drama therapy works with the client's body in relation to his/her heart, mind and soul. In this way, clients go beyond mental machinations, enabling them to discover important, new material in their transformational process.

4. Working with archetypes. The Transpersonal drama therapist holds an inner concentration on and identification with four archetypal roles, including healer, artist, educator and shaman or spiritual guide. The therapist is first and foremost a healer in leading the client back through the dense and dark matter of human experience to identification with his or her soul. The therapist is an artist in using the arts to help the client access the imaginal realm and find symbolic expression (i.e., balanced and healthy self), particularly for experiences so sublime–or so traumatic–that they defy words. He or she is an educator in teaching the techniques needed to maintain awareness of the essential Self, such as meditation, breath work, sound and light practices, visualizations, and in using Transpersonal drama therapy as the vehicle to educate the body, mind, heart and spirit. Finally, the Transpersonal drama therapist is a shaman or spiritual guide in working in the twilight worlds between the conscious and unconscious, matter and spirit. The shaman part of us, as therapists, is able to see the client in his or her essential core self by using the tools of meditation and the intuitive arts. Eventually, it is possible to sit with a client, attune to his or her breath and experience him or her on many levels simultaneously. This, of course, requires training and practice.

Additionally, we help our clients draw on archetypal motifs in world mythology, such as gods and goddesses, heroes, masters, saints and prophets, as well as on the archetypal elements in nature, such as earth, water, fire and air, animal totems, oceans, forests, and mountaintops, to help them work through their current issues and negative memories and find meaning in their life experiences. We also work with archetypal human themes such as finding love, overcoming great adversity, returning from grief, and rising from the ashes of devastating experiences. When people can recognize and identify with the archetypal symbols in their psyches, we can help them use these symbols to find healing and transformation.

5. Embracing love while holding all emotions as sacred. As Transpersonal drama therapists, we embrace the totality of the heart's experience: all emotions–even fear, anger, rage and frustration–have love as their base and can be used as guides back to our essential Selves. By holding all emotions as sacred, we honor all facets of emotional life as a natural part of the human life journey. In so doing, we can come to love ourselves and others authentically, thus overcoming loneliness and alienation. In our therapeutic work, we teach clients to honor their own emotions as well. We work with them in a way that feels sacred, rather than succumbing to programmed emotions such as shame and guilt. In this manner, healing can take place in a more fluid manner as clients come into their own authenticity. Holding the thought that emotions are sacred, the Transpersonal drama therapist works to facilitate the client's return to love, albeit through a hall of distorted mirrors. In truth, there is no split between the godly and ungodly, the holy and the profane: It is important to honor whatever feelings we experience as sacred.

6. Creating a sacred space. For healing to progress, it is important to enter a sacred space where we can reconnect to our soul essence, which is never tarnished by life experience. Beauty in the therapeutic environment helps to transmute the ugliness of emotional trauma. The atmosphere can become like a beautiful rose holding the client in her warm embrace and lovely fragrance. Whether working with an individual client, a therapy group, an educational group, or an audience attending a transformational theater performance, the Transpersonal drama therapist creates a sacred atmosphere to inspire people to connect with their essential selves and to allow for the possibility that the client will take a meaningful step in his or her own transformational growth and healing process. Physical beauty in the healing environment–flowers, soft colors, beautiful fabrics, and works of art also help people to feel better and to open to deep, dark places that need to be healed.

Creating simple warm-up exercises that awaken the body, mind, heart and soul help participants to build trust and develop a readiness to be present with themselves and the group. In the therapeutic, educational and theatrical settings, the Transpersonal drama therapist strives to create a *temenos,* or sacred container to hold the truth of the client's emotions and experiences. Through the therapist's compassionate, nonjudgmental witnessing, the temenos provides a sense of emotional safety that allows the client's deepest Self to surface, including suppressed and hidden aspects of the psyche, and to engage in the therapeutic process.

7. Fostering an experience of interconnectedness and unity. The Transpersonal drama therapist works to create experiences of the unity, connection, and interdependence of all living things, including human beings, animals, plants and the environment. It also relates to a holistic healing approach, working with the body, mind, heart and soul connection. Much of the work of healing concerns entering the consciousness of those with whom we are in conflict and working toward embracing their emotional experiences and points of view. We thus create exercises in nature that are designed to receive the healing power of Mother Earth and set up improvisations, meditations and creative exercises that relate a person's own experience (including challenges and future possibilities) to the experience of the earth and its cycles of birth, death and rebirth and the seasons. We also create experiences that allow one individual to see into the soul of another individual, gaining insight into old wounds and conflicts and come to resolution with the ones who wounded us, whether living or dead.

Transpersonal drama therapists also work with communities to help them experience that different religions, races, and ethnic backgrounds are all part of a larger system. Realizing that we are part of a larger, interconnected ecological system helps overcome the distinctions and differences that divide people and helps overcome our essential aloneness. We embrace and become part of a global culture and family. As we identify with larger sociopolitical concerns and issues, we realize that we exist together in an interdependent world.

8. Seeking mastery through self-discipline. The development of personal capacity to manifest our greatest potential depends on conscious thought and action. Discipline and focus lead toward the realization of the Self. Many great teachers and masters have taught us that mastery lies in stilling the mind and directing it toward what we desire. Whatever we think about, we will attract. If we're feeling and thinking positively, we will attract that, if we can master the discipline of becoming mindful of our thoughts. The lesson in this principle is that, although we work in the transpersonal realm and frequently process the contents of the unbridled imagination, the work of Transpersonal drama therapists–and their clients–must ultimately be grounded in the quest for personal mastery through self-discipline. This may involve compliance with recommended practices, stretching beyond our emotional comfort zone, and other forms of inner work. Mastery of our inner and outer lives ultimately produces harmony, health, balance, and the achievement of our life's goals.

9. Achieving balance. The essence of the message in many spiritual traditions today is balance: balance of receptive and expressive energies, yin and yang, activity and repose, inner masculine and feminine, spirit and matter, transcendence and immanence. As noted, mastery, self-discipline, and balance all work together to facilitate the client's evolution. Accordingly, the Transpersonal drama therapist nurtures experiences of balance in the therapeutic situation that can then be generalized to other aspects of the client's life.

10. Identifying and achieving our life purpose. Beyond working to heal family of origin challenges, we also want to help identify for ourselves our life purpose and help our clients to do the same. We want to guide our clients to use their unique gifts to serve the larger humanity, each in his or her own way. An ancient teaching says that our purpose is like the horizon, and the closer we get to it, the further it recedes. Our interests are clues to what our purpose is. One's purpose is continually evolving.

11. Creating life as a work of art. The culmination of this work is when we apply our learning creatively in our everyday life; then our lives can become shining works of art that draw their inspiration from the light within and interconnectedness to our higher source, which is reflected in family, community and the world around us. This is our ultimate goal for ourselves, as Transpersonal drama therapists, and for the people we serve in our work.

Techniques

Psychodrama

One of the foundations of drama therapy and Omega Transpersonal Drama Therapy is psychodrama. Psychodrama is a group therapy process with a specific set of techniques and forms within which the protagonist (client) works through challenging issues and relationships in his or her life. There is a warm-up procedure, the enacted drama and a process by which the group share issues in their lives, catalyzed by the protagonist's drama. My early training with Jacob and Zerka Moreno inspired experimentation in developing psychodramatic structures to access higher states of consciousness. In an early book, *Theater of Spontaneity,* Moreno (1947) includes many transpersonal concepts. Transpersonal dimensions of psychodrama include: the protagonist conversing with people who have already died, with angelic presences, with one's own higher self (as mentioned previously), or with a divine quality that someone role plays like a spirit of compassion, joy, forgiveness, inspiration or clarity. All of this is integrated into the Omega Transpersonal Drama Therapy approach.

Performances within a Transformational Theater Context

As the culmination of Omega Transpersonal Drama Therapy intensives, participants create biographical theatrical pieces based on their personal issues and sometimes on how their personal issues relate to larger social concerns, with healing and transformation as a goal. This can be done either as a one-person performance or as part of a larger ensemble work.

Storytelling

Dr. Carl Gustav Jung said that the mental health of a society is based on people's abilities to tell their stories. The proliferation of 12-step recovery groups, and the expansion of the storytelling field as an art form, are indications of the broad-based need for people to access and communicate their life stories. The Transformational Theater process is a development of this naturally occurring impulse in our culture at this time. By accessing one's source of strength or personal essential self, one is more able to access and communicate one's trauma history. This makes it possible to transform these earlier wounded patterns into the creation of a new story. The new story expresses one's wish to live unencumbered by a limited sense of self and feelings of inadequacy.

Music and Sound Healing

Music has been called the universal language of the soul that transcends individual religious, racial, and ethnic bias or identities. One of the most effective ways of creating an attunement within a therapy or training group or within a public transformational theater environment is by consciously working with vibrational resonance. Weaving beautiful sound and music textures that open hearts creates a safe and nurturing chalice to contain our sacred stories. This helps participants feel safe about opening themselves to attune to the deeper dimensions of their life experience.

My colleague, Sarah Benson, helps participants find their voice by singing their soul song. These songs are created spontaneously as an expression of the person's emotional state and transformational edge through pure sound expression. Often the client/trainee is sung to by the group as part of the process. Many times people are encouraged to move in relation to the sound, in order to fully embody the experience. In Sarah's words:

> There's no place to hide in the sound of our voice. It carries the vibration of the truth of the moment, of the life. Our fear, anger, guilt and shame–our love, joy, and delight are reflected in the sound of our voice. As we learn to release the fear, anger, guilt and shame through releasing the voice, blockages, both physical and emotional, are released and the energy begins to flow with greater ease. In the release of our emotions, we have more space to experience love, joy and soul integration, which can also be sounded by the voice. Songs of anger, songs of love walk hand-in-hand as we explore mysterious regions in the forest of the self. (Personal communication, 1995)

As we experience the retelling of our story, we open to another level of expression when we let our story become our song. Or after a particularly strong cathartic release, we can then translate the emotion into sound and allow the energy of the emotion to ride the current of music and movement.

SOUL SONGS. The group member is asked what name they would like to hear and a color with which they resonate. The person sits or stands in the middle of the circle. The group sings his/her name three times on the steps of an ascending major chord with harmonies. As the sound of the name rises, the arms rise with the sound. Group members are instructed to visualize that whatever that person does not need be released. As the arms come down, the group visualizes healing golden light flowing in and around that person. The person receives the energy and vibration that is mirrored to him/her. Then the person is encouraged to make sound from the energy they received and develop it into a soul song, in whatever way naturally evolves. There is no pressure to "sing a song" in tune. Each person's song evolves organically. Often the song moves naturally into a soul dance.

Archetypal Exercises for Healing

IDEAL MENTOR EXERCISE. First, people are guided into a relaxed, meditative state. Second, they are guided to journey to a mountaintop or other peaceful setting where s/he finds him/herself sitting opposite an ideal mentor. It cannot be anyone that a person knows in real life, but may embody the qualities of several beings that one knows or has heard of. Third, participants are invited to visualize the physical attributes of this being: age, sex and actual physical appearance. Then they are asked to visualize the qualities that are positive, since they represent the ideal. Examples may include: intuitive, intelligent, calm, compassionate, friendly, good sense of humor, responsible etc. Then they visualize the more subtle presence of this being. Next, they are invited to draw the being as they perceive him or her. The final step in the exercise is to physicalize this being and create a sound and movement language for him or her and to interrelate with the others in the space. People learn that what they created was a picture of their own soul qualities, essence or source of strength.

Sufi Purification Breath Practice and Improvisation Exercise

This breathing practice works with the healing magnetism of the earth, water, fire and air. (See *Sunsong,* above.) Each of the elements has a corresponding breath practice. Each is done five times:

EARTH BREATH (yellow). Filtering the impurities–Breathe in through the nose and out through the nose five times. Breathe in through the soles of the feet, up to the base of the spine, on up the spine to just above the crown center.

WATER BREATH (green). Washing the impurities–Breathe in through the nose and out through the mouth five times. Inhale through the soles of the feet and the crown center simultaneously and out through the finger tips. Feel the fluid magnetism that is continually circulating in the atmosphere, washing you clear, cleansing you of all impurities.

FIRE BREATH (red). Consuming the impurities–Breathe in through the mouth and out through the nose five times. Breathe into the fire in the solar plexus, consuming the impurities. Breathe out radiating light from the heart center, through the shoulder blades.

AIR BREATH (light blue). Dissolving the impurities–Breathe in through the mouth and out through the mouth five times. Inhale through the pores of the skin with palms facing out. Imagine you are porous. Expand into the vastness of space. Let the impurities dissolve.

Once people are familiar with the breathing practice, they are guided to embody these energies through walks in a circle that are practiced as an extension of each breathing practice, accompanied by the corresponding drum beat to maintain the correct rhythm. Out of the structured walk practices, people are invited to create free movement and sound. This evolves organically into the creation of improvisational archetypal characters and qualities that represent these energies. After invoking the pure elemental energies, the characters evolve from the unconscious and often become shadow or hidden energies that manifest in a variety of forms.

Mirrors: Body, Heart and Soul

BODY. In partners, one person is A, the other B. Partners are instructed to establish eye contact accompanied by dance music; person A leads a movement piece, person B mirrors the movement. Later the facilitator says, "leaderless," and the dance evolves without one person taking the lead.

HEART. In the same pairs, both people either standing or sitting maintain eye contact as they chant "Ahh," vibrating the heart center. Movement in the mirroring form evolves from the chant, still with eye contact.

SOUL. In pairs, sitting partners reestablish eye contact and mirror the same synchronized breath rhythm. The exercise becomes subtler and quite still. Here the people focus more intently on the eyes as windows to the soul.

Archetypal Enactment

Working with the archetypes of gods, goddesses, heroes, heroines, and power animals, people create masks that reflect the archetypes. They then create characters, and dramatic scenarios unfold using these masks. In another exercise, people are invited to select something from nature with which they identify in its pure form. They can then physicalize, move, sound, and poeticize it.

Videography

Finally, we were introduced to the power of video technology in transformational theater work by Ellen Burstyn, a wonderful friend and theater mentor. Placing a monitor next to the camera, the participant is invited to look at the image of him/herself on the screen, while being guided step-by-step from the physical to the soul level of awareness.

These are a few examples of techniques and exercises that have been developed to access a transpersonal identity that can be a source of strength in working with trauma, abuse, low self-esteem and limitation on any level.

COMPARISON WITH OTHER DRAMA THERAPY APPROACHES

Our Omega Transpersonal Drama Therapy approach can be applied to a variety of approaches and methods in drama therapy. This approach is as much a value system, an intentionality, and a belief about what may be possible in the healing process. It also offers methods to access a broader consciousness as well as principles and practices to help navigate clients through their healing processes, which can be used within other approaches. For example, in David Johnson's "Developmental Transformations," (Chapter 6), the therapist in the playspace, who is comfortable with the Omega Transpersonal approach, will be attuned to mirroring a client's spiritual wisdom guide, if that is what comes up in the playspace. In Robert Landy's "Role Method" (Chapter 5), his role of the *guide* could be developed in such a way that would help the client to role play their higher self more consciously and effectively.

Our Transpersonal drama therapy approach is very resonant with Pam Dunne's "Narradrama" (Chapter 9). As people tell their problem-saturated stories, she helps them reframe those stories into new stories that offer perspectives for healing. Omega

Transpersonal techniques have worked well in a Narradrama context, helping students and clients to reframe their stories in a different way, flowing easily, one from the other.

Many of the elements in Stephen Snow's "Ritual/Theatre/Therapy" (Chapter 7) approach reflect dimensions of our transpersonal approach. They include honoring the ancient traditions of shamanism, working with archetypes, and employing rituals and performances as an important part of the therapeutic process.

"Psychodrama" (Chapter 18) and "Sociodrama" (Chapter 19) are important foundational processes in the Omega approach. Moreno began with a vision of empowering everyone to heal the world. He taught that spontaneity leads to creativity and that everyone can become a player in creating and healing oneself and others. Fundamentally our philosophy honors the spiritual essence of every human being and the belief that recreating wounded lives is possible.

CASE EXAMPLES

Ray's Transpersonal Drama Therapy and Transformational Theater Journey: Freeing our True Self From the Bonds of Addiction

Many different modalities within our work in drama therapy have evolved with serious addiction and abuse cases. This case study is an example of a healing process in the challenges and triumphs of overcoming a 20-year, two and a half pack a day nicotine addiction. Excerpts from Ray's own journal will be used to describe our approach in The Omega Transpersonal drama therapy work. The brief summary will demonstrate how the integration of a Transpersonal Psychology approach into the therapeutic work with a serious addiction can make a significant difference in the treatment process. This approach not only facilitates the recovery process, but helps to foster the emergence of one's true identity. This new identity is the core essence of the person, which is uncovered, gently and creatively, from beneath the dark clouds of self-denigration, trauma and despair. What follows is Ray's own description about this therapeutic process.

Beginning

"Omega Theater was a new experience. Just move around, make sounds . . . this was so simple, almost child-like. It was like being a child. Liberating. I was taking deep breaths, relaxing, and then Saphira began to speak about breathing: there were four ways a body could breathe, and each way was tied to an element: earth, water, fire, air; and to an archetype: teacher, healer, artist, spiritual guide.

We were moving in a circle, practicing one of the breaths, the Fire breath, breathing in through the mouth and out of the nose, when my spine became warm, a rippling warmth up and down my spine, an emotional warmth to everyone in the room, wanting to love them, invite them into my heart; my heart opening to everyone in the room, unafraid. I was asked if I wanted to 'sound' what I was feeling, to create a soul song. I stood in the center of the circle and opened my mouth and my body began to move in a dance, the sounds shaping into a song, a tone poem expressing a deep love for everyone around me. I had overcome one of my greatest fears: being in front of people without having anything 'prepared.' The pure sounding created a vibrational resonance in me that opened my heart and made me unafraid. I did not care. I started to play with the sounds, modulating them, feel the vibrations in the chambers of my heart, soul and body.

I continued the weekly classes. It wasn't so much what we did but the safe and sacred space that was created to do it in. Stuff inside me kept loosening, floating up to my consciousness, taking shape in stories, poems. My next experience came during a meditation exercise. We were meditating on the chakras and when we came to the (third eye) chakra, I saw in my mind's eye this loving eye looking back at me. It was so conscious and loving. I was overcome with tenderness. There was a trust that was growing inside me for the process I was going through and where it was leading."

Core Unresolved Issues

"Where it was leading was not to a place, outside, but to a space, inside. My center, my core. I was terrified. Unresolved issues with my father floated up.

> My father–a good provider, loving and faithful, a good Christian example,
> A decent, kind, peaceable human being. It's been 22 years since my 21st birthday.
> Why am I writing to him for the first time in my life to express my true feelings?

I did not know where to begin, how to deal with this pain, anxiety. I had not the courage to deal with this, i.e., confront my father with these feelings: and even if I did, they were raw emotions, inexpressible.

> This has to do with my relationship to you . . .
> This has to do with being catholic . . .
> The role models you held up to me were St. Augustine and Thomas Merton . . .
> Did you hope and pray I would become a priest?

During a private session with Saphira, I was asked to imagine my father seated beside me. To tell him everything in my heart. I start, slow at first–this is hard!–but words, tears begin to flow. When I hit an impasse, to my astonishment, I am asked to reverse roles: be my father answering me. Then reverse roles again; and again until I (as my father) say "I'm so confused!" I am completely purged, relieved. This is followed by an assignment. Write a letter (which you may or may not mail) to your father. I start it that night and come up with seven pages! The words flowing freely. This letter became the ground, the raw material from which I shaped a dramatic presentation called *My Father.*

The disciplines I was learning in drama therapy and transformational theater were preparing me for one of my greatest challenges in my adult life: giving up an addiction–nicotine. For most of 20 years I had smoked two packs of cigarettes a day. I tried everything from sheer willpower to acupuncture to hypnosis, as well as various eastern and western medicines and nothing took hold.

The art of role playing and writing exercises (letter, diary and journal) provided a safe space for me to explore my terrors and fears about addiction. Not only did this give me confidence in confronting past traumas and resolving old wounds but it had the net result of embodying me in the present. It felt as if moral strength and courage had been added to my core/center where fear had resided.

Such Sufi concepts as befriending your pain, transforming your inner pain into a work of art and offering it back as healing to the community, the Sufi breath disciplines (which the act of smoking was a counterfeit of), visualization techniques of principal archetypes–Teacher, Healer, Artist, Priest/Priestess; group dynamics where other participants could role play different aspects of your self; storytelling and the creation and performance of a theater piece as a concrete goal and, most of all, the safe and sacred space to birth this in–all these disciplines were tools and weapons I used, with one hand, creating a work of art out of my withdrawal process, and with the other, fighting off the inner and outer demons that would pull me back."

The Cigarette Papers

"I began a journal called *The Cigarette Papers.* I set aside a specific time each day when I would not smoke. The gap would be long enough for the need of the drug to kick in. When the pain came forth from its hiding place, screaming for release, a threshold would be crossed and

> I began to yield to the pain
> let it seep into me
> up from my center to my chest and head
> down to my loins my legs my feet
> the pain becomes sweet, but it hurts so . . .
> but it is sweet and I marvel at this.

I would return to my studio to write, as accurately as I could, what was going on inside me. The discipline of journal-keeping and dialoguing with the pain provided me with a container to put the "withdrawal" in, transforming itself into cosmic and tragic poetic monologues which in turn would be acted out before the group and shaped into theater pieces.

Now into my third year with Omega Theater, I am beginning to realize the fruit of all I have learned and will continue to learn. I came to Omega Theater knowing a poet is not a person who only writes poems. Through the work there, I was reminded that a poet educates, heals, teaches, and shares the wisdom of life's path. This was confirmed through my experience in the training. I had the desire and the fire. What was lacking was the container to hold the fire, the disciplines to focus the flame and harness the energy into light and warmth.

It was in one of the group sessions, helping one of the members go through a particularly dark place in her past that began to open up the door in me to explore the same. Maybe it was seeing another make it through that gave me the courage; or the group functioning as a container, a net holding and helping her through the process; watching her come out the other side. During that session I felt something–a shadow rising in the back of my mind–some fear, terror reminding me of things/barriers I was unable to overcome in my past: about my family, my father, being catholic–shadowy stuff about guilt, sex, I wasn't able to break through; receded from the barrier only to pop up years later.

One worry that comes to mind: if I am healed of this dark place, this hole, will it take away from the energy/catalyst that is part of my creative process? Part of me worries that I will upset whatever internal balance I have–the dance I do with the dark and the light that enables me to midwife, bring to birth the poems I've created thus far.

During this time, dream journaling opens other doors. I recall all the times in childhood I froze when performing: in a play in second grade; little league baseball. Interesting that this comes up as I am thinking of the letter I am writing to my father."

Exploring the Hole

"I begin to explore the relationship between intimacy and addiction. During a private session, poems come up about nicotine/liquor/food. I explore the feel of the hole inside me that I keep stuffing with abuses. I explore the geography of the Hole/Whole. Intimacy related to my father–need unfulfilled–and trying other things–liquor, cigarettes, coffee–to fill it. My problems are in negative space. My father's sins were sins of omission. They are harder for me to locate and define. Finger–in the gaps, cracks, what fell through the holes, fell into the dark places.

What is a hole? Empty space. Gaps. Cracks. Hole. A vacuum–sucking light and healing, negating its effects. I went to a healer to be delivered of dependence on cigarettes. The hole in me was so powerful, it sucked in the healing powers!

But a hole can also mean something else. A dark place, the womb, the earth–the birthing process–out of a dark place, near death/shadow of death: the woman giving birth. The seed that must die in order to sprout. Maybe the hole in me isn't bad. Maybe I should stop seeding, penetrating it with abuses. Maybe I should let the Spirit, the Life/Creative force make love to that place in me, let the seed be planted, to give birth to poems, stories and give birth to a changed, new man, leaving behind my former self. It is the old self that hinders intimacy with all beings and things (relating to them only as objects). It is as if an intimate dialogue is a prerequisite for that being/thing to feel comfortable, trust you with its essence: you bring to the intimacy honor and respect so the being feels safe and trusting to share with you its essence, allow you to reveal it, give voice to it, say, in a poem or work or art. St. Francis comes to mind. And the native peoples of the Americas. The reason they are so eloquent, so poetic, is that they dwell in harmony with creation, and creation feels safe to share its 'speaking' through them as vessels.

So this hole is a sacred space that should be tended, nourished and respected. But this space inside me is in so much pain. Why I numb it with substances? Who wants pain! Yet I am reminded of what I am beginning to learn in transformational theater, what the Sufi's say: Start a dialogue with your pain. Embrace it as a friend. Let it speak, give it voice. It is a natural part of creation. Don't try to run away from it, numb it.

Now I am thinking of my letter to my father. This is what parents should be doing. Nourishing this space in the child. Being masks of the Creator until the child matures and can tend this space on their own. The soul spot. And this spot seems to be the most neglected. So what happens? Everything–good and bad–jumps in, a cacophony of mixed messages, static and general confusions running around inside.

Now my father tried to put God/the church into that space inside me, but it wasn't the living spirit of Christ, only the form. This is why it did not take hold and grow in me. Saphira suggests that the letter to my father/dialogue with the hole would be a good basis for a performance piece for the workshop.

Recording dreams, another tool used in transformational theater, helped me connect (again, a gap) the space between waking and sleeping states. What was too traumatic/dramatic to work out in the workshop was risked in my dreams: In one dream, I am performing one of my poems and all of a sudden, dance out on one of the lines right into conversation with the audience, then back to the text of the poem, then back out into improvisation. I began to lose the creative tension of the poem and the connection to the audience, but I kept at it and finished the poem. What was most important was that I did not freak out, freeze or get filled with stage fright. I just rolled with it. The weekly workshops, where I must improvise pieces two or three times during the course of the evenings have been good training. This would involve working with a partner in a performance piece that would require spontaneous dialogue. On the stage this discipline is transforming itself into conversing with the audience as I am performing the poem. This is like squaring the power. I am beginning to enjoy this.

The weekly workshop was also a way of keeping the internal dialogues out on the table, in the group. It is difficult to share my story with the group. I am nervous, embarrassed, but their support gives me courage. I am asked to:

Take the resistance (the present momentary struggle) and use it,
its energy to create with. Step inside of it and relax and it will help
transform, become the art. Trust your instinct. Jump into the piece.
The words and the art are waiting for you to shape them.

I try this with one of the members of the workshop, but spend most of my time running away, avoiding getting into my Hole where all the grief is. I resist doing an improv, but my partner is there to encourage me, so I give it a try. What happens is that I start off OK in centering myself in the Hole and the mood is serious and I am in character, experiencing the grief and somehow transmuting it to the audience, but at a certain point a split happens in me: I continue to verbally describe the Hole and my feelings, but my tone, mood and movement, facial expressions become radically altered: I shift into my playful/trickster mode with (as my partner describes) a smile on my face and begin to do hopscotch movements acting out the completely contrary emotion of grief. Up to the point of the split, I am speaking and acting in a calm, slow, deliberate manner in words and movement. Then I become hyper, speak quickly and move in a jerky, mimed fashion like a clown or a circus mime. I use the joyful face of the clown/elf/trickster to deal with (numb) the pain and sorrow in me, displacing it rather than dealing with it. The feedback is invaluable, enabling me to see into the mirror of my actual actions that are contrary to the emotions I am attempting to convey.

The inner self becomes a battleground now: the place in me fighting the healer who is approaching the Hole. I just want to dance, skate over the emotions, just going through the motions until I am safe on the other side. I sure do not want to sink into the Pain!

O Lord, please help me with this. I know you want me to deal with this.
Help me to acknowledge my pain, get to know it, accept it, experience it.
Grant me Grace to find the courage to endure the pain long enough to learn what it has to teach me.

I explain to a friend how frustrating it is, fighting myself, wrestling the angel to the edge of the Hole only to run away again. He says what I am really doing is wearing down a good path each time I try, making each successive time easier because I know the path. This will enable me to tolerate staying there longer and longer, to get to know the pain."

Ending

"What is this Core? It seems to have to do with Fear–fear of failure, rejection. The burden as a poet of not knowing each day if you're going to create, or the continual agony of holding within yourself the creative process, like grains of sand in an oyster, midwiving the poems to birth and then when you do, fearing it won't be good or strong enough. Perhaps this is Life. This is the everyday reality of the artist. To accept it, to get to know it, dialogue with it, learn to love it. It keeps coming back to the Sufi maxims I've been learning: Get to know and embrace your pain. This tells you your heart is alive. How these truths are beginning to resonate in me!

In my private therapy sessions with

Saphira I talk about fusing the apparent polarities in my life that keep running off in opposite directions–the monk and the lover, the poetry and the business, the need to live wild and free and the demand of Life to grow and mature, to nourish the Child within and the maturing Adult at the same time. How many artists have stumbled trying to do this, defaulted in areas of their life, failing to incorporate the entire vision.

There is a hunger in me to unite all these different parts and aspects of my life and experiences–the personal and political, the romantic and spiritual, the metaphysical and philosophical, the holy and profane, the chaos and the order, the wild and the sober–a passion to unite, meld, fuse all of this into a vision that will span my entire life, and the art I create along the way, a deep, rich, broad tapestry with many hues and colors that is as wide as it is high as it is deep–a life's work with all its many scenes and motifs, however individual and disparate from each other, but each one, each poem having within it the intimations, harmonies, and sympathetic vibrations of the whole."

Discussion

Ray has been nicotine-free now for 15 years. He developed *The Cigarette Papers* into a full one-man performance piece and went on tour with it, inspiring others with the possibility that they, too, could overcome a long ingrained addiction. As he wrestled with his demons, and opened more and more to his essential nature, his compassion, faith, inspiration and free spirit became more manifest. He truly embodied the artist as healer, educator and shaman through the vehicle of sharing his story with many audiences. He has told me that the stronger those identities became the more motivation he had to resist the temptation of returning to smoking cigarettes. He continues to be aware of this desire, from time to time, but how could this poet/priest/teacher/healer not "walk his talk" as he realizes part of his larger purpose is to be this messenger of an important story of faith, healing and transformation.

Aiko: The Recovery Process of a Japanese/Korean-American Woman

Aiko's Background

Aiko entered the Transformational Theater: Drama Therapy and Sound Healing program with great interest, but also with some reticence. She had grown up in a privileged Japanese class. Her early life was characterized by an appreciation for the beauty of Japan's countryside, the wisdom of her beloved grandparents, the intelligence, strength, rigidity and severe wounding of her mother. Her mother lived daily with the unacceptable situation of her husband's six concubines and her father's total preoccupation with his very successful business life and financial position. Over a period of hundreds of years, Aiko's paternal ancestors were forcefully brought from Korea to Japan as slaves. Gradually, over generations, they were able to climb the social ladder and build wealth and position, managing to erase their Korean heritage. But her father never lost the ancestral stigma of having been subjugated. Because of this, he identified with the abuser. It was an accepted practice among Japan's social elite for the men to have concubines, whom they fully supported financially. In this way, he became the "slave owner" and projected his "dominator" mentality onto these women. Aiko had been sent away by her mother to Canada to study music at the age of nine. She also studied dance, as she had done in Japan from an early age. One of the first things she shared in the group was how uprooted and split she always felt, in having been cast out of her homeland.

To work with Aiko therapeutically, it was important to understand the traditional Japanese values and norms with which she grew up. It was not within her cultural norms to share intimate feelings, especially about dark family issues. Euro-American values for healing, therapy goals and processes are frequently contradictory to Asian, particularly female gender-based values. Lee and Richardson in their book, *Traditional Japanese Values and Norms, Multicultural Issues in Counseling: New Approaches to Diversity* (1991), state that much of traditional Japanese culture can be traced to the philosophical precepts of life that were dictated by Buddhism. Within this cultural system, the individual is superseded by the family, specific hierarchical roles are established for all family members, and rules of behavior and conduct are formalized. An individual's adherence to this code of conduct is a reflection not only on the immediate family, but on the extended kinship network as well.

The father is the leader and decision-maker of the nuclear family. His authority is unquestioned. The welfare of the family rests squarely on the father's shoulders. He enforces family roles and is the primary disciplinarian. The traditional role of the mother is that of the nurturing caretaker of both her husband and children. The mother is clearly the emotionally devoted, nurturing parental figure. The stronger emotional attachments, therefore, tend to be with the mother.

In Aiko's case, the father was able to maintain his lifestyle despite great protests by his wife and uncomfortable, unexpressed feelings by his daughters. Aiko's mother, unlike the cultural norm, was not the emotionally devoted, nurturing parental figure, but was cold, angry and fearful. Aiko feels this was due, in part, to her unhappy marriage.

Highly developed feelings of obligation govern much of the personal relationships of Japanese-Americans. The often unspoken obligatory reciprocity within relationships is a serious consideration in the life of a Japanese-American. The individual is expected to express affection and gratitude as well as respect and obedience to parents and others in authority positions.

In a social structure where interdependence is so highly valued, the fear of losing face can be a powerful motivating force for conforming. The withdrawal of confidence and support by the family, community or society, and the exposure of an individual's wrong actions for all to see, is a profound shaming experience to be avoided at all costs.

When Aiko began this work, she was able to express to the group her discomfort with sharing her family secrets as well as her own issues. This made it possible for everyone, both leaders and group members, to actively encourage and support her in her current emotional dilemma. She soon was able to appreciate the opportunity to come to terms with and work through several significant issues.

Beginning with Psychodrama

In the first session, one of the group members enacted a psychodrama, which focused on that woman's relationship with her mother. Aiko role-played this woman's mother in the psychodrama. After the main drama, when everyone shares something of his or her own story that was catalyzed by the protagonist's drama, Aiko made a connection with her own mother. It was then suggested that everyone remember a moving moment with their mother and give expression to that moment by allowing a spontaneous song to emerge. By doing this, the participants created a positive container in which the more difficult object relations issues could be addressed.

Aiko referred to her mother in her first journal entry: "I wanted to remember only beautiful images of her today, and moments when she was in her elements, moments when she was joyful and vigorous. I remember her in her sunflower garden laughing in the sun. I remembered her in the Zen Village of Niigata (on the Northwest province of Japan, facing the Sea of Japan). I remembered her bicycling, running around, laughing again. Why did I want to remember mainly good and warm memories of her? Because I now see also the tragedy of her life, marrying someone too complicated for her to comprehend. Her family was all heart feeling. My father's family was almost all mind thinking, conniving and calculating how to survive. From joy to coldness and to madness. It was too much for her. In the end, she entered into the coldness and went mad. In this mad child-like state for a year, she took her own life."

Introducing the Transpersonal

From the time our work together began, it appeared that it would be most effective to relate to Aiko through a transpersonal/spiritual orientation. This was familiar to her from her Buddhist roots, which was naturally integrated into her early daily life. Zen Buddhism in its essence is the art of seeing into the true nature of one's being. It points the way from fear and desire to freedom from suffering. The goal of Zen Buddhism is to achieve Satori or enlightenment through zazen (emptying the mind) and Koan practices. The Zen Buddhist aesthetic of unselfconscious artfulness provides the basis of classical Japanese culture. Aiko told of Buddhist Monks coming often to homes in the community for different life events, to sit together with an awareness of their breath, and to meditate and chant. Since the transpersonal approach that is included in our work was especially helpful to Aiko, optimal opportunities were created to work on that level when it seemed appropriate. It was clear that every exercise and reference to spiritual language and experience opened Aiko to more easily face what was difficult for her, in her complex emotional history. It was natural for this Japanese woman to sit still, work with meditations and a variety of exercises that begin with an awareness of the breath including visualizations, voice and movement exercises, and the validation of transpersonal dimensions of consciousness. Reference to the purity of her soul's essence deeply resonated with her. It soon became clear that this approach did help to create the bridge from her reticence to build her trust and open her to deep, less familiar, emotional work. The transpersonal dimension can be significant in anyone's therapeutic process, but with Aiko, because of her cultural heritage, this became the key in opening to her buried pain.

In Aiko's Transformational Theater/drama therapy group, participants were invited to remember two dreams, one from early childhood and a meaningful recent dream. The dreamer then selects group members to enact each of the dream images from both of their dreams. The dreams come back to life before the dreamer's eyes, triggering memories of parts of the dream that were forgotten, often resurfacing emotional states from that time. At other times, new feelings surface as insights and connections are made, catalyzed by watching the dream images enacted. The dreamer is helped to see the inevitable relationship between both dreams in terms of core emotional issues and ongoing life challenges. A transpersonal dimension helps people to identify what are called soul qualities or essential parts of the human psyche that are our source of strength. Examples of these positive qualities are: clarity, magnanimity, sacredness, sense of humor, purity, majesty, creativity, peace, love, intuition. At least one and often more qualities can be seen in both dreams. The soul qualities can be identified as that place that we are able to turn to in ourselves that can never be tarnished from any abuse or life trauma. Helping people shift their identity from their sense of limitation, low self-esteem, shame, and feelings of inadequacy to these positive, essential parts of themselves is perhaps at the core of the healing process.

Participants are also helped to expand their identity to embrace the archetypes of Artist, Healer, Educator, Shaman or Spiritual Guide. Integrating these archetypes into their professional identities as well as into their general view of themselves becomes another source of strength and tool for transformation for group members. According to Jung, the experience of the archetype is often kept secret, since it so close to the core of one's being (Jung, 1977). When that archetypal shift in one's own identity genuinely begins to happen, a person's whole way of viewing him/herself shifts, influencing all aspects of the person's life.

Integrating the Cultural Elements

To create the accommodation for this to happen for Aiko, a basic Japanese value needed to be understood and addressed in subtle ways. For example, in many non-Western cultures, identity is not seen apart from the group orientation. The personal pronoun "I" does not exist in the Japanese language (Sue & Sue, 1990).

There were several things that happened in Aiko's therapy process that honored her cultural orientation. First, she was a part of a group process, where the group became very bonded as a kind of extended family. By enacting other peoples' dreams, for example, and participating in other group exercises, Aiko became increasingly comfortable in honoring and dealing with her own individual issues. Secondly, many process approaches were framed in spiritual language and values, so that if there was any sense of loss of one spiritual goal, in this case the valuing of the individual's privacy, other spiritual goals were honored and expressed. Thirdly, because this Japanese woman is naturally very creative with a distinct clarity of mind (perhaps reinforced through her meditation experience), she was fascinated by the depth of dream work and what was to be discovered in the rich terrain of the unconscious, as insights were revealed.

She wrote, "Dreams have power–my first discovery. Interpreting dreams have real power. Connecting two of my dreams, from childhood and adulthood was a surprise. Father image/male image certainly occupies me. My father certainly did and does have a profound effect on my life. All life revolved around him, when I was a child and even now. Saphira said, 'Honor the pain. In our society, we numb the pain by drinking, eating, drugs and working, among other things. Do not avoid the pain. Pain will naturally occur in life. When it does, simply embrace it and honor it. If we do not avoid the darkness, then one can also see the light. If not, then it's often more difficult to see the light.' She also said, 'Breath means inspiration. From breath, inspiration springs.'"

Participants are encouraged to identify, and to honor and dramatize shadow elements, in their psyches, within this work. In trying to make the unconscious conscious, people discover that there are many hidden things buried deep within. These things are not always negative and when they reach the light of our conscious self a power is unleashed in our healing and creative processes (Jung, 1977).

"My Truth: I do not digest my food well. Same with life issues–There is a black despair about everything I touch.–So many unresolved issues I carry in my constipated life–Running away literally from difficult issues has been my constant state" (Aiko).

Delving Into The Shadow

A number of drama therapy exercises were presented to help people discover their shadow characters and create them. These characters became an expression of hidden parts of themselves. For Asian people, overcoming the strong value of not sharing the dark side is often more of an obstacle than for Americans, as was mentioned earlier. In the safe atmosphere that was created, exploring this dark side seemed to flow quite easily, even for Aiko. Everyone sounded, sang, and danced their shadow. Questions helped the process: Who are you? Where do you come from? How do you move and sound? Why have you stayed hidden? They told their story, sang and danced and often cried. Further expression and more developed characters were encouraged to evolve.

Aiko learned from an early age to escape–escape from the bonds of her patriarchal, oppressive family and cultural roots. In so doing, she discovered that she was also escaping from the potential joys of her current life and the possibilities of deeper intimacy in her personal relationships.

She wrote:

> *Shadows are dark! My darkness was a hollow hole. Try as I previously did to fill it with harsh discipline of long hours of work it did not fulfill this emptiness. I needed a power greater than my human effort and sweat could provide. I needed to tap into source power. Grandmother was one who guided me into this power. In this power there flowed a steady, sustaining light. My grandmother was smiling as she led me to this river of quiet energy. River is one of the names given to me by a Burmese Monk. When I was totally stuck in my life, frozen and broken, he gave me this name so that I may defreeze. I discovered today that when I release from my unconscious, away from my head (which is quick and overactive), amazing things happen. Perhaps in my unconscious is hidden my real self.*

At this stage in the process, Aiko was able to receive a great deal of solace in connecting to her strong sense of peace and purity (soul qualities) which she experienced in nature, surrounding her aunt's country house, in which she spent her early childhood. However, images of her experience of men as violent, warlike, and powerful, symbolizing the oppressive patriarchal roots of her culture, presented itself in both of her dreams. These images suggest that owning her own female shadow and inner male (animus, in Jungian terms) is a key in her own healing process. Carl Jung also said that if we do not face our shadow, it will become our fate (Jung, 1977). If we do not own our own rage or violence we will play it out.

Aiko shared with the group that she had an abortion, without her husband's knowledge, which devastated him when he later learned of it. She described the process as being driven to do that by her own destructive impulse, without even thinking about all the pros and cons. She had told no one else about what she had done until working with the group.

Through a life incident improvisational exercise, in which participants recall significant incidents as a child, an adolescent and a young adult, another woman in the group revealed and dealt with the intense emotions around sexual abuse. This woman dramatized a powerful scene with her older brother, who had molested her. This triggered other sexual abuse memories in the group, many of which had been repressed and some of which had never been shared before. Through the other woman's drama, which the group helped to enact, Aiko got in touch with two traumatic events in her own life. One was an incident with her father, who took her away with him on a trip and tried to molest her as a young girl. The second situation was the abortion, which she first shared at this time.

Aiko's next two journal entries reflect her discoveries and experience with her sources of strength, the light and the dark, transpersonal dimensions and the nature of the healing process that she was experiencing at this time.

> Sources of strength–what a wonderful phrase and they are all already inside ourselves, waiting for us to tap into them. What are my sources of strength? My kind and merciful God, forest and animals surrounding our cabin, who constantly surprise and delight me with their resourcefulness. A thousand stars and the moon, who descend so close to me every night. My patient husband, who truly has embraced me with all my faults. Rekindling what I feel in my innermost being when I move. Transformational theater where we bring our darkness into light and make friends with them.
>
> Life challenges dissolved by source of strength. Darkness dissolved by light. Seriousness dissolved by play. Shutting down dissolved by love. Tonight I really felt the power of love. When P. [group member] put her hands on my heart and sang, her love breathed into my soul and body, and her intent of goodness towards me confirmed for me that life was good. Also, when we felt each other's aura emanating heat and whatever else, we confirmed for each other that we were creatures, not only of this earth but of places beyond. (Aiko)

Since overt expression of angry feelings are discouraged in the Asian culture, many Japanese people somatacize these feelings and are encouraged to present an appearance of peace and joy even when they are in conflict and pain. The combination of enacting one of the roles in another woman's drama, to help her, and then, from within the role, observing and identifying with the victim position, Aiko had a total, full-bodied, emotional experience. This is a striking example of the therapeutic value of drama therapy.

Final Performance

Participants were helped to create final performance pieces. They were to present their challenging life material as well as their transformational possibility, including their source of strength. They were encouraged to speak their truth. The final pieces were created by each individual and they could have other group members play the different roles in their drama, enacting people, environments, sound textures, as individuals or as an ensemble. People write their story as dramatic monologues, scenes, in prose, poetry, song, naturalistic or stylized, or a combination of the above. They can choreograph movement pieces within it. They can incorporate music in whatever way they choose. They can use costumes, props, masks, set pieces or whatever helps them tell their story more authentically. The group invites family and friends to be the audience. The process of objectifying the issues, after working through them in part, creating an artistic form to express them and then giving it away to the audience as a gift offering, has proven to be a very effective therapeutic tool. The process of creating the pieces takes everyone through struggle and creative tension, proving in the end, almost always, to be a very cathartic, healing and satisfying process for the participants. This was certainly the case for Aiko.

She chose to dress in a traditional Japanese costume and white face. She created her piece within a movement/dance structure. Aiko had not danced for some time, but had studied dance when she was younger, so it became important to her to work in that form. She also chose to insert phrases in Japanese at specific dramatic moments in her piece. Here is a summary of her final performance piece:

1. When I was born, I was immediately taken away from the warm breath of my mother. [movement]
2. She had already decided to leave my father. He had six concubines. (In Japanese, my mother speaking): How filthy! How disgustingly dirty! How long do you think you can continue to lie to me!!
3. Yes, the blood of incest and misguided sexual energy runs in my family. [movement]
4. When I was twelve, my father took me on a little trip, just the two of us. In the middle of the night, I felt Father's big hand descend on me. (In Japanese): What are you doing, Dad?! What are you doing?! [movement]
5. Today, I no longer feel, [movement] breathe, [movement] or play [movement].
6. (The group gathering around me.) Chieko-chan asobo, chieko chan asobo, little chieko, come and play! [movement]
7. Yes, sexual impurity appeared in me, too. I aborted my first child, my only child. I willed her death. [scream, movement]
8. (In Japanese) Please forgive me, please forgive me! [movement] I love you, I love you very much!
9. [As if holding the baby, sing lullaby in Japanese]
10. [With music accompaniment, dance improvisation]
11. [Bringing the cloth and the group across the stage, start the transformational dance-song] (The whole group rocking) Licking our wound, licking our wound.

> Burning in the fire, burning in the fire.
> Honoring our pain, honoring our pain
> Breathing dearly, breathing dearly.
> Looking into our darkness, looking into our darkness.
> Loving our soul, loving our soul
> Trusting our impulses, trusting our impulses.
> Forgiving ourselves, forgiving ourselves.
> Loving the God in us, loving the God in us!
> [Grab the cloth in the center and start the dervish whirl as light fades.]

Aiko expressed her feelings that with the new understanding she had gained, and through the surfacing and purging of so much pain and suffering, she now could forgive her parents. Our assessment was that she had done a significant piece of emotional work, but that most likely true forgiveness will take more time. In many sexual abuse cases, after the initial anger is expressed toward the perpetrator father, the often deeper feelings of abandonment by the mother surface: Where was she when I needed her and why did not she protect me? Aiko's feeling that she unconsciously blamed her mother needs to be further explored and those feelings validated, rather than dismissed. Concluding reflections written by Aiko, in her evaluation of her process:

> Externalization of my trauma enabled me to defreeze my trauma and start to move it and to be objective about it. Defreezing of my trauma enabled me to go deep into my darkness which subsequently allowed me to go into my light. A specific group exercise that was particularly transformative was the exercise in which I dramatized my family, by becoming my father one moment, my mother the next moment, and myself the next moment. This experience revealed to me how the whole world changes when one is in another's shoes. It allowed me to sympathize.

As a group, we became very close and caring for each other. In order to really help each other, our individual faculties as the artist, healer, educator, and shaman were demanded to be polished to the highest degree. My sympathies went to all members of the group who were struggling with their families. I was profoundly shocked and assured, at the same time, of our common human struggles on this earth. During this process, my patience with other peoples' struggles (outside the group) became larger.

Freedom to be who we each are
In the dance of searching, exploring
Laughing and crying
Up and down
Sideways and backwards
Can we be safe enough to not have the answers
While fully embracing the questions
Moving a single step closer
To a new becoming
Free to be our essential selves. (Aiko)

CONCLUSION

Transpersonal drama therapy is the process through which individuals transform their identity from a limited history-based sense of self to an experience of their essential soul self. From the experience of their essential self, individuals can access a relationship to the numinous and their unique life purpose. Transpersonal drama therapy utilizes the embodied arts in the recovery from abuse, addictions, dysfunctional relationships, outmoded survival behaviors and associated limitations acquired from personal history toward an experience of being fully present and whole, capable of intimacy with oneself, others and the transpersonal. From this relationship to wholeness, the process of individuation supports an individual's continuing development of self, deepening their connection to the deeper meaning of their lives and their potential service to humanity and the expansion of human consciousness.

In this chapter on Omega Transpersonal Drama Therapy, which reflects the theoretical foundation created by myself and Penny Lewis, I describe our work with institutionalized special needs children and adolescents, family systems therapy through participatory theater, organizational development/management training in corporations, diversity training, community healing events with a variety of sociopolitical concerns, womens' issues, geriatric healing, addictions and multicultural issues.

In the past ten years, our colleagues and students have taken the work into the world applying this approach to drama therapy in nursing homes, homeless shelters, foster care facilities, rehabilitation hospitals, mental hospitals, schools, after-school programs, autistic children and adolescent programs, community centers in the inner city, groups for the sexually abused, programs for addictions including dual diagnoses, grief groups, for people with life threatening illnesses, for communication training in corporations, for potential minority leaders in organizations, for developmentally delayed children and adults, for working with victims of natural catastrophes here and abroad, prostituted women and sex trafficking in India, Bangladesh, Taiwan, and Thailand.

We look forward to the development of programs for individuals, families and groups with a wide range of disabilities and wounds to find the way back home to their health and individuation, so that they may become their essential healed, balanced selves. We envision ourselves as drama therapists working together with our clients toward creating their lives as works of art, fulfilling our larger purpose in service to creating a better world.

REFERENCES

Grotowski, J. (1968). *Towards a poor theatre.* New York: Simon & Schuster.

Jung C.G. (1977). Psychology and religion: west and east. *Collected works,* 11. Princeton: University Press.

Lee, C., & Richardson, B. (Ed.). (1991). *Traditional Japanese values and norms, multicultural issues in counseling: New approaches to diversity.* Virginia: American Counseling Association.

Linden, S. (1997). A festival of light: a high school healing arts event celebrating the ethnic diversity of the school community. *The Arts in Psychotherapy, 24,* 255–259.

Moreno, J.L. (1947). *The theater of spontaneity.* Beacon, New York: Beacon House.

Portman, J., & Rollins, B. (1968). *Riot play,* unpublished.

Spolin, V. (1963). *Improvisation for the theatre.* Chicago: Northwestern University Press.

Sue, D.W., & Sue, D. (1990). *Counseling the culturally different: Theory and practice.* New York: John Wiley and Sons.

Walsh, R., & Vaughn, F. (1980). *Beyond ego: Transpersonal dimensions in psychology.* New York: Jenny Tarcher.

BIBLIOGRAPHY

Linden, S. (1972). Selecting and developing actors. Participatory theater for young audiences. In P. Hale-Whitton (Ed.), *A handbook for directors.* (pp. 48–61). Rowayton, CT: New Plays For Children, Inc.

Linden, S.B., & Bentov, M. (1973). *Improvisation in the classroom.* Roxbury, MA: Rice Printing.

Linden, S. (1977). Theater workshop Boston: An anniversary review. *Forum for Correspondence and Contact, International Center for Integrative Studies, 8*(3).

Linden, S. (1978). *Managing People.* Citibank video production, written, produced and directed by Theater Workshop Boston for Forum Corporation. Boston: The Video Picture Company, Inc.

Linden, S. (1978). The crystal chalice: Spiritual themes for women. In *Women in the world* (pp. 55–62). Taj Inayat: The Abode Press.

Linden, S. (1979). The nature of inspiration. *East West Journal, 12,* 82–84.

Linden, S. (1981). Free to create. *New Age Journal, 7,* 60–67.

Linden, S., & Litwin, G.H. (1988). *Visioning as a transformational process.* Unpublished. Available from the author.

Linden, S. (1989-90). Creating Gaia and ourselves as works of art. *Emergence: Journal for Evolving Consciousness, 3,* 19–20.

Linden, S., Moore, S., Inayat, T., & Tune, X., (Eds.). (1991). *Studies, reflections, reports from the chrysalis connection: The feminine council of the Sufi order.* Seattle: Sufi Order International.

Linden, S. (1986-1993). *The Omega Arts Network News,* Editor (six issues). Boston: Omega Theater.

Linden, S., & Inayat, T. (1996-7). An interview with Marion Woodman. *Heart and Wings Newsletter.* Seattle: Sufi Order International.

Linden, S. (1997). Aiko: drama therapy in the recovery process of a Japanese/Korean-American woman. *The Arts in Psychotherapy, 24,* 193–204.

Linden, S. (2007). The voice of Sophia: Feminine wisdom, revealing itself. *Elixir Magazine, 5,* 50–54, 80.

Theater and Television Productions

Awakening. (1978). (S. Linden, Director; S. Hanan, playwright; OM Theatre Company, Boston).

Barbara Linden, Artists in America Series. (1971). R. Hauser, producer; WGBH/PBS, Boston.

Coming Home. (1987). Play. (S. Linden, Director; Omega Theater Company, Boston.).

Cosmic Celebration. (1973–1983). Originally *The Cosmic Mass.* (Pir Vilayat Inayat Khan, author, & S. Linden, director; Boston).

Cosmic Celebration. (1983). Video tape/DVD production. (N. Ardalan, & H. Terk, producers).

Creation. (1970). Play. (S. Linden & I. Rosenberg, authors). Rowayton, CT: New Plays For Children.

Eartheart. (1995-present). Play. (S. Linden & S. Nisenbaum-Becker, creators).

How Can I Tell You? (1970). Teacher's guide to language arts, grades 1–6. (S. Linden, author; C.

Sarson, producer, Boston: WGBH).
Motherblood. (2004–present). Play. (S. Linden & S. Nisenbaum-Becker, creators, Boston).
Sunsong. (1976): A participatory people puppet pageant for children of all ages. (S. Linden, playwright, director; D. Sonneborn, musical director). Rowayton, CT: New Plays For Children, Inc.
The Finding Place: A Ceremonial Journey. (1992). (S.Linden, J. Grant, & H. Gebel, playwrights; Omega Theater Company, Boston). Sejecho Multicultural Arts Festival.
The First Earth Run. (1986). Ceremony. (S. Linden, director; OM Theatre Company, Boston).
Toward the One: A Family Board Game. (1974). (S. Linden, & B. Dym, creators; D. Hallowell, music director).
Tribe. (1969). Play. (S. Linden, playwright). Rowayton, CT: New Plays for Children, Inc.

FURTHER TRAINING

Omega Transpersonal Drama Therapy
Certificate Program
An individually tailored alternate route
training program
Co-Founders:
Saphira Linden, MA, RDT-BCT, LCAT, CP
Penny Lewis, PHD, RDT-BCT, LMHC, NCC,
ADTR

Address: Omega Theater
41 Greenough Avenue
Jamaica Plain, Massachusetts 02130
Telephone and Fax: 617-522-8300
www.omegatheater.org
email: info@omegatheater.org

Chapter 11

PSYCHOANALYTIC APPROACH TO DRAMA THERAPY

Eleanor Irwin

Throughout recorded time, drama and theatre have been the carriers of our deepest fantasies, portrayed through movement, sound, imagery and enactment. Because the arts have a unique power to invoke feelings and ideas, mental health practitioners have historically used art, drama, music, movement and poetry to understand and help those in psychological pain. Many years ago, convinced of the value of integrating drama in therapy, I began to look for dynamic, creative and effective ways of integrating these disciplines in my clinical work. Helping individuals to express emotions and ideas through spontaneous drama seemed natural and central to the process; understanding the deeper meanings of the elicited fantasies and behaviors, however, was much more complicated.

To decipher part of the puzzle, I sought psychoanalysis in the belief that the more we know about ourselves, the better prepared we are to understand and help others. In time, this valuable experience led to psychoanalytic training as I realized that more skill and knowledge in verbal psychotherapy would help to make drama and therapy co–creators of the process. Eventually this journey led to firmer ground, with a sense of deep satisfaction as an analytically-oriented drama therapist and a psychoanalyst, working with children, adolescents and adults.

In the course of training, I became familiar with different psychoanalytic theorists, including, of course, Sigmund Freud, the founder of the field and a genius who revolutionized modern psychology. Psychoanalysis, as a form of therapy, a theory of the mind, and an explanation of human development was very helpful in deepening my understanding of emotional development and functioning. These gains led to an interweaving of psychoanalytic knowledge with spontaneous drama, creativity, theatre, and psychodrama. I hope that the ideas presented in this chapter will illustrate how the core of this process is shaped by spontaneous drama, and understood through the lens of current psychoanalytic theory.

IMPORTANCE OF THE UNCONSCIOUS AND THE RELATIONSHIP

Some of Freud's core concepts that have withstood the test of time will be evident in the material in this chapter. This includes the theoretical bedrock (Wallerstein, 1992) of many of Freud's early theories: *the unconscious mind, symptom formation, resistances and defenses,* and *transference,* all concepts that can guide one's work in drama therapy. Freud's major contribution may well have been his discovery of the impact of unconscious mental processes in our lives, inasmuch as the unconscious inexorably shapes our lives and exerts a powerful influence on all aspects of our personality. Freud's second major contribution was his theory of neurosis, in which he conceptualized a dynamic relationship between the repression of unacceptable impulses, the creation of defenses, and ensuing symptom formation. Finally, Freud left us with a beginning understanding of transference, spelling out how identifications with significant others can lead us to transfer old imprints into new relationships, for better or worse.

Some may be surprised to find that certain aspects of psychoanalytic theory, while rooted in Freud's work of more than a century ago, are given renewed respectability in an emerging rapprochement between psychoanalysis and neurobiology (Fonagy, 2001; Shore, 2003b; Siegel, 1999), especially in the areas of affect regulation and body-mind relations (Shore, 2003b). While these new findings have developmental and clinical implications for the theory and practice of all therapies, it is not surprising that many of these concepts are already part and parcel of how drama therapists work. Calling the unconscious "Freud's major contribution to science," Shore wrote that a "deeper understanding of the fundamental problems of human emotion, motivation, behavior, and cognition can only be achieved by further investigations of this unconscious realm" (2003a, p. 277). The right brain, described by Shore as "the neurobiological substrate of the unconscious," is affect and bodily based, and in touch with the world primarily through emotions and the senses, presenting a kind of map of the mind-body. When drama therapists work in this area, they are primarily working in a preverbal mode in mind-body-emotion states that are out of conscious awareness. It is this work in the unconscious realm that accounts, in part, for the power of drama to access deep feelings and buried memories.

Of equal importance to drama therapists is recent research that emphasizes the therapist-patient relationship. This dyad, in many ways, is similar to that of the infant/young child in the caretaking environment, a topic that D.W. Winnicott (1960, 1965), a pediatrician and a psychoanalyst, addressed many years ago. Drama therapists emphasize this interpersonal aspect of treatment when they create a safe play space that promotes mirroring, empathic attunement and identification, mechanisms that are necessary for the development of a true self.

The importance of this period of early development has been widely emphasized by multidisciplinary studies that underscore the centrality of infancy/childhood, when genetics and interpersonal relationships interact to shape the brain, the mind, and ultimately, one's personality (Main, 1993; Shore, 2003 a, b; Siegel, 1999). This research, with roots in attachment studies (Cassidy & Shaver, 1999) indicates that positive early relationships with caretakers are crucial to stimulate pathways in the brain that can facilitate body awareness, memory, empathy, self-regulation, identification with others, self-control, and the ability to deal with stress (Bowlby,

1973, 1978, 1988; Shore, 2003a, b; Solomon & Siegel, 2003). When these developmental steps are compromised, there can be fundamental interference with healthy living. Work on some of these areas of arrested development is illustrated in the case examples of Lois and Zoey in this chapter, demonstrating how the power and pleasure of drama therapy became the "emotional glue" that intensified the transference, helped to repair emotional dysregulation, and promoted development.

Psychoanalysis, drama therapy, and indeed all forms of psychodynamically-oriented treatment stress the fundamental need for a psychologically safe climate that can make empathic, intimate, and respectful connections possible. As Winnicott (1960, 1965) points out, facilitating environments are crucial for the maturation of affects in the mother/infant relationship as well as the therapist/ patient one, in what is often called the *transference/countertransference* situation. Winnicott wrote that there can be no baby without a mother; Racker, suggesting a similar interactional effect in the transference, wrote that there can be no action on the part of the patient without a counterreaction from the therapist (Racker, 1974, p. 137).

CONTRIBUTIONS OF FANTASY AND PLAY

An astute observer, Freud based much of his conceptualizations of adult psychopathology on early childhood development, the unconscious, and trauma. Freud had a healthy appreciation of child play and what could be learned from it. To illustrate the importance of dramatic play in helping the child to resolve psychological problems, Freud gave an example of his grandson's repetitive play with toys (Freud 1920, p. 17). By continually throwing away and then retrieving his toy, the toddler was able to gradually deal with, and master, his separation anxiety about his mother's departures. The repetitive play with a reel, symbolizing the action of mother's coming and going, was followed by dramatic play in which the child made himself appear and disappear in the mirror. These spontaneous play activities helped the toddler to soothe himself, enabling him to master his worries about separation. Freud called this behavior the *repetition-compulsion* which, he wrote, was an impulse to mastery. "We see," Freud wrote, "that the children repeat in their play everything that has made a great impression on them in actual life, that they thereby abreact the strength of the impression, and so to speak make themselves masters of the situation" (Freud, 1920, pp. 16, 17).

Repetition in play that can lead to mastery was discussed by another early psychoanalyst, Robert Waelder (1933), who, like Freud, wondered why painful traumatic experiences are compulsively enacted in dramatic play. Waelder noted that when overwhelmed, children turn to play to relive and rework the experience, thereby assimilating piecemeal an experience which was too large to be assimilated instantly, all at once (1933, p. 217–218). Waelder noted that the pleasure and the need to play it out helps the child to shift from a passive to an active position; aids the abreaction of powerful emotions; provides wish fulfillment; and restores a sense of mastery. Through pretend play children can take a "leave of absence from reality as well as the superego" (1933, p. 224). That is, in reliving and replaying a traumatic experience, the child in play, and the individual in therapy, can bypass the superego and avoid guilt, because it is, after all, "just pretend!" There is a suspension of disbelief in the *as if* situation that adds to the psychic safety and pleasure of the experience.

Since Freud's time, free association through play and fantasy continue to be at the core of psychoanalytic therapy and, similarly, at the center of spontaneous drama. The value of the creative imagination as a channel for pleasure, sublimation, communication, abreaction, and as a stimulus for healthy development has been noted by many in the helping professions, including arts therapists. The relatively recent phenomenal growth of the arts therapy professions, including drama therapy, can, in fact, be attributed to the recognition that the arts provide a unique access through which individuals can express and explore deep-seated feelings, emotions, ideas and (conscious and unconscious) fantasies.

In distilling and representing conflicts that are portrayed through action and affect, drama presents universal truths that speak to the essence of our humanity, blurring boundaries, and crossing time, space, and cultural differences. Freud, acutely aware of the power of drama to symbolize the universality of unconscious conflicts, chose Sophocles' Oedipus Rex as a cornerstone of psychoanalytic theory. This powerful Greek tragedy depicts the child's intense feelings of love and hate, need and desire, jealousy and competitiveness toward parents, conflicts that Freud believed to be applicable to all. Myths and tales of this kind have historically been carriers of the deepest images and impulses within us, making drama therapy an immensely helpful channel through which hidden wishes and fears can be safely explored.

The core of drama therapy is rooted in our fantasies, revealing the content and coloration of our personal stories. Ubiquitous fantasies rapidly float in and out of our conscious and unconscious minds daily, invade our dream life at night, and dominate, guide, and control our lives without our conscious awareness (Person, 1995; Singer, 1966). Stimulating our creativity and passion, fantasies give us pleasure and pain, and reveal our desires and hatreds, even as they relentlessly shape our behavior in unconscious ways. As Gabbard (1990) put it ". . . we are but characters living out a script written by the unconscious" (p. 7). It is no wonder then that fantasy, and day and night dreams are central in drama and theatre, and indeed in all the arts.

THEORY AND PRACTICE

In an early paper (Irwin, 1979), I defined drama therapy as "a therapeutic modality in which dramatic activities, within a therapeutic relationship, are used to help individuals or groups make changes in personality and achieve a higher level of functioning," a definition that still seems valid. Although the NADT definition of goals in drama therapy speaks of "symptom relief," my own view is that "changes in personality" is more applicable because it implies internal structural change which is necessary for lasting results from therapy (i.e., resolved or lessened conflict, healthier alteration of defenses, increased capacity for sublimation, and the ability to love, work, and play, all psychoanalytic concepts).

In the above definition, the therapeutic relationship may be the single most important part of therapy (Shore, 2007), regardless of theoretical approach. The therapist can only help others deepen their capacity for self-awareness and self-regulation to the degree that s/he intimately knows himself/herself. This self-awareness needs to be present throughout the treatment process, with its cycles of organization/disorganization and disruption/repair that are part and parcel of our work. The capacity to tolerate the strong feelings and raw emotions expressed by patients depends on our ability to know ourselves and monitor our own reactions in the countertransference. Since each of us is a product of our past history, including our past attachments, the best way we can be of help to others is to have our own personal therapy, becoming familiar with the ghosts in our past. The kind of self-awareness that results from personal therapy is a crucial factor in one's capacity to help others because what we, as therapists, have to offer is, at core, ourselves; everything else, including theory and techniques, is secondary.

Drama therapy is the marriage of two well-defined disciplines, with each component part being crucial to the newly forged identity. In defining drama therapy for myself, I thought that both partners in the dyad needed to have equal consideration. Having had many experiences in formal and informal drama, I was pulled in the direction of spontaneous drama, believing that this approach provided the widest opportunity for self-expression and self-exploration. And as for the therapy part, influenced by psychoanalytic supervisors and mentors, I began to think in an analytic way about my clinical work. Psychoanalytic training consisted of a tri-partite program: (1) a personal analysis (four or five times/week on the couch); (2) four or five years of course work covering child and human development, theory and technique, electives and clinical case conferences, and (3) ongoing weekly supervision of cases.

Over time, I realized that there were individuals and groups for whom the spontaneous dramatic experiences, augmented by tact, empathy and respectful interventions, were effective in bringing about positive changes in their lives. Examples of this kind of supportive work (Winston et al., 2003) include adolescent groups and Tammy, cases to be discussed later. But other cases, like Lois and Zoey, were more complicated and needed more intensive work (Emunah, 1994; Irwin, 2006; Johnson, 1982, 1992). An insight-oriented psychoanalytic approach, with a focus on understanding dynamics, seemed necessary in these cases to bring about long-lasting change. By a psychoanalytic approach, I am not referring to 3–5 sessions per week psychoanalysis, but rather to a psychoanalytically-oriented approach that attempts to explain symptoms by examining underlying causes of behavior.

Freud technically defined psychoanalysis as a psychotherapy based on the interpretation of transference and resistance, concepts that are still central to the field. Psychoanalysis has changed radically over the last 100 years, and currently reflects changes that assure a healthy diversity and an open system. But for all these revisions and new schools within psychoanalysis, some concepts continue to be central to the work. These include the conceptualizations mentioned earlier: the *unconscious, resistance/defense; transference and countertransference; and interpretation* (Wallerstein, 1992, pp. 223–224). These core concepts, born and nourished in psychoanalytic soil, are now taken for granted in many, if not most, psychodynamic psychotherapies and pervade our culture.

Psychoanalytic and Psychodynamic Therapy

While the term psychodynamic is often thought to be synchronous with psychoanalysis, in actual practice many therapeutic approaches are psychodynamically-oriented, and share similar psychoanalytic concepts, including, among others, Gestalt, Jungian, Interpersonal, and Lacanian. Some of the similarities (and differences) within a psychodynamic approach can be seen in a comparison of my work and that of the late Penny Lewis, a former colleague and the co-author of the first edition of this book.

Whereas my training was in psychoanalysis, Penny initially trained with Judith Kestenberg, M.D., a Freudian analyst, and later she trained in Jungian psychology. Although Penny and I have different theoretical backgrounds, we are both psychodynamically-oriented in our work. That is, we both understand psychic development using a dynamic framework, informed by concepts such as unconscious conflict, defenses, transference and countertransference. Additionally, we also share a focus on attunement and measure growth through a developmental continuum. Our work, however, illustrates differences in a psychoanalytic and a Jungian approach in drama therapy.

Psychodynamic and psychoanalytic approaches are alike in that both affirm the power of the unconscious and the role of symptoms as a signal of conflict. Ego psychology, one of the first schools of thought in psychoanalysis (A. Freud, 1966), defines symptoms as the sign of emotional difficulties that are reflections of unconscious processes that defend against repressed memories, feelings and ideas. Symptoms might be expressed as anxiety, depression, inhibitions, eating disorders, panic attacks, sexual perversions, or school failures.

A core psychoanalytic understanding is that symptom formation occurs when the individual is caught in an unconscious conflict that he/she is unable to resolve. To protect against painful anxiety, the individual develops defenses that can lead to a compromise formation between the pressure of the underlying feelings (id) and the ego. A symptom, then, is a *compromise formation* that both defends against the forbidden wishes of the id, and yet gratifies the wish, albeit in a neurotic form. Conflicts that lead to symptom formation can be very debilitating, fundamentally interfering with the ability to love, work and play (Brenner, 1982).

Psychoanalytic Principles in Drama Therapy Practice

The psychoanalytic literature is a valuable resource, especially helpful when working with patients with complex symptoms. Winnicott (1960, 1965, 1971, 1975), mentioned earlier, is one of the most enigmatic yet helpful writers on this topic. He coined many terms that are equally applicable to the maternal and the therapeutic environment. Winnicott stressed the importance of creating a *holding environment* and a *play space* that is attentive to, and in synchrony with, the patient's needs. In addition to the crucial ingredients of spontaneity, empathy and reliability, a holding environment requires that the therapist behave in a way that creates an attitude of respect for, and appreciation of, the patient (Gerson, 1996). If a secure play space can be created, the individual can be helped to nonverbally transmit deep information about his/her needs, furthering healthy development. As with the young child, the patient in the play space can move from dyadic pairings in sound, images, pictures and patterns, to more verbal symbolic modes of communication (Johnson, 1982). This kind of progress can only be made, however, when the patient is ready to move forward, and when both parties are fully engaged in the work. In time the patient can be helped to communicate raw emotion and known-but-unknown (right brain) feeling states, into (left brain) language that can deepen therapy through verbal understanding. In all this, what the therapist says is less important than mirroring, being attuned to the patient, and sensing and articulating emotions (Irwin, 2004, 2006). The assumption of psychoanalytic therapy is therefore that individuals can be helped to work through factors that contribute to unresolved anger and despair, thus gaining greater control in life, becoming better emotionally regulated.

There is broad agreement among psychodynamic theories that the inability to regulate one's emotions (i.e., affect dysregulation, Shore, 2003b) is an underlying fundamental deficit in all emotional disorders. Thus it is likely that, despite our different orientations and techniques in drama therapy, we share common goals, because: first, when drama therapists focus on the expression and understanding of feelings, we work toward helping patients broaden their range of emotional tolerance; and second, in doing so, we help individuals modify maladaptive behavior and work toward achieving a more comfortable inner life. I have frequently said that it may not matter so much what theory a person espouses, as long as one has a theory, and as long as one's theory and practice are congruent. If so, one can explain to others with some degree of certainty and authenticity what one does in drama therapy and why. This kind of articulateness is as needed in our field as it is needed in all mental health disciplines.

METHOD AND TECHNIQUES

Many years ago I attended a performance by an improvisational theatre company that was similar to, but different from, both drama therapy and psychodrama. Much the way *Playback Theatre* works now, an improvisational theatre company invited audience members to tell their dreams, which were then enacted by trained actors (for further details on "Playback Theatre" see Chapter 20 by Jo Salas). I was fascinated by this way of working with dreams and the unconscious, but there was something unsettling in seeing the actors interpret the dream of another (something that Playback Theatre is careful to avoid). I wondered if, in such sessions, the dreamers could enact and associate to their own dreams, thus discovering their own personal idiosyncratic dream meanings. Later, in-depth training in psychoanalysis and psychodrama (becoming a TEP–Trainer, Educator, and Practitioner) made this kind of work possible, as illustrated by the later example of work with teenage girls.

I was impressed with the genius of Joseph Moreno, a psychoanalyst and the founder of "Psychodrama" (Chapter 18), "Sociodrama" (Chapter 19), encounter groups, and other modalities that emphasized the here-and-now (Blatner, 1988). While gratified to see how quickly psychodrama could both reveal and conceal crucial psychological issues, I also appreciated the need for careful application of this in-depth method. What I learned from this training continues to be a regular part of my clinical repertoire with children and adults.

In individual and group drama therapy I use many psychodramatic techniques such as: role reversal, doubling, the empty chair technique, the soliloquy, and writing a fantasy letter to articulate and/or resolve a conflict. I found psychodrama to be especially effective with short-term hospitalized patients, long-term incarcerated teenagers, women in residential treatment centers with drug and alcohol problems, and dependent and neglected teenage girls in a group home. These groups enjoy psychodrama and are comfortable with an action style of treatment, rather than one that depends upon verbal reflection. Similarly, sociodramatic techniques are helpful with families and groups, and are valuable teaching aids, especially when teaching skills via role play (Johnson, 1988) and problem solving. The goal in training sessions is not to train psychodramatists, but to heighten empathy for, and gain a deeper understanding of others, work that is very well described in detail by Garcia and Buchanan (Chapter 18), Sternberg and Garcia (Chapter 19), and Landy (Chapter 5) in this volume.

There are inevitable questions about the differences between drama therapy and psychodrama. Drama therapy, with improvisation at its core, focuses on process and usually begins with relaxation and body awareness exercises, movement, nonverbal activities and pantomime, and fantasy enactments. In psychodrama, the therapist, called a director, tends to direct the patient; while in drama therapy, the therapist tends to follow the patient, waiting for the latter to take the lead in the emerging process. Both modalities focus on the elucidation and understanding of fantasies and are used with all ages and populations, and in all modes of treatment. Although my understanding of group process is filtered through psychoanalytic lens, in practice, I frequently blend spontaneous drama and psychodrama, as illustrated in these two examples of supportive group drama therapy.

CASE EXAMPLES

Drama Therapy with Male Delinquents

Working with hard-core, incarcerated delinquent teenage boys, I gained instant rapport when I asked them to show what they had done to bring them behind bars. Without hesitation, Joey, a tough scrawny kid, volunteered:

"Yeah, well, I was drunk, I guess, and my old man beat the crap out of me. My mom watched. When I ran outta' the house, I jumped some old bitch in the alley."

(Me: "Jumped?")

"Yeah, well, I beat the crap out of her (nervous laugh, long pause) and . . . you know . . .

("Raped her!" someone yelled)

"Yeah, well, she was in the wrong place at the wrong time."

After more nervous laughter, I suggested we act it out and the kids greatly enjoyed practicing mock pantomime for the fight scene. Joey picked the players and momentarily took the role of each, then sat back to watch. When the beating was pantomimed, Joey, caught up in the drama, yelled, "Yeah! Give it to him!" The "him" turned out to be not his fellow player, but his father, who was the object of Joey's rage.

With little psychological awareness, Joey had never before thought about his mother's passive collusion with his father's brutality, nor was he aware of the displacement of rage from his parents onto the innocent woman passing by in the alley. Tragically, each adolescent had a similar story to tell of dysfunctional families, physical and/or sexual abuse, addiction, loss of self-esteem, and violent acting-out in an effort to regain power through the discharge of their internalized violent feelings. Enacting individual stories helped the group members talk about their delinquent behaviors. Many had, perhaps for the first time, an opportunity to understand that behavior has meaning, as they tried to explain to themselves and to others the possible reasons for their rage and self-destructiveness.

Drama Therapy with Females in a Group Home

A similar blend of drama therapy and psychodrama took place with a group of dependent and neglected teenage girls in a residential setting, many of whom had been physically and sexually abused. As a trusting and cohesive group emerged, anxiety-laden confidential material began to be explored. Talking openly about their worries, the girls shared terrifying dreams, afraid they would come true. To help them to express this material, I suggested that they keep a dream journal, elaborating on dream images in a drawing book if they wished. The group members were eager to tell, enact, and understand their dreams, which were always followed by sharing. Analysis or interpretation of another's dream was discouraged on the firm belief that only the maker of the dream knows its meaning, as is the rule in psychodrama as well.

Janie's dream was typical: "I was visiting my friend and left to go home after dark. It was late. I took a shortcut across the field. From nowhere a man came with a knife and he chased me; I was frozen and couldn't run. He cut me. I thought I was dead. When I got home, no one noticed the blood on me. They were laughing, watching TV."

In the lively discussion that followed, Janie, shocked, suddenly realized that the attack was probably a reference to a (repressed) memory of a sexual attack by her brother's friend when she was about 13. Remembering how she was unable to protect herself from the rape-like attack, Janie began to cry, and then talked of other times when she felt helpless and enraged in a family where alcohol and physical abuse were daily staples. Sexual and physical abuse went unnoticed, dismissed, or denied ("no one noticed the blood on me"). Enactments of the dreams served an important therapeutic function for these girls, who were astonished and relieved to find deep meaning in their otherwise frightening nighttime images. Journaling and dramatizations of the dreams fascinated these eager learners. The material that emerged from the group was channeled into the girls' individual sessions, and weekly collaboration with the staff helped deepen clinical understanding for all.

Work with these teenagers illustrates how arts experiences often become multimodal, as the arts blend one into another (Emunah, 1994; Rubin et al., 1981). Full of pride about their work, they wanted to present a play and invite everyone to see it. I was hesitant, concerned about the possible negative effects of performing such powerful confidential material, worried about revealing family secrets and possible covert retaliation from parents. Eventually we agreed to present some of the dreams as a play typical of this age group, disguising any material that might identify the dreamers.

The young women proudly performed *Once I Dreamed: A Play in Six Acts.* After the play, we talked with the audience about some of the issues depicted in the dreams, much as Playback Theatre does. We discussed themes of emerging self, sexual, and racial identity; need for closeness and separation; importance of emotional and physical protection from parents and friends (in spite of the adolescent's perceived independence); need to clarify boundary crossings and boundary violations; importance of appropriate choices about boyfriends, alcohol, and drugs. The discussion was not an analysis of the dreams per se, but an educational reframing that focused on the issues within the dream. Participants and audience alike were delighted with this experience, and the play was repeated in three-month intervals with new dream material, and sometimes toured to other group homes.

The theatre experience provided the girls with a sense of deep pride and self respect. They enjoyed the sense of accomplishment in being able to participate in a serious theatre experience and, seeing this, the staff arranged for other theatre trips for them. Eager to continue, the girls enjoyed preparing for and taking roles, working through inevitable stage fright, behaving responsibly as members of cast and crew, and participating in the post-play discussion groups in ever-more articulate ways. This was, altogether, a powerful, growth-enhancing learning experience, similar to that of Playback

Theatre and the work reported by Emunah in her 1994 book and in Chapter 4 in this volume.

CORE PSYCHOANALYTIC CONCEPTS IN DRAMA THERAPY

The Unconscious

One of the core concepts of psychoanalysis is the unconscious, which, as Freud pointed out, is timeless, exerting its influence in the here and now, connecting present reality to past reality. While this is most apparent in dreams, it can be seen in accidents, slips of the tongue, and, indeed, in all aspects of normal and abnormal behavior. Unconscious thinking (sometimes called primary process) is revealed in symbolic behavior, as in this tragic example:

Tammy was eight when her parents were killed. An intruder had entered the house intent on robbery; when Tammy's mother surprised him, he shot her and Tammy's father. In the morning, Tammy went downstairs and found her parents dead on the kitchen floor. Not surprisingly following such a trauma, Tammy was not able to speak about the terrible event with anyone. Instead, avoiding interactive play in her therapy, she repetitively went to the sandbox, and week after week, she depicted sudden disasters that wiped out everything. Constructing an elaborate village in the sandbox, for example, Tammy, without warning, suddenly poured water over the construction, obliterating and killing everything–houses, people, dogs. Or, if not a flood, then a hurricane, a sandstorm, a volcanic eruption, or some other terrible event took place. Tammy was not able to talk about these sudden disasters, nor ready to leave the realm of the symbolic. As though shell-shocked (PTSD), she shrugged, saying the play was just "stuff I made up . . . I don't know why." It was as though this suffering child was in a state of anticipatory anxiety, reliving and reexperiencing the event with a sense of profound helplessness. Seeing her pain, I simply mirrored her shock and empathized with the victims in the villages: e.g., how horrible to have everything wiped out so suddenly, to lose, without warning, the things you loved the most.

For a long time Tammy showed no conscious awareness that her play was connected to her own psychic disaster. The play seemed to reflect raw emotions, as though she was lost in time and space. Slowly, however, Tammy's depression lifted as she emerged from her "dark hole" (as she titled the darkness in one of her paintings). The unspeakable tragedy of her parents' murders needed to be metabolized first (Waelder, 1933) before her inner balance could be restored, and this once-emotionally healthy child could go on living her life. Sand play, and then puppet play and enactments gave Tammy further opportunities to symbolically reenact the sudden wiping out of life as she knew it, albeit in ever less disguised ways. Hesitantly, she began to talk sadly about how things used to be when she was little, with remembrances of happy times–birthday parties, first communion, and the like. Disasters in play began to be slowly replaced by enactments of good times with her beloved mother always present in the drama. But it was many months before Tammy could talk directly about waking, hearing her dog bark, going downstairs and finding her parents dead. This verbal recall, however, happened only after the painful reworking of the trauma in her nonverbal sand play.

Tammy's play reflected derivatives of unconscious thought. Symbolism, displacement, condensation, and other aspects of primary process thinking were evident in her play, similar in some regard to primary process thinking in dreams. Almost as though reliving a nightmare, she became wholly absorbed in grief and mourning. In most sessions Tammy seemed almost oblivious of anything around her. Her profound sadness affected me; I felt her pain so intensely that for many weeks I, too, was mostly silent, as though we were both in mourning. I was reminded of Freud's evocative statements about melancholia (now called depression), when "the shadow of the object falls on the ego," leaving the world–and the ego–poor and empty (Freud, 1917, pp. 243–258).

Transference manifestations were muted, but in the countertransference, I felt her unspeakable grief. I seemed to be a kind of helper (a real object more than a transference one) who accompanied her on a journey of despair and mourning. Verbal interpretations were unnecessary and might also have been intrusive, as Tammy worked through the metaphor in the play, clearly affirming that children have the capacity to recreate and find self-cure in play, "the most natural self-healing measure childhood affords," as Erikson has written (1950, p. 222).

Resistance/Defense

Another core concept in psychoanalysis is that of resistance/defense, an unconscious attempt to preserve the status quo, no matter how painful life is. Often people fear change and cling tenaciously to what they know. Sometimes patients are anxious about the unknown; others unconsciously need to suffer and find hidden ways to punish themselves (A. Freud, 1966). Whether visible in acts big or small, defenses and resistances unconsciously act in opposition to the treatment process, as in the following example:

Twenty-six-year-old Lois had multiple physical and emotional problems. Terrified and traumatized for most of her life, she was afraid of her own (unconscious) aggression which was reflected symptomatically as intense shame and low self-esteem. Lois married at 17 to escape a chaotic family life, and six years later, divorced, depressed and anxious, she became addicted to pain killers. Verbally attacking herself but afraid to confront her parents or ex-husband, she tried to hide from herself the extent of her shame and rage.

Initially in outpatient drama group therapy, Lois brought presents of food, as though to buy a place for herself. She overslept and thus (unconsciously) avoided what she feared. Often she seemed shamed and frightened, as though someone might see her bad, hidden self, sure she was beyond help. All of these behaviors were understandable resistances to treatment. Eventually she confessed that she feared opening Pandora's Box, certain she could not stand the pain or the shame of exposure.

After six months, Lois gained courage and became more involved in relaxation, movement, and theatre exercises, then entered more energetically in group dramas. In time, emboldened, she enacted fantasies that were centered on her hated parents, ex-husband, or the diseased/addicted part of herself. These reality-based memories were her attempts to explore the genesis of her problems and expressed retaliatory (and fearful) wishes towards those who had hurt her. Becoming more direct in the expression of feelings, she apologized to the child she had hated, aborted, and still mourned; wailed at her ugly body; expressed feelings of shame/rage toward the ex-husband who beat her; and chastised her neglectful mother. Sometimes Lois spoke to pictures she had drawn of the despised disfigured self; other times she bravely used the empty chair to rehearse talking to others, or enacted dramas of hoped-for future experiences.

Adopting more mature defenses and better coping skills, Lois showed less dependency on denial and projection and there were fewer instances of aggression turned against the self. The alteration of her defensive structure, in turn, enabled her to achieve greater gratification and self-pride in her new relationships, and ultimately she gave up her addiction to pain killers. After several years of therapy, this once inhibited and frightened woman found her voice, became less fearful of her own aggression, tamed her punitive superego, and was better able to be a more verbally mature young adult, resuming her thwarted development.

Transference

The power of transference and countertransference is astonishing, difficult to describe if one has not discovered it for oneself. Although common in everyday life, it is generally only in therapy that one attends to it and tries to understand its influence. Freud, puzzled and frustrated at first by transference, wrote that many patients claimed their love for him, but he realized this could not be real love, only transference love (Freud, 1915, pp. 157–171). Understanding more about the power and pervasiveness of these awakened "new editions of old feelings," analysts saw that transference could be an ally in treatment but could also be a powerful resistance to insight and change (McLaughlin, 1981).

First seen as an impediment to treatment, transference and countertransference eventually became one of the major ways of understanding how the patient was reenacting the past in the present. Normally, in once or twice/week therapy, the transference is not analyzed, the adage being that one does not "mess with the transference unless the transference messes with you." Nevertheless, a sensitive therapist will be alert to transference phenomena, using this information to better understand and help the patient. Transference reactions are invaluable in understanding what is being enacted clinically; i.e., seeing what roles the patient is taking, what is being projected/displaced clinically (Irwin, 2006; Irwin & Curry, 1983; Johnson, 1982, 1988; 1992; Landy, 1993). Whatever role is projected, it is helpful to have an understanding of this ubiquitous phenomenon in order to help the patient and track the treatment process, as happened with Zoey, in the final example to follow.

Interpretation

The last psychoanalytic core concept to be discussed is interpretation, often called an intervention. Simply defined, an interpretation means to explain or make understandable. Interpretations take place when the therapist says in words what the patient and therapist have come to understand in their work. By putting into words the heretofore inchoate emotions or ideas, and by linking cause and effect, the patient can be helped to understand more of his/her behaviors, and feel more in control (Schlesinger, 2003).

Interventions that promote insight or self-awareness include the use of such techniques such as clarification, confrontation, catharsis, and interpretation. Questions, used too liberally, may inhibit spontaneity and a deeper search for meaning, all the while subtly shifting control to the therapist. Since tact and timing are important, interpretations are worded as tentative hypotheses (e.g., "perhaps" and "I wonder if"). This sensitivity is more than a word game, however. Although the therapist likely has an educated hunch about what is going on, s/he really does not know the right answer or have the exact explanation for another's behavior or feeling. Preferably, both parties work together to figure things out, in what, clinically, is called a therapeutic alliance. The example of Zoey illustrates the use of transference and interpretation in weekly therapy.

Case Example: Zoey

Twelve-year-old Zoey was deeply troubled, diagnosed with borderline personality disorder. Unable to modulate her affect, with poor reality testing, she often lost control and behaved in wild and chaotic ways that compounded her problems. At times intense transferences became real, and made imaginative work impossible until boundaries and self-control were reestablished (Irwin, 1998). When enraged, she lost control and seemed to show her identification with her hated, enraged mother (her bad introjects), bringing the therapeutic process to a standstill. Nevertheless, because this bright child was now in a stable home, spoke often of her need/wish for help, and demonstrated the ability to pull herself together after an explosion, we decided to try twice/week insight-oriented drama therapy (Fonagy & Target, 2000, 2002).

In individual therapy for six months, Zoey clearly demonstrated difficulty tolerating changes and transitions. Any interruption, including the end of a session, was cause for a "meltdown" (her grandmother's words). Desolate and enraged, Zoey often "stole" (her word) something from the playroom as a kind of transitional object, as though this concrete reminder of the session helped her to symbolically hold on until the next session. "If you don't give it to me, I have to take it, otherwise I won't get it," she announced, showing insight into her need to take (steal) because she felt empty and deprived of love, certain her needs would not be met.

Fortunately, Zoey relished the opportunity to enact stories and greatly enjoyed coming to drama therapy. The pleasure afforded by drama therapy reinforced her attachment to me and to therapy, helping her contain herself in times of stress. The themes of her dramas were repetitive, with only a few plot changes. Splitting into good/bad was one of her major defenses: i.e., I was the bad, helpless and abandoned child, jealous of others with a warm and loving family; Zoey was the powerful, aggressive, cruel depriver. In her dramas, I was left alone, with no money or food, in a cold warehouse with a leaky roof, infested with bugs, terrified by noises, storms, and lightning. I thought this metaphor well-described Zoey's sense of inner desolation, as she relived the loss of her (addicted) mother who simply disappeared to the "treatment house," leaving the bereft child and her brother in the care of a wealthy but distracted grandmother. Although I had started to make tentative connections between the images/feelings in the play (representing her psychic reality) and her historical reality, Zoey was unable to tolerate any review of the drama. All interpretations or interventions, therefore, were made within the play itself, rather than in a discussion afterward.

With about 20 minutes left in a session, I reminded Zoey that I would be away for two weeks, something that had been previously discussed numerous times. Startled, she immediately became enraged and lost control. Wailing and yelling, Zoey shouted that it was unfair; I was a bitch and had no right to go away; she would "get me" for it! Wildly throwing things around the room, she shouted that since I didn't care about her, she didn't care about me and wanted to break my things (i.e., me). My first (countertransference) reaction was to feel annoyed about the mess rapidly accumulating everywhere. Then I worried about the big and little things being thrown in my direction, as well as the yelling and screaming. What would her waiting grandmother and my colleagues think? But a few minutes later, when tears alternated with choking sobs, I responded to the deep fear that was covered by her rage, barely concealing her acute pain and desperation (Ekstein, 1966).

In bits and pieces, I worked to repair the disorganization that erupted. I said that I could see that she was mad and sad about my leaving. I wondered if she was worried about my leaving because it would be as though part of her would be gone as well. For awhile she tried to shout me down, her voice at top volume. Then her rage slowly abated and she seemed to deflate, her voice less harsh. Although she covered her ears and insisted that she didn't care, she wiped her face and gradually quieted. Empathy for her pain and the mirroring of her intense feelings in an interpretation helped her to slowly contain her inchoate state, her toxic-like rage and almost unbearable hatred in the transference. When she said she didn't care, I wondered if she was saying that she thought I didn't care about her or her feelings. With that, she asked if I was going to the "treatment house." I said that perhaps she worried that I would go away and not come back, like her mom. Suggesting words for feelings helped the situation to feel more manageable; using words to name feelings made it possible for negative feelings to be tolerated (Irwin, 1998).

When the storm passed, I wondered if she would like to make a picture of her feelings, something that had helped her in the past to regain a sense of control. Scribbling a picture titled *The Dilapidated House* (perhaps a self symbol), she said she missed her mother; everything was unfair. Dejected but calmer, Zoey left the session clutching her picture tightly, along with two pieces of cotton: transitional objects to help her tolerate the emotional separation from me, the needed but hated mother in the transference (Winnicott, 1965, 1975). The interpretation helped her to gain greater emotional control for the moment, helping her to weather another crucial upset. Somewhat soothed, she was better able to regulate her emotions, hear words that named the un-nameable and still unknowable, as she tried to digest the hated news of the separation.

Experience with severely troubled individuals like Zoey, regardless of age, underscores the need for the therapist to serve as a container in emotionally overwhelming situations. If the intolerably painful state can be taken in and internalized by the therapist, then it can be re-presented to the patient, who, we hope, can internalize it, reducing anxiety. With lessened fears of abandonment and destruction, the patient can work toward a more cohesive self, less vulnerable to fragmentation (Kohut, 1977). In the process, the child can see that her worst fantasy, that of destroying the therapist and by extension, the therapy, did not come to pass.

CONCLUSION

This chapter briefly describes instances of psychoanalytically-oriented drama therapy, as well as examples of admixtures of drama therapy, psychodrama and theatre. The importance of having a theory that is congruent with one's therapeutic practice is stressed. Using psychoanalytic theory as a guide can help the drama therapist to find his or her way through rough and sometimes unknown territory, especially with severely ill patients. Alertness to the psychoanalytic concepts of unconscious, resistance/defense, transference/countertransference issues can help the drama therapist to become more aware of the therapeutic process, and chart the progress of treatment. Emphasized throughout is the importance in drama therapy of fantasy, the unconscious, the relationship, and playing in a safe space, for, as Winnicott has written, "It is in playing, and only in playing, that one can become real" (1971, p. 236).

REFERENCES

Blatner, A. (1988). *Acting in: Practical applications of psychodramatic methods.* New York.

Bowlby, J. (1973). *Attachment and loss: Vol. II. Separation.* New York: Basic Books.

Bowlby, J. (1978). *Attachment and loss. Vol. III. Loss, sadness, and depression.* New York: Basic Books.

Bowlby, J. (1988). *Attachment and loss: Vol. I. Attachment.* New York: Basic Books.

Brenner, C. (1982). *The mind in conflict.* Madison: International Universities Press.

Cassidy, J., & Shaver, P.R. (1999). *Handbook of attachment: Theory, research, and clinical applications.* New York: Guilford Press.

Ekstein, R. (1966). *Children of time and space, of action and impulse.* New York: Meredith.

Emunah, R. (1994). *Acting for real: Drama therapy process, technique, and performance.* New York: Brunner/Mazel.

Erikson, E. H. (1950). *Childhood and society.* New York: Norton.

Fonagy, P. (2001). *Attachment theory and psychoanalysis.* New York: Other Press.

Fonagy, P., & Target, M. (2000). Mentalisation and the changing aims of child psychoanalysis. In K. v. Klitzing, P. Tyson & D. Burgin (Eds.), *Psychoanalysis in childhood and adolescence* (pp. 129–139). Basil: Karger.

Fonagy, P. (2002). Early intervention and development of self-regulation. *Psychoanalytic Inquiry,* 307–335.

Freud, A. (1966). *The ego and the mechanisms of defense* (Rev. Ed.). New York: International Universities Press.

Freud, S. (1915/1978). Observations on transference love. In J. Strachey (Ed. & Trans.), *The standard edition of the complete psychological works of Sigmund Freud (12),* (pp. 157–173). London: Hogarth Press.

Freud, S. (1917/1978). Mourning and melancholia. In J. Strachey (Ed. & Trans.), *The standard edition of the complete psychological works of Sigmund Freud (14),* (pp. 239–258). London: Hogarth Press.

Freud, S. (1920/1978). Beyond the pleasure principle. In J. Strachey (Ed. & Trans.), *The standard edition of the complete psychological works of Sigmund Freud (23),* (pp. 3–64). London: Hogarth Press.

Gabbard, G. O. (1990). *Psychodynamic psychiatry in clinical practice.* Washington, D.C.: American Psychiatric Press.

Gerson, B. (1996). *The therapist as a person.* New York: Analytic Press.

Irwin E. (1979). Drama therapy with the handicapped. In A. Shaw & C. S. Stevens, (Eds.), *Drama, theater and the handicapped* (pp. 21–30). Washington, DC: Arts for the Handicapped Foundation.

Irwin, E., & Curry, N. (1983). Role play in child therapy: An object relations point of view. In C. Schaefer (Ed.), *Techniques of play therapy* (pp. 157–187). New York: Jason Aronson.

Irwin, E. (1998). Child dramatic play as viewed from two perspectives: Ego psychology and object relations. *Journal of Clinical Psychoanalysis, 4,* 505–533.

Irwin, E., (2004). Facilitating play with non-players: A developmental perspective. In A. M. Weber & C. Haen (Eds.), *Clinical approaches of drama therapy in child and adolescent treatment* (pp. 3–23). New York: Brunner Rutledge.

Irwin, E. (2006). Peter: From robot to regular guy. In L. Carey (Ed.), *Expressive and creative arts methods for trauma survivors* (pp. 93–113). London: Jessica Kingsley.

Johnson, D. R. (1982). Developmental approaches in drama therapy. *The Arts in Psychotherapy, 18,* 183–190.

Johnson, D.R. (1988). The diagnostic role-playing test. *The Arts in Psychotherapy, 15,* 23–36.

Johnson, D.R. (1992). The drama therapist 'in role. In S. Jennings (Ed.), *Dramatherapy theory and practice 2* (pp. 112–136). London: Tavistock/Routledge.

Kohut, H. (1977). *The restoration of the self.* New York: International Universities Press.

Landy, R. (1993). *Persona and performance: The meaning of role in drama therapy and everyday life.* New York: Guilford Press.

Main, M. (1993). Discourse, prediction, and

recent studies in attachment. Implications for psychoanalysis. *Journal of the American Psychoanalytic Association, 41,* 209–244.

McLaughlin, J. (1981). Transference, psychic reality, and counter transference. *Psychoanalytic Quarterly, 50,* 639–665.

Person, E. S. (1995). *By force of fantasy.* New York: Basic Books.

Racker, H. (1974). *Transference and counter-transference.* New York: International Universities Press.

Rubin, R., Irwin, E. & Borrero, G. (1981). *The green creature within: Art and drama in group psychotherapy.* Video. www.Expressivemedia.org.

Schlesinger, H. J. (2003). *The texture of treatment: On the matter of psychoanalytic technique.* Hillsdale: Analytic Press.

Shore, A. N. (2003a). *Affect regulation & repair of the self.* New York: W. W. Norton.

Shore, A.N. (2003b). *Affect dysregulation and disorders of the self.* New York: W. W. Norton.

Shore, A.N. (2007). Psychoanalytic research: Progress and process. Developmental affective neuroscience and clinical practices. *Psychologist Psychoanalyst.* Summer, 6–15.

Siegel, D. J. (1999). *The developing mind: How relationships and the brain interact to shape who we are.* New York: Guilford Press.

Singer, J. L. (1966). *Daydreaming: An introduction to the experimental study of inner experience.* New York: Random House.

Solomon, M. F., & Siegel, D. J. (2003). *Healing trauma: Attachment, mind, body and brain.* New York: W. W. Norton.

Tronick, E. Z., & Weinberg, M. D. (1997). Depressed mother and infants: Failure to form dyadic states of consciousness. In L. Murray & P. J. Cooper (Eds.), *Postpartum depression in child development* (pp. 54–81). New York: Guilford.

Waelder, R. (1933). Psychoanalytic theory of play. *Psychoanalytic Quarterly, 2,* 208–224.

Wallerstein, J. (1992). *The common ground of psychoanalysis.* New York: Jason Aronson.

Winston, A., Rosenthal, R.N., & Pinsker, H. (2003). *Introduction to supportive psychotherapy.* Washington, DC: American Psychiatric Publishing.

Winnicott, D. W. (1960). The theory of parent child relationship. *International Journal of Psychoanalysis, 41,* 585–595.

Winnicott, D. W. (1965). *The maturational processes and the caretaking environment.* New York: International Universities Press.

Winnicott, D. W. (1971). *Playing and reality.* New York: Basic Books.

Winnicott, D. W. (1975). *Through paediatrics to psycho-analysis.* New York: Basic Books.

BIBLIOGRAPHY

Journal Articles

Tisza, V., Irwin, E. & Zabarenko, L. (1969). A psychiatric interpretation of children's creative dramatics stories. *Cleft Palate Journal, 6* (3), 228–234.

Irwin, E., Levy, P. & Shapiro, M. (1972). Assessment of a drama therapy program in a child guidance setting. *Group Psychotherapy and Psychodrama, 25* (3), 105–116.

Irwin, E. (1975). Facilitating children's language development through play. *The Speech Teacher, 24* (1), 107–116.

Irwin, E. & Malloy, E. (1975). The family puppet interview. *Family Process, 14* (2), 179–191.

Irwin, E., Baker, N. & Bloom, L. (1976). Fantasy play and language: Expressive therapy with communication handicapped children. *Journal of Childhood Communication Disorders, 1* (2), 99–115.

Irwin, E., & Rubin, J. (1976). Art and drama interviews: decoding symbolic messages. *Art Psychotherapy, 3,* 169–175.

Irwin, E., & Frank, M. (1977). Facilitating the play process with learning disabled children. *Academic Therapy, 1,* 435–444.

Irwin, E., (1978). Play, drama, and symbols: Drama with emotionally disturbed children. *American Journal of Psychotherapy, 31,* 426–436.

Irwin, E., (1978). Expressive therapy with a communicationally handicapped deaf adolescent. *Arts for the Handicapped: Why?* (pp. 12–29). Washington, DC: National Committee: Arts for the Handicapped.

Irwin, E., (1984). The role of the arts in mental health. *Design for Arts in Education, 86,* 43–47.

Irwin, E., (1984). Externalizing and improvising

imagery through drama therapy. *Journal of Mental Imagery, 9* (4), 33–42.

Irwin, E., (1985). Puppets in therapy: an assessment procedure. *American Journal of Psychotherapy, 34* (3), 389–400.

Irwin, E., (1986). Drama therapy in diagnosis and treatment. *Child Welfare, 65,* 347–357.

Irwin, E., (1986). On being and becoming a therapist. *The Arts in Psychotherapy, 13,* 191–195.

Irwin, E., (1987). Drama: the play's the thing. *Elementary School Guidance & Counseling, 21* (4), 276–283.

Irwin, E., (1998). Child dramatic play as viewed from two perspectives: ego psychology and object relations. *Journal of Clinical Psychoanalysis, 7,* 505–533.

Chapters in Books

Irwin, E., & Shapiro, M. (1975). Puppetry as a diagnostic and therapeutic tool. In I. Yakab (Ed.), *Art and Psychiatry,* Vol. 4, (pp. 86–94). Basil: Karger Press.

Rubin, J. & Irwin, E. (1975). Art and drama: parts of a puzzle. In I. Yakab (Ed.), *Transcultural aspects of psychiatric art: Art and Psychiatry,* Vol. 4, (pp. 193–200). Basel: Karger Press.

Irwin, E. (1979). Drama therapy with the handicapped. In A. Shaw & C. S. Stevens, (Eds.), *Drama, theatre and the handicapped.* (pp. 21–30). Washington, D. C.: ATA Publication.

Irwin, E. (1983). Enlarging the psychodynamic picture through dramatic play techniques. In K. O'Laughlin & E. Nickerson (Eds.), *Helping through action: Readings on action-oriented therapies* (pp. 53–59). Amherst: Human Resource Developmental Press.

Irwin, E., (1983). The diagnostic and therapeutic use of pretend play. In C. E. Schaefer & K. L. O'Conner (Eds.), *Handbook of play therapy* (pp. 148–173). New York: John Wiley and Sons.

Irwin, E., & Curry, N. (1983). Role play in child therapy: an object relations point of view. In C. E. Schaefer (Ed.), *Techniques of play therapy* (pp. 157–187). New York: John Wiley and Sons.

Irwin, E., (2000). The use of a puppet interview to understand children. In C. E. Schaefer, K. Gitlin & A. Sandgrund (Eds.), *Play diagnosis and treatment,* 2nd Ed., (pp. 682–703). New York: John Wiley and Sons.

Irwin, E., (2005). Facilitating play with non-players: A developmental perspective. In A. M. Weber & C. Haen (Eds.), *Clinical approaches of drama therapy in child and adolescent treatment* (pp. 3–23). New York: Brunner Routledge.

Irwin, E. (2006). Peter: a study of cumulative trauma: from "robot" to regular guy. In L. Carey (Ed.), *Creative arts methods for trauma survivors* (pp. 93–119). London: Jessica Kingsley.

Eleanor C. Irwin, Ph. D., RDT
Park Plaza Apts., Suite 212
128 N. Craig Street
Pittsburgh PA 15213
412-681-7020
eleanor.irwin@verizon.net

Chapter 12

THE DEVELOPMENTAL THEMES APPROACH IN DRAMA THERAPY

PENNY LEWIS

From birth to the final rite of passage we humans journey through life's meta-dramas. Unresolved childhood dramatic themes and their prescribed roles interweave and repeatedly overlap, recreating the past as if it were the present. The work of the drama therapist is to not only view the fabric of the drama as a momentary gestalt, but also to identify the repetitive phenomena. Once identified, their origins can be traced back etiologically where thematic scripts along with their associated roles and settings group themselves in developmentally based constellations. When these immature themes are cleared from unconscious habituation, archetypal life themes become available to healthy children, adolescents, and adults in their unfolding personal quests.

GENESIS

Conceptual Origins

Through the theories of ego psychologists (Erikson, 1963; A. Freud, 1966), therapists have come to understand that with each stage of life there are specific themes that manifest and dominate an individual's way of viewing and interacting in the world, requiring defined roles for that person and significant others to enact. For example, the theme of the development of trust, self-nurturing, and a sense that the environment is need satisfying (Erikson's first stage, trust vs. mistrust) is very different than the drama to be played in Erikson's second stage of autonomy where themes of power and control dominate. Dysfunction and pathology emerge when these theme-based stages have been unsuccessfully integrated due to role deviation or dysfunctional environment.

Greater sophistication in developmental theory emerged with the work of object relations therapists and neo-Jungians. Most therapists agree that the origins of their clients' dysfunctions began within the first three years of life. Ego psychologists covered these years but not with the specificity of object relations theorists such as Melanie Klein (1975), Margaret Mahler (1968), D.W. Winnicott (1971), and Ronald Fairbairn (1976), who held a magnifying glass up to the intrapsychic and interpersonal world of the infant. What they found were subtly changing themes within the mother-child drama which served with "good-enough mothering" to provide the child with a realistic sense of self and a constant internalized supportive and enabling object or inner mother.

Once object constancy has been achieved, life's drama expands. Here other theoretical constructs need to be introduced, as the dramas become far more complex and diverse given the sex and dominant characterological structures of the individual. The work of Jung (1977) and post-Jungians (Neumann, 1973, 1976; Von Franz, 1978, 1982) have taken culture's externalizations of universal life themes and characters found in myths, fairy tales, religious rituals, and stories of gods and goddesses, and provided a rich view of the powerful archetypal *mythelogems* in the life quests and cycles of individuals. In addition more recent investigations have refined adult life stages (Moore & Gillette, 1990; Sheehy, 1995), expanding and enriching our understanding of mid-life phases.

Author's Genesis of the Model

In 1971, I began work at Pittsburgh Child Guidance as a dance therapist, joining Eleanor Irwin (one of the founders of the NADT) and Judith Rubin (renowned art therapist). We became the Creative Arts Therapy Team working collegially in consultation and education. My work with the children had an improvisational drama base in which I entered into the child's imaginal realm, costumed in a created setting, which took up a large group room. I followed the children's improvisational dramas, identifying the symbolic developmental themes and related dysfunction. I intervened in a dramatic role within the symbolic imaginal realm to transform dysfunction and foster healthy development. I also had a private practice with adults and discovered that they, too, benefited from a developmental themes approach and were often struggling with the very stages that the children were. My work at this time was influenced by Anna Freud's concept of interconnecting developmental lines, utilizing both dance and drama media.

DRAMA THERAPY FRAME OF REFERENCE

Basic Concepts

Health

Health is seen as the successful integration of all previous developmental stages and the capacity to utilize all the themes and associated roles of those stages in an adaptive manner in service to oneself, respectful interaction with others, the environment, and other coexisting realms of reality. Additionally, successful functioning requires the ability to allow current life themes to further evolution and growth.

Dysfunction

Dysfunction occurs when healthy development is arrested due to trauma within the family system or the inability of the primary caregivers to create the required ontogenetic setting and associated role relationship. No matter what the etiology, if the healthy integration of a particular developmental theme has not been fostered, the individual will be stuck in the developmental phase that was not successfully completed. The role that individuals play as well as those roles transferred or projected onto others and the way in which the surrounding setting is viewed will be based upon the developmental theme in which they have been arrested. They repeat the theme with the associated roles over and over again, unable to utilize other themes or integrate new ones.

Techniques within the Therapeutic Process

Awareness

Individuals' arrested developmental themes are played out in their lives through repetition compulsions or repetitive childhood patterns originally utilized either for aborted attempts at integrating the phase or for the recreation of the trauma in order to perpetuate the familiar. These thematic recreations keep individuals from responding adaptively to the moment. The threads of the themes and roles are gradually revealed to the client through etiologically based exploratory role playing. These enactments may entail the interviewing of childhood survival patterns as to their origin or elucidating developmental themes through such venues as improvisational drama, authentic drama, dreamwork as theater, and embodied sand play.

Encouragement to delve developmentally into the source of the theme and its associated role occurs through redramatization of a typical formulating occurrence.[1] In this first state of awareness, the individual needs to get a sense of how these behaviors and interactions are internalized and projected onto their present life themes.

The Transformative Process

Drama therapists have long known that it is only through embodied enacted experience that change can occur. To understand the notion of healing and developmentally-based transformation in psychotherapy, the elusive phenomena of *transitional space* (Winnicott, 1971) in object relations theory and the *imaginal realm* (Lewis, 1985, 1988b, 1993; Schwartz-Salant, 1982; Turner, 1969) in Jungian theory need to be explored. Winnicott's transitional space and the imaginal realm described by Jung in the *Mysterium Conunctionis* (Vol. XIV) have a common experiential link. In both cases the individual is experiencing the moment in a realm that lies between reality and the unconscious. It is akin to the world of pretend play in childhood. This is the realm in which the internalized origin of the threads of repetitive drama lie. Thus, in order to transform them, the client and/or group and therapist must enter into the bipersonal field of the imaginal realm in a fully embodied, enacted manner.

The Bipersonal Field and The Role of the Therapist

Individual depth work allows for the subtle dramatic nuances associated with early object-related trauma to be monitored from moment to moment by the therapist and responded to through her subtle body and vocal responses, co-creating within the bipersonal field a transitional space of healing. The role of the therapist is paramount in healing early stages of development; for just as no infant can evolve a sense of self without the attentive ministering of the attuned mother, no adult can do so either. Additionally, just as children know if their parents truly love and know them deeply, clients are

---

1. Since embodiment is perhaps the most powerful expressive arts technique, memories or flashbacks of severe physical abuse are clearly less appropriate for this method. In these cases I suggest individuals use drawing as a means to recover and contain their child selves. In addition I do not believe in individuals re-experiencing the trauma that caused their fixation in a particular developmental theme- rather only the relationship between the theme and the age-related child self.

not fooled by therapists going though the motions of acting like they care. Thus the role of the therapist is that of genuine care and concern seeking connection (relational model), contact (Gestalt model), and genuine intimacy.

This means that the therapy room can become a nursery for old pathological scenes to be reexperienced. Here classic psychodrama techniques and structures are exceedingly helpful, particularly in the re-creation of history, confrontation and antagonist transformation. Then redramatization of healthy development is possible between the client and therapist or within a group.

Individuals' further development is, of course, curtailed when early phases have been disrupted. In these situations it is not so much the "re" enacting but providing the needed developmentally based setting for the client to integrate higher levels. This is not so much empirically provided as it is liminally and dramatically provided. Once childhood development is integrated, jungles are created for a hero to confront and individuate his or her inner instinctual beast. From a Jungian archetypal perspective, this means that numinous energy can enter the room through the embodied personification of a goddess or spontaneous enactment of a ritual or rite of passage. The therapist's repertoire of roles extends to all possible enabling and destructive characters in human development as described by the individual in their personal history or by individuals through culture's history in myths, fairy tales, literature, religious liturgy and other manifestations.

Being cognizant of adult stages of development allows the therapist to encourage and give meaning to archetypal life themes that emerge from the imaginal realm. For example, understanding the death, dismembering and putrefying cycle of the heroic quest can provide the needed support and encouragement for the client to undergo this sometimes frightening but necessary mid-life rite of passage.

Being in the Moment with the Creative Void

The third stage in the therapeutic process unfolds naturally. Clients observe, sometimes in retrospect, how their behavior has changed. They have choice as to whether or not they want to repeat an archaic dramatic theme when they no longer are fixed in an unconscious replay of a childhood role. They live in the moment and spontaneously respond to life's dramas.

Appropriate Populations for the Developmental Themes Approach

Because the approach is by definition developmental, all ages from infancy to aging and dying are appropriate. Those with functional diagnoses such as: personality disorders, PTSD, addictions including eating disorders, dissociative disorders, adjustment disorders, as well as nongenetic history-based mood and anxiety disorders; some forms of schizophrenia as well as many organic diagnoses such as mental retardation, developmental delay, autism, and learning disabilities have worked within this model. This approach has been used with individuals, couples, mothers and children and groups of all ages.

Limitations, Challenges and Growing Edges

Because this approach is developmental in nature, any problems that do not arise from unsuccessful development or do not influence development are less appropriate. Less relevance is seen with those with paranoid schizophrenia, sleep disorders or some cognitive and medically related disorders. Families and organizations may be best helped with systemic approaches. The challenge and growing edge is to provide outcome studies and to see how this approach can comingle with other approaches such as "Role Method" (Chapter 5), "Psychodrama" (Chapter 18), "Sociodrama" (Chapter 19), "Playback Theatre" (Chapter 20), "Developmental Transformations" (Chapter 6), and "Ritual/Theatre/Therapy" (Chapter 7).

Drama Therapy Techniques in the Developmental Themes Approach

The Internal Drama

Reclaiming preverbal memories that lie in the body and bodily sensations allow both the client and therapist the ability to reconstruct early pre-language experiences. Winnicott has stated that many memories are "pre-verbal, nonverbal and unverbalizable" (1971, p.130). Since many memories of abuse occur prior to language, they are often held in unconscious somatic schemata that can only be recalled by imaginal embodied reconstruction. Asking clients to imagine journeying inside their body and personifying sensations, feelings, viscera and other body parts begins to create a dramatic communicational bridge from the clients' early history to the present.

Core to the formation of a sense of self is the suggestion for the client to journey to his or her solar plexus to find the core of who they are or the child within. Relating to the imagined child allows for the clearing of abusive history and the beginning of healthy reparenting or co-parenting with the therapist entering into the bipersonal imaginal realm.

The Use of the Somatic Countertransference

Another aspect of the internal drama is the technique of the *somatic countertransference.* Based upon phenomenological research (Lewis, 1981), I began to conceptualize this bipersonal dialogue between therapist and client. I was further encouraged when I began my analytic training in 1984 at the C.G. Jung Institute of New York. Jung (CW vol. XVI) in his "Psychology of the Transference" discussed an unconscious to unconscious connection between the client and therapist. Jung suggested that not only are client and therapist communicating on a conscious to a conscious level or, as in psychoanalytic work, from the client's unconscious to the analyst's conscious level, but that there is also a direct unconscious to unconscious communication going on all the time. The therapist thus receives from the unconscious of the client into her somatic unconscious and can send back to the client's unconscious either through the conscious ego or the unconscious. In this realm, attending to the somatic countertransference it is possible, for example, to imaginally create dramas that transform projected split-off aspects of a person's psychology through remembering, and neutralize and detoxify transferred negative objects (Grotstein, 1981; Jung, 1977; Lewis, 1988a, 1988b, 1992, 1993; Racker, 1982; Schwartz-Salant, 1982, 1984; Stein, 1984). The therapist may receive the client's negative judgmental or engulfing parent from the client's somatic unconscious and may imaginally utilize themes from fairy tales or myths to heal and transform these feeling-charged personifications while still in the therapist's body vessel.

With other clients, their infant self may be imaginatively received for love and healthy gestation to be retransferred when the client is ready. This form of projective identification has been highly successful. Again, just as clients do not benefit from having a new role superimposed on them, it does not work for the therapist to conjure up what s/he thinks the character should act like. Nor am I suggesting something akin to Stanislavski method acting. I imagine I am playing the role of my client's symbiotic good mother and based upon what inner child needs that I receive from the client's unconscious, I imagine a corrective drama. Because this unconscious to unconscious connection travels both ways, this imagining can be received by the client's unconscious. This imagined enacted dialogue has a powerful effect and is always received by the client. I have had many confirmations of this through clients' dreams, poetry, drawings or statements, such as, "I know you've been holding me all along" or "my inner child feels your constant encouragement of her assertion" (Lewis, 1983, 1993, 1994).

Re-dramatization of Object Relations

Healthy infant and toddler care is conducted on a relational sensori-motor level. Mahler (1968), Kestenberg, (1975), Stern (1985), and Winnicott (1971) discuss concepts such as attunement, rhythmic synchrony, holding and handling by the mother, as conveying to the infant relatedness, appropriate boundaries and a sense of trust, safety, identity and internalized other. All of these are crucial in the foundation for healthy development. They are learned in vivo through the actual enacted experience and cannot be conveyed by talking about them. Therefore the thematically-based developmental re-dramatization of the mother/child embodied relationship by the client and therapist is often a sine qua non of transformation.

Dreamwork and Projective Techniques: Art and Sandplay

Dreamwork as theater, embodied art and sandplay work are drama therapy techniques based upon the premise that the purpose of dreams and art expressions are not only to inform but also transform the dreamer/artist (Lewis, 1993). For this reason, dream and art interpretation is found to curtail the full value of this unconscious expression. If a dream is interpreted, it serves to separate the dreamer from the dream. It has the same effect as interpreting a work of art does. In both cases the observer looks at and intellectually assesses the work rather than experiencing it.

With dreams that are symbolic in nature and emerge from the personal unconscious, the technique of dreamwork as theater can be used. This technique keeps the dream and the dreamer in the imaginal realm. The dreamer can then understand the dream though the experience of it and can frequently use the dreams as a vehicle of transformation.

In dreamwork as theater, the dreamer is asked to become different characters and symbols in the dream. The drama therapist interviews the dreamer in character and then, taking on roles, role reverses when needed in service of the client's integration of these parts of the self.

At times the dream appears to have a beginning and a middle, but no ending. After interviewing the characters I suggest that the client imagine an ending. Since the responses and story endings emerge from the imagination, there is no wrong response as the dream has come from the same source (Lewis, 1993). Dreams invariably reflect history that needs to be revealed or new life themes and the associated shadow and animus/a aspects that seek recognition and integration.

Sandplay, sometimes called *the world technique,* is a Jungian technique in which an individual moves or shapes sand in a box or arranges small symbolic figures in the sand. Usually individuals allow their imagination to select from figures that range from animals (magical, domesticated or wild), human figures (all ages and character types), environmental objects (trees, containers, walls, stones, shells), dollhouse furniture, vehicles, sacred icons, and other small objects of symbolic significance. Often the result is a symbolic representation of their psyche or a map of their developmental psychological and spiritual journey. These figures are then given imaginal life and the small sand space is treated as a world in and of itself. The figures are interviewed and converse among themselves, with the client playing all the parts. Because the clients are within the imaginal realm, they can experience the transformative power fostering healthy developmental growth as they come to understand the symbolic meaning through the experience of living in it (Lewis, 1993).

The role of the drama therapist is to assist in the recreation of the art, dream or sandplay world. On occasion I, too, enter into the dream, art or sandplay world to further reveal the meaning and foster development. The experience of being in the bipersonal field can be expanded to include others in a group and can serve to continue to extend the drama of the developmental themes or related characters (Lewis, 1988b, 1992, 1993). In doing so, characters can transform for the purpose of integration or union. Developmental themes can unfold a map of a person's entire life journey or therapy process, and the archetypal life themes can propel the individual through the adult life stage process.

Authentic Sound, Movement and Drama

Authentic Sound, Movement, and Drama is a technique of active imagination that was influenced by Mary Whitehouse (Lewis, 1982, 1986, 1996). It is an experience of being moved by the imaginal metaphoric realm of the unconscious. The technique of authentic sound, movement and drama began its infancy in 1966 and reached full form in 1971. About this time I heard of Mary's technique of *Authentic Movement* and decided to employ the name she had created. But the technique is slightly different than Whitehouse's classical approach as it is taught by those who trained with her. In the Whitehouse approach, participants engage in the technique with the therapist acting as stationary observer. The therapist is identified as a witness who is not encouraged to interact on a movement level with the mover(s). Additionally, classical Authentic Movement is based upon a somewhat parallel process group style. Although interaction among the participants is not taboo, it is also not considered an integral part of the work. Authentic sound, movement and drama however encourages the interaction between therapist and individual mover when it supports relationally-oriented healing and developmentally-based growth. Additionally, it advocates group interaction in which individuals can co-participate in each other's imaginal realm. Group members are encouraged to spontaneously transfer or project any role onto any member. Thus one member may transfer his engulfing space-invading parent onto another member and explore separating and maintaining healthy boundaries by finding and embodying the part of him that, although still in instinctual animal-like state, can growl and snarl. The other person may project her distancing biting, snapping childhood survival pattern onto the man who is transferring on to her. In her case she may attempt to soothe him, telling him there is no reason to be so snappy and angry. He in turn, viewing her as attempting to cajole him back into enmeshed complacency, continues to growl. Thus each are reinforced positively: he in claiming his differentiating instinctual self, she in claiming her core self and desire for externalizing and attempting to transform her off-putting survival mechanism.

Authentic sound, movement, and drama is employed with individuals and with groups. Some movers prefer silence, others prefer white noise such as ocean or wind recordings, while others prefer the many New Age tapes available. With those individuals who are unfamiliar with authentic movement, I offer an initial guided imagery to assist them into a deeper imaginal state.

Some individuals feel various sensations and are moved in response to them. Most however create imagistic environments and move and sound within them. These can be re-creations of the past that emerge from the unconscious realm to be consciously known or reclaimed by the enactor, or they may be new experiences that are unfolding for individuals to embody and integrate into their personality.

Developmental Theme-Based Improvisational Drama

Developmental theme-based improvisational drama is akin to authentic drama. The only difference is that a suggestion is made by the therapist, and then taken by the client into the imaginal realm. For example, I have frequently offered the suggestion to explore a developmentally-based thematic process that has emerged in a dream or in the client's life to increase the individual's experience of adaptive integration.

Ritual Drama

Ritual drama taps into the archetypal universal pool of transformational theater. The creation of sacred dramatic rites of passage, typically carried out in communities, help honor and support the transition from one developmental stage to another.

METHOD OF ASSESSMENT AND/OR INDIVIDUAL EDUCATION PLAN

Knowledge of the key themes that dominate each stage of development, or resulting maladaptive ontogenetically-related themes, which are created due to unhealthy development, gives the drama therapist a built-in assessment tool that also serves as a natural treatment or education planning structure. It is vital to remember that each successful integration of a theme builds upon the themes from the former stages. The proceeding thus represents the metadrama of human developmental themes delineating within the various stages, examples of the optimum settings and roles that are needed to be played in order for a healthy and rich life tapestry to be woven. Culture's externalization of the unconscious via archetypal mythic stories of gods and goddesses, stories from the old and new testaments, as well as fairy tales are employed. Examples are also given of pathological dramas and developmentally based drama therapy processes that provide the needed roles and enacted dramatic themes for the individual to weave into their life.

Pre-Symbiosis Themes

Described here are undifferentiated ego-

Age/Stage	*Healthy Developmental Themes*	*Dysfunctional/Developmental Themes*
Presymbiosis	Floating in life-giving fluid Being held Feeling at one with the All Being a part of the Light Being in heaven: endless love	Drowning Falling forever in endless space Overpowering ominous archetypal presence(s) due to size, power, or multiplicity Being chaotic within chaos Being in hell: endless torture
1-Symbiosis	Being able to care for oneself Allowing self to be appropriately cared for when needed Trusting others appropriately Retaining and digesting what is received that is positive and life enhancing Seeking & experiencing attuned mirroring Listening & responding to self needs Caring for self and others mutually	Needing others to care for self Filling an endless void through needing love, attention, food or other addictions Not wanting to leave a paradisiacal state Not trusting oneself, humans and/or a higher power Merging or enmeshed with others, their ideas or ways of being Being a baby or little animal looking for mommy or a caregiver Being wounded or otherwise helpless Being wantless, needless or numb Feeling less than or better than (narcissistic)
2-Differentiation	Discriminating between self and others Discriminating between fantasy & reality Demonstrating healthy ego boundaries Demonstrating healthy body boundaries Allowing only healthy touch and being touched Separating mine and not mine Restraining from projection, displacement & transference Holding on & letting go appropriately Competing when appropriate Claiming and transforming imaged creatures with teeth who can protect "Spitting out" what is not one's own nor digestible	Lacking discrimination between self & others Confusing fantasy and reality Lacking or faulty ego boundaries: Possessing the ego by complexes Touching or being touched inappropriately Touching fear: wall-like body boundaries Confusing whose is whose through projecting, displacing & transferring Holding on or letting go inappropriately Envying and being rivalrous Seeking to destroy via out of control toothy monsters and creatures Swallowing everything without discrimination

Figure 12.1. Developmental themes.

Age/Stage	*Healthy Developmental Themes*	*Dysfunctional/Developmental Themes*
3-Practicing	Practicing going away and returning Refueling when empty Inspecting the mother Letting go pleasurably Measuring and smearing playfully Pleasuring in one's products	Committing inability Leaving ambivalence Returning ambivalence Repeating approach/avoidance– come here/go away in relationships Fearing close inspection of the other Fear of letting go Devaluing one's own products
4-Rapproachment	Asserting of self Knowing who you are and what you want: independent thought & action Saying no when appropriate Presenting & representing self realistically Standing up for self Claiming power when appropriate Demonstrating healthy external boundaries Respecting one's & other's personal space	Asserting belief inability Being powerless or power & control obsessed Being unable to say no in some or all areas Being unable to realistically present self (either better or less than) Being unable to stand up for self Bullying & identification with aggressor Having wall-like, faulty, or external boundaries Disrespecting self & other's personal space
5-Self & Object Constancy	Maintaining sense of self Sustaining a connection to the inner child Having realistic whole sense of self: "both good and bad" Carrying out tasks in timely fashion Demonstrating initiative Utilizing imagination to mediate instincts Maintaining healthy realistic constant inner parent Delaying gratification Demonstrating object constancy	Being unable to sustain sense of self Being unable to sustain a connection to the inner child Maintaining a split self; either is the good one or the angry two-year-old Being unable to carry out tasks Lacking impulse control Being caught in guilt; unable to move forward Presenting imaged themes of uncontrollable monsters Losing the significant other Searching for the other
6-Identification & Relationship with parents	Identifying with mother as creative Creating with pleasure Building, constructing, and making Penetrating & surprise themes Killing the mother dragon for boys & animus Confronting the obstacle & gaining the treasure Presenting themes of three into four, chaos into organization	Blocking creativity Experiencing pain & ambivalence regarding creativity Being unable to be proactive Sexualizing relationships Seeking to perpetuate triangular relationships Seeking to separate one from couple Being possessed by the power of the mother complex

Figure 12.1–*Continued.* Developmental themes.

Age/Stage	*Healthy Developmental Themes*	*Dysfunctional/Developmental Themes*
7-Latency & Peer Relationships	Focusing on rules & structure Forming chumship groups Creating themes of life at home Domesticating self or others Moving from wild or instinctual to more civilized in dramas Maintaining same-sex roles Reflecting industry themes	Being unable to relinquish adultified or parentified roles & associated themes Disregarding rules & structure Being unable to sustain membership in a group Sustaining wild, untamed, feral characters in dramas which require civilized behavior Being unclear on sexual identity Repeating themes of guilt
8-Puberty	Subduing wild beasts Mediating aggression of sexual or purely physical nature Letting go of childhood behavior toward adult behavior Experiencing body transformation toward adult Experiencing pubertal rites of passage Descending into the underworld for rebirthing Leaving what was, entering into a liminal realm Being initiated into a mystery Seeing the light from darkness Gaining power or special abilities Gaining courage, intuition, wisdom Heightening spiritual awareness or relationship to transpersonal	Having wild beasts being victorious Unmediated sexual or nonsexual acts of aggression Acting out behavior which is illegal Threatening life and freedom behaviors: such as, DWI & other addictions & behaviors which are illegal Experiencing non-transformative depression Being held in captivity Descending without meaning or possible transformation Being cast out of group without reentry Being unable to see the light Losing power to special abilities Experiencing fear which cripples courageous acts Lacking relation to the transpersonal
9-Adolescence	Trying on various adult roles and their associated life themes Trying on idealized role & life theme Searching for the beloved: Stories of romance Finding, rescuing & joining with the beloved Presenting themes of hostility to old authority Dethroning old rule Claiming the authority for self rule Striving to better oneself within socially acceptable venues	Being stuck in childish roles and dependency themes Maintaining projected idealized role on other Lacking in sexual exploration Blocking relation to inner feminine or inner masculine due to history Confusing or abstaining from sexual preference Repeating rapprochement issues with authorities Repeating need to dethrone realistic authority figures Being unable to claim one's locus of self rule Blaming others in authority for lack of success (given realities of minority societal discrimination)

Figure 12.1–*Continued.* Developmental themes.

Age/Stage	*Healthy Developmental Themes*	*Dysfunctional/Developmental Themes*
10-Young Adulthood	Claiming of shadow (same sex) aspects of the self through role and associated archetypal life themes Claiming of contra sexual animus/i (inner masculine for women) and anima/ae (inner feminine for men) aspects of the psyche and their associated archetypal life themes Experiencing themes of the hieros gamos (the union of opposites)	Being unable to expand ego through shadow integration and relationship and the lack of claiming shadow aspect archetypal life themes Being unable to claim and expand the integration of contra-sexual aspects of psyche and their archetypal life themes Projecting shadow and animus/a on to others continuously Lacking themes that join opposites of the psyche
11-Midlife	Experiencing aspects of love, work, and life to be up for question Letting go of who one is Losing of self and life Revisiting history for healing and release Descending into death Being held in suspension Being impregnated symbolically Experiencing gestation Rebirthing and new birth Experiencing being more fully oneself Discovering of who one truly is Serving the core of who one is–integrity	Fearing questioning who one is, unsuccessful relationships and/or work Holding onto unsuccessfully aspects of who one is, relationships and work Repeating history; unable to let go of archaic unsuccessfully roles and themes Experiencing being captive Escaping or flying: an inability to descend or enter uncharted settings Serving others without serving the core self Behaving in a way that supports a lack of connection to oneself and one's path

Figure 12.1–*Continued.* Developmental themes.

Age/Stage	*Healthy Developmental Themes*	*Dysfunctional/Developmental Themes*
12-Middlesence	Letting go of young adult self image gracefully Mourning the loss of fertility (women during menopause) and physical competitive edge (men) Letting go of aspect of identity based upon work, power, and status Experiencing another "Great Round": letting go, death, descent, rebirth Experiencing deeper androgyny Shifting from "my will be done" to "Thy will be done" Expanding spiritual consciousness "I-Thou" or Mystical "Atonement" Being able to see and respond to the "bigger picture" Self-actualizing themes Experiencing ego-self axis & soul connectedness	Behaving in ways which inappropriately hold on to youth Being unable to accept and mourn loss of fertility or diminished virility Holding onto aspects of identity that have passed Worshiping at the alter of false gods: money, power, status, external beauty and youth Holding onto personal will and self needs over the greater good Blocking the expansion of consciousness Limiting view of existence Lacking capacity to evolve from being ruled by basic needs and their derivatives Lacking a relationship to self and one's eternal life force
13-Aging	Accepting aging process without losing inner eternal youth Entering another "Great Round": death–rebirth process Experiencing themes of "aging into saging": Becoming the wise wo/man Disidentifying with that which is not eternal Experiencing ego integrity Living in Love and Grace	Being unable to accept aging process Losing eternal youth and associated themes Being unable to surrender into another "Great Round" Experiencing themes of rigidity and death of capacity to grow and expand consciousness Holding onto worldly possessions and identities Living in bitterness, despair and/or fear of death
14-Dying	Going through the stages of dying Denial, bargaining, anger, grief and acceptance in a responsible realistic manner Completing unfinished business Saying good-bye Receiving grace and spiritual transitional help Surrendering to death rite of passage	Being unable to move into acceptance of death Being unable to complete unfinished business Being unable to say good-bye Being unable to receive grace and spiritual transitional help Being unable to surrender to the death rite of passage

Figure 12.1–*Continued.* Developmental themes.

less themes of archetypal and mystical states of union. Dysfunctional themes are of psychotic proportions and may appear in dreams, collective or individual delusional or hallucinatory processes. With the former, individuals are encouraged to experience the "atonement" as it often heralds a rebirthing of a higher state of consciousness. With the latter, drama therapy that focuses on the development of the ego, ego boundaries and, in cases of psychoses, the capacity to reality test is in order. Here role playing reality-based activities of daily living and life skills are helpful.

Symbiosis Themes

Margaret Mahler (1968) describes the first stage of development of object relations as symbiosis in which there exists a dual unity between mother and child. The mother's role is to merge with her infant, to attune to his/her body, to hold and fondle the baby, giving him or her a sense of entity and existence, personhood and uniqueness. The mother mirrors and reflects the child with love and acceptance and begins the process of filling the infant with a sense of self. When this does not occur, pathology replaces a positive sense of self and a realistic trust in the environment as capable of being safe and need satisfying. Many oral-associated addictions such as food, smoking, and alcohol develop as "false mothers" attempting to fill the endless void. This dysfunctional theme habitually replays as a result of a lack of early object-related ministering.

One client had spent his whole life shut down. He was driven by the role of being a need-less and want-less work-addicted perfectionist within the dysfunctional life theme of accumulating wealth, power and material goods in order to fill him with his missing inner substance. He came to see me because he felt something inside of him was beginning to sabotage his strategy. I suggested he journey imaginally into himself to find the origin of the saboteur. When he did, he discovered a screaming infant. He treated this infant with disdain, and stated he had no time for such antics. I suggested that this was perhaps how he had been treated as an infant by an overwhelmed mother. Since he had children, I asked if he treated them in the same manner. He then began to sink into a deeper understanding. I suggested a role reversal dialogue between his adult self and infant whom he eventually held and rocked tearfully.

There are some who are clueless about how to effectively parent because the parental experiences they had were so abusive that there is no positive internalized object–no inner good parent. One woman in my authentic sound movement and drama group typified this phenomenon. For months she found herself lying on my floor drifting back to her infancy. Here she found herself harnessed in a crib unable to move. She struggled to free herself. Since developmentally she could neither stand nor talk, she was often helpless to prevail over her bondage. There were times when I entered into her imaginal realm and assisted her. Finally, over time, the harness dispersed from her body memory as did the unemotionally attuned mother. Now she lay alone on the floor sounding weakened monosyllabic repetitive cries in an oral sucking rhythm (Lewis, 1986, 1990, 1993, 1999a & b).

Since her wounds were relational in origin they were best healed relationally. She needed to experience healthy object relations. Since much of the mother-infant interaction is nonverbal, the redramatization of object relations was one that focused upon attunement to sound and movement, along with touch and proper holding. I began by mirroring her longing sounds from a distance. Then I gradually approached her, crawling to her on a diagonal. Now our synchronous repetitive sounds were more like coos. I touched her shoulder and moved slowly behind her. She was lying on her side in a semi-fetal position. I moved so that she could rest her back into my chest and nuzzle her head under mine. Now we were rocking and cooing in the same rhythm. I gently touched her graying hair. Two other members were alternatively singing and playing with words. Toward the end of the hour of this redramatization of object relations, she began to connect with these two participants, responding to their sounds spontaneously–something she had never been able to do before. Indeed, it is difficult to feel free to spontaneously play if there was a lack of empathetic mirroring and reflection during symbiosis.

Separation and Individuation: Differentiation Sub-phase–Body and Ego Boundary Formation

Mahler describes the next phase in development as separation and individuation, beginning with the sub-phase of differentiation in which the infant experiences boundaries and the fundamental capacity to discriminate. This stage emerges with teething and is associated with the capacity to "chew over things and spit out what isn't digestible." A "me-not-me" body boundary paves the way for healthy touch and knowing the difference between one's own thoughts and feelings and those of others. Projection or the "ejecting out of what is part of the self onto or into another" demonstrates incomplete differentiation. Additionally, clients who fear sustained physical intimacy and who repeat themes of separating and pushing away in their interpersonal dramas did not have a mother and/or a developmental setting that allowed for them to successfully integrate the separation drama (Lewis, 1993).

On an intrapsychic level, this phase heralds the development of ego boundaries required to maintain the integrity of the ego's rationality against the onslaughts of invasive complexes such as addictions, inner critics, outmoded parental internalizations and uncivilized, unconscious materials such as hallucinations and flashbacks which have the potential of flooding the ego if faulty boundaries exist.

One woman came to me complaining about everything in her life. A sharp derisive critic, she bit and chewed up anyone who approached her. Countertransferentially, I felt any suggestion to enact or embody the work was ripped apart and spit out. I became as helpless as I was sure her mother had felt. She had come to me because I was a dance and drama therapist; she did not want to talk about her problems, but when I suggested these techniques, she said she did not trust me. She sat with her legs drawn up barring access and placed a pillow between her and me. Clearly, she was stuck in the teething, oral aggressive differentiating phase (Lewis, 1990, 1993). Angered by what she did not get, she could not move on. But the clearest indication came when I gently began inquiring about the amount of boundaries she needed to put between her and me. It was then that she stated she felt she had been metaphorically dipped in an acid bath at birth. She had no skin boundaries. How could she feel safe? No wonder she had to fend people away with biting retorts.

It was in the second hour that she was able to embody her vulnerable child self. I suggested she or I could move a greater distance apart until she felt comfortable. She chose to move, and crawled behind my sand tray table peering out at me sheepishly. I asked if she wanted a blanket to put around her and extended my arm with it so as to not invade her space. She wrapped it around herself. Peeking into the sand she asked where the sand was from. I meanwhile sat very still so as not to scare her and answered her questions gently, simply and concretely. We were redramatizing object relations.

The development of healthy body boundaries cannot be done in one hour or in six hours; it takes time. Trust must be built through enacted relational experiences of "coming up against the other" and serve the purpose of establishing healthy skin boundaries rather than feeling that one is being violated.

One man in my authentic sound movement and drama group spent several months imaginally feeling enveloped by his enmeshed parents. "Get out of my room!" "Leave me alone!" were constant refrains from his favorite side of the therapy space. At times I or others received the projection of the engulfing parent. One session I responded as his mother, "I need you. I need to devour your soul. I'm starving. Please let me breathe your air and consume what you do to make it mine." Repeatedly yelling, "No!" he shoved me along the floor until I was out of his space. The next series of sessions had him literally struggling to eject the object internalization from his body. Coughing and gagging over time brought forth a full baritone voice, one that had not been heard before. Now instead of remaining in his designated corner, he began to crawl around the room making instinctual animal-like sounds. Testing his new-found body boundaries, he bumped up against others, annoying them. They in turn either joined him in animal play or projected onto him their own violating objects.

A four-year-old boy was referred to me. He raced into the room, immediately spat in my face and bit my knee. His mother had recently given birth and this little fellow, struggling with the shift in his mother's attention, had angrily regressed to the first stage of separation. A few sessions were spent with him "being the baby and me the mommy," and then a gradual age-appropriate improvisational shift developed in which we became construction workers like his dad, building tall edifices.

Separation and Individuation: Practicing and Rapprochement Sub-phases

Practicing and rapprochement are the final sub-phases in separation and individuation. Practicing entails the experience of spatially leaving and returning to the mother for refueling. Rapprochement involves asserting one's autonomy and joining the good and bad self and object. This final phase results in the experiencing of a realistic whole self and a caring, internalized mother. The capacity for a healthy external boundary denoting one's personal space and awareness of others is also organized in this phase.

This line between paradise and independence is a struggle many borderline clients face. A client redramatizes the practicing phase of separation by spatially moving toward me and farther away. In one session she asked me to go into the smaller sand tray room and close the door. In another she asked me to shut my eyes while she moved about. In another I was covered with material. At times she sat in my lap and at other times beside me. During rapprochement, she drew huge pictures of devouring dinosaurs, symbolic of her rage. Her rageful split-off self then began to appear and finally to be claimed and enacted. Claiming both sides of the self in relation to the other is vital in therapy with the rapprochement client, as is healing the split in the transferred mother object.

Another client role played a dialogue between her symbiotic needy self and her separating, wall-like boundaried rapprochement self. This split-self needed to be joined so that she could experience both her relationally-oriented vulnerability and her capacity for boundaries simultaneously. "I need a man; I'll do anything, be anything just to be with him" was followed by "who needs anyone? They're all just takers. Be alone." Finally she reached an agreement and moved to blend the two. Subsequently she began and sustained a relationship without the "come here- go away" practicing phase dramatic theme she had repeatedly enacted.

Self and Object Constancy

In this final phase of Mahler's, the individual begins to internalize the mother so that full separation can occur without the fear of abandonment. If good-enough mothering was present, individuals will experience a whole, full realistic sense of self. They will also experience being held, supported and loved for who they are. They will be internally encouraged to feel pride in their productions, confidence in their doings and interest in exploring their creativity.

All too often a negative parental object is introjected. A witch mother may want to smother the child, keeping her debilitated and infantile, as in Rapunzel. She may demand that only part of the self be allowed to come out into the light of consciousness while the bad parts must remain in shadow. She may be submerged in the oceanic unconscious, as in Cinderella, or she may inflate the child self to a grandiose state of narcissism to feed off the child's accomplishments, as in Hansel and Gretel.

When this cannibalism occurs, all products are rendered to the primary caregiver–not only the sense of self, but who one is and what one does. This creates tremendous ambivalence within their victims. I have had numerous clients, most of whom are males in their mid to late thirties, who have had one great aspiration crash after another. These men were adored by their mothers who told them early on that they were going to be great, and that, unlike others, they would never have to work for anything. Such was the case with one depressed man who was part of a men's group. He never seemed to be able to sustain any intimate relationship nor maintain any job stability. Enacting the mother-child drama, I as mother, said to him, "You are wonderful, my boy, no one can see how marvelous you are but me. Stay with me always, my little phallus." He moved toward me, drawn to the mother-witch seduction. I clutched him. "You're mine and everything you do is mine. I'm hungry, you must do for me. So I can brag about my son and what he does."

The other men in the group were now getting agitated: "Get away from her!" "They're just jealous of our special relationship," I responded. The men were disgusted, but the man I was clutching appeared deep in thought with furrowed brows as if he was struggling to understand what appeared so obvious to the other men.

I decided to intensify the scene: "everything you think, say and do is mine. You're mine. Since everything you produce is mine, I want your balls." Now the men were yelling, "Get away from her!" Consciousness started to dawn, and he shoved me away saying, "No, you can't have them! Get your own!" Feeling my power diminish I crouched to the floor, becoming an old beggar crone, "Please, I need you. Don't leave me." Now the men huddled around him and then covered me with huge pillows for an early burial.

Mediation of the Instinctual, Identification, and Triangular Relationships with Parents: Magic Warlike and Magical Creative Phases

In the next stage delineated by Eric

Neumann (1973), the child must integrate much of his/her instinctual life in order to be socialized into the community of playmates. This instinctual realm is still viewed as related to the matriarchate. At this time, a child's dramatic skills naturally awaken to aid in this process within the mundus imaginalis. Nightmares begin around three and a half. Here the realm of the nightstalkers emerges from the earth and sea (mother realms); bats, devils, witches, and zombies manifest themselves in order to devour, smother or poison their prey. In this phase clients enact rageful, powerful creatures who have long been repressed for fear of retaliation or envy from the parents. These creatures from the deep can be mirrored and engaged by the therapist.

One woman dreamt that a tiger leaps into her car. She woke up screaming. Utilizing the technique of dreamwork as theater, I interviewed her as the tiger while I played the dream ego. "What are you doing in my car? You frighten me! Get out!" I exclaimed. "Do you want to eat me?" I asked. "I should. You're a little wimp," she responded. "Well, I had a rough childhood. If I stood up to my dad he would have clobbered me worse." I retorted, "Well, I don't see him around here now. I'm tired of your wimping out." She growled as the tiger. As the dream ego I asked, "Well you're no wimp. Maybe you could help me." "Yeah, I could help but you have to let me speak up." "Then nobody will mess with me," I affirmed. "Yeah," she reaffirmed. Giving her homework, I suggested she walk and think like this tiger. She found this instinctual part of her becoming gradually civilized, but the "don't mess with me" core remained underneath.

During the fifth year the triangular relationship with the parents expands. In this magic warlike phase, it is vital for the male to kill off the inner mother no matter how wonderful she may appear to be in order for the Oedipal crisis to be resolved and for him to have access to his anima or inner feminine side. Without this act, a man will forever transfer his mother onto the women he is with, resulting in his fearing commitment or symbolically clinging, depending on whether his mother was controlling or abandoning.[2]

This phase, which I have called the *magical creative stage,* is much different among women. She does not kill the mother because they are of like sex, but she must learn to mediate the powerful feminine and to experience the father not as bestial, under the power of the dark feminine as in Beauty and the Beast, but as human and approachable.

One couple complained that they have drifted apart. We spent the first hour identifying the players. The wife appeared warm and loving with compassionate eyes, but her husband's response to her was clearly through a distorted lens. With some exploration he was found to have a mother (I named her the Ice Queen) who was emotionally and physically unavailable. His father, although more loving, was a harsh taskmaster and beat him with a paddle. Touching, caressing and feeling loved and safe did not come naturally to him. The wife

2. Eric Neumann (1973) was able to delineate male stages of development, but he decided that the ego was also masculine for the female as well. I disagree. I believe as did Jung that there are contrasexual aspects to both male and female psychologies, i.e., men have inner feminine complex(es) called animae and women inner masculine called animi. I feel that a woman's ego is feminine and that her quests and development are centrally different than that of the males. I do feel, however, that both men and women must undergo developmental stages for both their ego and animus/a, with both moving toward the goal of androgyny in later life. I have, therefore, added female stages of development to Neumann's male ego stages. Thus the "magic warlike" is Neumann's and the "magical creative" is mine.

had a more nurturing childhood, but inside her was a critical father judge who convinced her that her husband was unavailable because there was something wrong with her. Her critic protected her by asking the husband a myriad of questions devised to discover the truth, i.e., that he did not really love her. Her husband, meanwhile, experienced male relational dread (Bergman, 1991) and felt unable to respond with the needed emotionally-laden, relationally-oriented verbal processing of which most women are adept. Since he was raised without access to a communicating female and by a father who trained him to compete among males, he remained silent, ill-equipped to engage. She was sure he was hiding something.

With the roles identified as ice queen mother and critical father, I began to role-play their transferences. At times I physically put my body between them so they had to struggle to see and touch each other. Their goal in the drama was to connect; my task was to keep them from intimacy. "All women are cold and unavailable; don't touch her, she'll freeze your fingers off," I exclaimed as the husband's ice queen mother. As her critical father I said, "Don't listen to him, he's not safe. Only I can protect you."

Through the externalization of these intrapsychic phenomena, I was also able to capture the transferential and projective material, thereby keeping it from contaminating their capacity to see each other. Intimacy was able to follow with a good deal of loving tenderness.

Latency, Peer Relationships and Puberty

With latency comes a shift in themes to those that reflect learning and living within the social realms of home and society. The industry of play and school become the precursors to adult work.

Pubertal rites of passage herald the next phase in the development of ego consciousness. Jung felt that this was the time of psychic birth. For the boy, as well as for the animus in girls, this means being separated from the collective, undergoing pain or deprivation, and undertaking tasks that entail empowerment and mastery over masculine instinctual phallic energy. As boys develop, their bodies become stronger. Their brute force can kill; it thus needs to be mediated. Control over drives and fear is rewarded with spiritual consciousness. For the maturing girl and the boy's anima, their rite of passage entails a descent and sacrifice of girlhood toward the search for embodied empowered feminine soulful wisdom.

One woman was in the process of reclaiming her inner children. Near termination, she reported having had an image of a pubescent young girl while on the way to the session. This girl had asked to be welcomed into her consciousness. She and I had previously discussed how her mother had felt shame and disdain for all aspects of female reproduction and sexuality. Her pubescent sensual self went underground, hidden under weight and layers of clothing to protect herself from the growing attention of the men around her. Menarche came and went in hidden shame. There was no pubertal rite of passage. Now in her forties, she and I enacted a pubertal rite for her embodied pubescent self. This woman then blossomed with creative ideas and ventures.

An eleven-year-old girl was referred to me for individual and group work. She lived with her stepmother without her salesman father much of the time. In the girl's improvisational drama group, she repeatedly took on angry male roles until the other girls encouraged her to enact female roles. As she began to claim her femaleness she came in one day with her beautiful hair butchered by her stepmother into a boyish cropped length. In individual work that day, she requested we dramatize Snow White with her as the heroine and myself playing the other roles. With much self-hate, she insisted I "cut her heart out" even though the story dictated otherwise. I suggested a time-out, and had her interview me as the evil stepmother who, with Wonder Woman's sash around her, had to tell the truth about her jealousy toward her stepdaughter.

Adolescence and Young Adulthood

Moving further in the transition between childhood into adulthood requires the exploration of new roles and the testing of familial and societal ruling principles. The striving for identity within one's peer group is carried out through costuming, roles and thematic enactments. Mythically, real identity can only emerge if one is willing to undergo a personal quest. If undertaken, the individual stands alone from the tribe and is identified as the hero or heroine. This journey frequently commences with a relationship with both the masculine and feminine sides. Thus, a man's male ego must join with his anima and a woman's female ego with her animus. Frequently, the contrasexual sides are projected into a lover for an embodied experience of the sexual union. However, the libido that belongs to the inner anima or animus must eventually be reowned and internalized or the individual will forever feel that s/he is only half a person without the other. Additionally, shadow aspects now emerge from the unconscious to be claimed. These same sex parts of the self often appear on more purely archetypal levels and can be readily dramatized and integrated into the psyche.

One client in her early forties brought in the following dreams. The first entailed her floating away from the reality she knew and becoming an instinctual Artemis figure. As she enacted her, she squatted on my green rug making gathering motions. She then brought her cupped hands upward through her body and extended them upward and outward from her heart–an ancient archetypal gesture (Lewis 1988b, 1993). As Artemis, she spoke to the dreamer, telling her to trust her instincts and profound intuitive ability and to continue to connect to nature to find a grounded energy source to fuel her busy day.

In the next dream a baby boy was born to her and placed in a bassinet which was too big for him. She was told his heart was broken. She woke up crying. This newly emerging relationship to her masculine had been injured at infancy and not allowed to develop. I suggested she reenter the dream, hold and verbally soothe her baby and heal his heart through love and nurturance.

In the following session, it became apparent that her positive caretaking had paid off. The infant had grown to manhood. She dreamed that she said to a priest, "I really love you." This figure represented a highly developed inner masculine and an agapé experience of spiritual love. I encouraged her to return to the imaginal realm of the dream to continue the experience. This brought her to a higher *conuinctio* (Jung, 1977; Lewis, 1993) or spiritual union. She reported feeling greater compassion and wisdom.

Mid-life Stage I: Heroic and Heroinic Quest: Death, Rebirth, and the Mid-life Crisis

Once both contrasexual natures have been differentiated out of parental complexes and joined together toward a united purpose, the quest begins its most treacherous phase. Because of this, many are unwilling to pursue it and stay frozen in the solar realm. But if the hero and heroine take on the quest, there are many myths of gods and goddesses that serve as guides; and through this relationship to the archetypal life themes, individuals can feel deeply connected to all of humanity–past, present and future–thus instilling meaning to their suffering.

This cycle of descent and death and ascent toward rebirth is typically undergone in mid-life and is often identified as a mid-life crisis. It spans a period of time between 35 and 45 years of age. During this time, individuals begin to be aware of their own mortality. During the next five years they slowly take stock of their lives: "Do I really want to spend the next half of my life with this person, job, or way of being?" Individuals often become preoccupied with aging signs. They may try to counteract the inevitable, by having affairs with younger individuals, buying youthful sports cars or clothing. They may attempt to curtail the results of age on their body by getting into heightened physical exercise at health clubs. Others compete with their now adolescent children or younger colleagues at work only to find the inevitable, i.e., that their football player son beats them at arm wrestling or their daughter really does look much better in that dress than they do. Frequently old behavioral patterns begin to be questioned. For example, one woman said, "I thought if I was nice to everyone, then they'd be nice to me. For 20 years I thought that if I just loved my husband more, he would stop undermining me." A man reflected, "I thought all I had to do was get this full professorship then I would have it all, but I'm still missing something. Status and money aren't 'it' like I thought."

This initial period is followed by an experience of breaking down or letting go of who one was. This occurs generally around ages 38–42. Described as "disassembling ourselves," (Sheehy, 1995), it is a dark time which is often precipitated by a crisis e.g., an affair being discovered, loss of a job or promotion, divorce, or the death of a parent. Some get into accidents or have their first experience with a life-threatening medical problem such as cancer or a heart attack. In any case, this is a time of suffering the insecurity of not knowing where one will end up. It is a time of grieving the years that were wasted not being truly oneself. At this time in therapy men and women are more willing to recognize and feel the pain from their past and let go of repetitive developmental themes that have not been helpful to them in their life. This frees up energy for the final phase. The final phase of the mid-life crisis is one of experiencing the development of a new, more authentic, expanded sense of self. Terms such as renewal and rebirth are employed here.

A 39-year-old man presented as the classic male in mid-life crisis reassessing his life. He was the oldest child of an alcoholic, physically abusive father and a narcissistic mother who parentified him since age six at the time of their divorce. He remained shut down and dutiful throughout his childhood, graduate school and marriage.

In one session, he began by dragging around a huge imagined excaliber sword–symbolic of his overresponsible ACOA behavior. He entered a forest and transversed a bridge. He sat down to rest and reported seeing a fox. Entering the imaginal realm I become him and he the fox. As the fox he said, "I'm free; you can live here too." Reversing roles repeatedly, the drama continued. Darkness came and he became afraid. The fox then attempted to teach him other ways to see.

He returned the next week and reentered the imaginal realm. He became possessed with despair. In the center of the despair was his inner 6-year-old. Over the course of several sessions I frequently portrayed the despair along with his survival mechanisms of cynic, Mr. Responsibility and "Shut down," while he as his adult/ ego and I battled for the possession of his soul/child. Finally he dreamed and subsequently enacted a descent in which he rescued a submerged boy. In the following week, he brought in a dream of a laughing baby dropping from the sky into his arms. In one of the last sessions he and his inner child fended off all my/his strategies in a playful drama improvisation. At one point I dressed in a witch cape and hat with a halo and pretended to be "only there for his best interests." I was perfunctorily dismissed.

Mid-Life Stage II: Middlessence

Working-class men identify middle age at 40; white-collar workers at 50. This author takes the mean of these two. Thus the middle years span between 45 and 65. Menopause is considered a ten-year cycle from 45 to 55 years or the onset of climacteric (the cessation of menstruation).

This is a time when the new-found self from the resolution of the mid-life crisis manifests itself. Individuals in this phase are often free from their childhood history and from attempting to be like anyone else but themselves. They become far more outspoken about their own personal beliefs and care less about what other people think. Greer (1992) notes, regarding women during "the change," that as they become less sexually attractive to men; and many, after mourning the loss of being able to trade on their appearance, feel a new-found freedom. One woman in her latter 50s said in session, "I don't have to defer to men anymore and pretend I'm less than who I am to reinforce their fantasy that they're better than I."

Male menopause, beginning around 45, is marked by decreased testosterone. Some men have insomnia, chronic fatigue and headaches. Research also demonstrates the more anxious a man is, the more his testosterone decreases (Sheehy, 1995). This can produce a downward spiral. Diminished sexual activity for males in Western culture is often equated with a decrease in power in general. This equation frequently makes a man more anxious which in turn decreases the hormone. Nervousness, irritability and depressive phases can be part of male climacteric.

Menopausal women, who have traded on being pretty, experience what Greer (1992) identifies as a "free fall which brings with it panic" (p. 8). Until she can realize the freedom this gives her, she will feel she has been thrown in to the scrap heap of a youth culture that is fearful of the aging process. Regardless, women in this phase mourn the loss of their fertility and capacity to give birth. One client remarked, "It's not that I want to have another child. Lord, no. I don't have the energy or the patience anymore. But it is the loss of being fertile. It's a feeling I've had ever since I was 13. It was so much a part of me that until it was gone I never knew it was so infused in me. It's in the way I walk, the dresses I wear. I did not realize it, but I was saying to all who could see, 'I am fertile.'"

In this final phase, a woman is able to let go of the child bearer and love goddess images, and claim her croneship. Clarissa Pinkola-Estes says about women that in their earlier years they shed blood to have children and now they hold blood to store wisdom (Greer, 1992). The postmenopausal woman has acquired deep serenity, power, wisdom, depth of love and spirituality.

In men, too, being able to let go of the burden of pretending to fit the male stereotype is freeing. Gone is the strength, gone the lithe body and tight stomach, gone the competitive edge. Contemplative, observant and knowing, he has come through the retirement panic, i.e., that he was what he did.

Now he is truly free. Men have no need for excuses anymore and women need to make no more apologies.

Often clients have a series of spiritual dreams at this time in their life which when explored and experienced in an embodied way, can result in the client being deeply moved. A 58-year-old woman related the following dream four months into her depth therapy: "A Chinese man in a limousine hurls a plastic bomb into an old, dark fortress. One of my daughters dressed in a white clerical gown is pushing a woman on a hospital gurney toward a church." Through dreamwork as theater she role played this Chinese figure, and as I interviewed him, she experienced him as symbolic of ancient wisdom and the rising sun of Consciousness. She learned he was bombing her rigid body and archaic defensive behavior (old fortress).

In the next scene with her daughter, she realized she was the body lying on the gurney. I then encouraged her to enact lying on the moving bed. A suggestion was also made that she imagine continuing the dream and experience what would happen next. She then laid down on the couch and closed her eyes. "I am entering this church," she related, "and there is this dome with an opening at the center. There is light pouring down at the center point." "Allow your daughter to wheel you into the Light," I responded gently but firmly. Her breathing changed and became deeper. Her eyes teared. Her mouth opened with a sigh. No words could describe this feeling of the Holy Other. The therapy room and I were also transported into the sacred space of her dream. Both she and I felt surrounded by Grace. Deeply moved she left with an expanded vision of the many realms of existence.

This expanded vision is yet another by-product of the mid-life aging process. Now the focus of a person's life can shift away from self in relation to one's immediate environment and attempts to attain what Western culture has deemed of value. Usually the more an individual has achieved these worldly plateaus, whether they are relationships, family, money, status and/or professional success, the easier it is to let go of what has been acquired. Many that failed, for whatever reason, to meet their ideals of the good life, have difficulty letting go of their sine qua non place in their consciousness. These individuals often live out their lives in a quiet despair.

But for those who can shift their attention, their view expands. They see the bigger pictures of humanity, planetary existence and spiritual consciousness.

Aging and Dying

Wisdom comes with the aging process. Those who live long enough see that trends in life among humans and in nature have a tendency to repeat themselves. The commonality of experience among all peoples becomes clearer. They come to know more deeply that all humans experience joy, anger and suffering. All share concerns over territory and survival. Thus greater consciousness concerning oneself provides a foundation for interpersonal consciousness which in turn provides a springboard for greater transpersonal or spiritual consciousness.

The same man described in mid-life crisis returned years later for five months with a very different focus. He reported that he had not been depressed or cynical since our work, but something had happened. He was diagnosed with cancer and was scheduled for chemotherapy. He knew that chemotherapy not only kills any possible cancer cells, but just about everything else draining one's life force. He felt he wanted to know his path in life more clearly.

For the next several sessions, synchronistic phenomena occurred during his therapy hour in the form of animal appearances never before seen in my office. In one session two seals appeared at river's edge in front of us. With a shamanic frame in mind, I suggested he enter into the imaginal realm with the seals and dialogue with them. "Be harmonious with nature, and joy and pleasure will be yours," was their response.

In the next hour, he looked up to find a magnificent eight-point stag in the meadow out front who appeared and stayed for his hour only. I knew from my research that the stag is one of the major power animals of shamans and is a symbol of Christ (Lewis, 1993). Through dramatic dialogue with the buck he received, "Get rid of fear. This is filling your mind with useless thoughts. Get off your butt. Don't waste time looking for outside guidance through books. Be open now."

In the following hour, he reported a dream, "I am in a medieval inner courtyard–like a circular paddock. The stag goes through a big dark wooden door. I feel I'm supposed to follow, but I don't want to. Then I'm aware there is a huge male figure dressed in white robes. He is laughing." I role played the white figure who was clearly a trickster and he was the dream ego. I told him he must go through the door, and that if he did not, all his suffering from the chemotherapy would have no meaning.

He returned a month later racked with pain and nausea from the chemotherapy. He reported seeing two hawks facing in opposite directions on the same branch in the front of my office. He lay down, and I suggested he connect with the hawks. During this time I sensed something unusual occurring. He later reported that the hawks helped him leave his body. "Now I know I have a body; I am not a body." "Yes," I responded, "it is easier for people to be willing to have out-of-body experiences if they are in physical pain."

Three weeks later he returned with the following dream. He was in a monk's habit leading a group in the wilderness. He came upon a rock impasse. Before him appeared five angels. Each sent him their names: Love, Compassion, Truth, Understanding, and Humility. He extended his hands and radiant beams of light emanated. He then told me he was not religious and felt unworthy. I instructed him to ask the angels. He stretched out his arms and then began to laugh. "They say that is beside the point," he reported. I then instructed him to reenact his dream. During this drama he began to cry. "This may sound corny," he reported later, "but to touch people . . . we're all suffering . . . to touch with kindness. . . ."

After a hiatus in which he was recovering from the chemotherapy, he returned. I suggested he imagine and reconnect through improvisational drama with the animals that had appeared to him. Moving about the room he reported, "The hawk is circling above and the stag is entering a forest." "Follow him," I said. He comes to a circular clearing with a 20-foot stone circle with a fire in the middle. He sees many faces in the fire. "Step into the fire," I said. He stepped in and reported, "I'm looking out. Everything is dark. I sensed there is something beyond, something green, but I'm afraid of the dark." My insistence for him to continue was to no avail. At this point all the electricity in my office went off and stayed off until he left.

In the next session, I returned him to his incomplete journey. He stepped into the flame and saw a dark hole in the middle. Reminding him to let go of his fear, he was able to descend. The hole got smaller and he crawled until he saw large teeth in front of him that kept him from proceeding. He said finally, "You know this is funny but if I were a snake I could slither right through." "Be a snake," I said. He proceeded and learned he can shape shift.

In his last session he reported that the

president of his company wanted to place him in a managerial position, one in which he would be speaking nationally. But he told me he was afraid of what he will say. "They might ask questions that I don't know the answers to." I said, "Ask the angels." The angels said, "It's not what you say. It is your being, your compassion and your love which is the message." He then said to me, "All my life I've always judged myself as being a 'jack of all trades master of none.' I've never reached the pinnacle of accomplishment in any field. Now I realize this is not the direction at all. It is not what you do; it is who you are." "Yes," I responded, "Manifesting your soul is truly the most important accomplishment."

CASE EXAMPLE

Laura, a bright woman in her early thirties with a strong ego, was referred by a former client. She entered the room and quickly held me with intense riveting eyes. I felt immediately moved into a state of idealization. I then began to receive the full transference of a mother that needed to be put on a pedestal or there would be no chance of receiving any attention, let alone love. I pondered internally as to whether she unconsciously felt she needed to heal me, the mother-therapist, first, i.e., to fill me with narcissistic supplies in hopes there would be enough to send back to her. I immediately began to send support, care, and valuing back to her through the imaginal realm of the somatic countertransference. I learned from her that her mother was empty and enmeshed and her father narcissistic. She was ignored or engulfed by the mother and sexualized by the father. Neither parent instilled in her a sense of self. I wrote in my notes from this first hour, "must have very good boundaries with her. She needs to have her new sense of self encouraged and supported as she claims more of herself."

Developmental Themes of Symbiosis

The only one who noticed her was her father, but only in relation to what she looked like and what she did to enhance his own aggrandizement. He had sexualized her and now her sexuality was split from her inner substance and used to seduce in order to be seen. As she role-played her mother while I interviewed her, I began feeling as if I were in the presence of a mannequin who consisted solely of an outer shell. It became exceedingly difficult to make sure I did not get caught in her excellently trained ability to mirror what the other wanted. Much of my response to her was on a nonverbal level. I sat in opened posturing and attuned to her breath and traced self-nurturing movements. In this type of transference, however, who is mirroring whom can be a very subtle, and at times, confusing pas de deux.

In five sessions her trust was sufficient enough to begin the work of self-formation. During this hour she realized that she had given up her soul's manifestation in return for the hopes of parental love. I asked her if she was willing to let me in, i.e., for my soul to find her soul. Would she let me look inside her? She was intrigued; and looking into my eyes, she allowed me to look into hers. This suggestion brought us into the transpersonal. I connected to my soul and began looking inside her for a spark of I-ness. Eventually she allowed me to find her. She said, "I feel like we weren't the only beings in this room. I felt someone saying 'wake up'." I responded, "Let those words be your mantra."

The next week she brought in a dream in which she was lead by a psychopomp figure into "seeing the light in the darkness, like the light that shines at the bottom of the sea." I encouraged her to enact this experience. She began by kneeling with her head downward. She then said, "I need to do this with someone." I moved toward her, and I supported her as I mirrored her in this birthing. In this way we began the redramatization of object relations. We finished the sequence by her indulging in eye-to-eye contact. I felt her beginning to receive and digest my genuine care. She questioned, "Will you receive my anger too?" I smiled back and imagined her whole and sent the image back to her through the somatic countertransference.

In the next hour she reported dreaming that she was "deep in liquid–like a womb, and I feel my center." I suggested that she enact the dream. She lay on the floor. I sat next to her and supported her back with my hand gently following the flow of her breath. Role playing her fetal self, she began to speak, "I feel empty." I respond soothingly, "Yes little one, that is because there was no one to feed you, but we will fill you with love and care and you will feel full."

Developmental Themes of Differentiation

"I need to see myself" was Laura's first comment at the beginning of the next session. I brought her a mirror and encouraged her to look into her own eyes. "I am worried. I need space; I am empty." She continued to use the mirror and then became aware of her inner judge that we had explored in earlier sessions. I role played her judge to externalize it, and she was able tell it/me to leave her alone. Her inner mother then appeared in this imaginal process and her developmental themes changed from symbiotic to those of differentiation. She growled and snapped and clawed the rug as she struggled to claim the needed differentiation from her. In the next hour, her persona charming false self emerged through her telling her to stop expressing anger, that no one would like her, that it's not safe. Feeling that this survival mechanism needed to be externalized so that she could more fully claim her nascent self, I took over role playing it while she embodied her angry self.

Throughout the next few months she continued to enact the growing infant-toddler self. She often began the session connecting to the early infant. In one hour she said she imagined an egg that was between us; I then created a nest of pillows around her. She became concerned that the pillows barred access to me. So I moved next to her and extended my arm into the nest like an umbilical cord. In the nest she began to posit the concept of whole parents: "I have hated both my parents and stayed away to separate from them, but I now think that they are neither all good nor all bad."

The next session she crawled everywhere in the drama space. Embodying this differentiating self she related that she felt more energy, and that she wanted to "rip at the veils that keep me from being more here." She then related this to her mother and became angry once again at her mother's lack of connection. I elected to receive the negative transference and veiling myself in a parachute, I began to role play her mother, "If you become real, I will leave you; or make you go; or make you wrong or bad." Laura responded with more differentiating themes: demonstrating healthy body and ego boundaries serving to separate intrapsychically from her mother's toxicity.

With each session she continued to enact the differentiating toddler creeping and crawling while separating and discriminating her thoughts and feelings from her mother's. In one session she repeatedly reached out and grabbed. She then became contaminated by the negativity of her inner mother. "My mother is surrounding me with her disgust. I shouldn't grab or want or need!" I mirrored her sounds of exclamation while placing the parachute around her to externalize and objectify her experience of her invoked mother surrounding her with disgust. Additionally I placed a pillow between her and me. Laura continued to moan. As the shamed child she said, "I am yucky; my mother said I was disgusting." "It's a good thing," I responded using metaphors from this developmental stage; "because otherwise she would have devoured you." "Yeah," she returned, "It was safest to hide." Gradually she removed the parachute and risked being present in the room with me. For several minutes she looked into my eyes and received my good will toward her "a drop at a time" while I reassured her that her needs were not yucky but normal.

Developmental Themes of Practicing and Rapprochement

She began to crawl and roll about the room smearing the rug. Utilizing practicing developmental themes she stated, "I can be yucky and you won't push me away." I meanwhile sat some distance away honoring her entrance into the distancing aspect of this stage. In processing, I suggested she needed to sort her mother's and father's "yuckiness" from her own good shit, as the power to have pleasure in one's own bodily products paves the way for creativity.

It was four months before she moved developmentally from crawling to standing. She brought in a powerful dream. "I am at my mother's childhood home. The sky gets dark, ominous. The wind comes. The house collapses. It's snowing and icing. I only have time to grab one thing–my sturdy walking shoes. I leave and fall into the ice flows. I call for help, but a friend of mine (who has gone through a lot of recovery) says, 'You can stand,' and I do." I suggested that she dramatize the dream. She was able to stand but tried to walk prematurely. Her arms were unable to move in a reciprocal manner to her gait. In the next session she again moved to a standing position and this time asserted herself utilizing rapprochement themes as she invoked her mother in the room. "I hate you! You could not see me. I wasn't allowed to get angry or say you weren't mothering me. You told me I was mean. I felt I could not leave you because I would never get your love!" I again maintained a vertical position and imagined her whole with pride within the somatic countertransference. Following this session she arrived wearing a pair of red slacks and exclaimed, "My life has been about standing up."

About this time there was a hiatus in the work due to a vacation. Upon return she embodied her toddler self and yelled at me. "It was too long; I am angry. You know I do fine without you but inside it was too long." "Your adult self functions well; but this is about the child self inside you that is developing. You were just standing up and beginning to practice leaving, and I left you instead. It is you that should be leaving." "Yeah!" she affirmed. She continued, "I need the physical. It's physical how I feel. My body misses you. It's like I begin to feel empty again." "Yes," I responded, "It's like I am a part of you that creates a holding place for the you inside you so that you can be filled with yourself." "It's like when you left, there was a hole, and I began to drain out of me," Laura replied.

During this conversation she is rocking on all fours. I am next to her with my hand on her back. Laura continued, "This mom stuff is so important to me. My life is really shifting." She then sat up to vertical, and I responded by giving her more spatial distance and shifting from the horizontal to the vertical. She then adjusted her body into the forward plane and began to describe a highly creative work in which she was engaging with another woman.

Developmental Themes of Self Formation and Identification and Relationship with Parents

Subsequently she had several dreams that she was pregnant. Her creativity began to expand at work as she was given new projects. Her sexuality that had been split off in service to gaining her father's and subsequent men of authority's value and approval began to be reclaimed. In one session she gathered several figures from the sandplay shelves and arranged them on the rug. Her libidinal needy self, her boundaried rapprochement self, her ego, and two Aphrodite statutes: one white, one brown. As the white goddess, she addressed her inner psyche's personifications, "I will seduce men and give them whatever they want." As the brown Aphrodite, "All men just want sex; they don't ever see me. So I'll give it to them and have power over them." Her symbiotic child self responded to the split-off sexuality, "Oh take me with you; maybe I'll be loved too." But the new rapprochement self said to the needy child, "Wait! Just wait! I am the one to help and protect you, not the sex vamp. She can't take care of you; she can't take care of herself."

Developmental Themes of Puberty and Adolescence: Claiming her Sexuality and De-throning the Old Rule

The overlapping interrelationship between her rapprochement assertiveness and her awareness and experience of her pubertal sexuality continued for several sessions. Her capacity to claim her sexuality was contingent upon her integration of the rapprochement developmental themes of self-assertion and independent thought and action, as it is in this phase that healthy external boundaries are formed. Her sexual interiority had been perpetrated upon in early years by her mother's sexually competitive narcissism and her father's sexualization of her. Later during puberty and early adolescence, her parents had violated her personal space through highly inappropriate interest in her desire, orgasmic performance, and intimate encounters with boys.

In one session she began via the improvisational technique of authentic sound, movement and drama. She writhed on the floor and discovered that she only felt comfortable moving from her shoulders upward. She had sheathed the rest of her body with an imaginal barrier in order to bar her parents' access to her embodied sexuality. To get greater insight into her mother's abuse, I suggested she role play her mother while I interviewed her. With each response I encouraged her to remove a layer of her mother's false-self persona until her raw blood-curdling competitive and provocative nature was revealed.

In the following week she reported a dream of waves or orgiastic energy moving through her body. She recalled saying in the dream, "I am preparing myself to be a virgin; this is what Penny meant." She then arranged pillows around her external boundary and spends 45 minutes shoving away the imaged holograph of her parents that existed in her personal field. Additionally she toned in differentiating and rapprochement sound reinforcing external and body boundaries. She then formed a word, "Neeeeeed . . ." I added, "I need . . ." She responded, "I need floor, earth to be mothered. I need to be human." I responded, "You need to be fully in your body all the way to your skin." "Yes!" she exclaimed and began to sob. I then brought a box of tissues over to her. She said,

"Don't go." I sat next to her on the floor. She lay down with her head next to me on a pillow. I stroked her head. She said calmly, "I trust you."

Developmental Themes of Young Adulthood

Gradually she shifted her work from healing through the redramatization of earlier developmental themes to exploring adult life stage themes. She began to have dreams and do sandplay depictions of shadow (same sex) and animi (inner masculine) aspects seeking to be claimed. Employing dreamwork as theater and embodied sandplay she role played these complexes. In one dream a woman "who has always been watching from a distance" pushes her into a pool. Enacting the woman with me interviewing her she, in a punk style, complained that the dreamer had always kept her away. Role playing the dreamer I responded, "well you would have gotten me into big trouble had I listened to you. Your 'nobody messes with me' attitude is just too 'uncivilized.'" "Well it's what you need, you've been a wuss!" We made a deal: I encouraged her to embody her throughout the week and, with her shadow's influence, begin to alter her responses to situations. Later she role played and subsequently joined two other shadow aspects–one a blitheful puella (eternal youth) and another a responsible, maternal archetypal woman caught in tribal tradition.

In sandplay, she placed an animus figure next to her inner mother. She then realized that, instead of supporting her, he had become her mother's henchman as in Sleeping Beauty. She role played him and I her. I encouraged him to come and be in relation to me. As he shifted, his personality developed demonstrating strength, gentleness, thoughtful caring and responsibility. Soon she began dreaming of archetypal unions with her inner masculine.

CONCLUSION

From birth to the final rite of passage we humans explore developmental themes that build upon preexisting stages. If unintegrated, these themes become dysfunctional and perpetuate themselves, keeping the person from moving forward and responding spontaneously. The drama therapist identifies the repetitive phenomena and their developmentally associated roles; and through the techniques of inner drama, the redramatization of object relations, dreamwork as theater, sandplay embodiment, dramatic improvisation, and authentic sound, movement and drama, resolves and clears the habitual patterns. Then mythelogems or archetypal life themes become available to healthy children, adolescents, and adults in their unfolding personal quests.

A client's recovery into wholeness means that s/he can fully experience the uniqueness of each moment. It means that the inner masculine and feminine are balanced and integrated. It also means s/he has the potential to be in relationship to the archetypal Self, to that which can continuously provide the stage for involvement in developmentally stimulated life themes.

REFERENCES

Bergman, S. (1991). *Men's psychological development: A relational perspective, Work in Progress.* Wellesley: The Stone Center. No. 48.

Erikson, E. (1963). *Childhood and society.* New York: W.W. Norton and Company.

Fairbairn, R. (1976). *Psychoanalytic studies of the personality: The object relation theory of personality.* London: Kegan Paul.

Freud, A. (1966). *Normality and pathology in childhood.* New York: International Universities Press.

Greer, G. (1992). *The change: Women, aging and menopause.* New York: Alfred Knopf.

Grotstein, J. (1981). *Splitting and projective identification.* New York: Jason Aronson.

Jung, C.G. (1977). *Collected works, Vol. XVI, and XIV.* New York: Bollengin Foundation.

Kestenberg, J. (1975). *Children and parents.* New York: Jason Aronson.

Klein, M. (1975). *Writings of Melanie Klein* (Vols. 103). London: Hogarth.

Lewis Bernstein, P. (1981). Moon goddess, medium, and Earth mother: A phenomenological study of the guiding archetypes of the dance movement therapist. *Research as creative process.* Columbia: ADTA.

Lewis Bernstein, P. (1982). Authentic movement as active imagination. In J. Hariman (Ed.), *The compendium of psychotherapeutic techniques.* Springfield, IL: Charles C Thomas.

Lewis Bernstein, P. & Singer, D. (Eds.). (1983). *The choreography of object relations.* Keene: Antioch University.

Lewis Bernstein, P. (1985). Embodied transformational images in dance-movement therapy. *Journal of Mental Imagery, 9,* 1–9.

Lewis, P. (1986). *Theoretical approaches in dance-movement therapy Vol. I.* Dubuque: Kendall/Hunt Pub.

Lewis, P. (1988a). *Theoretical approaches in dance-movement therapy, Vol. II.* Dubuque: Kendall/Hunt Pub.

Lewis, P. (1988b). The transformative process in the imaginal realm. *The Arts in Psychotherapy. 15,* 309–316.

Lewis, P., & Loman, S. (Eds.). (1990). *The Kestenberg movement profile–Its past, present and future applications.* Keene, NH: Antioch-New England Graduate School Pub.

Lewis, P. (1992). The creative arts in transference-countertransference relationships. *The Arts in Psychotherapy, 19,* 317–324.

Lewis, P. (1993). *Creative transformation: The healing power of the expressive arts.* Willmette: Chiron.

Lewis, P. (1996). Authentic sound movement and drama. *A Moving Journal.* vol. 3, no. 1.

Lewis, P. (1999a). The clinical interpretation of the Kestenberg movement profile with adults. In J. Amaghi, P. Lewis, S. Loman, & M. Sossin (Eds.), *Understanding personality through movement: The role of movement in development.* New York: Gordon & Breach Pub.

Lewis, P. (1999b). Healing early child abuse: The application of the Kestenberg movement profile and its concepts. In J. Amaghi, P. Lewis, S. Loman, & M. Sossin (Eds.), *Understanding personality through movement: The role of movement in development.* Newark: Gordon & Breach Pub.

Mahler, M. (1968). *On human symbiosis and the vicissitudes of individuation.* New York: International Universities Press.

Moore, R., & Gillete, D. (1990). *King, warrior, magician, lover: Rediscovering the archetypes of the mature masculine.* San Francisco: Harper.

Neumann, E. (1973). *The origins and history of consciousness.* Princeton: Princeton University Press.

Neumann, E. (1976). *The child.* New York: Harper & Row.

Racker, H. (1982). *Transference and countertransference.* New York: International Universities Press.

Schwartz-Salant, N. (1982). *Narcissism and character transformation.* Toronto: Inner City Books.

Schwartz-Salant, N., & Stein, M., (Eds.). (1984). *Chiron: Transference/countertransference.* Wilmette, IL: Chiron.

Sheehy, G. (1995). *New passages: Mapping your life across time.* New York: Random House.

Stein, M. (1984). *Power, shamanism, and maieutics in the countertransference.* Wilmette, IL: Chiron.

Stern, D. (1985). *The interpersonal world of the infant.* New York: Basic Books.

Turner, V. (1971). *The ritual process.* Chicago: Aldine.

Von Franz, M-L. (1978). *Interpretation of fairytales.* Dallas: Spring.

Von Franz, M-L. (1982). *Individuation in fairytales.* Dallas: Spring.

Winnicott, D.W. (1971). *Playing and reality.* New York: Penguin Books.

BIBLIOGRAPHY

Books

Amaghi, J., Lewis, P., Loman, S., & Sossin, M., (Eds.). (1999). *The meaning of movement: Developmental and clinical perspectives in the Kestenberg movement profile.* Newark: NJ: Gordon & Breach.

Lewis Bernstein, P. (1975). (Ed.). *Therapeutic process movement as integration.* Columbia: ADTA.

Lewis Bernstein, P., & Singer, D., (Eds.). (1982). *The choreography of object relations.* Keene: Antioch University.

Lewis, P. (1986). *Theoretical approaches in dance-movement therapy, Vol. I.* Dubuque: W.C. Brown-Kendall/Hunt.

Lewis, P. (1987). *Theoretical approaches in dance-movement therapy, Vol. II.* Dubuque: W.C. Brown-Kendall/Hunt.

Lewis, P., & Loman, S. (Eds.). (1990). *The Kestenberg movement profile: Its past, present and future applications.* Keene: Antioch University.

Lewis, P. (1993). *Creative transformation: The healing power of the expressive arts.* Willmette: Chiron.

Lewis, P. (1994). *The clinical interpretation of the Kestenberg movement profile.* Keene: Antioch New England Provost Fund.

Lewis, P. (1999). *Schopfennshe Prozesse. Kunst in Der Therapeutis Chen Praxis.* Zurich/Dusseldorf: Verlag.

Articles and Chapters

Lewis Bernstein, P., & Cafarelli, E. (1972). *An electromyographical validation of the Effort System of notation. Writings on Body Movement and Communication. Vol. II.* Columbia: ADTA.

Lewis Bernstein, P., (1972). *Range of response as seen through a developmental progression. What is dance therapy really?* B. Govine (Ed.). Columbia, MD: ADTA.

Lewis Bernstein, P., & Bernstein, L. (1973-4). *A conceptualization of group dance-movement therapy as a ritual process. Writings on body movement and communication. Vol. III.* Columbia: ADTA.

Lewis Bernstein, P. & Garson, B. (1975). Pilot study in the use of tension flow system of movement notation in an ongoing study of infants at risk for schizophrenic disorders. *Dance Therapy–Depth and Dimension.* D. Plunk (Ed.). Columbia, MD: ADTA.

Lewis Bernstein, P. (1975). Tension flow rhythms: As a developmental diagnostic tool within the theory of the recapitulation of ontogeny. *Dance Therapy–Depth and Dimension.* Columbia, MD: ADTA.

Lewis Bernstein, P., Rubin, J., & Irwin, E. (1975). Play, parenting, and the arts. *Therapeutic process movement as integration.* P. L. Bernstein (Ed.). Columbia, MD: ADTA.

Lewis Bernstein, P. (1980). Dance-movement therapy. In R. Herink (Ed.), *Psychotherapy handbook.* New York: The New American Library Press.

Lewis Bernstein, P. (1980). A mythic quest: Jungian movement therapy with the psychosomatic client. *American Journal of Dance Therapy. 3,* 44–55.

Lewis Bernstein, P. (1980). The union of the Gestalt concept of experiment and Jungian active imagination within a woman's mythic quest. *The Gestalt Journal, 3,* 36–46.

Lewis Bernstein, P. (1981). Moon goddess, medium, and Earth mother: A phenomenological study of the guiding archetypes of the dance movement therapist. *Research as creative process.* Columbia, MD: ADTA.

Lewis Bernstein, P. (1982). Authentic movement as active imagination. In J. Hariman (Ed.), *The compendium of psychotherapeutic techniques.* New York: Charles C Thomas.

Lewis Bernstein, P. (1986). Embodied transformational images in dance-movement therapy. *Journal of Mental Imagery, 9,* 1–9.

Lewis, P. (1987). The expressive therapies in the choreography of object relations. *The Arts in Psychotherapy, 14,* 321–332.

Lewis, P. (1987). *The unconscious as choreographer: The use of tension flow rhythms in the transference relationship.* A.D.T.A. Conference Monograph. Columbia, MD: ADTA.

Lewis, P. (1988). The transformative process within the imaginal realm. *The Arts in Psychotherapy, 15,* 309–316.

Lewis, P. (1988). The dance between the conscious and unconscious: Transformation in the embodied imaginal realm. *The moving dialogue.* Columbia, MD: ADTA.

Lewis, P. (1988). *The marriage of our art with science: The Kestenberg Profile and the choreography of object relations.* Monograph 5. Columbia, MD: ADTA.

Lewis, P. (1990). The Kestenberg Movement Profile in the psychotherapeutic process with borderline disorder. In P. Lewis, & S. Loman (Eds.), *The KMP: Its past, present application and future directions.* Keene: Antioch University.

Lewis, P., & Brownell, A. (1990). The Kestenberg Movement Profile in assessment of vocalization. In P. Lewis, & S. Loman (Eds.), *The KMP: Its past, present application and future directions.* Keene: Antioch University.

Lewis, P. (1991). Creative transformation: The alchemy of healing, individuation and spiritual consciousness. *Shadow and light: Moving toward wholeness.* Columbia, MD: ADTA.

Lewis, P. (1992). The creative arts in transference-countertransference relationships. *The Arts in Psychotherapy, 19,* 317–324.

Lewis, P. (1993).The use of reflection, reciprocity, rhythmic body action, and the imaginal in the depth dance therapy process of recovery, healing and spiritual consciousness. In S. Sandel, S. Chaiklin, & A. Lohn (Eds.), *Marian Chace, Her Papers,* 2nd Ed. Columbia: ADTA.

Lewis, P. (1993). Michael Jackson, Analysiert Mit Hilfe Des. Kestenberg-Bewegungsprofils in Tanztherapie. In K. Hormann (Ed.), *The application of the Kestenberg movement profile and its concepts.* Zurich: Beitrage zur Augewandten Hogrefe.

Lewis, P. (1993). *Kestenberg movement profile interpretation: Clinical, cultural and organizational application.* American Dance Therapy Association Proceedings. Columbia, MD: ADTA.

Lewis, P. (1993). Following our dreams: Dance therapy as transformation. *American Dance Association Proceedings.* Columbia, MD: ADTA.

Lewis, P. (1994). *Die Tiefenpsychologisch Orientierte Tanztherapie in Sprache der Bewegung.* Berlin: Nervenklinik Spandau Publication.

Lewis, P. (1996). Depth psychotherapy and dance-movement therapy. *American Journal of Dance Therapy, 18* (2).

Lewis, P. (1996). Authentic sound movement and drama: An interview with Penny Lewis. *A Moving Journal, 3,* no.1.

Lewis, P. (1996). The Gestalt movement therapy approach. In L. Tsung-Chin (Ed.), *Dance therapy.* Taipei, Taiwan: Publisher identified in Chinese.

Lewis, P. (1996). Authentic sound, movement, and drama: An interactional approach. In M. Robbins (Ed.), *Body oriented psychotherapy,* Vol. I. Somerville, MA: International Scientific Community for Psycho-Corporal Therapies.

Lewis, P. (1996). The Kestenberg movement profile. In M. Robbins (Ed.), *Body oriented psychotherapy,* Vol. I. Somerville, MA: International Scientific Community for Psycho-Corporal Therapies.

Lewis, P. (1997). Multiculturalism and globalism in the arts in psychotherapy. *The Arts in Psychotherapy, 24,* 123–128.

Lewis, P. (1997). Appreciating diversity, commonality, and the transcendent. *The Arts in Psychotherapy 24,* 225–226.

Lewis, P. (1997).Transpersonal arts psychotherapy: Toward an ecumenical worldview. *The Arts in Psychotherapy, 24,* 243–254.

Lewis, P. (1999). Healing early child abuse: The application of the Kestenberg movement profile. In J. Amaghi, S. Loman, P. Lewis, & M. Sossin (Eds.). *The meaning of movement: Developmental and clinical perspectives of the Kestenberg Movement Profile.* Newark: Gordon & Breach.

Lewis, P. (1999). The embodied feminine: Dance and drama therapy in women's holistic health. In E. Olshansky (Ed.), *Woman's holistic health care.* Gaithersburg, MD: Aspen Press.

FURTHER TRAINING

Kim Burden, Drama Therapy Advisor
kimberley_burden@antiochne.edu
Alternate Route Drama Therapy Training
Dance Movement Therapy Program,
Department of Applied Psychology
Antioch University New England
40 Avon Street
Keene, NH 03431
603-357-3122

Chapter 13

THE ENACT METHOD OF EMPLOYING DRAMA THERAPY IN SCHOOLS

DIANA FELDMAN, FARA SUSSMAN JONES, AND EMILIE WARD

HISTORY

Since 1987, *ENACT* has been recognized as a specialized New York City arts in education organization that excels in working with troubled youth. Reaching thousands of students each year, ENACT delivers customized workshops that employ theater and drama therapy techniques to teach vital social emotional skills to students, parents and teachers. Now in its twentieth year, ENACT has expanded its programming to offer several long-term models that respond to changing school needs. At the heart of the ENACT program lies its signature methodology. In the ENACT model, two highly-trained teaching artists partner to run three 45-minute theater-based classroom workshops each week for a period ranging from ten weeks (short-term work) to forty weeks (full-year program). ENACT ensures that each teaching artist–with his/her particular style and skill set–is appropriately matched with each participating school–with its own distinctive culture and environment (Feldman, 1997).

Over the years, ENACT has grown to serve all five New York City boroughs, working mostly in high-risk classrooms with the neediest students. With years of experience using creative drama and drama therapy techniques with students of all ages and abilities, we have come to believe that many of the children we serve in the New York City school system suffer from unrecognized trauma resulting from the effects of poverty and dangerous and unstable living environments. ENACT's partnering schools are located in neighborhoods in which poverty has contributed to high rates of violence, crime, and drug and alcohol abuse. Seventy-five percent of ENACT's current work is in the South Bronx, a region in which more than 40 percent of the residents live below the poverty line. Almost all of ENACT's remaining work takes place in high poverty areas in Queens and Brooklyn. To date, ENACT has a cadre of 50 teaching artists trained in the ENACT method and has served over 100,000 students in the neediest neighborhoods of New York.

Changing perspectives on the arts and drama therapy in the school system and how they are funded have played a direct role in

ENACT's development. For years, given ENACT's theater-based approach and use of drama therapists and professional actors as actor-instructors, city arts funding proved the best source of revenue for a program that integrated theater arts and drama therapy techniques in the classroom. ENACT, like other school arts-related programs, depended on city budgets that annually determined the scope of arts programming in the schools. As is often the case, the arts were viewed as enhancements to core curricula and funding was tenuous from year to year.

Over the years, ENACT staff have seen the climate in our schools change. Students, especially those labeled with behavior problems, were so responsive to ENACT's methods that teachers increasingly requested ENACT to help them learn creative approaches to managing chaotic classroom behavior. To accommodate requests from both teachers and students, school principals had to seek innovative ways to secure additional funding for ENACT programs. In addition, funding for arts programs began to see a rapid decline in the 1990s, while educators and policy makers were beginning to recognize the link between mental health services and learning. Before drama therapy was a recognized or credentialed field, however, ENACT had to work hard to define itself in a changing climate and had to negotiate both traditional arts and traditional mental health funding. Furthermore, funds coming from the state level were disseminated to more traditional social service agencies with licensed therapists.

The World Trade Center tragedy of September 11, 2001 had an important impact on this situation. Many students who had been affected by the disaster were not requesting counseling services. They did not want the stigma of being in therapy. In response, schools were worried and looking for alternative approaches that would be less stigmatizing. By this time, ENACT had earned a reputation for reaching and empowering troubled students. Many in New York City schools had come to see us as the "resource of choice." As a result, more and more teachers were requesting ENACT programs in their classrooms to work with students to address their feelings of shock and fear. New York City's Central Board of Education awarded ENACT a contract to specifically address prevention and intervention in response to the effects of the disaster on students. The tragedy had given many in the school system a new understanding of trauma and its documented effects on student functioning.

After the September 11th tragedy, ENACT continued to be the only organization in the New York City school system that used the arts and drama therapy techniques to teach social-emotional skills. The agency was honored by the American Group Psychotherapy Association (AGPA) for its "creative approach to group counseling." Foundations that had funded more traditional arts or mental health programs in the past were now looking at ENACT and drama therapy with new eyes. More and more opportunities finally were becoming available to work in schools, aided by New York State's decision to certify creative arts therapists and grant licenses to organizations in the field.

Around this time, ENACT received a grant from the Ford Foundation to evaluate its best practices. ENACT had grown rapidly in a few years, and there was a need to closely evaluate programs and monitor quality. Staff also needed ongoing training and support. ENACT responded by providing staff with enhanced supervision and a series of specialized trainings. The grant from the Ford Foundation, which viewed our program as a unique addition to the arts education field, helped ENACT to hire specialists in education, psychology and the arts. Together, they took a focused look at ENACT's best practices for working with troubled youth, as we continued to adjust and improve classroom climate. At about the same time, the United Way of New York was seeking to fund programs that were successful in preventing school drop-out in the city's highest risk schools. They awarded ENACT a multi-year contract to address this growing issue. In addition, ENACT responded to the changing needs of the school system by expanding its program design to include individual and small group work. These new programs were facilitated by social workers and/or drama therapists. We also developed another integral component of ENACT: developing original plays that explored current social issues and brought professional theater performances with ENACT's professional actors to the schools. This component of our programming expanded to include a repertory of plays for elementary, middle and high school students that were presented in school auditoriums. On occasion, plays were also performed for the broader public in an effort to increase community awareness around major issues, such as the effects of September 11th on students.

ENACT's 20-year evolution has coincided with both the growing needs of New York City public schools and the emergence of the field of drama therapy. Recent breakthroughs in the field of social-emotional education, spearheaded by Daniel Goleman (1995), have been instrumental in increasing awareness of the important link between social-emotional functioning and academic achievement. In fact, a bill recommending the inclusion of social-emotional education in the New York State school curriculum was signed by former New York State Governor Pataki in January, 2007. Social-emotional education seems to share quite a few goals with drama therapy, such as building self-awareness, developing social awareness and relationship skills, improving self-management, fostering responsible decision-making skills, developing the capacity for empathy and effecting behavior change. We are grateful that the New York City school system has become increasingly aware of the mental health needs of all students, including inner-city youth–a group that we believe has long suffered from unrecognized trauma.

ENACT has always held true to its mission to address the needs of struggling students by engaging them at their own level of development within the school environment. Drama therapy and the theater's powerful tools engage students in a process of emotional integration, which is especially important for the students we serve. Today, ENACT continues its work in poor urban neighborhoods with high rates of crime, drug and alcohol abuse. In these environments, we can reach students who may never otherwise have the opportunity to access much-needed services.

THEORY AND PRINCIPLES

The ENACT Method Draws from a Cross-Disciplinary Approach

When ENACT began teaching in the New York City School system, we were asked to work in special education classes within a regular school setting. The classes were small and contained, and were run by both a teacher and an assistant teacher or paraprofessional. This setting proved to be quite conducive to drama therapy work, because it already was a supportive and contained environment. We began working with students labeled developmentally-delayed, with difficulties ranging from autism to mild retardation. Additionally, some students were severely physically and emotionally challenged. Working consistently with these young people, we had the opportunity to learn how to connect with them and endeavored to respond to their needs in an authentic way. As a result, the students began to guide us, through their responses, showing us the level at which they could learn and we should teach. To this day, we are thankful for their guidance. Our work with these students became the basis for the founding principles upon which much of ENACT's work is based.

It was through this experience that we at ENACT learned about and began to implement a developmental approach to teaching (Wenar, 1994). As we worked to join students (work with them at their emotional and physical level of development), to connect authentically with their ongoing needs, and to move at a pace that was developmentally appropriate for them, we began to see profound improvements in social and emotional functioning. Our experience with these students also made clear the importance of creating a therapeutic alliance. As time went on, the ENACT approach that we developed included creative applications of joining and working with every student at their level of development–in terms of age and functioning. Today, ENACT staff are trained in this methodology, and they continue to utilize and teach these concepts and practices as necessary foundations for facilitating growth and change with any population.

Joining: The Discovery of Theater as a Powerful Means of Connection

Before we could thoughtfully teach our methodology to others, including classroom teachers anxious to reach their students, we felt the need to explore more closely why it was that students were responding so quickly to our work in such a meaningful way. We had already identified and named some key concepts–such as working developmentally, joining, and forming a safe space or what we call the *creative container.* However, we needed more analysis of our work. Through this examination, we found that the importance of joining and empathy seemed to underpin much of our particular application of theater games and role playing techniques.

In our work at ENACT, the drama therapist/actor-instructor must be open and receptive to the thoughts, feelings, and needs of the client/student in order to create scenarios and characters that reflect the client's/student's feelings and experiences. In much of our work, the drama therapist and actor-instructor becomes a vessel that both holds and reflects back students' feelings in the characters they portray in the scene work. As a crucial element of the therapeutic alliance, empathy validates the students' experiences and forges a connection. We found this empathetic connection was an essential element in our work. In fact, understanding the importance of this connection led us to a discovery of one of our key dramatic role play techniques, which we call *externalizing the unspoken* and which we have used with individuals of various ages and abilities, both in verbal and nonverbal ways. By bringing to surface unspoken thoughts and feelings in a distanced creative or metaphoric way, clients feel seen and heard and ultimately safe enough to speak (if they can) about an experience, because the group leader has already revealed it in the scene work in a nonjudgmental way. In our experience, this approach has had a profound impact while working with characteristically unreachable, nonverbal autistic children, as seen in the Moon Man example below.

Working with Autistic Children: A Visit to the Moon Man

A group of about 12 severely autistic,

nonverbal children were wandering around the classroom when the ENACT drama therapist and actor-instructor entered their classroom. The children did not seem disturbed by our presence, because they continued wandering around the room, spinning in circles and playing with toys in cognitively disconnected ways. Despite their teacher's efforts to get their attention, they continued what they were doing. Finally, the three of us, the teacher and ENACT staff, were able to guide the students into a circle by having them hold hands to keep them from wandering away. We started the session by moving together. Some children made little sounds, others just swayed back and forth. We moved together in the circle, round and round in slow motion, and did various other simple exercises and techniques, using sound and movement, to assess the kids' level of functioning and to see how we might connect with them.

We did connect to some extent, but we wanted to connect in a deeper way. We sensed the feelings of isolation that these children seemed to be experiencing, and we wanted to join them, to let them know that we understood. After the class, we brainstormed about the best way to do this, and we came up with the following day's main activity. We were going on a journey to outer space to visit a man in the moon who was very sad, because no one understood him and he could not speak anyone else's language. One instructor was the pilot of the rocket ship. The other took up the rear, and the teacher stood in the middle, helping the kids get on the ship. We stopped and started several times, imitating the rocking back and forth as the ship slowed and accelerated. The children loved the movement. Once we reached our destination, we journeyed out of the spaceship and onto the moon, moving in slow motion as we looked for the moon man.

Suddenly, we heard sounds coming from behind a large rock (the desk). It was the moon man (the ENACT actor-instructor hidden under a flowing, purple piece of material). He was making soft longing sounds. We asked the students if they heard it, and told them that the moon man was very shy and that they would have to be gentle with him. The moon man cautiously came around the rock and continued to make calling sounds. Then we asked one of the more outgoing students if he wanted to come up and greet the man in the moon.

Excited, the student came forward and gently touched the moon man, who jumped back in fear. The student seemed very concerned for the creature. Knowing that this child could make sounds, we suggested that if he repeated back what the moon man said, the moon man might feel more comfortable. The moon man said "aah," and the student repeated the sound. The moon man laughed and jumped up and down. The student was very happy. Another student then came forward and greeted the moon man. We were very surprised when he presented the moon man with an imaginary gift, and the moon man jumped with joy. The student smiled. One by one on their own, other students stepped forward. They each presented the moon man with a gift and the moon man responded with joy. Finally, we encouraged another student who made sounds to repeat the sounds of the moon man and see what would happen. The moon man said "ooo"; the student said "OOO." The moon man said "hello"; the student (who normally only makes sounds and does not speak) said "hello." The moon man jumped for joy. We then explained to the students that the moon man was happy, because someone on earth was communicating with him. It was a very moving experience. Soon after, it was time to return to earth. The moon man said good-bye, and, in unison, all of the students said good-bye. The moon man disappeared behind the rock, and we journeyed back to earth.

Although, as a class, we could not really talk about what had just happened, there seemed to be an authentic understanding and a true connection in the room. The ENACT actor-instructor came out from behind the desk and removed the material, showing the students that the moon man was not real. They each got under the purple cover and made believe they were the man in the moon, moving and making sounds.

Over the years, we have had many experiences like these, which have led us to conclude that students respond to ENACT work in a meaningful way, because our drama therapists and actor-instructors use their empathy and artistry to gauge what the children are feeling and to reflect those feelings back to students on an emotional level–this, of course, is an essential skill for any instructor. In the moon man exercise, we externalized the students' feelings of isolation through the metaphor of the lonely moon man, with whom they then communicated. This joining technique helped them feel validated and understood which propelled their willingness to learn to communicate.

Role Playing as an Opportunity to Connect

Much of ENACT's work takes place in inner-city schools with middle school students who have been labeled as having various behavior problems, ranging from acting out to withdrawal. Normal adolescence is a period of rapid change and turmoil (Caissy, 1994). Since individuals at this stage in life generally have not mastered how to express their inner turmoil, they often display defensive behaviors that can be destructive and counterproductive. This often results in conflict. While many of the artful defenses these students have developed serve to block out strong, unwanted feelings (such as intense anger and fear), they also keep students locked into unhealthy behavioral patterns. Over the years, we have seen time and again how these defensive masks and roles are adopted when students feel the need to guard against particularly distressful emotions, such as shame, embarrassment and grief.

The inner-city students ENACT works with are exposed to higher than average levels of crime and report that they are exposed to violence on a regular basis. Some are in gangs. They often live in housing projects, foster homes and/or neglectful living conditions (Ravitch & Viteritti, 2000). In our opinion, these young people are victims of their circumstances. Fighting against both internal and external obstacles on a regular basis can cause anyone to become highly anxious or depressed. A combination of age, culture, socioeconomic circumstances and failure in school tend to cause students to display behaviors that are inappropriate. This occurs not only because students have not mastered a positive means to express their inner turmoil, but also because their environmental conditions are not conducive to healthy and adaptive functioning. These students get labeled "at risk" and often label themselves as "bad students." They anticipate the type-casting or labeling that routinely occurs within the school system. Knowing they are bound for a label, students will be the first ones to say, "We are the bad ones, right?" They begin to see their bad behavior as who they are, as who their peers are. These negative, narrowly-defined labels are roles that, from a drama therapy perspective, could benefit from rethinking.

Drama therapist Robert Landy's "Role Method" (1993, 1994, Chapter 5) offers clients the opportunity to expand, revise and seek balance within their *role system.* It is a very useful approach to draw from in helping adolescents see that they can both get stuck and expand the repertoire of roles they play in their lives. ENACT's role play methods gives students the chance to both observe and revise their limited self-perceptions in a protective, shame-free environment. In ENACT scene work, for example, students have the chance to see themselves in a safe way, as the actors portray students in nonjudgmental ways. In this way, ENACT instructors guide students, helping them to discover more effective ways to manage troubling feelings.

In chaotic classrooms that do not have adequate support systems in place, well-meaning teachers often contribute to the escalation of bad student behavior. Teachers "throw salt in students' wounds" by punishing them for acting out, while at the same time not helping them learn new coping skills. These types of teacher-student confrontations often and unfortunately shame students in front of their peers; ironically, it is students' desire not to feel shame that precipitates acting out in the first place. Because students may not have the emotional tools to understand and regulate their behavior, they typically rely on the defensive behavior they know for protection. ENACT has always been interested in reading adolescent behavior as a protective role and an indicator of the level of distress a student may be experiencing. In fact we see these roles as opportunities to connect with and gain access to our students by portraying these behaviors nonjudgmentally in our scene work. In this way, we use theater as an agent for change that helps students access their creativity and transform their lives. When working with a group of students for a long period of time, we often create *culminating performances,* an empowering process that redirects and transforms student behavior.

Our three-year research/evaluation grant from the Ford Foundation allowed us to study our best practices and confirm these beliefs. Experts in child psychology and movement therapy, cultural specialists and theater artists worked together to help define verbal and nonverbal indicators of emotional distress and all agreed on one thing: the observable behavior some students exhibit such as acting out and withdrawal are most likely more serious indicators of trauma, such as dissociation or the fight/flight response, which are most effectively addressed in a safe, nonthreatening environment. The role play and safe space we create in our work were studied and seen as conducive to behavior change, brought about by the combination of artistic and therapeutic means.

A Case for Reading Behavior as an Indication of Trauma

According to research by child trauma experts at Stanford University, "as many as one-third of children living our country's violent urban neighborhoods have PTSD . . . Children who survive urban warfare suffer from PTSD, too. The violence, layers of it overlapping year after year, can eventually take up residence in the children's minds. Like combat veterans, they develop post traumatic stress disorder, the soldier's sickness" (Tucker, 2007).

Peter Levine, a highly respected somatic trauma expert and author of the book *Waking the Tiger* (Levine, 1997), gives examples of life events that without proper treatment result in traumatic symptoms: the loss of a parent or close family member; physical injuries; sexual, physical and emotional abuse, including abandonment or witnessing violence. Unfortunately, these are common events for many of the students with whom we work.

Levine's theories show how the body not only internalizes trauma, but tries to release it. This may explain some of the behaviors students exhibit, including acting out. Levine, who based his findings on years of research on animals' reactions to trauma, shows that symptoms of trauma stem from a residue of energy that has become frozen and not been resolved or discharged. He explains the confusion that accompanies human response to trauma and sets the stage for what he calls the "Medusa Complex- the drama called trauma." Levine states, "We may literally freeze in fear, which will result in the creation of traumatic symptoms" (Levine, 1997). This kind of dissociation is commonly seen in students who seem to space out or appear quite disconnected from the classroom experience.

Levine's work and that of other somatic therapists, as well as multicultural experts, can help us interpret the behavior of students who act impulsively and with exaggerated physical reactions to what seem like the smallest incidents or events. Clearly, those who work with students and who may not have experience with trauma need better ways to observe, note and respond to behavior that is itself a response to trauma. At ENACT, we often witness in our students a compulsive desire to replay traumatic events. We see students choose to play out the same roles and violent situations, over and over again, whenever they have an opportunity to create original scene work. For example, they may want to replay the drive-by shooting in an attempt to negotiate the trauma.

As drama therapists, we must exercise caution in these instances so as to avoid the possibility of retraumatization. By redirecting student energy, offering alternative roles, and empowering students with new choices that help them release their frozen energy, students begin to discharge energy in healthier ways. Studying physical behavior as an expression of internal forces reinforces our belief that the defensive armor (body language) that students use to form their own protection can actually be used to help them develop a conscious awareness of their feelings, which eventually leads to opportunities for transformation.

The Body as an Emotional Storehouse

When the path to awareness is blocked, individuals are less likely to experience healthy social and emotional functioning. When individuals are not in touch with their feelings, they are less likely to be spontaneous in movement and action. In fact, sometimes physical ailments develop in response to repressed feelings. We have heard many times students say they "don't feel well" or put their heads on their desks and complain of stomach aches. Ultimately, these students habituate these locked physical patterns and become cut off from their own bodily experience (Upledger, 1996).

Observing body language and understanding its origins is very useful in building self-awareness. At ENACT, our actor-instructors, in the characters they play during scene work, use their own bodies to portray the masked feelings or defended body armor of our students. We recognize the behavioral problems as signs of unresolved stress and trauma and use theater arts and drama therapy approaches as opportunities to portray the student experience so that we may help them connect to their feelings as a first step of therapeutic intervention.

Resistance

During our work with students, we have observed that *resistance* is common, especially during adolescence. Adolescents will go to extreme measures to protect themselves from shame and other intense feelings. Any therapeutic or teaching process aimed at increasing self-awareness can trigger heightened resistance. Resistance in adolescents can manifest in any number of ways, including a refusal to participate, highly defensive body language, irritability, and sabotage. In fact, ENACT drama therapists and actor-instructors monitor student resistance to measure how well they are joining the group. ENACT workshop leaders are trained to be aware of resistance and student affect level as a way of measuring their effectiveness in aligning with students. ENACT activities are adjusted according to the readiness and responsiveness of a group. In our view, students' responses to an activity are a reflection of their ability to tolerate both the emotional and intellectual challenge of the exercise. It is very important not to infantilize group members by choosing an activity that is not appropriate to their intellectual or emotional developmental level or their culture.

Overcoming Resistance: The Story of Tina

When ENACT's creator, Diana Feldman, first met Tina, she would not say hello or acknowledge her at all. She appeared quite angry and distrustful as demonstrated by her lack of eye contact, vocal tone and disregard of Diana's presence. Tina was in a special education class as a result of her behavior, but she clearly appeared quite intelligent. She was very resistant to learning and acted out often. In addition, English was her second language, and this added to her frustration. Each day, when Diana entered the room, she said hello, and Tina made a point of turning her back to her and ignoring her. Her body language was her armor. Her arms were always crossed, and her lips clenched tight. "Don't mess with me" was what she exuded. Diana kept her distance, respecting Tina's boundaries. However, every day she invited Tina to participate. Every day, Tina declined.

One day during the scene work, Diana created a character that was a student who was extremely defensive when her teacher asked her to come up and write on the blackboard. This behavior reflected many students in the class, so as not to put Tina on the spot. With exaggerated body language (crossed arms and shutdown emotions), the character refused to do what the teacher asked, saying, "Leave me alone!" Following the scene, Diana asked the class if they knew why this character was acting this way on the outside and how she was feeling on the inside. Tina's arm went up. She said that the character did not trust anybody, that she had the right to be that way, that the teacher was embarrassing her and that the teacher did not know what the student had been through. Diana agreed with Tina, validating her feelings.

Over the next few days, Diana worked with students on many scenes that explored the idea of trust. One day, Tina volunteered to be part of the scene work. She wanted to do a scene about living in a group home. She played the counselor that kept putting a young woman on the spot, asking her, in front of others, to clean up. In the discussion that followed, Tina revealed that she had been moved from group home to group home and was now back at her birth home taking care of her elderly father. She had come to the United States from another country and never really had a solid living situation. English was not her first language. As she talked about her situation, her body language became more open. Her defenses melted away as she was able to verbalize her feelings. That year ENACT performed one of their plays off-Broadway. We asked Tina if she would like the topic of group homes to be in the show, because we realized that it might heighten awareness for some audience members. We asked if we could use the scene that she created. Tina was delighted. After the play, during our group discussion with the audience, Tina stood up and talked about the difficulties of caring for an elderly parent and living in a group home to an audience of 200 adults. She had found her voice. At the end of the year, Tina said to Diana, "Thank you, this was the best thing that ever happened in my life!" That was unexpected.

Distance, Connection, and Catharsis

Recognizing the importance of ensuring that students feel safe and protected, the ENACT method asks instructors to make careful judgment calls on the degree of distance they use in scene work to safely address students' core feelings. Instructors assess the distance that is required based on the amount of trauma associated with a given situation. Students confirm that the right amount of space for safe emotional connection has been achieved when they begin to feel comfortable naming and talking about their feelings.

ENACT's drama therapists and actor-instructors work together carefully to construct scenes that are inspired by student experiences, but are also removed from the particulars of any given situation, so as not to risk putting any student on the spot. In the composition of a scene, the drama therapist and actor-instructors carefully examine a given situation to find the *aesthetic distance* that is required to effectively engage students. According to sociologist T. J. Scheff, "At aesthetic distance, there is a balance of thought and feeling. There is a deep emotional resonance, but also a feeling of control" (Scheff, 1979). On many occasions we have seen how a safe connection creates a *catharsis.* According to somatic body workers, this indicates a release of frozen or blocked energy.

A group that has a similar approach to ENACT is "STOP-GAP," a California-based nonprofit theater that uses professional actors and drama therapists to deliver their programs (see Chapter 14). While their work takes place in more clinical settings, they make use of the art of theater to help clients ultimately become more self-aware. Both ENACT and STOP-GAP recognize that actors (with proper training) can be used as a safe vehicle to stimulate clients' feelings. What STOP-GAP calls *empathic embodiment* is similar to the technique used by ENACT actors who must take on the feelings of the group or client in order to stimulate self-awareness and discussion. ENACT's specific approach to distancing involves artists creating a specialized kind of parallel scenario to help youth unearth core feelings without exposing or shaming anyone. In a similar way, STOP-GAP never plays out a client's direct story. Instead, STOP-GAP uses their *Make the Menu* technique to lay out the scene. Both groups make use of the collective group experience to help stimulate self-awareness and offer tools to manage feelings.

Distance, Connection, and Catharsis: A School Shooting

A middle school principal asked ENACT to visit her school to help address an event that had occurred a few days earlier: a shooting of a neighborhood child in the school parking lot. The students were confused, because it appeared that some parents were telling their children not to come to school without protection, while the school instructed the students not to carry weapons and to report any students who were. Moreover, the students were shutting down and noncommunicative when teachers and counselors attempted to talk about the incident.

When drama therapist Diana Feldman

entered the school to meet with the principal and find out more about the situation, she was told that the principal was in the auditorium addressing angry parents who were threatening to bring in baseball bats to protect their children, unless the school took more action. Diana met the principal in the hallway as she was striding towards the auditorium. "The kids are all clammed up," the principal said, "they will not discuss the event and many are not showing up for school. Their parents are very angry and scared about the incident." The principal had no time to discuss it further; she continued to run down the hall back to the auditorium.

The bell soon rang, and Diana met her first group of students. They were very quiet when she entered the classroom. Diana had to find a way to connect with them, so she explained that she ran a theater group that worked in schools. With her actor-instructor partner, she demonstrated a scene and some theater games, and she asked the students if they would be interested in participating. She made sure to tell them it was optional. She spent this first day simply doing theater games and scene work, explaining that actors need to be in touch with their feelings.

The session went well, and Diana knew that the next day she would do a scene that would open up discussion. She needed to construct a scene that would give the students the right distance to feel safe enough to discuss their feelings about the shooting without feeling overwhelmed. That evening, she consulted with a child psychologist to help her hone in on a proper diagnosis, so that she could frame the scene around the students' core feelings. Based on the knowledge that students were receiving mixed messages from parents and teachers, the therapist and Diana concluded that mixed messages were causing a kind of cognitive dissonance or a conflicted emotional state that was holding students hostage and keeping them from moving forward. In response to the conflicting messages from teachers and their own parents, students were clamming up. A very skilled and long-time ENACT actor-instructor devised a scene that spoke to this cognitive dissonance. The scene would take place at a local Gap store where a student (the actor-instructor) was employed and up for a promotion and a raise. On the particular day that the scene was taking place, the employee was asked by his manager to move some damaged sweaters to a rack at the back of the store. As the employee was following his manager's directions, a regional supervisor entered the store and gave him a different directive, contradicting the store manager's order.

In presenting this scene, Diana froze the scene at the moment when the employee was weighing his options. In an inner monologue, the employee talked about his confusion, about not knowing what to do or which manager he should listen to. The students were fully engaged in the scene. In a process of careful facilitation, Diana asked the students to describe what was going on in the scene and whether or not they felt it was realistic. After agreeing that the scene was indeed realistic, the students talked about situations in which they got mixed messages. She asked them how the character was feeling, and they said, "confused." She asked them what they do when they are confused and feel at odds with different messages.

At this point, they began to describe the recent shooting. The conversation about their parents' and teachers' reactions was completely without judgment. The students talked about the pressure they felt in going to school unprotected or even showing up for class at all. They spoke about the pressure they felt in being asked to report anything that seemed suspicious, as if this was the only thing that the teachers wanted them to discuss. Diana asked the students what people do when they don't know who to listen to or which way to turn. "I don't speak," one student said, "When my teachers ask me my opinion, I stay quiet." This comment opened up the discussion for the rest of the group. They talked about the conflicting messages they were getting from their family and the school, as well as about peer alliances.

As they discussed the incident, one student explained that she gets stomach aches when she is really upset. By the end of the facilitation, the students felt validated and the group was able to identify some positive coping strategies, such as naming their feelings of confusion and speaking to a third party. Some students even volunteered to get direct counseling following the session.

ENACT METHOD AND TECHNIQUES

The Role of Actor Instructors and Drama Therapists

ENACT work in the classroom is facilitated by either a drama therapist and an actor-instructor or two actor instructors–a lead actor instructor and a supporting actor instructor–with specialized skill sets. Actor instructors are trained in the ENACT method by drama therapists, and they have core skills that include: acting, directing, behavior management (including prevention and intervention techniques), group management, the developmental use of theater games, and scene work and facilitation skills. To be most effective, actor instructors must have strong improvisational acting skills, as well as knowledge of the school, neighborhood and cultural make-up of the group with which they are working. In fact, every effort is made when casting an ENACT residency to match the cultural background of the actor instructors with the school's student population. In addition, ideally actor instructors must be able to play the ages of the students with which they are working. Their versatility, including the ability to play a wide range of characters with a variety of affects, is crucial. Actor instructors must also possess the spontaneity needed to adjust activities on the spot in order to respond to students' shifting needs and meet them at their level. This type of meeting is a first step in the joining process, which helps to preempt or ward off resistance from students.

Before scheduling each residency, ENACT staff conduct a teacher needs assessment, which gives the opportunity to assess the cultural make-up of each class, class dynamics, as well as any other pertinent issues or events that occurred at the school and in the neighborhood. This allows ENACT to select the best team of actor instructors for each residency. At times, if a given set of students is struggling with a particularly challenging situation (such as the school shooting discussed above), ENACT will staff a residency with an actor instructor and a licensed drama therapist, instead of two actor instructors.

Cultural considerations play an important role in every residency. In order to effectively assess students' responses, therapists and instructors must have an appropriate cultural lens through which to view the process. As part of ongoing training, ENACT drama therapists and actor instructors receive training from various professional advisors, including: drama therapists, child psychologists, movement therapists, conflict resolution specialists and multicultural specialists, in order to become more familiar with their students' cultures.

The ENACT Workshop

On the surface, ENACT's work in the

classroom resembles a typical New York City arts education residency that either teaches an art form or is used to enhance classroom curriculum. However, ENACT's end goal is different. ENACT uses the art form of drama as a vehicle to help students become more self-aware and to learn better ways to manage their feelings. In the ENACT model, two highly trained ENACT actor-instructors, supervised by drama therapists, engage students in interactive in-class workshops. ENACT classroom residencies are often scheduled during the English Language Arts or Social Studies class periods. Some program designs also include *pull-out sessions,* where students who have been identified as at-risk (for example, those with high absenteeism, those who are chronically late and those living in foster homes) are pulled out of class for special sessions and/or after-school workshops. In addition, when needed to strengthen the mental health component of our program, ENACT offers a more comprehensive wrap-around model. This model places a full-time social worker or drama therapist at the school to offer support to both students and their families. This model has been so successful in addressing the high drop out rate in New York City schools, that it was recently included in a New York City Council Bill.

The basic structure of ENACT work in the classroom is similar to that of many creative arts programs. Each session has a warm-up, a main activity, and closure. During the warm-up, we use theater games, metaphor, sound, and movement to introduce the social-emotional theme for the day, which usually grows out of prior assessment in the classroom. We use these exercises to bypass resistance and to help students reconnect with their own bodies. After the warm-up, the main activity is a scene performed by the drama therapist-actor and actor-instructor that explores an issue that is relevant to the entire group. The intention of the scene is to promote self-awareness as a first step toward transformation. During this phase of the session, we plant a core issue or feeling in a generalized, distanced context as a way of safely exposing it to students. A facilitated discussion and replay of the scene follows. This discussion period helps students become aware of their feelings so that they can ultimately learn positive tools for communication and expression. At the end, closure offers opportunities to use words and gestures to help students integrate the day's work and what they learned into their bodies and minds. Sometimes, we play additional games to assess the impact of the day's work and plan for the next lesson.

The Foundation of Protection: The ENACT Creative Container

Creating a sense of safety and support is an essential element of ENACT work and it permeates every aspect of what we do. This sense of safety is especially important for students who have experienced trauma. Since we do not work in a clinical setting, we take extraordinary measures to avoid overwhelming students and to create the best conditions for learning and healing to take place. Many of the school environments in which ENACT works are chaotic, with students banging on doors and running in and out of classrooms, constant interruptions over the school's public announcement system, students being pulled out of class, and the like (Glasser, 1990). As a result, it often takes time to establish a safe physical and emotional play space that allows for the deeper ENACT self-awareness work to take place. We build the ENACT *Creative Container* to create a secure and trusting environment that reassures students and gives them the freedom to explore and take creative risks as they learn important social-emotional skills and become more self-aware (Mackenzie, 1996).

In ENACT practice, we often work in a circle when possible, because this configuration gives us access to various built-in creative behavioral control elements. We also establish group agreements, which, out of respect for the classroom teacher, sometimes include already established classroom rules. In some cases, ENACT instructors will write contracts with the students that list group rules and consequences for breaking them. Consequences for rule-breaking are created to protect students, not punish them. ENACT instructors will also describe how to use creative directives, such as *freeze* and *focus,* which are terms used on movie sets as creative control techniques. All of these elements contribute to the development of a protected space that everyone in the classroom collaboratively creates. This collective effort proves effective as students become invested in following rules they co-created. These are all elements of the creative container, which includes the establishment of both personal and group responsibility and other ENACT core values, such as trust, compassion and nonjudgment.

Just as we draw from the theater world–using professional actors, stage directives, and improvisation to engage students–we also use many concepts and practices from drama therapy to inform and guide our work in ensuring that students feel safe. We employ joining practices such as reflecting students' feelings and behaviors in scene work, which enables us to build trusting, nonjudgmental relationships with students. In addition, the use of distance in scene work creates the space and safety students need in order to connect with the work at their own level of readiness. Finally, the developmental progression of in-class activities fosters class cohesion, which facilitates the assessment of students' functioning. All of these drama therapy concepts–joining, distance and working developmentally–help us to create a bridge from the external workshop experience to students' internal experiences.

The ENACT container is a carefully constructed safe space that provides the optimal conditions for expression and growth. In this safe space, students are supported and validated while they engage in theatre games and scene work that teach essential social-emotional skills and foster self-awareness. The container is a fundamental principal in our work, aligning us with our humanistic core values.

During the evaluation that was supported by the Ford Foundation, ENACT elected to use an action-based research model. During this process, evaluators observed ENACT practitioners in the process of creating the container. In this active way, evaluators examined and identified our best practices for safely engaging students in our work. The action research team ultimately defined the ENACT container as:

> . . . a safe space that values the human spirit and provides emotional boundaries that neither overwhelm emotions nor distances them, a key factor that can impede the learning process. The container ultimately acts as a bridge, calling on the use of external experience to connect to internal experience, ultimately allowing for self knowledge. Students are regularly given opportunities for self-reflection and an increase in self-awareness. In this environment, ENACT teaching artists deliver a social-emotional curriculum, whereby children are routinely given chances to express their emotions, make personal connections, learn new skills and modify their behavior. (ENACT, 2005, p. 1)

This evaluation revealed the advantages of creating a safe container in a classroom: the development of group cohesion and trust, which create the optimal conditions for learning. A good container provides a nurturing environment that decreases resistance, creating an avenue for growth and learning.

Warm-Up Games

For adolescents, especially those with behavioral problems, the warm-up period is essential. It sets up the boundaries of the safe, creative space that develops through the group dynamic. It creates community and introduces and enforces ENACT core values. In the warm-up phase of the workshop, we begin to form the creative container as we assess and address the group's needs by carefully gauging their physical and verbal responses to activities.

The work of drama therapist David Read Johnson, especially his "Developmental Transformations" (1982, Chapter 6), was influential in the development of ENACT's warm-up practice. In this phase of the workshop, warm-up begins with all students participating in unison, and then transitions to exploring interpersonal structures before any demands are placed on individual students. Group exercises involve all students simply imitating the leader. This is the safest way to foster group cohesion. Once instructors see that a group is able to complete an exercise in unison and without interruption, they know that they have created a contained environment and that the students are able to move to the next phase of theater games.

In the next phase, interpersonal games offer students a chance to relate to each other. This step, which occurs near the beginning of the session, gives students the opportunity to build trust without risking feelings of shame. In addition, these exercises do not overwhelm students by placing demands on them that they cannot tolerate. Once instructors see that students can relate well with each other, without making fun of each other and hopefully supporting one another, instructors move to the final phase, which involves the most risk-taking. This is the individual phase, where one student is called upon to demonstrate something for the group.

Overall, the warm-up phase in the ENACT model, like Phase One in Renée Emunah's "Integrative Five Phase Model" (Chapter 4), utilizes interactive techniques and exercises that engage students in a playful effort to build group trust.

Specialized Warm-Up Games to Address Resistance

Throughout our work, ENACT instructors strive to give students a sense of accomplishment. This is the first step in helping students to become aware of their behaviors and change them. Theater games are a great way to instill this sense of accomplishment and safety, which minimizes resistance.

Drama therapist Renee Emunah explains that "when the beginning exercises allow group members to express actual feelings, defenses are minimized" (Emunah, 1985, p. 73). Emunah suggests that "with this approach to drama therapy, clients have little to resist because they are allowed act as themselves; in fact they may even be encouraged to exaggerate their rebellious behavior" (p. 74). One of ENACT's theater games highlights defensive behaviors in a similar manner. In this game, instructors ask students to exaggerate their body language by showing the biggest attitude they can. They then ask students to bring their bodies back to a centered, grounded and relaxed position. In this way, highly defended students can become aware of their body language in a playful and safe way. Other games uncover the motivations that underlay defensive behavior. For example, instructors ask students to create tableaus that symbolize resistance. They encourage students to build group and/or individual statues that represent a variety of emotions, such as anger, sadness or fear. Once created, instructors work with students to find ways to uncover the underlying thoughts, needs and other feelings that precipitated the creation of these statues. Sometimes instructors ask students to interview members of the tableau, asking them what feelings their statues reflect. In this way, students learn to identify and name their own feelings, while becoming aware of similar and multidimensional feelings in others.

Instructors also use themselves as *reflective vessels,* meaning that they attempt to reflect what they perceive the group is feeling. They use metaphor, games, and reflective scene work. For example, if an instructor senses resistance in the room, he or she may employ a call-and-response exercise that externalizes the unspoken feelings of the group. In an exaggerated (distanced) way, the leader reflects what they are picking up from the room. The instructor might say, "I don't want to be here, it is so nice outside." The group repeats it. "I'm tired and hungry." The group repeats it. "I can't wait for lunch," and so on. As the instructor senses the group's resistance diminishing, he or she may say something like, "Well, I'm here anyway so I might as well have fun." The group repeats it. This exercise reflects and validates participants' feelings. Once these feelings are expressed and validated, students are ready to proceed with the activities.

Focusing on interpersonal skills, the next step in the process can be challenging, depending on the population. At ENACT, we often work with students who act out a great deal and have poor impulse control. Without structure, they often lose control and break all kinds of boundaries. The instructor must carefully design games that begin with a high level of structure and then "loosen the reins" as the group begins to feel safe and trust develops. In many cases, the initial introduction and the management of these games is the most challenging part for instructors, who must be persistent, strong, and patient. Without a sound container, it is almost impossible to move forward in any kind of productive way. With many groups, the instructor creates a contract with the students to elicit commitment and a sense responsibility in the work.

Since most adolescents fear looking or feeling infantile, especially in front of their peers, they often demonstrate a high degree of resistance. ENACT games are designed to safely redirect resistance. Once the instructor senses that resistance has dissipated, he or she can continue to build interpersonal skills, which include communicating, listening, cooperating, and resolving conflict. Adolescents must feel a sense of progress and accomplishment, and the instructor must artfully design games that both challenge students and allow for achievement. Conversely, games that are developmentally inappropriate may increase student resistance and spur increasingly problematic behavior.

In many ways, the ENACT warm-up is an opportunity to enlist students in building a new kind of community, one they might not have experienced at home or in school. It is a chance to create a supportive, responsible atmosphere that encourages creative expression and self-worth.

In summary, the ENACT warm-up:

- Creates a safe, structured container
- Addresses resistance
- Facilitates the assessment of the group dynamic
- Builds interpersonal and individual skills
- Instills a sense of accomplishment in students

Main Activity: Scene Work

Specialized scene work and the facilitation that follows it are the main activities in ENACT workshops. These activities make up the longest segment of the workshop (30 minutes). Facilitation usually includes a short period of reflective role play and discussion, a consciousness-raising phase.

ENACT scene work is the springboard for creating opportunities for self-reflection and awareness, which are essential to the process of fostering conscious change in students. In essence, the therapist and co-leader perform real-life scenes that are relevant to the group. These scenes are designed to resonate with the group and their life experience. Since we work in city schools, scenes usually focus on issues and conflicts typically seen in urban schools, such as peer pressure, violence, and teacher-student interaction. We usually survey teachers ahead of time to discuss common concerns–in the classroom, the school and the community.

ENACT role play and scene work are designed with a series of protective layers that are peeled away gently, to eventually and carefully expose students' core feelings. We begin by addressing student behavior, working from the external–the students' body armor. As the session continues, we gradually begin to explore core feelings that are buried under the armor. In scene work, by creating characters and situations to which students can relate, we attempt to *join* students. We validate their feelings, while increasing their awareness of their own behavior. Through scene work, we also give students a safe way to see that negative behaviors often lead to negative consequences. Students begin to see that type of behavior as self-defeating. Ultimately, students' defensive layers are peeled away and replaced by a new form of protection: naming one's feelings.

Through various creative methods, ENACT therapists and teaching artists carefully construct scenes that relate to student experience, but have enough aesthetic distance that they do not identify a given situation or put any particular student on the spot. During scene composition, drama therapists and teaching artists carefully approach a given scenario, balancing the need for distance with the need to engage students. If a scene does not have enough distance, we risk overwhelming students, flooding them with the very feelings they have been fighting to avoid. On the other hand, if the scene is too distanced, students will only relate to the scene from a cognitive place, which will not affect them in a meaningful way. Student responses tend to be very clear, and we use them to assess if scenes are on target. Once again, the body is a good indicator of connection.

Facilitation follows role play and scene work. This period gives instructors an opportunity to foster self-reflection in the students by asking questions that distance students from the scenes. In fact, instructors begin with questions that are more distanced and cognitive, like those that ask about particular facts and details in the scenes. The instructor then begins to ask less distanced and more affective questions in an attempt to bridge characters' emotions with those of the students. In each phase, the instructor seeks to create a safe space for reflection. Reflection leads to self-awareness, which triggers a cathartic release of held energy in the body. Outwardly, student response may seem small–a gesture, laughter or even a tear. However, this cathartic release indicates that the instructor has successfully facilitated a student's personal connection to the theme or core feeling in the scene. This level of self-awareness or connection is our central goal. At ENACT, we believe that removing a block to awareness creates a simultaneous shift or an opening up of perspective that makes true learning possible. As students are given the opportunity to name their feelings in the replay, the last phase of scene work, emotional integration, can begin to occur and can be read in the body.

Designing the Scene: Choosing the Context

We develop scenes around core feelings germane to the group or specific issues that emerge from our work with each group of students. Scenes are brief–less than two minutes. In presenting them, the therapist enlists the class in creating a safe container by asking them to say "quiet on the set," which makes them responsible for their own behavior. Carefully-designed characters in these scenes reflect inner behavior (needs and feelings) and outer behavior (physical defenses). Scene work is powerful, projecting behavior that is engaging, reflective, and affirming. Sara's story, above, is an example of this. Once again, creating the appropriate distance is key. Often this distance is achieved through characters and/or circumstances that parallel students' experiences.

To ensure that the therapist is in step with the group, she or he may ask the students if the scene seemed realistic and, if not, to say why. This is how the therapist begins to create trust, dialogue, and self-reflection. If she or he handles the discussion well, students feel seen, heard, understood, and respected. This discussion is one of the first ways a therapist can meet students where they are, bringing about self-awareness as thoughts, images, and feeling emerge. ENACT reflective scene work is a creative way to help students move past resistance and work toward behavior change. By enacting familiar situations that feature resistant (aggressive or withdrawn) characters, participants can safely see themselves. Sometimes, they even laugh at their own behavior. In addition, as the teaching artist/therapist verbalizes a character's underlying thoughts and feelings–saying things like "I am afraid I'll get in trouble," or "I am really angry"–underlying feelings are externalized, away from students' defense mechanisms and in a safe, validating space. Students feel less fear and are able to see and hear what they were defending against.

In summary, ENACT scene work:

- Evokes memories and emotions, while validating feelings
- Gives students a way to see and explore behaviors
- Safely externalizes core, unspoken feelings
- Creates opportunities for self-reflection by allowing students to safely explore a situation without judgment
- Highlights what students have in common and fosters bonding, which is very important to adolescents
- Creates an opportunity for real change as students feel joined and validated

The Facilitation Phase

The main goal of the facilitation phase is to use cognition to bring about conscious awareness of behaviors, needs, and feelings. The therapist is often aware of one or two specific students he or she wants to reach, but works with the entire group as a way to create group consciousness. After presenting a scene, through question and answer, the therapist gently guides students from a cognitive connection with the scene to a more affective connection to the material. Moving back and forth from cognitive and affective connections creates safety by providing cognitive distance from affect. The therapist moves from generalized to more specific questions like, "Does this kind of thing happen? Why?" or "Can you give examples of a similar situation?" and so on. Students have the opportunity to stop, think, and connect with their own experiences and feelings at their own pace and level of readiness. By focusing on more than one student's story and feelings, the leader avoids turning the session into work that would be more appropriate in a clinical setting.

ENACT leaders do not work in a clinical setting where students would be given follow-up to ensure safety and closure. As such, once students make a personal connection to a character, workshop leaders are very careful to focus on the character's experience, not the students'. The focus is always the character in the scene, encouraging students to come up with solutions and give the character suggestions. This engages students' intellect, not just their feelings. Triggering cognition is very important for students who have behavior and impulse control problems. It encourages them to think before they act and helps them avoid a quick regression to self-defeating behaviors, which often happens when students get lost in themselves or overwhelmed with feelings. The therapist asks students to come up with ideas for the character in the scene, exploring how the character could have more effectively handled the given situation. The therapist then distills these ideas, reframes them, and writes them on the blackboard. This prepares students for the final phase: replaying the scene, using new information and tools.

In summary, the facilitation process:

- Helps bring buried feelings to conscious awareness
- Validates thoughts, feelings and needs
- Helps the workshop leader identify indicators of connection
- Creates opportunities for transforming behavior
- Allows students to witness real-life scenarios in a supportive environment

The Replay

Replay occurs after a brainstorming phase, during which students explore how the scene they previously witnessed and discussed could change. During replay, students integrate the information they have learned in scene work and facilitation into their bodies and minds. One or more students usually volunteer to replace the actor and play the character that was the focus of the scene and discussion. The actor-student is set up to win, because the group discussed suggestions for a successful outcome to the scene in the facilitation phase. These suggestions were written on the board.

As students replay scenes, they practice naming feelings instead of choosing the less effective acting out behavior, demonstrated in the scene the first time it was played. Here, in this safe environment, students are able to practice making statements, for example, "I feel angry" instead of hitting. In some circumstances, when the therapist is aware that the student has poor impulse control, the therapist may stand behind the student as a coach, monitoring affect and control. The therapist may also decide to employ other drama therapy techniques, such as *role reversal* or *doubling,* both of which offer an empowering individual intervention for the student who has replaced the focus character.

It is amazing to watch students' behavioral transformations during replay. The most resistant and defensive students, when offered the opportunity to name their feelings, do so with bravery and pride. Often their extreme body language is replaced with an empowered verbal statement. The therapist also coaches students to develop other coping strategies, such as proper breathing and other relaxation techniques that will help them better express themselves, instead of acting out. By the end of the replay, the entire group responds with a round of applause, reinforcing the safe, supportive container that the leader is continually reinforcing.

In summary, the replay:

- Allows students to integrate the social-emotional skills they have learned
- Gives students an opportunity to learn how to express their feelings and needs
- Transforms resistance and creates a demonstrable, positive outcome
- Integrates in the student a feeling of felt-self
- Gives students a new sense of empowerment

The Closure

Closure brings each session to an end, instilling in participants a sense of completion. Closure gathers the emotional energy in the room and ritualizes it through theater games or affirmations, inviting students to use their minds and bodies to ground what they have just learned. Closure reinforces the group bond and leaves students with a sense of accomplishment and excitement. The students prepare to leave the safe container, a space that we hope they will internalize over time.

Special Concerns for the Drama Therapist

The drama therapist may encounter several challenges in a classroom setting. Just as the students want their peers to like them, the therapist may parallel that feeling and seek to be liked. While the therapist should be an ally to students, he or she is not their friend, nor should they pretend to be one. The nature of ENACT's aesthetic projective work can blur students' boundaries, so it is crucial for the leader to maintain his/her own boundaries. In addition, as in any therapeutic situation, countertransference can also occur. Many of the students are skilled at pushing buttons, and the therapist must be careful not to personalize student reactions or be reactive.

In addition to the blurring of boundaries, the precariousness of adolescence that the therapist sees in students often can remind the therapist of his or her own past. The therapist was once that age. Simply being back in a classroom, with its sights, sounds, and especially its smells, can create flashbacks and trigger memories. The therapist may have been teased or picked on as a child, or he or she may have been a bully. These dynamics can be even more challenging when the therapist suspects that a student may have suffered abuse or neglect. This can trigger the therapist's own fear and rage, driving him or her to want to be the student's savior. The therapist must remember that he or she is only a guide, helping participants to help themselves by transforming blocks that get in the way of authentic expression. The therapist cannot always create miracles. However, in doing this work, we believe that we support the creative potential and the divinity that each person possesses. Through drama therapy, we are able to help others. In many ways, this also allows us to tap into our own potential.

At ENACT, we have found that although the public school system is not always the optimal setting for drama therapy work, it is an environment where the application of drama therapy methods and techniques has great impact. If we believe our students are survivors of unrecognized trauma, they do not deserve to be overlooked or punished for their symptoms. One of our challenges at ENACT, then, has been to continually modify our approaches and techniques to meet the growing needs and challenges of the school system at large.

ENACT instructors also face many of the challenges classroom teachers face on a daily basis: small classrooms, large student enrollment, and administrative issues, such as scheduling conflicts and a lack of administrative support. All of these factors create obstacles in our work, especially in building and maintaining a safe container. For example, large numbers of students and highly chaotic classrooms pose a challenge to the establishment of group safety and trust, while also restricting therapists in providing individual attention and focus. As a result, we often spend a great deal of time continually creating and maintaining a safe container within the classroom. We also spend time on classroom management and coping with behavior difficulties before we can help individual students deal with their social and emotional needs. Furthermore, we must consider that the therapeutic solutions that seem appropriate in the classroom setting may not always be viable options in the daily lives of the culturally and economically diverse student populations we serve. The school system is changing rapidly in response to the growing needs of our children. The rise of school violence is our students crying out. Adolescents need attention in areas other than academics, and schools are desperately looking for solutions.

CASE STUDIES

Creating a Container for Safety and Growth: The Story of John

In 1991, we were working in a public high school's special education department with at-risk youth known mostly for acting out. We were asked to work with a class once a week for a double period. This was to be a full-year program, and we felt that we needed to work toward a culminating project. We planned to develop a performance piece that expressed students' needs and concerns.

The first day was not much of a challenge. Although students had a difficult time focusing their attention on the exercises for more than a few minutes, they seemed motivated by the process and excited about the goals. We explained that in order to meet the program's goals we had to set up agreements. We had been told that there was a big problem with absenteeism, so we decided to include regular attendance as one of the criteria for participating in the final production that was to take place at an off-Broadway theater.

On day two, John entered the room late, armed with a portable music player, a comb, and a lollipop in each hand. He was a very large teenager with an awkward walk and a focus that continually jumped from one thing to the next. Since John had missed the first day, he did not know about our class agreements. He continually interrupted and seemed hyperactive, unable to stand in one place for more than a minute. He was highly reactive. John had a way of upsetting everyone, including the facilitator.

As the year progressed, John continued to push the limits of the class. Each day was a struggle. John had a difficult time relating to other students and broke every rule set by the group. At the same time, he was a wonderful actor and had much to say. We wondered how we could get him to use his exceptional acting ability, while teaching him to contain his behavior at the same time. We spent a great deal of time redirecting and channeling his creative energy into the work, but he was still not willing to be a team player.

One day when John was late, one of the students suggested we kick him out. We knew that John really liked the acting process and felt this would be unfair without discussing it with him first. Just then, John entered the room. We discussed our concerns with him and told him we wanted him to be in the show, but could not continue to work with him this way. "What's going on?" we asked. John was honest. He explained that he had a really hard time controlling himself and that he would try to do so in the future. He pleaded with us to let him stay. We eventually drafted a contract and hung it on the wall. It included rules about not hitting, not cursing, being respectful, and being on time.

John agreed that after three warnings he, and anyone else who was disruptive, had to sit out of the acting circle until he was ready to participate productively with the group. If he continued to disrupt the class, he would be asked to leave. John did mess up a few times, but reigned in his own behavior and even stepped out of the circle before he was asked. He often apologized to the group and worked diligently on his lack of control. He was learning to take responsibility for his actions and began to see how these actions affected other people. He showed up every day and worked hard on improving his behavior. We continued to acknowledge him by reinforcing his positive attempts and successes. The work with John had a meaningful effect on the entire group as John's negative behavior was something to which each member could relate.

The night of the show, John stood backstage with the group. Everyone was holding hands. He had become an integral part of the group, and was saying a prayer for them all. For his work in the show, he got rounds of applause, and, in the audience discussion that followed, he was remarkable. One woman asked how everyone had worked so well as a group, and John volunteered a response, admitting, "At first it wasn't easy, but we all really tried." The group laughed. He had come through with shining colors, empowered with new understanding about his behavior.

This case story demonstrates how a contained environment that allows for choice, expression, and creativity can help a student who is labeled at-risk gain personal awareness and social skills.

Empathy in the At-Risk Classroom: The Story of Sara

Sara was a 16-year-old girl who was placed in a school day-treatment center at a hospital in New York City because of severe emotional problems. ENACT staff were told she almost never spoke. In fact, even when she worked with her psychiatrist, Sara used puppets to communicate. Sara always came to our workshops, but sat in the back, not saying a word. She held her head down, her body was turned into itself, and her eyes shot back and forth very quickly. We rarely saw her smile, but when she did, her entire face lit up. She vehemently refused to participate, although she took responsibility for her behavior by saying the agreed-upon word, "pass." She sat quietly in her chair, cautiously observing the activities of others. Although we always invited Sara to participate, we also respected her decision not to work. We assumed that when she was ready she would join us. Little by little, Sara participated in the group theater games and a smile broke out as she became a part of the group. She never participated in the scene work, though she watched intently.

One day, after speaking to the teacher about the students' needs, we agreed to do a lesson that dealt with abuse. Several of the girls in the group were in abusive relationships. We carefully designed a distanced scene that allowed the group to connect at its own pace and level of safety. The scene was about two old friends, who were going out to the movies. It was a date they had been planning for a long time, because it had been repeatedly called off. Amy's boyfriend, Jimmy, was very possessive and demanded that she be with him every Saturday night. This Saturday, Amy decided to spend the night with her friend Lisa, because she needed to feel more independent from her boyfriend.

Just as the two friends were about to leave, the phone rang, and it was Jimmy. He insisted that Amy drop her plans immediately and go directly to his house. Once again Amy was swayed, afraid Jimmy would leave her. She began to run out of the house. Lisa became furious, saying, "Why do you drop our plans over him? You don't care about me. He doesn't respect you anyway–he hits you. Why do you keep doing this?" The quarrel escalated, and the friends could not find resolution. At this point, the scene was frozen.

During the next part of the lesson, we began a question-and-answer session aimed at guiding the students to focus on relationships and feelings of dependency. Although the scene initially was developed to focus on the friends' relationship, the students quickly chose to tune in on the issue of abuse. As they made personal connections with the characters, they were anxious to name what was going on in the scene.

We stimulated further discussion by asking students what the friend who was being abandoned by Amy should do. Suddenly and unexpectedly, Sara murmured from her chair, "I know, it happened to me." We could barely hear her. "What?" we asked. "I know," she announced, in a much louder voice, "it happened to me!"

In order to maintain a safe aesthetic distance for Sara, we immediately refocused the discussion on the characters in the scene. I asked Sara if she wanted to role play the friend in the scene. She jumped up immediately and said to Amy in a voice that we had never heard from her, "Don't ever let anyone hit you. Do whatever you have to do, run away, call a hotline, but don't ever let anyone hit you!" Sara's entire body language had changed as she spoke in an empowered voice. Everyone in the group was surprised and moved, and applauded as Sara began to smile. Students came up and hugged her. Her teacher said Sara seemed like a different person. The school counselor was notified and continued to work with Sara.

When doing scene work with cases like Sara's, the therapist must carefully observe student behavior. When encountering resistance and acting out, the therapist must artfully employ distance as the scene is reflected back to the students, so that they can see themselves without judgment or feelings of shame.

CONCLUSION

Given the urgent need to reach resistant, often traumatized youth in inner-city schools–as well as the need to address alarming drop-out rates–schools are reaching out more and more for alternatives like ENACT. The ENACT model offers an engaging approach that compels students to reflect upon their lives and, drawing on their own creativity, learn vital social emotional skills. Through playful drama and drama therapy techniques, students find more productive ways to manage the feelings that often have derailed them in the past.

The ENACT creative container offers students a safe space to develop self-awareness and social awareness along with a host of other important life skills, including relationship and self-management skills. Developing scenes in the classroom that reflect students' life experiences, the ENACT approach validates students' feelings, fosters connections, and creates a nonjudgmental therapeutic alliance among teaching artists and students. Ultimately, facilitation helps students make connections with their own internal experiences. Within the safe space of the creative container, these connections are the foundation for reflection and growth.

Despite the challenges inherent in working in chaotic school environments that are not conducive to therapeutic growth, the ENACT method creatively externalizes and addresses the unspoken issues that plague students. With these opportunities, students who might otherwise languish have their rightful chance to develop increased self-awareness, growth and change.

REFERENCES

Caissy, G. A. (1994). *Early adolescence.* New York: Plenum Books.

Emunah, R. (1985). Drama therapy and adolescent resistance. *The Arts in Psychotherapy, 12,* 71–80.

ENACT. (2005). *Mid report to the Ford Foundation.* New York: ENACT.

Feldman, D. (1997). *ENACT workbook.* New York: ENACT Institute.

Glasser, W. (1990). *The Quality School: Managing students without coercion.* New York: Harper Collins Publishers, Inc.

Goffman, E. (1959). *The presentation of self in everyday life.* New York: Doubleday.

Goleman, D. (1995). *Emotional intelligence.* New York: Bantam.

Johnson, D. (1982) Developmental approaches in drama therapy. *The Arts in Psychotherapy, 9,* 183–189.

Landy, R. (1993). *Persona and performance.* New York: The Guilford Press.

Landy, R. (1994). *Drama therapy: Concepts, theories, and practices.* Springfield, IL: Charles C Thomas.

Levine, P. (1997). *Waking the tiger: Healing trauma.* Berkeley: North Atlantic Books.

Mackenzie, R. (1996). *Setting limits in the classroom.* Rocklin, CA: Prima Publishing.

Ravitch, D., & Viteritti, J. (2000). *City schools.* Baltimore, Maryland: John Hopkins University Press.

Scheff, T.J. (1979). *Catharsis in healing, ritual, and drama.* Berkeley: UC Press.

Tucker, J. (2007). *Urban warfare: America's shell-shocked children.* San Francisco Chronicle, August.

Upledger, J. (1996). *Somatoemotional release and beyond.* Palm Beach Gardens: UI Publishing, Inc.

Wenar, C. (1994). *Developmental psychopathology.* New York: McGraw-Hill, Inc.

FURTHER TRAINING

Diana Feldman, MA, RDT-BCT, Director
Visit our website at www.enact.org

Chapter 14

THE STOP-GAP APPROACH TO DRAMA THERAPY

Don Laffoon and Fionnuala Kenny

STOP-GAP is an interactive theatre company creating and delivering programs to a range of at-risk and in-need populations throughout Southern California. Having recently purchased an office in Costa Mesa, California, STOP-GAP operates as a not-for-profit corporation employing a company of directors, facilitators and independent professional actors, delivering over 1,000 programs each year. STOP-GAP programs are delivered to two distinct populations–educational programs (prevention) and drama therapy programs (intervention), which draw their funding from a range of sources, including foundations and corporations, individual donations and fee-for-service programs.

Not just live theatre, STOP-GAP is *LIFE* theatre–a theatre dedicated to working with people who wish to make a change in the way they understand, function in, and relate to the world around them. Based on ultimate respect for the individual and believing that individuals have the innate capacity to look into the heart of their situation and find their own answers, STOP-GAP is focused on using theatre to create the context for individuals to examine their situations and to pose creative solutions to the challenges they face. The theatre that STOP-GAP creates is spontaneous, dynamic and interactive. Each performance is unique, because a large part of each performance looks to the clients or students to create the narrative of the presentation. Each performance starts with a scene that may be scripted or suggested by the audience, but the audience is quickly invited to enter a dialogue with the actors and facilitators. This dialogue determines how events proceed–what the feelings of the characters are, what they want, what the barriers are, what their choices are and what resources they can draw on to make what they want to happen more likely to happen. Observing how different factors shape an interaction and how a character's actions can significantly affect their outcomes provides the audience with what STOP-GAP calls *Rehearsal for Life,* an opportunity to experiment with and see the results of a series of possible strategies before being faced with a real life situation.

STOP-GAP was co-founded in 1979 by Don Laffoon and Victoria Bryan. Don

Laffoon continues to act as Executive Director of the organization. Now approaching its 30th year of operation, STOP-GAP primarily serves two different client groups with two distinct programs: prevention and intervention.

PREVENTION

Educational touring plays are delivered in classrooms to school populations and serve a range from elementary schools to colleges. These programs are based on specially created scripts and are designed to be preventative. The plays deal with challenging subjects–violence in dating relationships, date rape, binge drinking, and alienation. Because of the sensitive nature of the subjects with which we deal, STOP-GAP performances in schools are delivered in classrooms to groups of between 30–50 students. Our current repertoire of unique plays stands at 23, and we are constantly developing new plays in response to requests from educators, parents and funders or in direct response to the students themselves.

The educational touring play department is under the leadership of Artistic Director Fionnuala Kenny, MA, who is also responsible for hiring and training the STOP-GAP company. All new plays are written in-house either by the Artistic Director or the Executive Director or as collaboration between them.

INTERVENTION

Drama therapy workshops are delivered on an ongoing weekly basis to: children with life-threatening diseases, women and children escaping abusive relationships, adults in recovery from substance abuse, children who are the victims of abuse and/or neglect and seniors and frail elderly populations. All drama therapy workshops are delivered by or under the direction of the Executive Director, Don Laffoon MA, RDT/BCT. The scope of each program area is considerable. For example in 2005–2006, STOP-GAP delivered over 600 Touring Plays to approximately 30,000 students and over 400 drama therapy workshops. Each year, STOP-GAP serves between 30,000 and 50,000 at risk and in-need populations with plays, weekly drama therapy workshops or specially devised presentations.

To provide for the wide range of client groups that it serves, STOP-GAP has a core of five full-time staff (Executive Director, Artistic Director, Development Director, Program Administrator and Administrative Assistant) and a company of approximately 16 professional actors and facilitators. All actors and facilitators are trained in the STOP-GAP method of interactive theatre, and training is provided on a continuing basis as plays are added to the repertoire.

In addition to the two major areas of work, STOP-GAP also functions as a training institute for students wishing to study the STOP-GAP method of interactive theatre for use in their own work, for students wishing to become a Registered Drama Therapist (RDT) through the alternative training route and as a creative workshop to design custom-made programs in response to special requests.

PHILOSOPHY AND PRINCIPLES

What's Stopping You?

The STOP-GAP philosophy with regard to the individual or client is one of ultimate respect. Drawing on the body of person-centered psychological theory that holds the individual to be the ultimate expert on their own needs, and on the schools of educational thought that place the learner at the center of the educational dynamic, STOP-GAP believes the individual to be the ultimate pilot of his or her own destiny. Many individuals, given the opportunity, are fully capable of comprehending their own situations, fully capable of identifying the choices that are available to them and fully capable of determining the steps that need to be taken if they wish to accomplish their personal journey towards the goals that they themselves have defined.

However, at certain times in our lives, something stops us from being able to access our own capabilities. We get bogged down. We become overwhelmed, we feel out of control, we lose our grip, we become unable to take effective action, we can no longer clearly identify our choices. In cases of consistent abuse or addiction, this way of living becomes habitual. Frightened of being punished or abandoned, frightened of making the wrong choice, or frightened of a future that is unknown, we may relinquish our power to make choices at all and "allow the choices to make us." Paolo Freire (1973) speaks of this as adaptation instead of integration–where an individual: ". . . loses his ability to make choices and is subjected to the choices of others . . . his decisions are no longer his own because they result from external prescriptions . . . the adaptive person is person as *object*" (p. 4).

By putting our lives on pause and reflecting on the challenges we face, by seeing our dilemmas played out dramatically, by taking time to focus on what is going on in our lives that is of concern and worry to us, by achieving perspective, we can take back the power that we have relinquished. We can find out what is stopping us and, having identified this, we can take steps to remove the obstacles and get back into the driving seat of our own lives.

Where's the Hurt? Where's the Help?

STOP-GAP's most basic philosophy can be described simply as: "Where's the hurt? Where's the help?" This simple question refers to STOP-GAP's philosophy that each person holds within the key to well-being, recovery and growth. STOP-GAP believes that individuals have the innate capacity to frame their own questions and, having framed these questions, to choose the appropriate answer for themselves from among the range of possibilities. This capacity is the sum of a person's experience, learning, self-knowledge, intuition, and will. In the STOP-GAP philosophy, difficult life circumstances cause these capacities to become clouded, unclear and unavailable to us. Barriers, both internal and external, are set up that prevent us from accessing our own powers to determine suitable courses of action for ourselves. A person may know that they are hurting, but may have temporarily lost the ability to truly choose from among the many sources of help that are available.

Through the power of the interactive drama therapy intervention, individuals can regain perspective, recover the ability to see their dilemma objectively, regain clarity and choose from the range of available options to begin the process of transforming themselves and their relationship with the world around them.

Life in your Face

STOP-GAP believes that all people deserve dignity, respect and trust. We believe that people hold the key to understanding their own situation. Within the STOP-GAP Method, the circumstances that have brought people to the crisis point are called *Life in your Face.*

Many individuals who attend our workshops have become overwhelmed with the circumstances of their lives. In recovery from addiction or abuse, beaten or maltreated, abandoned or ill, fearful, undermined and with no secure future in view, many of our clients have reached a state where they feel that the circumstances of their life are, quite literally, blinding them. In workshops, during the introduction, the facilitator will often demonstrate this physically by placing one hand over our face so that it covers our eyes, nose and mouth, saying: "We call this *Life in my Face.*" Then s/he will ask the question "When my life is in my face like this, what happens?"

The participants often answer that when their life is in their face like this, they cannot see clearly, cannot focus, cannot think and cannot function. In many instances, the participants will confide that when life is in their face, *they cannot even breathe.* The facilitator will then move that hand away from covering the face and, keeping it a full arm's length away, will explain that STOP-GAP will work to get life out of their face so that the participant can focus, can get some perspective and can fully see.

STOP-GAP does this by creating a spontaneous theatrical event in each workshop. The participants are invited to suggest scenes by writing from their own lives on the *Who What Where* cards. These scenes are then played out anonymously, using trained, professional STOP-GAP company members in both facilitating and acting roles. This allows the clients to observe the transactions and work out what is happening through dialogue with the actors, the facilitator and each other. The clients analyze the factors that are contributing to the current situation, suggest key alterations to the characters, the script or the interaction, introduce a new character or use one of the other available theatrical methods of altering the course of the action. They may even volunteer to become part of the action and become an agent for change themselves. It should be noted, however, that the clients are never pressed to get up and improvise with the actors. It is enough if the participation is in opening up their minds and hearts. Theatre is introduced to the clients as a powerful means by which we can step outside our own reality and by observing it, begin the process of transforming it.

Mirror Image

To hold, as 'twere, the mirror up to nature.
–Shakespeare: Hamlet

One of the principles on which STOP-GAP was founded was that theatre has the power to transform lives because it allows the individual to observe the feelings, behavior, conflicts and resolution that make up an interaction, to replay life in order to understand what happened and why, or to speculate on the consequences of a particular action. This power that theatre confers on humans, the power to see ourselves in action, makes us unique among living things. As Augusto Boal (1995) contends, no other living thing has the capacity to observe itself in action, to better understand its own reasons for doing what it does. "Observing itself, the human being perceives what it is, discovers what it is not and imagines what it could become" (p. 13).

Theatre is a powerful tool to inspire change because through the power of theatre, an individual is able to see the dilemma they are facing and achieve a measure of objectivity that is impossible in life. Theatre, being a magical context in which we can speculate with "what if" (the *Magic If,* in Stanislavski's words)–where actions can go forward or back, skip years, focus on one moment in time, create new characters, give voice and form to abstract ideas, even bring people back from the dead–provides STOP-GAP with the perfect vehicle for examining events by creating (or recreating) them. By encouraging the clients to draw on their experience, their intuition and their creative gifts to better understand the factors that have made up their lives so far, STOP-GAP invites the clients to creatively pause the trajectory of their lives and by changing key factors, to experiment creatively with how a different outcome might be achieved. Grotowski (2002) poses a question about what purpose art serves and then answers it by identifying that art is a process in which what is dark becomes revealed: "Why are we concerned with art? To cross our frontiers, exceed our limitations, fill our emptiness–fulfill ourselves. This is not a condition but a process in which what is dark in us slowly becomes transparent" (p. 21).

However, we also believe that theatre for therapeutic purposes is not just live theatre. It is *Life* theatre. It is this *Life* Theatre that STOP-GAP works to develop and grow. Drawing on the legacies of Boal (1995, Chapter 21), Brook (1968) and Grotowski (1968), and on the psychodramatic work of Moreno (1946; Fox, 1987; Chapter 18), STOP-GAP has created a dynamic and immediate theatrical experience which is available to all the participants served in the STOP-GAP programs and which is created, on the spot, using the input of the participating audiences. This theatre is team-focused, conceptual, process-based and interactive. There is no stage, no lighting and no props. There are no costumes.

> By gradually eliminating whatever proved superfluous, we found that theatre can exist without make-up, without autonomic costume and sceneography. Without a separate performance area (stage) and without lighting and sound effects etc. It cannot exist without the actor-spectator relationship of perceptual, direct, 'live' communication. (Grotowski, 2002, p. 19)

The decision to embrace the concept of the *poor theatre* ensures that the presentations remain at all times focused on the characters and on their situations with the goal of exploring who these people are, how they are feeling, what has brought them to this impasse that they are facing and what strategies, tools, and resources are available to them to bring about a resolution. Where the STOP-GAP experience deviates most sharply from traditional theatre is that it is process-based and not product-oriented and that the nature of its presentations is open-ended. Having identified the choices available to any particular character, STOP-GAP upholds and reinforces its philosophy of nonjudgment and non-prescription by entering only into a dialogue about the possible results of a particular set of actions for any particular character. A STOP-GAP presentation will never conclude with the traditional endings of either the comic or tragic tradition. There are no happy endings and no tragic outcomes. Closure is achieved by revisiting the choices that a character has in his or her given situation and by identifying, in general terms, what the consequences of each choice are likely to be. The farthest a presentation will go is by asking questions of the participants at the close of the interaction–questions such as "What might happen now?" or "If this character continues doing x, what do you think the outcomes might be?" A STOP-GAP presentation does not have the goal of tying up ends or solving problems. It is a device for assisting the participants to identify the range of solutions that are available to any character in any situation. By identifying the range of choices available to a character the participants are, by extension, reclaiming their own abilities to identify choices and select from these.

Safe Space–the STOP-GAP Promise

STOP-GAP believes in the commonality of the theatre experience and in the transformative power of theatre. The theatrical experience belongs to everyone, not just those who attend the performances of formally produced plays. "The theatrical profession, which belongs to the few, should not hide the existence and permanence of the theatrical vocation, which belongs to all. Theatre is a vocation for human beings; it is the true nature of humanity" (Boal, 1995, p. 14).

In the STOP-GAP philosophy we believe that given the vulnerability of many of our clients, no one should ever be required to do something that they do not want to do. For many of our clients, the fear that they might be required to perform would, in itself, inhibit their participation.

At the beginning of every performance, therefore, we give what is called the STOP-GAP promise–that no client will ever be required to volunteer to act, enact or role play unless they volunteer to do so. This is an essential component of the relationship of trust and mutual respect that we work to establish with the clients and is also, we believe, critical to the establishment of the *safe space.*

The principle of a safe space for the clients is essential to the proper functioning of the STOP-GAP processes. If the clients are concerned that they may be called upon at some time to perform, they may become inhibited, distracted or fearful. Fear that they may be called on may hang over them like the sword of Damocles, affecting their spontaneity and inhibiting their frank and open responses. Freed from this fear, we believe that clients can jettison their inhibitions and be confident that nothing they contribute on their cards or volunteer in answer to a question will precipitate a call to play it out. This respect for the safety and security of the clients leads to a level of honesty and frankness in their responses that is essential in giving the performances dramatic springboards with the necessary authenticity and tension.

Opening the Dialogue

All of STOP-GAP's presentations rely on the creation of a dialogue between the STOP-GAP team and the participating audience. As Paolo Freire (1973) describes, a dialogue is a "horizontal relationship between persons" in which both persons A and B share communication and regard each other as equals. He contrasts this with what he refers to as anti-dialogue in which A stands over B and the relation of empathy is broken. The dialogue matrix is identified as "loving, trustful, hopeful, humble and critical" (pp. 45–46).

This interaction, this dialogue, lies at the heart of the STOP-GAP experience. At STOP-GAP, relying as we do on the experiences of the clients and on their ability to determine their own future direction, we avoid any suggestion that we are there to tell them what to do, to identify desirable paths or actions, to save or deliver them from their life situations, to forgive them, to release them from their feelings or to–in any other respect–take the position of those who have power over the participants. STOP-GAP believes that many clients are in the life situation that Freire (1973) describes: "Unfortunately, what happens to a greater or lesser degree in the various worlds into which the world is divided is that the ordinary person is crushed, diminished, converted into a spectator" (p. 6).

Our role, therefore, is to empower clients to reconnect with their own internal, vibrant forces, and central to that empowerment is the necessity to open a dialogue in which the observations of the client are of equal value to the contributions of the team. For this reason we uphold and value the reciprocity of the interaction and we share responsibility for how the presentation develops.

Role Clarity/Role Confusion

While we never require anyone to enrole, part of the STOP-GAP philosophy has to deal with the roles that people wish to play in creating a presentation. Role clarity is an important aspect of working successfully at STOP-GAP where roles are often blended and where ability to function as a member of a team is an essential prerequisite. We believe in the principle of role change, and we celebrate the ability to be able to change roles quickly and easily to function as part of one team or another. This is demonstrated not just in our requirement for the Educational/Preventative work that all of our actors know all of our plays and that generic roles (Parent/Doctor/Teacher/Friend) can be played by either gender, but by the fact that 90 percent of our plays are written to accommodate lead characters who may be played by either gender.

However, when it comes to members of the audience en-roling, there are clear guiding principles that are observed whether the session is educational or therapeutic. Members of the audience, or clients, are always en-roled in positive, powerful roles and are never en-roled as a victim, as an aggressor, or as a character who is negative, passive or aggressive. Once a client volunteers, a role is immediately constructed for them that gives them the opportunity to access that within them which is powerful, experienced and wise. Thus, in the role of a positive, caring and wise person, the volunteer is able to give the character-in-trouble (always played by an actor) some helpful and constructive guidance. Frequently, the facilitator will gather suggestions of powerful and wise things to say from the audience and will let the volunteer choose from the range of ideas that have been given. Occasionally, if the volunteer is completely overcome when on stage, they will be guided into the effectiveness of simply listening. In each case, STOP-GAP wishes to reflect back to volunteers their best selves. Part of the STOP-GAP philosophy is to give the clients the opportunity to voice positive, assertive, wise, and affirming thoughts and ideas. We believe that all people have the capacity for constructive and creative dialogue with others and with themselves. We believe that the opportunity to assume a more powerful role is a momentary release from the role of victim, patient or addict. Projection into a powerful and effective role can confer status, authority, wisdom and respect and can help a person reconnect with these valuable attributes. A critically ill child, therefore, encouraged to take on the role as Chief Physician of the Hospital, may achieve a level of authority, resilience and wisdom that was quite hidden in the ill child who began the session. The wise, competent friend who is advising another woman to leave her abuser is often unrecognizable as the frightened, panicky woman who began the session.

Similarly, STOP-GAP strives to ensure that the focus of the scene remains on the character representing the client and on her/his dilemma. Clients often present cards in which someone else (the abuser, a parent, a substance) holds all the power in the interaction. They have cast that person or thing in the lead role and are in danger of allowing the focus to drift towards them. In order to avoid this happening, the facilitator will often employ the theatrical device of *Spotlight,* inviting the clients to visualize that the *Spotlight* is following the character who needs guidance. Part of the philosophy is to assist the client to *Take Back the Spotlight* and central to that is focusing on the character that needs the assistance, not on the drama that is being created by another character. A facilitator will often acknowledge how compelling the drama of another can be, and how some characters excel at getting the spotlight to shine on them. A facilitator may stress that a character is in danger of getting so involved with managing someone's anger, or their abuse that s/he has forgotten that it is s/he who is in need of the attention. The facilitator will then quickly work to focus the attention (Spotlight) of the group on the person who really needs the help. One of the principles at STOP-GAP is to remind clients at all times that they must be the focus of the attention if they are to make any progress. This is frequently a considerable shift of emphasis for the clients who are not used to thinking of themselves as worthy of any attention.

Rehearsal for Life

"The normal role of human beings in and with this world is not a passive one. Because they are not limited to the natural (biological) sphere but participate in the creative dimension as well, men can intervene in reality in order to change it" (Freire, 1973, p. 4)

The creation of dramatic scenes aimed at giving the participants the perspective to regain their internal coping abilities is known in STOP-GAP as a *Rehearsal for Life.* Through the dramatic presentation of situations that the clients have identified to us, using professional actors to take on the roles that have been described, clients are given the opportunity to revisit, replay, reappraise or predict a feared or troubling situation. But in the STOP-GAP scenario, it is the client who now has the power. A character on stage may be passive, fearful or a victim but the clients can now control the outcome of the scene by pausing it, by interacting with the actors and facilitator, by dialoguing, by changing the roles and/or behavior of the characters, by inventing additional characters or by drawing on additional resources either from within or without to assist the character in her/his dilemma. No longer individuals to whom something is happening, no longer passive accepters of roles that have been thrust upon them, the clients can assume the roles of observer with all the advantages that this role can bestow–clarity, empathy, judgment and perspective.

Participants in a STOP-GAP presentation have the advantage of being able to rehearse a range of situations so that they can experience some of the setbacks that may occur when they are faced with the real life situation. People may be determined to face their abuser, or their substance-abusing partner, but the ability to rehearse how this might go, including all the emotional blackmail and manipulation that are frequently part of these interactions, gives the participants the advantage of being able to see the situation before they are in it and to do a reality check on their responses with their peers and the STOP-GAP team. Life can be a tough teacher and trial-and-error learning can be too risk-laden in some of these life situations. The Rehearsal for Life format gives the participants the advantage of being able to practice and rehearse skills that will be invaluable tools for them in the challenging situations they face.

Although the STOP-GAP process is interactive and participative, the basic building block of all presentations is a team of facilitator and actor(s) who begin the process by playing out a scripted scene, or a scene suggested by the audience from the Who? What? Where? cards. Working with the facilitator, the audience then creates the characters that will play the scene, giving them names, character details and a first line to say. The actors take the assigned parts (frequently a protagonist and an antagonist) and play the scene, which is observed by the clients/audience. The audience then continues the dialogue with the facilitator and actors, analyzing the feelings, behavior, choices and decisions of the characters and identifying possible directions for the story to take. An audience member may suggest a direction, may introduce a new character, may even volunteer to join in the action to progress it. The performance will never become about the audience member, however. It will continue to be about the central character, which has been communally invented.

In STOP-GAP, the Who? What? Where? cards remain anonymous. One of the key components of the program is that once the cards are collected, they become communal. There is no longer any focus on the individual who wrote the card. The cards identify common problems, not individual ones. The cards now become the property of the group. The facilitator will often stress the need for the group to let go of the Who (whose card is this?) and focus on the What (what situation is being identified?).

All focus now goes to the creation of the characters that will play out the scene. The creation of a character to represent not only the person who wrote the card, but all people participating in the group is an essential distancing technique, helping STOP-GAP's intention to take specific interactions and give them general applicability. These *distancing* techniques have several purposes. They broaden both the character and situation from the specific to the general. This ensures that the scene is relevant to everyone. It also ensures that we do not get bogged down in the specifics. (We were in the kitchen and he was standing in front of the door.) What is relevant is what is occurring in the scene: Who are these characters? Why are they in this situation? How are they feeling? What are their choices? The final advantage of distancing is that any characteristic or feeling can be placed on a character (played by an actor) without fear for an individual who may already be feeling vulnerable.

All activities at STOP-GAP are team-based, and all teams must share a commitment to the philosophy and principles of STOP-GAP. Part of this commitment is a willingness to continue training to update and refine the skills of the delivery teams to ensure that the principles of respect for the client, and assisting the client to identify alternatives and choices continue to inform the work at every level. To assist in this, the STOP-GAP Five Point Method was formulated in 1997 by Fionnuala Kenny and Don Laffoon. It has been in use ever since both as a training method for actors and facilitators and as a springboard for professionals and/or students who wish to learn the STOP-GAP method to either support their own work or to develop different aspects of it.

THE STOP-GAP FIVE POINT METHOD

The STOP-GAP Method of Interactive Theatre is a form of improvisation comprising five distinct components. The five components of the STOP-GAP Method are:

- Make the Menu
- Focus on Feelings
- Cut to the Chase
- Swing the Pendulum
- Hit the Bull's-eye

These five components are used in different combinations in our interactive touring plays and therapy drama sessions to assist the STOP-GAP team and the audience participants to focus on the performance and ensure that the goal of the session (the Bull's-eye) is achieved.

Make the Menu

In *Make the Menu,* the facilitator invites participants to suggest characters, relationships, situations, reasons for the situation, and a first line for a character to say. This process lays the foundation for participant involvement. Make the Menu invites the audience to become actively involved in the development of the story. By naming the characters and providing details of the situations they find themselves in, the audience interest increases and their involvement is secured. Make the Menu is also the means by which the concept of choice is emphasized with the participants. The concept of making conscious choices is a vital underpinning of STOP-GAP's philosophy, and in all situations the characters will demonstrate that there are different options available to them. In the STOP-GAP tradition of "show, don't tell" the facilitator demonstrates that the participants can choose who will play a scene, where that scene will be played, who will speak first and what they will say. The facilitator is most active in opening a dialogue with the participants while practicing Make the Menu but the actors are required to listen to, and act on, the responses of the participants. The STOP-GAP Institute trains its actors and facilitators to listen to the responses, the names, places and relationships that are suggested by the audience and repeat them if they are unclear. If the facilitator asks for a first line, ("Who speaks first in this scene? Let's have a first line.") the actor must repeat that line exactly as it was spoken. Paraphrasing, adding or changing the sense of what is offered, is not permitted because it is essential for the audience to feel that their offering is used just as it was volunteered.

Focus on Feelings

STOP-GAP believes the things that human beings share are significantly more powerful than the things that, apparently, make us different. Most importantly, we believe that human beings share feelings and that the feelings that humans experience–sadness, joy, grief, anger, loss and pain–are common to all of us. These are what make us human and they transcend language, culture and status.

However, how these feelings are presented can differ from situation to situation and from person to person. Many of us are taught as children that showing certain feelings (anger, fear, anxiety) is not acceptable and showing too much of any feeling, even joy, is to be avoided. So, many of us become adept at hiding our feelings, or we learn to disguise them, particularly if they are troubling. When we are faced with identifying our true feelings, or those of others, we may have difficulty. We may feel irritable when we are deeply anxious or we may feel bored when we are, in fact, sad. In STOP-GAP, we believe that fear lies at the heart of much dysfunction, and that fear is often masked by anger. Sometimes, the true nature of our feelings causes inner conflict and we cover how we are feeling with behavior that draws attention away from the underlying troubling feelings. We find that we also do this with other people, focusing on their behavior, (She's always late. He's always breaking promises.) instead of looking deeper towards the feelings that are driving this behavior. Identification of our own feelings and the feelings of others is an important aspect of the STOP-GAP process. Therefore, central to the process is the technique of *Focusing on Feelings.*

In a STOP-GAP scripted or improvisational scene, the actors will invent characters whose feelings are being masked by inappropriate behavior. It will quickly become clear that each of the characters in the scene is experiencing strong and powerful feelings. The facilitator will pause the scene at the appropriate time and invite the audience to comment on what is happening in the scene and what the underlying feelings of the characters are by asking, "How is this character feeling?" or "How does it make her feel when this happens?" The audience will respond by interpreting the feelings of the character, not judging their behavior. Through exploring the feelings of the characters underneath their masks, participants are better able to identify their own feelings and the feelings of others. In a situation in which an individual may be apprehensive about expressing personal feelings in unfamiliar surroundings, the characters in the plays provide a safe means by which a participant can explore difficult and painful issues. The facilitator is trained to accept all responses without judgment. If an audience member hypothesizes that a character is expressing anger because they are really feeling sad, that will guide the facilitator in the framing of the next question, which might be "What is making this character sad?"

Focus on Feelings helps to remind the participants that feelings form a vital part of every interaction and that understanding how we are feeling and being able to express that feeling opens up new avenues for shared understanding and communication.

Cut to the Chase

Cut to the Chase means getting to the point effectively and efficiently. STOP-GAP sessions usually last between 45 minutes and one hour, and our goal is to perform the maximum possible number of scenes and involve as many participants as possible. It is particularly important in improvisational theatre that our actors do not spend time in elaborate set-ups, which may be both confusing and distracting to the participants. It is important for the participants to see their dilemma played out swiftly and for the conflict to become clear quickly. For this reason, we emphasize Cut to the Chase. Having invited the audience participation in setting up the scene, STOP-GAP uses Cut to the Chase to shortcut to what the participants already know about the situation being role played. In the therapeutic drama work, where ongoing weekly workshops are the norm, STOP-GAP is able to make certain assumptions about the client group–that they are all escaping an abusive relationship, for example, or that they are in recovery from substance abuse. Even in the educational touring plays, however, Cut to the Chase is a guideline for how quickly we want the issues to guide the improvisation.

For example, "My husband has promised that he will never hit me again," sums up what has been established and gets immediately to the heart of an issue for a woman who is considering returning to her abuser. It is up to the other character to now *Swing the Pendulum* to provide the necessary counterpoint to make the scene dramatic and involving. Another example of Cut to the Chase might be set in a restaurant (a favorite choice for participants). In a restaurant scene, the actors might spend many minutes debating what they will eat, how easy/difficult it was finding the restaurant, or what they see others wearing or eating. In Cut to the Chase the STOP-GAP actors know that the decision to drink or not is what the scene is really about, so within the first few seconds, one of the actors will make reference to that. "So, do you want to split a bottle of wine?" or "So, how long before you can have a beer?" might be typical ways to start the scene. In the STOP-GAP method of improvisation, a lengthy build up is not necessary–we know the characters; we have established the situation. We want to find out what is going to happen when these characters begin to interact with each other.

The facilitator also uses Cut to the Chase when s/he pauses a scene because the main point of a scene has been reached, whether that takes three seconds or three minutes. This keeps the play alive and gives the facilitator the opportunity to set up several improvisations which can include participants who volunteer to come on stage and take part in the action.

If the actors need more information about their character or the situation, they can either ask the facilitator or ask a direct question of the audience–for example "Is this happening in the shelter or outside it?" or "Is her husband a user?" Getting information from the participants helps to focus their attention; getting to the point quickly ensures that we can maintain it.

Swing the Pendulum

Strong conflict lies at the heart of drama. Two characters struggling to resolve a conflict from seemingly irreconcilable standpoints, or escalating a discussion into a conflict is a powerful jumping-off point for any theatrical piece. In the STOP-GAP Method, the actors are trained to take opposing positions at the commencement of a scene. This may be done in a number of ways. Here are some examples:

a. One character speaks and the second character responds by expressing vehement disagreement:
   Character 1: Bob has asked me to go on a date and I think I'd like to.
   Character 2: You must be mad to even think about it. Your last relationship was a complete disaster.
b. One character speaks and the second characters asserts that much more is needed in order to be effective:
   Character 1: My daughter is driving me mad. I feel like grounding her for a week.
   Character 2: That's not going to do any good. You need to take away every privilege and ground her for a year. That is all adolescents understand.
c. One character speaks and the second character asserts that much less is needed in order to be effective:
   Character 1: I feel that I should ask my doctor for a second opinion–what do you think?
   Character 2: You need to be very careful. They can be very sensitive about that. You don't want to upset your doctor!

This may be done in any combination of ways to avoid stereotyping of characters. Thus, the teenager may be assertive and strong against a parent who is irrational and angry, or a boss may vacillate and become distracted when interacting with a worker who is focused and decisive. How the characters interact is one of the ways that we can never quite predict and one of the things that makes a STOP-GAP presentation dynamic and unique. However, all STOP-GAP actors know that good scenes will come from two characters stating strongly opposing or contradictory views, or between characters who are approaching a situation with totally different attitudes. However, we are also careful to avoid typecasting, so we look for ways for characters to express themselves that do not reinforce stereotypes.

An example of Swinging the Pendulum (STP) in a scene between a parent and child might be:

Parent: I want you to come straight home after school today.

(Non-STP response: "OK" or "Do I have to?")

STP response: Why do I have to go to school at all if you are so scared?

Or between an abuser and their partner:

Partner: I need to go out tonight to see my mother. She's not well.

(Non-STP response: OK or Not again! That's the third time this month)

Abuser: You are just looking for an excuse to get out of the house. Who are you meeting? Tell me!

The energy of the responses–the fact that each response comes from the perspective of different individuals–sets the tone for the scene which will be charged emotionally and interesting to the observers. It also helps to establish that each character is coming from a definite standpoint, which is very helpful when we come to Focus on Feelings.

Characters expressing different points of view focus the audience interest and help to maintain their involvement. In a scene in which characters are broadly in agreement, simply responsive or in which the conflicts are too subtle, the scene may lose energy and grind to a standstill. STOP-GAP acting teams are trained to state strong positions in order to establish that there is a conflict and move to an exploration of what the feelings underlying the conflict may be. The participants are then well placed to contribute to the dialogue by suggesting alternatives that may move the characters forward and ease communication between them. In some cases, the participants may volunteer to come on stage and interact with the character to make the characters' transition even easier.

Hit the Bull's-eye

The Bull's-eye is the most vital component of the STOP-GAP method as it contains the central point of the play or scene. What is the scene really about? Underneath the behavior, the conflict, the attitudes–what are these characters trying to communicate to each other? What are they afraid of? How can they move beyond these barriers and recognize their own deep feelings and those of others? How can they enlist support? How can they discover what their choices are? How can they take effective action?

In the interactive touring plays, the Bull's-eye is determined and refined during the writing process, is known to the facilitator and the actors, and is revisited before each performance begins. An example of a Bull's-eye for STOP-GAP's presentation about violence in dating relationships would be "wanting to control a person is not the same as loving them." The facilitator keeps the Bull's-eye of the scripted piece in mind and uses it as a guide to focus the improvisations and discussion.

In the therapeutic drama programs, in which the entire session is improvised from scenes suggested on anonymous cards, it is the skill of the facilitator that determines what the Bull's-eye (known as the *IT* in therapeutic drama) of each scene really is. This is, to some extent, reliant on the context–for example, in a battered women's facility, the *IT* of a scene may have to do with fear of the abuser, fear of financial instability, feelings of guilt, feelings of inadequacy or apprehension. Working within the scene as suggested and the contributions made by the participants, the facilitator will dialogue with the audience to discover what the real dynamic of the scene is–what is really driving the behavior and fueling the conflict? In another context (a recovery center), a card depicting a scene about a recovering addict seeking support from apparently indifferent parents may turn out to be about the addict's need to blame other people for his/her continuing behavior, or it may turn out to be about a person's need to be accepted for who they are. A scene in which a rebellious adolescent expresses constant aggressive anger with a parent might be masking the adolescent's fear that the parent's decision to continue smoking is going to lead to his/her premature death.

The responsibility for hitting the Bull's-eye is held by the team and involves the actors and facilitator working closely together, listening and responding to the input of the participants. The exercise becomes one of close collaboration, active listening and interacting, peer referencing and drawing on relevant experience. The group creates each piece, guiding and shaping it until a resolution is reached. The group then works with the team to construct closure and identify all of the factors that have helped promote the growth and healthy development of the relationship between the characters and the factors that may have hindered this.

THE WHO? WHAT? WHERE? CARDS

In the educational touring plays, each session begins with a scripted play on a particular topic (violence in a dating relationship, underage or binge drinking, bullying or a hate crime in a school setting) which lasts between ten and twenty minutes. This is paused at frequent intervals by the facilitator, who asks relevant questions, (What is happening here? How are these characters relating to one another? How are these characters feeling) but is played out fully before the session is opened up to audience interaction.

In drama therapy, there are no scripts and each session begins with either a series of questions from the facilitator or by distributing the *Who? What? Where?* cards. The Who? What? Where? cards are, to some extent, a formalization of Make the Menu because it is through the device of the cards that the audience identifies the issues that are on their minds at the time.

By filling out a card, each audience member is given the opportunity to map out a situation that confuses, worries or concerns him or her. The situation can be in the past, present, future. It can be real or imagined.

First, in the *WHO* segment, participants are asked to identify the two principal characters by role rather than name (e.g., Husband, not "John") who can be "Me" and another (Mother, Boss, Judge, Spouse, Child), or it can be between two characters who have some connection to them (Spouse and Child, Counselor and Friend in shelter).

Second, in the *WHAT* segment, they are asked to identify what is happening. The *What* can be a general statement (e.g., Hitting me, Putting me down) or a specific (I'm frightened that when I have to go to court, I'll see him).

Finally, the *WHERE* segment asks where this might be happening. This can be a specific place, (The courtroom, the police station, my kitchen) or somewhere more abstract ("Right now," "In the future," or "In my dreams").

Here are some examples of cards that were completed during our workshops:

> *Who:* Me. My abuser
> *What:* He wants me back, give him another chance
> *Where:* Home (front of house)
>
> *Who:* Me and Me
> *What:* Wanting tomorrow makes it hard to concentrate on today. I want to

move on now
Where: in Life

Who: Me and daughter
What: Using drugs and not working and not taking care of her children but saying she will take care of responsibility and crying and never getting it done
Where: For the last year and now

At the start of each session, the facilitator introduces STOP-GAP and goes through some of the key elements of the STOP-GAP program, including the promise that no one will be made to do anything that they do not want to do. The actors introduce themselves and the facilitator introduces the cards, distributing these and answering questions about how to complete them. The actors and facilitator then collect the cards and the facilitator quickly scans them, grouping them together into cards that have similar themes–for example, the cards that deal with fears about going to court, the cards that deal with fears that the abuser will find them and/or gain custody of the children, the cards that deal with problems with the children's behavior since coming to the shelter. The facilitator then asks the participants to let go of whose card is chosen and to focus instead on the issues that the card presents, reassuring the participants that in every card there will be something of interest and relevance to the whole group.

The facilitator then selects a card and read it aloud, or tells the group that there were several cards dealing with the same concern, for example, "It seems that a number of us today are very concerned about meeting our abuser when we leave the shelter. Let's set up a scene in which this happens." The facilitator then proceeds to set up the scene:

"Let's have (Actor 1) play a woman who has just been discharged from the shelter. Let's have a name for this character. (Audience volunteers name.) Ok, so where is this happening? (Audience gives some possible venues.) OK, so this happens in a supermarket. Let's have (Actor 2) play the abuser. Let's have a name for him. Let's have a first line. Who speaks first? What does s/he say?"

The actors take their positions and the scene begins. The facilitator watches the action intently and also observes the audience to get a feel for their reaction. When the facilitator feels that a critical juncture in the improvisation has been reached, the facilitator will say "Pause" and stop the scene. The facilitator opens a dialogue with the audience. The dialogue progresses with questions based in the method–"What is happening here? How is this character feeling? How long has this been going on?"

Once the audience has framed what is happening in the interaction, (control, manipulation, persuasion, going back into old habits, becoming vulnerable again, being frightened again) the facilitator asks what the character might need. The audience suggests a range of strategies, (she needs to get out of there, she needs to talk to someone, she needs a friend to help her, she needs her family around her) and the facilitator selects from among these and sets up the next improvisation. If a scene is selected in which there is a wise, calm, mature and experienced person, the facilitator will turn to the audience and invite a volunteer to come on stage and take on that role. If no one volunteers, the facilitator will en-role the other actor, or will en-role herself, and the scene will progress. When that scene reaches a point, the facilitator will pause and again will dialogue with the audience, inviting their comments on what is happening and what the central character is feeling. Advice will be sought again from the audience on the range of choices that are available to the character, and one of these choices is selected. A scene is then set up in which the character makes that choice and the action moves forward again.

Although the narrative is often kept going in a forward momentum, the facilitator may at any point use one of the many theatrical devices that are available to give the scene or the character a different perspective. For example, the action may move back: the facilitator may suggest that the action move back several years and that we look at the character during a much earlier stage of life, (Let's have a look at this character when she was dating. What do you think her first boyfriend was like?). Or the action may move forward with the facilitator asking what might happen in ten or twenty years time, (If she stays with this man, what do you think will have happened in ten years time? Where will she be?).

There are several other devices that the facilitator may use. S/he may use the *voice in the head* technique (*doubling*), where one actor speaks the negative or destructive thoughts of another, or an alternative technique where conflicting voices in the same person's head (a constantly warring mother and father) reveal a character's ambivalence. Frequently, a facilitator will use the device of the *listening chair* in which one actor or participant simply listens to another without interruption. Often, the entire group is en-roled in the manner of a Greek Chorus to provide constant and unflinching support to a character going through a difficult decision.

The purpose of all these devices is to provide the participants a Rehearsal for Life, so that, in the safety of a familiar environment, surrounded by people they know and trust, they can share and rehearse strategies for dealing with the difficult and challenging situations that they will face when they leave the program, hospital or shelter and begin their lives again.

CASE EXAMPLES

Heliotrope House– Ties with Meaning

(This session took place at a local Orange County shelter for abused woman and their children. STOP-GAP delivers programs there on a weekly basis. This session was facilitated by Don Laffoon.)

The door at Heliotrope House opens to women escaping with their children from the nightmare of the closed, abusing relationship. The door opens onto a world of transition, where safety is the key. In this safe place, they can pause and catch their breath–a luxury they were never allowed while they lived in dread of the raised fist or the consistent threats–"I will take the children away from you and you will never see them again."

Don introduces STOP-GAP. "We are the theater company STOP-GAP. We work here every week and first, let me give you the STOP-GAP Pledge. I promise that I will never, never ever, EVER, make anyone in this room here do anything that they do not want to do. Today we are in a safe place. In a safe place, we can be honest. When we are not in a safe place it can be dangerous to be honest. When we are honest, we may say things that others disagree with. Here, in this safe place, we may agree with what others say, we may disagree or we may agree to disagree." (Don holds up his hand.)

Don: "Imagine this hand is your LIFE. I call this Life IN your face." (He places the hand over his face, covering his eyes, mouth and nose.)

"Do any of you have the experience of having *life in your face?*"

One of the women shudders, "Sometimes when my life is up there I can't even breathe."

Don: "Today, we get a chance to take this

hand OUT of our face and have a look at what is going on. What is going on is up to you. You can choose to explore something from the past, present or the future."

The *Who What Where* cards are distributed.

Don: "Please just put down something that is troubling you right now. Put down a brief description of the *What* and tell us *Who* you want to see in the scene. The actors will do the rest by improvising."

Card 1.
Who: Me and my son.
What: My son is becoming a young man. I can't accept that he is not a little boy any more. It is difficult for me.
Where: At home.

Don: "Who do you want to speak first?" The group decides that the Mother will begin.

Don: "Who has an opening line for Mom?"

"You need to listen to me" is chosen. (The actor playing Mom must begin by saying this line exactly like the client.) Actor 1 is enroled as the son and given the name Jose by the group (Make the Menu). Actor 2 is enroled as the Mother.

Scene:

Mother: "You need to listen to me."

Jose: "I told you before, Mom. I'm going out with Luisa." (*Swinging the Pendulum*)

Mother: "But we have to buy your clothes for the wedding!"

Jose: "Mom – I'm not going clothes shopping with you!"

Mother: "Oh yes you are. I'm not having you turning up to the wedding looking like a tramp."

Jose: "Luisa is going to help me to choose something."

Mother: "What does Luisa know? She's just a child herself. And the way she dresses . . ."

Jose: "Mom! Don't start. I'm beginning to wish I'd never agreed to go to this wedding. It's been nothing but a hassle!"

Don: "Pause. Well, what have we here?"

"Mom is having a problem–oh, yes!" There is general laughter.

"She is afraid," more quietly, from the woman to one side of the group.

Don: "What is she afraid of?" (*Focus on Feeling*)

"She's afraid that she is losing him."

"They have been through so much together–she has come to depend on him."

"She still thinks he's a child."

Don: "How will this be if this goes on?"

"If this goes on, she really will lose him."

Don directs the improvisation to continue. Mom becomes insistent, threatening even. She forbids him to see his girlfriend and ends up sending him to his room with the line, "We are going at 2 o'clock whether you like it or not!"

Don: "How is Mom feeling?"

"She's angry. She's trying to control him."

"She's frightened of not being the one to make the decisions."

"She wants to do what they used to do before."

"She doesn't want things to change."

Don: "Ah, yes. Change. Change is scary, isn't it? But what about Jose–what does he want?"

"He wants to do what he wants to do."

"He wants to change. He is changing, right before her eyes!"

There is a pause. Don looks at his tie. The base of the tie is almost black, and as you look closely you see that the grey shapes edged in pink are fish lying silently, just visible against the dark background. As the eye moves up the tie, the pattern made by the fish becomes more and more diffuse until somewhere around the midpoint, they disappear–as does the black background–and are replaced by flying black birds, still edged in pink, now on a grey ground.

Don: "Change. Transitions. They are hard. The fish on this tie are in the process of changing–they change and then they become birds. When they become birds, they can fly. Does Jose want to fly?"

"He wants to find his wings."

"But Mom is afraid that he'll fly away and she'll be left."

Don: "Is Mom in transition, too? What was Mom's *Bull's-eye* up to now?"

"To keep him safe from harm."

"To keep him protected."

"To make sure he was fed and clothed."

"To make him secure."

Don: "Has she done a good job? How is Jose?"

"Independent."

"Able to stand up for himself."

"Assertive."

"In a relationship."

Don: 'So, it sounds like she has done her job. He's a young man, confident and secure–she has got him through childhood. But now, it's the next stage–it's transition time. What does her *Bull's-eye* need to be?"

"To let him go."

"To help him to be independent of her."

"To help him find his wings."

Don: "How can she do that?"

"Trust him."

"Trust what she has given him."

Don: "She has to let go, or he'll be dependent on her all his life. He will never be able to make his way in the world with confidence. I heard a wonderful thing about parenthood, once. 'Give them roots. Give them wings.' What has Mom given Jose already?"

"She has made him secure–she has built a life."

"She has given him roots."

Don: "And now?"

"She needs to give him wings."

Card 2:
Who: Me/My husband.
What: Telling me I'm stupid. That I'm not fit to be anyone's mother, or wife. I know he's going to try to take my daughters from me.
Where: Kitchen.

The names of the husband and wife are given as "Michelle" and "Eddie." The scene is set in the kitchen. The actors are en-roled. The group decides that Michelle will speak first and her first line will be "How was your day?"

Michelle: "How was your day?"

Eddie: "Don't ask." (angrily)

Michelle: "Eddie - I need some money–I'm sorry–I have to go to the store and get some milk . . ."

Eddie: "Milk? Why do we need milk? You just want to get out to the house, don't you?"

Michelle: "No. The girls had some friends over after school and they made shakes . . ."

Eddie: "Who said they could have friends over? Don't tell me there were boys here, Michelle!"

Michelle: "No, Eddie–there were only girls–They were having a good time–I thought–it would be O.K."

Eddie: "Every time you 'think,' Michelle, something goes wrong. Why don't you just do what you are told? Who are you seeing at the store? That manager, is it? And you better not even think about lying to me because I have my ways to find out."

"Michelle" cowers, visibly afraid.

Don: "Pause. What's going on here?"

"He is jealous–he is insane."

"He is frightening her."

"He is suspicious."

"He is controlling her with his temper."

One woman has been watching the scene intently, her eyes flicking back and forth during the interchange with something resembling panic. She speaks rapidly to the translator, who repeats for the group. She says, "Now he will lock her in the house and he will not let her out for perhaps three days–she will not see anyone, speak to anyone."

Don: "Who is in control?"

"He is."

Don: "How is Michelle feeling?"

"Uncertain."

"Afraid."

"Terrified of what he will do next."

The woman speaks again through the translator, "She is trapped, like an animal." She bows her head.

Don: "Well, this is the theatre and we can just direct Eddie to exit the scene. Where shall we put Eddie for the moment while we work out what to do?"

As she understands, the woman lifts her head and her eyes shine. "The deep freeze," she says, longingly and then laughs out loud.

"Goodbye Eddie," shout the women as he retreats.

Don: "OK, we move forward in time. Michelle has left Eddie and has come to the shelter. What is she feeling now?"

Women: "She is still afraid."

Don: "Yes, she has good reason to be afraid–this is a violent and unpredictable man–and he is the father of her daughters. But Michelle needs support now, she needs help. Can we have a volunteer to talk to Michelle?"

A woman volunteers. She plays another person at the shelter, someone who has been there longer than Michelle. The name Lydia is given and the first line is "So, how are you doing?" She sits with Michelle while Michelle pours out how frightened she is of having her daughters taken from her–how powerful she feels Eddie is, how she feels he will convince the courts that he will make a good father. Lydia offers consolation and advice.

Don: "How is this going?"

Lydia: "She is really scared. It's like that Eddie has come into the shelter with her. He's not here, but he is–if you see what I mean."

Don: "What is happening?"

"She is still hearing him, in her head."

"She has brought him into the shelter with her."

"She's on a conference call–with him brainwashing her."

Don: "Let's have a look at that voice in the head."

Don en-roles Eddie to stand behind and over Michelle, repeating phrases that undermine her: "You can never get along without me." "You are a loser." "You can't get a job!"

Pause.

Don: "Sometimes, after we have left a bad relationship we still carry those damaging messages around, don't we? In our heads, in our hearts. Those messages are powerful and they are frightening. How can we stop those messages being the messages we listen to?"

The women take a moment while they think long and hard. Every woman in the room seems to be processing the difficulty of getting rid of that voice in the head: the one that tells you that this time it will be different, that tells you not to give up on the relationship, that tells you to go back and give it another try. The voice that always omits to tell you that this time, you may get killed.

Eventually, it is Lydia who responds. "In my case, the more I hear something, the more it becomes true. That's what kept me in the relationship for so long. He kept telling me I was stupid and eventually, I got to believing it too and started saying those things to myself. Getting away and staying away has made that message become weaker. Now, I am hearing other messages, positive messages and they are becoming more true for me. I am not what he said I was. I didn't deserve to be treated like that. I am becoming stronger and stronger. As long as I have no contact–absolutely no contact. No calls. No news of how he is. No places where he might be. Nothing. In my case, it's never being alone near a telephone, with the price of a call in my purse. It is an addiction. It is a sickness. It is hard. But you have to create the space for other messages to come in. You have to go far enough to seriously weaken the signal. That's what Michelle needs to do. She needs to seriously weaken the signal so that other messages–positive messages–can come in."

> Card 3:
> *Who:* Myself/my husband
> *What:* I want to learn to be strong because he is planning to be nice to convince me to go back to him. He is planning to take me back to Mexico and according to him to take good care of me there.
> *Where:* The shelter.

The names Elizabeth and Jonathan are chosen for the characters and the actors enroled. The actor who was Eddie has made a complete character switch. Jonathan is a wonderful creation–able to laugh, to charm, to cry, to plead and above all, to persuade. Elizabeth is at first skeptical but under the barrage of charm, begins to weaken. She has a huge investment in the marriage and desperately wants it to work. Jonathan produces some very good arguments. He claims he was under stress–the stress of being in a different country. When they get back to Mexico, it will all be different. There will be family there to take care of the kids. He will change. He paints a picture of the life they will have there with himself as the loving and considerate husband–the husband she always wanted.

Don looks around at the women, fascinated and intrigued with Jonathan.

Don: "Does Elizabeth believe him?"

"She wants to believe him–she wants to believe him so badly!"

"He is saying all the things that she wants to hear–he loves her, he is going to take care of her."

Don: "Does he mean it?"

"He means it now, at this moment."

Jonathan now adds fuel to the fire by declaring, passionately, that he will dedicate his whole life to winning Elizabeth back.

Don: "Is he telling the truth? How long will he really dedicate to getting her back?"

"About five more minutes."

Some of the women are laughing, but on some of the faces, there is strain and concern.

Don: "Is Elizabeth safe?"

"She's in danger of going back to give it one more try."

"She is in danger of feeling sorry for him–when he starts to cry, she might give in."

"She is in danger of going back just to show him that it's not going to work."

"She is in danger of letting him be the voice in her head again."

Don: "Ah! Maybe his voice has been there all along. What does she need?"

"She needs to hear some other voices–reminding her of how it really will be."

Don: "Will you all be those voices?"

One by one, the women are brought onstage to stand behind Elizabeth, who is now visibly faltering. Jonathan begins his onslaught again–he tells her how he intends to change, how he never meant to hit her and will never, never do it again, how he will be a good husband from now on, how different life will be in Mexico. He cries, he pleads. He tells her that she has taken everything from him and left him alone–how could she be so heartless? Each time he speaks, one of the women reminds Elizabeth of reality.

"Haven't you heard this a thousand times before?"

"Remember, he did not hit only you. He hit your daughters. Remember that."

"In Mexico, you will be like a prisoner. No friends. No one to talk to. Only his family who will take his side."

"He will lock you in–lock you in and not let you go out of the house."

"Why would he keep this promise? He breaks all of his promises."

"You deserve better than this."

"You deserve better."

The women are now a chorus of positive voices behind Elizabeth, who is growing visibly stronger. Jonathan is outmaneuvered as the women lay reason upon reason of why Elizabeth should not consider going back to him. Elizabeth ends the improvisation by repeating that she is beginning a new life, without him.

Don: "How does Elizabeth feel now?"

"Strong."

The women make strong gestures at each other, flexing arms. They are laughing with the actor, who has now de-roled and is acknowledging that everything Jonathan said was calculated to manipulate. Jonathan would have made any promise to get what he wanted–making promises is so easy.

Don: "Is Jonathan going to change?"

"No, why should he?"

Don: "Jonathan has no need to change–no need to transition. He's in total control–he has all the power. But was it working for Elizabeth?"

"No."

Don: "No. It doesn't work for the women trying to make a life with men like this. What does Elizabeth need to do?"

A small, silent woman raises her face to everyone for the first time. She is not biting her lip any more, nor covering her mouth with her hand, neither does she ask for help to translate. Her English is not perfect but it is good enough and she addresses Don directly, pointing to his tie: "I was like this fish, at the bottom of the sea, not able to move. It was dark. Now, here (she points to the middle ground) waiting to find my wing. Soon, fly." She spreads her hand like a wing. She laughs and, as the drama therapy session ends, the other women surround her, patting her on the back. Pretty much where her wings will be.

CONCLUSION

STOP-GAP has delivered interactive educational workshops and drama therapy interventions for the past thirty years and in that time, has developed and refined its own unique brand of intervention, using many educational and therapeutic techniques to make the intervention powerful and effective. STOP-GAP originated from the founders' conviction that theatre had the potential not just to entertain, but also to inspire positive change in individual lives. By observing their own patterns of behavior being played out by characters and by helping those characters to gain some perspective on their situations, clients work to change their lives. By identifying the choices available in a range of situations and by predicting likely outcomes from choices made, clients are able to learn and rehearse strategies that lead to different outcomes–often to outcomes that more closely resemble the lives that clients wish for.

The combination of therapy and theatre is not exclusive to STOP-GAP. Many individuals and organizations use theatre techniques as a means to explore the potential for individuals and groups to observe, develop and act out dramatic recreations or representations of events from their lives. However, the STOP-GAP method is unique in that it relies on the communal creation of characters who embody dilemmas that are common to the group, in its preservation and protection of the anonymity of the original card author and in its consistency in providing theatrical teams to ensure that participants are positioned to choose the level of their own participation. STOP-GAP also remains well-positioned to develop and refine the method through a constant and extensive process of rehearsal, training, delivery and feedback.

REFERENCES

Boal, A. (1995). *The rainbow of desire: The Boal method of theatre and therapy.* New York: Routledge.

Brook, P. (1968). *The empty space.* London: MacGibbor and Kee.

Fox, J. (Ed). (1987). *The essential Moreno.* New York: Springer.

Freire, P. (1973). *Education for critical consciousness.* New York: Continuum.

Grotowski, J. (2002). *Towards a poor theatre.* New York: Routledge.

Moreno, J. (1946). *Psychodrama. Vol. I.* Beacon, New York: Beacon House.

FURTHER TRAINING

The STOP-GAP Institute
2900 Bristol Street D-105
Costa Mesa CA 92626
Tel: 714-979-7061
www.stopgap.org

Chapter 15

THE BERGMAN DRAMA THERAPY APPROACH: CREATING THERAPEUTIC COMMUNITIES IN PRISONS

John Bergman

Prison cultures can be very dangerous. The anger that is part of prison life can become a deep and corrosive force stifling staff and prisoner alike. Geese Theatre Company USA has been involved with institutional change since 1980. It is our experience that challenges to institutional cultures are modified, and therapeutic communities are created through elements of drama therapy.

Geese Company has been involved in creating, running and training staff to work in total and modified therapeutic communities in prisons since 1988. We have created a practical set of principles using drama therapy to transform staff and prison cultures so that they can effectively and safely run therapeutic communities. There has been some evaluation of our work, including the effectiveness of one of the communities in Australia (Cook, Semmens & Grimswade, 1999).

This chapter reviews the issues that we faced and the processes that we used in two prison therapeutic communities in Australia and Romania. The issues were similar in both countries in that we were forced to deal with varying degrees of dense, angry resistance to change. In both sites we were attempting to challenge the cultures of the prisons. This meant understanding staff beliefs about prisoners, justice and punishment and using drama therapy to make it possible for these deep-rooted beliefs to change.

It has been our experience that staff beliefs increase or reduce the environmental support for inmate change. Therapeutic communities are environments for offenders to challenge and change their behaviors. Everyone involved in a therapeutic community must either believe or be able to maintain the belief that offenders can change. The staff in a therapeutic community are change agents, no matter what their rank or function.

In this chapter we hope to make clear that it *is* possible to make profound changes in institutional behavior. We are clear after all this time that certain mechanisms in the institution must be present for change to occur and we have tried to document them through the account of the processes at the two international sites. We also make clear that drama therapists who engage in this work must be prepared to endure countertransferential affect and allow time for staff to change. It is our belief that drama therapy can create the intense fuel necessary for old beliefs to be changed sufficiently to challenge dangerous prison cultures.

GENESIS

Geese Theatre Company, United States was founded in 1980 by John Bergman, an ex-patriot from England. Geese Company's mission was to use the arts to make change in criminal justice settings, especially penitentiaries. Currently, there is a Geese training/drama therapy component in the United States, in Romania in alliance with TRANSCAENA Company, and a very strong touring company and treatment component in the franchised Geese Theatre Company, United Kingdom.

One of Geese Company's basic premises is that prisons develop institutional thinking, metaphors, responses, and actions that are peculiar to them and to no one else. During its inception in 1980, Geese Company focused on how to acquire and convert prisoner images and metaphors (*Violent Illusion,* Bergman, & Hewish, 1996) through drama-based techniques. Many of our philosophic work practices are based on understanding the metaphors particular to special populations. We believe that the drama therapy worker is a skilled listener with a set of action tools that can convert what she/he hears into systemic growth. The drama therapist allows the practical work/life metaphors of the institution to be seen and worked with in a different way.

BASIC CONCEPTS

Interactive Performance Theatre and the Therapeutic Community

The success of some of our work is based in part on the fact that our metaphors, treatment processes and interactive psychoeducational performances have all been co-created through extensive listening and conversion of offender and officer perceptions into theatre-based modalities.

The strategies of work with staff in therapeutic communities that are outlined in this chapter follow our two basic precepts:

- Work with what you really hear, not what you would like the client to say or be
- All people can change if they get the opportunity to CONSCIOUSLY do so

Theatre can and does actively teach people more about who they are. Drama therapy does this by:

a. Providing participants with a temporary mechanism to enact significantly alternative versions of their life behavior.
b. Providing a dynamic learning experience that also acts as a potent memory or mnemonic device especially for participants who respond poorly to paper and pencil lectures.
c. Giving a tool for creating new organizing principles for institutions.
d. Making powerful connections between self, therapeutic insight and action. We use drama therapy to highlight every aspect of cognitive restructuring–affec-

tive memories in offender cycle work; experiential enactment of cognitive-based changes, and the real-time testing of skills in high-risk situations.

Drama therapy mimics situations in a way that is safe but sufficiently real that participants can experience or create changes that have powerful meanings both at that time and for the future. Our training increases awareness of how offenders and staff think. It draws from newer psychological practices (attachment theory, narrative therapy, Arnold Mindell's (1992) process-oriented physical work) and is connected to well-known game and drama work, as well as criminal justice specific theatre-based strategies to stimulate affective responses. We can therefore attack the profound resistance of prison cultures using a very wide variety of institution-specific tools.

Systemic Dysfunction: Officer versus Offender

Prisons exacerbate everyone's problems, including the jailers. The beliefs and myths about prisons and prisoners, supported by officers' potent beliefs about justice and punishment, can clash dangerously with the basic considerations of institutional safety and ethical relationships. The overriding concerns of security staff and their often unacknowledged states of anxiety create hostility towards prisoners even without the periodic acts of violence done by prisoners.

It is our experience that the more acutely the clients are feared the more intensely the physical environment is monitored, and stripped of any material (such as sensory material) that help make personal change. A prison of fear gradually becomes merely bare walls, bars and the combat of competing control. The inmate's limited sense of self is completely suppressed. This mimics his own past violence. He rebels. He is further monitored and suppressed. This combat may lead to an attempt to suppress all normative affect. At its worst this battle leads to violence.

In a recent article in the New York Times, there was a lengthy investigative article on current correctional practices on Riker's Island. The terms and actions have a war feel to them such as *cell extraction* for getting a prisoner to come out of his room, the common use of pepper spray for offender control, and the use of electric devices to give offenders massive electric shocks (50,000 volts) for control.

Fear reduces the available human surfaces for connection. Fear makes the other an enemy. Fear and fearful staff find ways to support institutional administrative bureaucracies that are conservative, cautious, reactive and maintain the status quo: the we/they of the Zimbardo prison roles (Zimbardo, 1973). Correctional facilities then spiral down into using more and more specialized facilities for the dangerous. In the Texas Department of Corrections, offenders can be sent to administrative segregation for endangering an officer. Administrative segregation can include being locked up for 20 hours or more a day for up to two years–alone. Endangering an officer may mean only talking back to him. It is not uncommon for staff in some institutions to have an unofficial goon squad that takes violent care of men that are perceived to be too mouthy, too dangerous.

This fear, in our experience, has a complex etiology. It is a fear that when you hear it close-up, it has the raw edge of anger, of righteousness, of past injustices made into a way of thinking. Many male staff, in our experience, have survived dangerous family experiences as children. It is not uncommon in our trainings for male staff to talk about the use of violent punishment by their parents or siblings. Many have, we believe, learned that bad behavior must be punished swiftly. They have learned that aggressive punishment means good control, and good behavior. From their own behavior, it seems that these staff have never experienced or learned tolerance.

In practice the power of dangerous beliefs about justice and punishment can translate into demeaning, harsh, derisive and cruel ways of communicating with the incarcerated. Beliefs alone can lead to lowering the bar of humane relationships with in-house punishments that are arbitrary, unjust, clearly favoring some rather than others, and applied differently from shift to shift.

The offender in this environment is pitted every moment against the officer and the administration–the officer who is certain that the offender is out to kill him, the inmate certain that the officer is waiting to take his very life spirit from him.

In this culture, the worst that a prison can produce, there is no possibility of change. It is not what we mean by justice, unless we really think that the convicted should experience hell as a just punishment for his/her crime. It is not a place of trust. These types of institutional settings are not conducive to change.

Systemic Dysfunction: How Administration Can Make it Worse

Prisons in particular are often run as paramilitary, top-down hierarchies. This applied in particular to Romania. Individual thinking, human rights, and ethical interventions were often ransomed to power relationships and allegiances that spelled temporary safety for lower ranked staff. Life in the administrative section of a prison or prison system can be Macchiavelian. New programs, or new thinking can become pawns in a game of influence and power. There are few steady loyalties. Without *total* support from the top no initiative has a chance.

Institutions work through repetition, imitation, and obedience to plans that support variations of suppression in the name of safety. These plans are rarely democratically created. They are generally enforced, either benignly or in some cases with emotional force. Perceived or imagined resistance is overcome by more rules or more force. Sometimes new ways of doing things are put in place through fake democracy–lectures with a "you must" message, fiats by e-mail or on notice boards at the officer's muster. This is met by resistance and disbelief from all.

Even administrators themselves feel helpless and frustrated since they may introduce new ideas that are rarely implemented or superceded by fiats from above or in central office. Sometimes staff who have made their allegiance to a program are told overnight that their program no longer exists. Staff from all ranks lose any sense of purpose. The resistance mounts. The difficulty of maintaining standards makes it possible for recalcitrant staff to hide in the crannies and crevices of the institution. No one is accountable, there are no firings; the staff run the institution in whatever way they interpret the rules.

Clearly this chaos trickles down the hierarchy to the offenders. As their fear mounts, the pressure to defy mounts. The offender survives through temporary links with other offenders, through intimidation and imitation and detached momentary relationships with institutional staff. The administration feels hopeless.

In Romania the infrastructure is very new, but the old administrative strata are still secretly in power. When they are not in power, staff still believe that they are. This makes Romanian staff very pessimistic. This in turn makes change even harder to create. Since the country also has no deep resources, change is triply difficult. In

Romania there was always the perceived problem of trying to work out people's loyalties. A question made in public to the administration is simply met by silence. As we found many times, it is still dangerous to speak. It is still not easy to understand the layers of the prison administration. There is, we believe, much more to unfold.

In Australia, many of the administrative problems had been breached by a very potent steering committee. But there was still a very significant resistance from "the good old boys" about the work. In short order the work was labeled as Spice World, Wobbies World, and so forth. One of the major goals early on was to try to persuade male administrators that the culture change was real, necessary and safe.

The Fundamental Task

A prison or a juvenile facility is a tapestry of connections, counterconnections, loyalties, counterloyalties, relatives, outcasts, tryers, destroyers, saboteurs, worriers, people sticking their heads in the sand, get by-ers, do my time-ers, nasty ones–and everyone is as Camus said–innocent: "We are all special cases. We all want to appeal against something! Everyone insists on his innocence, at all costs, even if it means accusing the rest of the human race and heaven" (*The Fall*, Camus, 1991).

This is critical. Neither those who make the institution survive from day to day nor those who make it fail see themselves as anything other than on the side of the angels. Unmindful of why they do what they do, many staff are simply people operating in accordance with what is congruent with their beliefs. No matter what the new or old mission statements really are, or how eloquent/elegant they are, staff often at heart find the pretty phrases irrational, ego dystonic, not congruent with the realities as they see them. The mission statements neither salve the edge of the authoritarian nightmare, redress the endless resentment of perceived random pronouncements from the hierarchy, nor seem attuned to the reality of privately held beliefs. Mission statements do not solve the ethical issues of problems on the job.

A crucial thread in the work of any drama therapist must always be understanding how staff or clients construct their realities. We have to find out what things mean in a prison before we can change or consider changing its meaning. Why is a belt a powerful resonant object in the mind of some staff or clients? Why do the words *good, safe, wrong,* or *bad* produce such a huge response? Why do so many correctional staff have such a mammoth response to the word *fair?*

We will go to war for the most extraordinary of things even though they are as abstract as a belief or as small as a nickel. A prisoner once told Geese USA how he had killed a man because he stole his last match. He actually said, "If you let someone get away with something like that, they'll never stop. They'll take everything you have. You'll end up with nothing. You have to teach people lessons. Get what you can, before they get you."

THERAPEUTIC PROCESS

Surfacing the Beliefs

Part of the task of cultural change is surfacing beliefs and changing them. You cannot change what you do not know. Most people in institutions are simply not aware of the power of their beliefs over their actions–and this is one of the most cherished tenets of cognitive behavioral change.

We create many exercises to surface the power of staff beliefs. In Romania, for example, there are two very famous football teams called Dinamo and Steua. In my first meeting with all of the officers in the Bucharest-based prison called Rahova, where we were due to open a therapeutic community, we asked the officers who supported which teams. After a show of hands we asked the 150 officers what they thought about their own teams and then about their rivals. Fortunately the differences were enormous–one is a team that represents the military and one a team that was the team of the justice department. In the old days that had included the feared Securitate, or special police force. Obviously when we asked staff about their teams, we also tapped into deep beliefs about the past, the state of the country and so on. Their responses were very lively for so early in the morning.

Then we asked the officers how much it would take to become an *ardent* supporter of the rival team. In a country where the average salary is $50–$75 per month, one officer finally said a million dollars, and a white Rolls Royce. He then rebutted himself and said that actually he would still really be lying and that nothing could ever make him change teams.

An absurd exercise? Football teams are not justice, beliefs about punishment or the small thoughts that make up the support for action. But those football teams are metaphors for complex beliefs. Administrations ask staff in institutional settings to change their teams on demand. At worst they neither bargain with them, nor help them adjust to the new beliefs. In Australia and Romania we asked the staff to go from custody roles to therapeutic relationships. It is not uncommon for trainers and administrators to present the new team and its philosophy overnight in a three-day training with an unwritten implication that if you go along you will be accepted and if you do not you will be ostracized. But the Dinamo supporter would not change to the Steua team because of what he believed, and asking staff to change from fear and control to supportive connection with offenders is as intense a demand.

The drama therapist must use the art to create the gateway for either a profound change of beliefs or for an acclimation to beliefs that are uncomfortable.

Changing Dysfunctional Beliefs

Drama therapy helps people see the other side, stripping long-held beliefs of their validity for a short time. It makes it possible to think that the enemy is human. The drama therapist's job is to help staff adjust the beliefs that they have, beliefs based on their own life experiences, so that they can deal compassionately with people whose behaviors have tended to evoke a judgmental or revengeful reaction.

One of the reasons that we also use cognitive behavioral change is that this therapeutic tool helps people to become conscious of how they think very quickly. Becoming conscious of every thought, feeling, physical sensation, picture and belief is at the heart of cognitive behavioral change and therefore an invaluable addition to drama therapy. In cognitive self-change for offenders one challenges beliefs that lead to old injurious behaviors. I am most grateful for the time that Dr. John Bush took while we worked together in Vermont, to teach me how to get staff and offenders to document their minds in the very simplest way possible. Perceived conscious thought, plus conscious feelings, plus the awareness of the power of a belief is the meat of action. If we are to be successful in changing and training staff and prisons we must become conscious of the power of our own thoughts and feelings. This is the task of the drama therapist creating cultural change in a prison.

The Therapeutic Community

Incarcerated clients can be resistant, defiant, dependent, anti-authoritarian, victims of violence. They may suffer from intrusive memories; they can be deeply conservative, active thrill-seekers, obsessive, secretive, hostile, aggressive, determined, curious, courageous, emotionally unattached, and very afraid. Violent clients will not let you close. They believe that the world is out to hurt them. These same clients paradoxically often have good humor, enormous insight into others, and a great argumentative tenacity in defending their own beliefs.

Prisons are often violent. Certainly prisons are filled with violent men with violent thoughts and beliefs. In antisocial environments, aggressively defensive adults and children adapt by competing against feeling overwhelmed. They use coping skills like rage, intimidation and deception to deal with violent environments that they consider a threat to their own safety. Bad prisons make prisoners emotionally and psychosocially worse. Adult and adolescent incarcerated clients need at a minimum carefully crafted environments in which they can learn and practice alternative ways of responding. They need environments that challenge their thinking and engage them to try alternatives.

"The therapeutic community movement implicitly adopts the view that deviant behavior, much of which is deemed criminal, represents a breakdown of the relationship between the individual and the structured society of which he is . . . a member" (Roberts, 1997, p. 5). Strong therapeutic communities create whole societies with strong prosocial values against which offenders can measure their current new behaviors. In these types of environments nothing is overlooked. All behaviors are subject to scrutiny. Any one action can be seen as symptomatic of the entire behavioral outlook. In 1991, during a visit to the Missouri State penitentiary therapeutic community, a young prisoner told us how he came to break out of his old behaviors. He had been in the community kitchen and had failed to wash his cup–the older peers in the TC simply confronted him until he saw how this represented his longstanding unwillingness to be responsible and respectful. "Successful socialization gives an ability to empathize with and place a value on other beings" (Roberts 1997, p. 7).

Therapeutic communities are high tariff environments. They are emotionally hot, intensive, and confronting. These environments do not give offenders their traditional means of escaping either responsibility or the emotions that they find so threatening. TC s force offenders to interact with others, potentiating the long march towards empathy.

"TC learning experiences consist of a combination of natural and logical consequences which can be viewed as behavior therapy or social learning within the context of a positive peer culture and experiential framework" (Yokley 1999, p. 2).

In the Romanian and Australian TCs we insisted that staff look at punishment in a new way. For offenders to change they must be made conscious of their actions in an environment that actively mimics the real world but highlights positive reinforcing value behavior. TCs cannot work in an atmosphere of distrust, violence, changing standards and arbitrary pictures of punishment. It was paramount in Australia that we break the old culture of using enforced isolation to change behavior. Changed behavior must be practiced, supported, encouraged and made the norm.

Significant decreases in criminal involvement after treatment has been demonstrated for both adults and adolescents in the community setting (DeLeon, 1984, 1987; Pombi,

1994) and for inmates in the correctional setting (Wexler & Love, 1994; Yokley, 1999).

The therapeutic community serves many purposes. It is a place where unlike any other unit in an institution, the focus is self-change and growth rather than mere incapacitation. It is a place where all people are expected to take on far more responsibilities than they do in a regular setting and even than in the real world.

It is an environment in which people are encouraged/expected to respond to things in a nonviolent way. It is an environment in which the new, the unexpected, the direct, the honest, the caring, the crying, the feeling, the hurting, the attempting, the getting there way of life is supported and created.

TCs are famous for being vital, creative, intense and hugely rewarding environments to work in. They put staff in diametrically new relationships with clients. The demands of a real therapeutic community are so intense that they automatically raise the caring standards of the workers in the unit. This type of configuration is a remarkable strategy for creating a new culture in a facility.

The Institution's Role

Beginnings are critical. Drama therapists, like any visitor making changes, should pay attention to what the institution, or system, or central office leader actually sets in place. The institution must take on part of the task from the outset of supporting, alerting, and informing the system that there is going to be a huge cultural change. For big changes one will need:

a. A management team that is organized, aware of the issues, has cleared, booked, found people, arranged for backfill and personnel support. This team may become one's closest friends during the work. They must maintain their enthusiasm during the dark days when the new ideology is attacked.
b. Total support from the top of the system. I cannot stress this enough. If one is attempting to combat an entrenched prison culture and one's authority is dependent on whims, favors, power plays, the process will be at risk. The top person must be prepared to stand and deliver, to publicly support the work.
c. Real funding that will cover a therapeutic community after the drama therapist has gone. Nothing will get staff attention more than the knowledge that there is a budget for a return visit and for the materials that they will need.
d. Real time to do the work. A measure of the seriousness of the institution or correctional system is their willingness to bend the rules, adequately ensure that staff have a real grounding in the work through lengthy training. Three-day trainings rarely accomplish much.
e. A high-placed person in the process to maintain the integrity and real meaning of the work hour to hour on the ground in the unit. Our success in Australia is in great part due to Di Garner, a youth worker administrator who remained committed to the process, maintained connected with us and dealt at every turn with vital issues of personnel and client distress.
f. Staff who are prepared in some ways to create a new culture. One of the key components of a resistant culture is the ongoing resentment of many staff at feeling forced to do yet another initiative that they have neither chosen nor debated. Staff and offenders must be polled, challenged, informed. They must have free will or they will not fight for the new culture and will crum-

ble when the old guard fights back.

g. Someone who will manage the staff during your training. Staff can be rude, antagonistic, even insulting. There must be a staff supervisor who will effectively discipline the trainee. I had to ask an officer in the Romanian training to leave when he insisted that "there is nothing good about inmates." I explained to him that the therapeutic community simply would use different values and beliefs from his own and that it looked as if it might be too hard to align them.

CASE EXAMPLES

The Romanian and Australian facilities in which we created these modified therapeutic communities seem on the surface enormously different. The maximum-security penitentiary in Bucharest where we created the TC is situated in a suburb of Bucharest called Rahova. It is a 1500 bed, soon to be 2000 bed, prison for adult prisoners who have committed everything from theft to murder. On average, the men are serving five to ten years, and have either been sent directly to the prison or sent from other older prisons.

The prison is less than two years old. It is run by Dr. Florian Gheorghe who was both a high ranking member of the older prison system after Ceaucescu and is also a clinical psychologist. Dr. Gheorghe is a personable man in his forties with a deep passion about this work. He has written about the psychology of prisoners and was entrusted with the running of this prison as soon as it was conceived. He unfortunately inherited its less than useable design. He also inherited many of the staff, some of whom have come from prisons such as Gelava, a prison that has a notorious and dangerous reputation.

During his tenure as commandant he has seen a number of system bosses, but the current head of the prison services named the Direction General Penitenciar or D.G.P. is a former magistrate called Mr. Marian Eftimescu. He is the current General Director of the entire Romanian prison system. He is a warm and genuinely caring man who speaks openly about the problems that present-day Romania has inherited from the Ceaucescu days. This in itself is an act of great courage since there still exists a culture that represses open talk about anything that could be conceived of as controversial. One quickly learns, or believes, that it is normal to have spies working with you while you teach or train, reporting what one does to whoever thinks they need to know. It is normal for the staff to believe that there is always some type of Macchiavellian plot going on. Suspicion deeply permeates any work and relationships, and engenders cynicism and hopelessness. It is quite common in Romania for people to tell a trainer that there is not much point in doing any work. "It will only be sabotaged and destroyed."

Dr. Florian Gheorghe and I had begun discussions together in 1997. At that time his major concern was how to create a new, caring and humane cadre of officers and subofficers. He had taught some of his new staff to listen to the inmates' concerns, a revolution in its own right in Romania. As we continued the discussions I spoke about the first unit for violent men that I had co-created and run with Jack Bush in the Vermont Department of Corrections in 1988. This unit was run by correctional officers as well as Jack and myself. It was our shared belief that correctional officers could make creditable prison group leaders using cognitive restructuring strategies and high risk role work. These are fundamental strategies for working with men convicted of violence.

This appealed strongly to Dr. Gheorghe and the objectives were to train five psychologists and 12 correctional staff to work together to run a therapeutic unit of 30 incarcerated men. There were also long-term comprehensive goals. We determined that the unit was to become a training centre for best practices and to be an experiential center for other staff from other penitentiaries. Dr. Florian was very concerned with how officers can do the right thing after many years of not doing so.

The beginning was not auspicious. Many of the Romanian staff were completely unprepared for the work. The officers volunteered themselves on the very day that we began. Money, always a crucial issue, had not been allocated for translators, nor was there money for supplies. We simply bought what we needed on the first days.

Dr. Florian was unavoidably on holiday for one of the weeks that we worked. It is sometimes critical that the boss be present when large changes are happening. Of much greater gravity very early on in the work, three officers put on hoods and beat an inmate very badly. We had no idea if this was a threat or a violent coincidence. But it cast a shadow over the work.

The impact of the commandant's absence was quite large, even though there was little that he could have done about this. One shift seemed very proactive, ushering us politely through daily checks. Another held us up, asked for papers, kept other staff waiting. Senior officers did not always come to training. When it came to getting special packages for offender participants in the proposed new community the discussions became quite murky, especially without having the commandant to work with us. Paperwork, constructive meetings, equal discussions, feedback, constructive criticism, and reviews were almost nonexistent. To the credit of the Romanian team who worked with us, whatever we suggested they tried to do or get.

Many staff were unable to believe that change was possible and harbored deep angry beliefs about the prisoners. The language difference was sometimes too huge. But we were reassured by our meetings with General Director Marian Eftimescu. It was he who told us that inmates who participated in the therapeutic community would get packages and visits. In doing this he told us that the work would be supported.

In Australia, this support was clear from the outset and became crucial when the resistance to change became very ugly. The initial preparation for the work at the facility had been impeccable. Melbourne Juvenile Justice Centre is a prison for adolescents; it classifies, detains, imprisons and releases. The CEO, Diana Batzias, had gradually transformed the institution from a hard core imitation of an adult prison, contained a staff riot, let older youth workers go, supported a steering committee and its recommendations for change.

When we began our work there, Diana Batzias said the situation was ripe. There was a significant core of administrative staff, and members of the chaplaincy and senior staff, overwhelmingly women, who wanted change. The pump had been primed by Patrick Tidmarsh, a noted sex offender therapist in Australia who had worked in the 1980s with Geese UK. We gave an introductory workshop on-site with the senior staff who then made recommendations that Melbourne Juvenile Justice Centre (MJJC) should create a new therapeutic unit.

In the case of MJJC, there were plenty of problems to deal with–entrenched notions of what the children could really do (or not do), a lack of trust in the children's ability to self govern, real ignorance about newer methods of working with defiant and oppositional behaviors, and in some cases a sense that the children were on a revolving door journey and that therefore nothing could work. Some staff felt that there was no point in doing anything, that it would be better to "lock 'em up since it's the only thing they understand." In a few cases there was also a culture of restrained and unrestrained violence towards the children, the arbitrary use of the "slot"–isolation for children who were considered too defiant. In a few cases the violence and threats to the children were a permanent way of mind.

Each adolescent unit houses between seven and fifteen children, ages roughly 13 to 18. The crimes committed by the adolescents range from murder and rape to theft and repeated arrests for drug and alcohol use. The sentences in American terms are very low–2 years served for murder, generally serving no more real time than a year. In South Bank, one of the housing units at MJJC, the average time served by the children was under three months.

We found the basic ideologies and philosophies of understanding and working with children at MJJC confused and flawed. The most common that we first encountered was a notion of benign neglect that said "these children have suffered too much already, so they must be looked after and then returned to the community with as little interference from us as possible." Post Martinson, the architect of the notion that "nothing works," suggests this had even been the law. The downside of this benign approach is that the heroin in Melbourne is cheap and powerful. Too many children were leaving the facility without self-restraint skills, or any conscious strategies for self-change and either reoffending or dying of overdoses. Many of the adolescents had simply not had a chance to try out any alternative behavioral responses to any stimuli.

When we finally wrote to Di Garner who became one of the administrators most central to the success of the therapeutic community, we said the following:

The Premise:

1. Security and treatment are complementary.
2. Punishment alone is ineffective as a mode of change.
3. Treatment is not an alternative to taking responsibility for dangerous actions.
4. Treatment and security are part of a three-cornered hat that includes the children.
5. Security is the application of rules in a way that makes children understand their relationship with authority and encourages them to make change through treatment and behavioral experiment.
6. Children are smart enough to make their own choice to change.
7. Children must change their relationship with authority, which requires treatment to help with their thoughts and feelings, and behavioral practice, which is created in their relationships with the youth workers and the treatment community.

The Aims of this Training are:

1. To teach the methods of behavioral change using the security/treatment principles.
2. To teach youth workers how to apply these principles with youth in a treatment community.
3. To teach children how to reflect on their dangerous beliefs about authority and begin the process of seeing and taking responsibility for their relationships with authority.
4. To teach treatment staff their role in this model.

Institutions must know that change is

coming. MJJC took a huge responsibility for making the ground as fertile as it could. The working drama therapist must make sure that he/she does the work that she/he is really responsible for. The institution must let the entire facility know what is going on, mobilize support all the way to the top, inform and educate.

Melbourne Juvenile Justice Centre was a full experiment in shifting the culture so that the whole institution could move on. Rahova, on the other hand, was a great juggling improvisation to make one corner of the prison map a decent place.

How Did It Happen?

The creation of change in both the Australian and Romanian systems was similar in one way because time for both was so limited–ten days, eight hours a day, to train staff, and five days to get the system up and running with the clients. We had to start quickly.

In both countries, the central issue was to break through staff disbelief and resistance as quickly as possible. In Australia, part of the change was accomplished before we even started.

All the staff was alerted, no secrets were kept, a steering team kept the ball rolling and there were people who were accountable for introducing the entire process to the facility. The center was put on notice in a clear and professional way that change was coming in six months–a reasonable amount of time for any forewarning of change. For our purposes as the change agents, we had a clear picture of what was happening, what we had to do and the knowledge that there would be people left on the ground who would make it their responsibility to create and maintain the work after we left. Di Garner, who was point person, the communicator, had a good line of authority to the CEO, and therefore enough authority to make the work happen. This is critical. We strongly recommend that drama therapists trying to take on an entire institutional culture look clear-eyed at whether they have any of the above processes and people in place. Changing institutional beliefs will raise resentment and defiance. Without the determined support of the type we received from Di Garner and the CEO Diana Batzias, the work will become corrupted and marginalized afterwards.

The Process

The management team made sure that they knew what the work was and also wrestled with the issues. It was the management team that came to a one-day intensive that we did and fully participated in the experiential training. It was they who wrestled with the interviews and what good practice might really mean.

Many of the staff members in Romania and Australia were nervous from the very beginning. At both sites some of them looked at our mask, dolls and toys with a mixture of fear and scorn. It is the norm for corrections. Our first task was to listen to the officers and administrators, empower them by recognizing their real knowledge, hear them out and make them feel as safe as possible.

Romanian staff members were harder to read in the beginning and the language issues played against us. In the first days the novelty of the situation seemed to overwhelm the Romanian staff. Discussions were harder to maintain and the staff was more anxious to be led, to take notes. The drama games were a relief, but not a way to deal with truth. The trust issues were significantly greater and there was a greater sense of opacity of the staff. Romanian staff were poorly prepared in terms of information, the *why* and the *what* of the training. They had more to catch up with, though this was balanced by the newness of some of them. The new staff had not had time to create hard and fast beliefs. Of the basic training principles the most crucial was that they had at least volunteered to take part in this training.

Check In

We always begin trainings by asking people what they want from the sessions, what they actually do at the institution and what they think the real issues are. We do this whether it is a conference, a training, or a three-hour workshop. It is democratic and it is a powerful moment for some of the staff. It sets a tone and in Romania signifies democracy. We believe that once people have been doing their prison job for a while they have something important to say. They are at least more expert about the stress and problems of their respective jobs than the outsider who comes to teach and visit. It is a hallmark for trainers working in criminal justice that 65 percent of the success of any training is getting the trust of the staff. They have to believe that you have been there, that you can take it, have confronted the violence and made it through. It is an unspoken challenge. When the staff share or smile or confront each other in the presence of the trainer, then you have begun to win.

Warm-up Theater Games

Once the check-in is done we go straight to theatre games. Theatre games change atmospheres, loosen attitudes, affect and cognitions. But games may be threatening to some. In prisons, play means letting down one's guard and so it is unusual and dangerous. Games mean losing face, appearing silly and out of control. In Australia, staff were far more sensitive about looking stupid and seemed strongly influenced by the "tall poppy syndrome," a culturally shared idea that people do not try to stand above or be different from each other.

Romanian staff, on the other hand, took to theatre games with gusto and great invention. They seemed to find the exercises an immediate relief from discussions about the prison. There is a greater fear of discussion in Romania, of naming truths. But Romanian staff was also considerably more comfortable in using metaphors and masks. It is safer in Australia to talk, though discussions about institutional violence were never honestly dealt with. But the real point of the games was the start of the assault on dangerous institutional beliefs. Even to play is the start of giving some staff a key to other types of thinking–kinetic, visual, auditory.

The choice of theatre exercises was crucial. Officers in our experience seem to relate strongly to action exercises. They are in action work. They are strongly responsive to running and chasing games. So the first exercises in both countries included:

1. Calling out five things to be touched in seven seconds, then shortening the time to five seconds and so on.
2. A blind conga line with a sighted leader who took the followers out of the space altogether and in Australia out into the street. This helped to foster the idea of safely breaking rules and that there would not be too much sitting down and being lectured to. The game also sent a message of excitement, and that there was less to fear than people expected.
3. Walks leading to jumps, touching backs, sudden turns, freezes. In other words kinetic action that focused staff on listening, responding quickly and giving up some of their control to us. Trust without saying the words.

4. Red light/Green light, an exercise that encourages silent kinetic control. We played a version of this exercise in which the entire group had to work together to get a large set of keys back to the "beginning" without being seen by the one who is "it." This game is also a way to break up cliques, and set people to work with those who are not accustomed to doing so. It was the first exercise in which the staff had to figure out a problem together. There would be hundreds more.

As we taught we let staff know what the pattern of work every day would be–physical games and exercises first, then more intensive work, then more drama work, then theory and so on. We did not do any large scale trust work on the first day because we did not know who people could trust. In Romania in particular we were still very uncertain who the participants were and felt that it was our responsibility not to put the participants in jeopardy.

Much of the early days consisted of action exercises followed by discussions. We challenged the staff to think about what the TC would be, how it would operate with the clients. We used sculpts to start the ball rolling into the dangerous territory of perceiving the clients in new ways. Rather than discussions that might make staff feel like they had to defend an institutional way of doing things, we wanted the ball in our dramatic court, away from resistance about theories of correctional change, and tired discussions of punishment. Using theatre exercises allows for discovering new ways for people to think about problems. Physical sculpts invariably give staff a way to express the sense of a thing, making the old facility suddenly exciting again. It is this excitement that we knew we had to generate in order to make an affective and experiential platform that would support change.

We used standard sculpts that we began from an exercise in which groups had to first get specific numbers of feet and hands on the ground while leaning on each other, and then a smaller number of feet and hands and so on. This physically connected staff and gave them another problem to solve, while masking fears of creativity. Once the staff were used to being kinetically connected we transformed the exercise into creating sculpts about Tower Bridge, broken bridges, blocked dreams, and finally shared pictures of the old unit as it had been and the perceived blocks to change this. We gave the staff very little time to talk to each other. We wanted to avoid their blocks about the work and to continue the idea of brainstorming in small groups, trusting the first best idea and acting on it. This work seemed to excite the staff in both countries and gave them an acute sense of solving problems.

Deepening the Process

It was at this point that we asked the groups to create sculpts about clients' issues. We focused the groups on creating sculpts with affectively intense titles such "Outcast," "I hate you," "Unwanted." Each sculpt was interpreted by the staff with little comment from us to give everyone the sense that they could create in their groups without interference. When staff asked what a title referred to we said, "Whatever comes to mind is correct. There is no right or wrong answer."

From the outset we had watched some staff, especially those we suspected had more issues with violence in the unit, trying to gauge how other staff were responding to the work. In Australia and to some extent in Romania the more defended staff repeatedly sent fearful or questioning looks to each other or rolled their eyes looking for an answering nod. Some for a short while hovered on resisting doing the work altogether. The great efforts of the steering committee really panned out for us here. The breaks were filled with fast-talking cliques, some of whom looked very angry and gave us cold looks.

Working With Resistance

This is a pattern of response that we have seen repeated many times in Australia. Staff can get ruder (than they are to offenders) to the trainers, and challenge our ethical stances about offenders in very aggressive ways: "You can't do these things with crims." "They just won't change." They back away from the exercises, or openly attempt to sabotage a game or role play. As a trainer, you have few choices. You must face this resistance directly, call the bluff, name the action, keep working and maintain focus with those who are trying hard to overcome their anxiety or fear. At the worst, you may have to ask for a staff member to be put out of the training as we did in Romania and nearly did in Australia. It is why getting the staff to audition for the training and the unit was so crucial to its success. People who have competed to be in a training/unit will work far harder to challenge themselves.

Exploring New Beliefs

We asked each group to present their sculpt work to the others. This is a very dangerous moment especially for prison officers. It is the first time that staff can look at each other's drama work outside the collective identity of the prison. It is the first time that staff can show other identities. The rapport created from the work of making the sculpts can be easily jarred. In Australia we heard the phrase "comfort zone" used time and again. It was used as a wall against any experience that challenged the known. As the work progressed the phrase disappeared.

The intensity of the sculpt titles also gave us our first opportunity to see what staff thought when they heard these words, how they saw the prisoners, how they saw themselves. We used these exercises to start the work of getting staff to understand how people make decisions in their lives. It was a way to start the discussions about *other,* about the realities of working with violence, about the fears that any reasonable person would have and what our vision and experience of violent people was. The outcast sculpt represented some of the staff who could not tell friends about their vocation, or the agony of the adopted and forgotten child/adolescent offender, or pictures of the worker versus the administration. But these sculpts helped set the tone–cruelty out, respect and connection in. The debate got hotter.

In Romania we had each staff member describe something good about the prisoners. One of them said there was nothing. At the break I asked him to leave. We talked about the fact that his values and those of the new community conflicted, and that there was no blame here. I cannot condemn a man for his beliefs, but I can challenge them in fair debate or ask someone to leave when they are antithetical to our work practices. In this new environment we demanded that people use an attitude of respect for the offenders. It meant finding something that one can believe about all humankind.

Foundation Principles for the Therapeutic Community

The work on sculpts and on understanding the dynamics of the outcast lead easily to the next phase–to get staff to work on the foundation principles for their therapeutic community. The foundation principles are a high-toned way into the concepts of therapeutic change and of modeling new beliefs and attitudes. The principles are like a United Nations charter of beliefs. They are the spine for any new community. They also release staff from the feeling that they are being led. The creation of the principles is high energy, intense small group work.

Therapeutic communities take a huge amount of energy, and a lot of responsibility and personality. Therapeutic communities are not places for "shrinking violets" and because they are environments in which the offenders have much more overt responsibility for the gist and running of the experience, staff must be more quickly engaged and present. They must have a set of principles to guide the new environment. We push the staff to work on the ideas for the TC.

We encouraged the staff to create these principles in the simplest language they could. We broke down the use of the mission-statement-type language of Australia and the patriotic language of Romania so that the language could be something that adolescents could cope with and prisoners trust. We prepared the ground by asking the staff to do the *Island Exercise.*

Staff members first drew everything that they would want on their own island. Then they wrote the rules of their islands and what happened if anyone broke the rules. Then we asked the staff to pair up and share islands. This was hard. Some people had peaceful open islands without rules or punishment. Some staff had intensely private islands with rules for everything and a long list of punishments for breaking the rules. The parallels with the staff's lives were very obvious. Staff who hardly knew each other cautiously bared themselves through a game that had real meaning. We reminded them–*it is just a game,* and then contradicted this by reinforcing the need to work the problems out as if they were actually real problems. In small groups the staff discussed and challenged their own isolation.

These early days were jammed with break-off groups, action assignments and homework. The walls of the training space were covered with group thoughts, questions, new ideas for working with clients. This modeled the environment that we hoped the staff would create. We continued to monitor the resistance and resentment. The sculpts had opened the door to the beliefs about the clients. The foundation principles were too high-minded to allow ordinary prison-based resentment to occur. But we knew the rage would come.

This was the base work for the making of the foundation principles. From the Island exercise we asked people to create the most decent bases for co-existence in the TC. The principles were the drawing board for the functions of the TC. They were demanding, romantic and utopian. They were simple and nonbureaucratic. Some of the principles created for Eastern Hill in Australia and the Descatus area in Romania were remarkably similar and simply breathtaking. For instance:

"Anyone from anywhere is the same as anyone else."
"All life is sacred."
"In this place all people must be safe."
"Change is possible for every person."

The romance of these principles, the work of creating these principles together and of experiencing difference without violence created a growing sense that all things were possible, and a growing sense of fear and resentment. On the third day the Australian staff openly questioned our assertion that whatever we all created in this off-campus space would be the map for the work in the therapeutic community. It was as Australians say a "full on" confrontation. It was a mixed message challenge. It was a veiled way to sabotage the work and it was a way for some to say this is really stupid, nobody believes this work you are doing. It was a critical moment. It meant that some of the staff members, especially the most anxious, were feeling too threatened and too far away from the institutional norms. This is a classic moment in the confronting of prison culture, and the creation of these types of communities. (The Romanian version of this moment was far more muted.)

Fortunately and by design the CEO was present. Diana Batzias got to her feet and in front of all the staff reaffirmed that she would support whatever we did in this preparation (rehearsal) stage. This affirmation is of huge importance. One simply cannot be successful without it. I believe that this was one of the Australian TC turning points. The angry staff got the point, felt the weight of the authority. Staff must get the message that this work is for real and supported by the authority vested in the institution. For the CEO this moment was a complete leap of faith. If the experiment had gone wrong she would have been badly hurt by the failure. So the drama therapists who take on these tests must be able to deliver. We bear a huge burden of responsibility. One should not do this work if one does not have the confidence, knowledge, or ability to withstand the pressure and continue on with some degree of grace.

Changing Belief Crises

Throughout the next days all staff went through crises of belief, resistance and distancing. We overtly sympathized with this resistance but we tried to keep working, answer and send the issues back, minimizing the analysis. We let the staff think about things without our interpretation, saying instead, "What does this mean to you?" We encourage respectful honesty. We try to model that it is all right to disagree, that kids and adult offenders will disagree and that this is human, not a sign of a rebellion to be crushed. We model listening, trying to get staff to tell us what they mean in what they say, sometimes playing back what we hear and so sending the message that what people say, think, and believe is of critical importance to us. When it is safe I name the resistant thoughts that might be inside staffs' minds, so that they feel safe to defy. We repeat our philosophy over and over–your values may be different from ours–but how can you change what you believe, or moderate it to do this work. We did not compromise our beliefs no matter what exceptions the staff came up with. People are won and lost sometimes in these daily tests and debates.

Lateral thinking is a vital part of the work of providing a base for beliefs to change. The drama exercises incite the staff to learn to use their innate creativity, create metaphors and venture into the world of the impossible and illogical. This is a critical need in order to cope with the multiple demands of a TC. The usual prison environment encourages staff to be too concrete. Concrete thinking supports resistance to change and institutionalized answers. That is, staff relies on the well-worn paths of the institutional hierarchy and the reasoning associated with the status quo. Training must address this. We work very hard to introduce alternative thinking at every stage of the work, whether through using dolls and getting staff to create dialogue, humor, drawings and the constant use of improvisations, role play and the sense of sudden change. The idea is always to keep the staff a little unbalanced.

The Development of Creative Thinking

If the staff are to create very emotive environments, find alternatives for clients about violent beliefs, and even challenge their own beliefs about offenders and punishment, they must have the skill of making quick lateral idea changes. A staff member in a TC cannot rely on "this is the rule so you do it like this or else." S/he has to be able to say, "Have you tried thinking about it in another way, what if . . ."

But lateral thinking is a safe *what if* way to experiment with the shock of new beliefs. We got the staff into the habit of free associating from games, setting up word plays without the idea that there was an expected answer. We began a session from a single sentence–"my horse has just eaten . . . what?" and ask the staff to act or fill in the blanks. We played many variations of "Why are taxis painted yellow?" over the training period, pushing them to come up with more and more outlandish answers to these types of questions until they got used to jumping off the logic of the previous idea.

The effect of this work was cumulative. At first these lateral devices supported the staff in mocking, making jokes, playing safely in front of each other and therefore making the work less threatening. As we continued these processes, the staff creativity grew, and they began to make suggestions bringing paints, paper, books, photographs into the proposed unit where once this material had been considered a security issue. The lateral devices created a "theatre of all possibilities." On the final day of the work, one of the staff members came to see me. An adolescent in the unit had defaced a book. I expected her to say that he needed to be punished. Instead she said, "You know this will make a great group discussion with all the unit."

The drama therapy exercises deepened the focus of the training experience and the ability of staff to tap into their affect consciously, safely and publicly. The whole focus of the training is to challenge and change the unspoken or unacknowledged and dangerous assumptions, especially about prisoners, punishment and anger. Every tool the drama therapist uses must be for this conscious goal.

Matching Drama Therapy Interventions to the Needs of the Institution

Change in institutional settings is somewhat counterintuitive for many staff. They rely on routine, predictability, the imposing of order on adolescents or adults who enter in chaos and emotional distress. This, we believe, is a set-up for conflict that may end up resolved only with force and intensified opposition.

We had to give staff a mechanism to disengage themselves from old reactivities. In many cases we used the simplest techniques. We found that basic drama exercises and games gave staff the opportunity to step away from themselves, and to entertain that *other* was possible. Theatre, and the exercises that all actors and directors have used in theatre rehearsals, have a power that is easily underestimated.

For a non-theatre person to do an exercise as simple as five different greetings in a circle setting, can be very frightening, exciting, or freeing. If then we add in the multiplier of culture, for instance the many ways in which Australian staff felt easily confronted by the emotions engendered for them in the simplest of theatre exercises, you can well see why it was often unnecessary to use more intensive drama therapy exercises. Forbearance and simplicity are often more effective. It was sometimes simply ineffective to do very intensive drama therapy style exercises with these staff because simple work sufficed.

But in Romania we dealt more often with fear, repressed trauma, and that lack of trust that was a result of living under the autocratic rule of Ceaucescu. Officers were much less able to access their own angry thoughts, let alone their own feelings about anger. The staff combined fear of authority with what often looked like frozen attachment. The staff clearly found it difficult to speak about their grief and even shame at some of their experiences during the communist period. It was common for staff during trainings there to simply freeze, not be able to remember, dissimulate and ask not to answer.

We had begun a session on thinking disorders by doing a series of role plays about resistance and deception. Using the interpreter, we asked the staff to create what they thought were common reactions on the part of offenders to being approached by the police. Mostly the reactions appeared to be fearful, with heads held low, or lowered as the staff playing police approached. We then set up a series of empty chair exercises in which staff attempted to imagine what the offenders might be thinking. This produced many freeze reactions. We then used a double to try to elicit some of the unspoken scripts that the staff could not get to. Obviously at this point it was clear that the freeze responses were also those of the staff, as well as what they imagined the responses of the offenders to be. Using a hand pushing exercise that is a very common strategy for eliciting affect, we put the staff in pairs and asked them to try again with the double to articulate what they thought the offender was experiencing when approached by the police. Finally the interpreter spoke of what some people might believe: "here it comes, this same old . . . again, now it's time to shut up, don't say anything , these people are no good." When she articulated this, the entire staff group became very quiet. Later that day, as we processed Potter-Effron's (2004) *anger ladder* for the curriculum of Descatusarea, one of the staff was able to make reference to the first level of anger–sneaky anger–and that perhaps this might be one of the experiences of the offenders.

While we titrated drama therapy's power to fit the international circumstances, mixing theatre games with role plays and with sculpts, we also used some more intense strategies when staff were seemingly stuck. It was a delicate walk.

Cognitive Exercises and Homework

We also worked in part through the use of nondramatic cognitive exercises. In the earliest days of the training we had taught the basic tools of cognitive behavioral change: close attention to one's interior conversations and sensations–thought, feeling and action, and then record this data without censoring anything. This we buttressed with focused homework assignments consisting of phenomenological cognitive reports of real life events. The process begins by first splitting staff into pairs and asking them to create role plays based on conflicts that they have experienced within the last two weeks. We made one stipulation: no conflicts from home or from work. Each pair then enacted two role plays–some of which were emotionally quite hot. The themes of the situations in both sites were quite similar–conflicts with storekeepers, telephone operators, drivers, bus conductors, etc. But we knew that any focus on conflict gave us access to beliefs and thoughts that are relatively similar to the way in which staff dealt with any conflicts including with offenders. The assignment was to write down all the thoughts, feelings, sensations and beliefs that they remember having at the peak moment of the conflict. These were then objectively discussed in class.

This *thinking report* is a tool that we teach staff to teach to the clients. It is used as a major strategy to make prisoners mindful of their own thoughts. Publicly discussing the thoughts and actions of conflict is a very intimate act. It is a way for all the participants to see into the thoughts and feelings of their work friends. It is an unvarnished look at the beliefs that support anger, revenge, and even small acts of violence.

It is also the first time for many of the staff that someone else has listened to them think with total attention. All the group members listen. We teach how to listen without critiquing, without pretending to be therapists. They are not in therapy. They are just officers and youth workers. We do not do analysis with the thinking reports. We do not interpret. They note the meaning of their own thoughts. They note how their beliefs affect them. They see their hot thoughts, the interventions that they sometimes have not used. We make no comments. We return to the foundation principles.

Staff is mesmerized by the simplicity of cognitive work. We teach the message of change like this: "What I think, feel, believe affects what I do. If I change what I think, I can change what I do." It is elegant and surprisingly persuasive. Staff cannot change others if they do not have this tool. We can teach them to use cognitive behavioral change tools because of their great simplicity. Cognitive change directly feeds our notions of fair consequences versus aversive punishment. It is the ideological reinforcer of the training.

We often found that this was the first time that most staff ever stopped to listen to what they really think in their heads. Some of the staff came back the day after they had done a thinking report in training and talked about how they had stayed up all night, how they had been thinking and remembering, how they realized that they had bad tempers. Some staff talked to us privately about their difficulties with their own children at home and their fear about whether they were good parents.

Punishment

The cognitive tools raised the issue of punishment. People do what they do, in part, because of what they think and believe. Arbitrary punishment will not change people's acts because the beliefs that fuel the acts are so potent. This is central to what we teach. But we also teach that offenders must be given logical consequences for persistent rule breaking. The offenders must find a way to mute or change their thoughts and beliefs. Only by holding firm can we give the offenders a stationary target of change.

This is the hottest area of changing a prison culture. Some staff members are so conflicted about using punishment and about how to use it. In many cases the guidelines in the prison are too flexible, unclear or subject to peer pressure. Some staff fear that without their old arsenal of control and punishment that they will be naked and vulnerable.

At this point we had intense disagreements with some staff in both sites about how to deal with inmate violence, verbal aggression and angry outbursts. Although we did not concentrate at this point on how to change beliefs with offenders, we discussed interventions, how to stop violence, how to create respectful environments without resorting to the punishment slot. We focused repeatedly in Romania on the idea of respect, and in Australia on making connection with children who are radically unattached.

To make the point we used a psychodramatic exercise that reenacted old embarrassing experiences with violent teachers at school. When staff once again experienced the old humiliation of teenage school days, it was not hard to turn the debate to connection and respect. The experience of once again having those shamed, angry thoughts poignantly skewered those who held out for punishment versus controlling consequences. We used the same exercise many years earlier with high ranking Central and South American policemen, and it worked to remind them of the hell they endured before they became powerful.

Then we deepened the challenge. Building on role plays we asked the staff to begin to experience the beliefs of the prisoners. We split the staff into pairs giving them each single phrases like "I want you to stay/I want you to leave," or "there's something I want to tell you/I do not want to hear it." We asked each pair to speak using only the assigned sentence. These are obviously the phrases of rejection, abandonment and anger. But we used the exercises as a way to start a practical discussion of what to do for children who have gone through violent experiences and how to counter their global beliefs, thoughts and feelings towards anyone who is an enemy. All staff began to see what their clients were doing on a daily basis, rather than just attributing their actions to being bad, or morally flawed. They used lateral thinking skills to imagine the thinking behind many of the offenders' actions. It was as if they were all in on the game of imagining.

Deepening Empathy

After much discussion amongst ourselves we decided that it was time for the staff to deepen their empathy toward the clients. We had stressed that children cannot change without connection. We insisted that punishment was an ineffective tool to counter resistance. We repeated the need for consistent consequences as a way to focus children's thoughts. We created pictures of the children's fearful lives using full masks and mimed scenes of family violence.

We wanted to intensify the staff's understanding of the fragility and strength of the connection they needed to make in the therapeutic community. We created a mass improvisation in which half the staff, seated and with eyes shut, first created a safe place to be in their minds. Then they were slowly led to connect to the hand of someone else using only their fingers. When the connection was established, on cue the standing staff suddenly withdrew their hands. It was shocking. Some of the seated staff cried, some tried to follow the hand, some withdrew entirely. We reconnected the seated staff with their own personal place of safety through their visualization. Once the seated staff had been calmed everyone processed together. They talked for a long time.

We had needed to give staff a radical experience that gave them a picture of those clients whose lives have been so bitterly ripped apart. We no longer experienced the antagonism of any of the staff. Intriguingly it was decided that the Romanian staff were simply too fragile to do this exercise. The long history of the fear and reality of people being snatched, taken, seized and never coming back was just too close to the surface. There are many anomalies in Romania. Many of the work issues we faced pointed back to Ceaucescu. For instance, asking each group to come up with one best answer for the group seems to mimic the old Ceaucescu demand of sublimation to the group and an enforced loss of autonomy. We had the experience of being confronted for using this group strategy and told that we were communists.

We had to win the trust of the staff. In Romania one of the turning points in the training was our willingness to go out on limbs of responsibility, to go to General Director Eftimescu and to get materials for the offenders such as writing materials, to entrust the youngest officers with intellectually challenging tasks, to practice democracy and not champion a hierarchical world. We had to actually prove that we were safe fathers.

Romanian culture in the main still sees the father as the dominant figure. Thinking otherwise has very limited roots. An example of this was the issue of the "chef de camera." Some staff are wed to the old way of having in each camera or cell block a "chef de camera" who organizes the inmates for the staff. We had to challenge this strong father idea even though the new rule put in place by Dr. Gheorghe was that the "chef de camera" was illegal. It took not just our insistence that this old kapo system was outmoded, dangerous and illogical but the dawning belief that we were going to get this community to work without it. The work created mantras. In Romania our mantra was that respect led to keeping the channels of communication wide enough to change and that without respect prisoners would simply not even believe. Descatusarea is still working and experiencing significant growing pains over basic issues such as dealing with the concept of boss, or no boss, or who will have information, or who is controlling information. The experiment that is Descatusarea is a meta-strategy for the ongoing battles for change in the Rahova/DGP culture.

As Mihaela Sasarman, a famous Romanian prison theatre specialist and drama therapist who co-works extensively with us in our shared company Transcaena said: "There is no history at the moment of making community. The sense of community created by the experience was very new for this staff. They know brutality from the hands of bosses and that at any time anything can change. It is hard to fight, because there is so much hopelessness. The training gave them a sense of life. But life is so dark for us. You can see that we do not have much, and that we cannot say. When I work with puppets and masks and ask the officers to speak, then they can do this. They can speak. We live in symbols and we are trapped by them. You make them speak aloud. It is dangerous. It is the way. Your work is full of hope. Hope is dangerous. But everyone is fighting to do it, to learn something, and to succeed. To build the new experience we fight to win this new way. We are very excited."

Working with the Offenders

At some point the staff at both sites became like gladiators. It was time to work with the offenders. This meant for some the reigniting of their fear and anxiety and for us the test.

In Romania we carefully orchestrated the respectful meeting of the offenders and the newly trained staff. Working with the mantra of respect we interviewed each prisoner in the presence of all the trainee staff. The offenders were as unsure as the staff. We openly modeled listening, not analyzing, asking if what we had heard was what they thought they said, explaining the ideology of the community and its voluntary basis. And respect! The prisoners responded with as much surprise, wonder and suspicion as the officers.

Gradually we handed the interviews over to the staff after we modeled and discussed what we were doing. Like a giant role play, staff learned how to play the atmosphere, look for the "yes" opening, keep the ball in the air and not let the interaction with the offenders go flat. The staff were enormously excited. Two days of interviewing and explaining confirmed the simple idea that respect worked, that respect can keep the door open. For both staff and offenders this was the first time that they had met in this way. It was the cap to the attack on old beliefs. The proof was there. They believed. Descatusarea means "Break the chains." A few chains broke.

In Australia it was equally dramatic but in another way. On the very first day of the new unit, before we the trainers even got there, the staff sat down with the children and ate a huge breakfast together. They had already connected, and broken the old belief-based actions. The children were as amazed as anyone.

The staff watched closely as we went through the new ideas with the children. They watched as we coped without violence with the young offenders' fear, intransigence and anger at the new notions. We modeled that this could work even when the children rebelled. When one staff member went back to the old ways we took over. But the staff connected with the children–played, talked, listened, and asked. In fact their real skills simply took over. Many of the staff members know these young adolescents very well. They knew their parents, their homes, their lives. They taught themselves how not to scapegoat, and not to give in to fear. They reveled in the new and they looked proud. I have never seen anything quite like that moment of watching the staff play, talk, work to break through. It is the hallmark of Eastern Hill 22 months later.

Evaluation

Eastern Hill, the Australian therapeutic community at Melbourne Juvenile Justice Centre, was evaluated by Latrobe University for one year using both qualitative and quantitative research methods. In addition, the researchers from LaTrobe University and the University of Melbourne, Cook, Semmens and Grimswade, used the Moos Correctional Institution Environment Scale. Data was collected pretraining, during training and at the conclusion of the work, roughly from March 1998 to December 1998.

The evaluation's focus was to assess the impact on clients, staff, management and the environment. Information was analyzed from various sources including:

a. Incident reports before and after the work
b. Staff absences before and after the work
c. Taped interviews
d. The Moos scale
e. Observations by the researchers

The Moos scale developed by Rudolph Moos in 1975 is a measure of institutional climate. Moos defines this as the way that the "organizational context of correctional institutions may shape individual behavior" (Cook, Semmens, & Grimswade, 1999, p. 73). The authors refer to Moos' reference to Stern who defines climate as "the private percept that each person has of the events in which he takes part." They go on to say: "Moos' definition is intended to include not only each individual's private world but also the point at which this private world merges with that of others to form a common interpretation of events. Such common interpretations may differ from those of a detached observer because the ongoing interaction of the participants and their perceptions develops a dominant culture within the institution, and this is the prevailing institutional climate" (Cook, Semmens, & Grimswade, 1999, p. 73).

In Geese Theatre Company, we were particularly excited at this use of the Moos because it supported our beliefs about the need to change institutional beliefs in order to change culture. In addition, the subscales of the Moos include measures of institutional relationships, treatment programs and system maintenance.

A modified Moos was given to the staff, clients and administration. In all cases the Moos notes the following: during the changeover to the new system of the therapeutic community the climate dips and then recovers and finally overtakes the original preprogram scores. In terms of administrative satisfaction the change is startling from a minus 10 to plus 26. For the clients the change is a nearly 50 percent change in satisfaction. The staff after 8 months shows a smaller increase in their satisfaction in the climate.

Prison life is measured in part by trouble, or lack of trouble. When we were asked by the interviewers we predicted that the frequency of incidents would increase in the new system first especially as staff changed their old disciplines and clients tested the new regime. We also predicted that over time the frequency of incidents would decline. (There is some issue as to whether reporting prior to the training was accurate or whether incidents were underreported. Certainly staff hinted that this might have been so.) But the statistics show that there was a high point of violent incidents immediately following the first training, and that after the second training this gradually trailed off.

Similarly we made predictions that there would be a drastic reduction in the use of the isolation cell as punishment. Prior to the training 86 percent of incidents resulted in isolation being used. This figure reduced over a period of 8 months and after the next training to 46 percent (Cook, Semmens, & Grimswade, 1999, pp. 76–77).

Furthermore, when isolation was used it was often in tandem with other disciplinary strategies such as counseling, group meetings, thinking reports, management reports, consequences and/or debriefing. In fact, isolation was rarely used on its own to a reported incident in the first 6 months after the initial training (3.8%) and was not used at all as a singular response during the second training session and after (Cook, Semmens, & Grimswade, 1999, p. 77).

There are also statistics indicating that verbal altercations eventually decreased quite dramatically. The statistics show a similar trend throughout: after the first training there was a highly complex and anxious turn-around, which showed in increased aggression and dissatisfaction which was resolved some few months after the second training when staff actually received further training and a manual of community therapeutic activities.

CONCLUSION

Changes in prison culture must be driven by powerful modalities since there is so much resistance to change. Drama therapy has a built-in advantage over many strategies in that it intensifies the affect necessary to challenge beliefs, and gives staff a rehearsal of new ways of relating that is more dimensional than those that can be learned in pen and paper lectures.

Therapeutic communities have intensive demands. Because many clients respond well to the learning principles and opportunities of the therapeutic community, it is a good rehabilitative environment. The demands are such that staff must learn to operate at much more intensive levels of participation and creativity. The action methods of drama enhance responses so that staff can become acquainted and comfortable with rapid change and being in focus all the time.

Drama therapy accommodates prison staff well by blending theory and action. Prison staff responds well to action-based work. Changing prison cultures requires a format that is unexpected, challenging and relentlessly honest. Drama therapy is driven by people in relationship with each other. It is alive. It is not an ideology but a praxis. For cultural change in prison to be effective there must be a real democracy, a freedom of choice. Drama therapy operates by accepting all choices, seeing what happens when everything is tried.

For the drama therapist to be effective there must be at the minimum a courageous prison administrative leader with real power, access to the entire system and a person on the ground who will help drive the changes. We therefore acknowledge strongly General Eftimescu, Dr. Florian Gheorghe, Mihaela Sasarman, Diana Batzias, Johan Top, Di Garner and Patrick Tidmarsh. Ultimately, people make systems change.

REFERENCES

Bergman, J. (1995). Life, the life event and theater–A personal narrative in the use of drama therapy with sex offenders. In B.K. Schwartz & H.R Cellini. (Eds.), *The sex offender: Corrections, treatment and legal practice* (pp. 17; 1–24). Kingston, NJ: Civic Research Institute.

Bergman, J., & Hewish, S. (1996). The violent illusion. In M. Liebmann, (Ed.). *Arts approaches to conflict* (pp. 92–117). London: Jessica Kingsley Publishers.

Bergman, J., & Hewish, S. (1996). Pin point–The precise fit of drama therapy and cognitive restructuring, in creative therapies and programs in corrections. *Correctional Issues,* American Correctional Association, Maryland.

Camus, A. (1991). *The fall.* New York: Vintage Books.

Cook, S., Semmens, R., & Grimswade, C. (1999). Evaluation of Melbourne Juvenile Justice Centre Behavioural Program. LaTrobe University and University of Melbourne. Unpublished manuscript. Melbourne: Australia.

De Leon, G. (1984). *The therapeutic community: Study of effectiveness. Treatment Research Monograph Series.* DHHS Publication No. 84–1286. Washington DC: US Government Printing Office.

De Leon, G. (1989). Psychopathology and substance abuse: What we are learning from research in therapeutic communities? *Journal of Psychoactive Drugs 21,* 177–188.

Mindell, A., & Mindell, A. (1992). *Riding the horse backwards: Process work in theory and practice.* London: Penguin.

Pombi, K.F. (1994). Adolescents in therapeutic communities: Retention and posttreatment outcome. In F. Tims, G. DeLeon, & N. Jainchill (Eds.), *Therapeutic community: Advances in research and application,* no. 144 (pp. 159–185). Rockville, Maryland: NIDA.

Potter-Effron, R. (2004). *Angry all the time.* New York: New Harbinger Publications.

Roberts, J. (1997). History of the therapeutic community. In E. Cullen, L. Jones, & R. Woodward (Eds.). *Therapeutic communities for offenders* (pp. 3–22). Chichester: John Wiley.

Wexler, H.K., & Love, C.T. (1994). Therapeutic communities in prison. In F. Tims, G. DeLeon, & N. Jainchill (Eds.), *Therapeutic community: Advances in research and application,* no. 144 (pp. 186–213). Rockville, Maryland: NIDA.

Yokley, J.M. (1999). The application of therapeutic community learning experiences to adult abusers. In B.K. Schwartz, & H.R. Cellini (Eds.), *The sex offender* (pp. 25; 1–26). Kingston, NJ: Civic Research Institute.

Zimbardo, P.G. (1973). On the ethics of intervention in human psychological research: With special reference to the Stanford prison experience. *Cognition, 2,* 243–256.

FURTHER TRAINING

John Bergman
macflap@www.aol.com

Chapter 16

REHEARSALS FOR GROWTH: DRAMA THERAPY WITH COUPLES

DANIEL WIENER

INTRODUCTION

Rehearsals for Growth (RfG) is a therapeutic application of improvisational activities (improv), particularly the use of interactive theatrical games (Spolin, 1963; Johnstone, 1981). While RfG may be applied to individual therapy, its primary uses have been to improve interpersonal relationships and develop relationship skills. Since 1985, a growing number of therapists have been applying improvisational theater games to the practice of relationship therapy with couples, groups, and families as well as to work with special populations such as substance abusers (Ramseur & Wiener, 2003).

As will be demonstrated in this chapter, RfG provides therapists with a powerful resource to address three broad tasks in the successful therapy of relationships: (1) changing dysfunctional yet stable transactional patterns; (2) broadening the range of displayed social identities and expressive behaviors that clients present to others; and (3) altering the affective climate during therapy sessions. RfG is not in itself a comprehensive method of therapy but rather an approach that provides tools for enhancing the effectiveness of therapy.

RfG methods consist of offering client dyads or groups the opportunity to enact brief tasks and scenes that involve unusual conditions or rules (termed *exercises*) and/or the playing of characters different from those that the clients ordinarily identify as themselves (termed *games*). Such offers, made in the spirit of invitations to play or experiment, serve as therapeutic tools for both assessment and intervention. Numerous theater games have been adapted, modified, or invented to serve these therapeutic ends (Wiener, 1994).

The key insight that led to the creation of RfG is that competent stage-improvisation shares a number of characteristics with good interpersonal relationship functioning. These include:

- attentiveness to others' words and actions.
- flexibility in both initiating and accepting others' directions and suggestions (giving up over-control).
- making others right (validation of their

reality, thereby supporting them to look good).

In addition to those benefits common to all action methods, such as broadening sensory, emotive, and movement expressiveness, the therapeutic advantages of RfG may be summarized as follows:

1. *Encouraging novelty and playfulness.* RfG games involve pretense and are clearly marked as imaginary adventures. They shift the context of therapeutic reality to a more playful and fantastic mode, thus encouraging exploratory behavior and lessening fear of real life consequences of change. They also provide opportunities for clients to access playfulness (which is unavailable to many adults and even some children) within a safe, nonjudgmental context, to face fear through fun.

2. *Experiencing spontaneity and taking risks.* Clients engaged in theatrical enactment are referred to as *players.* Effective improvisation requires that players give up their conception/expectation/script concerning what is expected to be there and to attend to what is happening here and now, both intra- and interpersonally. Improvisation thus entails spontaneity, defined as "an ability to experience fully, express without inhibition, and respond to new situations in an immediate, creative, and appropriate manner" (Wiener 1994, p. xviii).

The major obstacle to being fully present in the moment is the overriding tendency of the human mind to prepare for the future. Because improv places people "on the spot" to respond spontaneously without knowing what will come next, the mind interprets the situation as dangerous; the improviser feels anxious and at risk of failing. Keith Johnstone, founder of the theatrical form of improv which RfG is based upon, observes that spontaneity is socially threatening because it reveals one's natural self as opposed to the self one has been trained to present to others (Johnstone, 1981). Anxiety and defensive behavior, then, are likely responses to the demands of improv. When clients are encouraged to overcome the risks of failing and looking foolish by improvising playfully, they awaken to an enjoyable and expanded use of self. Paradoxically, the spontaneous use of pretense also leads to the discovery and expression of therapeutically useful truths.

3. *Building and expanding interpersonal trust.* RfG exercises are constructed so that their tasks can be accomplished only when players put aside their willfulness, defensiveness, and competitiveness in order to attend fully and receptively to their partner(s). Because of the previously noted sense of being on the edge of danger when improvising, people who improvise together share an adventure which provides a social bonding experience that results in enjoyment, friendship, and trust.

4. *Co-creating new realities with others.* RfG games provide opportunities for clients to stretch themselves by incorporating and rehearsing new roles. Analogous to the way theatrical performance of a scripted scene is enhanced by theatre directors who guide actors toward new possibilities, RfG therapists use improv with clients to explore less familiar choices than the ones habitually made in their lives. Such dramatic role rehearsals provide relationship partners with the opportunity to try on complementary identities in scenes that bring forth novel patterns of interaction. In this way, established relationships can be expanded safely beyond their existing habitual limits.

RfG games also can be used to promote the restorying and performance of individual and relationship narratives. Improv does not constitute an escape from reality but rather permission to create and explore new realities.

5. *Developing flexibility in life.* Improv is not only a tactical skill with broad social application but promotes an adaptive stance for dealing with change. As life circumstances are ceaselessly changing and our capability to foretell the future is highly limited, flexibility is a virtue that can be cultivated through improvisational practice. Among the benefits of such practice are: confidence in facing the unknown, greater appreciation of the present moment, and heightened powers of observation.

THEORY AND PRINCIPLES

RfG is not, to date, rooted in any unitary conceptual or theoretical framework. Soon after its inception in 1988, I began viewing RfG from a Social Constructivist perspective, one in which reality is understood as co-created (invented) through people's interactions with one another. From this perspective, both a person's identity and the relationships one participates in are formed and continually shaped through interpersonal process; both are organized by others and by oneself as narratives (stories). However, by the late 1990s, it had become clear that a number of clinicians were using RfG techniques quite effectively without adhering to a Social Constructivist perspective. Consequently, Social Constructivism's place in the story of RfG has itself become an optional (yet useful to some) metaphor linking theater with psychotherapy, as has the importance of theory itself.

While working extensively with interpersonal relationships viewed from a Social Constructivist perspective, my RfG praxis is strongly informed by training in Family Systems Therapy (for a similar viewpoint, see Hoffman, 1988). One basic systemic principle is that relationship dynamics cannot fully be accounted for by characteristics of the individuals who comprise them. Thus, a relationship is more than the sum of the individuals who participate in it. A relationship's uniqueness brings forth ever-varying experiences of self for each of its individual members, though such variance is patterned and considerably constrained by habitual, co-created interaction. This may be illustrated by considering a hypothetical couple, Mr. and Mrs. Smith. As individuals viewed during times they are apart, they each engage in different pursuits, present distinct preferences and styles, and interact differently with other people. Knowing only one of them, one finds it difficult to infer the personality or characteristics of the spouse. When viewed together, the Smiths are far more predictable; they spend more of their time in a limited number of places, engaged in mutual activities with each taking circumscribed, often reciprocal roles, co-regulating their emotional interchanges.

Four interrelated clinical concepts useful to the practice of RfG couples therapy are: *stories,* which describes both the initial content and the ongoing process of co-creating the couple's common story out of each partner's individual narrative; *rules,* which includes both explicit and implicit procedures for interpreting actions as either fitting or not fitting the couple's story; *intimacy/expressiveness,* which attends to the dynamic quality of the couple's affect; and *status and gender,* which deals with the ways that power is distributed and displayed in the relationship (for descriptions of these concepts in considerably greater detail and analysis of their interrelationships, see Wiener 1994, pp. 185–190). While RfG's primary application lies in enhancing relationship functioning and improving the affective climate of relationships systems, some of the work in relationship therapy is also directed toward expanding the possibilities and choices available to individuals, meaning that RfG is not practiced as a pure systems approach.

When used with families or couples, improvised enactments promote the adventure of moving into unfamiliar territory, thereby bypassing familiar sequences and habit patterns that often defeat intended change efforts.

Around 1998, I articulated a *Dramaturgic model* [based on the ideas of both David Holt (1992) and Brissett & Edgley (1990)], that linked psychosocial life functioning (labeled as the theatrical meta-roles of Director, Performer, Author, Spectator and Producer) to improvisational performance (Wiener, 1999). This model has proven useful in assessing individuals and matching the patterns of choices clients make in life to those observed when these clients improvise. The Dramaturgic Model also is consistent with the point of view that people do not have psychological disorders but are living badly performed lives that can be improved by expanded social skills and better integration of meta-roles. As each relationship's uniqueness precludes drawing valid inferences about an individual's contribution, the use of the model for the assessment of individuals requires repeated observation of the client improvising with different partners. In clinical practice, the opportunity to apply the model arises only in group therapy.

METHODS AND TECHNIQUES

The techniques (games and exercises) used in RfG are either adaptations of improvisational theater games or inventions that share many characteristics with these games. Used both for assessment and intervention, these techniques may be classified as serving one or more of the following purposes: accepting/blocking offers; freeing the imagination; expanding emotional range; storytelling; and using status transactions. When *Rehearsals for Growth* was published in 1994, about 150 variations were included as clinically useful; currently, several hundred more could be enumerated. In practice, responding to the interplay between their own creativity and the in-the-moment clinical circumstances, experienced RfG therapists devise new variations and combinations continually. While beginning training in RfG emphasizes using specific techniques, more advanced training encourages therapist invention and improvisation.

In expounding RfG methods below I have separated assessment and intervention for the sake of conceptual clarity. In clinical practice, these two areas overlap considerably.

Assessment in RfG Couples Therapy

The process of assessing the couple system, begun during consultation, is a continual one throughout therapy. Assessment covers several aspects and areas, as outlined below. Most aspects that are initially assessed through observation and verbal inquiry will be assessed later on in the therapy through enactments and homework assignments.

Assessing the Couple System

a. The fit between the operating styles of partners–symmetrical (similar) or complementary (opposite)–across different areas of functioning (e.g. for work, result-oriented or process-driven; for verbal presentation of information, metaphorical or literal).
b. The affective climate- initial and subsequent impressions, comparing verbal reports of at-home with in-session observations.
c. The emotional range exhibited in the couple's interchanges with one anoth-

er, compared with their individual ranges of expression shown when each interacts with the therapist.

d. Manifest control issues, such as: acceptance/validation; over/under functioning (e.g., one speaking for other); and status maneuvers (including competing for the loyalty and sympathy of the therapist).

Assessing the Treatment System

Consistent with systemic principles, the therapist, though outside the couple system, is nonetheless a member of the treatment system, as is each of the clients. Therefore, the therapist attends to the following areas:

a. The fit between the operating style of the therapist with the couple-as-entity and with each partner.
b. The affective impact of the couple's/each partner's presence on the therapist's emotions (e.g., becoming tense/relaxed; humorous/literal during interaction). This includes emotional triggers (i.e., countertransferential reactions) of the therapist and includes the therapist's accommodation to clients' interpersonal demand(s) (e.g., for reassurance, availability in crisis, "air time" during verbal exchanges, and respect for privacy).
c. Coalitions and/or triangles[1] that pull in the therapist.
d. Control issues in the therapy, primarily the clients' acceptance of the therapist's leadership as well as the collaborative potential/alignment with the purposes and methods of the therapy. The latter is estimated by the couple's responsiveness to the therapist's questions and, later, to therapist directives.

Assessment of Rules and Boundaries Operating in Couple's Relationship

Throughout therapy, the therapist acquires an ongoing, growing knowledge of the rules and boundaries operating in the relationship, including those rules and boundaries outside the clients' awareness. The main classification on initial assessment is of the degree of structure in rules and boundaries.

a. At the chaotic extreme, the relationship is characterized by too little structure–rules are infrequently articulated; there is frequent heightened emotional reactivity when one partner's expectations of the other's behavior are unmet; frequent arguments erupt about control/power issues; there are escalating threats and/or repetitive attempts to change the partner.
b. At the rigid extreme, there is an avoidance of conflict, with fixed cognitive/emotional/behavioral positions (and often unstated judgments); patterned predictable interaction, routinized emotional co-regulation; and, often, highly compartmentalized lives with little shared activity and/or communication.

Assessment of Interactive Process Revealed through Improvisational Enactment

Applied to the assessment of couples and other relationships, RfG enactments reveal

1. Triangles are relationship patterns in which one person becomes emotionally invested in the relationship between two others.

and locate relational deficits manifested by:

a. difficulty in entering or leaving the play context.
b. players ignoring or undermining the choices made by their partners, or long hesitations indicative of overcontrol[2] and risk-avoidance instead of spontaneity.
c. expressed emotionality that is inhibited or contextually unjustified.
d. breaking character or breaking dramatic action.
e. incapacity to play together in a way that both partners experience as satisfying.
f. role hunger (a desire to take up a particular role) and role nausea (a reluctance to taking up a particular role).

Additionally, attending to how clients interpret the therapist's instructions for enactments is as much a part of assessment as the content, style, skill level, or outcome of the enactment.

Intervention in RfG Couples Therapy

RfG therapy occurs in the following sequence: 1. preenactment discussion and warm-up; 2. instruction; 3. enactment; 4. post-enactment processing; and, optionally, 5. video feedback, usually in a subsequent session.

Since few clients enter therapy with either an expectation of, or experience with improv, during consultation I include a brief mention of using improvisational enactment and typically defer its offer until the joining phase of therapy is well underway. I usually present offers of enactments as opportunities to try something new or learn in a different way. Therapists should offer these without expectation that the client will accept; play is always voluntary, so there should be no pressure or persuasion. Even when therapists plan in advance to offer clients a specific technique, it is important that they be inwardly receptive to their own spirit of adventure.

Once they have accepted the offer to enact, clients are reminded that they need to limit physical movement of their bodies to avoid injury and to notify their partner of any physical limitations. They are then invited to move from their seating to a stage area, a space set aside for enactment, where they are designated players. Any space will do so long as players move physically from their prior places as clients. The characters they take up in RfG games are put on and taken off on stage to maintain the segregation of the stage as the exclusive physical location in which the *playspace* (Johnson, 1992) is invoked. With some exceptions, the progression is from exercises (nondramatic enactments) to games (dramatic enactments).

In addition to enacting characters and using imagination, clients can reenact real situations that are conflictual, first from the perspective of one partner, then from the other's experience. While such scenes are not improvisations (being closer to psychodramatic enactments) they usefully demonstrate, in action, the impact of differences in perception and value on memory, thereby driving home to clients the Social Constructivist point that what is taken as reality in relationship is only that which is

2. Overcontrol refers both to the intention and to the actions taken either to control others or to defeat the control of self by others. Overcontrol goes well beyond the normal human preference for having influence with others and autonomy from them; at its extreme, it supercedes all other social motives and becomes an identity-defining "master motive."

consensually created and validated. As a practical matter, such scenes also offer partners dramatic experience to anchor intellectual insight regarding the nature, extent and implications of their differences.

Displacement scenes are dramatic enactments designed to: (1) replicate an existing dynamic of a relationship (primarily to heighten awareness of habitual transactional patterns); (2) reverse roles or positions in order to heighten empathy for the other partner; and (3) offer roles that encourage exploratory choices that go beyond familiar ones, including ones that expand clients' emotional range. Displacement scenes are usually created through the therapist's improvising in the therapeutic moment; familiarity with RfG greatly facilitates their creation and fashioning them artfully to fit the clinical situation. The therapist's calibration of the degree of displacement to be offered is guided both by the need to make the scene's conditions or setting unfamiliar enough so that clients do not revert to playing themselves in overly familiar circumstances, yet sufficiently relevant emotionally and dynamically to engage clients with their therapeutic issues. Displacement scenes are often staged in sequences, sometimes with repeated variations, to alter their outcome, affect, or power dynamics; they are often key enactments that provide breakthroughs that lead to changes in dysfunctional patterns of behavior, affect and cognition.

Homework is used in RfG couples therapy in three ways: first, as directives to record behavior, cognitions and/or affect that is either habitual or exceptional (in order to heighten awareness of underlying relationship patterns); second, as suggestions to repeat an in-session enactment at home (in order to strengthen a more desirable pattern of interaction); and third, to deepen a client's connection to a character that had recently emerged during an in-session enactment (in order to facilitate the emergence of a new resource that may expand the relationship's possibilities).

During enactments the therapist functions in the several role(s) of: theatrical director, side-coach, in-scene or offstage commentator, audience, and, occasionally, another actor (in a minor role). These functions are activated in order to encourage and support clients to enter and remain in the playspace, stay in character, advance the scene's action, and fulfill initial instructions.

For chaotic relationships, structured enactments (exercises) are helpful in experientially teaching the principles of good relationship functioning. For rigid relationships, displacement scenes and games that expand emotional expressiveness or vary status maneuvers are useful to induce novelty and surprise. For both types of relationships, enactments to explore exceptions or counterplots (i.e., alternatives to familiar moves and outcomes) can be helpful. Their usage is similar to the psychodramatic technique of enacting fantasies based on hopes and fears (Chasin, Roth & Bograd, 1989), though in RfG, more rewriting and sequential exploratory improvising is used, with greater emphasis on shifting the affective climate than on enacting an altered outcome.

COMPARISONS WITH OTHER DRAMA THERAPY METHODS

At the time RfG originated I was largely ignorant of drama therapy as a field, having only had training in psychodrama and some acquaintance with a few writings of Robert Landy and David Read Johnson. What follows is an attempt to connect RfG to selected other drama therapy practices, all of which (excepting Harvey's *Family Dynamic Play*) are therapies with individuals and groups.

"Psychodrama" (Chapter 18): The major influence of psychodrama on RfG lies in its explicit Warmup–Action–Sharing process sequence, which is adhered to in every RfG therapy session. RfG also borrows the use of physical movement to and from a defined, set-aside stage or space used for the Action (enactment) phase. In RfG group therapy one member may emerge as a protagonist around whom the enactment is centered with others playing supporting roles. Unlike psychodrama auxiliary egos, these supporting actors are encouraged to improvise and develop their own characters.

Emunah's "Integrative Five Phase Model" (Chapter 4): The progression from nondramatic exercises to dramatic games in RfG corresponds roughly with the movement from Emunah's Phase One (Dramatic Play) to Phase Two (Scenework), which involves playing roles other than those reflecting one's own life. In Emunah's Phase Three (Role Play), interactions between clients and others are explored through theatrical versions of actual events, played by auxiliaries who are not in actual relationship with the protagonist outside of therapy. By contrast, the RfG therapist develops displacement (fictional) scenes that are dynamically similar to real-life issues in the clients' actual relationship; these scenes are then enacted by the relationship members themselves.

Johnson's "Developmental Transformations" (DvT; Chapter 6): In both DvT and RfG, improvisation is the underlying, distinctive therapeutic technique. Both methods induce clients to take up dramatic roles and enter into playful exploration in-role. In DvT, improvisational play is the entire method, with no verbal interpretation during the session; in RfG, each improvised enactment is episodic and relatively brief, with more session time given to verbal therapy and post-enactment processing. DvT enactments are spontaneous and flow in and out of themes emerging and submerging during continuous enactment, while RfG enactments are intentional directives offered by the therapist, along with instructions for their performance, in the course of verbal therapy. Unlike DvT, in which the therapist improvises in-role and is a co-equal play partner at all times except when (briefly) in the Witnessing Circle, the RfG therapist is seldom in-role and rotates between the role functions of Director, Side-coach, and Audience/Witness.

Harvey's "Family Dynamic Play" (FDP; 2000): FDP is the only other drama therapy approach centering on direct work with client relationships, particularly families with young children. There are many similarities between FDP and RfG: (1) systematic observation of play activity for assessment; (2) stimulating and encouraging naturally-occurring playfulness in relationships; (3) cultivating mutual, cooperative interactions in relationships through play; (4) offering structured tasks/games as tools for both assessment (e.g., play flow and play breaks) and intervention; (5) alternating between play and verbal episodes that provide reflection and consolidation of insight; (6) active use of the presence of the therapist; (7) use of between-session homework; and (8) moving through successive stages of assessment, directive coaching, and the creation of "core scenes" (in RfG, displacement scenes) that ". . . defines and addresses a family's specific emotional issue and characteristic interaction patterns" (Harvey 2003, p. 23). FDP's final stage, the successful generation of the family's own play(ing), is not an explicit part of RfG, although it frequently occurs outside of therapy.

Apart from FDP's application solely to family work, some differences between RfG and FDP include: (1) setting (FDP makes considerable use of props and art media, requiring the use of a large, safe space that allows chase games and hide-and-seek; (in RfG props are mimed or minimal); (2) physicalizion of enactment (FDP games include occasionally strenuous activity–e.g., swinging a child into a pile of pillows–and physical contact; in RfG, physical contact is mimed or negotiated in advance); (3) theoretical foundation (FDP's goals are related to attachment theory [Bowlby, 1980], unlike RfG's); and (4) centrality of play (in FDP, play enactment is the clinical method; in RfG playful enactment is a tool in the service of therapy that progresses also by verbal means).

CASE EXAMPLE

While RfG techniques can be utilized as adjunctive techniques in a wide variety of therapies, there is a distinct though flexible process developed in working with couples (Wiener, 1997; Wiener, 1999; Wiener & Cantor, 2002). This process is explained through the alternation of description and commentary in the detailed couples therapy case example that follows.

The initial session or two is termed a consultation, during which the therapist obtains sufficient history and current information about the couple and each partner. Consultation signifies that therapy has not yet begun and permits: (a) the therapist to learn how feasible work with this couple is likely to be; (b) the clients to learn how therapy is conducted; and (c) both to estimate the fit between therapist and couple, so that all parties can make an informed choice whether to move on to therapy.

Tony and Sara, married six years, lived with their biological daughter, age four and two other daughters, ages 10 and 12 from Sara's previous marriage of nine years. Sara, who had initiated therapy, was worried about Tony's recently increased emotional distance, and suspicious of his recent preoccupation with health (he had increased the frequency of his visits to a health club). Tony's father had had a stroke seven months earlier; when Tony reported being anxious over his own health, Sara invalidated Tony's health concerns as overblown. In their families of origin, Tony (41) was an only child with an overprotective mother and a distant father; Sara (38), the eldest of three sisters, had witnessed her mother's divorce of her unfaithful father when she was eight. Significantly, Sara's middle sister, married fourteen years, had separated from her husband two months earlier over his affair, replicating their parents' marriage.

It was clear from the start that their marriage was a complementary fit; at our initial session Tony presented as expressive and hearty while Sara appeared restrained and more intellectual. Tony was impulsive, starting a lot of projects without completing them; Sara, by contrast, was focused and detail-oriented. Tony was outcome driven; Sara, more process oriented. The initial affective climate was strained but respectful; both Tony and Sara took pains to avoid giving the other offense. Their exhibited emotional range appeared curtailed, with not much humor, a few warning glances, and distant, closed-off body postures and no touching while seated on the office couch. In their accommodation to me as their therapist, Sara, though responsive to questions about herself, appeared chiefly motivated to remind me of my function to keep Tony on task in revealing himself; Tony seemed only mildly interested in the therapy process and was initially more aloof, going along with therapy just for Sara's sake. He didn't volunteer information except when an opportunity presented itself to joke with me at Sara's expense.

Regarding control and power, Sara displayed a high-status position as hurt and entitled, but dignified. Tony took a defensive, lower-status position that signaled, "I'm really a good guy but need you to validate me." *Status* in RfG refers to behavior that signifies a degree of importance relative to others, rather than referring to social position or to self-esteem. Operationally, status is the social expression of power. In RfG clinical and social skills training, emphasis is first placed on detecting both status cues (indicators of status) and status maneuvers (patterns of behavior from which attempts to achieve a desired status may be inferred). Therapists are then trained in intentionally maneuvering their own status with clients to achieve tactical therapeutic objectives (Wiener, 1994; Wiener, Yagaloff, Alexanian & Larose, 2004).

My initial assessment of status was that Sara was maneuvering to place me in a subordinate status position to herself but over Tony, while Tony's maneuvers attempted to isolate Sara in her high status, while offering me solidarity as an equally downtrodden male.

Notwithstanding these status maneuvers, I experienced a fairly good fit between myself and these clients. I felt I could connect to each of them without uncomfortably stretching my own presentation of self. In their presence I was at ease, inclined to join with them through the relaxed display of humor. I was aware of my slight tendency to side with Sara (in my family of origin, I had aligned more with my overresponsible mother than with my underresponsible father) but was confident I could be evenhanded in working with them and get them to accept my leadership. As the initial phone contact by Sara had been a bit anxious and lengthy, I was careful to set boundaries on my availability outside of sessions. I thought it quite possible that she would deem their quarrels as emergencies that would result in frequent after-hours phone calls.

Although Tony and Sara quarreled frequently in my presence during the first three sessions, their process lacked vitality, seeming routine. I noted how Sara's sharp, critical tone was predictably followed by Tony's soft, resigned tone, while on the content level Sara's direct questions were regularly met by Tony's short, nonvolunteering-of-additional-information answers. Based mainly on these predictably co-regulated exchanges (in vocal dynamics and content) I classified Tony and Sara nearer the rigid end of the "operating rules and boundaries" spectrum.

When asked about their satisfaction with their sex life, Tony became quite animated, stating that Sara had become progressively less sexually available over the past three years. Sara agreed that was true, but countered that Tony had become less tender and more demanding, which turned her off. This exchange had all the earmarks of a familiar impasse, so I shifted to ask each the scaling question, "how important is it that your sex life improve?" This was to be rated on a 1-to-10 scale, "1" being "completely unimportant" and "10" representing "the most important thing in life." Handing each a piece of paper and a pencil, I asked them to write both their own answer and what they thought their partner's rating on this question would be. Sara wrote "9" for Tony and "7" for herself; Tony wrote "2" for Sara and "8" for himself. Tony seemed surprised by the disparity between Sara's self-rating of "7" and his own expectation of a "2." I knew we'd come back to this issue later in therapy.

Action Phase after Consultation

Following an involved discussion in the third session of each partner's dissatisfactions across a range of practical issues, I proposed the exercise *Mirrors* both to learn more about how their partnership functioned nonverbally and to warm them up to further enactment.

In Mirrors, two players stand facing one another at a distance of about five feet, looking into each other's eyes without speaking. One, designated as Leader, begins to move slowly from the waist up and the other, as Follower, mirrors the Leader's action until "change" is called (after about 30 seconds); they then switch roles. "Change" is called twice more and then they are instructed to give up leading and following and move simultaneously (mutuality). Care should be taken by the Leader to move slowly and in such a way that the Follower can keep up and be able to maintain the mirror.

The couple did well, looking attentively into each other's eyes and moving in accordance with the mirroring instructions. When asked afterwards, Tony expressed a preference for leading, as he then didn't need to pay close attention to Sara, while she expressed no preference. During the Mutuality phase, they each did some micro-leading which they knew wasn't mutual–Tony (but, surprisingly, not Sara) seemed slightly frustrated at their failure to attain true mutuality. I congratulated them on their displayed cooperation (it is actually rare that willing adults fail to coordinate their movements approximately) and asked them what they noticed about their cooperation. Both reported that they felt assured by being followed faithfully when leading and by attending closely to the leader when following. Mirrors, being simple to understand and requiring a very modest level of skill, reliably produces a success experience that can be built upon in more demanding exercises and games.

After further discussion of relationship cooperation during that same session, I proposed another exercise, One Word at a Time, to explore cooperation in the verbal, rather than movement dimension. In *One Word at a Time,* two players stand alongside one another with arms around each other's shoulders. Looking frequently into each other's eyes, they narrate an improvised story, alternating words with each other while creating grammatical sentences. This is a clear demonstration of co-control, where the dyad cannot function successfully without each player giving to and receiving support from the other. It is necessary for players to give up preconceived associations and storylines as the other player will often give the wrong (i.e., unexpected) word; if this is accepted and built upon, surprising sentences and stories spring forth, to everyone's delight. Since every time a player gives a word she or he is anticipating a specific direction for the sentence to go toward, this game places the players in the interesting position of blocking their own word associations in order to accept their partner's offer.

Tony tried to throw in grammatically appropriate but unusual words on some of his turns. Though Sara took long pauses on her turns after these, the couple was able to produce coherent, grammatical sentences. It was initially unclear to me whether Tony was being competitive with Sara, trying to throw Sara off, thus getting her into trouble playfully; or attempting to impress me. In accordance with RfG's dramaturgic perspective it is not so important to assess motive as to note what effect these choices have on the current relationship climate. Sara displayed neither annoyance nor surprise and both seemed mildly pleased with their capacity to carry out the task, yet Tony still appeared dissatisfied.

In light of the high degree of predictability to the emotional exchanges observed between Sara and Tony, I next proposed that they play *You Will, I Won't* (Wiener, 1994). Originally a Gestalt therapy exercise, in You Will, I Won't (also known as *Line Repetition,* Emunah, 1994), two players face off in dialogue, each player stating repeatedly a short command that blocks (contradicts) the command given by the other player, as exemplified by the name of this exercise. Sara was first given the "You will!" line to repeat, which she varied by becoming more insistent, though only slightly louder starting around the third repetition. Tony's "I Won't!" was initially delivered in a matter-of-fact tone which grew more irritated and sounded nearly angry as the repetition continued. After six repetitions I stopped them, and asked them to repeat the exercise with lines reversed. This time, Tony's "You Will!" started as matter-of-fact but grew steadily louder and more emphatic, accompanied by jabbing his index finger at Sara. For her part, Sara grew more emotionally distant, broke eye contact and repeated her line with decreasing volume.

In the post-enactment discussion that immediately followed, both had rich associations of their performances to their real-life interactions. Sara reported that she experienced a kind of resignation the first time; she hadn't believed she could get Tony to comply. Her sense of futility was sufficiently unpleasant, she reported, that she would have quit soon beyond the point I stopped it. Tony appeared very interested, even surprised to hear this; he had felt she was succeeding at wearing him down and had been desperately trying to hold off giving in to her. Sara, in turn, was greatly surprised to hear this from Tony. In neither the exercise nor in real life had she ever suspected she had all that much influence with him. The results of this enactment and its subsequent processing made two important things clearer: First, the couple's emotional co-regulation was fairly strong, with constricted affective range; less rigid couples display greater variety of tone, loudness and flexibility of intentions (e.g., demanding, pleading, seducing). Second, they were locked into mutual projections which prevented each from reading the actual intentions and motivations of the other.

Regarding the second round of the exercise, Tony reported that he had felt strong at first by making his demands increasingly emphatic, but that Sara's distance was unsettling, undermining his initial sense of power. Sara shared how the exercise had transported her back to a preschool age when her mother would first berate and then punish her. Early in life she had learned to tune out so that the coming punishment would affect her less. Further questioning on this recollection established that she had not been abused by her mother, nor had she fully dissociated at those times; I concluded from this that she had not been truly traumatized. Although undertaken for purposes of assessment, what was revealed by this exercise became an intervention whereby Sara and Tony each experienced a shift in their understanding of their own and each other's position regarding personal power and interpersonal influence.

In the next session I devoted half of the time to repeating You Will, I Won't with them, now presenting this exercise as an opportunity to discover how they could playfully try out interesting variations. Accordingly, I coached them by calling out such ongoing stage instructions as "Louder!," "Softer!," "Be seductive!," "Sound apologetic!," "Don't take 'no' for an answer!," and "Think yourself entitled!" By coaching them I took responsibility for the stance they took, lessening their inhibitions about owning these positions and facilitating their shift into performing. After some initial hesitation on Sara's part, both took up the enactment, playing the exercise with increasing involvement and evident enjoyment. In the processing that followed, Sara reported that she felt hopeful and energized in a way she had not felt in a long time. Tony agreed, adding that their relationship was honeymooning again.

Shifting the affective climate toward pleasurable excitement, even temporarily, acts to instill hope and counter the demoralization with which couples enter therapy. Such shifts do more for the progress of therapy than does the verbal processing of substantive issues without affective change.

In the next session, wishing to explore the extent of competitive impulses in their relationship, I introduced Tony and Sara to *Tug of War,* an exercise that appears to be a competition between its players.

In Tug-of-War (Wiener, 1996), two persons face one another, three to six feet apart, with some room behind each of them. These players are told that there is an imaginary rope on the ground between them and that, on the therapist's signal, they are to pick up the rope and have a tug-of-war with their partner. The players need to treat the rope as a reality of their interaction; one's hauling in rope implies the other's being pulled toward the center. Blocking often takes the form of a "rubber rope" which is seen as stretching or going slack when the players are inattentive.

Tony, looking uncomfortable, leaned backward slightly, arms away from his body, his gaze averted from Sara. Sara, puffing and indicating strenuous effort, began slowly hauling in the rope hand over hand. From the sidelines, I reminded Tony that, for the rope to appear real, her pulling back would result in him being pulled forward. All at once, Tony launched his body toward Sara, falling headlong at her feet. Rather than being gratified at having won, Sara snapped at Tony that he had spoiled things by making her winning too easy. Startled, Tony replied that it would have "gotten him in trouble" if he had used his greater size and weight to have defeated her (overlooking that, with an imaginary rope, he had no advantage in effecting the outcome). "Let's save this discussion for later and try another variation," I suggested. "This time, the outcome will be scripted and your task is to make the contest look convincing by closely watching your partner and making the rope behave realistically. So, this time, Tony will win within 30 seconds. Now, pick up the rope, make eye contact, and GO!" In contrast to the first variation, this one makes it clear that the exercise is not a contest but a performance that requires coordination of effort between partners to be convincing. This time, there was a palpable connection between Tony and Sara as both leaned away, grunting and pretend-straining. Tony appeared to be slowly winning at first, but Sara fought him to a standstill and started to pull him over. Then, with a loud grunt, Tony yanked strongly and Sara came flying over the line, falling on top of him. Grinning, they helped each other up. I applauded the drama and gestured them back to their seats.

In the post-enactment processing that followed, both reported enjoying the second contest. Tony was surprised that Sara didn't care about losing; Sara said that their connecting the second time was what made the exercise enjoyable for her. Instead of pleasing her by losing in the first Tug of War, Tony' s actions felt patronizing and phony to Sara, a pattern she readily connected to Tony' s accommodations to her in everyday life. Sara saw these accommodations as evidence of Tony's desire to placate her for what he must be feeling guilty about. Tony, dumbfounded upon hearing this, protested that he had nothing to feel guilty for. Moreover, he said (showing some anger for the first time in therapy) he was tired of being damned when not nice (as being selfish and insensitive) and damned when nice (for concealing some guilty secret). Sara acknowledged that she equated accommodation with guilt, as this was her father's pattern. I gave Sara the homework to make daily entries in her diary of all the instances she saw Tony as concealing guilt. Tony's homework was to note instances of doing things to please Sara and whether she acknowledged these as helpful. In our next session, Sara came in with four instances of Tony's accommodation that she associated with guilt. Tony had counted six instances, of which he recorded only one which she had positively acknowledged.

Given Tony's aversion to displeasing Sara, I decided to offer the couple a displacement scene to explore alternative choices. I invited Tony to play "Mr. Wilkins," a customer trying to return a defective toy to Sara, who was to play "Ms. Coles," a clerk working at the Customer Service Desk of a department store. Handing Tony a tissue box, I told him that he, Wilkins, didn't have the receipt but to be persistent in getting a refund, while coaching Sara as Ms. Coles that store policy required a receipt. With a high-backed chair between them as a counter, I established the scene location. Wilkins, a tissue box under one arm, strode purposefully up to the chair-back counter. Without any pleasantries and in a stern tone, he thrust the box at Ms. Coles, stating that this doll was defective. Ms. Coles gazed impassively at Wilkins; without touching the box and in a formal tone, she asked for the store receipt. Wilkins gruffly said he couldn't find it and launched into a description of the doll's several defects. In the middle of his third sentence, Ms. Coles cut in to state store policy requiring a receipt, pointing behind her to an imaginary sign. Wilkins, in an angry voice, stated it was obvious from the carton that the doll had been bought at that store and accused Ms. Coles of behaving rudely to him. In a restrained, yet tight, voice, Ms. Coles asked Wilkins to lower his voice and reminded him that she did not make store policy. Wilkins coldly insisted on speaking with Ms. Coles' manager; she replied evenly that the manager was out and that Wilkins was welcome to speak with him upon his return from lunch. Snatching the box and walking away, Wilkins turned his back on Ms. Coles, calling over his shoulder that he'd have words with her supervisor about her rudeness when he returned. I motioned them back to their seats. Tony was smiling, but Sara looked upset.

"So, what was happening to your Mr. Wilkins character, Tony?" I asked. It is important, post-enactment, to indicate to clients that they are no longer in role. "Oh, he was a grouchy guy and knew he wasn't gonna get anywhere with that snippy broad, so he might as well ruin her day," Tony answered easily. I turned to Sara. "And what went on with Ms. Coles?" "I . . . she didn't like her job 'cause of jerks like him," Sara snapped, gesturing toward Tony. "Sara, are you upset?" I asked. She nodded. "Are you upset at Tony or only at the character he played?" I gently asked. Sara hesitated, then glared at Tony. "You can be mean, sometimes," she said flatly. Tony, startled, protested that he had just taken the enactment as an opportunity to play someone who he saw as quite unlike himself and that he didn't hold her accountable as being the snippy character she played. Sara looked uncertain. I said to her: "Sara, what came up for you during that scene?" After a pause, she replied, "I guess I didn't see Tony as capable of such rudeness. He's not usually like that." "Are you the same person as Ms. Coles, the character you played just now?" I asked. Sara shook her head. "Actually, I set you guys up by having you play a scene where there was bound to be conflict. As I see it, we're all capable of displaying every trait," I put in, "only we ordinarily bring forth only a small fraction of our potential. In good relationships, both partners like who they become around each other and tolerate unwelcome exceptions. Would you now be willing to play another scene where Tony' s character came home to his daughter after trying to return a defective doll he had bought her for a present?" This scene was offered in order to have the clients explore potential tenderness rather than inevitable conflict. Sara thought for a moment and then nodded. "Okay, then, come up here, both of you," I gestured toward the stage, placing a chair for Sara to sit in. "Wilkins, you're coming home to your daughter . . ." I paused, looking at Sara . . . "Amanda," she said. ". . . Amanda," I continued, "right after the encounter at the Complaint Department. The door is here." I gestured, gave him the tissue box, and then left for the other side of the room.

Wilkins entered, went to Amanda, and gave her a gentle hug, still holding the box. "Hi, Honey, how's it going?" he began. "Did you get me a new dolly, Daddy?" Amanda asked eagerly. "Well, no, not yet, Honey," Wilkins replied softly. "The lady told me she couldn't help me and that I had to come back another time to see her boss." "But Daddy, you told me you'd bring home a new one," Amanda exclaimed. "Well, Honey," Wilkins replied, sitting next to her and putting an arm around her shoulders, "sometimes these things get complicated. But I promise, one way or another, you'll have a good doll by tomorrow." "Okay, Daddy," said Amanda, laying her head against her father's chest, "Fiona'll be coming over to play with me."

I applauded, ending the scene, and motioned them back to their seats. "Sara, what was different for you this time?" "Oh, I liked how gentle Tony was and liked playing his little girl," Sara said, smiling. "Yeah, that was nice," Tony allowed, "but now I'm scheming how to get a refund or exchange from the store, so the pressure's on." "Fortunately, this is improv, so you can come home with a working doll even if you had to get it at gunpoint," I said. Everyone laughed.

In the ensuing discussion, both Tony and Sara reported that the tenderness and protectiveness of Wilkins and Amanda's trust in her daddy had felt particularly welcome. I then asked Sara to reflect again on her feelings toward Tony's character during the first scene. "Well, it's really different. I didn't like being on the receiving end of that, but now I see he was just trying to do right by Amanda," she said. Tony added: "I like being a hero, but it's also fun to play the bad guy, if no one really gets hurt."

In subsequent sessions, we returned repeatedly to these two scenes which provided rich insight. Both came to see how the premise of the scene had influenced, yet not determined, their choices: in the first scene, Tony could have portrayed a determined, yet polite customer, and Sara could have played her character with sympathy for him. In the second, Sara as Amanda might have been whining that she didn't have the doll and Wilkins could have blamed the clerk to exonerate himself as a good-guy father. Tony even stated that, in retrospect, it was his security in their marriage that had allowed him license to play at being rude and aggressive, a point that Sara found intriguing. These enactments appeared to have induced a greater degree of openness between Tony and Sara, who had both become more emotionally expressive in sessions and, by later report, at home.

From my point of view, both were now more practiced in validating each other's reality through co-creating these scenes as well as sharing the adventure of fictionalizing together. It was also apparent that Tony and Sara's emotional expressivity in my presence had expanded. Both seemed less careful and more open in a way that suggested they were now occasionally interacting more spontaneously. However, we had not addressed the core issue of Sara's fear that Tony might be having an affair. I decided to offer another enactment to detoxify that issue.

Once again, I proposed a scene in a complaint department, but this time with Sara as the customer without a sales receipt for the defective merchandise. The added premise here was for Sara's character to attempt to seduce Tony, a married clerk, to get him to bend the rules for her benefit. This was not intended as a test of Tony's actual fidelity, I pointed out. We then engaged in a fairly detailed discussion of whether Tony felt safe to play his character as succumbing to Sara's character's seduction. Interestingly, Sara was fairly eager to allow this possibility, not as a test of Tony, but to explore the temptress role for herself, while Tony was fearful that this would not end well. I suggested that, as with the second Tug-of-War enactment, we could partially script the drama in advance. They agreed. This is an example of creating high-stakes enactments collaboratively with clients; even though discovery through improv is thereby curtailed, the clients then feel safe enough to attempt the enactment. I also pointed out that they might become self-conscious enacting a seduction scene in front of me, so there should be some agreement as to how far to enact any seduction. I left the room to give them privacy for this discussion of limiting physical contact in my presence. While therapists are often privy to intimate details of their client couples' relationships, it is important to strengthen the boundary around their intimacy so that they experience their connection as deeper than either has with the therapist. After they signaled their readiness I returned and they began.

Sara, as Janice, strolled up to the counter, gently placing the box down. "Sorry, I've got to return this," she purred, while tilting her head and briefly licking her lips. Tony, as Frank, stared at her, motionless. Finally, in a soft voice, he said, "How can I help, Miss? "Well," Janice answered slowly, "this isn't really what I want. Can you help me?" Frank asked to see the receipt. Janice mimed fumbling in an imaginary purse for a few seconds, then looked up at Frank wide-eyed, saying, "I can't find it" in a helpless tone. Looking uncomfortable, Frank had started to recite store policy when Janice lightly touched his forearm and told him it would make her very happy if this could be worked out somehow. Frank looked Janice over and, glancing around him, leaned forward, suggesting they could discuss this further over lunch. Janice smiled at him, saying how much she appreciated good customer service. After trading a few more innuendos, they agreed on a meeting place and Janice left, smiling as she glanced over her shoulder at Frank.

As they returned to their seats, it was evident that they had both enjoyed playing the scene. Even before they were seated Tony exclaimed that he found her irresistible. "Who was it that found whom irresistible?" Sara demanded. But she was smiling. "Well, both," Tony answered ambiguously, sitting close to her on the couch and putting his hand atop hers. When the joking evasions and genuine confusion had cleared, Tony had let Sara know that he loved her seduction and that his character Frank had had no reason to resist her character Janice. "What about that he was a married man?" Sara asked. Well, he's that kind of guy, Tony answered. "I promise you, I'm not!"

I then inquired as to Sara's experiences; she reported that she had felt both energized and uneasy while playing Janice and seemed anxious to know whether she had appeared "slutty." Tony assured her that he had not seen either her or her character that way. I stated that she appeared to be judging herself, inviting her to reflect further on her experiences. Sara then connected her experience with the Janice character to doubts she had about her own image; while she wanted to be sexually adventurous with Tony she held back out of her fear that expressing this impulse would somehow undermine her right to his fidelity. Further exploration of her family of origin revealed that Sara had been closer to her emotionally warm father prior to the divorce and had felt pressure to maintain an outward loyalty to her emotionally cold mother following the divorce of her parents. Tony then chimed in that he wanted the passionate woman he had married to show up more often and that she fully satisfied him; he had no interest in an affair. Ending the session early, I gave them the assignment to each do some journaling concerning the issues that had surfaced, sharing any writings with one another on a voluntary basis. I also suggested that, if they wished, they could play another version of this last scene at home, unrestrained by my presence. Insights are often triggered by displacement scene enactments, and can be articulated during the post-enactment process; clinical experience shows that their value increases when slowly absorbed through reflection, rather than by the piling on of immediate further enactments.

When Tony and Sara came to the following week's session it was apparent that they had achieved a breakthrough. Not only had they made love at Sara's initiative (in which she had reprised her role as Janice) but they had transformed the beginning of a fight over Tony's visit to his health club into a post-workout "date" which they had both enjoyed considerably and were now planning to schedule regularly. Therapy ended two sessions later. In a follow-up call four months later I learned that they were still doing well.

CONCLUSION

RfG is a method of relationship therapy that utilizes improvisational tasks assigned by the therapist to playfully explore alternatives to clients' problematic patterns of interaction. The RfG method first establishes conditions that ensure both physical and psychological safety for clients as a precondition to their venturing into the territory of unfamiliar roles and novel interactive behaviors. Brief in-role enactments, played by client relationship members, are then staged at the direction of the therapist. Next, clients are de-roled and engaged in off-stage processing (as themselves), gaining a constructive learning experience by juxtaposing their adventuresome in-role forays with reflections. Finally, the process is repeated, with clients and therapist co-constructing further dramatic enactments.

Therapists wishing to use RfG are advised to first gain personal experience with improvisational enactment and to learn the rudiments of systemic therapy. Drama therapists who are comfortable with an active and collaborative style of working with relationship systems and who are open to continually examining their own use of self will likely find themselves successful in applying RfG.

REFERENCES

Bowlby, J. (1980). *Attachment and loss: Vol. 3.* New York: Basic Books.

Brissett, D., & C. Edgley, C. (1990). The dramaturgical perspective. In D. Brissett & C. Edgley (Eds.) *Life as theater* (2nd ed.) (pp. 1–46). Hawthorne, N.Y.: Aldine de Gruyter.

Chasin, R., Roth, S., & Bograd, M. (1989). Action methods in systemic therapy: dramatizing ideal futures and reformed pasts with couples. *Family Process, 28,* 1, 121–136.

Emunah, R. (1994). *Acting for real: Drama therapy process, technique, and performance.* New York: Brunner/Mazel.

Harvey, S. A. (2000). Family dynamic play. In P. Lewis & D. Johnson (Eds.), *Current approaches in drama therapy* (pp. 379–412). Springfield, IL: Charles C Thomas.

Harvey, S. A. (2003). Dynamic family play with

an adoptive family struggling with issues of grief, loss and adjustment. In D. J. Wiener & L. K. Oxford, (Eds.), *Action therapy with families and groups* (pp. 19–43). Washington, DC: APA Books.

Hoffman, L. (1988). A constructivist position for family therapy. *Irish Journal of Psychology, 9,* 110–129.

Holt, D. (1992). Enactment, therapy and behaviour. In S. Jennings (Ed.), *Dramatherapy: Theory and practice 2* (pp. 68–81). London: Tavistock/Routledge.

Johnson, D.R. (1992). The dramatherapist in-role. In S. Jennings (Ed.), *Dramatherapy: Theory and practice 2* (pp. 112–136). London: Tavistock/Routledge.

Johnstone, K. (1981). *Impro.* London: Metheuen.

Ramseur, C. A., & Wiener, D. J. (2003). Using Rehearsals for Growth in group therapy with substance abusers. In D.J. Wiener & L.K. Oxford (Eds.), *Action therapy with families and groups: Using creative arts improvisation in clinical practice* (pp. 107–134). Washington, DC: APA Books.

Spolin, V. (1963). *Improvisation for the theatre.* Evanston, IL: Northwestern University Press.

Wiener, D.J. (1994). *Rehearsals for growth: Theater improvisation for psychotherapists.* New York: W. W. Norton.

Wiener, D.J. (1997). Presents of mind. *Journal of Family Psychotherapy, 8,* 85–93.

Wiener, D.J. (1996). Tug-of-war: A theatrical technique for marital therapy. *Dialog, 27,* 37–43.

Wiener, D.J. (1999). Rehearsals for Growth: Applying improvisational theater games to relationship therapy. In D.J. Wiener (Ed.), *Beyond talk therapy: Using movement and expressive techniques in clinical practice* (pp. 165–180). Washington DC: APA Books.

Wiener, D.J., & Cantor, D. (2002). Improvisational play in couples therapy. In C. Schaefer (Ed.), *Play therapy with adults* (pp. 62–77). New York: Wiley.

Wiener, D. J., Yagaloff, C., Alexanian, J., & Larose, D. (2004). Status: a sociometric tool for understanding intra-familial conflict. In Wiener, D.J., *Rehearsals for growth: Collected papers, 1991-2004* (pp. 247–269). Leverett, MA: self-published. Available from the author.

BIBLIOGRAPHY

Wiener, D.J. (1991). You wanna play? Using enactments in couples therapy. *Journal of Feminist Family Therapy, 3,* 213–219.

Wiener, D.J. (1994). *Rehearsals for growth: Theater improvisation for psychotherapists.* New York: W. W. Norton.

Wiener, D.J. (1994). Rehearsing for growth: Improvisational group therapy. *Tele, 5,* 3–4.

Wiener, D.J. (1995). The gift of play. Family Therapy Networker, 19, 65-70. Reprinted in R. Simon, L. Markowitz, C. Barrilleaux, & B. Topping (Eds.), (1999). *The art of psychotherapy: Case studies from the Family Therapy Networker* (pp. 203–214). New York: Wiley.

Wiener, D.J. (1995). Use of RfG in facilitating basic skills (Part I). *Rehearsals for Growth Newsletter, 1,* 12–13.

Wiener, D.J. (1996). Assigning "home play" in family therapy. *Rehearsals for Growth Newsletter, 5,* 7–9.

Wiener, D.J. (1996). Improv games: Games and variations not included in rehearsals for growth. *Rehearsals for Growth Newsletter, 5,* 10–12.

Wiener, D.J. (1996). Tug-of-war: A theatrical technique for marital therapy. *Dialog, 27,* 37–43.

Wiener, D.J. (1997). Presents of mind. *Journal of Family Psychotherapy, 8,* 85–93.

Wiener, D.J. (1997). Rehearsals for growth: A methodology for using theater improvisation in MFT. *The Family Journal, 5,* 309–314.

Wiener, D.J. (1997). Using dramatic enactment in MFT supervision. *The Supervision Bulletin, 10,* 1.

Wiener, D.J. (1998). Feeding the relationship by feeding each other. In L. L. Hecker, S. Deacon & Associates, (Eds.), *The therapist's notebook: Homework, handouts, & activities* (pp. 163–166). New York: Haworth Press.

Wiener, D.J. (1998). Mirroring movement for increasing family cooperation. In T. S. Nelson & T. Trepper (Eds.), *101 more interventions in family therapy* (pp. 5–8). New York: Haworth Press.

Wiener, D.J. (1999). Rehearsals for Growth: Applying improvisational theater games to relationship therapy. In D.J. Wiener (Ed.), *Beyond talk therapy: Using movement and expressive tech-*

niques in clinical practice (pp. 165–180). Washington DC: APA Books

Wiener, D.J. (1999). Using theater improvisation to assess interpersonal functioning. *International Journal of Action Methods, 52,* 51–69.

Wiener, D.J. (2000). Rehearsals for growth: Activating clinical change via theater improvisation. *Journal of Systemic Therapies, 19,* 43–54.

Wiener, D.J. (2000). Struggling to grow: Using dramatic enactments in family therapy. *Journal of Family Psychotherapy, 11,* 9–21.

Wiener, D.J., & Cantor, D. (2002). Improvisational play in couples therapy. In C. Schaefer (Ed.), *Play therapy with adults* (pp. 62–77). New York: Wiley.

Wiener, D.J. (2003). Creating a participating role for adolescents in family therapy. In C. Sori & L. Hecker, (Eds.), *The therapist's notebook for children and adolescents* (pp. 180–184). New York: Haworth.

Wiener, D.J. (2003). From the outside in. *Psychotherapy Networker, 27,* 55–61.

Oxford, L.K., & Wiener, D.J. (2003). Rescripting family dramas using psychodramatic enactments. In D.J. Wiener & L.K. Oxford (Eds.), *Action therapy with families and groups: Using creative arts improvisation in clinical practice* (pp. 45–74). Washington, D.C.: APA Books.

Ramseur, C. A., & Wiener, D. J. (2003). Using Rehearsals for Growth in group therapy with substance abusers. In D.J. Wiener & L.K. Oxford (Eds.), *Action therapy with families and groups: Using creative arts improvisation in clinical practice* (pp. 107–134). Washington, DC: APA Books.

Wiener, D.J. (2004). *Rehearsals for growth: Collected papers, 1991–2004.* Leverett, MA: self-published.

Wiener, D.J. (2004). Treating depression with Rehearsals for Growth. In L. Harrison, (Ed.), *Natural healing for depression* (pp. 68–70). New York: Kensington.

Wiener, D. J., Yagaloff, C., Alexanian, J., & Larose, D. (2004). Status: a sociometric tool for understanding intra-familial conflict. In Wiener, D.J., *Rehearsals for growth: Collected papers, 1991–2004* (pp. 247–269). Leverett, MA: self-published. Available from the author.

Wiener, D.J. (2007). Rehearsals for growth: Applications to therapy and personal development groups. In A. Blatner (Ed.) w. Wiener, D. J., *Interactive and improvisational drama: Varieties of applied theatre and performance* (pp. 174–183). New York: iUniverse.

Wiener, D. J. Assessing trust in action: (in press). The couples leaning exercise. In L. Hecker & C. Sori, (Eds), *The therapist's notebook III: Homework, handouts, & activities* (pp. 137–142). New York: Haworth.

FURTHER TRAINING

At the present time, training in RfG is offered only by the author or by one of the three other certified RfG trainers. A 60 contact-hour RfG Certificate Training Program for clinicians is offered annually as are various briefer workshops, some focusing on more specialized applications. Up to 2007, about 2000 clinicians have attended at least one of the 175 RfG workshops (lasting from 1.5 hours to four days) offered in eight countries. 65 clinicians have taken the 60 contact-hour RfG Certificate Training Program, of which 24 are RfG-Certified Therapists. The book *Rehearsals for Growth* has been translated into Italian; a Japanese translation is currently in progress.

REHEARSALS FOR GROWTH, LLC
81 Long Plain Rd.
Leverett, MA 01054
Tel: (860) 490-3337
e-mail: Dan@rehearsalsforgrowth.com
website: www.rehearsalsforgrowth.com

Chapter 17

PERFORMANCE IN DRAMA THERAPY

SALLY BAILEY

INTRODUCTION

The creation and performance of plays by clients is an approach to drama therapy that offers many opportunities for personal growth, exploration of a wide variety of therapeutic issues, and the development of social skills. Performance can be used as the primary undertaking of a group or serve as the culminating project for a group that has been working in a process mode. This chapter will review why performance is effective therapeutically, the difference between fictional and nonfictional approaches to performance in terms of providing appropriate therapeutic distance, and a few useful methods for creating theatre pieces with clients.

Lou Furman (1988) notes, "Theatre has been accepted as a therapeutic agent since its first appearance." In *Poetics,* the first treatise written on theatre, Aristotle (1954) identifies theatre as an agent of catharsis–the purging of negative emotions. Aristotle was not referring to purging emotions of the actors, but of the audience members watching the play. However, actors, as the vehicle through which the emotions of the characters are expressed, necessarily experience catharsis, too. Part of an actor's training focuses on stage techniques, voice and diction, stage movement, and script analysis, which involve primarily cognitive and physical skills. However, since the beginning of the twentieth century, with the introduction of Stanislavski's psychological methods developed at the Moscow Art Theatre (Brockett, 1968), a good portion of actor training has included learning how to get in touch with the emotions felt by the character in order to portray them realistically and faithfully. Many of Stanislavski's (1936, 1961) techniques work from the inside out while others like Michael Chekhov's psychological gesture (1953) or Susana Bloch's Alba Emoting (2003) work from the outside in.

The experience of the character's emotions through the medium of acting a role can enrich the actor's understanding of his/her own emotions and motivations as well as understanding those of other people. T.D. Noble, a physician at Sheppard and Enoch Pratt Hospital in the 1930s, recognized that psychiatric patients who participated in plays learned how to identify emotions (Phillips, 1994). Through rehearsals, they developed the ability to connect their character's emotions with the character's biography, behavior, thoughts, and motivations. This led to being able to generalize these skills and make those same connections in their own lives during therapy sessions. Once patients were able to link their present state to past traumas, they were better able to resolve their emotional crises (Phillips, 1994). Noble felt that playing a character in a play "released repressed emotions" (Phillips, 1994, p. 232). He also recognized the socializing value of the rehearsal and performance process as the patients worked together toward a common goal (Phillips, 1994, p. 232). Growth in intrapersonal understanding and interpersonal skills are two main outcomes of performance.

Emunah and Johnson (1983) have written about their experiences creating original theatre performances with patients in residential psychiatric treatment centers as well as with ex-psychiatric patients in transition between institution and community. They observed that "self-image is expanded through experimentation with a variety of roles within the safety and boundaries of the structured group" while the play is being created (p. 235) and the performance allows the clients to "present themselves in a new way" to the audience (p. 236). They note that the performance provides a model for dealing with life's stressful situations as it "is like a planned crisis: one knows when it is coming, but no matter what one does to prepare . . . the safety and structure of that moment can only come from within" (p. 236). Snow, D'Amico, and Tanguay (2003) highlight "the power and influence of group dynamics that are always involved in a play production," which can be further put to therapeutic use as the group simultaneously works toward therapeutic goals under the direction of a drama therapist who understands both how to direct a play and how to facilitate change through dramatic means.

NARRATIVE, HEALING, AND MEANING-MAKING

Narrative is basic to the way the brain makes sense of the world around it. The left hemisphere is believed to have a narrator function, taking autobiographical memories from the right hemisphere and articulating experiences into words, which are used to make meaning of our existence. In therapy, clients must go back to that raw right hemisphere material to reframe, restructure, and then relanguage the past through their left hemisphere functions in order to understand it in a new way (Cozolino, 2002, 2006; Siegel, 2007). Neuropsychiatrist Daniel Siegel (2007) notes, "The mindful telling of our tale can be greatly healing of unresolved issues in our life" (p. 309).

Another aspect of narrative that seems to have therapeutic implications is that narratives are time-bound: they have a beginning, middle, and end. We experience life-in-process as an ongoing series of unrelated events: we do not remember the beginning of our own life; the middle often seems to extend formlessly before us with little to no connection between many of our experiences. We cannot truly understand the ultimate meaning of our life until we can look back at the whole from the end. Narratives select a discrete sub-section of experiences within a life which together create a plot or a causal linkage from the first event to the last. A narrative is understood only through reviewing its contents backwards from the end: the final consequence lets the storyteller and the audience make meaning from the whole (Mattingly, 1998). David Ball explains in *Backwards and Forwards,* "Going backwards exposes that which is required," while going forwards only "allows unpredictable possibility"(1983, p. 15). One must clearly know not only what happened sequentially, but why it happened and how each event was connected.

Clients in therapy are in the middle of the healing process. Encapsulating experiences in the form of a story allows them to choose an ending they would like to achieve, evaluate all the relevant events in their healing process so far, and, through understanding the relationship between the actions they took and could take, create a plot (a planned series of actions) that gets them where they want to go. Studying that story from beginning to end (and backwards from the end to the beginning) allows clients to come to a new understanding or a new perspective on their life. As Mattingly says, "To have a story at all is to make a whole out of a succession of actions. This 'making a whole' is also making meaning. . . . Narratives give meaningful structure to life through time" (Mattingly, 1998, p. 46). Utilized in therapy, narratives allow clients, in conjunction with the therapist, to work toward endings they desire. They can make actions cumulative rather than a collection of unpredictable possibilities.

The drama therapist who understands dramatic structure can help clients structure a narrative that cumulatively builds action upon action to create a coherent, meaningful whole. Drama therapist Pam Dunne taps into these qualities of narrative through her "Narradrama" method (Chapter 9) which is improvisational and process-oriented in nature. As clients explore their past life stories through drama and creative arts techniques, "the therapist invites the client to compare the old story with the new to decide which direction suits better and to build on exceptions to problem behavior in constructing a new story" (Dunne, Chapter 9).

The oral tradition of storytelling is a means of connecting individuals with a community by constructing shared messages and linking the feelings and actions of one person to others. When a group creates and rehearses an original play, they are co-constructing a group narrative through which they form and share a common meaning. Social and emotional bonds are forged among the group members, providing a sense of connection and acceptance which is essential to the healing process (Cozolino, 2002, 2006). The performance of the play allows the actors to reach out beyond the confines of their group and transmit their story to the outside community. Extending social bonds builds the connections which neuroscience has begun to prove are essential to all humans for a long and healthy life (Cozolino 2002, 2006; Goleman, 2006; Siegel, 2007).

THE STAGE AS A HEALING SPACE

Performing the story on a stage adds a formal sharing and witnessing aspect that provides another level of healing to the co-constructed group play. Susana Pendzik (1994) points out that theatre is a form of sacred space. Sacred space is qualitatively different from other mundane spaces and, as a result, anything that happens within it is invested with extreme significance. Reality becomes *more real* or *extraordinary,* just as fantasy becomes *more fantastic.* Within the microcosm of the stage, the macrocosm of the world can be represented. There is what Pendzik terms a magical flexibility because "the stage has no limitations. As a container of the cosmos, it encloses all spots on earth, heaven or hell, and can manifest them at any moment without breaking its credibility" (1994, p. 28). Any role, any emotion, or any experience that can be imagined can be tried out. In the act of performing or of watching a performance, the willing suspension of disbelief, which is basic to theatre, allows what is not-real to be transubstantiated into the imaginary-real.

In her analysis of stage spaces, Pendzik (1994) goes on to connect the sacred stage space with therapeutic space, citing the connection between sacred spaces and healing rituals. Pendzik identifies the stage as providing a metaphor for the client's capacity for constructive risk-taking and a symbol of his being able to stand apart from others in order to develop an identity and achieve individuation. She sees the stage space as able to activate unconscious archetypes which "may account for its [the stage's] ability to amplify emotions, sharpen conflicts, accelerate time and make any action that occurs on it look meaningful" (1994, p. 32), and, in fact, for the actor and the audience, those acts do become meaningful.

From the theatre perspective, Peter Brook agrees (Brook, 1968). Given that theatre began in religious ritual, he believes theatre that excites an audience and brings them in touch with the truth of being alive could be called the *Holy Theatre* or "The Theatre of the Invisible-Made-Visible: the notion that the stage is a place where the invisible can appear" (1968, p. 38). In this space a living confrontation–the drama–takes place. "The focus of a large group of people creates a unique intensity–owing to this, forces that operate at all times and rule each person's daily life can be isolated and perceived more clearly" (1968, p. 90). But it is not enough to have actors present the essence of a truth and make it visible–there must also be a witnessing of that truth by an audience. He says, "Until the audience is present, the object [the play or performance] is not complete" (1968, p. 115). In terms of drama therapy, the witnessing of the explorations and discoveries of the actor-clients by an audience in a theatre setting validates their discoveries.

From the therapeutic perspective, D.W. Winnicott (1971) identified *potential space* as a place and a time in an interpersonal interaction in which healthy relationships can develop through play. Winnicott's potential space has come to be commonly called *transitional space* in therapeutic circles. The creative arts therapies have extended this concept to the space/time of a creative arts therapy session. McNiff calls it *ritual space,* Johnson calls it *playspace,* Lewis calls it *liminal space,* and Robbins calls it *therapeutic space* (Johnson, 1999, p. 146). Johnson goes on to say, "the notion of *transitional space* provides an excellent description of the environment that is recreated in the creative arts therapy session; that is, an aesthetic, imaginal, metaphoric space in which inside and outside, self and other, are mixed" (1999, p. 146).

The stage is a transitional space. In fact, one could say the stage is one of the greatest potential or transitional spaces available–the place where anything can happen–among the actors on stage and between the actors and the audience. In a process-oriented drama therapy session, the play and healing involve the clients and the therapist inside the therapy room; in performance-oriented drama therapy, the clients create the play in rehearsal while the therapist guides its creation, and the audience is brought in to share the performance and serve as witnesses at the end of the process.

DRAMA THERAPY CONCEPTS IN PERFORMANCE

Role theory, first proposed by Jacob Levy Moreno (Fox, 1987) and developed further by Robert Landy in his Role Method (1993, 1994, 1996, Chapter 5), is integral to drama therapy performance. Every client in a performance takes on the role of actor as well as that of at least one character in the play.

Within a play, clients have the opportunity to move from their usual role as sick person into the role of actor who learns lines and blocking, follows stage conventions, and moves into the thoughts, behaviors, and emotions of the role they are portraying.

Role repertoire is the number of different roles that a person is able to take on and play out comfortably in life. As Emunah says, "Our real-life roles, responses, and dynamics in interaction with others are limited; we become imprisoned by our own patterns and the expectations held by others that we behave in certain ways. In drama, however, the possibilities are limitless. . . . An expanded role repertoire equips us to deal with a broader range of life situations, to cope with new tasks, and to respond to old tasks in new and creative ways" (1994, p. 32).

Casting actors in roles as characters whose issues contrast with their own can help clients expand their role repertoire by challenging them to try out new behaviors, thoughts, or emotions in a safe situation. The script provides a reliable, stable structure to work within. At the end of each rehearsal and performance, the actor takes off the role (de-roles). New roles or new ways of playing old roles, once practiced, become available for clients to try out later in their real lives. Someone who is afraid of taking risks could play the hero; someone who is shy could be the outspoken one; someone who always makes excuses and complains could be the can-do character; someone who avoids conflict in real life could be the one who confronts other characters directly. Taking on a different perspective can open up the possibility of a new way to perceive or approach other people.

Actors taking on characters whose issues do not contrast as much with those in their own lives can also work on their issues through the play in a safe way. They have the opportunity to experiment with their problems or look at life from a different perspective. However, the script needs to reframe their options or offer new positive alternatives for behavior so the client is not reinforcing unhealthy habits.

In a nonfictional context, actors can explore their own personal life story through *self-revelatory performance* (Emunah, 1994). Past experiences, present predicaments, and future hopes can be embodied by the actor directly. The story is witnessed, honored, and validated by the audience, providing positive feedback and acceptance. Embodying one's own story directly allows the self to be seen openly in public–a powerful experience for those who are ready for it. Emunah (1994) cautions that autobiographical or self revelatory performance must avoid self-indulgence and must translate the experience of the actor into universal truths that offer meaning to the audience in theatrical form. Clients need to have attained a certain amount of insight and resolution of the therapeutic issues they are performing in order for there to be emotional safety for both the actors and the audience.

Distancing is an important concept in drama therapy and in theatre. As defined by Robert Landy, distancing in drama therapy at an intrapsychic level relates to the client's sense of closeness to or alienation from feelings, thoughts and physical self-image (1996, p. 13). When clients feel overwhelmed or too close to their feelings and/or body, they are said to be *underdistanced* and when too far away, *overdistanced*. Little therapeutic work can be accomplished if a client is under- or overdistanced because his connection to self is incomplete or unbalanced. To be able to heal on an emotional, cognitive, and physical level simultaneously, a client needs to find a place of balance called *aesthetic distance*. This is a state in which one can feel and think and experience being connected to one's body/mind/emotions all at once.

This intrapsychic place is where healing and meaning-making can happen.

Likewise, actors in the theatre must perform in a place of aesthetic distance or they cannot portray the character in an effective manner. Too much emotion/too little distance and the sense of self is lost, becoming totally engulfed in the emotions and psychological reality of the character. Actors will not be able to handle the technical aspects of the performance, such as remembering blocking, projecting their voice so the audience can hear, or speaking clearly enough to be understood. With too much distance/too little emotion actors give a stilted performance that does not embody the character with any emotional life or truth.

The drama therapist must carefully select the appropriate intervention to bring a particular client (or group of clients) into balance. For instance, if a client enters a session over-distanced (not emotionally connected), the drama therapist might facilitate a very physically active and thrilling drama game to encourage a better integration of physicality, cognition, and emotion.

On the distancing continuum within performance, creating fictional characters and situations typically creates more distance between the actor-client and character being portrayed, while autobiographical performance or self-revelatory performance typically create less distance. For clients to experience aesthetic distance in performance and really learn from the role they are playing, they must feel safe enough to embody the character or parts of self openly and fully. Feeling safe enough might require acting a fictional character in a drama therapy setting where what is autobiographical and what is invented remains unclear. Behind the mask of the character, clients often feel free to take bigger risks and explore new emotional or behavioral territory. This relates to Phase Two of Emunah's "Integrative Five Phase Model" (Chapter 4) and to the fictional role playing used in "Sociodrama" (Sternberg & Garcia, Chapter 19). On the other end of the continuum, acting one's own story might feel safe if the client has good ego strength and feels secure enough to reveal oneself to others.

Ultimately, what matters is the amount of distance that is appropriate for each client in order to arrive at aesthetic distance and achieve insight into the issue being worked on. Emunah says her clients referred to drama therapy groups both as "the place where we get out of ourselves" and the place "where we really get into ourselves," indicating the range of distancing a group experiences over time (Emunah, 1983, p. 79). She talks in terms of heightening or containing the emotion when relating client work to distancing (Emunah, 1994). This image can help the therapist grasp in which direction the client(s) needs to go.

Actors playing a character unlike themselves often feel challenged by the distance they must go to find the character. Once the characterization is achieved, playing the role can feel very liberating because the actors experience themselves as outside of their normal way of being. On the other hand, actors playing a character very similar to themselves can heighten their self-awareness, discover new insights, and deepen their connection with themselves.

PLAYS AS MEANING-MAKING AND MEANING-SHARING DEVICES

A play created by a group can synthesize personal and interpersonal learning that has happened during the group's process. Drama therapy groups I worked with at Second Genesis, a long term residential drug and alcohol rehabilitation treatment program in the Washington, DC area, created plays about their journeys to recovery, summarizing the skills they had developed in avoiding negative people, places, and things that would take them off the path to sobriety. Through the plays they were able to demonstrate how they could pro-actively stay on the straight-and-narrow. Those actions, which they honed in rehearsal, often were of benefit off stage. Several times graduates from my drama therapy group have reported, "I was back in my old neighborhood visiting my mother when my old drug dealer came up to on me on the street and said the exact same thing that the dealer in our play said! And I said to him, 'I don't do drugs anymore! I'm clean!' just like I did in the play and walked away. I didn't feel any cravings for drugs. I just felt really proud of myself!" Emunah reports similar reactions from her clients: "The way I'm acting in my life now is catching up with the way I act in drama" (1994, p. xiii).

A play can become a way to tie together or explore further themes and issues that have come up in groups. For instance, one group of recovering addicts was very concerned about future jobs and responsibilities once they finished treatment. Their play, *My Workshop,* became a realistic fantasy of potential careers and workplaces where they could successfully use their strengths and talents. The play helped each group member set goals, imagine the steps for getting there, and experience an embodied preview of coming attractions. It is hard to work for a future that seems vague and ephemeral; the clearer the future is imagined, the easier it is to hold onto one's dreams and commit to the work that is necessary for making it happen.

Through performance, discoveries that have been made within the group are shared with others outside the group. My drama therapy groups of recovering addicts performed for family, friends, and other residents of the facility on Family and Friends Nights or at graduations, sharing stories and strong visual images that provided insights for our audiences into how difficult dealing with addiction is and how they could support that struggle. When we had an appropriate play, we sometimes performed for school groups, and followed the performance with a talk-back in which the students asked the actors about how they were introduced to drugs and how hard it is to reach sobriety.

Plays can make a difference in how clients are viewed by their community. Adolescents and adults with disabilities in performing companies I directed have created plays that provided them with opportunities to entertain others and show how able they were. Parents, teachers, relatives, and friends who came to our public performances often saw abilities, strengths, dreams, and imaginations they otherwise would never have realized existed. One parent of a young man with cerebral palsy said in an after-show discussion, "I always learn new things about my son when I come and see him in these plays!" (Personal communication, 1990). Another mother who has a daughter with Asperger's Syndrome told me:

> I have seen the child we knew was inside, but which we rarely saw at home, come out on stage. In real life my daughter is very shy and quiet in social settings, but during the plays she is not afraid of the audience. On stage she is at her most confident, most assertive, her most centered self. Being in the plays gives her something *entirely* her own. . . . It is extremely hard for us to find something that the *whole* family can participate in and enjoy together. . . . Our family and friends and neighbors can come to see our daughter in the performances and celebrate her success. After they see her in a play, they begin to see her in a whole new light. (Personal communication, 1990)

BUILDING SKILLS THROUGH PERFORMANCE

Rehearsing a play enhances self-discipline. Actors must show up on time for rehearsals and performances, learn their lines by set deadlines, focus, and work hard during rehearsals. Team skills are developed. Actors need to support each other and work together toward the common goal of the performance. All involved in a production may have their own individual ideas about how a scene should be staged or how a moment should be played. To resolve the conflicts that inevitably come up requires flexibility, patience, and willingness to compromise.

Actors will feel the difference between coming to rehearsal prepared or unprepared. The therapist-director can highlight this difference and underline its value in terms of the individual and the group. Sometimes it is not easy to communicate to an actor-client that being prepared and willing to work in rehearsal is a necessity. Actor-clients who have spent their lives failing often do not know how to be responsible, choose positive actions, or put them in a sequence that will lead to success. Many times this process has to be taught step by step. Therapist-directors cannot forget that actors with strong theatrical work discipline are made, not born. However, once learned, these lessons can be accessed again in other life situations.

A positive rehearsal process will generate respect among cast members and eventually a tight-knit, caring feeling will develop. Casts and crews from all types of theatre experiences (professional, educational, community and drama therapy alike) report that working on a play creates a family. When it is a positive experience, guided by a drama therapist, the rehearsal and performance process can model for clients how a healthy, loving family functions. For clients from dysfunctional families, this may be the first positive holding experience they have had in their lives.

Acting in a play is one way to practice taking the stage and getting up in front of others. Actors learn how to make eye contact with each other, speak loudly and clearly, stand and deliver. Performing is a wonderful way to experience positive attention. Many clients only know how to seek negative attention because that is the only kind they have ever received. After awhile, generating negative attention becomes habit-forming. Performing in a play, hearing the positive reactions of the audience, and receiving applause can be a client's first experience with receiving positive attention. Once clients know how good this feels, they will tend to seek positive attention again. Drama therapy performances allow clients to be contributing members of their community, doing something of value, sometimes for the first time in their lives. This is no small accomplishment.

Actors can physically feel the electricity, focus, and aliveness generated when they are performing with energy. Emotional connection and rapport develops between the actors on stage and between the actors and the audience. A good therapist-acting coach can help client-actors learn how to reproduce this energy whenever they need it on stage or in other aspects of their lives.

As the date of the performance gets closer, actors begin to feel nervous. Stage fright essentially is the result of the brain sending a message to the adrenal glands to release adrenalin in response to the impulse, "I sense risk!" The experience of this rush of adrenalin is a physiological sensation which the person recognizes as a feeling and then translates into an action (Bilodeau, 1992). When an actor translates this adrenalin-based feeling as fear, they may panic, run away, or freeze and go blank. Sometimes an actor-client will misinterpret this feeling as anger and provoke a fight with another company member. However, if clients learn how to translate this feeling into excitement, they can channel this adrenalin rush into concentration and energy that can be used in their performance.

Dealing with stage fright and opening night nerves give actor-clients excellent practice for handling the anxiety and fears that come up in real life situations like job interviews, work presentations, or even personal confrontations. Often when someone is nervous, they breathe very shallowly. Without enough oxygen their muscles tense up. They panic, resulting in the classic stage fright reaction. When coupled with oxygen, adrenalin releases energy into the body that can be used to enhance performance. Actors learn how to breathe slowly and deeply and to focus on the task at hand (the performance). Suddenly the world comes into focus and the actor feels tremendous power flowing through him, resulting in that natural high that all actors love to feel.

If actor-clients are warned about opening-night nerves ahead of time, they can be gently reminded what to do when their nerves flare up on opening night. One aspect of stage fright is that actors disengage from the moment and experiences themselves as disembodied (a version of freezing or dissociating when faced with danger). Then they are not able to process verbal and visual information well. Practicing beforehand is the best preparation.

Post production depression is something all actors experience to some degree when a show ends; however, client-actors often experience this loss of the theatrical family as highly alienating and rejecting. Emunah and Johnson (1983) stress the importance of continuing therapeutic support for the actor-clients after the final performance. While working as drama therapists in psychiatric hospitals, both recognized that clients experienced severe feelings of loss, depression, and other clinical symptoms in the immediate post-production period. This pattern was identified in the writing of earlier directors of dramatic productions in psychiatric settings as well (Brookes, 1975; Gibson & Brookes, 1976; Mazor, 1966). All discovered that continuing the support of the group after the final performance through round table discussions, focus groups, or continuation of the group process helped clients assimilate the lessons learned without feeling abandoned. Johnson (1980) states, "Important therapeutic work begins with the end of the play. . ." (p. 271). No opportunity to provide a complete healing experience should be left unexplored.

CONSTRUCTING A PLAY WITH A DRAMA THERAPY GROUP

Plays can be created through improvisation, interviewing, editing clients' written work, adapting a story that holds therapeutic meaning for the group, or by the drama therapist sitting down and writing a play specifically for the clients. Clients who are not physically able to write or who lack literary abilities and confidence will have difficulty writing their own stories to dramatize; however, they may be very able to create a play through improvisation or to act out a play that has been written with their themes, strengths, and abilities in mind.

The first skill the drama therapist-playwright needs to understand is how a well-made play is constructed. Plays are typically about conflict between characters and how that conflict is resolved. (Sometimes plays are about internal conflicts within a character.) Conflicts are caused by obstacles created by other characters or circumstances that are placed in the path of the main character(s). There are many models for building a play, but they all can be boiled down to a simple formula, identified by drama therapist Norman Fedder during his years of writing plays and teaching playwriting at Kansas State University (Personal communication, 2000). He calls this formula *Fedder's Four:*

I Want–But–However–So . . .

Within any dramatic unit–be it play, act, scene or beat–action follows the dramatic structure of:

a. A character WANTS something
b. BUT there is an obstacle of some kind in the way
c. HOWEVER, the character takes action in an attempt to get past the obstacle
d. SO he gets past the obstacle and the play ends or he moves on to the next obstacle in the play or he doesn't get past the obstacle and must try again

If Fedder's Four is followed, any narrative can be shaped into a dramatically satisfying play that has a beginning, middle, climax, and end.

Another important ingredient in playwriting is starting with the end and working backwards (Ball, 1983). Without beginning with the end in mind (what the main character achieves), chances are you will never get there. The clearer your end is, the more interconnected you can make each action in the plot so the only direction the play can take is where you want it to go. That doesn't mean the audience always knows what is going to happen–a well-made play always has twists, turns, and surprises, but at the final curtain, when the audience thinks back, they realize the journey they took with the characters makes sense. In a therapeutic play, this end and how it is achieved is doubly important because the therapeutic play is a blueprint for the client's life.

What makes a play therapeutic and how can the drama therapist guide the creation of plays that will heal rather than retraumatize actors? The healing aspect of plays–and, in fact, the healing aspect of the therapeutic process–is inherent in the Fedder's Four structure: healing or transformation happens when the main character/client has a dream of a better life or a goal which will make him/her more whole or more complete (I WANT), (BUT) a trauma of some kind–addiction, disability, depression, or death of a loved one, etc.–has blocked that dream or goal. As a result the main character/client takes an action (HOWEVER)–usually a number of successively culminating actions–to resolve or remove the obstacle, (SO) he/she can reach the goal and become whole again. All well-made plays (and successful therapies) move from a state that is out of balance through a series of trials to a new state of balance at the end (Downs & Wright, 1998; Mattingly, 1998). The main character/client must be responsible for transforming the situation and there is no guarantee that the goal will finally be achieved, so danger, suspense, and uncertainty are experienced in the process.

> So narrative time is marked by change, or by the attempt at change. It is time characterized by an effort at transformation. Things may be changed in an outward, public way or there may be an inward difference. People may come to think and feel differently . . . the agency which most matters in creating change is human agency. (Mattingly, 1998, p. 94)

In other words, a well-written play should not end with a *deus ex machina* (literally translated from the Greek as "god from a machine") where some greater power swoops in to solve the problem for the main character at the last minute. The characters/clients must do the work themselves! They could have help from a wise mentor; however, the healthiest way characters can overcome their adversity is ultimately through their own labor and insight.

The first step in creating a play is to decide what it will be about. One way of guiding a group toward play formation is to brainstorm issues and struggles that they find in their lives, about which they have questions and want to know more, or about themes they want to explore. Groups of adolescents tend to come up with topics like The Wild West, Cops and Robbers, Pirates, Time Travel, Soap Operas, or Dating–themes that symbolically express rebellion, independence, identity, and the search for acceptance and love. Groups of addicts select topics like The Road to Recovery, The Search for Success, Exploring the Wilderness, or My Future, which symbolically allow them to explore their issues of staying sober, finding what is valuable and worthwhile in life, facing the unknown with courage, and evaluating vocational, financial, and social goals. If there is a groundswell of support for one particular topic, you are on your way. If not, consensus needs to be reached so that everyone will buy into the work ahead.

If the group has been working together in a process drama therapy mode before moving into performance, the issue to be dramatized might have already been identified. If the drama therapist presents this in an open, nonjudgmental manner (e.g., "I've noticed that the theme of the search for spirituality keeps coming up. A lot of people seem to have questions and opinions about it. What if we work on a play that can present the different sides of that?"), chances are that the group will come to consensus quickly.

Once the theme has been identified, the play can be developed through improvisation to generate characters, plot ideas, and dialogue. Remembering that a well-made play starts with the end in mind–an end achieved by the main character–the drama therapist and clients must make sure they know where their dramatic destination is before they start filling in the details of the journey. For instance, if the play is about the Road to Recovery, the end probably needs to show the main character arriving at the Land of Recovery (or Sobriety, Wisdom, or Reunification with Family). If the play is about a crew of pirates in search of treasure, the end is probably going to be Finding the Treasure.

It might be useful for a play to be a tragedy and highlight all the worst choices that might be taken. *Romeo and Juliet* is a perfect case study on teen suicide as it shows all the wrong ways to handle depressed adolescents: isolating, not listening, keeping secrets, giving double messages, resorting to deception, teasing and ridicule, giving superficial advice (Barton, 1985). However, it is usually therapeutically more useful to work on the proactive steps for getting past life's obstacles in order to generate a sense of hope and power in actor-clients.

Groups that are highly verbal and articulate can be audiotaped or videotaped to save rich details of improvised scenes. This allows the drama therapist to stay focused on setting up and coaching the improvisations–helping the clients maintain the flow of the scene–instead of getting bogged down taking notes or trying to remember things to write down later. If actors are particularly articulate, the tape can be later transcribed so dialogue can be used verbatim.

Another way to develop a play is through writing and drawing exercises. Through guided imagery journeys, clients can go on parallel adventures in which the "I WANT" is given ("I want to reach the top of the mountain") but each client in his own imagination creates the specific obstacles–the

"BUTs"–as well as the "HOWEVERS" of getting past them. After imagining their journeys, clients write about or draw their adventure. Their poems, stories, maps, and scenes become the raw material from which the drama therapist forms the play.

The basic journey suggested by the guided imagery provides the bare bones of a plot structure, ensuring there are obstacles and direct confrontation with them which work toward a final goal. Thc play that results is truly a group collaboration with contributions from everyone. The drama therapist as playwright can pick the most therapeutic conflicts, actions, and words to help illustrate positive ways of dealing with life problems. For example, one group of recovering addicts faced a gigantic spider web blocking the path in a dark forest. Some group members destroyed the web, some went around it, some climbed over the trees, one even climbed onto the web and got stuck, but one person who didn't want to be destructive humbly asked the spider for help. The spider was delighted and showed him how to unhook the web from the tree, walk underneath, and rehang the web. This was the episode chosen for the play because it demonstrated "how to do your business the right way."

Documentary theatre (also called nonfiction theatre, reminiscence theatre, verbatim theatre, ethno-theatre, or reality theatre) allows real people to tell their stories directly. The group chooses an issue or event to explore and they interview each other, or they interview people outside of the group who have experienced the issue or event to get first person testimony which–edited and shaped–will become the words of the play. A good example of this process is *The Laramie Project* (Kaufman, 2001). The Tectonic Theatre Project, a New York City-based acting company, interviewed over 500 people in and around Laramie, Wyoming about the murder of Matthew Shepherd, transcribed the tapes, and edited together the testimony into a play that portrayed the reaction of the community to a controversial tragedy in its midst. *The Laramie Project* is a portrait of the issues of violence, justice, homophobia and hate crime, but also a snapshot of a contemporary Western town grappling with its multiple reactions to a specific event at the end of the twentieth century.

Actor-playwright Anna Devere Smith (2000) has created a series of solo performance pieces, such as *Twilight: Los Angeles, 1992* and *Fires in the Mirror,* based on interviews with real people who experienced race riots in LA and Boston, respectively, as she has searched for personal understanding of what she terms the American character. She has found that the verbatim use of pause, syntax, grammar, and word choice helps crystallize the psychology of the interviewee-characters, making it easy to capture their personality and move it from the page to the stage. Jessica Blank and Erik Jensen, who created *The Exonerated* from interviews with individuals who had been exonerated from death row, also report experiencing this phenomenon (Blank & Jensen, 2005).

Johnny Saldana (2005), who advocates ethno-theatre as a method of qualitative inquiry and a viable alternative manner of documenting and presenting data, stresses the necessity of transferring the words from interviews to the stage in aesthetically and theatrically exciting dramatic structures. Too many ethno-plays evolve into boring, didactic readings instead of stories that come to life on stage. As he says, "Theatre's primary goal is to entertain–to entertain ideas as it entertains its spectators" (p. 14). He advocates the use of effective playwriting methods, as those outlined previously, to create works that have artistic integrity as well as ethno-dramatic validity.

Reminiscence Theatre has been used

extensively in Great Britain and Europe with older adults for therapeutic purposes, community building (specifically intergenerational and intercultural explorations), and educational projects (Schweitzer, 2007). Interviews with older adults about life experiences are edited into either verbatim plays performed by professional actors or developed into improvised dramas performed by acting companies comprised of older adults, providing occasions for validation, affirmation, and life review, a specific form of narrative meaning-making identified by Erikson (1997) and others as an important task of the final stages of life.

Drama therapist Stephen Snow and his colleagues have moved from creating therapeutic theatre based on folk tales, chosen because of inherent archetypical themes that relate to their clients' therapeutic needs, to ethno-dramas that reflect the life experiences of their developmentally disabled clients at the Centre for the Arts in Human Development at Concordia University in Montreal (Chapter 7). Their first ethno-drama, *The Story You Need to Hear Now,* was premiered at the Opening Ceremony of the 2007 National Association for Drama Therapy Conference.

Another example of how ethno-drama can positively affect interviewees and their community occurred recently in Manhattan, Kansas in response to the work of two drama therapy students. Martha Crouse interviewed young gay men who were afraid to come out to their families and wrote a play called *If Truth Be Told.* The same year, Jemmie Godwin wrote *You Belong to Us* from the testimony of parents of lesbians and gays whose children had come out to them. Both plays were produced by the Flinthills PFLAG (Parents and Friends of Lesbians and Gays). In each production a few of the interviewees chose to play themselves, while other roles were assumed by actors. The rest of the interviewees who lived in town came to be part of the audience. A few even came to each performance and participated in the talk-backs after the shows. Because the plays were written, rehearsed, and produced by drama therapists who were aware of the vulnerability of the interviewees as cast and community members in a conservative Kansas college town, great care was taken to provide education, process emotions, and share other stories that came up in rehearsals and in the talk-backs. The goal of these two productions was to create a safe and healing environment in which members of the gay and lesbian community and their families came together to have their pain and experiences witnessed, validated and respected. This goal seems to have been accomplished as both women received the 2007 Human Rights Award presented by the Flinthills Human Rights Commission and the 2007 National Award for Outstanding Educational Programs given by the National PFLAG organization for their work.

CASE EXAMPLE

One year my Pegasus performing company at the Bethesda Academy of Performing Arts decided to create a hospital drama. Pegasus actors were teens with and without disabilities who worked together for seven months to create a play based on their own ideas through improvisation. The recorded improvisations, their ideas, and their choices for the roles they wanted to play were fashioned into a one-act play. This particular year the actors were interested in the topic of hospitals. All of them had spent time in hospitals: some had had short stays while others had had years of operations and doctors visits. All felt they wanted to explore the power differential between doctor and nurse and between medical staff and patient as well as the frustrations of being sick, the struggle to get well, and the powerlessness they often felt while in the care of the medical establishment. In addition, they had been exposed to hospital soap operas on TV that highlighted the romantic intrigues that could go on in a hospital setting. This allowed us to deal with attraction, flirtation, love, jealousy, and betrayal–all favorite adolescent themes. A doctor character was created who romanced two nurses at the same time and got into big trouble when his two-timing ways were discovered.

Gretchen, one of my actresses who had spina bifida, was struggling in her life with not being accepted by her typically developing school peers. The girls excluded her socially and the boys were not interested in her romantically because she wore braces on her legs and used a wheelchair. She wanted to create a character with a disability who stood up to the bullying and condescending behavior of her peers. The character she chose to play–a psychiatrist with a physical disability–became a wonderful example of using a role that is fictional–but close to oneself–to release frustrations, change perspective, and explore ways of overcoming the obstacles life puts in one's way.

In improvisations, when Gretchen as the psychiatrist tried to have a serious conversation with the other doctors and nurses, she was treated like she did not have a brain in her head. They dismissed her ideas and diagnoses as worthless. In one scene they started taking everything she said literally. For example, when she tried to express her frustration by shouting, "Look!" they all turned and looked out the window.

If Gretchen had not felt safe in her role–and in the group–her response might have been to cry as she did in real life. Instead, she started to giggle and then laughed uproariously because for the first time in a situation like this she felt in control. She had set up the situation and she knew she could explore it any way that she wanted: she could stop it, she could exaggerate it, she could replay it. She knew she could ask the other actors to play out their roles in any specific way because they were trusted friends who accepted how wonderful and talented she was. In that moment of laughter she experienced aesthetic distance and began to see her real life predicament from another perspective. She began to come up with new ways of getting past her obstacles in improvisations than she had never thought of before–which, of course, were incorporated into the play. In the final version, the other doctors and nurses dismissed her character because of her disability, but the audience witnessed her character continually making very astute diagnoses and interventions which cured her patients, proving how little insight the other medical professionals had. In the final scene even her coworkers had to acknowledge her competence because she saved the day in the operating room when no other doctor knew what to do. Through the play Gretchen had the chance to confront her obstacles and overcome them fictionally, which raised her confidence in her ability to overcome the obstacles in her own life.

CONCLUSION

Performing plays is a dynamic drama therapy approach which allows clients to expand and practice their role repertoire; gain confidence; be witnessed for their creativity, expressiveness, and strengths; share their stories and ideas; and learn how to work more effectively with other people toward an end product that makes a difference. Whether the play is created through improvisation or is scripted, whether it is based on fictional characters and situations or nonfiction ones, new insights can be achieved at every point in the play-making process through the careful guidance of the drama therapist who has expertise in theatre processes and psychotherapy.

REFERENCES

Aristotle. (1954). *Aristotle's rhetoric and poetics.* New York: The Modern Library.

Ball, D. (1983). *Backwards and forwards.* Carbondale: Southern Illinois University Press.

Barton E. (1985). *Romeo and Juliet: Friends for life.* Washington, DC: Youth Suicide Prevention Center.

Bilodeau, L. (1992). *The anger workbook.* Minneapolis, MN: CompCare Publishers.

Blank, J., & Jensen, E. (2005). *Living justice: Love, freedom, and the making of The Exonerated.* New York: Simon & Schuster.

Bloch, S. (1990). Alba Emoting: A psycho-physiological technique to help actors create and control real emotions. In H. Conrad, (Ed.), (2003). *The development of Alba Emoting: The work of Dr. Susana Bloch and collaborators* (pp. 90–105). Idaho: Brigham Young University.

Brockett, O. G. (1968). *A history of the theatre.* Boston: Allyn & Bacon.

Brook, P. (1968). *The empty space.* New York: Avon Books.

Brookes, J.M. (1975). Producing Marat/Sade: Theater in a psychiatric hospital. *Hospital and Community Psychiatry, 26*(7), 429–435.

Chekhov, M. (1953). *To the actor: On the technique of acting.* New York: Harper and Row.

Cozolino, L. (2002). *The neuroscience of psychotherapy: Building and rebuilding the human brain.* New York: W. W. Norton.

Cozolino, L. (2006). *The neuroscience of human relationships: Attachment and the developing social brain.* New York: W.W. Norton.

Downs, W.M., & Wright, L.A. (1998). *Playwriting from formula to form.* Fort Worth: Harcourt Brace College Publishers.

Emunah, R. (1983). Drama therapy with adult psychiatric patients. *The Arts in Psychotherapy, 10,* 77–84.

Emunah, R. (1994). *Acting for real: Drama therapy process, technique, and performance.* New York: Brunner-Mazel.

Emunah, R., & Johnson, D.R. (1983). The impact of theatrical performance on the self-images of psychiatric patients. *The Arts in Psychotherapy, 10,* 233–239.

Erikson, E. (1997). *The life cycle completed.* New York: W.W. Norton.

Fox, J. (Ed.). (1987). *The essential Moreno: Writings on psychodrama, group method, and spontaneity by J.L. Moreno, M.D.* New York: Springer Publishing.

Furman, L. (1988). Theatre as therapy: The distancing effect applied to audience. *The Arts in Psychotherapy, 15,* 245–249.

Gibson, W., & Brookes, J.M. (1976). The drama group. In J. Erikson (Ed.), *Activity, recovery, growth* (pp. 101–125). New York: W.W. Norton.

Goleman, D. (2006). *Social intelligence: The new science of human relations.* New York: Bantam Books.

Johnson, D.R. (1980). Effects of a theatre experience on hospitalized psychiatric patients. *The Arts in Psychotherapy, 7,* 265–272.

Johnson, D.R. (1999). *Essays on the creative arts therapies: Imaging the birth of a profession.* Springfield, IL: Charles C Thomas, Publisher.

Kaufman, M., & Tectonic Theatre Project. (2001). *The Laramie project.* New York: Dramatists Play Service, Inc.

Landy, R. (1993). *Persona and performance.* New York: Guildford.

Landy, R. (1994). *Drama therapy: Concepts and practices,* 2nd ed. Springfield, IL: Charles C Thomas, Publisher.

Landy, R. (1996). *Essays in drama therapy: The double life.* London: Jessica Kingsley Publishers.

Mattingly, C. (1998). *Healing dramas and clinical plots: The narrative structure of experience.* Cambridge: Cambridge University Press.

Mazor, J. (1966). Producing plays in psychiatric settings. *Bulletin of Art Therapy, 5*(4), 135–148.

Pendzik, S. (1994). The theatre stage and the sacred space: A comparison. *The Arts in Psychotherapy, 21* (1), 25–35.

Phillips, M.E. (1994). Looking back: The use of drama and puppetry in occupational therapy during the 1920s and 1930s. *American Journal of Occupational Therapy, 50* (3), 229–233.

Saldana, J. (Ed.). (2005). *Ethnodrama: An anthology of reality theatre.* Walnut Creek: AltiMira Press.

Siegel, D.J. (2007). *The mindful brain: Reflection and attunement in the cultivation of well-being.* New York: W.W. Norton.

Schweitzer, P. (2007). *Reminiscence theatre: Making theatre from memories.* London: Jessica Kingsley Publishers.

Snow, S., D'Amico, M., & Tanguay, D. (2003). Therapeutic theatre and well-being. *The Arts in Psychotherapy, 30*(2), 73–82.

Smith, A.D. (2000). *Talk to me: Listening between the lines.* New York: Random House.

Stanislavski, C. (1936). *An actor prepares.* New York: Theatre Arts Books.

Stanislavski, C. (1961). *Creating a role.* New York: Theatre Arts Books.

Winnicott, D.W. (1971). *Playing and reality.* London: Routledge.

BIBLIOGRAPHY

Bailey, S. (1993). *Wings to fly: Bringing theatre arts to students with special needs.* Rockville, MD: Woodbine House.

Bailey, S. (1997). Drama: A powerful tool for social skill development. *Disability Solutions, 2* (1), 1, 3–5.

Bailey, S. (2003). Drama therapy for behavioral change. *Social Spectrum, 3,* 14–17.

Bailey, S. (2006). Ancient and modern roots of drama therapy. In S. L. Brooke, (Ed.), *Creative arts therapies manual: A guide to the history, theoretical approaches, assessment, and work with special populations of art, play, dance, music, drama, and poetry therapy* (pp. 214–222). Springfield, IL: Charles C Thomas, Publisher.

Bailey, S. (2007). Art as an initial approach to the treatment of sexual trauma. In S.L. Brooke, (Ed.), *Creative arts therapies in the treatment of sexual abuse* (pp. 59–72). Springfield, IL: Charles C Thomas, Publisher.

Bailey, S. (2007). Drama therapy. In A. Blatner, & D. Wiener, (Eds.), *Interactive and improvisational drama: Varieties of applied theatre and performance* (pp. 164–173). New York: iUniverse, Inc.

Bailey, S. (in press). Developing identity through drama therapy. In S.L. Brooke, (Ed.), *Creative arts therapies in the treatment of addictions.* Springfield, IL: Charles C Thomas, Publisher.

Bailey, S. & Agoglioti, L. (2002). *Dreams to sign.* Bethesda, MD: Imagination Stage, U.S. Department of Education.

Carmody, M. (Producer), Bailey, S. & Pascale, B. (Directors). (1993). *Making Connections* [video]. Washington, DC: Choices, Inc.

Carmody, M. (Producer), & Pascale, B. (Director). 1993). *Roots and Wings* [video]. Washington, DC: Choices, Inc.

Timmons, N. (Producer/Director). (2007). *Art is Life* [video].

FURTHER TRAINING

Sally Bailey, MFA, MSW, RDT/BCT
Associate Professor
Director, Drama Therapy Program
129 Nichols
Communication Studies, Theatre and Dance Department
Kansas State University
Manhattan, KS 66506
Email: sdbailey@ksu.edu
Office phone: 785-532-6780
Website: http://www.dramatherapycentral.com

Section III

RELATED APPROACHES

Chapter 18

PSYCHODRAMA

ANTONINA GARCIA AND DALE RICHARD BUCHANAN

Psychodrama is a deep action method developed by Jacob Levy Moreno (1889–1974), in which people enact scenes from their lives, dreams or fantasies in an effort to express unexpressed feelings, gain new insights and understandings, and practice new and more satisfying behaviors.

HISTORY

The history of psychodrama to a great extent is also the history of its founder, Jacob Levy Moreno, M.D. This chapter could not possibly document all of Moreno's contributions. An in-depth review of his work can be found in two fascinating and well-documented biographies (Hare & Hare, 1996; Marineau, 1989).

While Moreno is best remembered for his creation of psychodrama, sociodrama and sociometry, his legacy lives on as a pioneer and innovator in other fields as well. Corsini (1955) credits Moreno with being one of the founders of group psychotherapy, and Thomas and Biddle (1966) credit Moreno as one of the founders of role theory. Compernole (1981) credits Moreno with being the first family therapist and Maslow (1968) attributes many of the Human Potential Movement exercises to Moreno.

Moreno was born and educated in Europe and received his medical degree from the University of Vienna. During the years 1908–1925, he formulated his theories of psychodrama, sociometry and group psychotherapy. From 1908–1911, he played spontaneous theatre games with children in the parks of Vienna and discovered the importance of spontaneity and creativity. In 1913, he organized and did group work with prostitutes. He dates this as the beginning of group psychotherapy. This experience revealed the power of the group, and he discovered that each member is a therapeutic agent for the other.

Sociometry, the measurement of groups, had its beginnings when Moreno was Superintendent of a World War I resettlement camp at Mittendorf. Observing the unrest in the refuge camp, he petitioned his superiors to reorganize the camp along the lines of choice. He wanted to empower the refugees, torn from the comfort of their homeland, to make here-and-now choices of the people with whom they worked and lived, thus maximizing their chances for positive human interaction in an already difficult situation.

Between the years of 1921–1923, Moreno returned to Vienna and developed his Theatre of Spontaneity. Moreno dated the first psychodrama session as occurring on April 1, 1921.

Finding Europe to be too conservative for his revolutionary ideas, Moreno emigrated to the United States where he hoped his ideas would be better received. During his early years in the United States he coined the term group psychotherapy, conducted sociometric studies at the Hudson School for Girls and in Sing Sing Prison, opened a private sanatorium and founded and published several journals. He also wrote several books.

In 1942 he met Zerka Toeman, who became his wife, his muse and his equal partner. She organized and edited his writings and maintained and nurtured his professional connections. While Moreno was a visionary thinker and prolific writer of great breadth, Zerka made an enormous contribution to the theory and practice by expanding upon his ideas and deepening them as well as developing practical applications for everyday use. After a prolonged illness, Moreno chose to die by abstaining from all food and water. At his request, his epitaph was "the man who brought laughter to psychiatry."

Since Moreno

Since Moreno's death the field of psychodrama continues to thrive with scores of books on psychodrama and sociodrama published worldwide. Moreno's influence can also be clearly seen in the work of others who have developed offshoots and/or transformed psychodrama into new modalities. Some of these are Robert Landy's "Role Method" (Chapter 5), Jonathan Fox's "Playback Theatre–"(Chapter 20), Kate Hudgins' (1998) Therapeutic Spiral Model, Peter Pitzele's (1998) Bibliodrama and Renée Emunah's "Integrative Five Phase Model of Drama Therapy" (Chapter 4). Emunah's article, "Drama Therapy and Psychodrama: An Integrated Model" (1997) offers both a comparison and integrative perspective on drama therapy and psychodrama. For an in-depth comparison and contrast of Psychodrama, Role Method, and "Developmental Transformations" (Chapter 6), see Robert Landy's *The Couch and the Stage* (2008).

PSYCHODRAMA FRAME OF REFERENCE

Underlying the practice of psychodrama is a strong theoretical foundation that informs the work. Moreno developed four cornerstones of psychodrama: (1) role theory; (2) sociometry; (3) the theory of spontaneity/creativity; and (4) psychodrama intervention constructs. Each of these interlaces and interfaces with the other. While each can be used independently, and often is, Moreno created and envisioned them as interdependent parts of an organic whole.

Role Theory

Moreno believed that each person is a composite of the *roles* he/she plays. Human beings are known and evaluated by self and others through the roles they play. When we say someone is a nice person, what do we mean? We mean that we have observed the person acting in a positive way toward someone else or toward ourselves. The father picked up the fallen child, comforted her, cleaned up the cut on her knee, and put a bandage on it. We notice he is a father (role), she is a daughter (role), and from his behavior in the role, he appears to be a "good father."

In *Psychodrama: First Volume,* Moreno (1946) said, "Role can be defined as the actual and tangible forms which the self takes" (p. 153). He also considered role as a cluster of behaviors that is culturally recognized and labeled. A particular behavior may be utilized in a variety of roles, but isolated behaviors do not make up roles. For example, the behavior of reading may be present in scores of roles: student, teacher, researcher, or secretary. The specific joining together of behaviors is what makes one role different from another.

The cultural aspect is important as well, since all cultural groups do not have the same roles. Nor do all cultural groups have the same expectations for how roles should be played. The roles of husband and wife, for example, may carry different cultural expectations among different ethnic groups. Clinically, it is essential to treatment to understand the role expectations members of a couple have of each other, particularly if they are from different ethnic groups.

Attitudes and emotions also add personal descriptors to role enactment. Although there are collective components to every role we play (and it is through these that we recognize a particular role), each of us has our own unique way of playing a role.

For every role that we play we have expectations of how we should play the role. Our expectations come from how we have seen the role modeled by others, by our own personal dynamics, and the demands of our culture. Functionality exists when a person has a wide range of roles available to him or her and flexibility in playing those roles. One measure of dysfunction is a limited *role repertoire.* This can occur when individuals become locked in a particular role, thereby excluding other roles from their repertoire. Burnout is an example of role-lock. Other examples of dysfunction include role fatigue, role confusion, role conflict, role tension, role crisis, and role stripping.

Moreno said that there are three types of roles: the psychosomatic, the social and the psychodramatic. These are hierarchical in nature in that our psychosomatic role needs must be satisfied before we can warm up to our social and psychodramatic roles. Our *psychosomatic roles* are those which manifest physically, e.g., roles like eater, runner, sleeper. These roles may or may not have a psychological component. For example, in the role of eater, I may have a larger breakfast than usual because I've just come back from a seven-mile hike (physiological) or I may have a larger breakfast because I'm nervous about the interview I'm to attend in an hour, and I'm eating from anxiety (psychological).

The *social roles* are those that we enact in relation to other people, e.g., mother, friend, lover. They exist in the social sphere. These roles are always reciprocal, requiring others to take roles in relation to us: husbands need wives in order to enact their roles, and vice versa. One of the reasons that people seek psychotherapy is that they are in unsatisfying role relationships or are mourning the loss or lack of a reciprocal role partner.

The *psychodramatic roles* are those that are enacted inside our heads. They are the interior or intrapsychic roles of imaginer, problem solver, and creative thinker. They also comprise wished-for roles that exist in our minds until they become externalized in social reality. They are a manifestation of the imaginative process of who we think we are and who we would like to become.

For example, if I want to enact the role of ice skater, I may imagine myself in the role long before I actually take ice skating lessons. On the other hand, if I imagine myself a Rock star and neither sing well nor have any intention of working to become a Rock star, I am also engaging in a psychodramatic role when I play out in my mind and take pleasure from a scenario of myself singing before thousands.

Robert Landy, in *Persona and Performance* (1993), further differentiates the concept of roles through his *Taxonomy of Roles.* His views about *role, counter-role* and *guide* provide not only theoretical structure, but also offer an action method for therapeutic intervention. Psychodramatic methods are integrated into his work. Phase Three of Renée Emunah's "Integrative Five Phase Model of Drama Therapy" (Chapter 4) is also based on role dynamics and Phase Four is psychodramatically based.

Role Dysfunction

Dysfunction occurs when a person has a lack of either social roles or psychodramatic roles, and function is seen as having a balance of both. One of the aims of psychodrama is to activate the birth of psychodramatic roles by stimulating the imaginative processes through play and fantasy. Another aim is to assist individuals to give birth to social roles through behavioral rehearsal and therapeutic role assignment.

Another type of dysfunction comes from inaccurate role perception. For example, a husband buys his partner a vacuum cleaner for a special birthday and is shocked that she does not seem to appreciate it and wants to know why he couldn't give her something more personal. He has perceived her in her role as housekeeper, but has ignored her role as romantic partner. Functionality comes when one accurately perceives the role of the other as well as one's own role.

Dysfunction comes also when a person accurately perceives a role but is unwilling or unable to enact it. For example, take the worker whose boss tells her to complete certain tasks by a particular deadline. She has the time to complete the tasks, but she would rather do something else. She does not like to be told to do things so she balks and does not adequately enact her role.

Role Development

Moreno believed that the self emerges from the roles we play. He postulated that when people learn a new role, they follow a particular pattern of role development. The arc of the learning curve begins with role taking and proceeds to role playing and role creating.

Role taking refers to an enactment of the role in a routinized, somewhat stilted way. When people are just learning to play tennis, for example, they are likely to appear awkward as they try to coordinate their stance with their arms and both of these with the racket and the ball. They may have to practice long hours simply to get the ball over the net, or to serve to one spot on the court. As they progress with experience, they will gain ease and will be able to move around the court freely making choices spontaneously as the ball comes their way. They will not have to think every minute about the basics of the game. These will have become second nature. They have entered the phase of *role playing* in which a person enacts a role with comfort, flexibility and spontaneity. Literally, they infuse the role with a playfulness that is lacking in role taking.

Finally, when people have mastered the rudiments of the role and has become comfortable enacting it, they are ready to move into the phase of *role creating.* When one role creates, one is able to add new and sometimes unique elements to the enactment of the role and to think beyond its confines to develop unexpected solutions for difficulties that emerge in role enactment. At this point, the tennis player may devise a new method for serving the ball, and the method of role enactment becomes a model for others.

Sociometry

As was said earlier, each of us is a composite of the roles we play. Many of those roles are social roles, and social roles have reciprocal partners. This aspect of reciprocity brings us to another of Moreno's basic contributions: *sociometry.* Put simply, sociometry is the assessment of social choices and a set of intervention tools designed to facilitate social change.

In life, each of us is engaged in making many choices daily. When we make a choice that places us in proximity to others, in avoidance of others or in a neutral relationship to others, we are making a sociometric choice. Moreno was very interested in the choices we make and the criteria upon which we base our choices.

Clearly, families and communities function or dysfunction in part as a result of the choices individuals in the system make in relation to each other. Moreno believed that the more options a person has available to him or her, the more opportunity for satisfaction for the individual and the collective.

All choices that we make are related to our perception of the role of the other. If someone were to ask, "Whom do you choose?" one might ask, "For what?" Choice of a person is always connected with at least one role-related criterion: "Whom would you choose to accompany you to the movies to see a romantic comedy?" Based upon specific criteria, we have reasons for our selections. For example, functional people may choose to invite one friend to accompany them to a romantic comedy film and another to accompany them on a backpacking trip in Appalachia. They may make these choices because the first friend considers camping out to be staying at a motel and ordering in a pizza and the second talks incessantly during movies.

A colloquial meaning of sociometry is the invisible and visible network of connections in any group. Although the connections among the individuals may not necessarily be observable to us if we step into a room, the connections are there nevertheless. Two people with whom one is chatting at a party may have been in the same geometry class in high school, but one will not know about that connection unless one of them reveals it. Moreno referred to this aspect of sociometry as social reality.

A successful group leader understands that there are invisible connections among group members and facilitates the rising to the surface of these connections so that the group may work together to accomplish its goals. This is in part the function of the warm-up in a psychodrama session.

The instruments of sociometry make visible some of the invisible aspects of social reality. One of these instruments is the sociogram. A *sociogram* is a map of the connections that people have with one another. The sociogram can be completed in action or on paper when working with groups. One example of an action sociogram in a group is to ask the group members to place their hands upon the shoulder of the person with whom they would like to have lunch at the session's end. Another is to ask group members to place their hand on the shoulder of the person whose issue is most closely related to their own. Conducting sociometric explorations often stimulates strong feelings in participants and, therefore, should be used with caution.

There are a variety of sociometric instruments and exercises that have been devised for promoting social change. Among these are the social atom, role diagram, spectrogram, social barometer, and diamond of opposites (Buchanan, 1984b; Carlson-Sabelli, Sabelli, Patel, & Holm, 1992; Edwards, 1996; Hale, 1986; Sternberg & Garcia, 2000). The limitation of traditional sociometry is that it is unsuccessful in melding intensity of feeling with choice of a person. While one can make a choice in a sociogram, that choice does not indicate the intensity of feeling that the person has in making that choice. For example, if Joe chooses to ask Marlene to go out to lunch, we do not know from the sociogram if he is excited about that choice or if he just figured, "Well, why not?" Nor does the sociogram, which is linear, provide the opportunity to chart ambivalence. Carlson-Sabelli et al. (1992) developed a new instrument, the *diamond of opposites* that can chart both ambivalence and intensity of feeling and is three-dimensional. It also charts neutrality.

Sociometry can be used descriptively to describe intra- or intergroup relations at any given time. It can also be used prescriptively to make changes in the system. For example, during World War II a study was conducted in which fighter pilots chose their copilots. A significant number of those who chose returned alive as opposed to others who were randomly assigned copilots.

Moreno and other social psychologists researched sociometry extensively and found that left to their own devices a group tends to overchoose some individuals and underchoose others. This is called the sociodynamic law. Moreno felt that the psychodramatist's work is to assist groups in sharing the sociometric wealth. Moreno also noted that just as individuals without intervention revert to homeostasis, or the status quo, so does a group seek to return to *sociostasis,* even if the status quo is dysfunctional. In one way psychodramatists are always revolutionaries, in that they seek to facilitate change in the status quo in assisting a group to more spontaneous functioning.

When looking at sociometry, one can view it from the perspective of the group or the individual. When using sociometry in a group, there are four basic positions that individuals occupy: positive star, rejection star, isolate and star of incongruity. All of these positions have benefits and liabilities. The functioning individual and group rotates through all these positions over time. The psychodramatist assists the group in shifting sociometry in positive ways.

Those who receive the largest number of choices based on a particular criterion are called stars. A positive star receives the most positive choices, and a rejection star receives the most negative choices. On the surface it may seem that it is far better to be a positive star than a rejection star. However, as wonderful as it is to be regarded highly for some gift, quality or competence, to be consistently overchosen is a burden. If a star is incapable of saying no to the role demands of others, both the individual and the group become stuck. If taken too far, sometimes a star who cannot say no becomes physically ill as a way of removing himself from over-responsibility.

At the same time, while it may seem unpleasant to be rejected, the rejection star is freed from the responsibilities the positive star carries. They are also freed from the norms, rules and expectations of the group. It has been said that the positive star belongs to the group and the rejection star belongs to him or herself. If taken too far, the rejection star becomes an outcast whom the group engages in scapegoating.

Even grammar school children are aware of sociometric stars, rejection stars, and isolates. The work of the psychodramatist is to provide opportunities to share the sociometric wealth of the group in a group setting and to assist individuals in shifting their personal sociometry in positive ways in individual psychotherapy. A person may also be an isolate when he or she neither chooses, nor is chosen based upon a particular criterion. An example of functional isolation is a group member, Joe, who is undergoing a chronic fatigue episode. He may choose not to participate in a particular sociometric exercise, and other group members may respect his decision and, not choosing him, select another member of the group. On the other hand, if for every exercise in nearly every group, Joe, whether sick or well, neither seeks anyone out nor does anyone seek him out, his isolation will be dysfunctional for him and the group. Those who persistently choose isolation and who are persistently not chosen are true isolates. These people are found among the homeless, the mentally ill and in prisons. Incongruous choices are those that lack reciprocity. What we seek is mutuality. In groups when there are high levels of incongruity, group members will express dissatisfaction, feel disconnected, and the group may fall apart if interventions are not made to increase mutuality. Regarding tenor of feeling between people, Freud talked of transference and empathy. Moreno said that there is another phenomenological experience between two people. This he termed *tele*. *Tele* is a deep, accurate knowing of the self and the other. Tele is present between two people when each sees the other as the other truly is and accepts the other as the other is. One does not try to change the other even though he or she knows the other is not perfect.

Moreno believed that each relationship has some degree of tele and some degree of transference. There are some people with whom we have very high tele: we are comfortable with them almost immediately, and feel we have known them forever. As we get to know them better and have more concrete information about them, we feel reinforced in our original perceptions. Even though they have just as many faults and foibles as the next person does, we accept them and they accept us. We feel at home when we are with them and can pick up where we left off when we see them after a long time.

Many of our relationships may have more transference than tele at the outset. Ideally, over time we can diminish transference and increase tele. Moreno felt that sociometric, sociodramatic, and psychodramatic interventions can help people to remove the veils of transference and reveal the true person underneath.

Moreno had a tremendous interest in the concept of the *encounter*. He believed that each of us is at our best when we live in the *here and now,* a term he coined. Further, if we live in the moment, not in our past or future, we can fully relate to those whom we meet and they to us. The encounter occurs when two people meet in as honest a way as they are able. The Encounter Movement of the '60s was based on this concept but went awry as people confused confrontation and attack with encounter. In psychodramatic encounter, both people make room for each other and respect the other, while taking responsibility for their own feelings and actions. Good will is a necessary ingredient as is speaking from an "I" position and accepting that what the other person says is his/her personal truth.

Moreno said that we are wounded in relationship and can be healed in relationship. He devised psychodrama and sociodrama as modalities to accomplish that healing.

Theory of Spontaneity and Creativity

The third and key cornerstone of psychodrama is spontaneity/creativity theory. It is based on Moreno's belief that all humans are fallen gods.

The Godhead

While other methods of psychotherapy have either been silent about or shunned the very concept of God, Moreno was deeply interested in spiritual issues. Of course, readers should be clear that there is distinction between organized religious practice and spirituality as a base of human behavior. Moreno focused on the spiritual aspects of behavior.

As Kraus (1984) has noted, the psychodramatic process attempts to bridge the paradoxical relationship between humanity and divinity. Moreno said that the central paradox for humans is the wish to be God and the reality that we are not: the fantasy of omnipotence and the need to face reality.

Moreno coined the term *Meglomania Normalis* for that human state of wanting to be at the center of our universe and wanting the rest of the human race to be our auxiliaries. In other words, our desire to create the perfect world for ourselves from our perspective.

As infants we all begin with the experience of being at one with the world and in perfect harmony with all that is. We do not know where we leave off and the other begins. We are boundaryless. He called this the *First Universe,* and it is a state to which we often wish to return. When we are old enough to realize a separation between the self and the other, between illusion and reality, we enter what Moreno called the *Second Universe.*

In Morenean philosophy anxiety is caused by the breach between the First and Second Universe. Moreno referred to anxiety as a cosmic hunger to maintain identity with the entire universe. One of the objectives of psychodramatic treatment is to help individuals become less anxious and more fearful. This means replacing an individual's generalized anxiety about separation/connection with specific fears about people, places and things. For example instead of an overwhelming anxiety about a job interview, it is far better to be fearful of being asked your employment history. Spontaneity training and role playing can be used as rehearsals for life to lessen our cosmic anxiety and increase our mastery of our everyday fears.

Moreno's philosophical solution to bridge the breach is to live in the here-and-now. Unlike many other schools of psychotherapy, Moreno believed that enlightenment can be found only in community.

The Canon of Creativity

Moreno developed the *Canon of Creativity* to describe how spontaneity and creativity work. The Canon of Creativity (see Figure 18.1) shows the interrelationship and interaction of spontaneity and creativity with the *cultural conserve* (e.g., status quo). It also demonstrates that it is necessary to warm up to our spontaneity and creativity.

According to Moreno (1953) spontaneity-creativity is the most important problem in psychology. In the midst of the Great Depression, Moreno hypothesized that only the creative and spontaneous would survive and that the rest would be relegated to the dustbin of history.

Moreno viewed spontaneity and creativity as an open system with limitless potential that cannot be stored for future use. He further postulated that spontaneity and creativity are available to everyone and that all our success is directly connected with our ability to be spontaneous.

Spontaneity can be thought of as the readiness for an action and creativity as the idea. The twin concepts of spontaneity and creativity are responsible for the formation of our cultural conserves. Cultural conserves are the given patterns, relationships, or products of our society. Cultural conserves define the norms, mores, and folkways of our culture and help transmit these normative patterns to future generations.

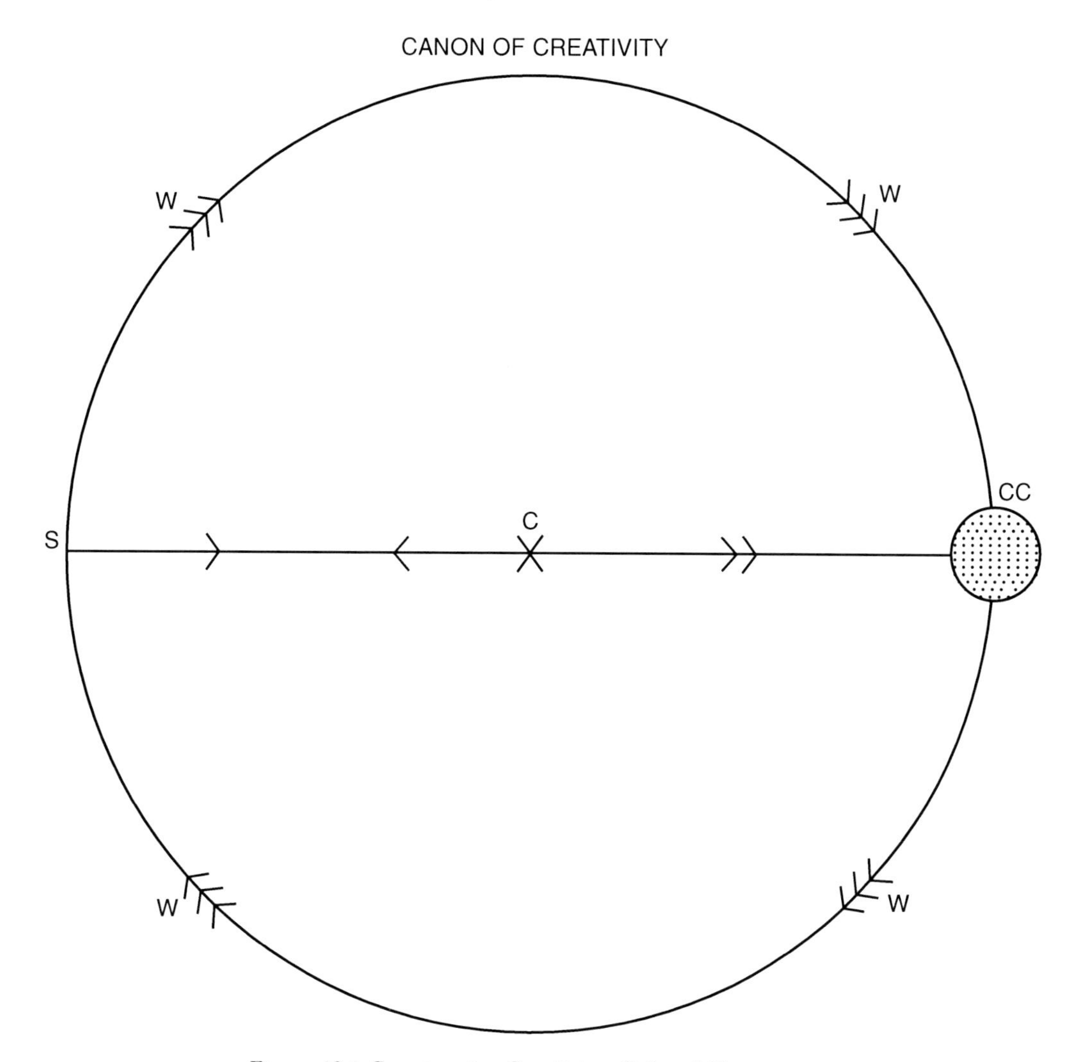

Figure 18.1. Spontaneity–Creativity–Cultural Conserve.

Field of Rotating Operations Between Spontaneity–Creativity–Cultural Conserve (S–C–CC)
S–Spontaneity, C–Creativity, CC–Cultural (or any) Conserve (for instance, a biological conserve, *e.g.*, an animal organism; or a cultural conserve, *e.g*, a book); W–Warming up is the "operational" expression of spontaneity. The circle represents the field of operations between S, C and CC.

Operation I: Spontaneity arouses Creativity, C. S — > C.
Operation II: Creativity is receptive to Spontaneity. S < — C.
Operation III: From their interaction Cultural Conserves, CC, result. S — > C — > > CC.
Operation IV: Conserves (CC) would accumulate indefinitely and remain "in cold storage." They need to be reborn; the catalyzer Spontaneity revitalizes them. CC — > > > S — > > > CC. S does not operate in a vacuum, it moves either towards Creativity or towards Conserves.

Total Operation
Spontaneity–creativity–warming up act < actor / conserve

God is spontaneity. Hence the commandment is: "Be Spontaneous!" (Moreno, 1920). Moreno (1953) stated that spontaneity propels the individual toward an adequate response to a new situation or a new response to an old situation. Adequacy encompasses the concerns of appropriateness, competency, and skill in interacting within any given situation.

Our spontaneity is highest when we are infants and decreases with age. As noted earlier in the history section, The Theatre of Spontaneity was designed to increase the spontaneity of the actors and the audience.

Moreno called those times when we are most spontaneous as being in the *moment.* The moment may last for a few seconds or it can last hours or days. The moment is the experience of living in complete harmony and unity while staying connected to the social realities of the here-and-now. Csikszentmihalyi (1991) has called this concept flow. According to Csikszentmihalyi, this moment of peak spontaneity is the point when the ego disappears, the time space continuum evaporates and there is a sense of connection and flow with the entire universe.

Creativity is the spark from whence the novel comes. Creativity is the ability to think beyond our own personal limitations and see the world in a new way. To be creative means to risk, to see people and things differently than as we might normally view them and to experiment with the new and different. Not all of us are up to the challenges posed by this endless quest for creativity and some of us retreat to pathological creativity, violence and destruction, or passive ascription.

Spontaneity and Creativity Dysfunction

Moreno viewed life as a series of spontaneity tests. All dysfunction is caused by a lack of spontaneity and/or creativity, while all functionality can be attributed to an adequate amount of both. The reason that people come into treatment is that they either do not know what to do about a given situation or they cannot spur themselves into action in the situation, or both. There are three threats to our spontaneity: paralysis, impulsivity and reactivity.

Paralysis occurs when we are faced with a new situation and we become frozen and are unable to act. The situation passes us by and we feel disappointed in ourselves that we were unable to find an adequate response for the situation. Impulsivity is simply action without reflection. Our act hunger is so great that we act without contemplation or reflection about the act's appropriateness or its consequences. Reactivity is reflection without here-and-now action. In reactivity we are so mired in the past that our actions today are based upon our experiences of the past. When we are reactive we are unable to be proactive and simply react to the world and the situations around us.

The litmus tests for spontaneity and creativity are novelty and adequacy. Many of us are stopped dead in our tracks because we cannot bear to engage in an activity in which our behavior will merely be adequate. In striving to be brilliant, we sometimes do not even begin an activity for fear of being average or of failing. The Morenean way is to strive for adequacy rather than brilliance. If we strive for brilliance we are often inadequate, and if we dare to be adequate we are often brilliant.

One retreat from creativity is pathological creativity. Pathological creativity is a compulsive drive for creativity that becomes so great that the quest of the new overwhelms the need for adequacy. Pathological creativity is caused by the lack of tangible and challenging creativity in our everyday life; this lack of usable creativity festers into a compulsion for novelty. Another retreat from creativity happens when we become frustrated at our inability to create new roles and role relationships. Blocked creativity can lead to violence or destruction as the last resort for the impotent creator. In the Morenean philosophy, all rage is viewed as crushed creativity. All intrapersonal and interpersonal violence is correlated with an increase in frustration that stems from failing to produce a creative and spontaneous response.

A third threat to our creativity is becoming overwhelmed by the sheer number and complexity of choices in our everyday life and looking for someone or something external to make those choices for us. The responsibility involved in assuming the role of creator and engaging with spontaneity and creativity is too frightening for some. So instead of embracing the role of creator, they retreat to a passive role and vest their creative power to some authoritarian figure. Erich Fromm (1941) brilliantly discusses this concept in his seminal work *Escape From Freedom.*

Cultural Conserves

A cultural conserve is any finished product of the creative process. Cultural conserves operate on both individual and collective levels. Whether created by an individual or a group, the cultural conserve preserves the values of its creators.

As individuals each of us creates our own cultural conserves of affective, cognitive, behavioral and spiritual states. We have habits and routines and particular ways of doing things or interacting with others. These interactions become our cultural conserves. When others say that we are not being ourselves today, what is really being said is that we are not enacting our usual cultural conserves.

As collectives, whether in families, small groups or societies, there are also cultural conserves of how we as a collective should interact with one another and our environment. When individuals say that is how we should act, they are saying that is what the cultural conserve prescribes.

In the beginning what is now called a conserve was a spontaneous/creative act that met the needs of the situation. The repetition of the act is what institutionalizes the conserve. Cultural conserves are the springboard for new spontaneity and creativity and inherently are neither good nor bad. Cultural conserves are good when they contribute to our creativity and spontaneity and bad when they stifle or repress any individual or group. As individuals we can thrive through change or thrive by changing.

Spontaneity Theory of Child Development

Moreno created a complex theory of child development, based on scientific observation. A complete discussion of the theory can be found in *Psychodrama: First Volume.* According to the spontaneity theory of child development, Moreno points out that when we are born, we need others in order to stay alive and to flourish. He termed these others *auxiliaries* and noted that their method of relating to us and us to them warms us up to our first social role. As was said before, humans are most spontaneous in infancy. The reason for this is that all of the situations that the infant encounters are new and require new responses. Our auxiliaries help us to develop roles by their interaction with us. Auxiliaries also help us to put names to what we experience.

In order to develop functionally, Moreno believed that each of us must first be doubled when we are newborns. In doubling, our caregiver joins with us and accurately interprets our cries and body language and responds to those cues. Later, we are mirrored by our caregivers when we make a face or a sound and they make that same face or sound, not to mimic us but to reflect our experience back to us. The final stage is role reversal in which the child in a rudimentary way role reverses with the caregiver and the caregiver takes the reciprocal role, as when a child initiates a peek-a-boo game that they have seen their caregiver initiate.

Psychodramatists believe that if people have not been adequately doubled or mirrored, they will be unable to role reverse with others. Treatment may consist in part of doubling and mirroring for the client so that they may learn to role reverse.

Theoretical Constructs of Psychodrama Methodology

The theoretical constructs form the fourth cornerstone of the practice of psychodrama. Moreno began to write about his philosophy in the 1920s. In 1966, he discussed the nub of his theory. He said, "The objective of psychodrama was, from its inception, to construct a therapeutic setting which uses life as a model, to integrate into it all the modalities of living, beginning with the universals–time, space, reality, and cosmos–down to all the details and nuances of life" (in Fox 1987, p. 3).

Time

As was said earlier, Moreno was a great proponent of living in the moment and participating in the ever-evolving present. As a result, in psychodrama all time is present. It is as if all time were liquid in a large bowl. Although you may float a little boat sending it from one point to another, the boat is still in the liquid, all of which exists simultaneously and which has no start or finish.

As with all other events, when a traumatic event occurs in a person's life, the information about that event is stored in the body, mind, emotions, and spirit. Moreno believed that when we get trapped in our past, it is because our spontaneity and creativity were insufficient to help us at the time, so that a piece of us is snagged on the past as a sweater would be snagged on a bramble bush.

In psychodrama the protagonist has the opportunity to recreate the past, and correct the scene, changing history so that one disentangles the snag from the bramble and moves more freely in present-day life. One may correct the scene by expressing emotions unexpressed until now; one may gain a new insight into the experience; and one may find another, more satisfying way to end the scene than the way it occurred in the literal past. One might say, "How can you change what actually happened?" The fact is that in reexperiencing the situation in a new way kinesthetically through the body in action, the protagonist is implanting new information about the prior experience in the neural pathways. The aspect of changing history is profound as it neutralizes traumatic incidents and builds a new frame of reference.

One may ask how psychodrama is about the present, if a protagonist is dealing with a scene from the past. The answer is that the protagonist is asked to recreate and step into that past as if it were now the time the event is happening. For example, if a protagonist reenacts a scene from when he was five years old in 1992, he is asked to imagine that it is now 1992 and he is five years old. He is asked to describe what is happening in 1992, not what happened.

In the same way that the past becomes present in psychodrama, so, too, does the future. Through future projection the protagonist steps into a wished-for or feared future, as if it were here today, to explore its possibilities, to role rehearse for future situations and to find advice in dealing with current concerns.

One of the most powerful aspects of psychodrama is the collapsing of time. In one psychodrama, the person from today can receive advice, support and encouragement from their future self and then go back to care for their younger self and help heal an early trauma.

Space

Moreno was acutely aware of the evocative nature of place in therapeutic work. Not only is what happened to the client important but where it happened. While it would be painful and difficult for a child to endure being slapped in the face by his parent, it would be even more humiliating if this happened in front of friends at school. Further, we experience some places as safe while others feel less safe. If we want to have a private, intimate conversation with someone, we might not choose the local diner to initiate it.

When setting up a psychodrama, the client and director decide where the scene will take place and set it carefully, using props and furniture in the therapy room to set the scene. Scene-setting warms the protagonist up to the work and anchors the action in space. Further, it quickens the imagination of the audience and warms them up as well. It is not uncommon to hear someone a month or two later say something like this, "You know, whenever I'm feeling stressed, I think of that tree by the stream from your psychodrama. In my mind's eye, I imagine I'm sitting under the tree, and listening to the water flow over the stones. It's so restful."

Reality

Moreno believed that reality was larger than that which is observable via the five senses. He discussed three levels of reality: *infrareality* which is our own subjective experience of the world, e.g., megalomania normalis; reality, which is the group's consensus map of the world; and *surplus reality,* which incorporates a perspective beyond our collective and ourselves (Moreno, Blomkvist, & Rutzel, 2000).

One of the aims of psychodrama is to make our personal world bigger by helping us to integrate other's perceptions into our own world. Every time we have a conversation with friends and imagine ourselves in their position, we are engaging in surplus reality. Our daydreams and night dreams are also forms of surplus reality as are the fruits of our imagination. In fact, all theatre games, plays, and most play activities are vehicles for creating surplus reality.

In some ways all of psychodrama exists in the realm of surplus reality. Someone reenacts a segment of his life experience onstage. They choose people from the group to play the roles of others who were present at the time, and the role players assist them successfully even though they were not present when the event occurred originally. While the original father or mother is not onstage, the protagonist steps into the scene and experiences the reality of the portrayals nevertheless, and is thereby able to suspend disbelief and experience the reality of the moment. It is through the use of surplus reality that the client is healed.

If clients are unsatisfied with the manner in which they play a role in life, they may through simulation and role rehearsal train themselves to play the role differently. They can in this way utilize surplus reality to expand their everyday reality.

One of the most powerful surplus reality techniques is *role reversal.* Clearly, we cannot literally step into another person's shoes and become the other. However, we can come to a close approximation and expand our view of reality by changing places and changing roles with another. The perspective shift is enlightening.

Cosmos

Moreno believed that, while each of us is an individual and a social being, we are also all cosmic beings, connected to the universe and seeking to find our purpose in relation to all that exists. He felt that a psychotherapy that does not address man's teleological and cosmological concerns is incomplete.

As a result, gods and heroes appear on the psychodrama stage. Reality is expanded and we connect beyond the flesh with others as men portray women and women portray men. An older person may play a younger and vice versa. People can play animals. The unborn and the dead are alive on the psychodrama stage.

Psychodrama explores the cosmos within us and the cosmos outside us; the visible world and the invisible. It helps us to find our place in the universe and restores soul and spirit to those who have misplaced those vital entities.

PSYCHODRAMATIC GOALS

All of us are physical beings with bodies, minds, emotions and transpersonal aspects. Moreno believed that psychotherapy should be broad enough so that its interventions can touch all of these factors that make us human. Therefore, there are four primary goals: Affect, Behavior, Cognition, and Spirituality (ABCS).

"A" for Affect

In the realm of affect the goal is catharsis, a deep expression of feelings. There are two primary types of *catharsis*–the catharsis of abreaction and the catharsis of integration. Catharsis of abreaction occurs when the client regresses to a difficult experience and re-experiences an expression of emotion that is associated with that time. The catharsis of integration is not simply the expression of deep emotions, but also contains a simultaneous action insight. Catharsis of integration occurs when the client is able to gain a new understanding of the situation and imprints a new experience of the situation through the expression of emotion as a new action. Thus, the catharsis of integration is a vital part of the working through process.

In psychodrama, a person may experience a catharsis of laughter as well as of tears. These are equally valuable in promoting healing and lasting change. If clients are embarrassed at or fearful of their tears, the authors remind them that tears water the seeds of the soul.

"B" for Behavior

Behavioral rehearsal allows people to practice new and more satisfying ways of handling situations. Sometimes in life it feels unsafe or frightening to experiment with new behavior. Psychodrama provides a safe setting where people can role train, adjusting their behavior as they learn through trial and error. They can learn to restore spontaneity and creativity to areas of their lives in which they feel blocked.

"C" for Cognition

The goal of cognitive insight occurs when the client achieves an epiphany, or enlightenment, regarding the situation at hand. Because it happens holistically, rather than just in the mind, when one gains insight in a psychodrama, the person will often look startled, or the mouth will drop open or the person literally steps back as if taken aback. One can almost see the light bulb lighting up over the person's head as in a cartoon. There is a reorganization of perceptions that takes place as a result of action insight.

"S" for Spirituality

The process of psychodrama is a transpersonal one. Whether in groups or in individual therapy, the whole is greater than the sum of the parts. In a group, when a member plays a significant other of the protagonist, the auxiliary ego also learns and grows from the experience. The audience, as active observers of the drama, step into the protagonist's life and step into their own as well. They are healed through the work of the other. The protagonist encounters the group both through means of the story of the drama and through the help of group members in co-creating his world in the enactment. Many times the goal of spiritual connection is overtly a part of the contract as when a protagonist says, "I feel so alone. I've lost my faith in people and in a Power greater than myself. I want to stop feeling so empty. I want to feel full again."

It's rare that clients have deficits in all four areas–ABCS. An overarching goal is to help clients to integrate these four areas in their lives. When behavior and affect are at variance, for example, the goal is to bring both to consciousness and develop a new solution that encompasses both.

Act Hungers and Open Tension Systems

Moreno said that the body remembers what the mind forgets. *Act hungers* are connected with Moreno's theory of human development. The act hungers are strong urges or desires for expression, for understanding, for mastery in a situation or for connection. *Open tension systems* are the context within which we have an act hunger. Open tension systems are the unresolved issues that are emergent in a group at any given time. They may be intrapsychic or interpersonal dealing with people inside or outside the group.

For example, Elise had a terrible argument with a friend the night before the group meets. She is still upset about it when she comes to the psychodrama session. She feels that her friend didn't listen to her and cut her off and walked away. Because of the argument, Elise has an open tension system about abandonment. The act hungers are what we want to do about the open tension systems. Elise is upset and seeks resolution of her problem and relief from her fears. Her act hunger may be to tell her friend off, to reconcile with her friend, to understand her better, or to practice other ways to relate to the friend.

The psychodrama director works to help a group to close at least one of its open tension systems and satiate its act hungers through interventions made in the psychodrama enactment. This is done so that the protagonist can restore spontaneity and begin again to live in the here-and-now. In fact, the contract which the director makes with the protagonist is essentially an agreement to do just that. The ABCS are accomplished by facilitating the fulfillment of the protagonist's act hungers.

INSTRUMENTS OF PSYCHODRAMATIC TECHNIQUES

Moreno adapted many of the psychodramatic techniques and methods from the theatre. In a speech to the American Psychiatric Association, Moreno (1946) noted that drama is a translation of the Greek word which means action, or thing done. He defined psychodrama as the science which explores the "truth" by dramatic methods. He went on to elaborate the five instruments of the psychodramatic process–the stage, the protagonist, the director, the auxiliary egos and the audience (i.e., group).

The Stage

Moreno (1969) envisioned and created a therapeutic theatre where men can play women and women can play men; where a black person can play a white person and the white person can play a black person; and where an old person can play a child's role and a child can play an older person's role. Moreno concluded by saying that as a result of psychodrama, a healthy person may live more effectively, a sick person may learn to bear his misery, and the dead may continue to play a part in our lives. On the therapeutic stage people can act out not only their ordinary everyday lives, but also their dreams and desires.

Moreno knew that each space evokes memories and expectations. Psychodramatists can transform an ordinary space into the sacred space of the therapeutic theatre through rituals such as the forming of a circle of chairs, the placements of a few colored scarves, music, or incense.

The Protagonist

The *protagonist* is the term given to the person who is the focus of the psychodrama. The protagonist is encouraged to be as spontaneous as possible. The goal is for protagonists to enact their story in the here-and-now, not merely be the spectator or teller of the story. Protagonist are also given the freedom to undo the past, redo the present and create a different future for themselves.

While protagonists are encouraged to have maximum involvement and to enact their story with vitality and passion, psychodrama is just as much a method of restraint as it is of expression. For example, protagonists will not only learn new behaviors, but will also learn to contain feelings or thoughts so as to be more spontaneous. They are also encouraged to expand their perceptions and encounter the unknown or rejected parts of themselves and others.

The Director

The preferred term for the group leader is the director rather than the therapist. Moreno said that the director was a member of the group with directorial responsibilities and that all members of the group are therapeutic agents for each other. The director must be the most spontaneous member of the group. Kellerman (1992) has discussed the four main roles of the director: analyst, producer, therapist, and group leader.

As an action analyst (Haskell, 1975), the director analyzes not only the intrapsychic and interpersonal issues of the group but also the transpersonal issues. The critical function of this role is the empathizer who brings understanding and affirmation to the protagonist and group members.

As a producer, the psychodramatist is responsible for the dramatic action that unfolds during the course of the group session. There are many sub-roles to the producer role including: scene-setter, choreographer, coach, dramaturge, and timekeeper.

As a therapist, the director must maintain that role for both for the protagonist and all the other group members. In the role of therapist it is essential to distinguish good therapy from adequate drama. The director as therapist observes, monitors and guides the protagonist's production. Kipper (1986) states that the two major vehicles of change in psychodrama are catharsis and role training.

While the drama is unfolding the director must also assume the role of the family therapist and mentally role reverses with each person from the protagonist's social network. The therapist structures the drama in such a way that all the characters in the drama become real, complex human beings rather than stereotypical projections of the protagonist.

As the group leader, the psychodramatist is the manager and facilitator of the group process who helps to co-create a supportive sociometry that maximizes freedom in choice of roles and people. Since sociometry is the base of all the work a psychodramatist does, in a group session the director notes the currents of feeling that flow between participants and in relation to the director. Directors note what issues emerge as the group members interact and how the members feel in relation to those issues. They make interventions to include silent members and to encourage participation from everyone. They help the group to warm-up enough that a protagonist will emerge, and then make interventions based on their observations.

The Auxiliary Ego

Auxiliary ego is the term given to other group members who play roles for the protagonist in the psychodrama. The auxiliary ego brings life to the protagonist's world. Auxiliary egos may play parts of the protagonist's self (e.g., double, shy and afraid me, the loud and abusive me) and/or interpersonal and transpersonal roles. The auxiliary egos may play wished-for, dead or absent others in the protagonist's social network.

The auxiliary, in service to the protagonist, is called upon to connect on a deep, inner personal level with the role assigned and to communicate the experience of that role to the protagonist, director and group members. The auxiliary ego serves as a bridge between the protagonist and the director, the protagonist and the group and the protagonist and his drama.

The auxiliary must match the spontaneity and creativity of the protagonist and gently encourage the protagonist to embrace deeper levels of experience. An auxiliary who assumes the role too quickly and too strongly can extinguish production from the protagonist, while an auxiliary who takes the role too cautiously and too slowly can deaden the protagonist's production.

As a general rule it is easier to contain an auxiliary who is too creative rather than to expand an auxiliary who is too cautious. The auxiliary ego has the greatest freedom to challenge, promote, extend and expand the protagonist's perceptions.

The group member also personally benefits from the playing of an auxiliary role. Playing the auxiliary role provides access and opportunity to become connected to another dimension of the self and the other. Auxiliaries may be called upon to play a role that is foreign, unknown or disclaimed by themselves. If the individual makes a total commitment to the role, that very role will transform the auxiliary's life as they connect with and incorporate new information gleaned from playing the role.

There are several tips for being an auxiliary ego:

1. *Trust your intuition.* Trust that you will do a good enough job for the protagonist and embrace the role.
2. *Bring everything you have to the role.* A good auxiliary learns to go inward and pull forth experiences, expectations, behaviors and verbal responses that are congruent with the role assignment.
3. *Maximize production.* Use both verbal

and nonverbal communication to embody the role.

4. *Stay in role.* Once assigned a role, the auxiliary should respond to all situations from that role. If you are chosen to play the father in a drama, do not look to the director and say, "What I am supposed to do?" but use those feelings and speak directly to the protagonist and say "I do not know what I'm supposed to do with you."
5. *Role Reversal.* In the role-reversed position, assume the body posture, voice and gesture of the protagonist and repeat the last few lines of dialogue from before the role reversal. This will anchor you in your new role and provide continuity to the drama for the protagonist.
6. *Maximize the creativity of the protagonist.* Encourage and support the protagonist in the production of new affect, thoughts, behaviors and spirituality.

The Group

The group serves as a microcosm for the larger community. The group members serve as both social lubricants and social irritants. They are the witnesses and provide existential validation and objective confirmation for the protagonist. The group functions in both individual and collective roles.

On an individual level the group can represent the struggles within the protagonist. It is one of the major tasks of the director to establish connections between group members (see sociometry). When the protagonist is a mirror for the individual members of the group, there is an experience of awareness and connection with the protagonist's story. The individual group members discover parts of themselves and their relationships within the protagonist's drama.

As a collective, the group is a microcosm of society and serves as a stand-in for the world at large. The group acts as a mirror for the protagonist. The roles that are present in the protagonist's life are reflected back by the group members: the critical parent; the annoyed sibling; the supportive friend, the loving partner.

THERAPEUTIC PROCESS

While the time for a psychodrama group may range from 30 minutes to three hours, all psychodrama sessions are divided into three parts: warm-up, enactment and sharing. Generally 50 percent of the allotted time is used for the enactment phase. The warm-up and sharing phases equally share the remaining time.

Warm-up

The *warm-up* is an essential component of every psychodrama session. It is highly unlikely for group members to enter the therapy room and be instantaneously ready to leap into a psychodrama. The warm-up provides them with a gradual readying for the enactment. In psychodrama, the concept of resistance does not exist. Instead, a client's reluctance is perceived as being connected to an incomplete warm-up. Rather than trying to force the client to go where they do not want to go, the psychodramatist meets and joins the client where they are and assists them in the warming-up process.

The warm-up is the time when group members begin focusing on the issues that they may wish to explore during the session. The warm-up may be either structured or unstructured. With a structured warm-up the director leads the group in an exercise designed to facilitate the emergence of issues of importance to group members. The warm-up may be cognitive, as with a brief didactic about relapse prevention in a substance abuse recovery group. Or the warm-up may be affective as putting an empty chair in the center of the room, telling the group that alcoholism is in the chair and asking members to tell the disease what it has done to them.

There are literally thousands of structured warm-ups (Dayton, 1990; Schutz, 1967; Sternberg & Garcia, 2000; Weiner & Sacks, 1969). Prior to selecting a structured warm-up, the director should review the history of the group, the overall goals for the group and the developmental stage of group process.

An unstructured warm-up occurs when group members discuss their issues and the director focuses the group on themes that spontaneously emerge from their discussion. The *Central Concern Model* (Buchanan, 1980) is one way of looking at a group's warm-up and providing a structure and method for selecting a protagonist when the group is unwilling or unable to select a protagonist.

Selection of the Protagonist

The four ways a protagonist is selected are: (1) system, (2) director, (3) group; and (4) self-selection. Prior to the session the director should have already developed a plan about the method of protagonist selection. If the protagonist is identified prior to the session (system or director choice), other group members should be informed early so that they do not become too warmed up to their own issues and so that they do warm up to the preselected protagonist.

The system selects approach usually occurs when the psychodrama group is sponsored by an agency. The selection can be an institutionalized process such as providing an opportunity for each new patient in an acute care psychiatric program to enact a psychodrama as a method of assessing the strengths and weakness of that client. The system selects approach may also be used when a case manager requests that a client be chosen (e.g., the case manager of a substance abuse program requests that Mr. Jones do a psychodrama to see if he is ready to go for a home visit).

The director selects approach occurs when the director of the group chooses a protagonist. The director can routinely choose the protagonist, or this approach can be used on an as-needed basis. An example of an as-needed basis occurs when a group member has a crisis and the director wants to ensure that the person and issue are addressed.

The director selects approach can also be used routinely in the group when the group members are either unwilling (nonvoluntary clients such as prisoners and juvenile delinquents) or are unable (psychotic or schizophrenic patients and abuse victims) to participate in a voluntary process. Psychiatric clients and people in crisis may simply not have the ego strength to risk volunteering to be chosen and deal with the consequences of not being chosen. As noted in the warm-up section, the Central Concern Model was developed for use at Saint Elizabeth's Hospital precisely because group members were incapable of making choices and withstanding the rejection of the group selection process.

The director selects approach is also useful in groups that have become fixed and stagnant in their sociometric processes. The director can select a rejection star or isolate to facilitate greater spontaneity and creativity among the group members. For example, the director may choose an underchosen, emotionally expressive person to be the protagonist in a group that is stuck in intellectuality and avoids dealing with emotions.

When a group member volunteers to be the protagonist, usually that protagonist is used for short enactments or demonstrations. The director asks for a volunteer who highlights the training issue or the group's issue (e.g., "Who would like to enact a ten-minute drama with a significant other to demonstrate how to use a double?" or "Who would like to do a ten-minute drama where you practice some new behavior you'd like to introduce into your life?"). The first person who volunteers is the protagonist.

The group selecting a protagonist is the most common technique for selecting a protagonist in ongoing personal growth and therapy groups. Following the group warm-up, the director informs the group members of the time limit for the drama and opens the process to volunteers. Group members who wish to be the protagonist come forward and gather in a circle. One at a time the potential protagonists briefly speak about the issues they would like to explore in the drama.

The director instructs the audience members to place a hand on the shoulder of the potential protagonist whose issue is closest to their own issue. The person who receives the most choices is the protagonist. Following the selection of the protagonist, some of those who chose the other potential protagonists tell these volunteers why they chose them–what in their own lives is similar.

It is helpful for the director to commend the volunteers on their courage and encourage them to be persistent in continuing to offer themselves as protagonists in future sessions. The director may state, "Each story has a time to be told. We need to be ready to tell our story, and we need others to be ready to witness it and participate in the telling of it."

The authors have observed that virtually all groups have the innate wisdom to know in what order stories should be told in order to provide maximum benefit to the group and to the protagonist. Telling our story before someone is willing to listen is as bad as not telling our story at all.

Action Phase

After the protagonist is selected the *action phase* begins. This, too, has a kind of warm-up with the Walk and Talk, Casting and Role Training the Auxiliary Egos, and Scene-Setting. These activities further warm up the protagonist and the group to the specific issues and relationships that will be explored in the drama.

Walk and Talk

After the protagonist is selected, the director and the protagonist walk side by side in a circle and discuss the contract for the drama. The *walk and talk* serves to deepen empathy between the director and the protagonist, to clear up any distorted expectations, to warm-up the protagonist and group to the drama, and to establish a contract for the drama. The director and protagonist will negotiate appropriate boundaries for the enactment. For example, the director might say, "Since we have only twenty minutes available, I do not feel comfortable directing a four person enactment with two scenes. Is there a way to do your drama with one character in one scene?" The director also focuses the protagonist on his own work rather than on changing others. The director might say, "No, I can't get your father to understand you, but you could tell your father your side of the story and your feelings about his lack of support for you." At the end of the walk and talk, the director should clearly and succinctly restate to the protagonist and the group the contract for the work. If the protagonist concurs, the scene setting and auxiliary training begins.

Casting and Role Training the Auxiliary Egos

The first order of business after the establishment of the contract is to cast the characters for the drama. Usually protagonists are asked to choose group members whom they would like to play the roles.

It is imperative that group members have the right to decline any role. Also, the director encourages spontaneity in the choice of auxiliaries so that group members are not role locked into playing the same types of roles every time they are auxiliaries. Occasionally, directors will suggest a therapeutic role assignment, by recommending a specific group member to play a role because they feel it will be particularly useful for the person.

If a protagonist has difficulty casting a role because they believe it is a role no group member wants to play, the director may ask the group who is willing to play the role. This is done so that the protagonist will know that these people are not afraid to play the role and are willing to assist in the drama. If several people raise their hands, the director will ask the protagonist to choose from among them.

One by one the characters are chosen and the formal role training of the auxiliaries begins. There is a basic assumption that the protagonist casts the roles for both overt (you look like my mother) and covert (undiscovered sociometric connections) reasons.

Role training can be done "Hollywood Style" with all the roles being cast simultaneously and role training for one role at a time, or each role being selected one at time with role training prior to the selection of the next character.

The protagonist begins with a physiological description (height, weight, age, posture, etc.) and moves on to include qualitative issues such as personality characteristics or how the protagonist feels treated by the person.

After the verbal description by the protagonist, the protagonist is role reversed and assumes the role of the other through posture, movement and comments. The director may ask, "What are some things you generally say to the protagonist? Use the tone of voice you tend to use with her." The auxiliary egos are asked if they have sufficient information to play the role or if they have any questions for the protagonist. To summarize, the protagonist first describes the role of the significant other and then assumes the role. After the auxiliary egos are assigned and role trained, the first scene is set.

Scene Setting

The scene setting begins with the director asking the protagonist where the action occurs. The first question generally will be, "Where does this scene take place?" When the protagonist is unsure or uncertain of where the scene takes place the scene may be set in the "mists" (i.e., the unknown, the area between heaven and earth).

Setting the scene for the drama is important in that it anchors the protagonist in time and space. If the scene is set in the protagonist's family home, is it occurring when the protagonist was ten years old or in the home as it is today? The setting may be much the same or quite different.

One of the first tasks of the director is to decide on the time limits that will be allocated to the scene setting and each particular scene. Although it is possible and sometimes desirable to use an entire thirty-minute enactment solely for the purpose of exploring in depth the details of the scene and that scene's relationship to the protagonist, it is an exception to general practice to do so.

After the place of the scene has been chosen, the protagonist is asked to set the scene. In setting the objects within the scene it is important to allow the protagonists time to create their own space. Unless the protagonist is physically challenged, the protagonist is responsible for moving all the objects in the scene. The actual physical creation of the space is the protagonist's warm-up to the scene and the warm-up to the creation of their own world.

Whatever objects are available in the group room are transformed by surplus reality into the objects in the scene. The protagonist speaks aloud in the present tense and says, "This chair is my father's armchair." The protagonist is encouraged to provide texture and flavor to the object. "My father's armchair is big and well worn. The cushions are faded brown corduroy, and they sag. You can see the rings from my father's beer can on the right arm of the chair and the cigarette burns from when he falls asleep in front of the television."

Although it should be used sparingly, a director may request that the protagonist reverse roles with an object. Nonverbal cues from the protagonist and cultural sensitivities may indicate a role reversal with an object could be useful. If the protagonist states that her mother was a devout Catholic, a role reversal with a statue of the Virgin Mary may yield significant results.

After the scene is over, the protagonist is asked to strike the set. Again, neither the director nor any of the group members participate in the dismantling of the scene, unless directly asked by the protagonist. The speed and order with which the protagonist clears the scene are additional cues to the protagonist's psychological state.

In these days of managed care and shorter sessions most psychodrama sessions are from 60 to 90 minutes and thus the number of scenes during the action phase are reduced.

Common Production Techniques

Zerka T. Moreno (1965) provides a full description of basic and advanced psychodramatic production techniques that are designed to increase the protagonist's creativity and spontaneity. The five basic and most frequently used production techniques are the *soliloquy, double, aside, role reversal,* and *mirror.*

SOLILOQUY. The soliloquy is a moment between reflection and action. It brings the protagonist out of their head and into the moment so that the covert is made overt and we can all hear the running commentary in their mind. The soliloquy is most often used as a bridge in beginning or in ending a scene.

The protagonist is asked to perform a soliloquy by walking in a circle and speaking aloud the thoughts and feelings in their head. A protagonist may also be asked to leave the scene for a moment and soliloquize on their experiences within that scene. The soliloquy is analogous to the free association technique in psychoanalysis except that the individual is asked to move while speaking. The soliloquy is done in action so that the protagonist's movement patterns and gestures are visible.

ASIDE. The aside is another term that comes from theatrical tradition. This technique is used when the protagonist is acting within a scene, but appears to be someplace else. The protagonist is instructed to turn their head to the side (an aside) and speak the thoughts they are thinking but not saying. During the aside, the action continues, but the other characters are instructed that they cannot hear the aside.

The aside technique is most commonly used when the protagonist is disassociating from the enactment and is engaged in a residual warm-up. The aside gives voice to the residual warm-up so that the residual warm-up can be incorporated into the scene.

A visible indication for the need for the aside occurs when protagonists' body language is significantly different from their words, or when protagonists are distant from the scene and appear to be lost in their own thoughts.

It is also used when the person's affect seems incongruent with the words and the protagonist seems constrained from speaking by social mores of the situation. An example of this is a person not wanting to admit feeling rejected in a situation where the auxiliary is ending a relationship with the protagonist.

DOUBLE. The double is the most frequently used technique in psychodrama. The primary purpose of doubling is to provide the protagonist with an awareness and integration of a domain of self that has previously been underdeveloped (e.g., emotion, mind, body and spirit).

Classical doubling occurs when an individual, chosen by the protagonist, literally reflects the protagonist's physical posture and brings a voice to the underdeveloped domain. There are many kinds of doubles: Affective, cognitive, somatic, amplifying (speaks louder for a quiet protagonist), and containing doubles are the most common. Paradoxical and antagonist doubling is less often used.

Doubles begin by assuming the same posture and gestures as the protagonist. They stand beside and slightly behind the protagonist in a place where they can see the protagonist's affect, yet not upstage the protagonist. The double first establishes rapport with the protagonist by stating the obvious and giving expression to the unexpressed manifest content. After establishing rapport, the double slowly and gently begins making statements that deepen the protagonist's awareness of these unexpressed thoughts and feelings. The best doubling statements are direct, pithy and evoke a response from the protagonist. Sentence stem doubling statements are often useful as well, e.g., "I'm feeling. . . ." or "What I would like to tell you is. . . ."

The protagonist and other group members are informed that only the protagonist can hear the double. All other auxiliaries respond only to words and actions initiated by the protagonist. It is a disservice to the protagonist, and reinforces "magical thinking" that an individual can be heard without speaking. The protagonist must incorporate, change or disavow the words of the double so that the protagonist deepens his internal experience. During the doubling, the director must be vigilant in monitoring the protagonist and directing the protagonist either to repeat aloud, clarify or disavow the double's statements.

In spontaneous doubling, rather than having a particular double assigned to the protagonist for the entire drama, group members are encouraged to rise, stand in the double position, make one doubling statement, wait for the protagonist's response and then sit back down in the group. Spontaneous doubling is excellent for developing emotional intelligence in other group members and providing the protagonist with a deep feeling of connection with the group.

Doubling can also be used as a method of restraint. Clients with impulse control disorders often benefit from cognitive doubling. A cognitive double builds introspection, reflection, and future projection within the protagonist. For example, a cognitive double of an impulsive, aggressive client might say "I'd like to hit this person but hitting others results in my going to seclusion and losing my phone privileges. I want to call my girlfriend tonight, so I'd better not hit him."

An assignment of a double is contraindicated when the protagonist is fully experiencing the drama.

ROLE REVERSAL. Zerka T. Moreno has called role reversal the sine qua non of psychodramatic techniques. A role reversal occurs when the protagonist reverses with another and becomes the other (when A becomes B and B becomes A). The protagonist and the auxiliary literally change places in the room and switch roles.

When directing multiple role players it is essential that the protagonist is role reversed back to home base before assuming another role reversal (if the protagonist (A) is in the role of B, the protagonist is reversed back to his own role (A) before being reversed with C).

A role reversal is indicated under any of the following conditions:

1. when the protagonist has information that the auxiliary does not have.
2. to provide an opportunity for the protagonist to see themselves from the role of the other.
3. when the protagonist lacks empathy or understanding of the role of the other.
4. to avoid physical harm to the auxiliary.
5. when the protagonist lacks spontaneity and role reversing will increase affect, cognition or performance.
6. to verify the accuracy of the statements from the other.
7. when the protagonist asks a question. The idea here is that all that we need to know is within.

Role reversal is contraindicated when the protagonist is highly codependent and routinely and automatically assumes the role of the other and abandons the role of the Self. Role reversal with abusers is contra-indicted for abuse survivors until the final stage of treatment.

MIRROR. The protagonist is asked to step out of the scene and choose someone to take their role. The protagonist then observes the "mirror" enact the scene. The mirror technique allows protagonists to see themselves as others see them.

Mirroring was created before audiovisual feedback and can be an excellent way for group members to gain a perspective on their own actions. This technique is useful when the protagonist becomes overheated or overwhelmed and a cool down is indicated so that the enactment does not get too chaotic. A mirror is also useful in unblocking protagonists who have distorted images of themselves. For example, from the mirror position the protagonist might note that rather than being assertive, they are instead being docile.

This technique is contraindicated when it would be used to shame or embarrass the protagonist or in situations when the protagonist might feel ridiculed rather than supported.

Other Specialized Production Techniques

In addition to the five most commonly used psychodramatic production techniques, a variety of specialized techniques have been developed.

EMPTY CHAIR. The *empty chair* technique, while coined and first used by Moreno, was popularized by Fritz Perls, who borrowed and adapted the empty chair as a Gestalt Therapy technique.

The protagonist is asked to place a person or object in an empty chair and to begin a dialogue with that person or object. This technique is often used as a warm-up for a group. The director can also suggest who should occupy the empty chair. The subject in the empty chair can be someone from the past, present or future, or it can be a part of the Self or someone transpersonal (e.g., St. Peter, Buddha, Hercules).

In general the dialogue begins with the protagonist speaking to the empty chair. The director can prompt the protagonist by asking the protagonist to make a statement, ask a question or speak a feeling. When appropriate, role reversal is used with the protagonist becoming the person in the chair and speaking back to themselves.

FUTURE PROJECTION. As noted earlier in the theoretical constructs section, time collapses in psychodrama; thus the drama can include a scene from the future. According to Moreno (1946), the future is a better motivator for the present than the past. The future projection technique can be used as one scene within a psychodrama, as a warm-up technique and for separate one-scene enactments.

In the future projection the protagonist is asked to imagine what a specific future might look like. Auxiliary egos are chosen to play the main characters (real or fantasy) and are trained by the protagonist to take the roles. A person is chosen to play the present self while the protagonist plays the future self. At the conclusion of the future projection, the director instructs the future self to role train the present self to identify concrete behavioral actions that will create the wished-for future.

The future projection technique is best used to instill hope, provide motivation, and to assist the protagonist in creating a plan to solve a current dilemma. The future projection technique is contraindicated when it may break through a protagonist's denial and cause trauma to the client (e.g., a client who is in denial over a terminal illness).

PSYCHODRAMA A DEUX. *Psychodrama a deux* is psychodrama for two (Stein & Callahan, 1982). Psychodrama a deux is often the focus of individual therapy when provided by a psychodramatist. It is accomplished through use of as many empty chairs as there are auxiliaries in the drama. The protagonist places them in the room as they would set the scene in a group session and is asked to imagine that the chairs are filled with their auxiliaries. The director reverses the protagonist into each role to learn more about the role. When the protagonist is sufficiently warmed up, they begin the drama. If they do not want to use chairs, scarves or props may be used to mark the spots held by the auxiliary roles. Unlike in Developmental Transformations, it is considered best for the director to refrain from playing roles, but to be an active double for the protagonist.

The director can also interview and coach the protagonist in the role of the other at various moments in the drama. For example, if the protagonist is in the role of an unusually critical mother, the director may say, "I know that you do not like Mary to be overconfident, yet she's feeling that you do not love her and you think she's seldom competent. Do you love her? Do you want to help her? Would you be willing to tell her that you love her? Can you tell her one thing about her that you admire?"

There are some pitfalls to avoid when using psychodrama production techniques in individual therapy. One of the great benefits to the psychodramatic group process is that more of the transference is projected onto other group members and less is projected onto the director. However, in a one-on-one setting all the transference will be placed upon the director. The danger in psychodrama a deux is in the director assuming roles within the process. Assuming the role of an antagonistic other in psychodrama a deux heightens the negative transference towards the director and often results in a client's premature termination.

Another danger in psychodrama a deux is that experiential methods can too quickly cut through defense systems and can lead to premature breakthroughs or breakdowns of natural defense systems. In using psychodrama a deux on a regular basis, the director should spend considerable time working with supportive relationships and supportive parts of the self rather than focusing mainly on dysfunctional role relationships (internal or external).

Sharing

The final phase of a psychodrama session is the *sharing*. The sharing is a vital and integral part of the session. The sharing phase incorporates the protagonist back into the group and offers the group members an opportunity to connect, on a personal level, with the issues and concerns explored in the drama. It is a time for closure and integration. It is a time for group members to acknowledge how the drama has affected them personally and what they have learned about their own lives through the protagonist's journey.

Prior to the sharing the auxiliary egos are de-roled from their assigned roles and resume their membership in the group. Just as it is important to warm-up the auxiliary egos to play a role, so, too, is it essential for the auxiliary egos to formally discard the assigned roles and return to themselves. After the de-roling is concluded, the sharing portion begins.

Sharing is unique in that the verbal statements by the other group members to the protagonist are based on identification and connection rather than evaluation or interpretation. Group members are encouraged to identify with rather than critique or interpret the protagonist. To facilitate this process group members are encouraged to begin their sharing statements with an "I" statement: "When watching your drama, I thought about my own rocky relationship with my partner, and I felt a sense of hope that we could work something out too." The depth and level of sharing from the group members can also serve as an assessment of how adequately the drama met the needs of the group members.

If a group member becomes critical, judgmental or advice-giving rather than sharing, it may be because that group member has identified with the role of the other rather than the role of the protagonist. For example, "You know, you are very sensitive and as your partner I would have a hell of a time putting up with you." It is best for the director to nip these statements in the bud and refocus the group member to share with the protagonist. The director might say something to the group member, such as, "It would be helpful to the protagonist and to you to share from your own experience and say what the drama brings up from your life." After the group member responds, the director might say, "You noted you feel the protagonist is sensitive. How does sensitivity play out in your own life?"

The director monitors the group members and establishes sociometric connections among the protagonist and other group members. The director can ask for clarification or elaboration from group members who are finding it difficult to make a bridge between themselves and the protagonist. If a group member is having difficulty in finding something to share, the director can gently guide them to a similar issue (e.g., the group member might say, "I've never been married, so I do not have anything to share." The director could respond, "I know you have never been married, but have you ever had a relationship with someone you loved and feared losing that relationship?").

Depending on the time allotted for sharing and the number of people in the group, there are several ways to conduct the sharing. If the group is small and there is sufficient time, the group can share as a whole, with each group member sharing with the protagonist. If there is limited time or if there is a large group, sharing can be done in small groups with the auxiliary egos sharing with the protagonist and other group members forming small groups for sharing. After the small groups have shared, the director asks a few group members who have not already shared with the protagonist to share with the protagonist in the larger group.

It is important that the auxiliary egos have time to share with the protagonist both their experience in playing the role (e.g., "as your father I felt . . .") and from their own personal life. Sharing from the role often provides invaluable feedback to the protagonist.

In an ongoing group the sharing illuminates the next phase of the group and highlights issues that may be on the agenda at the next meeting. It is to be remembered that sharing is an absolutely essential part of a psychodrama session. It helps a group to cool down from the action, to reach closure, to deepen connections with one another and the self, and provides time for introspection and reflection on the drama.

POPULATIONS AND SETTINGS

Psychodrama has been used with a broad range of people in a variety of settings, including but not limited to: the severely and chronically mentally ill (Buchanan, 1984b); alcohol and substance abusers (Fuhlrodt, 1990); both normal and emotionally challenged children and adolescents (Hoey, 1996); eating disordered clients (Hornyak & Baker, 1989); clients and staff of the criminal justice system (Buchanan, 1981); and in individual and group therapy (Blatner, 1996; Garcia, 1984; Holmes & Karp, 1991; Holmes, Karp & Watson, 1994; Williams, 1991).

Psychodrama can be used successfully with virtually every population, provided that the psychodramatist is skilled enough to modify treatment to suit the population. Psychodrama can be preventive. With psychodrama, one can help clients cope with stressful situations and learn how to enact alternative solutions to repetitive problems. Psychodrama can also treat specific symptoms. For example, psychodrama is highly effective in the treatment of phobias. It can also be used for personal growth, such as improving relationships and restoring a sense of joy in life. Psychodrama treatment can be brief (1–6 sessions) or of longer duration. Psychodrama is the original brief therapy. Goals and interventions are specific and behaviorally-oriented and tested. While practically any client can benefit from psychodrama, careful screening must be done so that the person can be placed within the appropriate psychodramatic treatment setting. A client with a substance abuse problem, for example, is best treated in a homogeneous substance abusers group rather than a generic group. Clients with fragile ego boundaries are best placed in groups where the treatment focus is on behavior and interpersonal skills development rather than in a group dealing with strong emotions and regressive early childhood drama.

Moreno cautioned against the use of psychodrama to rehearse homicidal and suicidal fantasies. Psychodrama should also be used judiciously with individuals with severe impulse and acting-out disorders so that they do not rehearse destructive actions. While van der Kolk (1987) has stated that psychodrama may be helpful in working with abuse survivors, Hudgins and Drucker (1998) caution that psychodramatists working with abuse survivors need specialized training.

CASE EXAMPLE

Psychodrama in a Group Setting

Joan had been dating a wonderful man who had asked her to marry him. She had also been dating another man off and on over a period of years. She felt that this man, too, was finally ready for marriage. Tom, the first suitor, was a civil servant, a sweet and loving man with a wonderful sense of humor. Andre, the second suitor, was handsome, exciting, and charming. Joan and Tom loved the same kinds of activities and shared basic values. Joan and Andre went to chic nightspots and had differing views on life.

Joan was in a quandary. What to do? Which man to marry? In the walk and talk it seemed clear that she was in love with Tom, but the lure of excitement with Andre was compelling, especially since she felt that her deceased mother would have wanted her to marry Andre. Her mother had known Andre and liked him and would be disappointed if Joan didn't marry him since he was so handsome and charming, apparently a mover and shaker. The contract made in the walk and talk was to help Joan move closer to a decision. She decided that she wanted to encounter both men in the drama as a way of clarifying her feelings about both. As she brought them in she continued to talk about what her mother wanted her to do. We decided to bring her mother in too and give her a chance to encounter Mother about choice of mate. Joan placed the men in a tableau and in a surplus reality scene talked to her dead mother about both men. As Joan spoke to her mother she began to realize that Tom was very much like her father, whom she deeply loved and admired. It became clear in the scene through role reversal that Mother did not share Joan's love and respect for Father. Joan's mother would rather have married a debonair and handsome man like Andre.

The director reversed Joan back into her own role to hear her mother's statement and respond to it. Then the director doubled, "Well, if you think he's so great, you marry him." Joan said, "Yeah, you marry him" and began laughing at the thought of her mother marrying Andre. The director asked her if she would like to see that happen. Joan's mouth dropped open at the prospect of such an odd event, but she quickly decided she would love to see her mother walk down the aisle with Andre since they seemed "perfect for each other."

The scene was quickly set up and Joan watched gleefully as her mother greeted churchgoers and asked them if they were impressed that she had finally landed such a great catch. Joan stood at the side with Tom. In a soliloquy she noted her relief at seeing her mother happy.

She recognized that she had been hanging on to her unsatisfying relationship with Andre as a way of making up for her mother's unhappy relationship with her father. Up to that moment she had been a bit ashamed that she was in love with Tom, a sweet, ordinary guy like her dad, rather than the exciting Andre.

The truth was she couldn't make herself love Andre as she loved Tom. "I do not really trust Andre. He does not have much substance. And I do not think he's as financially stable as he implies. I think it's all flash. And–I think he'd spend the rest of our life together running after other women."

When she saw her mother as Andre's happy bride, she felt relieved of the burden of her mother's wishes and unmet needs. She ended by telling her mother how much she loved her and how delighted she was that Mother was now happy. She asked Mother for her blessing with Tom. Reversing Joan into the mother role, she told her daughter that now that she was so happy, she wanted Joan to be happy too and gave her blessing for the marriage to Tom. Joan reversed back to her own role to receive her mother's blessing. She ended the drama by telling Tom how much she loved him and why she did. Within a couple of months after the session,

Joan and Tom were married. When the director saw her some years later, she said how happy she was that she had married him and that they were still very much in love. She had found a soul mate.

CONCLUSION

Psychodrama is a powerful treatment modality and has a unique ability to heal. It has a rich history, philosophy, theory of human development, and set of interventions and techniques. It also has many qualitative and quantitative research studies. In a meta-analysis of 25 experimentally designed studies on psychodrama, Kipper and Ritchie (2003) found that psychodrama had an improvement effect similar to or better than that commonly reported for group psychotherapy in general. The techniques of role reversal and doubling emerged as the most effective techniques.

The trained psychodramatist will have the knowledge, skills, and abilities to design the right treatment for each specific client rather than rely upon a cookbook of structured techniques. A skilled practitioner understands dramas can range from the behavioral (role rehearsal) to the affective (catharsis for release of tension) to the cognitive (reorganization of perceptual patterns) to the spiritual (establishing and deepening transpersonal connections).

For issues regarding competency, the American Board of Examiners in Psychodrama, Sociometry and Group Psychotherapy has set standards of professional practice and certifies individuals based upon these standards with a written and an onsite examination. While it is not essential that all individuals who use psychodrama are certified, it is essential that they have received proper training, education and supervision for its use.

REFERENCES

Blatner, A. (1996). *Acting-In: Practical applications of psychodramatic methods,* 3rd Ed. New York: Springer Publishing.

Buchanan, D. R. (1980). The central concern model: A framework for structuring psychodramatic production. *Journal of Group Psychotherapy, Psychodrama and Sociometry, 33,* 47–62.

Buchanan, D. R. (1981). Action methods for the criminal justice system. *Federal Probation, 45,* 17–25.

Buchanan, D. R. (1984a). Moreno's social atom: A diagnostic and treatment tool for exploring interpersonal relationships. *The Arts in Psychotherapy, 27,* 173–183.

Buchanan, D. R. (1984b). Psychodrama. In T. B. Karasu (Ed.), *The psychiatric therapies* (pp. 781–800). Washington, DC: American Psychiatric Association.

Carlson-Sabelli, L. C., Sabelli, H. C., Patel, M., & Holm, K. (1992). The union of opposites. *Journal of Group Psychotherapy, Psychodrama and Sociometry, 45,* 147–171.

Compernole, T. (1981). J. L. Moreno: An unrecognized pioneer of family therapy. *Family Process, 20,* 331–335.

Corsini, R. J. (1955). Historic background of group psychotherapy: A critique. *Journal of Group Psychotherapy, Psychodrama and Sociometry, 8,* 219–225.

Csikszentmihalyi, M. (1991). *Flow: The psychology of optimal experience.* New York: Harper Collins.

Dayton, T. (1990). *Drama games: Techniques for self-development.* Deerfield Beach: Health Communications, Inc.

Edwards, J. (1996). Examining the clinical utility of the Moreno Social Atom Projective test. *Journal of Group Psychotherapy, Psychodrama and Sociometry, 49,* 51–75.

Emunah, R. (1994). *Acting for real.* New York: Brunner/Mazel.

Emunah, R. (1997). Drama therapy and psychodrama: An integrated model. *International Journal of Action Methods, 50,* 108–134.

Fox, J. (1987). *The essential Moreno: Writings on psychodrama, group method, and spontaneity by J. L. Moreno, M.D.* New York: Springer Publishing.

Fox, J. (1994). *Acts of service: Spontaneity, commitment, tradition in the nonscripted theatre.* New Paltz, NY: Tusitala Publishing.

Fromm, E. (1941). *Escape from freedom.* New York: Harper Collins.

Fuhlrodt, R. B. (Ed.) (1990). *Psychodrama: Its application to ACOA and substance abuse treatment.* Caldwell, NJ: Promises Books.

Garcia, A. (1984). Psychodrama: Creative approaches to human growth. *Design for arts in education, 86,* 40–42.

Hale, A. E. (1986). *Conducting clinical sociometric explorations: A manual for psychodramatists and sociometrists.* Roanoke, VA: Blue Ridge Human Relations Institute.

Hare, A. P., & Hare, J. R. (1996). *J. L. Moreno.* London: Sage Publications.

Haskell, M. R. (1975). *Socioanalylsis: Self-direction via sociometry and psychodrama.* Long Beach, CA: Role Training Associates, Inc.

Hoey, B. (1996). *Who calls the tune? A psychodramatic approach to child therapy.* London: Routlege.

Holmes, P. H., & Karp, M. (Eds.). (1991). *Psychodrama: Inspiration and technique.* London: Routledge.

Holmes, P. H., Karp, M., & Watson, M. (Eds.). (1994). *Psychodrama since Moreno: Innovation in theory and practice.* London: Routledge.

Hornyak, L. M., & Baker, E. K. (Eds.). (1989). *Experiential therapies for eating disorders.* New York: Guilford Press.

Hudgins, M. K., & Drucker, K. (1998). The containing double as part of the therapeutic spiral model for treating trauma survivors. *International Journal for Action Methods, 51,* 63–74.

Karp, M., Holmes, P., & Tauvon, K. (1998). *The handbook of psychodrama.* London: Routledge.

Kellerman, P. F. (1992). *Focus on psychodrama: The therapeutic aspects of psychodrama.* London: Jessica Kingsley Publishers.

Kipper, D. A. (1986). *Psychotherapy through clinical role playing.* New York: Brunner/Mazel.

Kipper, D., & Ritchie, T. (2003). The effectiveness of psychodramatic techniquers: A meta-analysis. *Group Dynamics, 7,* 13–25.

Kraus, C. (1984). Psychodrama for fallen gods: A review of Morenian theology. *Journal of Group Psychotherapy, Psychodrama and Sociometry, 37,* 47–65.

Landy, R. (1993). *Persona and performance.* New York: Guilford Press.

Landy, R. (2008). *The couch and the stage: Integrating words and action in psychotherapy.* New York: Jason Aronson.

Marineau, R. F. (1989). *Jacob Levy Moreno 1889–1974, Father of Psychodrama, Sociometry and Group Psychotherapy.* London: Tavistock/ Routledge.

Maslow, A. (1968). Letter to the editor. *Life Magazine,* August 2, 1968, 15.

(Moreno) Levy, J. (1915). *Einladung zu einer begegnung heft 2 (Invitation to an Encounter, Part 2).* Vienna/Leipzig: Anzengruber/Verlag Bruder Suschitzky.

Moreno (published anonymously), J.L. (1920). *Das testament des vaters (The Words of the Father),* in Die Gefahrten, 3:1–33. Berlin/Potsdam: Kiepenheuer Verlag.

Moreno, J.L. (1946). Psychodrama and group psychotherapy. Paper presented at American Psychiatric Association Meeting May 30, 1946 in Chicago.

Moreno, J.L. (1946). *Psychodrama first volume.* Beacon, New York: Beacon House.

Moreno, J.L. (1947). *The psychodrama of God: A new hypothesis of the self* (revised edition). Beacon, New York: Beacon House.

Moreno, J.L. (1953). *Who shall survive?* Beacon, New York: Beacon House.

Moreno, J.L. (1966). Psychiatry of the 20th century: Function of the universalis: Time, space, reality and cosmos. *Journal of Group Psychotherapy, Psychodrama and Sociometry, 19,* 146–158.

Moreno, J.L. (1969). *The magic charter of psychodrama.* Beacon, New York: Beacon House.

Moreno, Z. T. (1965). Psychodramatic rules, techniques, and adjunctive methods. *Group Psychotherapy, 18,* 73–86.

Moreno, Z. T., Blomkvist, L.D., & Rutzel, T. (2000). *Psychodrama, surplus reality, and the art of healing.* New York: Routledge.

Pitzele, P. (1998). *Scripture windows: Toward a practice of bibliodrama.* Los Angeles: Torah Aura Productions.

Schutz, W. (1967). *Joy, expanding human awareness.*

New York: Grove Press, Inc.

Stein, M. B., & Callahan, M. L. (1982). The use of psychodrama in individual therapy. *Journal of Group Psychotherapy, Psychodrama and Sociometry, 35,* 118–129.

Sternberg, P., & Garcia, A. (2000). *Sociodrama: Who's in your shoes?* 2nd Ed. Westport: Praeger.

Thomas, E. J., & Biddle, B. J. (Eds.). (1966). *Role theory: Concepts and research.* New York: John Wiley & Sons.

van der Kolk, B. (1987). *Psychological trauma.* Washington, DC: American Psychiatric Press.

Weiner, H. B., & Sacks, J. M. (1969). Warm-up and sum-up. *Journal of Group Psychotherapy, Psychodrama and Sociometry, 22,* 85–102.

Williams, A. (1991). *The passionate technique: Strategic psychodrama with individuals.* London: Tavistock/Routledge.

FURTHER TRAINING

The American Society of Group
Psychotherapy and Psychodrama
301 N. Harrison Street, Suite 508
Princeton, NJ 08540
(609) 737-8500, email: asgpp@ASGPP.org.

and

The American Board of Examiners in
Psychodrama, Sociometry, and Group
Psychotherapy
PO Box 15572, Washington, DC 20003
(202) 483-0514

The Society has been the general membership organization for over 50 years and publishes a newsletter, sponsors an annual conference and several regional meetings. The official journal of the Society is *The International Journal of Action Methods,* which is published quarterly.

The Board of Examiners publishes an annual directory, which includes the standards for certification and names and addresses of those who are certified. The directory is available free of charge to individuals who request it. The Board also maintains an ethics committee to oversee the professional conduct of all certified psychodramatists.

Chapter 19

SOCIODRAMA

PATRICIA STERNBERG AND ANTONINA GARCIA

Sociodrama concerns itself with the role aspects that people share. For example, all students are expected to study; most nurses encounter dying patients in the course of their careers; most charter boat captains encounter rough seas; all employees have bosses with whom they must deal. Jacob Levy Moreno, M.D. originated sociodrama between 1921 and 1923. One of the reasons that sociodrama works so well is that Moreno was able to tap into the truth about humanity: that we are more alike than we are different.

In *Who Shall Survive?* Moreno said, "The true subject of sociodrama is the group. . . . Sociodrama is based upon the tacit assumption that the group formed by the audience is already organized by the social and cultural roles which in some degree all the carriers of the culture share. . . . The sociodramatic approach deals with social problems and aims at social catharsis" (1993, p. 59–60).

Basing itself on the premise of shared experience, a sociodrama group might seek to define a problem that the members would like to solve. If they are social workers for example, they might want to be better able to deal with a situation in which family members disown a child's misbehavior at school. If they are police trainees, they may want to enhance their understanding of a rape victim's feelings. The members of a sociodrama group will work with a situation in which they would like to gain greater understanding. The members may also define and work with a decision that they would like to be able to make–for example, high school students trying to decide whether or not to go away to college rather than live at home and commute. Members may seek to train themselves in certain role aspects about which they may feel uncomfortable. Thus, if they are a group of the long-term unemployed, the members may want to role-train interview decorum.

Sociodrama is an action method in which individuals enact an agreed upon social situation spontaneously. The participants volunteer or are assigned roles by the director of the sociodrama. After every enactment there is a sharing in which group members discuss the enactment, the solutions or ideas it presented, and sometimes generate new material for future sociodramatic clarifications. The sharing is a time to begin the process of cooling down and integrating what has taken place moments before in action.

Sociodrama, with its action/reflection

components, speaks to both sides of the brain. It is a kinesthetic, intuitive, and cognitive modality. Unlike simple role playing, sociodrama employs many specific techniques to deepen the action of the enactment. These techniques include: the *aside, doubling, role reversal, soliloquy,* and *mirroring.* It is important to mention that theatrical training and/or interest in theatre are unnecessary for sociodrama. The modality is not meant to train actors but rather to draw upon a person's innate need and ability to learn with his whole body, mind, and intuition.

GENESIS

Moreno was born in Bucharest, Romania in 1889. His parents moved their family to Vienna while he was a small child. As a young man, Moreno completed a degree in philosophy, then received his MD from the University of Vienna. Throughout the time when he was a student, he was developing the ideas that ultimately blossomed into sociodrama.

Between the years of 1908 and 1911, Moreno experimented with dramatic play in the parks of Vienna. He gathered children around him, told them stories from fairytales and theatre, and then enacted the tales with the children. After a while, he encouraged the children to enact stories from their own imaginations. As he watched children take on and practice roles from the culture and work through their issues via play, Moreno hypothesized about roles and the educational and therapeutic benefits of role playing.

In 1913, while he was a medical student, Moreno began to explore the sociodynamics of groups. One day, Moreno met a prostitute on the Praeterstrasse. Because she was away from the red light district and wearing gaily-colored clothing rather than the more sedate apparel of a proper lady, a policeman carted her off to jail. Moreno, rather stunned by this occurrence, searched out the woman when she was released. He discovered from her that prostitutes had no legal rights and were not entitled to public medical care. Ever the social activist, Moreno interested a newspaper editor in the women's plight, got them medical care and organized the women into a kind of guild of prostitutes. The ladies met weekly to discuss their concerns. Moreno dates these gatherings as the inception of group psychotherapy.

As he observed the women and what they discussed, he began to realize what made groups work: that we are more alike than we are different. He noticed that for every role a person plays there are both collective and private aspects. The prostitutes were able to communicate with each other well because they shared difficulties and joys that were role-related. They all had to worry about aging, pregnancy, and venereal disease. These are some of the collective role aspects. At the same time, each prostitute had her own personality, personal concerns, and way of playing the role. These are the private aspects of the role.

Between the years of 1921 and 1923, Moreno developed and ran the Theater of Spontaneity. He loved theatre but was put off by the theatre of his day because he felt it had become sterile. He felt the actors and plays did not reach the community the way the theatre of the ancient Greeks did. Moreno believed that there should be interaction between audience and actors. Further, he believed that the theatre was lifeless because it did not explore issues that were of vital importance to the general public.

Moreno gathered together a group of professional actors and trained them both in spontaneity work and as sociological researchers. He wanted them to be actively aware of the current issues of their culture so that the audience members could mention a current event and the actors and audience could explore that issue onstage. As enactors and audience joined together spontaneously to examine social problems and discover possible solutions to them, sociodrama was born.

Moreno came to the United States in 1925. He had been invited to come to the States to develop a prototype of the tape recorder that he and a friend had invented. Once in the U.S., Moreno worked using threads of sociodrama with children in New York schools and with racial issues in Harlem.

In the years from 1929–1931, Moreno again created a theater company called the Impromptu Theater and began experiments with his actors in developing the Living Newspaper format. They performed in New York City at Carnegie Hall. Audience members were encouraged to come up on stage and interact with the actors. Moreno abandoned the Impromptu Theater when, as part of the Work Projects Administration, the company expanded to include playwrights. Moreno felt that playwriting was an anathema to spontaneity and interaction between audience and actor.

Since Moreno's initial creation of sociodrama, role play has developed as an offshoot and is a standard part of many forms of training in business and education. Role play enjoys wide usage because it is easy to do and does not require much training. It differs from sociodrama in that it does not utilize the many techniques of sociodrama, which widen and deepen the scope of the action, providing a more profound learning experience. Simulation games also have their roots in sociodrama.

There are two more developments that deserve further mention. One is Peter Pitzele's (1998) development of *Bibliodrama,* a form of sociodrama that explores scenes and characters from sacred scripture. While Pitzele's work often doesn't entail full enactment of scenes, group members embody roles from the Bible and interact with each other from the roles they play. Linda Condon (2007) has expanded bibliodrama to include the sociodramatic enactment of secular text as well.

The other development is Jonathan Fox's (1994) "Playback Theatre" (see Chapter 20). Playback Theatre is a form that combines elements of Moreno's Theater of Spontaneity, sociodrama, psychodrama, and drama therapy in that a member of the audience comes forward to tell a story that is then enacted by a trained troupe of actors. What is similar to sociodrama is that the performances are frequently open to the public and are often devoted to social issues. For example, Armand Volkas utilizes Playback Theatre in his "Healing the Wounds of History" approach (Chapter 8).

Sociodrama has developed primarily in terms of specific techniques and varied populations to fulfill Moreno's idea of healing all of humankind. At present, sociodrama is utilized in education, business, industry, psychotherapy, religion, spirituality, and theatre.

BASIC CONCEPTS

Spontaneity

Moreno believed that each of us is potentially a spontaneous, creative genius. He said that rather than focus on the worst aspects of human behavior, we should instead study the geniuses, artists, inventors and saints, those who achieve the highest of what it means to be human. Through this examination, social scientists can discover what the rest of us can do to develop ourselves as fully as possible. Thus, Moreno did not follow the medical model in relation to human growth, development, function and dysfunction. He believed that each of us is a work in progress and that psychotherapy and sociotherapy are methods for assisting people in their personal evolution. In *The Future of Man's World* (1947), he said,

> Man must take his own fate and the fate of the universe in hand, on the level of creativity, as a creator. It is not sufficient if he tries to meet the situation by technical control–defense weapons–nor by political controls–world government–he should face himself and his society in *statu nascendi* and learn how to control the robot not after it is delivered, but before it is conceived (creatocracy). . . . The future of man depends upon counter weapons developed by sociometry and sociatry. (p. 21)

Moreno believed that functionality had to do with the degree of spontaneity and creativity the person engages in the playing of life roles in relation to both the self and others.

Moreno's Role Theory

Moreno began looking at roles and role relationships as early as 1913 in his work with prostitutes in Vienna. He developed his *role theory,* which serves as the basis for using sociodrama. He defined role this way:

> Role can be defined as the actual and tangible forms which the self takes. We thus define the role as the functioning form the individual assumes in the specific moment he reacts to a specific situation in which other persons or objects are involved. The symbolic representation of this functioning form, perceived by the individual and others, is called the role. The form is created by past experiences and the cultural patterns of the society in which the individual lives, and may be satisfied by the specific type of his productivity. Every role is a fusion of private and collective elements. Every role has two sides, a private and a collective side. (as quoted in Fox, 1987, p. 62)

Role is a unit of behavior that reflects socially agreed upon boundaries. These behaviors clustered together create the broader category called role. Roles are important to us as a society, since we often identify people by the roles they play. For example if a person says, "Betty is a secretary," we have a pretty clear idea of that role. We may ask for more details as to what Betty's specific job is as a secretary, but her role is clearly understood.

When we identify the people we know it is difficult to obtain any meaningful description of the person without considering his or her behavior. If I say, "Linda is a workaholic," what do I mean? Did that label come out of the blue? No, every time I see Linda, she is busy with at least two or three projects going at once. She is frequently called upon by others and is always willing to take on another task to help someone else. Her actions tell a lot about her personality. Looking at the roles others play, as well as those we ourselves play, helps us understand ourselves.

Each of us plays many roles in our lives. Moreno pointed out that each role a person plays has two parts to it: a collective component and a private component. The collective component of the role is the common denominator or aspects of the role that are similar to all that play it. For example, Jack, Tom, and Barry are all police officers. All of them arrest suspects; all are proficient in the use of firearms; and all have concerns about being injured on duty. It is easy for them to converse with each other because they have the same frame of reference in role.

However, sooner or later they will probably begin discussing their own experiences. When that happens, they are moving from the collective to the private role components. It is the private component that distinguishes us in our own personal way. For example, Tom may work out of the 18th precinct and work on the beat, while the others work at the 20th precinct and ride in a patrol car. Jack especially likes lecturing kids in grammar schools on safety, while Barry feels he has a gift for intervening in domestic disputes.

Moreno felt, as the authors do, that as individuals we have much more in common than we are different. Beginning with those commonalities, or collective role components, group members can find a common ground on which to interact. In fact, communication, identification, and empathy are impossible in a group without people's recognition of collective role elements and, therefore, shared experience. Sociodrama emerges from that focus and explores in action aspects of our collective components. The focus of sociodrama is the group and the common threads of members' concerns.

Role Types: The Psychosomatic, The Social, and The Psychodramatic

Moreno further categorized roles into three types: the psychosomatic, the social, and the psychodramatic, or intrapsychic roles. The psychosomatic roles come first. Those are the physical roles that we see in newborn infants and continue in us throughout life, e.g., the eater, the crier, the eliminator. Moreno used the term psychosomatic to indicate a psychological connection with bodily functions. If a lightning flash frightens a child, he may cry out in fear. The crying out is a physical manifestation, while the response of fear is an emotional one.

Moreno noted that newborns are unable to differentiate between themselves and others. He felt that infants do not know where mother or father begins and they themselves end. The newborn is the center of his universe, experiencing himself as one with everything else in existence. In fact, Moreno termed this state the First Universe.

As the child interacts with those around him, he begins to develop social roles and an imaginary life that are independent of reality. At about two and a half, the child becomes aware of himself as a separate being. Moreno called this phase the Second Universe. The I and Thou are totally separate, and illusion and reality are recognized as two different phenomena.

Social roles come from our interaction with others: mother, father, doctor. The first social roles emerge slowly: the baby cries and the mother feeds him. The toddler smiles and the father plays with him. This action and response continues as we develop a sense of role reciprocity.

Psychodramatic roles are interior roles, such as the imaginer, the planner, the humorist. Among our psychodramatic roles are those which we play in our fantasy lives: the super hero, the prima ballerina, the baker, the novelist, the ruler of a new nation. These roles are important in our lives. We can imagine those roles and some perhaps are roles we would like to perform in the future.

Moreno noted that we are warmed up to different types of roles at different times in our lives. That realization can be important to the sociodrama leader. At times people may be more warmed up to psychodramatic roles rather than social roles. For example, the planner may be deeply involved with his next project, listening to his own inner dialogue and not listening to what his fellow group member is saying. At these times the leader can address those psychodramatic roles and bring the members back to group interaction by asking them to discuss what happens when distractions prevent them from focusing on what is occurring in the here-and-now. From this discussion a drama may emerge on managing distractions or scheduling time to devote to planning.

Role Taking, Role Playing and Role Creating

According to Moreno there are three ways of assuming roles in life: role taking, role playing, and role creating. *Role taking* is the most rigid or routine form. When someone role takes, he follows the parameters of a role as the culture established it with little or no deviation. *Role playing* offers a greater degree of freedom and responsibility and implies comfort in role enactment. Finally, *Role creating* offers the highest degree of spontaneity and creativity. When a person role creates, she adds something new to that role or creates a totally different version of the role. For example, if one were to take the role of a substitute teacher, that teacher would follow the syllabus given to him verbatim (role taking). If he were role playing, he might switch the first topic on the syllabus to the third or add an item for discussion that was not included on the syllabus (role playing). However, if he were role creating, he might decide to forget the syllabus entirely and take the class in an entirely new direction with the material (role creating).

Every role that we play proficiently has aspects of all three: role taking, role playing and role creating. When we learn a new role we usually begin with role taking. As we learn the role more thoroughly and become comfortable in it, we move to role playing, and finally when we see a new way to perform that role, we move to role creating. The understanding of how we engage in various stages of role development can help us find satisfaction in what we do well and spark us to try new ways (role creation). Through sociodrama we can explore the various roles we play and experiment with new roles, thus increasing our role repertoire. We can examine and practice ways to play our life roles with greater flexibility and tap into our inner creativity in dealing with our own lives.

Sociometry

Sociometry is the measurement of social choices. Throughout our lives we constantly make choices, choices that join us with one person or group and choices that separate us. Some of our choices are visible to others, such as which social club or community action group we belong to, or with what group of friends we spend time. Other choices may be invisible to other people, such as who our favorite coworker is or what political party we vote for.

Moreno was fascinated by this constant choice-making. He was even more intrigued by visible and invisible networks of choice, connection and rejection. He noticed that a person has his own individual criteria for choosing, rejecting or remaining neutral to another person. Moreno developed the science of sociometry to study the circumstances and reasoning that motivate social choice. He further saw sociometry as an opportunity for providing direction in making positive changes in the future based upon what was uncovered through sociometric examination. In *Who Shall Survive?* Moreno (1993) says,

> Sociometry deals with the mathematical study of psychological properties of populations, the experimental technique of and the results obtained by application of quantitative methods. This is undertaken through methods that inquire into the evolution and organization of groups and the position of individuals within them. (p. 51)

Sociometric Instruments: Sociogram and Spectrogram

Moreno developed several measuring instruments to map social choices and interrelationships among people, including the *sociogram,* the *social barometer,* the *spectrogram* and the *social atom.* The sociogram is a graphic representation of the social choices a group has made based upon a particular criterion. For example, a group may be asked, "With whom in the group do you have the most in common?" The sociogram can be written down or offered as an action sociogram. The director asks the group hypothetical questions such as, "Who would you like to accompany you mountain climbing? Who would you ask to help you pick out a wedding present for your fiancée? Whom would you seek out to assist you in setting up a cooperative day care center?"

The action spectrogram is a sociometric device that measures what people "like most" and "like least." It gives the leader and the group a reading of the group's tenor of feeling at a given time. When administering it in action, one end of the room represents "likes most" and the other end represents "likes least." One is to imagine there is a line on the floor that goes from one end of the continuum to the other. The area in between represents gradations of the feelings between the two poles. In a group devoted to exploring the ramifications of technology in everyday life, the director might ask the group questions like. "How do you feel about using cell phones while driving?"

A variation of the spectrogram is the social barometer. This technique focuses on the group's feelings regarding social issues. Once again the continuum line is used, but this time one end represents, "Pro or Yes" while the other end represents "Con or No." The center of the continuum represents "No opinion" or "Undecided." Again, the director calls out questions, but this time the questions are about social issues. For example, "How do you feel about prayer in the schools? Or welfare rights for noncitizens?"

In observing the interaction in the group and listening for the issues, sociodrama directors routinely employs sociometry. They encourage participation from all members of the group and value all contributions to the discussion. Group members see where others stand on certain issues, and lively discussions begin. Each of these sociometric devices mentioned above can serve as an excellent warm-up for a group. From there it becomes obvious which issues the group members are warmed up to and what it is they want to explore in a sociodrama. Sociometric connections build through the enactment and continue to strengthen in the sharing segment of the group experience.

Theory of Spontaneity and Creativity

Moreno developed a theory of *spontaneity* and *creativity* that underlies the practice of sociodrama, the spontaneous enactment of group concerns. Creativity is the seed of the idea, and spontaneity is the get up and go that impels us to actualize the idea and give it life outside the mind. In *Who Shall Survive?* Moreno (1993) postulated that, "There were many more Beethovens born than the one who created the sonatas. However, although they may have had the ideas for a symphony, they did not have the spontaneity to actualize the idea" (p. 39). Thus, spontaneity and creativity are partners in moving us through life. When only one of them is operating, we become stuck. We either have the idea with no push to bring it to action or we are ready to move but cannot think what to do. Sociodrama helps people to gather the forces of spontaneity and creativity to utilize those partners in solving problems and finding new ways to play roles and view situations.

Moreno hypothesized that warm-up and cool down were necessary functions in life. In the morning, the alarm clock rings. As we wake up, we warm up to getting out of bed and begin a longer warm-up to our day by performing our daily wakeup routines.

Many of us do not like it when our warm-up is broken by outside circumstances, as when we reach for the coffee in the cupboard, there is none left, and we need that coffee to wake up fully.

Throughout the day we warm up to various activities and cool down from those activities when they are over. Moreno found the warming-up process to be integral to the spontaneity/creativity cycle. If either our spontaneity or creativity is blocked, we need to warm up to it. For example, a group is questioning how to manage anger. If members have had difficulties with anger management and have become explosive when angry, they may need to warm up to the desire (spontaneity) to handle the situation differently or they may need to generate ideas (creativity) for how to manage their anger differently.

People's reluctance in a group is viewed as connected with the warming up process rather than resistance to doing the work. In sociodrama the concept of resistance has no place. Moreno instead said that the person's warm-up is inadequate. This view takes away the perjorative aspects inherent in the concept of resistance that implies a certain willfulness that may in fact be absent.

The sociodramatist evaluates friction or dysfunction in individuals and groups through testing the sociometry of the group and individual. How do people play the roles they play? What degree of spontaneity and creativity do they display? How warmed up are they to the roles they will play? If they want to make shifts in their behavior, how warmed up are they to doing this? What is the nature of their role relationships with others in the group? How do group members relate to each other in particular circumstances? What interferes with their warm-up if their warm-up is blocked? How warmed up are they to fulfilling the goals of the group?

Sociodrama/Drama Therapy Interface

As the authors think about the similarities and differences between classic drama therapy and sociodrama, the similarities far outweigh the differences. In both sociodrama and many manifestations of current drama therapy, there is enactment of metaphorical, nonprivate materials. People tell their personal stories through metaphor or role rather than directly playing out scenes from their lives. The enactments are issue-focused. The sessions are structured to provide a warming up to action and a cooling down segment with feedback, processing and/or sharing from group members.

The primary differences, as far as we can tell, are the following: In sociodrama, many action intervention techniques have been developed to facilitate the goals of the group, particularly in the warm-up and enactment phases of the session. These intervention strategies and techniques come primarily from Moreno and his followers and grow out of Moreno's theories. In drama therapy, the enactments employ more theatre-based interventions developed by many practitioners from a variety of theoretical frameworks. For example, one aspect of drama therapy is the creation of scripted works and their theatrical production, whereas, in sociodrama, enactments are wholly spontaneous and never scripted. Over the years there has been much crossfertilization between drama therapists, psychodramatists and sociodramatists, so that many drama therapists integrate sociodrama and psychodrama techniques into their work routinely.

THE THERAPEUTIC PROCESS

Every sociodrama session has three components: *the warm-up, the enactment,* and the *sharing.*

Warm-up

The warm-up is the time when group members leave behind their extraneous concerns and focus on what is happening in the group at the time. During the warm-up, issues emerge that the group wishes to explore.

In *Psychodrama: First Volume* Moreno (1985) says,

> This 'warming up' process of an entire group to a reexperience of a perennial social problem unsolvable by conventional means, as newspaper reporting, books, pamphlets, social casework, interviews, religious sermons, and so forth, is opening new roads for social *therapeusis.* It is inherent in the method that all phases of the sociodrama, even the most technical preparatory steps are initiated *within* the group situation and not outside of it. As nothing whatsoever is left out from observation and action, everything which happens is available to research and analysis. (p. 361)

During the warm-up directors are observing connections among group members and the building of connections where they are absent. They are also making interventions to bring in isolated or under-active members. They are listening for issues to which the group is warming up so that they may facilitate the group's exploring these issues later in action. They may help the group to move toward action by creating a structured warm-up or may facilitate group discussion of a topic brought up by a participant (unstructured warm-up).

In the course of the warm-up group members will decide what issue they wish to explore and will decide upon a situation that illuminates that issue. Members volunteer to play roles in the enactment and choose a setting for the first scene. Once this occurs, the session moves to the enactment stage.

The Enactment

The enactment is characterized by the action of the sociodrama. The director readies participants to play their roles by interviewing them in role. The director may also ask group members to contribute suggestions as to how the role should be played. After the enactors have received this warm-up to the specific situation of the drama, they spontaneously interact.

During the enactment directors utilize various techniques to assist the group in accomplishing its goals. If, for example, directors feel the characters need to develop empathy, they may call for a role reversal. Or if they see that several members of the group have suggestions for the enactors regarding how to solve a problem, they may freeze the action, ask the enactors if they would be open to suggestions, and facilitate the interaction between audience and enactors. If group members wish to rehearse behavior, they may take turns, practicing in action, making corrections as they go along. Some examples of this are a group of patients from a day treatment center practicing job interview skills, or a lower functioning population practicing how to give a compliment or make a request for service.

The Sharing

After the enactment is complete, the sharing begins. The director asks the enactors what they were feeling in the role and/or what they learned from playing the role. This serves as an opportunity for the enactors to derole as well to integrate back into the group. During the sharing, group members may express what they felt watching the enactment. Then the director asks them to relate what they learned from the enactment, and to make suggestions for further enactments or the testing of alternate solutions.

The sharing is not a time for criticizing the acting of the enactors in any way, nor is it a time for claiming that the portrayal was not true to life. If the latter occurs, the director may first point out that there are many ways to deal with a situation. Perhaps the dissenting person has a different way of doing so and would like to share it. This makes room for both the enactor's style of relating as well as that of the person criticizing his behavior.

ROLE OF DIRECTOR

Throughout the session the director's role is to assist in the group's warm-up to each other and the issues emerging in the group. The director must ensure a safe, nonjudgmental environment where people can express their thoughts and feelings with impunity, and where they feel comfortable enough to risk new learning. The director facilitates conflict resolution if conflict emerges in the group and to help build positive connections among members. The director needs to be cognizant of sociometry so that they can facilitate group process and move the group toward sociodramatic action that is group-centered and nonpersonal.

Frequently, deep feelings emerge in relation to issues enacted. It is important for the director to remember that all emotions are role related and that it is appropriate for feelings to arise if the chosen issue is affect-laden, as with euthanasia, abortion, and gun control. Ethically, the director needs to uphold the contract and not switch over to psychodrama just because the group members are expressing strong feelings.

The director is also responsible for helping the group achieve its stated goals. In addition to facilitating the action segment of the session the director assists the group in the process of integration of learned material after the drama has ended. As the session draws to a close, the director facilitates the cool down of the group by helping members to share feelings so that they may leave the room in a cognitive place rather than a raw, affective place. (For a lengthier discussion of application of techniques and how to conduct a sociodrama session and master skills, see Sternberg and Garcia's (2000) *Sociodrama: Who's in Your Shoes?*) When observing a skilled facilitator, the modality looks easy. The danger is that someone without training and sufficient knowledge of group dynamics and of her own limits may inflict harm unwittingly on others.

GOALS

Every sociodrama has three goals: catharsis, insight and role training. One or all three of these goals may be achieved through the enactment and/or sharing.

Catharsis

The term *catharsis* comes from the ancient Greek theatre. Aristotle defined the term in his book, *Poetics,* as the purging of the emotions of fear and pity. He used the term to describe the emotions the audience feels when they watch Oedipus Rex blind himself for the sin of marrying his mother and murdering his father. In sociodrama, catharsis can occur both with the enactors participating in the session as well as with the audience observing.

Sometimes catharsis comes as a surprise to the participants who are unaware of their feelings, or who are holding a tight rein on those emotions dealing with a certain issue. The opportunity to express these feelings spontaneously offers an immediate relief to those involved. It also provides an opportunity for a better understanding of the specific emotions brought into play. Therefore, when an enactor expresses his emotions fully and achieves catharsis, he is freed to explore alternative solutions to the situation he faces.

Insight

Everyone has had that feeling of "Oh, now I understand!" That is the experience we call insight. It is that "Aha!" moment, when one understands the full meaning behind what one said or what someone else said. This new understanding usually gives us a different way of viewing or comprehending a problem. In sociodrama, however, because insight occurs with the whole body in action, it tends to be profound and holistic. For example, a student came to the director after a sociodrama in which he played the role of someone who was unheard by a co-worker and did not hear the requests of his co-worker. He said, "Now, I know how my wife feels when I say I have to go out with the guys. We're not really communicating with each other." Prior to this, they had simply tried to convince each other that each was right in his or her request, but they were not really listening to what the other was saying and meaning. As a result of his insight, he reported that he was able to tell to his wife how he felt about spending time with his friends who go out on Friday nights. It had nothing to do with her or with looking for women. "It's a thing with the guys," he said. When he went on to explain, she understood his need to spend time with his old friends, and he came to understand her need for companionship. They compromised and found ways to accommodate both their needs.

Role Training

Role training is a rehearsal for future life situations. We all practice role training in our heads. We say to ourselves, "I'll say this, then he'll answer with. . . . Then I'll say. . . ." We all feel a need to try out new behaviors and practice our actions before we encounter new or unfamiliar situations. But many of us do not have the option of practicing before stepping into a new environment. Moreno felt we should have that chance.

He advocated role training as a way of providing an opportunity for people to try on new roles and situations in a safe environment. Since sociodrama recreates those feelings and emotional reactions that occur in real life situations, role training offers a way to practice a variety of behaviors to meet any given situation. With the help of other group members, trainees can receive feedback on which areas of their behavior are most effective, or which action solves the problem most effectively. They can replay their actions until they feel comfortable in their role and confident that they are ready to meet whatever challenges come their way. Simply put, role training offers a rehearsal for life situations, for the desired behavior or action one chooses.

Role training in sociodrama serves many purposes, from rehearsing for job interviews to dealing with a bomb threat in crisis intervention training. Most employee orientation classes use role training especially in those areas of the job where an employee has to deal with the public. Recognizing potential problems, difficult situations, and typical client questions can go a long way in creating confidence in the new employees.

While sociodrama can be and is used in psychotherapy, it can also be utilized in many other venues. Moreno considered sociodrama to be more of a socio-therapeutic than a psychotherapeutic modality because sociodrama helps to heal the rifts between and among people not merely in the psychotherapy office but in other settings in the community as well. He felt that as sociodrama focuses on group issues rather than personal ones, it can be used anywhere with positive results.

TECHNIQUES

Sociodrama and psychodrama share techniques although there are some differences in their uses.

Role Reversal

The concept of role reversal derives from perhaps the most brilliant of Moreno's observations. He recognized that most humans over the age of seven are capable of figuratively putting themselves in someone else's shoes and imagining what the other feels like in a given situation. People do this inside their heads all the time and request that others do it too: "Put yourself in my place. How do you think I feel?" What is especially noteworthy is that it occurred to Moreno that if one could reverse roles in one's mind and gain new understanding and empathy, much more could be gained by asking people to actually change physical places and their roles with each other.

As it turns out, the result of external role reversal (as opposed to that done in the mind) is profound. When enactors reverse roles, they see the world from the perspective of the other person. They can develop empathy and understanding by seeing themselves as others see them. After a sociodrama in which enactors have experienced role reversal, they routinely report that they gained new realizations, a broadening of understanding of others, a new compassion for others' behaviors and a new tolerance for others' viewpoints. They also say that they were able to see a problem in a new light and from the perspective of the other role could generate new solutions.

When the director calls for a role reversal, two enactors switch places and exchange roles. This shift in space is essential to achieve the full benefits of the technique.

Enactor A says, "You never listen to me." The director says, "Reverse roles." After enactors A and B have reversed, the director instructs B to repeat the last line before the reversal. Enactor B (in A's role) says, "You never listen to me." This repetition of the last line is important because it picks up the action where it left off. It also offers the enactor who is speaking an anchoring in the new role. Further, it re-anchors the audience and reminds them that Enactor A is playing B's role and vice versa.

Some of the reasons a director will use role reversal are:

- To increase understanding
- To develop empathy
- To facilitate insight
- To shift perspective
- To help the enactor see self in role as others see him or her
- To facilitate cool down if the enactor is overly engaged in role
- To increase spontaneity

A director may call for role reversal many times in a sociodrama. It should be mentioned that at the end of an enactment, enactors must be back in their original roles.

The Double

The concept of the Double also derives from Moreno's observation of the way the human mind works. There are many times in life when we are conversing with someone and saying one thing while feeling another. We tell our boss, "Sure I do not mind staying late at work tonight," when we feel, "I'm exhausted! This is the third time in two weeks he asked me to stay late. How annoying!" Or we may say to our friend, "I really like you," when we feel, "I love you and want a more committed relationship."

Everyone has an inner voice. Moreno chose to invent a technique, the Double, that is designed to externalize that voice so that everyone can hear it in a sociodrama. The Double expresses the unexpressed thoughts and feelings of an enactor. The director or any member of the group can act as a Double for an enactor. In order to double, the person doubling stands to the side of and slightly behind the enactor in the drama. The Double speaks the unspoken, and the enactor repeats what was said if it correctly reflects their feelings or corrects it if the expression is inaccurate. Although everyone in the drama can hear what is said by the Double, it is a sociodramatic convention that one responds solely to the enactor who has repeated or corrected the Double's statement. If you have several enactors and a few people doubling it becomes chaotic if everyone is responding to everyone else.

Sometimes a permanent Double is assigned to an enactor as in a sociodrama about what a shy person experiences at a party where they do not know anyone. Sometimes there are several permanent Doubles who interact with the main enactor as in a sociodrama in which a student is torn between one part that wants to quit school and get a job; another part that wants to stay in college; and another part that wants to live in the wilderness. Each of the enactors playing the interior roles is a Double.

The Double has several functions:

- To offer support
- To verbalize nonverbal gestures, movements, and sounds
- To maximize the feelings expressed by the enactor
- To question the self
- To make self observations
- To provide sentence stems (I feel –) that the enactor can complete (as appropriate)

Aside

This term comes directly from the theatre and is performed by an enactor in the same way that an actor in a play does it. When enactors are thinking or feeling something that they want to acknowledge but do not want to say directly to the other person in the enactment, they turn to the side and speak, often starting with, "I would not tell her this, but . . ." The other enactor is to ignore the aside as if they never heard it being spoken.

Soliloquy

This term also comes from the theatre. The soliloquy is essentially a monologue in which an enactor speaks aloud thoughts and feelings at some length. The soliloquy is sometimes used if the enactor seems confused, overwhelmed or stuck. The director may freeze the scene and ask the enactor to step out of the scene for a moment and talk about how they are feeling and how they view what is happening in the drama. The director may also ask the enactor to brainstorm aloud some solutions if the enactment is problem-focused. After the soliloquy the protagonist returns to the drama. In a drama about a family in denial about the mother's alcohol relapse, a teenager confronts the problem by challenging the mother about her drinking. An argument ensues with other family members supporting the mother and shouting down the teen. The director freezes the scene and takes each member of the family out of the drama one at a time to soliloquize about feelings and figure out what to do. After all soliloquies are complete, the action resumes.

Walk and Talk

In this technique, the director walks around the stage with the enactors one at a time and discusses with them the parameters of the roles they are to play. This helps the enactors to warm up to the roles, to develop the roles and to discuss the issues of the drama as the group wishes to explore them. For example, the director may ask the enactor playing the new employee how glad they are to be working for the company and how they like their co-workers. If the group defined the issue as how to cope with sexual harassment, the director may also ask how they felt when the supervisor asked them out for a drink after work.

The *Walk and Talk* most often occurs at the beginning of a drama, but it can also occur in the middle of the drama if the enactor loses spontaneity and gets stuck, overwhelmed or confused. The director takes the person out of the scene and walks and talks with them about the situation. If the enactor wants assistance from the group, the director may ask audience members to make suggestions for handling the problem in the scene. If the enactor playing the new employee cannot figure out how to deal with the supervisor's advances, they may walk and talk with the director, ask for and receive suggestions from the audience. When spontaneity is restored and the enactor decides what they want to do, they return to the scene.

The Walk and Talk is also useful in conflict situations in which enactors are getting overheated. Freezing the action and taking the enactors out for a minute gives them a chance to cool down and reflect on the triggers of their emotional reactions as well as to find new and more satisfactory approaches to the situation.

Empty Chair

A chair is put before the group or an enactor, who are asked to imagine that someone or some abstract quality is in the chair. Group members are then instructed to speak to whomever or whatever is occupying the chair. For example, Benjamin Franklin is in the chair. The director may instruct the group to say something to him or to step in and occupy the chair for a moment and speak to the group from the role about what it was like to be a great inventor and great wit. One can also put an emotion in the chair (anger) or an abstraction (alcoholism).

Freeze Frame

This term comes from film vocabulary, meaning to stop the action of a single frame on the screen. In sociodrama there are times when one wants to stop the action and view it as a tableau. The facilitator calls, "Freeze!" and the enactors do just that. This technique is used for a variety of situations. The director may want to take an enactor out of the scene in order to use additional techniques such as Soliloquy or Walk and Talk. Perhaps the structure of the action is lost because there are too many people in the scene all talking at once. One can freeze an area of the group and focus the action on another or call for a freeze and elicit audience reaction to the scene. "What do you see happening in this scene? What can they do to make things better?" It is important to remind the audience that this is not a time to judge or analyze the acting of the participants but simply to observe and discuss the situation.

Concretization

A concretization is a literal portrayal of figurative or symbolic language or feelings. Often the director notices a physical response to something that is occurring in the sociodrama and asks the enactors to concretize the feelings they are experiencing. For example, if in a sociodrama Maria says, "I feel like I'm being pulled in two different directions," the director can ask two other enactors to take hold of Maria's arms and each pull her in opposite directions. Therefore, the statement of being pulled in two different directions becomes literally true and is made concrete by the action.

Sculpting

This term describes a living tableau scene. It is a kind of concretization of interrelationships. In a work-related sociodrama, Nick volunteers to be the manager, and Sally says she will play his overworked secretary. Jerry will be the desk clerk and Donna volunteers to be his assistant, who feels she is experiencing gender discrimination from the manager. Each takes a position in the tableau. As a further warm-up for the enactors in their roles, the director asks each enactor to sculpt his co-workers in relation to themselves, placing each of the others in a position that symbolizes how they feel about the relationships. Donna places Nick very far away from her, while Nick places Donna on her knees next to Sally. Sally turns her back on them both, and Jerry places himself close to the manager.

Another use of sculpting is to stop the action when the enactors seem stuck or appear to have lost their spontaneity. The facilitator asks the enactors to sculpt the scene as it feels to them, or how they perceive the relationships or the emotional tone occurring in the scene.

Sculpting is also useful in setting up a sociodrama in which internal voices or parts of the self are present, such as the studious self, the lazy self, the enthusiastic self, the stressed self. The enactors playing the internal roles can position themselves in relation to the enactor playing the role of the external person. Emunah (1994, 1999) further developed this technique in drama therapy as "Self-Sculptures."

Mirror

The mirror is used to show enactors how they look and sound to others. A player comes into the action and takes the enactor's place, mirroring the enactor's verbal and nonverbal communication. The enactor steps out of the action and observes how the other player looks and sounds to others. This gives the enactor the opportunity to figure out what is going on in the situation and what to do next.

Additionally, if enactors display an especially revealing body position, the director can take them out, and ask for a volunteer to assume that posture. The enactors are asked what they observe and how they interpret the body language. A word of caution when using this technique: direct the mirror to take the role of the enactor accurately and without stereotype, so that the enactor does not feel mocked or judged.

Future Projection

This technique takes the action to a future scene. This may be a scene in which the enactors play out their projection of what would happen if they were to continue on the same course in a conflictual situation or their fantasy of an ideal ending to the conflict. This gives them the opportunity to try out the scene the way they hope it will happen or wish for. This is akin to Pam Dunne's "Narradrama" (Chapter 9) in its emphasis on creating positive outcomes and wished-for scenarios. It also offers the opportunity to play the scene in a way they fear it may happen, so they can respond in an appropriate manner.

For example, in a sociodrama regarding poor safety conditions in a work environment, Michael enacts a future projection in which he playfully approaches his boss about instituting the new safety rules in the workplace. He then returns to the present scene, and practices other methods of encountering his boss about his concerns. Although the final action ends the way Michael hopes for, he had to overcome several obstacles put in his path by the enactor playing the boss in order to make a case for the value of the new rules. In this instance, future projection stimulated role training.

POPULATIONS SERVED

Because of the nonpersonal nature of sociodrama, it is suitable for virtually any group. What is wonderful about sociodrama is that it can go just about anywhere since the focus is on group issues and common concerns rather than one person's story. It is appropriate as a modality for business, schools, churches and synagogues, psychotherapy, and for the community. It works well with both high and low functioning people, including the developmentally disabled, and people without vision or hearing, and those without speech or mobility (see Case Examples). For a lengthier discussion of sociodrama usages by leaders from around the world, see Sternberg and Garcia (2000).

LIMITATIONS, CHALLENGES, AND GROWING EDGE

Sociodrama is by nature a group modality and is seldom done with individuals. At the other end of the spectrum it is challenging to find ways to manage extremely large groups in facilitating sociodrama. The logistics present a problem in mobilizing the entire group in an organized fashion.

It is our belief that the sociotherapeutic aspects of sociodrama will become particular areas of growth and study in the next decade. For example, the authors believe that sociodrama will become a staple intervention in conflict resolution programs. It will find greater usage in the training of trial lawyers (Leach, 2003), labor negotiators, managers and executives. While David Swink has been using sociodrama for years in the training of corporate executives and staff (Sternberg & Garcia, 2000), the authors believe this is a fertile field for future sociodramatists to pursue. More problem-solving skills groups will utilize sociodramatic techniques and more community-based groups will employ sociodrama to enhance positive connections among diverse people. For example, Mario Cossa (2003) utilizes sociodrama with teens as a way of helping them resolve conflict, improve social skills and increase tolerance of differences.

CASE EXAMPLES

Example One: Aphasia Group

Aphasia is a disorder in which a person is unable to understand and use the symbols that comprise language. It may occur as a result of a traumatic head injury, a cerebrovascular accident, or from some other brain disorder. Whether because of stroke, encephalitis, head injury, or surgical accident, patients who have lost their use of speech find themselves isolated. They are incapable of communicating in ways that were previously commonplace.

In addition to loss of speech, many aphasics experience other concomitant disabilities, such as paralysis of one side of the body or spasticity. Their inability to use both hands in addition to their difficulty in understanding language symbols makes it hard to teach them traditional sign language. Aphasics who are in long-term treatment facilities tend to interact primarily with staff. Interactions with other patients often seem to be minimal.

Adult aphasics, because of their communication problems, tend to be treated individually or allowed to passively participate in a group setting. While individual treatment is appropriate for redevelopment of speech skills and physical therapy, group-oriented approaches provide an opportunity to reduce feelings of isolation, helplessness, and withdrawal, while improving communication skills. The question is how to implement group sessions with people who cannot speak.

The Director of Occupational Therapy at a local hospital had some acquaintance with the value of sociodrama in improving communication skills and interpersonal competence. She approached the author (AG) to work with a group of aphasic patients who were long-term residents at this public hospital that housed people who were chronically physically ill. Most patients were elderly or confined to wheelchairs and had multiple disabilities.

The occupational therapy director and the author organized a group that was composed of aphasic patients, relatives of patients, and staff members. It was felt that staff members' presence was essential, since the entire patient population of the group was confined to wheelchairs, and except for one, the patients were incapable of moving their own chairs because of paralysis of a least one arm. The staff, in short, could move the chairs during exercises and enactments. The OT director and the author (who led the group) also felt that staff members could provide verbal doubling and sharing, thus increasing the chances for group cohesion. Further, they could potentially take information about the aphasic patients' newly learned communication skills back to the rest of the staff.

Prior to the first session with patients, the author led two in-service sociodrama training sessions with hospital staff, doctors, nurses, occupational therapists, and medical technicians. These sessions were designed to acquaint the participants with basic sociodrama techniques so they could easily double for the patients and take roles if called upon to do so. The goals of the group were to improve communications skills, promote patient interaction and venting, to train spontaneity, and to improve patient/patient and patient/staff relations.

Content of the Sessions

At the first session, everyone was given a 4″ x 6″ matte board name card and a choice of a colored felt tip pen. The leader asked the patients to choose a color that represented how they felt that day. Then she asked them to draw a picture or make lines or shapes that represented how they would like to be seen by the group. There was space on the cards for a drawing. After the drawings were completed, the leader walked around the circle, showing the first, which was a flower. Some members responded with sounds, gestures, and showing of cards to indicate that they, too, had drawn flowers. Someone suggested arranging the flowers on the floor in a circle. Next came abstracts; those were arranged as leaves. There were also human shapes, a tree and a butterfly to be fitted into the picture. Finally, the picture of a sun shining over all, and the group had begun the making of sociometric connections. To further feelings of connection, the leader asked the members to make gestures expressing how they felt. She asked the other members to mirror the gestures. Later, members spontaneously added sounds to accompany the gestures and worked on changing the gestures and accompanying facial expressions to indicate various nuances of feeling.

In subsequent sessions patients continued to express, mirror, and double each other's feelings. As was mentioned earlier, chronic aphasics are thought to be unable to learn sign language because of their difficulty in symbolizing language. Also, most of the patients in the group had use of only one hand. Some also had impaired body image. Thus, if the leader said, "Put your hand on your chest," a patient might touch his leg. Nevertheless, since patients did seem to be able to be expressive through gesture, the leader sought to devise simple signs that the patients could learn and that could be understood and responded to in the closed system of the hospital.

After teaching the patients a sign for, "How do you feel?" the group divided into dyads to ask the question of a person whom they wanted to know better. They took in their partner's response, mirrored it and represented their partner's response to the whole group when the group reformed after the exercise. In later sessions, patients developed other signs to express feelings, (e.g., I'm sad, I'm happy; I'm hungry; I'm sleepy), and finally developed a complete sign exchange: "Please give me a blanket which is over there. Thank you." Patients readily expressed negative as well as positive feelings and expressed relief at having an accepting forum for presenting themselves honestly in the moment.

Many of the sociodramas dealt with hospital issues. In every instance group members chose the subject for and parameters of the enactment: dealing with a noisy neighbor, making clear your need to use the lavatory and convincing staff to take you there; dealing with hospital administration relative to room changes; getting the love and support you need in a hospital. Role reversals were particularly helpful when the participants were role training how to interact with staff and other patients. While the content was nonpersonal, the role reversals helped participants to experience what it was like to be in the role of the other, and to begin to understand what others might feel, want and need. At holiday time, there was a sociodrama of a family meal set in the past: patients enacted both a noisy family and a quiet family.

One of the group's and the leader's favorite sociodramas took place when it was snowing outside. As everyone watched the ground grow whiter, people began to remember snowfalls of their childhood. The group decided to enact a drama about playing in the snow. Sessions were held in a large space with large windows. All the patients were in wheelchairs. They designated one end of the room for the top of a hill. With wheelchairs as sleds and staff as wind to help push the sleds, the patients zoomed across the room, shouting, laughing, talking, and holding on for dear life. They made snowballs and had a snowball fight and made a snowman. By the end of the sociodrama, their cheeks were as rosy as if they had actually been outside in the falling snow. What fun!

Throughout the group's life, doubling was essential for adequate functioning. The leader and group members with any measure of speech doubled in all segments of the session. The members without words doubled nonverbally or through sound production. Those members who were doubled made very clear when they were doubled accurately and when they were not.

As the weeks went on, patients began to bring issues to the group that they wanted to work on. For example, the room change and family sociodramas were ones introduced by two patients who haltingly spoke and repeated, respectively, "Move me," and "Go home!"

During the last two of the seven weeks the group met, the members dealt with termination issues. They reviewed signs they had learned, expressed their feelings regarding what the group meant to them, what they had learned, what sociometric connections they had made, what surprised them about belonging to the group, what expectations were met and unmet and how the members felt about the group's concluding.

Staff and group members reported that the group had been useful in decreasing feelings of isolation among the patients. This was further evidenced by patients going out of their way to greet each other and wait for a response, and by their gestures and sounds during sessions indicating that they felt the same as another patient in a given situation. This was in direct contrast to the beginning of the group life when patients related solely to staff. Staff and participants noticed an increase in the repertoire of communication skills used by the patients. They also felt the sessions provided an opportunity for a safe and supportive environment in which to express feelings.

Example Two: Health Care Professional Group

The following example was conducted at a large metropolitan teaching hospital. There were 12 health care professionals who participated in the sociodrama group. However, the number at each session averaged between 8 and 10, since not all participants were able to leave their units during the time scheduled for the group.

Eight nurses, two male therapists, and two female administrators made up the group. Only six of the participants attended every session; eight attended three; ten attended two; and one attended only the initial session. The group met once a week for five weeks for two hours each session.

The sociodramatist (PS) met with the supervisor first for an initial meeting to discuss her needs and the needs of group before the sessions started and once again for an evaluation after the five sessions were completed. At that time there was a verbal assessment of the value of this type of training.

The sessions scored exceptionally high and sociodrama was rated as one of the best instructional tools the hospital had ever employed. This assessment ranked sociodrama highly successful both from the attendees' point of view and the supervisor's. In the weeks that followed, feedback from the attending physicians further reinforced the positive value of the sociodrama experience for the participants. Doctors reported that nursing support to patients and their families had dramatically increased the comfort level on the unit.

Background and Brief Overview of the Sessions

The supervisor of nurses in a large metropolitan teaching hospital became concerned about the young nurses in training there. Those that worked on the oncology unit with young children were especially vulnerable to their own emotional reactions. Very often, talking to the parents or siblings of these young children was even harder than dealing with the patients. The times that were especially difficult for the student nurses were when the first cancer diagnosis was given or the estimated length of life left was first discussed with the families. That was the moment when everyone had to face the reality of a dying child.

The supervisor was pleased that her young charges were showing so much empathy for their patients and their families, but she was also fearful that they were becoming too emotionally involved to function as a source of strength in the situation. She knew from experience that one had to maintain a professional demeanor even when she felt like crying herself.

This balance between empathy and professionalism was vital for a nurse to be able to do her job on the unit adequately. Frequently, the nurse was the one who was in attendance after the doctor had broken the news to the family. She had to offer both sympathy and courage to the family members and frequently a shoulder to cry on. In order to do that, these nurses had to learn to put their own feelings on hold, while assisting others with their grief and/or denial. Nurses had to be strong enough to offer as much support as possible in the situation. Although the main purpose was to help the young nurses deal with the feelings mentioned above, several of the other staff members, including some older nurses, chose to participate also.

The first sociodrama the group chose to enact was set up primarily to offer role training, but a great deal of catharsis and insight occurred as well. During the sharing that first day, a question came up that was quickly echoed by several members of the group: "What do I say when a child asks me, 'Am I dying?' I know the old line that says, 'We're all dying,' but that's no answer. What do I say?" This question prompted a great deal of discussion among the group. Some answers given were: "No one can be sure of that;" "We're trying as hard as we can to keep you with us for as long as possible;" "The doctors and scientists are coming up with new drugs and treatments everyday. They may find one tomorrow for you too."

One insightful moment occurred during the next sociodrama session when one of the older male nurses played a young patient. "I do not want everyone walking around here like death warmed over," he said. "I know I'm going to die, but can't we do something with the days I have left?" In the sharing the nurse explained that he'd heard those lines or similar ones frequently over the years. "And they want to talk about it–about dying," he added. "They ask questions like, 'What happens when you go to heaven? How do you feel when you die?'"

One of the therapists agreed that he too had heard those kinds of questions often from children on that unit. "Sometimes I think it's harder for us to talk about it than it is for them. They need to see we're not afraid to talk about it." Thanks to his comments, one of the young nurses had a new insight: "I never thought about it that way. I guess talking about the unknown makes it easier."

The third and fourth day's sociodramas moved in the direction of dealing with the families of the patients. One of the young nurses played a distraught mother. She adamantly denied that there was anything wrong with her child. "It's all a mistake," she said over and over again. When feelings were discussed later, everyone thought she was probably a mother herself. "I'm not yet," she said, "But I certainly felt like it in the sociodrama. It's amazing how you have all those real feelings when you are in a role."

Each succeeding day brought greater depth to the work and greater understanding among the participants. At the fifth and last session, one of the young nurses volunteered to be the one to break the news to a young mother in a sociodrama. She handled it with such compassion and strength that after it was all over, during the sharing, one of the older nurses told her that she had handled the situation much more sensitively than many of those who had done it for years. "I really feel like I have gained tremendous insight into my own feelings and those of others," the young nurse said. "We are all so much alike and have so much in common."

CONCLUSION

Sociodramas have been enacted for almost a century in such places as theaters, civic auditoriums, schools, religious venues, corporate headquarters, agencies and on street corners. Sociodrama works with small groups or large. It is a vital method designed to help people learn life skills and social skills through action. It can also facilitate the exploration of sociopolitical and moral issues that face us as members of the human community. Moreno's method anticipated by many decades the current interest in addressing social problems through role-play and dramatic means.

REFERENCES

Condon, L. (2007). Bibliodrama: Exploring the written word through action. In A. Blatner (Ed.), *Interactive and improvisational drama* (pp. 13–22). Lincoln, NE: iUniverse.

Cossa, M. (2003). Taming puberty: Using psychodrama, sociodrama, and sociometry with adolescent groups. In J. Gershoni (Ed.), *Psychodrama in the 21st century* (pp. 135–150). New York: Springer Publishing Company.

Emunah, R. (1994). *Acting for real.* New York: Brunner/Mazel.

Emunah, R. (1999). Drama therapy in action. In D. Wiener (Ed.) *Beyond talk therapy: Using movement and expressive techniques in clinical practice* (pp. 99–124). Washington, D.C.: American Psychological Association.

Fox, J. (Ed.). (1987). *The essential Moreno.* New York: Springer.

Fox, J. (1994). *Acts of service: Spontaneity, commitment, tradition in the nonscripted theatre.* New Paltz, NY: Tusitala Publishing.

Leach, J.D. (2003). Psychodrama and justice: training trial lawyers. In J. Gershoni (Ed.), *Psychodrama in the 21st century* (pp. 249–264). New York: Springer Publishing Company.

Moreno, J.L. (1985). *Psychodrama: First Volume.* Ambler, PA: Beacon House, Inc.

Moreno, J.L. (1947). *The future of man's world. Psychodrama, monograph 21.* New York: Beacon.

Moreno, J.L. (1993). *Who shall survive?* (Student Edition). Roanoke, VA: Royal Publishing Co.

Pitzele, P. (1998). *Scripture windows: Toward a practice of bibliodrama.* Los Angeles: Torah Aura Productions.

Sternberg, P. (1998). *Theatre for conflict resolution: In the classroom and beyond.* Portsmouth, NH: Heinemann.

Sternberg, P., & Garcia, A. (2000). *Sociodrama: Who's in your shoes?* 2nd ed. Westport, CT: Praeger.

FURTHER TRAINING

American Board of Examiners in Psychodrama, Sociometry and Group Psychotherapy
Website: www.psychodramacertification.org
Email: abepsychodrama@yahoo.com

Chapter 20

PLAYBACK THEATRE: A FRAME FOR HEALING

Jo Salas

GENESIS

Playback Theatre began in 1975 with Jonathan Fox's vision of a theatre in which ordinary people acted out the stories of their community (Fox, 1994). His vision combined aspects of tribal ritual–people whose lives are intertwined in everyday life coming together to celebrate, explore or heal through ceremonial and artistic action–and storytelling, an oral tradition in which wisdom and truth are embedded in *stories* told aloud. Jonathan was also inspired by Moreno's "Psychodrama" (Chapter 18), a therapeutic approach that draws its strength from the body-and-soul involvement not only of the protagonist but of the group.

Jonathan and others, including myself, spent several years developing a viable form for this vision (Salas, 1993). The idea eventually spread internationally: there are currently 200 registered groups in over 55 countries, doing Playback in many different settings. To this day Playback Theatre challenges the customary divisions of our society. It is theatre with the power and intention to heal and transform individuals and social groups. Playback's attention to process, to inclusivity, to the well-being of the performers as well as the audience distinguishes it from more familiar forms of theatre in which the artistic success of the production is the only thing that matters. On the other hand, its commitment to aesthetics places it firmly in the realm of art.

So Playback Theatre is not primarily a therapy, but a versatile theatrical form that is equally at home in public theatres, in schools, hospitals, and institutions, corporate settings and conferences, and in forums for social change–on the streets of southern India with Dalit people telling stories about police brutality, or at an outdoor community event exploring diversity in a small American town.

At the same time, since Playback's early years, drama therapists and psychodramatists have recognized Playback Theatre's potential as a therapeutic approach. There has been a rich cross-fertilization between Playback Theatre and therapy: many Playback practitioners are also trained as therapists, usually drama therapists, psychodramatists, or creative arts therapists.

They use Playback in their clinical work with trauma survivors, couples and families, adolescents, people in recovery from addictions, and other populations.

My own experience using Playback Theatre therapeutically has been with severely emotionally disturbed children ages 5 to 14, and it is this application that I will be describing in this chapter (Salas, 1994; 2007). Working as a music therapist at a residential treatment facility, I trained a group of staff members in Playback Theatre. We formed an in-house company, performing every month or two for groups of children. Later, hoping to give children the additional therapeutic benefits of acting as well as telling stories, I co-led (with a member of the staff Playback group) Playback Theatre therapy groups, with groups of four or five children meeting weekly for six sessions.

THERAPEUTIC PROCESS

In a cleared space–a stage, or one end of a large room–two chairs are set up on the side, facing the empty space. The chair nearest the audience is for the *Conductor,* Playback's onstage director or emcee. Across the back of the stage area, four or five actors sit on crates, boxes, or chairs. A musician with instruments is positioned further to the side, opposite the Conductor. Upstage, there is a collection of large fabric pieces for the actors to use as elemental costumes or props.

The Conductor invites someone from the audience to come and tell a story. Seated beside the *Teller,* the Conductor asks questions to find out what happened, who was there, how did it end–all from the Teller's point of view. The Conductor asks the Teller to choose actors to play the key roles, starting with the Teller herself. The actors stand up as they are chosen, not acting yet but preparing inwardly as they listen to the rest of the story.

The interview ends and the Conductor hands the story over to the actors with an injunction: "Let's watch!" As music plays, the actors silently position themselves for the opening of the scene. There is no discussion. The actors act out the story as accurately and creatively as they can. The Teller and Conductor watch from the side. When the scene is over, the actors pause in place, looking toward the Teller. The Conductor invites the Teller to comment, or perhaps just to pause before returning to the audience.

If the enactment was not true enough to the essence of the story to satisfy the Teller, the Conductor may ask the actors to redo some or all of it, incorporating the Teller's corrections. Occasionally, with a story that has been accurately portrayed but has left the Teller troubled, the conductor may invite him to imagine a new outcome, which the actors bring to life–a *transformation,* as it is termed in Playback Theatre. Another Teller comes to the chair, and the process continues.

This is how Playback looks in a performance context, with a trained company of performers and a defined audience. In my work with children in residential treatment, it was *performance Playback* that we began with–the children were audience and Tellers, not actors. But Playback Theatre may also follow a workshop model in which one or two experienced Playback leaders guide participants in enacting stories for each other: everyone has the chance to become an actor. The basic format remains the same, but without the emphasis on artistic competence that is required for public performance.

Workshop-model Playback is most often used in therapy. The therapy groups at my institution followed this model, with the children taking turns acting for each other as well as telling stories. (In both models, Playback includes a variety of "short forms"–briefer structures for responding to a Teller's experience or feeling.)

BASIC CONCEPTS

Playback Theatre is based on a constellation of beliefs and values. Practitioners generally share the following convictions:

- The characteristics of both a fully-realized human being and of an ideal culture include the capacity for connection with others, compassion, and creativity.
- People need stories in order to know who we are as individuals and as a society. The stories we tell of ourselves and our world crystallize and communicate social and personal self-knowledge.
- Personal stories hold wisdom and beauty for others, including strangers.
- Witnessing each others' stories fosters understanding and empathy.
- All human experience, including extreme suffering, finds meaning when it is communicated in aesthetic form.
- The connection that arises from sharing personal stories is a counterforce to increasing isolation and alienation.
- Given the right context, all people have the innate capacity and spontaneity to respond with empathic creativity to another person's story.

HEALING EFFECTS

These convictions have clear implications for Playback as a broadly healing experience in both performance and nonperformance settings. It is my observation that taking part in a Playback Theatre event creates movement toward wholeness for individuals and groups as they tell, hear, and watch stories about what is significant in their own and others' lives (Hoesch, 1999). This movement is apparent in the comments of Tellers about the lasting meaning and change that came from telling their stories; in the visibly empathic response of audience members as they watch and listen; and in the common Playback phenomenon of audience members–strangers two hours before–lingering to talk to each other and to the performers after a show.

In addition, there are a number of specific effects for the storytellers: the profound affirmation and validation of having your story enacted according to your subjective perception; the certainty that you have been fully heard by performers and audience; the relief from aloneness that comes with bearing witness in a public or semipublic setting; the sense of distance or mastery in relation to a difficult past experience; new perspective or insight into a life situation and the catharsis of laughter or tears.

For the people who enact the stories, whether they are members of a company or a group doing workshop-model Playback, Playback's intrinsic healing effects go further. Taking active part as an actor helps to develop spontaneity (in the Morenean sense of having full access to all one's resources). It also promotes expressiveness, receptiveness to others, self-confidence, self-esteem, creativity, teamwork, playfulness, and the capacity for aesthetic mastery and pleasure.

Two further healing aspects of Playback are profound and pervasive: one is the atmosphere of respect and acceptance that is fundamental to any Playback event. The other is the presence of ritual, by which I mean the establishment of a ceremonial frame in space (the simple but formal arrangement of the stage), time (the protocols of eliciting and enacting a story), and demeanor (the attentiveness of the actors, the inspired leadership of the Conductor), in which the stories of ordinary people are told and remembered.

PLAYBACK AS A DRAMA THERAPY METHOD

It is a natural step to go from the inherent healing effects in Playback Theatre to the use of Playback in clinical contexts. Most mental health clients are people who can clearly benefit from Playback's capacities to affirm subjective perception and experience, strengthen identity, increase awareness and compassion, express emotion, and respond creatively to the expressions of others.

A therapist integrating Playback into clinical practice will make choices about which particular aspects are most helpful and suitable for her clients. She may also need to modify or simplify Playback's structures according to client needs and capacities, as well as practical considerations such as limitations of time and space, and the availability of co-leaders.

When I first decided to bring Playback Theatre into the Neville School (name is fictional), my intention was to give the children a chance to tell their stories–to provide Playback's accessible stage as a forum where they could speak and be heard. I knew that they had remarkable stories to tell, that they were full of lively responses to the world around them, and that in the rough-and-tumble of institutional life there were few opportunities for them to be heard other than in one-on-one therapy sessions. I thought that the ritual of Playback might prove a strong enough frame–even in this environment–for the children to bear witness in front of their peers.

After I had taught the staff group enough of the basics of Playback, we began with after-school performances in the gym for groups of about 15 children, the maximum number we thought we could manage successfully. Soon, teachers in the Neville's school invited us to do shows in their small classrooms. Although our performances followed the traditional Playback format, we learned quickly which aspects needed adapting or emphasizing. We found that the children responded better to enactments that were literal and concrete rather than metaphorical. The Playback form called *Pairs,* in which actors portray the struggle between two feelings at the same time, required so much explanation that we stopped using it, realizing that its demand for emotional self-awareness was beyond the reach of most of the children. Special attention to openings and endings was needed: we sang with the children at the beginning to settle them into receptiveness and keep them occupied as latecomers straggled in. As the show ended we allowed time for verbal sharing, more singing, or art activities. More children wanted to be Tellers than we had time for, and our closing activities gave the disappointed ones a chance to express a small part of the story they had not told.

In spite of occasional frustration over not telling their stories, the performances brought joy to the children–a healing effect in itself. They were happy to come to the shows and thought of them as a pleasurable activity whether after school or during the school day.

Examples

In one classroom performance, six-year-old Courtney told a nightmare about a witch who came to her while she was asleep and put horrible stuff on her nails and pricked her skin.

"What was the scariest thing, Courtney?"

"I'm scared I'll be like the witch."

During the enactment she yelled at the

witch–"I'm over here!" I reminded her that Diane, the actor she had chosen, was being Courtney in the story, that she herself was just watching. She was very excited. I held her closely on my knee. When it was over, I asked her if she would like to make up a different ending for her story. It was at first hard for her to understand the possibility I was offering. Then she got it. Her eyes lit up. "I want to kill the witch, and I want my mom to hug me and say 'Good girl.'" With satisfaction she watched this amended scenario acted out.

Gary, who had been full of scathing complaints earlier, wanted to be the next Teller. But when he came to the chair, he did not have a story. It was not unusual for children to long for the experience of being a Teller while being not at all clear about what they wanted to tell. It was our job to find a story, however minimal, in whatever elements they could offer.

"Who's someone who might be in your story?" I asked Gary.

"My grandma," he responded immediately. I had heard that Gary's grandmother had died recently after a long illness. Soon a story emerged about the time she had entrusted him and his brother to go to the store for her. "She wasn't sick, she just too busy. We got everything and we gave her some change and she was real pleased."

As we acted out the story, Gary called out additional details from the side as he remembered them. "She wanted *soup!*" he yelled. Without missing a beat, the Teller's actor added soup to the grocery items he was putting in his imaginary basket.

"Thank you for telling us about your grandma, Gary," I said when the scene was over.

"Thank you for acting my story," he said, peaceful and gracious.

In another school experience, we met in the staff library to do a show for Leah's class. They were all about eight or nine years old, though, like most of the Neville kids, they seemed far younger than their chronological age. The library, used less for reading than for staff meetings or occasional events for the children, was a cozy book-lined room with a long and massive table occupying most of the floor space. We moved things around as best we could to clear a stage area at one end of the room.

Ernestine's hand shot up as soon as I asked for a story, but I passed over her to Omar, whose hand was up as well. I was remembering an earlier time when Ernestine had been the Teller. An angular little girl with darting eyes, she was one of the children who sailed close to psychosis. Her story a couple of months ago had been chaotic and without discernible relationship to reality. After Omar's story was over, Ernestine's hand was in the air again, waving urgently. Inwardly crossing my fingers, I invited her to the Teller's chair.

"What's your story about, Ernestine?" "It's about how I became an artist," she said. She was emphatic and clear. I listened, moved. She went on to tell, with perfect cogency, how she had started on the artist's path when she was five, thanks to a helpful teacher. "And I've been an artist ever since," she finished triumphantly.

Ernestine watched the scene intently. "Yes, that's right," she said, turning to me when it was over. She was smiling broadly, delighted to share this sense of herself with all of us in the room.

For Courtney, Gary, and Ernestine, there were somewhat different healing outcomes from telling and seeing their stories. For Courtney, the experience was a way to gain mastery over a troubling dream, first by seeing it externalized and physically separate from herself, and then by the opportunity to reimagine the scenario. (In Playback, this transformation is always generated by the

Teller, in response to the Conductor's invitation after the scene is first played as it happened. If a child needs help understanding such a profoundly creative possibility, the Conductor may offer a "for example" or two. But it is only the Teller's imagined scene that is acted out.) For Gary, telling a story about his recently-deceased grandmother was a chance to remember her as she was in life; it was his choice not to focus on her illness or death. In the company of witnesses, he honored her and his relationship with her–a primary function of any mourning ritual. Ernestine's story claimed the part of her that was creative and functioning. It was also an articulation of inner life unlikely to take place in any other context at the Neville.

Like all Playback audiences, the children told stories about things that were important to them. Sometimes a story revealed an aspect of the grievous history that had brought the child to the Neville–stories about a drug-addicted mother, an abusive stepfather, or violence on the streets or home. It was clear that telling and watching such a story helped in comprehending a painful reality; and letting others know about it lightened the burden of carrying such pain alone. But we neither encouraged nor discouraged the children from telling such stories. We conveyed our openness to whatever they wished to tell. We felt certain that there was a different and equally important healing taking place when the story was about a reward trip to get pizza or about being chosen as someone's friend. Such a story was an affirmation to the child that she was a person with success and happiness in her life as well as trouble.

Whatever the content of the stories, the most therapeutic effect of all was the experience of being heard, fully, respectfully, and without analysis or judgment. Interpretation in the psychological sense[1] is not constructive in Playback Theatre, even in clinical applications. Playback Theatre works like art or dream, presenting images, patterns, associations, allusions that are best comprehended on their own terms. Playback speaks the language of story, a right-brain language that holds potent meaning for the subconscious. It would have actually diminished the healing effectiveness of Courtney's story, for instance, to try to make explicit the relationship between her dream and her history. A relationship undoubtedly existed; but allowing it to remain embedded in the events and symbolism of the dream gave Courtney's emotional processing far more power than any discussion of feelings or facts could have had. Older Tellers often spontaneously express cognitive insights after seeing their stories; but it is still important that such insights come from the Teller and not from the Conductor or actors.

Playback Therapy Groups

The children were eager to act as well as tell, and sometimes we invited one or two of them to join us onstage in a minor role. But in general we knew it was too risky to give these very volatile children the responsibility of enacting the stories–at least in a performance context. On the other hand, I was aware of the potential therapeutic benefits to be gained from the experience of acting as well as telling in Playback: the chance to develop expressiveness, empathy, connection to others, a sense of teamwork and belonging. I organized therapy groups of four or five children in which they took part

1. Artistic interpretation, on the other hand, is legitimate and essential especially in performance Playback: the actor interprets the story the way a pianist interprets a Bach prelude, enriching it with her or his artistic vision.

in workshop-model Playback Theatre, learning how to enact stories as well as telling them. Over the period of a year and a half, I and a co-leader led eight different groups, each one meeting for six 45-minute sessions.

I knew from the outset that I needed someone to lead with me, for logistics–escorting children in different directions before and after sessions; for occasional crisis management–a reasonable likelihood with the Neville's population; and, most importantly, to support and guide the children's acting while I conducted. In the early phases of each group, Lisa, the co-leader, played whichever role required the most delicate handling, usually that of the Teller. Later, as the groups gained cohesion and confidence, I invited the Teller to choose freely from any of the actors. We made other adaptations as well, aimed at maximizing the children's success. We omitted music during the scenes since it was too difficult for them to create sensitive improvised music, and not practical to bring in another staff member. We also stopped using the fabric props when we saw that they were more distracting than helpful. As the Conductor I gave far more direction to the actors than I did for adults, including, sometimes, a brief narration to begin the story, to move it along in the middle if it got stuck, or to cue an ending. We routinely debriefed with sharing after stories so that actors as well as Tellers could speak about their experience during the enactment.

Each session followed a similar sequence, creating a predictable container for the creativity and openness that we were invoking. The quality of ritual in the structure of each session echoed the framing of the enactments themselves. We began with a song of greeting as we sat on the circle of pillows, sometimes followed by another fill-in song in which each child contributed a line expressing a feeling, an experience, or a wish. The warm-up phase often included one or two carefully chosen drama games designed to develop expressiveness and connection. Such activities were structured to make them as accessible and enjoyable as possible, for example in a game that required partners, we paired the children with Lisa and me until they were ready to work successfully with each other.

When it was time for stories, we set up our stage with plastic milk crates along one wall for the actors, the piano bench on one side for Teller and Conductor, and the pillows moved back for the audience. The children readily learned the simple Playback procedure of the enactment itself: the telling of the story, the standing of the actors as they are chosen, the "Let's watch!" injunction of the Conductor to signal the beginning of the action, the pause at the end when the Teller is acknowledged by the actors, and the Conductor's invitation to the Teller to make a final comment.

After one, sometimes two stories, we returned to the circle of pillows for several minutes of sharing–how was it for the Teller, for the actors, and for the children watching. As in the psychodramatic practice of sharing, the emphasis was on expressing any feelings or memories that had been stirred, not offering analysis or counsel. (Sharing was another adaptation–in nonclinical Playback Theatre, we do not pause to share after enactments, instead trusting in the natural dialogue that occurs between people and their own stories). We ended with another song to acknowledge each child and say good-bye until next time.

This routine, of course, was liable to change shape as each session evolved. Sometimes a warm-up activity expanded to take up most of the session (as with the role-playing activity I describe in the illustration below). At moments of particular intensity we sometimes paused and returned to the pillows for a song to help everyone express, contain, and integrate emotion. Singing became such a key element in these groups that the children sometimes initiated improvised songs, individually or as a group, as another way to tell their stories.

The Success of the Groups

Group therapy of any kind at the Neville was rare because of the children's instability: We were prepared for our experiment to fail as many others had. But it did not. The children relished the opportunity to tell stories in a more intimate setting. As in the performances, their stories often spoke of normality and humor, hope and love. But the intimacy and continuity of the group also allowed them to tell more tender stories, stories of loss or vulnerability that could be told only to trusted listeners–though still avoiding the stories of their worst traumas, sensing that even the relative safety of these groups was not enough to hold the extreme disclosures that many of them could have made. Their enactments were generally without artistic polish, but they were fully able to replay a story with enough accuracy and sensitivity to satisfy the Teller.

They responded gleefully to the acting games and songs, often using them to express feelings in somewhat oblique and therefore unthreatening forms. There was also a subtle change in their sense of themselves as people, citizens of the Neville. Day and night the message of their environment was that they were burdens, misfits, the cause of trouble for everyone around them–"emotionally disturbed." As actors in each other's stories they found an unfamiliar and precious opportunity to be the agents of comfort and learning for each other: helpers, not problem-causers. Their tolerance and understanding toward each other grew with their willingness to take on roles that crossed racial and gender divides.

Perhaps most significant of all was the growth of empathy. As they acted in or witnessed each others' stories, they found themselves stepping into another person's feelings in a way that they had seldom done before. A tough, violent boy watched a girl's story about being terrorized by a stepfather when she was two years old. "I felt bad for Sharelle. I wish her mom had come and helped her," he said afterwards, a rare expression of pity and identification. A black boy balked at playing a white grandmother in another boy's story, then did it with such effectiveness that the Teller was moved. "How did you know what she's like?" asked the Teller. "Just thought about my own grandma," was the answer. Taking roles in each other's stories, witnessing and reflecting each other's experiences, engendered a compassionate fellow-feeling that was generally absent from the interactions of children who had had little chance to learn about empathy from the adults in their lives.

In spite of numerous chaotic moments and occasional crises, the groups more than met our expectations as well as those of the children. Many expressed a wish to continue longer than the six weeks limit placed on us by the school authorities, understandably concerned as they were about the children missing too much of their academic studies.

I believe that to a large degree it was the ritualistic structure, both the protocol of enacting a Playback scene, and the design of each session itself, that accounted for the success of these groups. We organized time and space so that the children felt not only safe, generally, but invited and honored. They instinctively recognized the age-old presence of ritual, of a frame in which their personal experiences were communicated and held. Our circle of pillows on the floor, where we sat to greet each other and sing, embodied this framing of our time together, as did the creation in each session of the stage.

Playback Theatre is above all built around this sense of ceremony, the deliberate creation of an artistic and truth-telling space that is distinct from ordinary life. It is the element of ritual that accounts for Playback's power in any circumstance. The Neville children recognized and responded to it, telling their important stories to each other and enacting them with compassion, creativity, and respect.

Limitations and Growing Edges

We encountered difficulties as well as successes. The most challenging aspect was the lack of integration with the rest of the Neville program. It seemed difficult to gain a general acceptance from the staff, both for the performances and the groups. A number of them did appreciate its therapeutic value and were enthusiastic supporters. The attitude of these staff members–teachers, therapists, childcare workers–greatly enhanced the effectiveness of what we were doing. They took Playback seriously and made themselves available to follow-up where needed, for instance after a story that exposed a vulnerable experience. They sat with the children during performances, keeping them company, helping them to stay focused and involved, modeling the kind of respectful attention we were asking of the children. But other staff considered Playback Theatre to be at best an entertainment and at worst a subversive encouragement for the children to believe their own faulty versions of reality. It had been, in part, to improve this perspective that I initiated the therapy groups. My hope was that by inviting staff members to refer children, and by providing ongoing progress reports on what transpired, there would be an increased and synergistic understanding of the Playback approach. Although there was indeed some improvement, I remained unsatisfied with the place of Playback Theatre within the program as a whole.

The other challenge was the precariousness of the children's interactions. The atmosphere at the Neville was often fraught with violence. Many children were prone to losing control, at risk of hurting themselves, each other, or staff members. Although the ritual structure of Playback itself and of our sessions created a context of safety to a surprising degree, there were also occasions when one or more children had to be removed to avert conflict. We had to resort to a physical restraint once, when a girl became hysterically giggly as she acted out a story and could not regain control, spiraling rapidly toward violence.

We learned that for children to succeed in Playback Theatre therapy they needed enough ego strength to step into another role without losing the awareness of their own identity: some of the younger children, especially, could not cope with acting out even brief moments or feelings told by other group members. The Playback groups were also not suitable for the few near-psychotic children at the Neville. For someone who is unsure of the boundaries of reality, it is not safe to venture into the zone of *as if.* However, with careful clinical framing, such fragile children could and did tell their stories in performances.

From my experience, as well as that of other therapists whose work I know of, Playback Theatre has proved to be an effective therapeutic approach–when in the hands of people who have thorough training in both Playback and clinical practice. Playback Theatre's apparent simplicity is deceptive. It is a method of considerable power and subtlety. There are dangers to using it without adequate training, just as there are dangers in using Playback in clinical contexts without clinical training.

On the other hand, with a team of fully-prepared leaders, there are exciting potentials still to be fulfilled. One day there may be other places like the Elsinore Children and Youth Center in Denmark, where most of the staff are trained in Playback Theatre, allowing a synergistic relationship between the Playback work and every other aspect of the program–to the great benefit of the young clients.

CASE EXAMPLE

The Story of a Playback Group: Excerpts from Six Sessions

It was the first time. Like a pair of Pied Pipers, Lisa and I collected children from their various classrooms, our string growing as we progressed toward the Space Room, the small recreation room where the group was to meet. The children came in, curious and a little shy, and sat down on the circle of pillows. From staff referrals we had chosen two girls and three boys: tall, quiet Elizabeth, pixie-ish Kiki, Malcolm, calm and mature-seeming, with a habit of ducking his head to avoid eye contact; Albert with red hair and a touch of rakish glamour about him, and Ronnie, small and messy with shirt hanging out and glasses held together with Scotch tape. Malcolm and Kiki were African-American, the others white. All were 12 or 13 except Kiki, a precocious 9-year-old. Ronnie looked and behaved much younger than his actual years.

Sitting on the pillows, we sang a song of greeting. The kids joined in, briefly self-conscious, then relaxing into enjoyment. We sang around the circle, naming everyone.

"Here we are, it's another day,
Just one thing that I would like to say,
Oh Kiki, and Albert, hello to you."

I explained to them that in this group everyone was going to have a chance to tell stories and to act them out for each other. "And when you're not being an actor you can be a witness," I said. They looked at each other, confused.

"A witness?" asked Kiki. "You mean like in court?"

I realized this was the wrong term for children who were all too familiar with courtroom lingo. "I mean, you can be the audience. It's good to have someone to watch." They nodded.

"Is this therapy?" asked Elizabeth.

"Yes," said Lisa. "We want it to be helpful to you. We want it to be fun too." They nodded again, accepting.

Malcolm volunteered to tell the first story, after we had played a couple of warm-up games.

"When I was home last time," he began, "me and my cousin got into trouble because we took eggs from his mother's refrigerator and we threw them at kids in the street. So she got mad–she gets really mad sometimes but she don't hit us–and she made us go to the store and get some more eggs for her, with our own money. When we were in there, this kid, he was an older kid that my cousin knew, he told us to give him the eggs, but we wouldn't. So he waited for us outside the store, and he had a gun. So we gave him the eggs."

I asked Lisa to play Malcolm and invited him to choose actors for the other parts. As the Teller's actor, Lisa helped keep the story on track.

They acted it out, Malcolm and I watching from the side. The kids surprised me by how well they remembered what their characters said and did. Albert was the bully with the gun. He managed to rein in his restless energy until the right moment, when he stepped into the scene with a menacing swagger. Malcolm was riveted.

"Yeah, that's what it was like," he said,

shaking his head. "Man!" He was quiet for a moment. "Then later on, my other cousin, John, he really did get shot a couple of blocks from there. They killed him."

The other kids stared at him. Lisa and I waited. Malcolm's eyes were far away.

"Malcolm?" I said after a minute. "Do you want to tell us more about that?"

He turned to me, back in the room again. "Nope."

We came back to the circle of cushions for the last ten minutes of the session. I invited the kids to tell us what Malcolm's story might have reminded them of in their own lives. "Or you could tell us what it felt like being an actor."

"My grandma was shot in the stomach," said Ronnie. He seemed more proud than upset.

"I got shot in the arm. Look." Albert pulled up his sleeve to show a scar. "My brother's friends were fooling around. They were trying to scare me and they sure did."

I was taken aback. I could not get used to the dreadful familiarity so many of the children had with guns.

I asked Albert what it was like to play the threatening teenager in Malcolm's story.

"I felt bad! That guy was ugly." I thanked him for doing it. I told them that it was a kind of a gift they could give each other, to play the tough roles in each other's stories.

"I got something to say," said Malcolm, who had been listening without comment. "I hate guns. I hate people who use guns. They spoil everything for everyone. It's not fair." Malcolm was passionate. "My aunt, she belongs to Mothers Against Guns, and I think they're really cool. They want to make things safe again. They're sick of kids being killed."

It was time to go back to class. "Our plan is to meet every week for six weeks," I reminded them. "But it's your choice now. What do you think? Do you want to keep going?"

"Yes!" they all chorused. Lisa and I looked at each other, pleased.

The children wanted to talk about Malcolm's story when we met again.

"It was a sad story," said Kiki, wrinkling her nose. "I don't really like sad stories."

"It wasn't so sad, though," said Elizabeth. "At least Malcolm didn't get shot."

"What I think is, if something bad happens, it's better to tell people about it. At least they get to know about it," said Albert.

"Yeah," said Malcolm. "Anyway my story wasn't that bad, not as bad as what happened to my other cousin." They were silent.

Later in the session Kiki had a story to tell. "I thought about this yesterday, that I would like to tell it when I came to the group. It's about when I was seven, and I was living with my mother and my little brother, Mason. He was four." Kiki, sweet and smart, had been removed from the dangerous care of her mother when she was eight. "My mom, she used drugs all the time, and her boyfriend too, and he used to beat her up when they got high." Once again I found myself trying to listen attentively while sickened inside by what I was hearing. "I was playing with my little brother in our room and I could hear them hunting everywhere for that thing that you use–you know, Malcolm, what's it called?" She mimed with her hands.

"You mean the cooker?"

"Yeah, that's it. Anyway, I was very scared because I had thrown it out the window. I knew they'd both beat me up if they found out. But then my mom told me to take Mason to the store. I sure was glad to get out of there."

The actors, with Lisa as Kiki, acted it out. Kiki snuggled in as close to me as she possibly could, gripping my arm tightly. "Yeah, that really did feel like my story," she said, letting her breath out at last when it was over.

The others talked about what it was like for them to play it. "Sad," was the comment of most of them. "I felt sad for Kiki," said Elizabeth.

"Kiki, did you think it was a sad story?" I asked her, remembering her comment about Malcolm's story.

"Yes, it was, but I'm still glad I told it."

We talked, and sang, and acted out one more story. But they were still stirred up. I showed them how to take deep breaths and let their bodies relax as they exhaled.

It was time to end. Kiki turned and hugged me. "Anyone else want a hug?" I asked. They all did.

Albert arrived to the next session in a strange mood, disheveled and hollow-eyed. "I'm on special alert," he announced to everyone. "I got restrained five times today. I'm not allowed to go home for more than three days over vacation." The ten-day Easter break was coming up. I had not heard what the special alert was about, but it was usually the result of suicide threats. I knew that the anguish in his family was more than enough to make a child question the value of living. Albert and his siblings had been raped for years by both their father and uncle. Now in puberty, he was in trouble himself for sexual threats to younger children. The father had recently died of AIDS. The children and their mother lived with the knowledge that they might be infected, though tests so far were negative.

I watched Albert for signs of depression, and to see if he wanted to use this chance to explore what was on his mind. He did not, instead sabotaging the other children's attempts to express anything serious.

"I was thinking about something this week," began Elizabeth.

"Hoo-wee! Elizabeth knows how to think!" interrupted Albert. "Make a note of that, will ya, Ronnie?" Ronnie was always ready to play along with Albert's clown, but their comedy act had never been as disruptive as it was today.

"Let's everybody take some deep breaths," suggested Malcolm at one point when tempers were rising. It helped, but only briefly. Lisa and I finally gave Albert an ultimatum: settle down or go back to class. Albert saw that we meant it. His demeanor changed. "OK, I'll calm down. Don't send me back." He tried hard for the rest of the session, lapsing sometimes but then catching himself. Ronnie followed his cues precisely.

We asked the kids, one at a time, to enter the room in the role of someone they knew well–"Think of someone who really likes you," was my instruction. Elizabeth went first.

"I'm Mrs. Tait, Elizabeth's mom," she announced, sitting down in a chair.

"Welcome to the Space Room, Mrs. Tait. Please tell us about your daughter Elizabeth."

"Well, I think she's wonderful," said Elizabeth as her mother. She told us about Elizabeth's ambition to become a schoolteacher. "And she'd be a good teacher. She really likes little kids."

We thanked Mrs. Tait and said goodbye. Malcolm went next. He came into the room with a ghetto walk and sat down in the chair with his arms folded and his legs splayed out.

"I'm Malcolm's cousin Leroy. Malcolm told you about me. We almost got shot when this kid wanted our eggs, remember?"

"Hi, Leroy. What can you tell us about Malcolm?"

"He's OK. We do everything together. We're like this." Malcolm held up his fingers firmly linked together. "I look out for him, he looks out for me."

"What do you like best about Malcolm?" asked Lisa.

"Leroy" was suddenly bashful. "Well, it's

like, it's just that he's my best friend, and my cousin too." He paused. "All I can say is, we stick together, and if one of us gets in trouble, we both get in trouble."

"So maybe you could help each other stay out of trouble, Leroy, what do you think?"

"Yeah, I guess."

We had time for one story. Ronnie told about getting sent to the crisis room during school the day before. For the first time in this group, I invited him to choose any actors he wanted. He chose Malcolm to play himself, Lisa for the teacher, Albert for the easygoing crisis room supervisor who played cards with him. Malcolm did a fine job.

In the next session, we played the *Lying Game,* a favorite in which each person tells something that may be true or a lie. Ronnie said: "Me and Albert are brothers." Everyone except Albert held up two crossed fingers to show they did not believe it. Ronnie and Albert protested in unison. "It's true!" For once they were not clowning.

"He's lived next door to me all my life," explained Albert. "We *are* like brothers."

"Yeah," said Ronnie. I had never seen him so intense and serious.

We had discovered too that there was another connection that Lisa and I had been unaware of when we chose children for this group: Kiki and Elizabeth had also known each other before coming to the Neville. These long-established friendships accounted, at least to some extent, for some of the unusual cohesion of the group.

Albert was eager to continue the interviews. I had heard meanwhile from his therapist that he had suggested this activity in their session. In the role of his friend Thomas, he had talked about how upset Albert was about the fighting that went on at home, with six wild children and a helpless mother. The next day he had written a note to the therapist–"Thank you for helping me express my feelings." She was astonished and moved.

In the Space Room, Albert decided to be his older brother Gary. His voice deepened and his body seemed to grow bigger.

"So what do you and Albert like to do together?" Malcolm asked him.

"Rough-housing, that's what I like. He squeals a lot but I don't care." Albert had told us before how he hated his brother's rough play.

"What do you think Albert wants more than anything?" I asked.

"Gary" looked thoughtful. "He wants to come home in the summer. He wants everything to be OK by then." When his turn was over, Albert had trouble letting go of the role, cuffing and teasing the others in a way that seemed unlike himself. We had to remind him two or three times–"Albert, you're Albert, remember? You're not Gary any more."

Ronnie surprised me by being able to take on another role consistently. "Hi, I'm Nicky," he said in a high voice. "I'm Ronnie's brother and I'm only three and a half." He looked convincingly like a small boy, swinging his legs under the chair and chewing on his hand.

"Do you and Ronnie get along?" asked Elizabeth.

"Well, he's always beating me up."

"How come he beats you up?"

"Because I always punch him."

"What does your mom do?"

"Sometimes she hits Ronnie and then he cries, then he beats me up again."

Kiki was last. She left the room and came back in smiling and dignified. "Hello, everyone. My name is Annabel and I'm Kiki's big sister. I'm nineteen. My job is managing a supermarket."

"Hi, Annabel. Tell us about Kiki."

"She's my favorite sister, she's very funny and I miss her. A lot. She's very smart, too. She wants to be a lawyer when she grows up." I was touched. I had no doubt that Kiki was bright enough to become a lawyer–but how was she going to get there from here? She was black, female, poor, the child of a drug addict, institutionalized for emotional disturbance at the age of nine. She would need more luck than seemed likely to come her way.

It was time to end. The role playing exercise had taken the place of stories this session: another way to act out personal truth. Malcolm, who had a gift for sensing what the group needed, suggested a song. "How about 'We shall overcome'?" he said. All the kids knew it. They added their own words, prompted by the invitation that was in the air, to dream about the future:

"We'll have lots of money," sang Ronnie.

"We will all go home," sang Elizabeth.

"We'll grow up and be happy," sang Kiki.

"We will have nice families," sang Albert.

"There will be peace in the world," sang Malcolm, a little embarrassed but determined to say it. When the song was over he shook everyone's hand.

By the next group, Albert was in trouble again in school. When Lisa and I came to pick him up, his teacher was reluctant to let him go. "Albert, I just don't think you can handle it," she said.

"I can! I'll be all right! I really want to go, *please,* Carmen." At length she agreed. But as soon as he was in the Space Room he reverted to being giggly and rude. As usual, Ronnie caught his mood, and even Malcolm was affected. The girls were exasperated. Elizabeth wanted to tell us about her grandfather's death during the week. She had gone home for the funeral. Albert tittered as she spoke and tossed a pen from his pocket across the circle to Ronnie.

"Catch!"

Ronnie caught it and tossed it back. I grabbed the pen.

"Stop!" There was silence. "Everybody breathe." They did. I waited before going on. "Albert, do you want to listen to Elizabeth? Or do you want to go back to class?"

His tension released a little by the deep breathing, Albert's hysteria was subsiding. "It's OK, I can listen. Sorry, Elizabeth. I'm sorry about your grandfather."

"It's hard to think about death," I said. "But it happens in all our families."

They all nodded. "I got something to say," said Malcolm. He paused, looking down. "I'm thinking about my cousin. The other one. John." His voice was very quiet. "He was 28 and he had three little kids, and now he's dead. I'm scared about living in the city again. My mom wants us to move somewhere safer when I go home in June."

I wanted him out of that war zone. Malcolm was a remarkable boy. The world needed the adult that he would become, if he survived.

"My grandmother died, too," said Ronnie. "I was sad, *and* I was glad, because she wasn't in pain any more and also I got to see all my relatives." He was direct, sincere; so different from the Ronnie of a few weeks ago.

"When my dad died I laughed," said Albert, hunched over his knees. "My mom told me I should cry. I didn't know what to do, because he'd been real mean to us. I'm not sorry he's dead."

I was ready for this somber theme to continue when we did a story. But Elizabeth told about a good time with her brother and cousin and friends, all of them having an uproarious waterfight in the park. All four of the other kids acted, being expressive and imaginative in their assigned roles. They were a team: cohesive, disciplined, creative.

It was our last session. Elizabeth was missing, kept in class by an unrelenting teacher. Carol listened with pursed lips to our pleas–this is the last of six sessions, we think this group has been very significant for all of the children, our closure together is important–and shook her head. "You can take Ronnie, but Elizabeth's not going." It was a familiar dilemma. We wanted Elizabeth to come, for her own and everyone's sake. But forcing Carol to let her go might backfire on us later. We needed the teachers' goodwill and cooperation. Promising Elizabeth that we would find her after school, we took Ronnie and left her sighing over the schoolwork she had refused to do earlier in the day.

The others were disappointed not to see her. They were troubled that the group was ending and showed it by being distracted and giggly. It took them awhile to settle down. We had brought art materials for a final activity: each of them was to make a card like a book cover bearing the title of her or his life story. Inside, the rest of us were to write good-bye messages.

The Space Room was quiet as the children worked, decorating their book covers with drawings and symbols. Kiki's title was *The Girl Who Wanted to be a Lawyer.* Albert wrote *Albert's History.* Ronnie, glancing over Albert's shoulder, called his book *Ronnie's Humor.* Malcolm's was *Malcolm's Adventures in Life.* They passed their books around. "You are a kind and good person. I will always remember your two cousins," wrote Kiki in Malcolm's. "Thanks for letting me show my feelings," wrote Albert in Kiki's. "I had fun with you and everyone," wrote Ronnie. "When we're grown up and you're a lawyer, you can help me," wrote Malcolm to Kiki. "Now I know that we have stories in our lives," he wrote to Albert.

A few weeks later I tape-recorded individual interviews with Albert, Elizabeth, and Kiki about the experience of being in the group. One of my questions was about its duration–how did they feel about meeting for six sessions?

"It was too short," said Albert emphatically.

"*Way* too short!" said Kiki.

"I wish it was longer," said Elizabeth. "I wanted to keep coming."

"How long would you have liked it to be?" I asked them.

"A year," said Kiki.

"Maybe four months or six months," said Elizabeth.

"How long? I think, every single week," said Albert. "Yup, every single week, that would be better."

CONCLUSION

Although Playback Theatre is not primarily a therapy, it embodies significant therapeutic effects for people who participate as Tellers, audiences, and performers, effects that can be applied and developed in clinical contexts. Performance Playback with institutionalized emotionally disturbed children gave opportunities for the building of identity; mastery over difficult experience; expression of concerns, perceptions, and feelings; and the relief of realizing that one's story may be shared by others. When the children took part in ongoing therapy groups as actors as well as Tellers, they gained additional benefits from belonging to an intimate group and acting out each others' stories, developing further expressiveness, confidence, a changed self-concept, and empathy.

The source of Playback Theatre's potency as a healing force is its basis in ritual and the language of story. The success of Playback in therapy depends on these qualities being fully recognized both by Playback-trained clinicians and by the institutions in which they practice.

REFERENCES

Fox, J. (1994). *Acts of service: spontaneity, commitment, tradition in the nonscripted theatre.* New Paltz: Tusitala Publishing.

Hoesch, F. (1999). The red thread. In J. Fox, & H. Dauber (Eds.), *Gathering voices: Essays on playback theatre* (pp. 46–66). New Paltz: Tusitala Publishing.

Salas, J. (1993). *Improvising real life: Personal story in Playback Theatre.* New Paltz: Tusitala Publishing.

Salas, J. (1994). Playback Theatre: Children find their stories. In B. James (Ed.), *Handbook for treatment of trauma-attachment problems in children* (pp. 240–247). New York: Lexington Books.

Salas, J. (2007). *Do my story, sing my song: Music therapy and Playback Theatre with troubled children.* New Paltz: Tusitala Publishing.

FURTHER TRAINING

For training in Playback Theatre, contact:
Centre for Playback Theatre
www.playbackcentre.org
Phone 845-255-8163

For information about the International Playback Theatre Network visit www.playbacknet.org.

Chapter 21

THEATRE OF THE OPPRESSED: DRAMA THERAPY AS CULTURAL DIALOGUE

NISHA SAJNANI

The smallest cells of social organization (the couple, the family, the neighborhood, the school, the office, the factory etc.) and equally the smallest incidents of our social life (an accident at the corner of the street, the checking of identity papers, a visit to the doctor, etc.) contain all the moral and political values of society, all of its structures of domination and power, all of its mechanisms of oppression. (Boal, 1995, p. 40)

The *Theatre of the Oppressed* (T.O.) is a system of theatre-based techniques, games and exercises which include Image Theatre, Forum Theatre, Invisible Theatre, Legislative Theatre, and the Rainbow of Desire. Fundamental to the philosophy and practice of T.O. is the inseparability and permeability of false boundaries between the disciplines of art, politics and psychology in the pursuit of progressive individual and social change. Cohen-Cruz and Schutzman (1994) propose that "T.O. exposes the insufferability of politics that are artless and dogmatic, the presumptuousness of art that lacks self or collective consciousness, and the ultimate futility (if not harmful ethnocentricity) of therapies devoid of playfulness or cultural contextualization" (1994, p. 2). Around the world, educators, political activists, therapists and social workers have responded to the call to interweave the personal and political which has resulted in a myriad of adaptations of Boal's methods, addressing issues ranging from racism and sexism to depression and political impotence. The active negotiation of the complex interplay between culture, politics and psychology is given center stage in the Theatre of the Oppressed, a dynamic approach to encouraging critical thought and action in the repair of individual and social suffering.

GENESIS

The history of The Theatre of the Oppressed is also a history of its founder, Augusto Boal, theatre director, playwright, politician, and theorist. While an exhaustive biography is beyond the scope of this chapter, thorough reviews of his life and work can be found in several texts including

Boal's recently published autobiography entitled *Hamlet and the Baker's Son* (2001) and the extensive biography written by Frances Babbage (2004). The evolution of his methods has been published in several texts in several languages; however, readers may find the collection of essays printed in *Playing Boal: Theatre, Therapy, Activism* edited by Jan Cohen-Cruz and Mady Schutzman (1994) a useful overview of the scholarship and practice that has grown out of Boal's initial articulation of his work. The collection is divided into three parts: case studies, essays that contextualize T.O. in terms of psychotherapy, political theatre, and body theories, and three pieces that contest claims that Boal's turn toward theatre and therapy compromises his initial social aims. The following account highlights several pivotal moments in Boal's life that have informed the development of his methods.

The Early Years

Augusto Boal was born August 16, 1931 in Rio de Janeiro. At the age of 11, just as Brazil was entering WWII, Boal began to work in his father's shop, the Leopoldina Bakery where he found his first observation post at the cash register from which to gain insight into daily human rituals. Under the advisement of his father, Boal was formally trained in industrial chemistry in Brazil. During his undergraduate studies, his interest in the mundane and extraordinary performances of human activity took form in a series of lectures, which Boal organized in his post as cultural director at the National Chemistry School, on the subject of theatre and playwrighting. Inspired by the work of Stanislavski, Brecht, Gorky, Turgenev, Chekhov, and Tolstoy, Boal and his colleagues founded a new theatre group called "O Teatro Artistico de Rio de Janeiro." During this time the political significance and function of theatre began to take shape in his imagination. His interest in the work of John Gassner, American playwright, incited him to attend Columbia University in the late 1940s and early 1950s where he received his doctorate in philosophy and participated in the Actors' Studio and The Writer's Group in Brooklyn, NY. After he finished his degree at Columbia, he returned to Brazil to work with the Arena Theatre in São Paulo. His work at the Arena Theatre led to his experimentation with new forms of theatre that entertained and educated the public and, in the end, have had an extraordinary impact on applied theatre practice.

The Arena Theatre (1956–1971)

Within the small space of the Arena Theatre, Boal began to envisage a theatre collective that placed emphasis on the interdependence of characters portrayed and the mechanics of society. He formed a company of actors and drew on his readings of Stanislavski to guide their rehearsal process. In his own autobiography, Boal likens the theatre director to Socrates who, as in the tradition of Stanislavski, "makes the student discover what s/he already knows, without knowing that s/he knows it, by means of questions that provoke reflection, thus opening up a path of discovery . . . helping the actors give birth to characters" (2001, p. 147). Boal writes of having invented the expression *selective realism* and *expressionist realism* to describe his choice of partial gestures, images, or objects to symbolize that which is absent.

In 1957, Boal directed Sean O'Casey's *Juno and the Peacock,* an epic piece about the civil war in Ireland. It was during the staging and run of this play that Boal's attention, already attuned to the daily performances and rituals of everyday life, began to center on the audience. He noted the contradiction between the audience's outpouring of emotion while they watched the irrationality of war and their comments in the lobby that suggested that they had not grasped the significance of the content. Boal began to question the value of beauty, such as that realized in the writing and staging of O'Casey's masterpiece and in many of the Arena's productions, in engaging audiences to think about important themes.

In 1961, amidst the hype of global technological advances and growing political tensions between the U.S and Russia, the Arena's company ardently pursued its inquiry into the relationship between politics and theatre. In Brazil, the Communist Party extended its influence into the theatres, meeting with the Arena to inscribe their political ambitions against U.S. imperialism. The Communist's Party's prescription was to ally with the nation's wealthy or risk being seen as a traitor loyal to the other side of an impossible conflict. Boal writes, "The Communist Party thought there were two capitalisms in our native conjuncture, one good, the other evil: the first was in the interests of the fatherland, the second the figurehead of the Yankees . . . not all of us followed this ratiocination" (2001, p. 175).

The changing political climate in Brazil which forfeited the rights of the poor in exchange for the advancement of the wealthy, galvanized and politicized Boal's practice and pushed him towards its currently popular formulation. Boal's company made a decision to produce plays by national authors in the hopes of shedding light on the zeitgeist of their own country. The audiences that frequented the Arena theatre along with company members themselves were mostly middle-class, although they felt that their understanding of the *people* diverged from that of the Communist Party who sustained the interests of the Brazilian bourgeoisie. Boal writes that they "did theatre from the perspective which we believed to be 'of the people' but we did not perform *for* the people! . . . What was the point of representing working class characters and serving them up, as a pre-dinner treat, to the middle-class and rich?" (2001, p. 175). This practical and moral dilemma incited the Arena theatre company to leave the theatre and to move out into spaces populated by the people. Their romantic vision of "the people" seemed to fade momentarily during this time as Boal and the Arena company staged utopian masterpieces by Brazilian playwrights only to have them received by the same paying middle-class ears who frequented the theatres in the cities. The company struggled with their self-prescribed challenge to fuel their utopian ideals and simultaneously feed themselves.

The Arena was visited by many playwrights and philosophers during this time. Among these were Jean-Paul Sartre and Simone de Beauvoir who were temporarily self-exiled from France on account of their polemic against French occupation in Algeria. Finding suitable allies in their guests, the Arena decided to stage Sartre's satirical screenplay L'Engrenage (In the Mesh), at Ipiraga, a monument to Brazilian independence. This became the Arena's first brush with government censorship that only supported domestic cultural production. Police surrounded the square and demanded that they stop the play. To the applause of onlookers, the company stuffed handkerchiefs in their mouths and walked out in a procession of gagged artists. They returned to stage the play a second time and were met with increased brutality from the government police who wielded their guns and threatened violence if the company did not cease production.

Boal concedes that many in the Arena, including himself, succumbed briefly to what he termed the *Chê syndrome* in reference to the Argentinian hero, Chê Guevara's courageous yet at times patronizing desire to free those under military and economic oppression by force if necessary and for reasons often defined by the rescuer, not the rescued. In theatres across Brazil, companies were forming political theatre pieces which Boal later regarded as evangelist attempts to convince the people of what was best for them without, as Chê put it, running the same risks. "'To be in solidarity is to run the same risks,' Chê used to say . . . we were running no risk chanting revolutionary hymns" (2001, p. 194). Nowhere was this lesson better learned than when the Arena company performed amongst the Ligas Camponesas (Peasant Leagues) in the early 1960s. The Peasant Leagues fought against their own slavery, which took the form of indentured labor and restricted mobility to the lands on which they worked. They lived in fear of being killed by the landowner's mercenaries.

In many of Boal's workshops today and in several publications about his work (1992, 1994, 2001), he tells the story of when his company moved to Northeast Brazil and created an agit-prop (i.e., politicized) performance for the League's local peasant farmers which ended, as their plays would, in a frenetic revolutionary chorus, left arms raised and clenched in a fist chanting "the land belongs to the people, we must spill our blood to reclaim our land!" Boal recounts that one farmer in particular, Virgilio, was very moved by the message and asked him and his cast to take their guns and join them in their fight against the landowners. Boal tried to rectify this misunderstanding by clarifying that their guns were not real and that they were artists. Undeterred, Virgilio stated that they had enough guns for everyone. Boal recounts feeling ashamed that they had to decline the offer to fight rather than just talking about it. He tried to explain again that they were not genuine farmers but rather, genuine artists. Virgilio responded that he understood that when the artists were talking about spilling blood, it was peasants' blood and not their own as they would return to their secure homes. Boal has often drawn on this example in his current teaching about the role of the artist in community and the complicity of the messenger in compromising political agency by inciting a course of action without willingness to follow suit themselves.

Imprisonment and Exile (1971–1981)

Boal's plays were increasingly censored by the government who saw his cultural activism as a threat. One evening in 1971, as Boal walked home from an Arena performance of Brecht's *The Resistible Rise of Arturo Ui,* he was kidnapped off the street, arrested, imprisoned and tortured for four months. When he was released he was forced into exile and spent fifteen years in Argentina, Peru, Portugal and France before returning to Rio. While in exile, Boal remained a cultural activist and continued to conjecture viable relationships between politics and theatre, ideology and practice.

While in Peru, Boal discovered that the cultural and economic situation was very similar to that of Brazil. Peru was ruled by a minority of wealthy white landowners descended from Spaniards who came to Peru for its gold. The majority of people were of Incan, other Native American, or mixed descent and had poor living conditions, often living in areas lacking basic sanitation, clean drinking water and electricity. There was also a high rate of illiteracy in the countryside. Boal began to use his theatre to teach literacy. He joined the People's Theatre in Peru and helped to found Operación Alfabetización Integral (Integral Literacy Operation), or ALFIN. During this period of time, Boal also became increasingly influenced by the work of his countryman, educator Paulo Freire. In 1970, Friere published his most famous work, *Pedagogy of the Oppressed,* in which he articulated a revolutionary Marxist class analysis of the relationship between colonizers and the colonized and the necessity of a liberatory philosophy of education, a dialogic process rooted in praxis, an iterative cycle of action and reflection that he referred to as *conscientização,* or the development of *critical consciousness* (Freire, 1970). From the influence of Friere and from Boal's own literacy work in Peru, Boal began to develop *Image Theatre,* a system of corporeal images designed to provoke reflection and stimulate action towards the disruption of oppressive systems of power.

In 1979, Boal published *The Theatre of the Oppressed,* which provided the philosophical basis of his explorations to date. After his encounter with Virgilio, Boal writes that "the idea of the active spectator, the protagonist who oversteps limits instead of resigning himself to sedentary participation was already on my mind when I went back to São Paulo . . . something beyond Brecht who only asked the spectator to think with his head, without giving him the stage space to express that thought" (2001, p. 200).

A legendary development occurred in Peru in 1973. Boal and his company had been experimenting with staging a scene depicting real life challenges and inviting audience members to stop the action to share their ideas for what the main characters should do to overcome their dilemma and then watch as the actor carried out different suggestions. Boal tells the story of how a woman in the audience once was so outraged that the actor could not understand her suggestion that she came onto the stage and showed them what she meant. For Boal this was the birth of the *spect-actor* (not spectator) and his theatre was transformed. He began inviting audience members with suggestions for change onto the stage to demonstrate their ideas. In so doing, he discovered that through this participation the audience members became empowered not only to imagine change but to actually practice that change, reflect collectively on the suggestion, and thereby to generate social action. This was the birth of *Forum Theatre.*

While in France, Boal continued to teach his revolutionary approach to theatre, establishing several Centers for the Theatre of the Oppressed. His experience in Europe and North America was pivotal in shaping the next phase of his work. Participants in his workshops were repeatedly problematizing Boal's techniques and asking how his techniques could address oppressions for which there was no tangible or visible oppressor. Boal was working in unfamiliar territory in that the daily lives of citizens were not being monitored by the military police. Their experiences did not easily fold into a simple binary of oppressor/oppressed and incited Boal to evolve his methods to address isolation, depression, and fear amongst other 'oppressions' suggested by workshop participants. Boal developed methods he termed *Cops in the Head* and *Rainbow of Desire* to facilitate an embodied exploration and externalization of internalized oppressions (1995). The Rainbow of Desire extends Boal's theory and practice of theatre as defined within the Theatre of the Oppressed. In the context of those under-represented in society, his methodology can be used as a weapon against oppressors. In the context of those who are marginalized in society as a result of their religion, ethnicity, language or ability for example, the techniques described in the *Rainbow of Desire* use strategies drawn from *Image Theatre* to empower individuals to break down the internal oppressions that hinder full integration and participation in society.

Augusto Boal Today

Following the removal of the military junta in Brazil, Boal returned to Rio de Janeiro in 1986 where he continues to reside. Boal established a Center for the Theatre of the Oppressed in Rio and in Paris and has supported the development of hundreds of companies globally which continue to refine and adapt his methods in the service of progressive individual and social change. In the fall of 1992, Boal ran as an at-large candidate for the position of Vereador of Rio, a position similar to a City Council seat in the United States. While in office, Vereador Boal developed *Legislative Theatre* (1998) to work at the local neighborhood level to identify the key problems in the city. Using the Forum concept, he employed the dynamics of theatre to discuss what kinds of legislation needed to be enacted to address community problems. The resulting discussions and demonstrations became the basis for actual legislation put forward by Boal in the Chamber of Vereadors. Because of the increased visibility brought about by his winning a seat, he was able to obtain funding to hold an international festival for the first time in Brazil in July, 1993. Since then annual conferences and festivals dedicated to practice in T.O. occur around the world and attract hundreds of Theatre of the Oppressed practitioners from around the world in a rich confluence of languages, theatre styles, and social issues (Boal, 2006). Training is offered through various centers throughout the world, and books about Boal's methods as well as adaptations to his methods are in wide circulation. Many of his theatre forms have been adapted for use in television and Internet media, and have been applied to qualitative social research and performative inquiry (Linds & Vettraino, 2008). His work in pioneering methods of using theatre to transform culture, conflict, and injustice have been noted most recently in 2008 when Augusto Boal was nominated for the Nobel Peace Prize.

THE THEATRE OF THE OPPRESSED

The Joker and the Spect-Actor

Two roles are central to the Theatre of the Oppressed: the *Joker,* in reference to the drama facilitator and the *spect-actor,* the active witness. The term *Joker* is in reference to its neutral role in a deck of cards but also references the trickster who disrupts and reveals the complexities present in the embodied and/or staged processes that comprise the Theatre of the Oppressed. The *spect-actor* is a term Boal developed to counter the passive receptivity associated with the traditional division in the theatre which had expert actors on the stage invoking and (re)-enacting potentially troubling social dynamics, while audience members remained seated with their gaze fixed upon the action. By conceptualizing people as spect-actors, Boal transgresses this divide and reminds his participants and audience members to act upon oppression rather than only observe it.

Games of the Oppressed

"All our senses, our perception of reality, and our capacity of feeling and reasoning, tend to become mechanical by every day repetition. We tend to become less creative, accepting reality as it is, instead of transforming it" (Boal, 1994). Boal's theatre games are a system of exercises designed to de-mechanize the body and restore its responsiveness. In Boal's compendium of techniques, *Games for Actors and Non-Actors* published in 1992, he describes a series of exercises that help to *feel what we touch, to lis-*

ten to what we hear, to see what we look at, and to restore the connection between memory, emotion, and imagination. *Response/ability* is the cornerstone of Boal's practice, to liberate one's ability to respond in word and action and, therefore, take responsibility for either seeking alternatives or remaining complacent and complicit in the maintenance of deficient familial, economic and political systems. Here are three examples of games which Boal has used to restore the senses.

Ritual Sound (Listening to What We Hear)

Divide a group into two parts, A and B. A moves while B makes a collective sound. After the group has mastered this, B continues to make sounds but must choose a commonly experienced situation such as waking up in the morning, a classroom, the workplace, or highway traffic. Reverse groups so that group A is making the sounds. Notice how many rituals are common to the group.

Civil Disobedience (Listening to What We Hear)

The Joker instructs group members to do the opposite of the directions they are given. The Joker then takes on an authoritative stance and shouts out orders such as "face the wall, jump up and down, be quiet, walk along the right side of the path" and anything else that may come to mind. Participants usually find humor in this exercise as they catch themselves trying to find an alternate response to automatically doing as they are told. The Joker can change positions with a participant, relinquishing the role as leader while another participant gives the orders. This game is playfully revealing of false, though not necessarily dangerous, equality in common workshop settings no matter how participatory, as it is still the Joker(s) who shapes the exercise and directs the action and inquiry.

The Mirrors Sequence (Seeing What We Look At)

In addition to physical sculpting exercises that draw participants' attention to the detail and expression of each other's bodies and surroundings, Boal has elaborated upon a mirroring exercise that is familiar to many drama therapists/facilitators. Boal proposes a twelve-step sequence of mirroring exercises which may be done individually or in a progression and which move from the collective to the individual and from harmony to distortion. The *Distorting Mirror* invites participants to shift their focus from accurately mirroring the actions of their partners to responding at will, enlarging, minimizing, slowing down, speeding up, and diverging entirely from the movements of their partner. In effect, both partners enter into an embodied dialogue with one another without a leader or follower.

Image Theatre

Image Theatre is a series of exercises and games (as described above) designed to reveal complex truths about a culture or society without immediately resorting to the architecture of spoken language, which is already laden with hidden investments and hierarchies of power. Images are derived out of a series of exercises which Boal uses to demechanize the body, unhinging it from its overdetermined performances of daily life. Participants in Image Theatre create still images from their own and other's bodies of their feelings and experiences. These images become the starting point for a series of interventions which Boal (1992) refers to as *dynamisations* that further reveal the multilayered meanings and intentions behind the images. Through his dynamisation techniques, Boal offers various ways of shaping the pedagogical culture of the group towards valuing an exploration between personal narratives and social experience, between the micro and the macrocosm of the cultures participants inhabit.

One Model of Image Theatre and Dynamisations

In a small group, participants are directed by the Joker to simultaneously depict a chosen subject (i.e. climate change, U.S. election, war) with their bodies only. Then, as a first dynamisation, they are instructed to hold their images and observe the images created by other group members. Boal remarks that "in this first part of the dynamisation, the object is no longer to know what each individual thinks but to see what everybody thinks . . . the individual presentation of images gave us psychological representation, now we are given a social vision; that is, we are shown how this particular theme influences or affects our particular community" (1992, p. 166). Secondly, at the signal from the Joker, participants are instructed to form a relationship with images created by other group members (i.e., by moving towards or further away from them). This interrelation of images reveals the macrocosm, as according to Boal "what we see is not merely the social vision but an organized, organic, social vision" (p. 166). Thirdly, Boal remarks that it often happens that groups will represent the effects of a particular subject of concern such as violence, and not its causes or origins. If the perpetrators of the oppression are absent from the social microcosm created by the group in their images, Boal offers a third intervention. On the signal of the Joker, group members are instructed to transform their images of the victims into the images of the oppressors of these victims, therefore "the young woman who has been raped must show her rapist; the beggar shows the person who gives him alms, the citizen plays the policeman" (p. 168). In this way, both poles of a conflictual relationship are represented and the ideologies of the group are further revealed to each other and to the facilitator. Regardless of these initial images, Boal asserts that further dynamisations are needed "in order to delve as deeply as possible into the vision of the image, and not simply accept it as a statement of evidence, one has to lead the actor to complete the image he showed at the start" (p. 169). Further interventions and their rationales are offered in Boal's *Games for Actors and Non-Actors* (1992).

Complete the Image

This is a classic *Image Theatre* exercise often begun with the Joker walking into the center of the circle and shaking hands with a participant and freezing, drawing attention to the image that has been formed. The Joker asks the group what the image might mean and elicits several possibilities. The group may stay together or may divide into pairs wherein one partner begins with a still image and the other completes it, suffusing it with their own meaning. The first partner then observes the image created by their partner's body and completes it. This can continue as an exercise to warm up the body, warm up to other group members, and can also be conducted with a particular theme such as power, family, violence, or desire. The exercise should continue for enough time to allow for the emergence of a variety of images as participants gain mastery over the exercise. A particularly salient image arising from this exercise may also be selected to launch into a series of dynamisations which allow the meanings of the image to be developed further.

The Great Game of Power

Six chairs, a table, and a bottle are needed for this exercise. Group members are invited, one at a time, to arrange the objects into a structure so that one chair is clearly more powerful than the rest. Participants may place the objects in any way they wish, on their side, upside-down, on top of one another. After some experimentation, participants are asked to notice the formations that have emerged and name the social spaces they inhabit which are organized in a similar fashion. A variation of this exercise invites participants to enter into one of these constructed spaces and to take up what they would consider to be the most powerful place. Another participant enters and tries to find a yet more powerful place in the space constructed and this continues. In another variation of this exercise, participants are directed to create common social spaces (such as a bus stop, an airport, a courthouse, a place of worship, a kitchen, a factory, a prison) using these power constructs.

Invisible Theatre

Invisible Theatre is a previously scripted and rehearsed play that is performed in a public space without the public's knowing that it is a play. It must, according to Boal, address an issue of importance to the public in the particular area it will be performed in and is intended to provoke discussion. Often the actors will not just consist of the main characters but also those pretending to be bystanders who voice strong and often contrasting opinions on the subject, as a means of encouraging the "real" bystanders or passers-by to do the same. Its aim is to reveal the violence that exists in society and to draw attention to recurring and common problems. Boal provides several examples of Invisible Theatre, addressing issues from sexual harassment, racism, and the privatization of health care which were performed on public trains, on the street, and on ferries. These can be found in his text, *Games for Actors and Non-Actors* (1992).

Boal offers an *ideological warm-up* for theatre collectives and audiences stating that "theatre is an ideological representation of social life . . . it is important that actors do not become alienated from society at large, however specialized their technique may be . . . the actor must always be aware of the progressive nature of his mission, its pedagogical and combative character, theatre is an art and a weapon" (1992, p. 210). This is also reiterated by theatre theorist and practitioner Baz Kershaw who, in his writings on theatre as cultural intervention, lists ideological compatibility as a condition that allows theatre to affect the social norms of the audience (Kershaw, 1992). As an ideological warm-up for actors, Boal suggests dedicating the proposed performance to a particular person, dead or alive, or significant event, so that actors remains aware of the personified and real connection their work has. He also suggests that a variety of newspapers and alternative media be read aloud during a portion of the rehearsal process and that guests be invited to stimulate conversation of varied topics. Boal also suggests that actors research and possibly include portrayals of historical events that bear resemblance to current disturbing social and political phenomena. In effect, the artist who attempts to intervene within culture must also have a certain cultural fluency in order to be effective.

Forum Theatre

Forum Theatre relies upon presentation of short scenes that represent problems of a given community such as access to water for a community facing drought or sexism in the workplace for a group of concerned employees in an organization or institution. A short scene is created either by an external group (such as the Arena Theatre) or by those directly affected; the latter requires time to workshop the creation of the performance with participants unfamiliar with theatre improvisation and the form. The performance, lasting between 5–10 minutes, is performed for an audience of those directly affected and, ideally, at varied levels of investment, complicity, and power over the situation presented. The scene must contain an identifiable protagonist and an antagonist though there may also be other characters present in the scene as bystanders, enablers, and witnesses. The play is performed once through and then a second time with the direction that audience members may stop the scene at any time they feel that the protagonist may do something different to achieve a desired outcome. Audience members interact by replacing the protagonist in the scene and by improvising new solutions to the problems being presented and in so doing, galvanize the desire to challenge the culture they have grown frustrated with. The role of the Joker in Forum Theatre is to incite an active dialogue and embodied search for solutions by inviting as many active suggestions as possible, providing a brief summation after each solution offered, and keeping the action going. However, Boal is careful to note that the Joker is not there to make things easy but is also a *difficultator,* pushing audience members to grapple with the complexities within the scene presented without frightening the audience into inactivity. Boal provides several examples of Forum Theatre in his texts (1992, 1995).

There has been much debate and discussion about the aesthetics of Forum Theatre which contests the troublesome binary of the oppressor and the oppressed, challenges who can be replaced in a forum, subverts the pseudo-neutrality of the Joker who can never truly be neutral (as it is s/he whose gaze, questions, and comments determine what can be discussed in the forum), and the ideological contradictions inherent in a form that supports collective action but traditionally affords only individual intervention (Boal, 1992; Cohen-Cruz & Schutzman, 1994; Dwyer, 2004; Sajnani & Nadeau, 2006).

Rehearsal Techniques

Boal offers a variety of rehearsal techniques to prepare the Forum Theatre performance and develop and cement the connection between the actors' *wave* and *undercurrent,* terms Boal uses to describe the overt and subtle forms of communication transmitted between actor and audience. Another way to describe the partnership of the wave and undercurrent is in the phrase *mind-body agreement.* Complete descriptions of these can be found in the *Games for Actors and Non-Actors* (1992). Here are two examples:

Playing to the Deaf

Staying in tune with the rhythm of the piece, actors move through the performance without words. The idea is not to mime the piece or to add any additional gestures, but rather to allow the internal process of the characters to surface naturally. Boal states that this technique "is vital to ensure that the masks do not become clichés, symbols or signs; the exercise helps to 'Stanislavskify' the masks" (1992, p. 211).

Analytical Rehearsal of Emotion

The piece is played through the lens of one emotion only such as love, hate, fear, cowardice, or nervousness. All movements and dialogue must be infused with this one complete emotion. The purpose of this rehearsal technique is to reveal the emotions that most suit each moment in the play. A variation on this technique is the analytical rehearsal of style in which the play is played through the lens of melodrama, comedy, or film noir.

Newspaper Theatre

Newspaper Theatre is Boal's term for the work he was doing at the beginning of the Theatre of the Oppressed. The techniques are devised to facilitate scene development using news from a newspaper, or from any other written material as a means of demystifying printed knowledge and developing critical media literacy.[1] This method of theatre practice is also an excellent way for theatre collectives to enrich their cultural fluency and awareness of the basic ideologies and concerns that may be relevant to their audiences.

Legislative Theatre

The purpose of Legislative Theatre was originally to give Boal's electorate the opportunity to voice their opinions. The concept is similar to Forum Theatre; however, the subject of the production is based on a proposed law to be passed. "Spect-actors" may take the stage and express their opinions, thereby helping with the creation of new laws. The technique has since been used and documented in countries including Canada by Headlines Theatre in Vancouver, British Columbia, led by David Diamond to address substance abuse and gang violence, and in the United Kingdom by Cardboard Citizens led by Adrian Jackson to address homelessness.[2] Both of these companies have accessible documentation of their process and outcomes using Legislative Theatre.

Rainbow of Desire

Rainbow techniques stem from Image Theater and involve the creation and interaction of images created by group participants depicting internalized oppression usually embodied by a protagonist in relation to one or more antagonists. Boal describes 15 *prospective techniques* to evoke personal and shared experiences of oppression in a group, nine *introspective techniques* that concentrate on the use of images to surface and process the relationship between two people or two groups of people, and two sets of *extraversion techniques* that provide variations to extend the processing of a particular image(s) and which prepare the group to extend their kinesthetic dialogue to the public sphere through public performance. A complete accounting of Boal's techniques is provided in his text, *Rainbow of Desire* (1995).

Beginning of a Group

Boal relies on the creation of nonverbal images to evoke personal experiences. He suggests the following stages of image creation with a new group to "establish a relationship between personal singular problems and the collective problems a group is experiencing" (1995, p. 77). The following complete four-stage process is the first of 15

---

1. For an excellent interview with Augusto Boal in which he references Newspaper Theatre, see www. http://www.socialistworker.co.uk/art, issue 2101, May 17, 2008.
2. See http://www.cardboardcitizens.org.uk/ for more information.

prospective techniques.

Stage One: The Individual Images

Prior to beginning the exercise, Boal demonstrates ways in which an image can be formed, through modeling by physical manipulation or by mirroring the creator of the image. Boal instructs group participants to form groups of four or five people and, in a short span of time, have each member of each group create a realistic or metaphorical image of an actual oppression which is currently happening or which could happen again and which is true to the personal experience of the protagonist, the one creating the image. He instructs the protagonists or creators of each image to place themselves within the image in the position they actually occupy. Therefore, other members in the image are represented as either allied or oppressive forces or characters. All of this is done without speaking in order to retain the polysemy (the multiple possible interpretations) of the image.

Stage Two: The Parade of Images

In this stage, groups are invited into a delineated aesthetic space to remake their images in front of the larger group. After each image, the Joker asks the witnesses to share objective and subjective commentaries, and then differentiates between the two. Objective commentaries are based on "observable fact such as this person is seated or standing . . . subjective commentaries are individual perceptions, feelings, memories, sensations evoked by the image which must not be taken as definitive interpretations" (1995, p. 78). The Joker comments on the commonalities between the images presented.

Stage Three: The Image of the Images

The Joker then proposes that the group form a single image out of all the images which will contain the essential elements of all the others. To begin, a principal oppressed is chosen by the group from all of the images created. The only guideline Boal offers is that the image of the principal oppressed, and up to two can be chosen, will be one that is most representative of the group for reasons that need not be explained. Next, other images are constructed that have a relationship to the central image and that draw on important elements from the parade of images in the preceding stage.

Stage Four: The Dynamisation

In order for the resulting image to be a viable conduit for useful group work, Boal suggests that the Joker "verify the degree of interrelation of actor and image" by asking three questions and making necessary adjustments (1995, p. 79). First, do all participants *identify* with the images they are presenting? Those who reply that they do identify with the images they have embodied remain in those images. If there are images remaining that are embodied by participants who do not identify with them, the Joker then asks the witnessing participants, those not in the image, if they identify with any of those images and if so, replace them in the collective image. There may still be images with which none of the participants identify. In this case, the Joker asks if participants *recognize* the image or characters, i.e., do they have some knowledge of this character even if they do not immediately and personally identify with it. The same process is repeated to ensure that the collective image is populated by people who identify or recognize the characters embodied. If there are still images that remain, the Joker can ask if participants *resonate,* or have any feelings or emotions evoked by the image they are embodying and if so, remain in place. If not, they are replaced by a witnessing participant who does experience some resonance with the image or character. *Identification, recognition* and *resonance* are necessary, in Boal's formulation, for the capacity of the group to usefully engage with images created out of this and any process described in the Rainbow of Desire.

FIRST DYNAMISATION: INTERIOR MONOLOGUE. For three minutes, the participants embodying the "image of the images" are directed to speak their internal thoughts as the characters they are embodying. Others not in the image are invited to approach the image to hear the internal monologues of each character in the process of emergence.

SECOND DYNAMISATION: DIALOGUE. For another three minutes the participants in the image begin a dialogue with other characters in the image without moving from their original position, using speech alone.

THIRD DYNAMISATION: DESIRE IN ACTION. For another three minutes, characters demonstrate their desires, where they would naturally move and what they would naturally do within the image, in slow motion.

This process may result in a group discussion on what has been revealed about the nature of the oppression depicted or may be developed further through a variety of other techniques.

The Rainbow of Desire Technique

The Rainbow of Desire is a set of techniques as well as the name of an *introspective technique* in Boal's exposition on the relationship between theatre and therapy. "No sensation, emotion, or desire exists in a pure state in the human being . . . love and hate, sadness and joy, cowardice and courage, mix and mingle in constantly different proportions . . . that which emerges socially, at any given moment, is only the 'dominant strain'[3] of all these forces at work in the human soul" (1995, p. 150). The purpose of this introspective technique is to clarify these multiple desires, emotions and sensations in order to emphasize the protagonist's will and freedom of choice. Boal suggests that the following sequence need not be followed in order, nor to completion, but rather in accordance with each person's and groups needs and aims.

STAGE ONE: THE IMPROVISATION. Protagonists are selected from the group based on the degree to which their experience(s) resonate with other group members as in the prospective technique described above. The protagonists share an account of when they felt oppressed or unable to attain their desired outcome(s). The oppressive scene is re/enacted with the protagonists playing themselves and a chosen antagonist.

STAGE TWO: THE RAINBOW. The Joker asks the protagonists to create images with their body as a model of each desire, state of mind, and all the forces they feel are in play in the given scenario. After each image, the group is asked if someone feels like they can identify, recognize or feel a resonance with the image created. If so, they replace that image for the protagonists. After the protagonists have completed the series of images, the Joker asks if group participants have other images they would add or suggest. If

3. Boal's use of the term 'dominant strain' is, according to him, analogous to its use in musicology, whereby various strains of music interweave and one rises to the surface as melody. Boal uses this analogy in the Games for Actors and Non-Actors (1992) to describe the struggle between the will (melody) and counter-wills (harmonies and dissonant strains) in Image Theatre.

so, each one shows the images with their body and the protagonists can accept or refuse them.

STAGE THREE: THE BRIEF MONOLOGUE, THE CONFIDENCES. In this stage the rainbow of the protagonist's desires goes to the side of the delineated aesthetic space (stage space) in a line-up. Protagonists approach each part of themselves embodied by other group members and make a statement about what this part is and how they feel about it. This provides the protagonists yet another opportunity to bear witness to their internal experience, the first being the creation of the sculptures, and also provides each part of the self more information with which to play their part.

STAGE FOUR: THE PART TAKES OVER THE WHOLE. Here, the antagonist comes to the stage and remains fixed center stage. The protagonists send in one part of themselves, fixed in a sculpture to face-off with the antagonist in the middle of the stage space. The images of the part and the image of the antagonist come to life and enact the scene previously described to the group. This is repeated with each part of the rainbow in an order decided by the protagonists until each part has completed one round of combat. Each part and the antagonist maintain their sculpted image but are free to improvise their dialogue.

STAGE FIVE: THE WHOLE RAINBOW. In this stage, protagonists send the images of their parts back into combat together and in any order they choos. They can arrange them, one at a time, to be as near or as far, facing or turned away, from the antagonist who remains at the center. In this way, "the protagonist can determine the proportionate impact of the characteristics that animate each image" (1995, p. 153). The antagonist still addresses each part as though they are the protagonist.

STAGE SIX: WILL VERSUS DESIRE. Here, protagonists assert their will with each desire, each color of the rainbow. They approach each image and initiate a dialogue towards magnifying or minimizing each desire. The desires are instructed to begin with their original quality, as though to convince the protagonists that it is still a necessary part in the protagonists' real situation with the antagonist represented. However, each desire is also instructed to respond, without making it too easy, to the protagonists' assertions of their will and to shift, becoming stronger or diminished as demanded.

STAGE SEVEN: THE PROTAGONIST TAKES THE ANTAGONIST'S PLACE. After the protagonists have organized the constellation and have boosted each desire as described above, the Joker asks them to move beside or behind the antagonist, and gain from that perspective. "When we talk to someone we know what we are saying, but we have very little idea of how it is understood . . . equally when we carry out an action, we know what we are doing, but we do not know how it is perceived, felt or experienced" (1995, p. 154). Here the protagonists have an opportunity to gain insight into how they are perceived. The combat begins again with the antagonist dialoguing with each part of the rainbow from its position center-stage. After a while, the Joker asks the protagonists to take the antagonist's place and for the dialogues to continue without interruption.

STAGE EIGHT: THE AGORA OF DESIRES. Here the images that form the rainbow are instructed to find their contradictory desire and to continue the debate with them. After some time, the Joker asks the images to find another partner and continue the dialogue. This can be repeated a third time. The protagonists are instructed to leave the image and to circulate among the images of the rainbow, paying attention to seeing and hearing the alternatives and opinions that arise from conversations between parts of themselves.

STAGE NINE: THE REIMPROVISATION. The desires are dismissed and a scene between the protagonist and the antagonist is reenacted with or without a different outcome.

STAGE TEN: THE DISCUSSION. In this stage, all those who participated in the images share what they experienced in the scene, and those observing share their observations and experiences witnessing. Boal is careful to note that the Joker must never try to interpret "or discover the truth . . . he must only signal the originalities, the curiosities, all the aesthetic aspects of each intervention–the signifiers, rather than the signified" (1995, p. 156). Again, this approach to the dialogue does not try to reduce the process into a set of valuable lessons or meanings but places emphasis on the continued, active process of collective meaning making.

CONCEPTS IN THE THEATRE OF THE OPPRESSED

For Boal, there are no spectators, only active observers (or spect-actors). The emphasis is placed on the audience and not on the stage as whatever is staged must have resonance for those witnessing it in order to be therapeutic. As with the larger body of theory and practice that comprises the Theatre of the Oppressed, the Rainbow of Desire shares the aim of a) facilitating the transition of the spect-actors into a dramatic scene or images in which they will be able to rehearse alternatives to a recurring problem and b) extrapolate these experiences into their daily lives. With these aims in mind, Boal offers several key concepts in considering the interplay of theatre and therapy.

The Aesthetic Space

"The human being not only makes theatre, it is theatre" (Boal, 1995). For Boal, the literal meaning of theatre, drawn from the Greek *theatron,* referring to the audience seeing the act on stage, is central to his understanding of the emancipatory properties of theatre. According to Boal, theatre is concerned with the interrelations of people in society and its dramatic action lies in the staging of subtle and grand variations of contradiction and conflict. It is relational even in a monologue, as the antagonist is present even when absent. The *aesthetic space* of the theatre is determined by the physical dimensions of the space, or platform, and by the mutual agreement of those who gaze upon it. Therefore, the theatre can occur in any place and at any time in one body or in many bodies. Boal writes:

> The aesthetic space exists whenever there is a separation between the actor's space and the spectator's, or dissociation of two times–'today I am here, but yesterday I was here' . . . we coincide within ourselves when we integrate, into the present we are living, our memory of the past and our imagination of the future . . . the theatre serves as means of separating actor from spectator, the one who acts and the one who observes, [roles] which can coincide in the same person. (1995, p. 19)

Therefore the observing self is also theatre, or an aesthetic space, and can occur within subjective, intersubjective, spatial, or architectural dimensions. Boal describes the aesthetic space as having properties that stimulate knowledge and discovery, cognition and recognition, and learning by experience. Boal delineates these properties of aesthetic space into three fundamental characteristics: *plasticity, dichotomy,* and *telemicroscopy.*

PLASTICITY. The plasticity of aesthetic space refers to the malleable nature of theatre to evoke and represent real or imagined, past, present and future fears and desires culled from the memory of one, or from a collective, and projected into imaginal space. Boal describes the emancipatory qualities of this creative space where realities can converge, be constructed, stretched, reduced, amplified and deconstructed at will. Boal further distinguishes the affective and oneiric (dream-like) dimensions of the aesthetic space which relate to the core process of aesthetic distance in drama therapy (Jones, 1996). The affective nature of aesthetic space evokes feelings, sensations, and thoughts in the spect-actor (observing actor or client in drama therapy) and from Boal's understanding, facilitates a distanced recognition of these experiences whereas the oneiric nature of aesthetic space reduces distance and brings these experiences, thoughts and feelings into closer proximity with what the spect-actor conceives to be reality.

DICHOTOMY. The aesthetic space is inherently a dichotomous space allowing one to experience two realities at the same time, that of the physical aesthetic space, its contours and dimensions as well the imaginal space which has no boundaries except those internalized by the spect-actor(s). Boal also uses the terms *protagonist-patient* to describe the dual roles occupied by a single body which concretizes overt and covert desires within a fictional frame. Boal's vision of theatre and therapy requires the repetition of a scene taken from one's own life. As in a forum theatre performance, the first enactment is not interrupted but intended to bring the protagonist-patient into closer proximity with the desires in the scene, towards a concretization or materialization of these desires. In reliving the scene, the protagonist-patient replays the scene with an audience of fellow group members or guests and, in doing so, reveals the desires as objects or chosen performances. This repetition and recounting of experience creates a dichotomy for the protagonist-patient who is, as a result of these enactments, faced with choices of who to be and how to live out these, now palpable, desires.

TELEMICROSCOPY. Telemicroscopic is the term Boal uses to refer to the amplification and magnification of everyday interpersonal dynamics when given a platform, such as that afforded in an aesthetic space.

Cops in the Head

From a Boalian perspective, the therapeutic process entails the identification and active negotiation of prohibitive and inhibitive messages or *Cops in the Head* which limit or circumscribe the degree to which one is able to experience freedom in addition to awakening the desire to find plausible alternatives in thought and action (Boal, 1990). These messages or cops are always already embodied by social actors (the parent, teacher, police officer, judge) and culturally reinforced through daily rituals and institutions (marriage, criminal justice system, education system). Boal draws upon the de/construction and dynamisation of physical images to facilitate this inquiry. He details the three assumptions central to the *Cops in the Head* as *osmosis, metaxis,* and *analogical induction.*

OSMOSIS. *Osmosis* refers to the propagation or interpenetration, in Boal's terms, of values, tastes and ideas through repression and seduction. That is, it is both by choosing through love, desire, promises and by negating through acts of repulsion, violence, constraint and fear that osmosis takes place. Boal (1995) asserts that osmosis of power hierarchies, relationship to money, ideas about differences, ideas about punishment and reward takes place at all levels of culture from the family, to the school, at work, in places of worship, and is reinforced in the mediated narratives that occupy and infiltrate our public spaces. Boal also asserts that osmosis takes place in the theatre where transitive learning occurs through the immobilizing, repeated ritualistic division of the audience and stage wherein social roles and behaviors are modeled on stage to a deactivated, passive audience. In his work, Boal states he tries to "invert this immobilisme, to make the dialogue between the stage and audience totally transitive, in both directions; the stage can try to transform the audience, but the audience can also transform everything, try anything" (1995, p. 42). The quote at the beginning of this chapter is central to the understanding of this concept whereby all thought and behavior, whether it takes place in the family between two siblings, or between world leaders, is informed by globally propagated cultural values and their implicit hierarchies of power which have, for example, inscribed men with more access to wealth and social resources than women, lighter skinned people with more options than the darker skinned, and preference for heterosexuality over other sexual orientations.

METAXIS. Boal defines *metaxis* as "the state of belonging completely and simultaneously to two different, autonomous worlds . . . her reality and the image of her reality, which she herself has created" (1995, p. 43). In traditional theatre, the relationship between the character on stage and the spectator is wrought with empathy. Boal posits that the vicarious emotions felt by audience members through this process creates a window whereby the moral world of the characters portrayed invades and is internalized by the audience. In the Cops in the Head, the protagonist-patients create images and scenes of their own difficult realities which, according to Boal, produces sympathy among witnesses, a feeling of solidarity rather than an alienated and displaced longing. Through metaxis, Boal attempts to upset the conventional relationship governing the re/production of social norms, especially those identified to have contributed to the isolation, depression and loneliness he was witnessing in his participants. He does not prescribe censorship of potentially harmful messages but rather chooses to suffuse the culture with images of those living the suffering which accompanies marginalization in all its forms. Furthermore, Boal (1995) also warns against the easy reduction of images into words and asserts that their complexity is better preserved in symbolic form. He has noted the tendency among workshop participants to quickly ascribe words to the images produced as though to restrain and minimize their significance.

ANALOGICAL INDUCTION. Boal has stressed the need to move beyond the singular and individual to the plural and communal in order to identify the structural mechanisms that contribute and shape individual experience. As in "Psychodrama" (Chapter 18), Cops in the Head, along with all forms within the Theatre of the Oppressed, begins with the sharing of individual stories. If a story is shared in a group and immediately finds resonance with the realities of others, the process may proceed as the experience is sufficiently pluralized. However, if the story does not easily call forth similarities among group members, Boal draws upon *analogical induction* to enlarge the story so that others in the group may become engaged, in sympathy rather than stopping at empathy. He does this by inviting participants to create images or scenes of their experiences as they relate to the original image derived from the original story. From this point, a more distanced analysis of action, and reflection on that action, can proceed including the multiple perspectives offered by group members. Boal stresses the importance of tellers to play themselves in these images in order for their transformation to extend into real life.

Dysfunction

Dysfunction in Boal's constellation of theory and practice occurs with the internalization of any message that limits, circumscribes, or otherwise mutes the totality of what an individual or community is able to be and do towards achieving a better quality of life in relation to and in solidarity with their neighbors. These discouraging messages persist against the individual and collective desire to shift, change, upset, disrupt or question the current order of things in one's family, communities, neighborhood, city, country and at an international level. The symptom of this dysfunction is primarily inactivity or a perceived loss of agency but could easily be extrapolated to include symptoms of depression and anxiety. The therapeutic response to these symptoms is *catharsis,* a purging in the Greek sense of the word. Boal delineates four definitions of catharsis to emphasize that which most closely resonates with his overall philosophical tendencies: *medical, Morenian, Aristotelian,* and *Theatre of the Oppressed* (Boal, 1995).

MEDICAL CATHARSIS. Boal describes the medical approach to catharsis as ridding the body of an invading harmful entity or deficiency. A doctor prescribes a purgative, a relevant chemical or psychological antidote, to eliminate the dangerous substance or phenomena.

MORENIAN CATHARSIS. Boal posits that the goal of Morenian catharsis (articulated by the renowned psychiatrist and originator of psychodrama, Jacob Levy Moreno), is the elimination of psychological barriers to happiness. He refers to Moreno's *Case of Barbara,* an actress in Moreno's group who experienced a catharsis of her violent impulses through her portrayal of a similarly violent character on stage, thus freeing her to reconsider her relationships more openly.

ARISTOTELIAN CATHARSIS. According to Boal, the Aristotelian catharsis is (a) tragic catharsis and a coercive theatrical form. "In Aristotelian catharsis, what is being eliminated is always the hero's tendency to violate the law, whether human or divine . . . Antigone asserts the rights of the family over the law and over the rights of the state . . . Oedipus affirms the power of defying fate . . . Mexicans affirm the possibility of contravening General Custer's law . . . and what happens to all these people? They fall!" (1995, p. 71).

Boal's primary charge against Greek theatre and current Hollywood production is that they seduce their audiences away from their instinctual desire to change by instilling a fear of transformation. Through the passive witnessing of these stories exalting the rise and inevitable fall of change makers, audiences are vicariously tranquilized. The protagonist ultimately confesses to their deviance, thereby restoring the sanctity of social and moral order.

CATHARSIS IN THE THEATRE OF THE OPPRESSED. Boal differentiates his use of catharsis, which transgresses the accepted passivity of the spectator, and states that "the goal is not to create calm, equilibrium, but rather to create disequilibrium which prepares the way for action" (1995, p. 72). Boal attempts to achieve this through a dynamisation of the audience, inviting it to intervene and propose actions within scenes that depict common, frequently troubling social behaviors and rituals. Rather than ending with a superficial resolution, the goal in this form of theatre is to cathart all blocks to action by creating the conditions that will support the desire to speak up and act. In this way, the repeated embodied acts of spect-actors getting out of their seats and moving onto the stage, twice-repeated outside the confines of the theatre, is the optimal result of Boal's catharsis.

CASE EXAMPLE

Boal provides several case examples that illustrate the possibilities for cultural dialogue and the negotiation of conflict (1992, 1995). One such example is provided here to illustrate the Rainbow of Desire technique.

In May of 1989, Boal decided to use a *Cops-in-the-Head* technique rather than Forum Theatre in a public performance to mark the end of a week-long workshop. That evening, at Guissen, Boal recounts that a woman had offered herself as a protagonist stating that she wanted to get a better understanding of her male partner. She hesitated in front of the audience of 200, as Boal prompted her with questions about what she might want from her lover, her husband, or her boyfriend. Eventually, she answered "an elephant." Everyone laughed and Boal thought of asking her to suggest something more concrete but then decided to keep the image, thinking that it may be more useful to retain the symbol and its many possible meanings. As this was a public performance situation, actors were chosen from the participants who had attended Boal's workshop. Over the course of her process, Boal noted that she was asking her husband for something he could not give her and that she was asking for something without offering anything in return. He came to this determination by supporting her in the development of and engagement with the arc of her desires. In Stage Two of the *Rainbow of Desire* process, she was instructed to create the colors or aspects of herself that she was aware of when thinking of her situation with her husband. Her seven colors included an image of a young child demanding an elephant, a frightened spouse, a self-pitying wounded spouse, a fighter with fists out ready to box, a woman facing herself in a mirror, a solitary woman seated by an imaginary river, and a distanced spouse looking at her husband, and murmuring in inaudible whispers. Boal directed her to provide each image with a few lines of dialogue fitting the image of her self (Stage Three).

It was clear to Boal that only the first and last of her images appeared to retain a connection to the husband figure while the rest were images of self-contemplation and isolation. In order to draw attention to his observation, Boal invited the woman to consider the distances she was placing between her images and the husband. Once her rainbow was complete, Boal invited her to send the images into dialogue with the husband (Stage Seven). His hypothesis was proven when he observed that dialogue only occurred with the first and last image, while the remaining images enacted a monologue and the "husband" remained an ignored spectator.

After the dialogues, Boal asked the woman to form an intentional constellation with the colors of her rainbow (Stage Four). She placed the child in front of the husband and the murmuring spouse the furthest away. Between these two images, she formed a line with the remaining five images. Boal then asked her to stand beside the husband actor, in his position, to get a sense of his perspective (Stage Seven). "My God," she exclaimed and immediately went about rearranging her constellation by eliminating the child, placing five images behind his back and outside of his range of vision, leaving the murmuring spouse in front of him, albeit at a distance. The husband continued his dialogue with this image when the woman interrupted stating "It isn't like that. . . ." The image of the murmuring spouse responded to her interruption as though it came from the husband and asked the woman to clarify what she meant. At this point and without instruction, the woman replaced the murmuring image and, looking at her husband and then to the man in the audience who was seated beside her, said "let's go!"

This example illustrates how one woman's dilemma was given form and voice through the construction, activation and embodied negotiation of her internal impulses and desires. The stages of the Rainbow of Desire technique were not completed in order but rather were drawn upon as the situation required. The conditions offered through this technique appeared to give the protagonist an immediate opportunity to gain insight into her frustrations as evidenced by her reaction when she viewed her rainbow from the perspective of her husband. The re/arrangement of her constellation provided her an opportunity to consider her options and choices of how she wished to be seen and which aspects of herself were supportive of her desired outcome. As Boal notes, "All we know is that 'let's go!' implies a decision by two people. 'Let's go!' is itself a movement. All the forms of relation which had gone before were about blockage, about self-satisfaction or permanent, insipid lamentation. Even in the last instance, where a dialogue was taking place, the man was virtually extinguished. 'Let's go!' was a departure, a beginning, a new stage: it was an action, a decision. The impossible demand–'I want an elephant'–had been replaced with a possible proposition–'Let's go!'" (1995, p. 164).

Furthermore, she was witnessed in this negotiation by an audience who, as a microcosm of society at large, attuned its collective attention to the inner mechanics of what is normally understood to be a private relationship. The *performance of attention* afforded by this and other Boalian techniques is the nexus of cultural dialogue and cultural change because it brings the public and the private into conversation.

THEATRE OF THE OPPRESSED AND DRAMA THERAPY

The Theatre of the Oppressed includes an analysis of the interplay of the social, economic and political ways of a particular people in a particular place at a particular time, when considering the internal and external challenges that may face an individual or a community. At the core of Boal's theory and practice is the urgent necessity for individuals and communities to overcome fear, and become aware of possible alternatives and already existing capacities to respond to real and perceived challenges/oppressions towards realizing greater equity and justice in their lives. For the drama therapist, Boal calls us to step back and examine our definitions of illness and health in the varied contexts in which we work and to question whose interests we serve and sustain in our daily non/verbal exchanges with colleagues, clients, insurance companies, social service and other government agencies. He reminds us to compassionately inhabit and simultaneously call these heavily invested identities into question. His is also a call to remain informed of the ebbs and flows of culture as it is narrated and mediated. Boal's methods provide a means to stage and interrupt minute everyday interactions which, together, create culture and in so doing, examine the microscopic building blocks of society, its celebrations and abuses of power, its pathos and its spaces of hope. The cultural microcosm of the group creates an apt medium for this form of inquiry. The aesthetic space within the group as well as in public performance becomes a platform for cultural negotiation and dialogue as existing realities are grappled with, challenged and confronted in vivo.

The development of the Theatre of the Oppressed can be regarded as a series of discoveries grounded in direct theatre-based practice originating with Boal and challenged and adapted by many educators, therapists, social workers and artists to suit their particular contexts around the world (Cohen-Cruz & Schutzman, 1994, 2006). It is also currently practiced by drama therapists in Europe, Canada and the United States. In considering Boal's guiding theoretical framework, it is easy to see that it shares similarities with the central action of several phases in Renée Emunah's "Integrative Five Phase Model" in drama therapy (1994, and Chapter 4) and the *life-drama connection* articulated as a core process in drama therapy by Phil Jones (1996). Furthermore, Boal's description of the aesthetic space bears resemblance to the *embodied encounters in the playspace* described by David Read Johnson in his method, "Developmental Transformations" (Chapter 6). Both of these methods also emphasize the role of the therapy to disrupt and destabilize encrusted forms of thinking and behavior, and to tolerate the multiplicity of desire. Where they diverge is in the emphasis Boal places on the necessity of the collective in effecting cultural change in repair of individual suffering. Here, Boal's work joins with that of "Healing the Wounds of History" (Chapter 8), "Sociodrama" (Chapter 19), and "Playback Theatre" (Chapter 20). Boal's methods can be effective alone and in conjunction with other methods familiar to drama therapists in rendering the varied cultures we inhabit available to dialogue and change.

CONCLUSION

At a time when collective rights such as clean air and water are increasingly privatized, when poverty is increasingly racialized and criminalized, when the tyranny of war and genocide is given global audience, when people continue to labor under the burden of violent repetitions in their families and across generations, Boal's methods provide an increasingly necessary avenue to negotiate the de/construction of collective trauma and its effects on individual and group psychology. Through the collectivization of personal stories, Theatre of the Oppressed provides several means to identify and interact with the cultural conditions that give rise to suffering, dislocating psychopathology from its dominant formulation as arising from individual weakness or deficiency. His methods also emphasize the necessity of unveiling culturally produced forms of political abuses of power that dissuade action by building false walls between public and the private spheres of life. Boal's methods are central to integrated learning and provide hopeful avenues that can restore individual and collective response/ability and account/ability to the everyday social actor who, in partnership and alliance with others, will be the architects of progressive acts of freedom and, thus, the artists of our future.

REFERENCES

Babbage, F. (2004). *Augusto Boal.* New York: Routledge Press.

Boal, A. (1979). *The theatre of the oppressed.* New York: Urizen Books.

Boal, A. (1990). The cop in the head: Three hypotheses. *The Drama Review, 34,* 35–42.

Boal, A. (1992). *Games for actors and non-actors.* New York: Routledge Press

Boal, A. (1994). Vindicated: A letter from Augusto Boal. *The Drama Review, 38,* 35–36.

Boal, A. (1995). *The rainbow of desire.* New York: Routledge Press.

Boal, A. (1998). *Legislative theatre.* New York:

Routledge Press.
Boal, A. (2001). *Hamlet and the baker's son.* New York: Routledge Press.
Boal, A. (2006). *The aesthetics of the oppressed.* New York: Routledge Press.
Emunah, R. (1994). *Acting for real: Drama therapy process, technique, and performance.* New York: Brunner/Routledge.
Dwyer, P. (2004). Making bodies talk in Forum Theatre. *Research in Drama Education, 9,* 199–210.
Freire, P. (1970). *Pedagogy of the oppressed.* New York: Continuum.
Jones, P. (1996). *Drama as therapy: Theatre as living.* London: Routledge.
Kershaw, B. (1992). *The politics of performance: Radical theatre as cultural intervention.* London: Routledge.
Linds, W., & Vettraino, E. (2008). Collective imagining: Collaborative storytelling through Image Theater. *Forum: Qualitative Social Research,* volume 9.
Sajnani, N., & Nadeau, D. (2006). Creating safer spaces: Performing the politics of possibility. *Canadian Women's Studies Journal, 25,* 45–53.

Selected Articles and Books About Augusto Boal

Albuquerque, S-J. (1986). Conflicting signs of violence in Augusto Boal's Torquemada. *Modern Drama, 29,* 452–459.
Bisset, J. I. (1982). Victims and violators: The structure of violence in Torquemada. *Latin American Theatre Review, 15,* 27–34.
Chamberlain, F. (Ed.). (1995). Working without Boal: Digressions and developments in the Theatre of the Oppressed. *Contemporary Theatre Review. 3:*1. (Includes ten articles on the work of Boal. Authors: Frances Babbage, Steve Ball, Alister Campbell, Lyn Ferrand, Andy Hickson, Mary Ann Hushlak, Tom Magill, Nick Otty, and Chrissie Poulter.)
Cohen-Cruz, J. (1990). Boal at NYU: A workshop and its aftermath. *The Drama Review, 34,* 43–49.
Cohen-Cruz, J., & Schutzman, M. (1994). *Playing Boal.* New York; Routledge Press.
Cohen-Cruz, J., & Schutzman, M. (2006). *A Boal companion: Dialogues on theatre and cultural politics.* New York: Routledge Press.
Heritage, P. (1994). The courage to be happy: Augusto Boal, Legislative Theatre, and the 7th International Festival of the Theatre of the Oppressed. *The Drama Review, 38,* 25–36.
Milling, J., & Lay, G. (2001). *Modern theories of performance: From Stanislavski to Boal.* New York: Palgrave.
Paterson, D. L. (1994). A role to play for the Theatre of the Oppressed. *The Drama Review, 38,* 37–49.
Schutzman, M. (1994). Activism, therapy, or nostalgia? Theatre of the Oppressed in NYC. *The Drama Review, 38,* 77–83.
Schutzman, M., & Cohen-Cruz, J. (1990). Theatre of the Oppressed workshops with women. *The Drama Review, 34,* 66–76.
Taussig, M., & Schechner, R. (1990). Boal in Brazil, France, and the USA: An interview with Augusto Boal. *The Drama Review, 34,* 50–65.

FURTHER RESOURCES AND TRAINING

Global (in multiple languages):
www.theatreoftheoppressed.org

United Kingdom:
Cardboard Citizens:
www.cardboardcitizens.org.uk

Canada:
Headlines Theatre:
www.headlinestheatre.com
Mixed Company:
www.mixedcompanytheatre.com
Creative Alternatives:
www.creative-alternatives.ca

United States:
Theatre of the Oppressed Laboratory:
www.toplab.org
Pedagogy and Theatre of the Oppressed:
www.ptoweb.org

BIBLIOGRAPHY

BOOKS ON DRAMA THERAPY

Anderson-Warren, M., & Grainger, R. (2000). *Practical approaches to dramatherapy: The shield of Perseus.* London: Jessica Kingsley Publishers.

Astell-Burt, C. (1981). *Puppetry for mentally handicapped people.* Cambridge: Brookline Books.

Astell-Burt, C. (2001). *I am the story: The art of puppetry in education and therapy.* London: Souvenir Press.

Ayalon, O., & Flasher, A. (1993). *Children and divorce: Chain reaction.* London: Jessica Kingsley Publishers.

Bailey, S. (1993). *Wings to fly: Bringing theatre arts to students with special needs.* Bethesda, MD: Woodbine House.

Baim, C., Brookes, S., & Mountford, A. (2002). *The Geese Theatre handbook: Drama with offenders and people at risk.* Winchester: Waterside Press.

Balfour, M. (2003). *The use of drama in the rehabilitation of violent male offenders.* Lewiston, NY: Edwin Mellen Press.

Balfour, M. (2004). *Theatre in prison: Theory and practice.* Portland, OR: Intellect.

Bannister, A. (1997). *The healing drama: Psychodrama and dramatherapy with abused children.* New York: Free Association Books.

Behr, M.W., Snyder, A.B., & Clopton, A.S. (1979). *Drama integrates basic skills: Lesson plans for the learning disabled.* Springfield, IL: Charles C Thomas.

Bergman, J., & Hewish, S. (2003). *Challenging experience: An experiential approach to the treatment of serious offenders.* Oklahoma City: Wood 'n' Barnes Publishing.

Blatner, A., & Wiener, D. (2007). *Interactive and improvisational drama: Varieties of applied theatre and performance.* New York: iUniverse.

Boal, A. (1995). *The rainbow of desire: The Boal method of theatre and therapy.* New York: Routledge.

Bouzoukis, C.E. (2001). *Pediatric dramatherapy: They couldn't run so they learned to fly.* London: Jessica Kingsley Publishers.

Casdagli, P. (1998). *Trust and power: Taking care of ourselves through drama.* London: Jessica Kingsley Publishers.

Casson, J. (2004). *Drama, psychotherapy, and psychosis: Dramatherapy and psychodrama with people who hear voices.* London: Brunner-Routledge.

Cattanach, A. (1992). *Drama for people with special needs.* New York: Drama Book Publishers.

Cattanach, A. (1993). *Play therapy with abused children.* London: Jessica Kingsley Publishers.

Cattanach, A. (1994). *Play therapy: Where the sky meets the underworld.* London: Jessica Kingsley Publishers.

Cattanach, A. (1997). *Children's stories in play therapy.* London: Jessica Kingsley Publishers.

Cattanach, A. (Ed.). (2002). *The story so far: Play therapy narratives.* London: Jessica Kingsley Publishers.

Cattanach, A. (2003). *Introduction to play therapy.* New York: Brunner-Routledge.

Cattanach, A. (2007). *Narrative approaches in play therapy with children.* London: Jessica Kingsley Publishers.

Cattanach, A., Chesner, A., Jennings, S., Meldrum, B., & Mitchell, S. (1993). *The handbook of drama therapy.* London: Routledge.

Chesner, A. (1995). *Dramatherapy for people with learning disabilities: A world of difference.*

London: Jessica Kingsley Publishers.

Chesner, A., & Hahn, H. (Eds.). (2001). *Creative advances in groupwork.* London: Jessica Kingsley Publishers.

Cohen, H. (1995). *Dramatically able: Making drama accessible to participants with disabilities.* Ann Arbor, MI: Wild Swan Theatre.

Cossa, M. (2005). *Rebels with a cause: Working with adolescents using action techniques.* London: Jessica Kingsley Publishers.

Cossa, M., Fleischmann, E.S., Grover, L., & Hazelwood, J.L. (1996). *Acting out: The workbook.* Washington, DC: Taylor & Francis.

Courtney, R. (1990). *Drama and intelligence.* Montreal, Canada: McGill-Queen's University Press.

Cox, M. (Ed.). (1992). *Shakespeare comes to Broadmoor: 'The actors are come hither': The performance of tragedy in a secure psychiatric hospital.* London: Jessica Kingsley Publishers.

Crimmins, P. (1997). *Storymaking and creative groupwork with older people.* London: Jessica Kingsley Publishers.

Crimmens, P. (2006). *Drama therapy and storymaking in special education.* London: Jessica Kingsley Publishers.

Dayton, T. (1990). *Drama games: Techniques for self development.* Pompano Beach, FL: Health Communications, Inc.

Duggan, M., & Grainger, R. (1997). *Imagination, identification and catharsis in theatre and therapy.* London: Jessica Kingsley Publishers.

Dunne, P.B. (1988). *Media in drama therapy: An exercise handbook.* Los Angeles: Drama Therapy Institute of Los Angeles.

Dunne, P.B. (1990). *The creative therapeutic thinker* (2nd Ed.). Los Angeles: Drama Therapy Institute of Los Angeles.

Dunne, P.B. (1993). *Drama therapy activities with parents and children: An exercise handbook* (Revised Ed.). Los Angeles: Drama Therapy Institute of Los Angeles.

Dunne, P.B. (1995). *Creative journal.* Los Angeles: Drama Therapy Institute of Los Angeles.

Dunne, P.B. (1997). *Double stick tape: Poetry, drama, and narratives as therapy for adolescents.* Los Angeles: Drama Therapy Institute of Los Angeles.

Dunne, P. B. (2006). *The narrative therapist and the arts: Expanding possibilities through drama, movement, puppets, masks, and drawings,* (2nd Ed.). Los Angeles: Drama Therapy Institute of Los Angeles.

Dunne, P.B., & Rand, H. (2003). *Narradrama: Integrating drama therapy, narrative, and the creative arts.* Los Angeles: Possibilities Press

Emunah, R. (1994). *Acting for real: Drama therapy: Process, technique, and performance.* New York: Brunner/Mazel (Taylor & Francis).

Eulert, C.H. (1998). *The magic chest: Where you are, where you've been, where you're going.* Bristol, PA: Accelerated Development.

Feldman, D. (1997). *ENACT workbook.* New York: ENACT Institute.

Fox, J. (1986). *Acts of service: Spontaneity, commitment, and tradition in the nonscripted theatre.* New Paltz, NY: Tusitala Publishing.

Fox, J., & Dauber, H. (Eds.). (1999). *Gathering voices: Essays on playback theatre.* New Paltz, NY: Tusitala Publishing.

Gale, J., Realpe, A., & Pedriali, E. (2008). *Therapeutic communities for psychosis: Philosophy, history, and clinical practice.* Hove, East Sussex; New York: Routledge.

Gallo-Lopez, L., & Schaefer, C.E. (Eds.). (2005). *Play therapy with adolescents.* Lanham, MD: Jason Aronson.

Gerity, L.A., (1999). *Creativity and the dissociative patient: Puppets, narrative and art in the treatment of survivors of childhood trauma.* London: Jessica Kingsley Publishers.

Gersie, A. (1992). *Storymaking in bereavement: Dragons in flight in the meadow.* London: Jessica Kingsley Publishers.

Gersie, A. (Ed.). (1996). *Dramatic approaches to brief therapy.* London: Jessica Kingsley Publishers.

Gersie, A. (1997). *Reflections on therapeutic storymaking: The use of stories in groups.* London: Jessica Kingsley Publishers.

Gersie, A., & King, N. (1990). *Storymaking in education and therapy.* London: Jessica Kingsley Publishers.

Gold, M. (1991). *The fictional family: In drama, education, and groupwork.* Springfield, IL: Charles C Thomas.

Gold, M. (2000). *Therapy through drama: The fictional family.* Springfield, IL: Charles C Thomas.

Grainger, R. (1990). *Drama and healing: The roots of drama therapy.* London: Jessica Kingsley Publishers.

Grainger, R. (1995). *The glass of heaven: The faith of the dramatherapist.* London: Jessica Kingsley Publishers.

Grainger, R. (2003). *Group spirituality: A workshop approach.* New York: Routledge.

Grainger, R., & Andersen-Warren, M. (2000). *Dramatherapy: Expanding horizons.* Philadelphia: Jessica Kingsley Publishers.

Jenkins, M. (1996). *The play's the thing: Exploring text in drama and therapy.* New York: Routledge.

Jennings, S. (1974). *Remedial drama.* New York: Theatre Arts Books.

Jennings, S. (1987). *Creative drama in groupwork.* London: Winslow Press.

Jennings, S. (1987). *Drama therapy: Theory and practice for teachers and clinicians.* Cambridge, MA: Brookline Books.

Jennings, S. (Ed.). (1990). *Dramatherapy theory and practice 1.* New York: Routledge.

Jennings, S. (1990). *Dramatherapy with families, groups, and individuals: Waiting in the wings.* London: Jessica Kingsley Publishers.

Jennings, S. (Ed.). (1992). *Dramatherapy theory and practice 2.* New York: Routledge.

Jennings, S. (Ed.). (1995). *Dramatherapy with children and adolescents.* New York: Routledge.

Jennings, S. (1995). *Theatre, ritual, and transformation: The senoi temiars.* New York: Routledge.

Jennings, S. (Ed.). (1996). *Dramatherapy theory and practice 3.* New York: Routledge.

Jennings, S. (1997). *Introduction to dramatherapy: Theatre and healing: Ariadne's ball of thread.* London: Jessica Kingsley Publishers.

Jennings, S. (1999). *Introduction to developmental playtherapy: Playing and health.* London: Jessica Kingsley Publishers.

Jennings, S., Cattanach, A., Mitchell, S., Chesner, A., & Meldrum, B. (1994). *The handbook of dramatherapy.* London: Routledge.

Jennings, S., & Minde, A. (1992). *Art therapy and dramatherapy: Masks of the soul.* London: Jessica Kingsley Publishers.

Johnson, D. R. (1999). *Essays on the creative arts therapies: Imaging the birth of a profession.* Springfield, IL: Charles C Thomas.

Johnson, D.R., & Sandel, S.L. (1987). *Waiting at the gate: Creativity and hope in the nursing home.* New York: Haworth Press.

Jones, P. (1996). *Drama as therapy: Theatre as living.* New York: Routledge.

Jones, P. (2007). *Drama as therapy: Theory, practice and research.* New York: Routledge.

Kottman, T. (2001). *Play therapy: Basic and beyond.* Alexandria, VA: American Counseling Association.

Lacher, D.B., Nichols, T., & May, J.C. (2005). *Connecting with kids through stories: Using narratives to facilitate attachment in adopted children.* London: Jessica Kingsley Publishers.

Landy, R. (1993). *Personna and performance: The meaning of role in drama, therapy, and everyday life.* New York: Guilford Press.

Landy, R. (1994). *Drama therapy: Concepts, theories, and practices* (2nd Ed.). Springfield, IL: Charles C Thomas.

Landy, R. (1996). *Essays in drama therapy: The double life.* London: Jessica Kingsley Publishers.

Landy, R. (2001). *New essays in drama therapy: Unfinished business.* Springfield, IL: Charles C Thomas.

Landy, R. (2008). *The couch and the stage: Integrating words and action in psychotherapy.* Lanham, MD: Rowman & Littlefield.

Langley, D. (1983). *Dramatherapy and psychiatry.* London: Croom Helm.

Langley, D. (2006). *An introduction to dramatherapy.* Thousand Oaks, CA: Sage Publications.

Langley, D. M., & University of Exeter. (2003). *Dramatherapy and psychodrama: Towards a relationship.* Exeter: University of Exeter.

Larson, R. (2004). *A stage for memory: A guide to the living history theatre program of elders share the arts.* Brooklyn: The National Center for Creative Aging.

Lewis, P. (1993). *Creative transformation: The healing power of the arts.* Wilmette, IL: Chiron Publications.

Lewis, P. & Johnson, D. (Eds.). (2000). *Current approaches to drama therapy.* Springfield, IL: Charles C Thomas.

Lindkvist, M.R. (1997). *Bring white beads when you call on the healer.* New Orleans: Rivendell House.

Link, A. (1992). *Mirrors from the heart: Emotional identity and expression through drama.* Ontario,

Canada: Snailworks.
MacDougall, P., & Yoder, P.S. (Eds.). (1998). *Contaminating theatre: Intersections of theatre, therapy, and public health.* Evanston, IL: Northwestern University Press.
McCurrach, I., & Darnley, B. (1999). *Special talents, special needs: Drama for people with learning disabilities.* London: Jessica Kingsley Publishers.
Mitchell, S. (1995). *Dramatherapy: Clinical studies.* London: Jessica Kingsley Publishers.
Nelson, L., & Finneran, L. (2006). *Drama and the adolescent journey.* Portsmouth, NH: Heinemann.
Newham, P. (1999). *Using voice and theatre in therapy: The practical application of voice movement therapy.* London: Jessica Kingsley Publishers.
Pearson, J. (Ed.). (1996). *Discovering the self through drama and movement: The Sesame approach.* London: Jessica Kingsley Publishers.
Peter, M. (1994). *Drama for all: Developing drama in the curriculum with pupils with special education needs.* London: David Fulton Publishers.
Pickering, K. (1997). *Drama improvised: A sourcebook for teachers and therapists.* New York: Routledge.
Piggins, C., & Thurman, A. (1996). *Drama activities with older adults: A handbook for leaders.* Binghamton, NY: Haworth Press.
Pitruzzella, S. (2004). *Introduction to dramatherapy: Person and threshold.* New York: Brunner-Routledge.
Rowe, N. (2007). *Playing the other: Dramatizing personal narratives in playback theatre.* London: Jessica Kingsley Publishers.
Salans, M. (2004). *Storytelling with children in crisis.* London: Jessica Kingsley Publishers.
Salas, J. (1993). *Improvising real life: Personal story in playback theatre.* Dubuque, IA: Kendall/Hunt Publishing.
Salas, J. (2007). *Do my story, sing my song: Music therapy and playback theatre with troubled children.* New Paltz, NY: Tusitala Publishing.
Schattner, G., & Courtney, R. (Eds.). (1981). *Drama in therapy: Volume one: Children.* New York: Drama Book Specialists.
Schattner, G., & Courtney, R. (Eds.). (1981). *Drama in therapy: Volume two: Adults.* New York: Drama Book Specialists.
Schechner, R. (1994). *Environmental theatre.* New York: Applause.
Scheff, T.J. (1979). *Catharsis in healing, ritual and drama.* Berkeley: University of California Press.
Schutzman, M., & Cohen-Cruz, J. (1994). *Playing Boal: Theatre, therapy and activism.* New York: Routledge.
Schweitzer, P. (2007). *Reminiscence theatre: Making theatre from memories.* London: Jessica Kingsley Publishers.
Shaw, A., & Stevens, C. (Eds.). (1979). *Drama, theatre, and the handicapped.* Washington, DC: American Theater Association.
Slade, P. (1959). *Dramatherapy as an aid to becoming a person.* London: Guild of Pastoral Psychology.
Sternberg, P. (1998). *Theatre for conflict resolution in the classroom and beyond.* Portsmouth, NH: Heinemann.
Strimling, A. (2004). *Roots and branches: Creating intergenerational theatre.* Portsmouth, NH: Heinemann.
Telander, M., Quinlan, F., & Verson, K. (1982). *Acting up!: An innovative approach to creative drama for older adults.* Chicago: Coach House Press.
Thompson, J. (Ed.). (1998). *Prison theatre: Practices and perspectives.* London: Jessica Kingsley Publishers.
Thompson, J. (1999). *Drama workshops for anger management and offending behavior.* London: Jessica Kingsley Publishers.
Tomlinson, R. (1989). *Disability, theatre, and education.* Bloomington, IN: Indiana University Press.
Verhofstadt-Deveve, L. (2000). *Theory and practice of action and drama techniques.* London: Jessica Kingsley Publishers.
Warren, B., & Dunne, T. (1996). *Drama games: Drama and group activities for leaders working with people of all ages and abilities.* Studio City, CA: Players Press.
Warren, B., & Simonds, C. (2004). *The clown doctor chronicles.* New York: Rodopi.
Way, B. (1972). *Development through drama.* New York: Humanities Press.
Weber, A.M., & Haen, C. (2005). *Clinical applications of drama therapy in child and adolescent treat-*

ment. New York: Routledge.

Weisberg, N., & Wilder, R. (Eds.). (1988). *Creative arts with older adults: A sourcebook.* New York: Human Sciences Press.

Wethered, A.G. (1997). *Movement and drama in therapy: A holistic approach* (2nd Ed.). London: Jessica Kingsley Publishers.

Wiener, D.J. (1994). *Rehearsals for growth: Theatre improvisation for psychotherapists.* New York: W.W. Norton.

Wiener, D.J. (1999). *Beyond talk therapy: Using movement and expressive techniques in clinical practice.* Washington, DC: American Psychological Association.

Wiener, D.J., & Oxford, L.K. (Eds.). (2003). *Action therapy with families and groups: Using creative arts improvisation in clinical practice.* Washington, DC: American Psychological Association.

Wilder, R. (1986). *A space where anything can happen: Creative drama in the middle school.* VA: New Plays, Inc.

Wilder, R. (1996). *Life drama with youth and elders: Come, step into my life.* Charlottesville, VA: New Plays, Inc.

Wilder, R. (1997). *The lifestory re-play cycle: A manual of activities and techniques.* State College, PA: Venture Publishing.

Wilson, G.D. (Ed.). (1991). *Psychology and performing arts.* Lisse, Netherlands: Zeitlinger Publishers.

Winn, L. (1994). *Post traumatic stress disorder and dramatherapy: Treatment and risk reduction.* London: Jessica Kingsley Publishers.

INTERDISCIPLINARY BOOKS THAT INCLUDE DRAMA THERAPY

Anderson, W. (Ed.). (1977). *Therapy and the arts: Tools of consciousness.* New York: Harper Colophon Books.

Bannister, A. (2003). *Creative therapies with traumatized children.* London: Jessica Kingsley Publishers.

Bannister, A., & Huntington, A. (Eds.). (2002). *Communicating with children and adolescents: Action for change.* London: Jessica Kingsley Publishers.

Bertman, S.L. (Ed.). (1999). *Grief and the healing arts: Creativity as therapy.* Amityville, NY: Baywood Publishing.

Betts, D.J. (Ed.). (2003). *Creative arts therapies approaches in adoption and foster care.* Springfield, IL: Charles C Thomas.

Bolton, G. (Ed.). (2008). *Dying, bereavement and the healing arts.* London: Jessica Kingsley Publishers.

Brooke, S.L. (Ed.). (2006). *Creative arts therapies manual.* Springfield, IL: Charles C Thomas.

Brooke, S.L. (Ed.). (2007). *Creative arts therapies with domestic abuse survivors.* Springfield, IL: Charles C Thomas.

Brooke, S.L. (Ed.). (2007). *The use of creative arts therapies with sexual abuse survivors.* Springfield, IL: Charles C Thomas.

Brooke, S.L. (Ed). (2008). *Creative arts therapies with substance abusers.* Springfield, IL: Charles C Thomas.

Brooke, S.L. (Ed.). (2008). *The creative therapies and eating disorders.* Springfield, IL: Charles C Thomas.

Camilleri, V.A. (Ed.). (2007). *Healing the inner city child: Creative arts therapies with youth at risk.* London: Jessica Kingsley Publishers.

Carey, L. (Ed.). (2006). *Expressive and creative arts methods for trauma survivors.* London: Jessica Kingsley Publishers.

Cattanach, A. (Ed.). (1999). *Process in the arts therapies.* London: Jessica Kingsley Publishers.

Davis, S., & Ferdman, B. (1993). *Nourishing the heart: A guide to intergenerational arts projects in the schools.* New York: Creative Ways.

Doktor, D. (Ed.). (1998). *Arts therapies and clients with eating disorders: Fragile bond.* London: Jessica Kingsley Publishers.

Erikson, J. (1976). *Activity, recovery, growth.* New York: W.W. Norton.

Fryear, J., & Fleshman, B. (1981). *The arts in therapy.* Chicago: Nelson-Hall.

Gladding, S. T. (2005). *Counseling as an art: The creative arts in counseling* (3rd Ed.). Alexandria, VA: American Counseling Association.

Hornyak, L.M., & Baker, E.K. (1989). *Experiential therapies for eating disorders.* New York: Guilford Press.

Jones, P. (2005). *The arts therapies: A revolution in*

healthcare. New York: Brunner-Routledge.
Karkou, V., & Sanderson, P. (2006). *Arts therapies: A research-based map of the field.* Edinburgh; New York: Elsevier Churchill Livingstone.
Kaye, C., & Blee, T. (1996). *The arts in health care: A palette of possibilities.* London: Jessica Kingsley Publishers.
Knill, P.J., Levine, G., & Levine, S.K. (2005). *Principles and practice of expressive arts therapies: Toward a therapeutic aesthetic.* London: Jessica Kingsley Publishers.
Le Navenec, C., & Bridges, L. (Eds.). (2005). *Creating connections between nursing care and the creative arts therapies: Expanding the concept of holistic care.* Springfield, IL: Charles C Thomas.
Levine, S.K., & Levine, E.G. (1998). *Foundations of expressive arts therapies: Theoretical and clinical perspectives.* London: Jessica Kingsley Publishers.
Liebmann, M. (Ed.). (1996). *Arts approaches to conflict.* London: Jessica Kingsley Publishers.
Malchiodi, C.A. (Ed.). (2006). *Expressive therapies.* New York: Guilford Press.
McNiff, S. (1998). *Art-based research.* London: Jessica Kingsley Publishers.
McNiff, S. (2004). *Art heals: How creativity cures the soul.* Boston: Shambala.
Meekums, B. (2000). *Creative group therapy for women survivors of child sexual abuse: Speaking the unspeakable.* London: Jessica Kingsley Publishers.
Nathan, A.A., & Mirviss, S. (1998). *Therapy techniques using the creative arts.* Ravensdale, WA: Idyll Press.
Rogers, J.A. (Ed.). (2007). *The art of grief: The use of expressive arts in a grief support group.* London: Routledge.
Rogers, N. (1993). *The creative connection: Expressive arts as healing.* Palo Alto, CA: Science & Behavior Books.
Schaefer, C.E. (Ed.). (2003). *Play therapy with adults.* New York: Wiley.
Waller, D., & Mahoney, J. (Eds.). (1999). *Treatment of addiction: Current issues for arts therapies.* London: Routledge.
Warren, B. (Ed.). (2008). *Using the creative arts in therapy* (3rd Ed.). London: Routledge.
Weisberg, N., & Wilder, R. (2001). *Expressive arts with elders: A resource* (2nd Ed.). London; Philadelphia: Jessica Kingsley Publishers.
Wigram, T. (2002). *Assessment and evaluation in the arts therapies: Art therapy, music therapy & dramatherapy.* Radlett: Harper House.

BOOKS ON PSYCHODRAMA AND SOCIODRAMA

Baim, C., Burmeister, J., & Maciel, M. (2007). *Psychodrama: Advances in theory and practice.* London: Routledge.
Blatner, H.A. (1973). *Acting in: Practical applications of psychodramatic methods.* New York: Springer.
Blatner, A., & Blatner, A. (1988). *Foundations of psychodrama: History, theory and practice.* New York: Springer.
Blatner, A., & Blatner A. (1997). *The art of play: An adult's guide to reclaiming imagination and spontaneity.* New York: Brunner/Mazel.
Blomkvist, L.D., Moreno, Z.T., & Rutzel, T. (2000). *Psychodrama, surplus reality, and the art of healing.* London: Routledge.
Bukowski, W.M., & Cillessen, A.H. (Eds). (1998). *Sociometry then and now: Building on six decades of measuring children's experiences with the peer group.* San Francisco: Jossey-Bass.
Dayton, T. (1994). *The drama within: Psychodrama and experiential therapy.* Deerfield Beach, Florida: Health Communications, Inc.
Dayton, T. (1997). *Heartwounds.* Deerfield Beach, FL: Health Communications, Inc.
Dayton, T. (1999). *Trauma and addiction.* Deerfield Beach, FL: Health Communications, Inc.
Dayton, T. (2004). *The living stage: A step-by-step guide to psychodrama, sociometry, and group psychotherapy.* Deerfield Beach, FL: Health Communications, Inc.
Dimmock, H.G. (1985). *How to analyze and evaluate group growth.* Ontario: Captus Press.
Djuric, Z., Veljkovic, J., & Tomic, M. (2006). *Psychodrama: A beginner's guide.* London: Jessica Kingsley Publishers.
Farmer, C. (1995). *Psychodrama and systemic therapy.* London: Karnac Books.
Feasey, D. (2005). *Good practice in psychodrama.* New York: Wiley.

Figusch, Z. (Ed.). (2005). *Sambadrama: The arena of Brazilian psychodrama.* London: Jessica Kingsley Publishers.

Fonseca, J. (2004). *Contemporary psychodrama: New approaches to theory and technique.* London: Routledge.

Fox, J. (Ed.). (1987). *The essential Moreno: Writings on psychodrama, group method, and spontaneity.* New York: Springer.

Fuhlrodt, R.L. (Ed.). (1989). *Psychodrama: Its application to ACOA and substance abuse treatment.* East Rutherford, NJ: Thomas W. Perrin.

Gendron, J. (1980). *Moreno: The roots and branches; and bibliography of psychodrama, 1972–1980.* Beacon: Beacon House.

Gershoni, J. (2003). *Psychodrama in the 21st century: Clinical and education applications.* New York: Springer.

Goldman, E.F., & Morrison, D.S. (1984). *Psychodrama: Experience and process.* Phoenix: Eldemar Corp.

Greenberg, I.A. (Ed.). (1974). *Psychodrama: Theory and therapy.* New York: Behavioral Publications.

Haas, R.B. (1961). *Psychodrama and sociodrama in American education.* Beacon: Beacon House.

Hale, A.E. (1981). *Conducting clinical sociometric explorations: A manual for psychodramatists and sociometrists.* Roanoke: Royal Publishing.

Hale, A.E., & Little, D. (2002). *Sociometric processing of action events.* Toronto: Toronto Centre for Psychodrama and Sociometry.

Hare, A. P., & Hare, J. R. (1996). *J.L. Moreno.* London: Sage.

Haskell, M.R. (1975). *Socioanalysis: Self direction via sociometry and psychodrama.* Long Beach, CA: Role Training Associates of California.

Hayden-Seman, J.A. (1998). *Action modality couples therapy: Using psychodramatic techniques in helping troubled relationships.* Lanham, MD: Rowman & Littlefield Publishers.

Heisey, MJ. (1982). *Clinical case studies in psychodrama.* Washington DC: University Press of America.

Hoey, B. (1997). *Who calls the tune? A psychodramatic approach to child therapy.* New York: Routledge.

Holmes, P. (1992). *The inner world outside: Object relations theory and psychodrama.* New York: Routledge.

Holmes, P., & Karp, M. (Eds.). (1991). *Psychodrama: Inspiration and technique.* New York: Routledge.

Holmes, P., Karp, M., & Tauvon, K.B. (1994). *The handbook of psychodrama.* New York: Routledge.

Horvatin, T., & Schreiber, E. (Eds.). (2006). *The quintessential Zerka: Writings by Zerka Toeman Moreno on psychodrama, sociometry and group psychotherapy.* London: Routledge.

Hudgins, M.K. (2002). *Experiential treatment for PTSD: The therapeutic spiral model.* New York: Springer.

Kellerman, P. (1992). *Focus on psychodrama: The therapeutic aspects of psychodrama.* London: Jessica Kingsley Publishers.

Kellerman, P. (2007). *Sociodrama and collective trauma.* London: Jessica Kingsley Publishers.

Kellerman, P., & Hudgins, K. (Eds.). (2000). *Psychodrama with trauma survivors.* London: Jessica Kingsley Publishers.

Kipper, D.A. (1986). *Psychotherapy through clinical role playing.* New York: Brunner-Mazel.

Leveton, E. (1992). *A clinician's guide to psychodrama* (2nd Ed.). New York: Springer.

Marineau, R.F. (1989). *Jacob Levy Moreno 1889–1974, father of psychodrama, sociometry, and group psychotherapy.* London: Tavistock/Routledge.

Moreno, J.L. (1969). *The magic charter of psychodrama.* New York: Beacon House.

Moreno, J.L. (1975). *The theatre of spontaneity, Volume 1.* New York: Beacon House.

Moreno, J.L. (1993). *Who shall survive? Foundations of sociometry, group psychotherapy, and sociodrama.* McLean, VA: ASGPP.

Moreno, J.L. (1994). *Psychodrama* (4th Ed.), Volumes I, II, and III. McLean, VA: ASGPP.

Moreno, J.L., & Jennings, H.H. (1945). *Sociometric measurement of social configurations, based on deviation from chance.* New York: Beacon House.

Moreno, J.L., & Jennings, H.H. (Eds.). (1960). *The sociometry reader.* Glencoe, IL: Free Press.

Moreno, Z.T., Blomkvist, L.D., & Rutzel, T. (2000). *Psychodrama, surplus reality, and the art of healing.* New York: Routledge.

Pitzele, P. (1995). *Our fathers' wells: A personal encounter with the myths of Genesis.* San Francisco: Harper.

Pitzele, P. (1998). *Scripture windows: Toward a prac-*

tice of bibliotherapy. Los Angeles: Alef Design Group.

Roine, E. (1997). *Psychodrama: Group psychotherapy as experimental theatre.* London: Jessica Kingsley Publishers.

Scategni, W. (2002). *Psychodrama, group processes and dreams: Archetypical images of individuation.* London: Routledge.

Shu, G. (2004). *Yi shu: The art of living and change: Integrating traditional Chinese medicine, psychodrama, and the creative arts.* Hong Kong: F.E. Robbins & Sons Press.

Smilansky, S. (1968). *The effects of sociodramatic play on disadvantaged children.* New York: Wiley.

Starr, A. (1979). *Psychodrama: Rehearsal for living.* Chicago: Nelson-Hall.

Sternberg, P., & Garcia, A. (1994). *Sociodrama: Who's in your shoes?* Westport, CT: Praeger.

Tauvon, K.B., Holmes, P., Holmes, P., & Karp, M. (Eds.). (1998). *The handbook of psychodrama.* London: Routledge.

Torrance, E.P., Murdock, L., & Fletcher, D. (1988). *Sociodrama: Creative problem solving in action.* Buffalo: Bearly Limited.

Wiener, R. (1997). *Creative training: Sociodrama and team-building.* London: Jessica Kingsley Publishers.

Yablonsky, L. (1992). *Psychodrama: Resolving emotional problems through role-playing.* New York: Brunner/Mazel.

IMPROVISATION THEATER AND THEATER GAMES

Blatner, A., & Blatner, A. (1988). *The art of play: An adult's guide to reclaiming imagination and spontaneity.* New York: Human Sciences Press.

Boal, A. (1979). *Theatre of the oppressed.* New York: Theatre Communications Group.

Boal, A. (1992). *Games for actors and non-actors.* London: Routledge.

Brook, P. (1968). *The empty space.* New York: Avon.

Frost, A., & Yarrow, R. (1990). *Improvisation in drama.* London: MacMillan.

Johnstone, K. (1979). *Improv: Improvisation and the theatre.* New York: Theater Arts Books.

Pasolli, R. (1970). *A book on open theater.* New York: Avon.

Schechner, R., & Schuman, M. (Eds.). (1976). *Ritual, play, and performance: Readings in the social sciences/theatre.* New York: Seabury Press.

Spolin, V. (1969). *Improvisation for the theatre.* Evanston, IL: Northwestern University Press.

Stanislavski, K. (1961). *Creating a role.* New York: Theatre Arts Books.

Stanislavski, K. (1970). *An actor's handbook.* New York: Theatre Arts Books.

Stanislavski, K. (1972). *Building a character.* New York: Theatre Arts Books.

Stanislavski, K. (1989). *An actor prepares.* New York: Theatre Arts Books.

Turner, V. (1982). *From ritual to theater.* New York: Performing Arts Journal Press.

BOOKS ON CREATIVE DRAMA AND THEATER IN EDUCATION

Bolton, G.M. (1979). *Towards a theory of drama in education.* Harlow: Longman.

Bolton, G.M. (1984). *Drama as education.* Harlow: Longman.

Courtney, R. (1974). *Play, drama, and thought.* New York: Drama Book Specialists.

Courtney, R. (1982). *Replay: Studies of drama in education.* Toronto, Ontario: Institute for Studies in Education.

Hermann, A., & Clifford, S. (1998). *Making a leap–Theatre for empowerment: A practical handbook for creative drama work with young people.* London: Jessica Kingsley Publishers.

Hornbrook, D. (1989). *Education and dramatic art.* Oxford: Blackwell.

Landy, R. (1982). *Handbook of educational drama and theater.* New York: Greenwood.

McCaslin, N. (1994). *Creative drama in the classroom and beyond.* New York: Longman.

Slade, P. (1954). *Child drama.* London: University of London Press.

Slade, P. (1995). *Child play: It's importance for human development.* London: Jessica Kingsley Publishers.

CHAPTERS AND JOURNAL ARTICLES ON DRAMA THERAPY

No author. (2007). Abstracts from 15th Biennial South African Association of South African Child and Adolescent Psychiatry and Allied Professions Conference. *Journal of Child and Adolescent Mental Health, 17*(2), 87–99.

Aach, S. (1976). Drama: A means of self-expression for the visually-impaired child. *New Outlook for the Blind, 70*(7), 282–285.

Adams, S. (2000). Combining teacher and therapist roles: Making the space and taming the dragon. In N. Barwick (Ed.), *Clinical counseling in schools: Clinical counseling in context* (pp. 81–95). New York: Routledge.

Allan, J.A. (1977). The use of creative drama with acting-out sixth and seventh grade boys and girls. *Canadian Counsellor, 11*(3), 135–143.

Antinori, D., & Moore, P. (1997). The controlled approach exercise in cultural diversity training with clinicians. *The Arts in Psychotherapy, 24*(2), 173–182.

Avrahami, E. (2003). Cognitive-behavioral approach in psychodrama: Discussion and example from addiction treatment. *The Arts in Psychotherapy, 30*(4), 209–216.

Bailey, S. D. (1997). Drama: A powerful tool for social skill development. *Disability Solutions, 2*(1), 1–5.

Bailey, S.D. (2006). Ancient and modern roots of drama therapy. In S.A. Brooke (Ed.), *Creative arts therapies manual* (pp. 214–222). Springfield, IL: Charles C Thomas.

Bailey, S.D. (2007). Art as an initial approach to the treatment of sexual trauma. In S.A. Brooke (Ed.), *The use of creative art therapies with sexual abuse survivors* (pp. 59–72). Springfield, IL: Charles C Thomas.

Barratt, G., & Segal, B. (1996). Rivalry, competition and transference in a children's group. *Group Analysis, 29*(1), 23–35.

Barsky, M., & Mozenter, G. (1976). The use of creative drama in a children's group. *International Journal of Group Psychotherapy, 26*(1), 105–114.

Basso, R. (1991). A structured fantasy group experience in a children's diabetic education program. *Patient Education and Counseling, 18*(3), 243–251.

Bergman, J. (1995). Life, the life event and theatre–A personal narrative in the use of drama therapy with sex offenders. In B.K. Schwartz & H.R. Cellini (Eds.), *The sex offender: Corrections, treatment and legal practice* (pp. 17; 1–24). Kingston, NJ: Civic Research Institute.

Bergman, J. (2001). Using drama therapy to uncover genuineness and deception in civilly committed sexual offenders. In A. Schlank (Ed.), *The sexual predator, Vol. 2: Legal issues, clinical issues, and special populations.* Kingston, NJ: U.S. Civic Research Institute.

Bergman, J., & Hewish, S. (1996). Pin point–The precise fit of drama therapy and cognitive restructuring, in creative therapies and programs in corrections. *Correctional Issues.* Maryland: American Correctional Association.

Bergman, J., & Hewish, S. (1996). The violent illusion. In M. Liebmann (Ed.), *Arts approaches to conflict* (pp. 92–117). London: Jessica Kingsley Publishers.

Bielanska, A., Cechnicki, A, & Budzyna-Dawidowski, P. (1991). Dramatherapy as a means of rehabilitation for schizophrenic patients: Our impressions. *American Journal of Psychotherapy, 45* (4), 566–575.

Bikales, V.W. (1949). Drama therapy at Winter Veterans Administration Hospital: A preliminary report. *Bulletin of the Menninger Clinic, 13,* 127–133.

Bikales, V.W., Ebert, G., Weil, R., & Howe, L.P. (1952). The effects of leadership upon morale in a group therapeutic setting. *Bulletin of the Menninger Clinic, 16,* 202–210.

Blatner, A. (2000). A new role for psychodramatists: Master of ceremonies. *International Journal of Action Methods: Psychodrama, Skill Training, and Role Playing, 53*(2), 86–93.

Bracha, Z. (2000). The use of psychodrama in adolescents with Downs syndrome. *International Journal of Adolescent Medicine and Health, 12*(1), 85–95.

Bratton, S.C. (1999). Group puppetry. In D.S. Sweeney (Ed.), *The handbook of group play therapy: How to do it, how it works, whom it's best for.* San Francisco: Jossey-Bass.

Brett, T., Maux, C., Quayla, M, & Reiss, D. (1998). Dramatherapy for mentally disordered offenders: Changes in levels of anger. *Criminal Behavior and Mental Health, 8*(2), 139–153.
Bromfield, R. (1995). The use of puppets in play therapy. *Child and Adolescent Social Work Journal, 12*(6), 435–444.
Brookes, J.M. (1975). Producing Marat/Sade: Theater in a psychiatric hospital. *Hospital and Community Psychiatry, 26*(7), 429–435.
Brunside, I. (1995). Themes and props: Adjuncts for reminiscence therapy groups. In B. Haight (Ed.), *The art and science of reminiscing: Theory, research, methods and applications* (pp. 153–163). Philadelphia: Taylor & Francis.
Buchanan, D.R. (1984). Moreno's social atom: A diagnostic and treatment tool for exploring interpersonal relationships. *The Arts in Psychotherapy, 11,* 155–164.
Burleigh, L.R., & Beutler, L.E. (1996). A critical analysis of two creative arts therapies. *The Arts in Psychotherapy, 23*(5), 275–381.
Burton, C. (1986). Peekaboo to "all the all the outs in free": Hide-and-seek as a creative structure in drama therapy. *The Arts in Psychotherapy, 13*(2), 129–136.
Bush, C. S. (1978). Creative drama and language experiences: Effective clinical techniques. *Language, Speech and Hearing Services in the Schools, 9*(4), 254–258.
Carter, R., & Mason P. (1998). The selection and use of puppets in counseling. *Professional School Counseling, 1*(5), 50–53.
Casson, J. (1996). Archetypal splitting: Drama therapy and psychodrama. *The Arts in Psychotherapy, 23*(4), 307–309.
Casson, J. (2006). The five story self structure on the Communicube. *Counseling Psychology Review, 21*(2), 3–11.
Cattanach, A. (1995). Drama and play therapy with young children. *The Arts in Psychotherapy, 22*(3), 223–228.
Cattanach, A. (2006). Narrative play therapy. In C.E. Schaefer & H.G. Kaduson (Eds.), *Contemporary play therapy: Theory, research and practice* (pp. 82–99). New York: Guilford Press.
Chesner, A. (2002). Playback theatre and group communication. In H. Hahn (Ed.), *Creative Advances in Group Work* (pp. 40–66). London: Jessica Kingsley Publishers.
Christie, D., Hood, D., & Griffin, A. (2006). Thinking, feeling, and moving: Drama and movement therapy as an adjunct to a multidisciplinary rehabilitation approach for chronic pain in two adolescent girls. *Clinical Child Psychology and Psychiatry, 11*(4), 569–577.
Christofferson, B. (2005). Performance creation as a mode of self-care: A participatory study of caregivers and the prevention of burnout. In C. Le Navenec & L. Bridges (Eds.), *Creating connections between nursing care and the creative arts therapies: Expanding the concept of holistic care.* Springfield, IL: Charles C Thomas.
Cohen, H.U. (1985). Conflicting values in creating theatre with the developmentally disabled: A study of Theatre Unlimited. *The Arts in Psychotherapy, 12,* 3–10.
Cossa, M. (1992). Acting Out: A pilot project in drama therapy with adolescents. *The Arts in Psychotherapy, 19*(1), 53–55.
Cossa, M. (2003). Taming puberty: Using psychodrama, sociodrama, and sociometry with adolescent groups. In J. Gershoni (Ed.), *Psychodrama in the 21st century: Clinical and education applications* (pp. 135–150). New York: Springer.
Count van Manon, G. (2003). Drama imagery processes as socialization: An interdisciplinary perspective. *Journal of Mental Imagery, 27*(1–2), 42–87.
Couroucli-Robertson, K. (1992). Cultural differences and similarities in drama therapy. *The Arts in Psychotherapy, 1992, 19*(2), 117–121.
Couroucli-Robertson, K. (2001). Brief drama therapy of an immigrant adolescent with a speech impediment. *The Arts in Psychotherapy, 28*(5), 289–297.
Courtney, R. (1989). Dictionary of developmental drama: The use of terminology in educational drama, theater education, creative dramatics, children's theater, drama therapy, and related areas. *British Journal of Aesthetics, 29*(1), 79–81.
Crenshaw, D.A., & Foreacre, C. (2001). Play therapy in a residential treatment center. In A.A. Drewes, L. Carey, & C.E. Schaefer (Eds.), *School-based play therapy* (pp. 139–162). Hoboken, NJ: Wiley.
Curtis, A.M. (1999). Communicating with

bereaved children: A drama therapy approach. *Illness, Crisis, and Loss, 7*(2), 183–190.

Davis, B. (1985). The impact of creative drama training on psychological states of older adults: An exploratory study. *Gerontologist, 25*(3), 315-321.

Davis, B. (1987). Some roots and relatives of creative drama as an enrichment activity for older adults. *Educational Gerontology, 13*(4), 297–306.

Davies, D. (1984). Utilization of creative drama with hearing-impaired youth. *Volta Review, 86* (2), 106–113.

Dayton, T. (2007). Emotional repair through action methods: The use of psychodrama, sociometry, psychodramatic journaling and experiential group therapy with adolescents. In V.A. Camilleri (Ed.), *Healing the inner city child: Creative arts therapies with youth at risk.* London: Jessica Kingsley Publishers.

Dent-Brown, K., & Wang, M. (2004). Pessimism and failure in 6-part stories: Indicators of borderline personality disorder? *The Arts in Psychotherapy, 31*(5), 321–333.

Dintino, C., & Johnson, D. (1996). Playing with the perpetrator: Gender dynamics in developmental drama therapy. In S. Jennings (Ed.), *Drama therapy: Theory and practice, Vol. 3* (pp. 205–220). London: Routledge.

Doyle, C. (1998). A self psychology theory of role in drama therapy. *The Arts in Psychotherapy, 25*(4), 223–235.

Dunne, L. (2007). Drama therapy with sexual abuse survivors with substance abuse issues. In S.A. Brooke (Ed.). *The use of creative arts therapies with sexual abuse survivors* (pp. 261–279). Springfield, IL: Charles C Thomas.

Dunne, P. (1988). Drama therapy techniques in one-on-one treatment with disturbed children and adolescents. *The Arts in Psychotherapy, 15*(2), 139–149.

Dunne, P.B. (1997). Catch the Little Fish. In C. Smith & D. Nyland (Eds.), *Narrative therapies with children and adolescents* (pp. 71–110). New York: Guilford Press.

Dunne, P (2003). Narradrama: a narrative action approach with groups. In D. Wiener, & L. Oxford (Eds.), *Action therapies with families and groups* (pp. 229–265). Washington D.C.: American Psychological Association.

DuPont, S. (1992). The effectiveness of creative drama as an instructional strategy to enhance the reading comprehension skills of fifth grade remedial readers. *Reading Research and Instruction, 31*(3), 41–52.

Dutton, S.E. (2001). Urban youth development–Broadway style: Using theatre and group work as vehicles for positive youth development. *Social Work in Groups, 23*(4), 39–58.

Eberle, B. (1974). Does creative dramatics really square with research evidence? *Journal of Creative Behavior, 8*(3), 177–182.

Eliaz, E. (1992). The concept of dramatic transference. *The Arts in Psychotherapy, 19*(5), 333–346.

Eliaz, E., & Flashman, A. (1994). Road signs: Elements of transference in drama therapy: Case study. *The Arts in Psychotherapy, 21*(1), 59–73.

Emunah, R. (1983). Drama therapy with adult psychiatric patients. *The Arts in Psychotherapy, 10*(2), 77–84.

Emunah, R. (1985). Drama therapy and adolescent resistance. *The Arts in Psychotherapy, 12*(2), 71–79.

Emunah, R. (1989). The use of dramatic enactment in the training of drama therapists. *The Arts in Psychotherapy, 16*(1), 29–36.

Emunah, R. (1990). Expression and expansion in adolescence: The significance of creative arts therapy. *The Arts in Psychotherapy, 17*(2), 101–107.

Emunah, R. (1995). From adolescent trauma to adolescent drama: Group drama therapy with emotionally disturbed youth. In S. Jennings (Ed.), *Dramatherapy with children and adolescents* (pp. 150–168). New York and London: Routledge.

Emunah, R. (1996). Five progressive phases in dramatherapy and their implications for brief therapy. In A. Gersie (Ed.), *Dramatic approaches to brief therapy* (pp. 29–44). London: Jessica Kingsley Publishers.

Emunah, R. (1997). Drama therapy and psychodrama: An integrated model. *International Journal of Action Methods,* 108–134.

Emunah, R. (1999). Drama therapy in action. In D. Wiener (Ed.), *Beyond talk therapy* (pp. 99–124). Washington, D.C.: American

Psychological Association.

Emunah, R. (2005). Drama therapy and adolescent resistance. In A. Weber & C. Haen (Eds.), *Clinical applications of drama therapy in child and adolescent treatment* (pp. 107–121). New York: Brunner-Routledge.

Emunah, R., & Johnson, D. (1983). The impact of theatrical performance on the self-images of psychiatric patients. *The Arts in Psychotherapy, 10,* 233–239.

Fink, S. (1990). Approaches to emotion in psychotherapy and theatre: Implications for drama therapy. *The Arts in Psychotherapy, 17*(1), 5–18.

Finneran, L., Unruh, D., & Bartscher, B. (1997). The therapeutic classroom: A cooperative effort between Lawrence Public Schools and Bert Nash Community Mental Health Center. *Continuum: The Journal of the Association for Ambulatory Behavioral Healthcare, 4*(2), 153–174.

Fisher, E.P. (1992). The impact of play on development: A meta-analysis. *Play and Culture, 5*(2), 159–181.

Fong, J. (2006). Psychodrama as a preventative measure: Teenage girls confronting violence. *Journal of Group Psychotherapy, Psychodrama & Sociometry, 59*(3), 99–108.

Fontana, D., & Valente, L. (1993). Drama therapy and the theory of psychological reversals. *The Arts in Psychotherapy, 20*(2), 133–142.

Ford, G. (2001). Playback theatre. In H.G. Kaduson & C.E. Schaefer (Eds.), *101 more favorite play therapy techniques* (pp. 390–394). Lanham, MD: Jason Aronson.

Forrester, A. M. (2000). Role-playing and dramatic improvisation as an assessment tool. *The Arts in Psychotherapy, 27*(4), 235–243.

Forrester, A., & Johnson, D. (1995). Drama therapy on an extremely short term inpatient unit. In A. Gersie (Ed.), *Brief treatment approaches to drama therapy* (pp. 125–138). London: Routledge.

Furman, L. (1988). Theatre as therapy: The distancing effect applied to audience. *The Arts in Psychotherapy, 15*(3), 245–249.

Gallo-Lopez, L. (2005). Drama therapy with adolescents. In L. Gallo-Lopez & C.E. Schaefer (Eds.), *Play therapy with adolescents.* Lanham, MD: Jason Aronson.

Gallo-Lopez, L. (2006). A creative play therapy approach to the group treatment of young sexually abused children. In H.G. Kaduson & C.E. Schaefer (Eds.), *Short-term play therapy for children* (2nd Ed.). (pp. 245-272). New York: Guilford Press.

Gallo-Lopez, L. (2007). Beyond survival: Play and creative therapy with adolescents who have been sexually abused. In S.A. Brooke (Ed.), *The use of creative arts therapies with sexual abuse survivors* (pp. 170–180). Springfield, IL: Charles C Thomas.

Galway, K., Hurd, K., & Johnson, D. (2003). Developmental transformations in group therapy with homeless people with a mental illness. In D. Wiener & L. Oxford (Eds.), *Action therapy with families and groups* (pp. 135–162). Washington, DC: American Psychological Association.

Geissinger, A. (1996). Authentic sound movement and drama: An interview with Penny Lewis. *A Moving Journal, 3* (1).

Gerity, L. (2006). Art and community building from the puppet and mask maker's perspective. In F. Kaplan (Ed.), *Art therapy and social action.* London: Jessica Kingsley Publishers.

Gersie, A. (1995). Arts therapies practice in innercity slums: Beyond the instillation of hope. *The Arts in Psychotherapy, 22*(3), 207–216.

Gerson, M.J. (2001). The drama of couples therapy. *Journal of Psychotherapy Integration, 11*(3), 333–347.

Gheorghe, C. (2008). The sacred and the profane food: Ritual and compulsion in eating disorders–Existential drama therapy with adolescents and their families. In S.A. Brooke (Ed.), *Creative therapies and eating disorders* (pp. 194–208). Springfield, IL: Charles C Thomas.

Ghiaci, G., & Richardson, J. (1980). The effects of dramatic play upon cognitive structure and development. *Journal of Genetic Psychology, 136*(1), 77–83.

Gibson, W., & Brookes, J.M. (1976). The drama group. In J. Erickson (Ed.), *Activity, recovery, and growth* (pp. 101–125). New York: W.W. Norton.

Glaser, B. (2004). Ancient traditions within a new drama therapy method: Shamanism and developmental transformations. *The Arts in Psychotherapy, 31*(2), 77–88.

Glass, J. (2006). Working toward aesthetic distance: Drama therapy for adult victims of trauma. In L. Carey (Ed.), *Expressive and creative arts methods for trauma survivors* (pp. 57–71). London: Jessica Kingsley Publishers.

Gomes, R., & Count Van Manen, G. (1984). Family Life Laboratory: The uses of creative dramatic processes in university social sciences settings. *Journal of Mental Imagery, 8*(1), 109–115.

Goodrich, J., & Goodrich, W. (1986). Drama therapy with a learning disabled, personality disordered adolescent. *The Arts in Psychotherapy, 13*(4), 285–291.

Graham-Poole, J. (2002). The creative arts: What role do they play? In S. Shannon (Ed.). *Handbook of complementary and alternative therapies in mental health* (pp. 475–495). San Diego: Academic Press.

Grainger, R. (1987). Evaluation in drama therapy. In D. Milne (Ed.), *Evaluating mental health practice: Methods and applications* (pp. 154–162). New York: Croom Helm.

Grainger, R. (1996). Artistic expression and the embodiment of social constructs. *The Arts in Psychotherapy, 23*(2), 137–140.

Gray, B. (1997). This is the story of Wicked: Community drama theatre with at-risk aboriginal Australian youth. *The Arts in Psychotherapy, 24* (3), 275–279.

Grayer, E.D. (2005). The story of Alex–An improvisational drama. *Clinical Social Work Journal, 33*(1), 21-36.

Green, M.Y. (1995). When art imitates life: A look at art and drama therapy. *Public Welfare, 53*(2), 34–43.

Greenberg, S. (2000). The play's the thing: Older people as actors in their own life drama. *Journal of Geriatric Psychiatry, 33*(2), 169–182.

Hackney, P. (1986). Education of the visually handicapped gifted: A program description. *Education of the Visually Handicapped, 18*(2), 85–95.

Haen, C. (2005). Rebuilding security: Group therapy with children affected by September 11. *International Journal of Group Psychotherapy, 55*(3), 391–414.

Haen, C. (2007). Fear to tread: Play and drama therapy in the treatment of boys who have been sexually abused. In S.A. Brooke (Ed.), *The use of creative arts therapies with sexual abuse survivors* (pp. 235–249). Springfield, IL: Charles C Thomas.

Haen, C. (2007). Make me wanna holler: Dramatic encounters with boys from the inner city. In V.A. Camilleri (Ed.), *Healing the inner city child: Creative arts therapies with youth at risk* (pp. 212–228). London: Jessica Kingsley Publishers.

Haen, C., & Brannon, K. (2002). Superheroes, monsters, and babies: Roles of strength, destruction, and vulnerability for emotionally disturbed boys. *The Arts in Psychotherapy, 29,* 31–40.

Hanec, B. (2004). Mesmerizing violent offenders with a slice of life: Drama and reflexivity in the treatment of men who abuse their spouses. In T. Strong & D. Park (Eds.), *Furthering talk: Advances in discursive therapies* (pp. 199–215). New York: Kluwer Academic/Plenum Publishers.

Harvey, S. (1990). Dynamic play therapy: An integrative expressive arts approach to the family therapy of young children. *The Arts in Psychotherapy, 17,* 239–246.

Harvey, S. (1991). Creating a family: An integrated expressive approach to adoption. *The Arts in Psychotherapy, 18,* 213–222.

Harvey, S.A. (1993). Ann: Dynamic play therapy with ritual abuse. In T. Kottman & C. Schaefer (Eds.), *Play therapy in action: A case book for practitioners.* Northvale, NJ: Jason Aronson.

Harvey, S.A. (1994a). Dynamic play therapy: Expressive play intervention with families. In D. O'Connor & C. Schaefer (Eds.), *Handbook of play therapy: Volume two, advances and innovations.* New York: Wiley.

Harvey, S.A. (1994b). Dynamic play therapy: Creating attachments. In B. James (Ed.), *Handbook for treatment of attachment-trauma problems in children.* New York: Lexington Books.

Harvey, S.A. (1994c). Dynamic play therapy: An integrated expressive arts approach to family treatment of infants and toddlers. *Zero to Three, 15,* 11–17.

Harvey, S.A. (1995). Sandra: The case of an adopted sexually abused child. In F. Levy (Ed.), *Dance and other expressive arts therapies:*

When words are not enough (pp. 167–180). New York: Routledge.

Harvey, S.A. (1997). Dynamic play therapy: A creative arts approach. In K. O'Connor & L. Braverman (Eds.), *Play therapy theory and practice: A comparative presentation.* New York: Wiley.

Harvey, S.A. (2001). Volcano. In H.G. Kaduson & C.E. Schaefer (Eds.), *101 more favorite play therapy techniques* (pp. 188–192). Lanham, MD: Jason Aronson.

Harvey, S.A. (2003). Dynamic play therapy with adoptive families. In D. Betts (Ed.), *Creative arts therapies approaches in adoption and foster care* (pp. 77–96). Springfield, IL: Charles C Thomas.

Harvey, S.A. (2006). Dynamic play therapy. In C.E. Schaefer & H.G. Kaduson (Eds.), *Contemporary play therapy: Theory, research, and practice* (pp. 55–81). New York: Guilford Press.

Harvey, S., & Kelly, E.C. (1993). Evaluation of the quality of parent-child relationships: A longitudinal case study. *The Arts in Psychotherapy, 1993, 20*(5), 387–395.

Herman, L. (1997). Good enough fairy tales for resolving sexual abuse trauma. *The Arts in Psychotherapy, 24*(5), 439–445.

Hickling, F.W. (1989). Sociodrama in the rehabilitation of chronic mentally ill patients. *Hospital and Community Psychiatry, 40*(4), 402–206.

Hickling, F.W. (2004). Popular theatre as psychotherapy. *Interventions: International Journal of Post Colonial Studies, 6*(1), 45–56.

Hiltunen, S.S. (1988). Initial therapeutic applications of Noh Theatre in drama therapy. *Journal of Transpersonal Psychology, 20*(1), 71–79.

Hiltunen, S.S. (2001). Seven stages of womanhood: A contemporary healing ritual from the Finnish mythology of the Kalevala. *Journal of Transpersonal Psychology, 33*(2), 113–129.

Hindmarch, T. (2005). Eating disorders: A psychodrama approach. In T. Hindmarch (Ed.), *Eating disorders: A multi-professional approach.* New York: Wiley.

Hodermarska, M., & Scott-Moncrieff, S. (2007). Operatic play: A drama and music therapy collaboration. In V.A. Camilleri (Ed.), *Healing the inner city child: Creative arts therapies with youth at risk* (pp. 242–253). London: Jessica Kingsley Publishers.

Hollins, S. (2001). Psychotherapeutic methods. In A. Dosen & K. Day (Eds.), *Treating mental illness and behavior disorders in children and adults with mental retardation* (pp. 27–44). Washington, DC: American Psychological Association.

Huddleston, R. (1989). Drama with elderly people. *British Journal of Occupational Therapy, 52* (8), pp. 298–300.

Irwin, E.C. (1971). Why play? *Children in Contemporary Society, 5*(2), 15–17.

Irwin, E.C. (1975). Facilitating children's language development through play. *The Speech Teacher, 24*(1), 15–23.

Irwin, E.C. (1975). Drama in education: Drama in therapy. *Children in Contemporary Society, 8*(12), 34–39.

Irwin, E.C. (1975). Dramatic play and therapy. *Children's Theatre Review, 24*(3), 8–10.

Irwin, E.C. (1976). Play in psychotherapy. *Children in Contemporary Society, 9*(3), 75–79.

Irwin, E.C. (1977). Play, fantasy, and symbols: Drama with emotionally disturbed children. *American Journal of Psychotherapy, 31*(3), 426–436.

Irwin, E.C. (1978). Observational guide for drama activities. In J. Carlson (Ed.), *Counseling in the elementary and middle schools: A pragmatic approach.* New York: William C. Brown Company.

Irwin, E.C. (1979). Drama therapy with the handicapped. In A. Shaw & C.S. Stevens (Eds.), *Drama, theatre and the handicapped* (pp. 21–28). Washington, DC: American Theatre Association.

Irwin, E.C. (1980). The projective value of puppets. In R. Herink (Ed.), *Psychotherapy handbook.* New York: New American Library.

Irwin, E.C. (1982). Enlarging the psychodynamic picture through dramatic play techniques. In K. O'Laughlin & E. Nickerson (Eds.), *Helping through action: Readings on action-oriented therapies* (pp. 53–59). Amherst: Human Resource Development Press.

Irwin, E.C. (1983). The diagnostic and therapeutic use of pretend play. In C.E. Schaefer & K.J. O'Connor (Eds.), *Handbook of play therapy* (pp. 148–173). New York: Wiley.

Irwin, E.C. (1984). The role of the arts in mental

health. *Design for the Arts in Education, 86*(1), 43–47.

Irwin, E.C. (1985). Externalizing and improvising imagery through drama therapy: A psychoanalytic view. *Journal of Mental Imagery, 9* (4), 33–42.

Irwin, E.C. (1986) Drama therapy in diagnosis and treatment. *Child Welfare, 65*(4), 347–357.

Irwin, E.C. (1986). On being and becoming a therapist. *The Arts in Psychotherapy, 13,* 191–195.

Irwin, E.C. (1987). Drama: The play's the thing. *Elementary School Guidance and Counseling, 21*(4), 247–283.

Irwin, E.C. (1988). Arts therapy and healing. *The Arts in Psychotherapy, 15,* 293–295.

Irwin, E.C. (1988). Further thoughts on understandings. *The Arts in Psychotherapy, 15,* 307–308.

Irwin, E.C. (1991). The use of a puppet interview to understand children. In C.E. Schaefer, K. Gitllin, & A. Sandgrund (Eds.), *Play diagnosis and assessment* (pp. 617–635). New York: Wiley.

Irwin, E.C. (1999). Child dramatic play as viewed from two perspectives: Ego psychology and object relations. *Journal of Clinical Psychoanalysis, 7*(4), 505–533.

Irwin, E.C. (2000). The use of a puppet interview to understand children. In C.E. Schaefer & K. Gitlins (Eds.), *Play diagnosis and assessment* (pp. 682–703). New York: Wiley.

Irwin, E., (2004). Facilitating play with non-players: A developmental perspective. In A. M. Weber & C. Haen (Eds.), *Clinical approaches of drama therapy in child and adolescent treatment* (pp. 3–23). New York: Brunner Routledge.

Irwin, E.C. (2006). Peter: A study of cumulative trauma: From "robot" to "regular guy." In L. Carey (Ed.), *Expressive and creative arts methods for trauma survivors* (pp. 93–113). London: Jessica Kingley Publishers.

Irwin, E.C. (1983). Learning to play: Playing to learn. In S. Stoner (Ed.), *Arts resources and training guide.* Washington, DC: National Committee, Arts for the Handicapped.

Irwin, E.C., & Baker, N. (1976). Fantasy, play and language: Expressive therapy with communication handicapped children. *Journal of Childhood Communication Disorders, 1*(2), 99–115.

Irwin, E.C., & Curry N.E. (1993). Role play. In C.E. Schaefer (Ed.), *The therapeutic powers of play* (pp. 168–188). Northvale, NJ: Jason Aronson.

Irwin, E.C., & Frank, M. (1977). Facilitating the play process with learning disabled children. *Academic Therapy, 1*(4), 435–444.

Irwin, E.C., & Kovacs, A. (1979). Analysis of children's drawings and stories. *Journal of the Association for the Care of Children in Hospitals, 8*(2), 39–45.

Irwin, E. C., Levy, P., & Shapiro, M. I. (1972). Assessment of drama therapy in a child guidance setting. *Group Psychotherapy and Psychodrama, 25* (3), 105–116.

Irwin, E.C., & Malloy, E.P. (1975). Family puppet interview. *Family Process, 14*(2), 179–191.

Irwin, E.C., & Malloy, E.P. (1980). Family puppet interview. In J.G. Howells (Ed.), *Advances in family psychiatry, Vol. 1* (pp. 191–203). New York: International Universities Press.

Irwin, E. C., & McWilliams, B.J. (1974). Play therapy for children with cleft palates. *Children Today, 3,* 18–22.

Irwin, E.C., & Perla, R. (1978). Expressive therapy with a communicationally handicapped deaf adolescent. In *Arts for the handicapped: Why?* (pp. 23–29). Washington, DC: National Committee, Arts for the Handicapped.

Irwin, E. C., & Rubin, J. A. (1976). Art and drama interviews: Decoding symbolic messages. *The Arts in Psychotherapy, 3,* 169–175.

Irwin, E. C., Rubin, J. A., & Shapiro, M. I. (1975). Art and drama: Partners in therapy. *American Journal of Psychotherapy, 29* (1), 107–116.

Irwin, E.C., & Rubin, J.A. (1976). Understanding play interviews. *Children in Contemporary Society, 9*(2), 5–10.

Irwin, E.C., & Shapiro, M. (1975). Puppetry as a diagnostic and therapeutic tool. In I. Jakab (Ed.), *Transcultural aspects of art: Art and psychiatry,* Vol. 4 (pp. 86–94). Basel: Karger Press.

James, M., & Johnson, D.R. (1997). Drama therapy in the treatment of combat-related posttraumatic stress disorder. *The Arts in Psychotherapy, 23* (5), 383–395.

James, M., & Johnson, D.R. (1996). Drama therapy for the treatment of affective expression in posttraumatic stress disorder. In D.L. Nathanson (Ed.), *Knowing feeling: Affect, script, and psychotherapy* (pp. 303–326). New York: W.W. Norton.

James, M., Forrester, A., & Kim, K. (2005). Developmental transformations in the treatment of sexually abused children. In A. Weber & C. Haen (Eds.), *Clinical applications of drama therapy in child and adolescent treatment* (pp. 67–86). New York: Brunner Routledge.

Janzing, H. (1998). The use of the mask in psychotherapy. *The Arts in Psychotherapy, 23*(3), 151–157.

Jenkins, R.L., & Beckh, E. (1993). Finger puppets and mask making. In C.E. Schaefer (Ed.), *Play therapy techniques.* Northvale, NJ: Jason Aronson.

Jennings, S. (1991). Legitimate grieving? Working with infertility. In D. Papadatou & C. Papadatos (Eds.), *Children and death* (pp. 277–282). Washington, DC: Hemisphere Publishing.

Jennings, S. (1992). The nature and scope of dramatherapy: Theatre of healing. In M. Cox (Ed.), *Shakespeare comes to Broadmoor: 'The actors are come hither': The performance of tragedy in a secure psychiatric hospital* (pp. 229–250). London: Jessica Kingsley Publishers.

Johnson, D. R. (1980). Effects of a theatre experience on hospitalized psychiatric patients. *The Arts in Psychotherapy, 7,* 265–272.

Johnson, D.R. (1980). Principles and techniques of drama therapy. *The Arts in Psychotherapy, 9* (2), 83–90.

Johnson, D.R. (1982). Developmental approaches in drama therapy. *The Arts in Psychotherapy, 9* (3), 183–189.

Johnson, D. R. (1984). Establishing the creative arts therapies as an independent profession. *The Arts in Psychotherapy, 11,* 209–212.

Johnson, D. R. (1984). The field of drama therapy. *Journal of Mental Imagery, 8*(1), 105–109.

Johnson, D. R. (1984). Representation of the internal world in catatonic schizophrenia. *Psychiatry, 47*(4), 299–314.

Johnson, D. R. (1985). Expressive group psychotherapy with the elderly: A dramatherapy approach. *International Journal of Group Psychotherapy, 35*(1), 109–127.

Johnson, D.R. (1986). The developmental method in drama therapy: Group treatment with the elderly. *The Arts in Psychotherapy, 13*(1), 17–33.

Johnson, D.R. (1987). The role of the creative arts therapies in the diagnosis and treatment of psychological trauma. *The Arts in Psychotherapy, 14,* 7–13.

Johnson, D.R. (1988). The diagnostic role-playing test. *The Arts in Psychotherapy, 15,* 23–36.

Johnson, D. (1989). The theatrical dimensions of psychotherapy. In A. Robbins (Ed.), *The psychoaesthetic experience* (pp. 77–92). New York: Human Sciences Press.

Johnson, D. R. (1991). The theory and technique of transformations in drama therapy. *The Arts in Psychotherapy, 18*(4), 285–300.

Johnson, D. (1992). The drama therapist in role. In S. Jennings, (Ed.), *Drama therapy: Theory and practice, Vol. 2* (pp. 112–136). London: Routledge.

Johnson, D.R. (1998). On the therapeutic action of the creative arts therapies: The psychodynamic model. *The Arts in Psychotherapy, 25*(2), 85–99.

Johnson, D.R. (2000). Creative therapies. In E.B. Foa, T.M. Keane, & M.J. Friedman (Eds.), *Effective treatments for PTSD: Practice guidelines from the International Society for Traumatic Stress Studies* (pp. 302–314). New York: Guilford Press.

Johnson, D. (2007). British influences on developmental transformations. *Journal of the British Dramatherapy Association, 29,* 3–10.

Johnson, D.R., & Eicher, V. (1990). The use of dramatic activities to facilitate dance therapy with adolescents. *The Arts in Psychotherapy, 17,* 157–164.

Johnson, D. R., Forrester, A., Dintino, C., Miller, J., & Schnee, G. (1996). Towards a poor drama therapy. *The Arts in Psychotherapy, 23*(4), 293–306.

Johnson, D. R., & Lubin, H. (1998). Healing ceremonies. *Family Therapy Networker, 22*(5), 38–39, 64–67.

Johnson, D.R., & Munich, R.L. (1975). Increasing hospital-community contact through a theater program in a psychiatric hospital. *Hospital and Community Psychiatry, 26*(7), 435–438.

Johnson, D. R., & Ryan, E. R. (1983). Freedom and discovery within the therapeutic bond.

The Arts in Psychotherapy, 10, 3–7.

Johnson, D. R., Smith, A., & James, M. (2003). Developmental transformations in group therapy with the elderly. In C.E. Schaefer, (Ed.), *Play therapy with adults* (pp. 78–103). Hoboken, NJ: Wiley.

Johnston, J. C., Healy, K. N., & Tracey-Magid, D. (1985). Drama and interpersonal problem solving: A dynamic interplay for adolescent groups. *Child Care Quarterly, 14* (4), 238–247.

Jones, C. B. (1991). Creative dramatics: A way to modify aggressive behavior. *Early Childhood Development and Care, 73,* 43–52.

Jones, P. (2008). Audience and witnessing: Research into dramatherapy using vignettes and MSN messenger. *Research in Drama Education, 13*(1), 39.

Keats, P.A. (2003). Constructing masks of the self in therapy. *Constructivism in the Human Sciences, 8*(1), 105–124.

Kedem-Tahar, E., & Kellerman, P.F. (1996). Psychodrama and drama therapy: A comparison. *The Arts in Psychotherapy, 23*(1), 27–36.

Keeling, J.A., & Rose, J.L. (2006). The adaptation of a cognitive-behavioural treatment programme for special needs sexual offenders. *British Journal of Learning Disabilities, 34*(2), 110–116.

Kellerman, P.F. (1996). Concretization in psychodrama with somatization disorder. *The Arts in Psychotherapy, 23*(2), 149–152.

Kerr, C. (2000). Eugene O'Neill: An American playwright's contribution to family therapy. *The Arts in Psychotherapy, 27*(2), 115–122.

Kidder, B. (2002). Healing through action. *Focal Point, 16*(1), 17–18.

Kindler, R. (1997). Lonely as a cloud: Finding daffodils in the house of terror: Transference and countertransference in drama therapy with a 10 year old boy. In A. Goldberg (Ed.), *Conversations in self psychology: Progress in self psychology.* Mahway, NJ: Analytic Press.

Kindler, R. (1997). Turning passive into active: Treatment of physically handicapped preschoolers. *Psychoanalysis and Psychotherapy, 14* (2), 323–348.

Koch, S. C. (2007). Review of arts therapies: A research based map of the field. *Body, Movement and Dance in Psychotherapy, 2*(2), 151–153.

Kolko, D.J., Luar, L., & Sturnick, D. (1989). Inpatient social-cognition skills training groups with conduct disordered and attention deficit disordered children. *Journal of Child Psychology and Psychiatry, 31*(5), 737–748.

Kouttab, A. (2007). Mapping the emotional terrain of peace: Palestinians and Israelis search for common ground. *Journal of Humanistic Psychology, 47*(3), 351–360.

Kruczek, T., & Zagelbaum, A. (2004). Increasing adolescent awareness of at-risk behaviors via psychoeducational drama. *The Arts in Psychotherapy, 31*(1), 1–10.

Lahad, M. (1999). The use of drama therapy with crisis intervention groups following mass evacuation. *The Arts in Psychotherapy, 26*(1), 27–34.

Laffoon, D., Diamond, S., Bryan, V., & Kenny, F. (2003). When the bough breaks: The STOP-GAP method in foster care. In D. Betts (Ed.), *Creative arts therapies approaches in adoption and foster care* (pp. 152–167). Springfield, IL: Charles C Thomas.

Landers, F. (2002). Dismantling violent forms of masculinity through developmental transformations. *The Arts in Psychotherapy, 29*(1), 19–29.

Landy, R. (1982). Training the drama therapist: A four-part model. *The Arts in Psychotherapy, 9,* 91–99.

Landy, R. (1983). The use of distancing in drama therapy. *The Arts in Psychotherapy, 10*(3), 175–185.

Landy, R. (1984). Conceptual and methodological issues of research in drama therapy. *The Arts in Psychotherapy, 11*(2), 89–100.

Landy, R. (1984). Puppets, dolls, objects, masks, and make-up. *Journal of Mental Imagery, 8*(1), 79–89.

Landy, R. (1985). The image of the mask: Implications for theatre and therapy. *Journal of Mental Imagery, 9*(4), 43–56.

Landy, R. (1990). The concept of role in drama therapy. *The Arts in Psychotherapy, 17*(3), 223–230.

Landy, R. (1991). The dramatic basis of role theory. *The Arts in Psychotherapy, 18*(1), 29–41.

Landy, R. (1991). A taxonomy of roles: A blueprint for the possibilities of being. *The Arts in Psychotherapy, 18*(5), 419–431.

Landy, R. (1992). The case of Hansel and Gretel.

The Arts in Psychotherapy, 19, 231–241.

Landy, R. (1993). The child, the dreamer, the artist and the fool: In search of understanding the meaning of expressive therapy. *The Arts in Psychotherapy, 20,* 359–370.

Landy, R. (1994). Three scenarios for the future of drama therapy. *The Arts in Psychotherapy, 21*(3), 179–184.

Landy, R. (1995). Isolation and collaboration in the creative arts therapies: The implications of crossing borders. *The Arts in Psychotherapy, 22* (2), 83–86.

Landy, R.J. (1996). Drama therapy and distancing: Reflections on theory and clinical application. *The Arts in Psychotherapy, 23,* 367–373.

Landy, R. (1997). Drama therapy: The state of the art. *The Arts in Psychotherapy, 24*(1), 5–15.

Landy, R. (1997). Drama therapy in Taiwan. *The Arts in Psychotherapy, 24*(2), 159–172.

Landy, R. (1999). Role model of drama therapy supervision. In E. Tselikas-Portmann, (Ed.), *Supervision and dramatherapy* (pp. 114–135). London: Jessica Kingsley Publishers.

Landy, R.J. (2002). Sifting through the images–A drama therapist's response to the terrorist attacks of September 11, 2001. *The Arts in Psychotherapy, 29*(3), 135–142.

Landy, R. (2003). Drama therapy with adults. In C.E. Schaefer (Ed.), *Play therapy with adults* (pp. 15–33). New York: Wiley.

Landy, R. (2006). Drama therapy and psychodrama. In C. Malchiodi (Ed.), *Expressive therapies* (pp. 90–116). New York: Guilford Press.

Landy, R. J. (2006). The future of drama therapy. *The Arts in Psychotherapy, 33*(2), 135–142.

Landy, R.J., & Hadari, A. (2007). Stories of destruction and renewal: A drama therapy experience. *Journal of Humanistic Psychology. 47*(3), 413–421.

Landy, R., Luck, B., Conner, E., & McMullian, S. (2003). Role profiles–A drama therapy assessment instrument. *The Arts in Psychotherapy, 30,* 151–61.

Langley, D. (1998). The relationship between psychodrama and drama therapy. In M. Karp (Ed.), *The handbook of psychodrama.* New York: Routledge.

LeBlanc, K., Curtis, A.M., & Linville, S. (2004). Coping with grief and loss: Helping children heal within the classroom community. *Montessori Reporter, 28*(3), 14–17.

Leeder, A., & Wimmer, C. (2007). Voices of pride: Drama therapy with incarcerated women. *Women and Therapy, 29*(3–4), 195–213.

Leveton, E. (1991). The use of doubling to counter resistance in family and individual treatment. *The Arts in Psychotherapy, 18,* 241–249.

Lewis-Bernstein, P. (1980). The union of the Gestalt concept of experiment and Jungian active imagination within a woman's mythic quest. *The Gestalt Journal, 3*(2), 36–46.

Lewis-Bernstein, P., Rubin, J., & Irwin, E. (1975). Play, parenting, and the arts. In P. Lewis-Bernstein (Ed.), *Therapeutic process movement as integration.* Columbia, MD: American Dance Therapy Association.

Lewis, Penny. (1984). Expressive arts assessment profile. In P. Lewis (Ed.), *Theoretical approaches in dance-movement therapy, Vol. II.* Dubuque: Kendall-Hunt.

Lewis, P. (1987). The expressive therapies in the choreography of object relations. *The Arts in Psychotherapy, 14*(4), 321–332.

Lewis, P. (1987). The unconscious as choreographer: The use of tension flow rhythms in the transference relationship. *ADTA conference monograph.* Columbia: American Dance Therapy Association.

Lewis, P. (1988). The dance between the conscious and unconscious: Transformation in the embodied imaginal realm. *The moving dialogue.* Columbia: American Dance Therapy Association.

Lewis, P. (1988). The marriage of our art with science: The Kestenberg profile and the choreography of object relations. *Monograph 5,* Columbia: American Dance Therapy Association.

Lewis, P. (1988). The transformative process within the imaginal realm. *The Arts in Psychotherapy, 15*(3), 309–316.

Lewis, P. (1990). The Kestenberg movement profile in the psychotherapeutic process with borderline disorder. In P. Lewis & S. Loman (Eds.), *The KMP: Its past, present application and future directions.* Keene: Antioch University.

Lewis, P. (1991). Creative transformation: The alchemy of healing, individuation and spiritual consciousness. *Shadow and light: Moving toward wholeness.* Columbia: American Dance Therapy Association.

Lewis, P. (1992). The creative arts in transference-countertransference relationships. *The Arts in Psychotherapy, 19*(5), 317–324.

Lewis, P. (1996). Authentic sound movement and drama: An interview with Penny Lewis. Annie Geissinger interviewer. *A Moving Journal, 3*(1).

Lewis, P. (1996). Authentic sound, movement, and drama: An interactional approach. In M. Robbins (Ed.), *Body oriented psychotherapy, Vol. I.* Somerville, MA: International Scientific Community for Psycho-Corporal Therapies.

Lewis, P. (1996). The Kestenberg movement profile. In M. Robbins (Ed.), *Body oriented psychotherapy, Vol. I.* Somerville, MA: International Scientific Community for Psycho-Corporal Therapies.

Lewis, P. (1997). Appreciating diversity, commonality, and the transcendent. *The Arts in Psychotherapy, 24*(3), 225–226.

Lewis, P. (1997). Multiculturalism and globalism in the arts in psychotherapy. *The Arts in Psychotherapy, 24*(2), 123–128.

Lewis, P. (1997). Transpersonal arts psychotherapy: Toward an ecumenical worldview. *The Arts in Psychotherapy, 24*(3), 243–254.

Lewis, P. (1999). Healing early child abuse: The application of the Kestenberg movement profile. In J. Amaghi, S. Loman, & P. Lewis (Eds.), *The meaning of movement: Developmental and clinical perspectives as seen through the Kestenberg movement profile.* Newark: Gordon & Breach.

Lewis, P. (1999). The embodied feminine: Dance and drama therapy in women's holistic health. In E. Olshansky (Ed.), *Woman's holistic health.* Gaithersburg, MD: Aspen.

Lewis, P., & Brownell, A. (1990). The Kestenberg movement profile in assessment of vocalization. In P. Lewis & S. Loman (Eds.), *The KMP: Its past, present application and future directions.* Keene: Antioch University.

Lewis, S. (1974). Creative drama in the treatment of emotionally disturbed children from six years of age to pre-adolescence. *Australian Occupational Therapy Journal, 21*(1), 8–22.

Linden, S. (1997). Aiko: Drama therapy in the recovery process of a Japanese/Korean American woman. *The Arts in Psychotherapy, 24*(2), 193–203.

Linden, S. (1997). A festival of light: A high school healing arts event celebrating the ethnic diversity of the school community. *The Arts in Psychotherapy, 24,* 255–259.

Lippe, W. A. (1992). Stanislavski's affective memory as a therapeutic tool. *Journal of Group Psychotherapy, Psychodrama, and Sociometry, 45*(3), 102–111.

Long, J., & Soble, L. (1999). Report: An arts-based violence prevention project for sixth grade students. *The Arts in Psychotherapy, 26*(5), 329–344.

Long, J., & Soble, L. (2007). Art and drama therapy in three settings. In V.A. Camilleri (Ed.), *Healing the inner city child: Creative arts therapies with at-risk youth.* London: Jessica Kingsley Publishers.

Lowenstein, L.F. (1982). The treatment of extreme shyness in maladjusted children by implosive, counselling and conditioning approaches. *Acta Psychaitria Scandanavia, 66,* 173–189.

Lusebrink, V.B. (1991). A systems oriented approach to the expressive therapies: The expressive therapies continuum. *The Arts in Psychotherapy, 18*(5), 295–402.

MacKay, B. (1987). Uncovering buried roles through face painting and storytelling. *The Arts in Psychotherapy, 14*(3), 201–208.

MacKay, B. (1989). Drama therapy with female victims of assault. *The Arts in Psychotherapy, 16*(4), 293–300.

Mackay, B. (1996). Brief drama therapy and the collective creation. In A. Gersie (Ed.), *Dramatic approaches to brief drama therapy* (pp. 161–174). London: Jessica Kingsley Publishers.

MacKay, B., Gold, M., & Gold, E. (1987). A pilot study in drama therapy with adolescent girls who have been sexually abused. *The Arts in Psychotherapy, 14*(1), 77–84.

Marinovic, M., & Carbonell, E. (2000). A psychological study of Chilean actors' views of their art. *The Arts in Psychotherapy. 27*(4), 245–261.

Mazor, J.L. (1966). Producing plays in psychiatric settings. *Bulletin of Art Therapy, 5*(4), 135–148.

Mazor, R. (1978). Drama as experience. *Language Arts,* 328–333.

Mazor, R. (1982). Drama therapy for the elderly

in a day care center. *Hospital and Community Psychiatry, 33*(7), 577–579.

McClure, B.A., Miller, G. A., Russo, T., & Thomas J. (1992). Conflict within a children's group: Suggestions for facilitating its expression and resolution strategies. *School Counselor, 39*(4), 268–272.

McKenna, P., & Hasta, E. (1999). Clinical effectiveness of dramatherapy in the recovery from neurotrauma. *Disability & Rehabilitation: An International Multidisciplinary Journal, 21*(4), 162–174.

Meldrum, B. (1999). The theatre process in dramatherapy. In A. Cattanach (Ed.), *Process in the arts therapies* (pp. 36–54). London: Jessica Kingsley Publishers.

Middelkoop, K. (2006). Design and evaluation of a drama-based intervention to promote voluntary counseling and HIV testing in a South African community. *Sexually Transmitted Diseases, 23*(8), 524–526.

Mier, D. (2008). Drama therapy as treatment for survivors of domestic abuse. In S.A. Brooke (Ed.), *Creative arts as treatment for survivors of domestic abuse* (pp. 247–268). Springfield, IL: Charles C Thomas.

Miller, J.G., & Hymovitz, L. (1969). Therapy through drama. *Educational Leadership, 26,* 475.

Mitchell, S. (1999). Reflections on dramatherapy as initiation. In A. Cattanach (Ed.), *Process in the arts therapies* (pp. 10–35). London: Jessica Kingsley Publishers.

Moffett, L.A., & Bruto, L. (1990). Therapeutic theatre with personality disordered substance abusers: Characters in search of different characters. *The Arts in Psychotherapy, 17*(4), 339–348.

Moriyama, M., Sakurai, N., & Kamata, K. (1995). Therapeutic drama activity for the cognitively impaired elderly in a nursing home. *Aging Clinical and Experimental Research, 7*(6), 441–450.

Morgan, V., & Pearson, S. (1994). Social skills training in a junior high setting. *Educational Psychology in Practice, 10*(2), 99–103.

Mosely, J. (1991). An evaluative account of the working of a dramatherapy peer support group within a comprehensive school. *Support for Learning, 6*(4), 154–164.

Mulkey, M. (2004). Recreating masculinity: Drama therapy with male survivors of sexual assault. *The Arts in Psychotherapy, 31*(1), 19–28.

Murray-Park, S.A. (2003). An adoptee's journey to self: Containing the liminality of the adoption ritual through drama therapy. In D. Betts (Ed.), *Creative arts therapies approaches in adoption and foster care* (pp. 62–76). Springfield, IL: Charles C Thomas.

Newman, G.W., & Collie, K. E. (1984). Drama therapy training and practice: An overview. *Journal of Mental Imagery, 8*(1), 119–125.

Nitsun, M., Stapleton, J.H., & Bender, M.P. (1974). Movement and drama therapy with long-stay schizophrenics. *British Journal of Medical Psychology, 47,* 101–119.

Noble, G., Egan, P., & McDowell, S. (1977). Changing the self-concepts of seven-year-old deprived urban children by creative drama or videofeedback. *Social Behavior and Personality, 5*(1), 55–64.

Novy, C. (2003). Drama therapy with pre-adolescents: A narrative perspective. *The Arts in Psychotherapy, 30*(4), 201–207.

Novy, C., Ward, S., Thomas, A., Bulmer, L., & Gauthier, M. (2005). Introducing movement and prop as additional metaphors in narrative therapy. *Journal of Systemic Therapies, 24*(2), 60–74.

Odell-Miller, H., Hughes, P., & Westacott, M. (2006). An investigation into the effectiveness of the arts therapies for adults with continuing mental health problems. *Psychotherapy Research, 16*(1), 122–139.

O'Doherty, S. (1989). Play and drama therapy with the Down's Syndrome child. *The Arts in Psychotherapy, 16*(3), 171–178.

Osoff-Bultz, B. (2005). A template for the multidisciplinary team-led social and life skills groups utilizing drama and other creative arts therapies: Its application for girls experiencing neurological challenges. In C. La Navenec & L. Bridges (Eds.), *Creating connections between nursing care and the creative arts therapies: Expanding the concept of holistic care* (pp. 335–354). Springfield, IL: Charles C Thomas.

Pendzik, S. (1988). Drama therapy as a form of modern shamanism. *Journal of Transpersonal Psychology, 20*(1), 81–92.

Pendzik, S. (1994). The theatre stage and the

sacred space: A comparison. *The Arts in Psychotherapy, 21*(1), 25–35.

Pendzik, S. (2003). Six keys to assessment. *The Arts in Psychotherapy, 30*(2), 91–99.

Pendzik, S. (2006). On dramatic reality and its therapeutic function in drama therapy. *The Arts in Psychotherapy, 33*(4), 271–280.

Petitti, G. J. (1989). Video as an externalizing object in drama therapy. *The Arts in Psychotherapy, 16*(2), 121–125.

Petitti, G. J. (1992). The operational components of drama therapy. *Journal of Group Psychotherapy, Psychodrama, and Sociometry, 45*(1), 40–44.

Phillips, M. E. (1996). Looking back: The use of drama and puppetry in occupational therapy during the 1920s and 1930s. *American Journal of Occupational Therapy, 50*(3), 229–233.

Pithers, W.D. (1997). Maintaining treatment integrity with sexual abusers. *Criminal Justice and Behavior, 24*(1), 24–51.

Porter, L. (2000). The bifurcated gift: Love and intimacy in drama psychotherapy. *The Arts in Psychotherapy, 27*(5), 309–320.

Porter, L. (2003). Death in transformation: The importance of impasse in drama therapy. *The Arts in Psychotherapy, 30*(2), 101–107.

Ramseur, C. A., & Wiener, D. J. (2003). Using Rehearsals for Growth in group therapy with substance abusers. In D.J. Wiener & L.K. Oxford (Eds.), *Action therapy with families and groups: Using creative arts improvisation in clinical practice* (pp. 107–134). Washington, DC: American Psychological Association.

Rana, Y. (2006). Drama therapy and refugee youth. In S.A. Brooke (Ed.), *Creative arts therapies manual* (pp. 244–247). Springfield, IL: Charles C Thomas.

Reed, M. A. (2000). Shakespeare's poetics of play-making and therapeutic action in "The Tempest." *Journal of Poetry Therapy, 14*(1), 25–39.

Rose, S. (1982). Producing Our Town: Therapeutic theatre in a psychiatric hospital. *Hospital and Community Psychiatry, 33*(12).

Rosenberg, H. S., & Pinciotti, P. (1983–1984). Imagery in creative drama. *Imagination, Cognition, and Personality, 3*(1), 69–76.

Rousseau, C., Benoit, M., Gauthier, M., Lacroix, L., Alain, N., Rojas, M. V., et al. (2007). Classroom drama therapy program for immigrant and refugee adolescents: A pilot study. *Clinical Child Psychology and Psychiatry, 12*(3), 451–465.

Rosseau, C., Gauthier, M.F., Lacroix, L. Alain, N., Benoit, M., Moran, A., Rojas, M.V., & Bourassa, D. (2005). Playing with identities and transforming shared realities: Drama therapy workshops for adolescent immigrants and refugees. *The Arts in Psychotherapy, 32*(1), 13–27.

Rosseau, C., Lacroix, L., Signh, A., Gauthier, M.F., & Benoit, M. (2006). Creative expression workshops in school: Prevention programs for immigrant and refugee children. *Canadian Child and Adolescent Psychiatry Review, 14*(3), 77–80.

Rubin, J., & Irwin, E.C. (1975). Art and drama: Parts of a puzzle. In I. Jakab (Ed.), *Transcultural aspects of psychiatric art: Art and psychiatry, Vol. 4* (pp. 193–200). Basel: Karger Press.

Rubin, S. (2007). Self-revelatory performance. In A. Blatner & D. Wiener (Eds.), *Interactive and applied drama* (pp. 250–259). iUniverse.

Rubin, S. (2008). Women, food and feelings: Drama therapy with women who have eating disorders. In S.L. Brooke (Ed.), *Creative therapies and eating disorders* (pp. 173–193). Springfield, IL: Charles C Thomas.

Ruddy, R.A., & Dent-Brown, K. (2007). Drama therapy for schizophrenia or schizophrenia-like illnesses. *Cochrane Database of Systemic Reviews, 1.*

Salway, A. (2000). Can we afford the extras? A creative response to care in the community. *Therapeutic Communities: International Journal for Therapeutic and Supportive Organizations, 21*(4), 261–270.

Schauben, L.J. (1996). Those who hear need listen. In M. Corker (Ed.), *Counseling–The deaf challenge.* London: Jessica Kingsley Publishers.

Schaverien, J., & Odell-Miller, H. (2005). The art therapies. In G.O. Gabbard, J.S. Beck, & J. Holmes (Eds.), *Oxford textbook of psychotherapy* (pp. 87–94). New York: Oxford University Press.

Schnee, G. (1996). Drama therapy in the treatment of the homeless mentally ill: Treating interpersonal disengagement. *The Arts in Psychotherapy, 23*(1), 53–60.

Seligman, Z. (1995). Trauma and drama: A lesson from the concentration camp. *The Arts in Psychotherapy, 22*(2), 119–132.

Senroy, P. (2008). Nourishing the inner child: The Sesame approach of drama and movement therapy with teens recovering from disordered eating. In S.A. Brooke (Ed.), *Creative therapies and eating disorders* (pp. 209–224). Springfield, IL: Charles C Thomas.

Senroy, P., & Senroy, S. (2007). Rediscover, reclaim and rejoice: The Sesame approach of drama and movement therapy with the exploited girl child in India. In V.A. Camilleri (Ed.), *Healing the inner city child: Creative arts therapies with youth at risk.* London: Jessica Kingsley Publishers.

Shapiro, D.E. (1995). Puppet modeling techniques for children undergoing stressful medical procedures: Tips for clinicians. *International Journal of Play Therapy, 4*(2), 31–39.

Silverman, Y. (2004). The story within: Myth and fairy tale in therapy. *The Arts in Psychotherapy, 31*(3), 127–135.

Silverman, Y. (2006). Drama therapy theoretical perspectives. In S.A. Brooke (Ed.), *Creative arts therapies manual* (pp. 223–231). Springfield, IL: Charles C Thomas.

Silverman, Y. (2007). Drama therapy with adolescent survivors of sexual abuse: The use of myth, metaphor, and fairytale. In S.A. Brooke (Ed.), *The use of creative arts therapies with sexual abuse survivors* (pp. 250–260). Springfield, IL: Charles C Thomas.

Simpson, J.L., & Adelman, R.B. (2006). Voice and "the other": Interactive theatre as a model for education and liberation on university campuses. In O. Swartz (Ed.), *Social justice and communication scholarship* (pp. 77–104). Mahwah, NJ: Erlbaum Associates.

Smeijsters, H., & Cleven, G. (2006). The treatment of aggression using arts therapies in forensic psychiatry: Results of a qualitative inquiry. *The Arts in Psychotherapy, 33*(1), 27–58.

Smigel, E.O. (1961). A note on audience involvement and role-playing in sociodrama. *Group Psychotherapy and Psychodrama, 14*(1–2), 66–67.

Smith, A.G. (2000). Exploring death anxiety with older adults through developmental transformations. *The Arts in Psychotherapy, 27*(5), 321–331.

Smith, J.D., Walsh, R. T., & Richardson, M.A. (1985). The clown club: A structured fantasy approach to group therapy with the latency-age child. *International Journal of Group Psychotherapy, 35*(1), 49–64.

Smith, M., Nursten, J., & McMahon, L. (2004). Social workers' responses to experiences of fear. *British Journal of Social Work, 34*(4), 541–559.

Snow, S. (1991). Working creatively with the symbolic process of the schizophrenic patient in drama therapy. In G. Wilson (Ed.), *Psychology and the performing arts* (pp. 261–268). Amsterdam: Swits & Zeitlinger.

Snow, S. (1996). Fruit of the same tree: A response to Kedem-Tahar and Kellerman's comparison of psychodrama and drama therapy. *The Arts in Psychotherapy, 23*(3), 199–205.

Snow, S. (1996). Focusing on mythic imagery in brief drama therapy with psychotic individuals. In A. Gersie (Ed.), *Dramatic approaches to brief therapy* (pp. 216–235). London: Jessica Kingsley Publishers.

Snow, S., D'Amico, M., & Tanguay, D. (2003). Therapeutic theatre and well-being. *The Arts in Psychotherapy, 30*(2), 73–83.

Stahler, W. (2006/2007). Prayerformance: A drama therapy approach with female prisoners recovering from addiction. *Journal of Creativity in Mental Health, 2*(1), 3–12.

Steinhardt, L. (1994). Creating the autonomous image through puppet theatre and art therapy. *The Arts in Psychotherapy, 21*(3), 205–218.

Stevens, S. (1984). A multidisciplinary day unit for the treatment of substance abuse. *British Journal of Occupational Therapy, 47*(4), 117–120.

Stirtzinger, R., & Robson, B. (1985). Video-drama and the observing ego. *Small Group Behavior, 16*(4), 539–548.

Strawbridge, S. (2005). Story: A personal reflection. *Counselling Psychology Review, 20*(1), 11–15.

Strongylou, N., & Woodard, V. (1993). Exploring images of the Greek-Cypriot woman through drama therapy. *The Arts in Psychotherapy, 20*(2), 161–165.

Stuart-Smith, S. (1994). Reaction to Hill End Adolescent Unit: Interviews with 20 ex-patients. *Journal of Adolescence, 17*(5), 483–489.

Tisza, V., Irwin, E.C., & Zabarenko, L. (1969). A psychiatric interpretation of children's creative dramatic stories. *Cleft Palate Journal, 6*(3), 228–234.

Tisza, V., Irwin, E.C., & Scheide, B. (1973). Children with oral-facial clefts: A contribution to the psychological development of handicapped children. *Journal of the American Academy of Child Psychiatry, 12*(2), 292–313.

Trafford, B., & Perks, A. (1987). Drama therapy in a child and family psychiatry unit. *British Journal of Occupational Therapy, 50*(3), 94–96.

Treder-Wolff, J. (1993). Brief Report: The use of interactive theatre in AIDS prevention education. *The Arts in Psychotherapy, 20*(4), 335–338.

Urspruch, I. (1996). Therapeutic work with actors at the theatre therapy of dynamic psychiatry and in the Russian theatre tradition by Stanislavski. *Dynamische Psychiatrie, 29*(1-2), 69–77.

Valente, L., & F. D. (1994). Drama therapist and client: An examination of good practice and outcomes. *The Arts in Psychotherapy, 21*(1), 3–10.

Van den Bosch, J.A., Hales, H., & Philpot, M. (2005). Dramatherapy with older people suffering from functional mental disorders. *Psychogeriatria Polska, 2*(4), 341–348.

Vorenberg, B. L. (1985). Drama in a supportive environment: It's more than just a play. *Activities, Adaptation and Aging, 7*(2), 45–48.

Waite, L. M. (1983). Drama therapy in small groups with the developmentally disabled. *Social Work with Groups, 16*(4), 95–108.

Walsh, R.T., Kosidoy, M., & Swanson, L. (1991). Promoting social-emotional development through creative drama for students with special needs. *Canadian Journal of Community Mental Health, 10*(1), 153–166.

Walsh, R. T., Richardson, M. A., & Cardey, R.M. (1991). Structured fantasy approaches to children's group therapy. *Social Work with Groups, 14*(1), 57–73.

Walsh-Bowers, R. T. (1992). A creative drama prevention program for easing early adolescent adjustment to school transitions. *Journal of Primary Prevention, 13*(2), 131–147.

Warger, C. L. (1984). Creative drama for autistic adolescents: Expanding leisure and recreational options. *Journal of Child and Adolescent Psychotherapy, 1*(1), 15–19.

Warger, C. L., & Kleman, D. (1986). Developing positive self-concepts in institutionalized children with severe behavior disorders. *Child Welfare, 65*(2), 165–176.

Warren, B. (1989). The hidden stage: The role of drama in teaching the unspoken rules of social interaction. In R.I. Brown & M. Chazan (Eds.), *Emotional and allied issues in the field of disability* (pp. 97–104). Calgary: Detselig.

Warren, B. (2003). Treating wellness: How clown-doctors help to humanise healthcare and promote good health. In P. Twoghig & V. Kalitzdus (Eds.), *Making sense of health, illness and disease* (pp. 201–216). Amsterdam: Rodopi.

Warren, B. (2004). Bring me sunshine: The effects of clown-doctors on the mood and attitudes of health care staff. In P. Twohig & V. Kalitzkus (Eds.), *Interdisciplinary perspectives on health, illness, and disease* (pp. 83–89). Amsterdam: Rodopi.

Warren, B., & Nadeau, R. (1987). Enhancing the quality of life: The role of the arts in the process of rehabilitation. In R. I. Brown (Ed.), *Quality of life for handicapped people* (pp. 184–213). London: Croom Helm.

Warren, B., Richard R., & Brimbal, J. (2005). Drama and the arts for adults with Down syndrome: Benefit options and resources book. In R.I. Brown (Ed.), *Down syndrome issues & information: Adults with Down syndrome.* Portsmouth: The Down Syndrome Educational Trust.

Wiener, D.J. (1991). You wanna play? In T.J. Goodrich (Ed.), *Women and power: Perspectives for therapy.* NY: Norton. *Reprinted in Journal of Feminist Family Therapy, 2*(3), 213–219.

Wiener, D.J. (1994). Rehearsing for growth: Improvisational group therapy. *Tele, 5*(1), 3–4.

Wiener, D.J. (1995). The gift of play. *Family Therapy Networker, 19*(1), 65–70.

Wiener, D.J. (1996). Tug-of-war: A theatrical technique for marital therapy. *Dialog, 27*(2), 27–43.

Wiener, D.J. (1997). Presents of mind. *Journal of Family Psychotherapy, 8*(2), 85–93.

Wiener, D.J. (1997). Rehearsals for growth: A methodology for using theater improvisation in MFT. *The Family Journal, 5*(4), 309–314.

Wiener, D.J. (1997). Using dramatic enactment in MFT supervision. *The Supervision Bulletin, 10,* 1.

Wiener, D. J. (1998). Family assessment using subjective genograms. In T.S. Nelson & T. Trepper (Eds.), *101 more interventions in family therapy* (pp. 411–414). New York: Haworth Press.

Wiener, D.J. (1998). Mirroring movement for increasing family cooperation. In T.S. Nelson & T. Trepper (Eds.), *101 more interventions in family therapy* (pp. 5–8). New York: Haworth Press.

Wiener, D.J. (1999). Using theater improvisation to assess interpersonal functioning. *International Journal of Action Methods, 52*(2), 51–69.

Wiener, D.J. (1999). Rehearsals for Growth: Applying improvisational theater games to relationship therapy. In D.J. Wiener (Ed.), *Beyond talk therapy: Using movement and expressive techniques in clinical practice* (pp. 165–180). Washington DC: American Psychological Association

Wiener, D.J. (2000). Rehearsals for growth: Activating clinical change via theater improvisation. *Journal of Systemic Therapies, 19*(3) 43–54.

Wiener, D.J. (2000). Struggling to grow: Using dramatic enactments in family therapy. *Journal of Family Psychotherapy, 11*(2), 9–21.

Wiener, D.J. (2003). Creating a participating role for adolescents in family therapy. In C. Sori & L. Hecker (Eds.), *The therapist's notebook for children and adolescents* (pp. 180–184). New York: Haworth Press.

Wiener, D.J. (2003). From the outside in. *Psychotherapy Networker, 27*(2), 55–61.

Wiener, D.J. (2004). Treating depression with Rehearsals for Growth. In L. Harrison (Ed.), *Natural healing for depression* (pp. 68–70). New York: Kensington.

Wiener, D.J., & Cantor D. (2002). Improvisational play in couples therapy. In C. Schaefer (Ed.), *Play therapy with adults* (pp. 62–77). New York: Wiley.

Wiener, D.J. & Pels-Roulier, L. (2005). Action methods in marriage and family therapy: A review. *Journal of Group Psychotherapy, Psychodrama and Sociometry, 52*(2), 86–101.

Wilkinson, N., Srijumar, S., Shaw, K., & Orrell, M. (1998). Drama and movement therapy in dementia: A pilot study. *The Arts in Psychotherapy, 25*(3), 195–201.

Woodward, G. (2005). Acting for change: The evolution of a psychodrama group. In B. Reading & M. Weegman (Eds.), *Group psychotherapy and addiction.* New York: Wiley.

Yeager, J. (2006). Theatre engagement and self-concept in college undergraduates. *Journal of Occupational Science, 13*(3), 198–208.

Yotis, L. (2006). A review of dramatherapy research in schizophrenia, methodologies and outcomes. *Psychotherapy Research, 16*(2), 190–200.

Zerin, E. (1983). Finishing unfinished business: Applications of the drama triangle to marital therapy. *Transactional Analysis Journal. 13*(3), 155–157.

Zerin, E. (1988). An application of the drama triangle to family therapy. *Transactional Analysis Journal. 18*(2), 94–101.

BOOKS ON CREATIVE ARTS THERAPIES

Alvin, J. (1978). *Music therapy.* London: Hutchinson.

Amaghi, J., Lewis, P., Loman, S., & Sossin, M. (1999). *The meaning of movement: Developmental and clinical perspectives as seen through the Kestenberg Movement Profile.* Newark, NJ: Gordon & Breach.

Anderson, W. (Ed.). (1977). *Therapy and the arts: Tools of consciousness.* New York: Harper Colophon Books.

Bettelheim, B. (1976). *The uses of enchantment: The meaning and importance of fairytales.* New York: Random House.

Blanton, S. (1960). *The healing power of poetry.* New York: Crowel.

Brand, A.G. (1980). *Therapy in writing.* Lexington: Lexington Books.

Fryear, J., & Fleshman, B. (1981). *The arts in therapy.* Chicago: Nelson-Hall.

Harrower, M. (1972). *The therapy of poetry.* Springfield: Charles C Thomas.

Hornyak, L.M., & Baker, E.K. (1989). *Experiential therapies for eating disorders.* New York: Guilford Press.

Hynes, A.M., & Hynes-Berry, M. (1986). *Biblio/poetry therapy: The interactive process.* Boulder, CO: Westview.

Johnson, D.R. (1999). *Essays on the creative arts therapies: Imaging the birth of a profession.* Springfield, IL: Charles C Thomas.

Kalff, D. (1981). *Sandplay: A psychotherapeutic approach to the psyche.* Boston: Sigo.

Kaye, C., & Blee, T. (1996). *The arts in health care: A palette of possibilities.* London: Jessica Kingsley Publishers.

Krauss, D., & Fryear, J. (Eds.). (1983). *Phototherapy in mental health.* Springfield, IL: Charles C Thomas.

Leedy, J.J. (Ed.). (1969). *Poetry therapy: The use of poetry in the treatment of emotional disorders.* Philadelphia: JB Lippincott.

Leedy, J.J. (Ed.). (1973). *Poetry the healer.* Philadelphia: JB Lippincott.

Levine, S.K., & Levine, E.G. (1998). *Foundations of expressive arts therapies: Theoretical and clinical perspectives.* London: Jessica Kingsley Publishers.

Lewis-Bernstein, P., & Singer, D. (Eds.). (1982). *The choreography of object relations.* Keene: Antioch University.

Lewis, P. (1986). *Theoretical approaches in dance-movement therapy, Vol. I.* Dubuque, IA: W.C. Brown-Kendall/Hunt.

Lewis, P. (1987). *Theoretical approaches in dance-movement therapy, Vol. II.* Dubuque, IA: W.C. Brown-Kendall/Hunt.

Lewis, P., & Loman, S. (Eds.). (1990). *The Kestenberg Movement Profile: Its past, present and future applications.* Keene: Antioch University.

Liebmann, M. (Ed.). (1996). *Arts approaches to conflict.* London: Jessica Kingsley Publishers.

McNiff, S. (1986). *Educating the creative arts therapist: A profile of the profession.* Springfield, IL: Charles C Thomas.

McNiff, S. (1998). *Art-based research.* London: Jessica Kingsley Publishers.

Morrison, M.R. (Ed.). (1987). *Poetry as therapy.* New York: Human Sciences Press.

Rogers, N. (1993). *The creative connection: Expressive arts as healing.* Palo Alto, CA: Science & Behavior Books.

Rubin, J. (1984). *The art of art therapy.* New York: Brunner/Mazel.

Rubin, RJ. (Ed.). (1978). *Bibliotherapy source-book.* Phoenix: Oryx Press.

Sandel, S., & Johnson, D.R. (1987). *Waiting at the gate: Creativity and hope in the nursing home.* New York: Haworth Press.

Ulman, E., & Dachinger, P. (Eds.). (1976). *Art therapy in theory and practice.* New York: Scholken.

Warren, B. (Ed.). (1994). *Using the creative arts in therapy: A practical introduction* (2nd Ed.) New York: Routledge.

Weiss, J.C. (1984). *Expressive therapy with elders and the disabled: Touching the heart of life.* Binghamton, NY: Haworth Press.

CREATIVE ARTS THERAPY JOURNALS

Art Therapy: Journal of the American Art Therapy Association
www.arttherapyjournal.org

American Journal of Dance Therapy
www.springer.com

The Arts in Psychotherapy
www.elsevier.com

International Journal of Play Therapy
www.apa.org

Journal of Music Therapy
www.musictherapy.org

Music Therapy Perspectives
www.musictherapy.org

Journal of Poetry Therapy
www.poetrytherapy.org

Journal of Group Psychotherapy, Psychodrama, and Sociometry
www.asgpp.org

INDEX OF DRAMA THERAPY CONCEPTS

[These are Key Concepts as identified by the authors in this book, listed by (Chapter) and the page they are first mentioned.]

W

SUBJECT INDEX

(Techniques are listed in italics.)

S

T

U